European
Problems in
General
Management

EUROPEAN PROBLEMS
IN GENERAL MANAGEMENT

by

EDMUND P. LEARNED, D.C.S.

Professor of Business Policy and General Management
IMEDE Management Development Institute, Lausanne, 1961–62
and
Charles Edward Wilson Professor of Business Policy
Graduate School of Business Administration, Harvard University

FRANCIS J. AGUILAR, M.B.A.
and
ROBERT C. K. VALTZ, M.B.A.

Research Associates in Business Policy and General Management
IMEDE Management Development Institute, Lausanne, 1961–62

RICHARD D. IRWIN, INC.
1963 · HOMEWOOD, ILLINOIS

First Printing, August, 1963

Library of Congress Catalog Card No. 63–16888

PRINTED IN THE UNITED STATES OF AMERICA

To
ENRICO BIGNAMI
and
JEAN-C. CORTHÉSY

Managing Directors of
Nestlé Alimentana Company (Sté An.)

Men of foresight and great diligence—
Sensing the need for more and better management talent to deal with the opportunities
and problems of rapidly changing and developing economies—
They were leaders in establishing IMEDE which
was designed to capture the best of managerial philosophy, practice, and knowledge
from both Europe and North America so as
to produce broad-gauged, world-minded, efficient corporate executives for private enterprises operating in a variety of national and
cultural environments.

Foreword

THIS pioneering book, *European Problems in General Management,* is an outgrowth of six years of teaching and research at l'Institut pour l'Etude des Méthodes de Direction de l'Entreprise (IMEDE).

IMEDE is an international school of business for young executives. The Institute, which was founded in 1957, is affiliated with and operates under the patronage of the University of Lausanne, but has its own board of trustees, administration, faculty, and buildings. The program of study is open to qualified men from any business firm or government agency who, after some years of business experience, have reached positions of responsibility and have the potential for substantial advancement. In IMEDE's first six years, participants (with an average age of 35) came to this eight and one-half month program from 42 countries and 88 organizations.

The basic objective of the IMEDE program is to broaden the understanding of men whose previous business experience has been mainly specialized, thus helping them to prepare themselves for greater administrative responsibilities. Within this broad objective the program seeks to help its students gain skill in the analysis of business problems and in decision making, an understanding and appreciation of the integrating and coordinating role of top management, a considerable amount of substantive knowledge and understanding of the major functional areas of business, and, finally, an awareness and understanding of the international and changing environment of business at all levels of management.

In light of these objectives, obviously a key course in the IMEDE curriculum is Business Policy and General Management. As is true in most of the IMEDE courses, the person responsible for this course each year has been a professor on leave of absence from a leading graduate school of business in the United States. In addition to teaching, one of his major responsibilities while at IMEDE has been research leading to the development of teaching materials which would be particularly relevant to and useful for a General Management course in a management-development institute with a strong international emphasis. Research of this kind has been under way at IMEDE since 1957.

In the academic year 1961-62, IMEDE was particularly fortunate to have on its faculty Professor Edmund P. Learned, on leave of absence from the Harvard University Graduate School of Business Administration. Professor Learned holds the Charles Edward Wilson Professorship of Business Policy at Harvard University, and for several years prior to coming to IMEDE served as chairman of the Business Policy course at the Harvard Business School. In coming to IMEDE he was able to draw on a wealth of teaching and research experience in almost all major areas of business administration at Harvard over a period of 35 years. Professor Learned has now returned to the Harvard Business School to resume his faculty position there.

Professor Learned was indeed fortunate, as was IMEDE, to have working with him in 1961-62 two research associates of the highest caliber: Francis J. Aguilar and Robert C. K. Valtz. Both young men hold the degree of Master in Business Administration from Harvard University. While at IMEDE, Mr. Aguilar was on leave from his position as industrial market research project leader and presidential assistant at Northern Research and Engineering Corporation and is now a candidate for the Doctor of Business Administration degree at Harvard. Mr. Valtz is now on the management consulting staff of Arthur D. Little, Inc.

During their year at IMEDE, Professor Learned and his two research associates undertook, with my encouragement, the major research task of bringing up to date and adding to the European teaching materials for the course in Business Policy and General Management. The effort they devoted to this assignment was prodigious, and the results were excellent, in terms of both quality and quantity. As their year at IMEDE drew to a close in the spring of 1962, it became clear that the teaching materials which would be available in the general management area at IMEDE by the time they left would be more than sufficient to form the basis for a casebook focusing on European problems in general management. Such a book had not been attempted before, and it seemed to both Professor Learned and myself that through such a medium IMEDE might make a modest contribution to the development of Business Policy and General Management courses in business schools throughout the world.

With the approval of the IMEDE Board of Trustees, and again with my support, the project was carried forward during the year following the authors' stay at IMEDE. Additions were made by Mr. Aguilar to the informative series of notes on the chemical industry in Europe, and the entire text was assembled and organized for publication. I believe that the results, in the pages which follow, speak for themselves. We at

IMEDE hope that this book may be of value to those who teach business, and an encouragement to those who do research in business, in placing increasing emphasis on the international problems of general management. To its authors, and to all the contributors to this book, IMEDE owes a sincere debt of thanks.

THOMAS A. GRAVES, JR.
Director of IMEDE

IMEDE
January, 1963

Preface

THIS IMEDE book on *European Problems in General Management* is a direct outgrowth of an invitation to the authors to spend the academic year 1961-62 (12 months) at the Management Development Institute in Lausanne, Switzerland. The objectives of l'Institut pour l'Etude des Méthodes de Direction de l'Entreprise (IMEDE) have been explained by Dean Graves in the foreword. The objectives of the course in Business Policy and General Management, taught by Professor Learned, will be more fully developed in Part I of the following text.

The three authors had a special mission during the year, namely, to add significantly to the European teaching materials for this course. IMEDE has depended principally upon Business Policy cases prepared at the Harvard Business School and on its own growing supply of General Management cases. Several of the latter cases, on the watch industry of Switzerland, have already been published in Learned, Christensen, and Andrews *Problems of General Management*.[1] The authors of the present book functioned as a closely knit team and traveled extensively throughout Europe gathering data for technical notes on industries and collecting information on business problems from businessmen in ten countries for use in general management training. Though Professor Learned had primary responsibility for directing the research effort and designing the cases, both Mr. Aguilar and Mr. Valtz have in his opinion earned recognition as full-fledged co-authors of the book through their diligence, creativity, and dedicated effort going well beyond the call of duty. Though all three authors worked either singly or in combination in several countries and on several industries, each one nevertheless had special responsibilities. Both Mr. Aguilar and Mr. Valtz were responsible for writing specific cases or notes. In addition, Mr. Aguilar conceived and developed a major plan for studying the chemical industry of Europe. Some of the results of his field work are included in this book; others will appear, we hope, in subsequent publications. Professor Learned acted as general coordinator for the IMEDE faculty in preparing a series of thirteen notes and cases based on a study in depth of the Galvor Company. Mr. Valtz was field coordinator for the entire faculty

---

[1] Homewood, Ill.: Richard D. Irwin, Inc., 1961.

on this project, wrote seven of the thirteen cases, and gathered data as requested by other professors for four more.

Though this book includes IMEDE cases on Business Policy and General Management prepared by our predecessors, it contains mostly our own cases in this field. We have also included six notes or cases prepared by our colleagues in other courses at IMEDE. On all cases except our own we have shown in a footnote the name of the field researcher and the professorial supervisor of the case. We are indeed proud to include these cases in this collection and thank the authors for their contributions.

The cases and notes in this book have been largely drawn from European countries; a very few are from the United States. Sometimes it is evident what country is involved; in other instances the geographic location has not been indicated so as to protect the source. Sometimes it has been desirable to disguise products for the same general purpose. Many cases are under the real name of the company. Those that are not contain a footnote showing that the name is fictitious. Executives of some of the companies with disguised names expected that the firm would be identifiable by knowledgable persons in their industry, but nevertheless preferred fictitious names for the very good reason that disguise made it easier for their executives to talk freely for quotation or summarization in the case. To the companies and executives who gave both time and data the authors are deeply indebted. The fact that these sources must remain nameless in no way reduces our appreciation of the contribution they have made to business education.

The authors wish to thank many persons at IMEDE for making this book possible. We wish to acknowledge the foresight of Mr. Enrico Bignami and Mr. Jean-C. Corthésy, joint managing directors of Nestlé Alimentana, who originally arranged for the establishment of IMEDE and for its affiliation with the University of Lausanne, subject to the supervision of the authorities of the Canton de Vaud. Their vital interest in the welfare of IMEDE was shown in many useful ways. Their appreciation of our need for freedom to develop our work according to a professor's conception of his responsibility, and their willingness to absorb the costs of our expensive field work through a Nestlé Alimentana (Sté An.) Foundation (IMEDE) grant, both deserve the highest recognition we can give. It was a pleasure, furthermore, to work under the leadership of Dean Thomas A. Graves, Jr., whom we had known as an assistant dean at the Harvard Business School; he gave us continuous support and encouragement. We are indebted, also, to Mr. Pierre E. Jaccard, Secretary General of IMEDE, and to his secretarial and administrative staff for processing our large volume of paper and arranging our travel plans.

Finally, we thank the Trustees of IMEDE for permission to publish these cases. Their ownership of the basic copyright and of the right to reprint by permission is shown on each IMEDE case. We are also indebted to the President and Fellows of Harvard College for their permission to publish certain cases prepared by Professor Learned and copyrighted by them.

The wholehearted interest in learning of the fifty-one participants in the 1961-62 class at IMEDE, their dedication to work over a long period of time, and their favorable response to the European cases that we gathered were all sources of inspiration to us. The fact that these participants came from twenty-two different companies in nineteen countries and spoke at least two out of eight basic languages—English, French, German, Italian, Swedish, Spanish, Japanese, and Egyptian— dramatically highlights the possibilities for international and intercultural training that only IMEDE provides to this degree. There are rich rewards for teachers, researchers, and participants alike in such diversity. Opportunity was provided for teachers as well as participants to learn from one another.

The two married members of this author team want to thank their wives for loyal support during our year of intensive activity. Both the young bride of Mr. Valtz and the wife of forty years of Professor Learned permitted them to give their field work very high priority even though it interfered with other possible uses of this time. Without such support this book would not have been possible.

Lastly, the authors want to acknowledge the high-quality assistance of Mrs. Audrey Sproat and Miss Audrey Barrett, both of Lexington, Massachusetts, in getting the manuscript to the publisher.

EDMUND P. LEARNED
FRANCIS J. AGUILAR
ROBERT C. K. VALTZ

January, 1963

Table of Contents

PART I

Business Policy and General Management

PUBLICATION in the United States of a Business Policy casebook based on European experience reflects a world-wide trend toward heightened interest in learning more about general management and the problems it faces in differing national environments. This trend is exemplified in the continued offering of United States cases in European institutes of management training—even after these have developed a sufficient number of cases of their own—and in the increased offering of European cases here in the United States.

In light of the widespread interest in foreign business operations, the purpose of this opening part of the book is not so much to explain the reason for an international casebook as to introduce a new casebook in Business Policy. In the remarks that follow, we shall try to orient the reader —be he student, executive trainee, or executive—so that he may more gainfully peruse the content of this book. In pursuit of this objective we shall touch upon the following: (1) the subject matter and objectives of Business Policy; (2) the role of top management in firms of varying size; (3) some underlying assumptions about the role of top management in business and society; (4) the outline of a course in Business Policy; (5) the learning experience involved in the case method; and (6) skills it is hoped that the student will develop.

Just as the reader at the end of any serious book or study should ask himself, "What did I learn? Was my study worthwhile?" so should the author or teacher at the beginning seek to give some useful understanding of the learning experience that the reader is about to undergo.[1] It is in the hope of filling this need that this introductory section has been written.

---

[1] Many readers of this book will be students, and the senior author, of course, is a teacher by profession. Accordingly, many of the points in this introduction are specifically addressed to students engaged in group learning and discussion. It is hoped, however, that most of these remarks will be found equally useful by other readers.

BUSINESS POLICY: SUBJECT MATTER AND OBJECTIVES

Business Policy is concerned with the top-management function of (1) shaping high-level, long-range corporate objectives and strategies that will be matched to both company capacities and to external realities in a world marked by rapid technological, economic, social, and political change; (2) casting up an effective well-meshed set of general policies for the pursuit of that strategy; and (3) guiding the organization in accord with that strategy. Considerable emphasis is given to the role of the chief executive or top executive group as leaders in the organizational and personal processes by which objectives, strategies, and major general policies are formulated, on the one hand, and executed, on the other.

Cases on Business Policy are complex since they deal with the many phases of the top-management job: (1) perception of industry and economic trends, both national and international, insofar as these bear on the prospects of the company under study; (2) discernment in the environment of significant needs, company opportunities, and future problem areas; (3) selection from among an array of opportunities of those which seem both to offer special promise and to lie within the scope of company capacities; (4) formulation of a strategy through the matching of opportunity and resources; (5) evaluation of resources—material, human, financial, and intangible, on hand or obtainable—necessary to realize the objectives and to pursue the strategy previously determined; (6) formulation or revision of policies in the light of the requirements posed by an evolving situation; (7) development of operating plans for the pursuit of the chosen strategy and policies—"what" and "how much" has to be done, "when," "where," and "how"; (8) design of the company's organizational structure to allocate responsibility and authority for action; (9) stimulation and coordination of efforts and activities; (10) creation of a system of organizational relationships and an "atmosphere" which facilitates both corporate evolution and development and personal growth and self-realization; (11) measurement of progress and performance; and (12) periodic re-evaluation of position in the light of ensuing developments within the organization and its environment.

A course in Business Policy is usually preceded or accompanied by basic courses in Marketing, Production, Finance, Accounting, Human Relations or Administrative Practices, and International Business. In such courses departmental or functional policies are discussed. Thus it may be said that the teaching of policy is not the exclusive function of a course called Business Policy. Such a course, however, has the special mission of integrating knowledge gained in the various functional courses into the study of the firm as a whole.

The Business Policy course aims to provide men with a "general management point of view" in contrast to a "departmental" or "functional" view. It is intended to give men an appreciation of the many pressures and the complex considerations involved in the decisions of senior executives, and to help men increase their personal capacity for top-level management.

Of course, it is not expected that every man who takes such a course will end up being a general manager or a president, for there are not enough potential vacancies to create the required number of opportunities. But there are more than enough high-level jobs—requiring great understanding, judgment, and general management skill—to absorb the men who are qualified to fill them. And as our economies grow, opportunities for such men will increase. The men who can learn to think as a highly qualified general manager thinks, who can see problems in the broad-gauged way that a general manager perceives them, who can see the cross-departmental implications of their work, who can deduce both short-term and long-term consequences of proposed actions, are the men who will enhance their opportunities for making contributions to their companies and, incidentally, to themselves. Even junior executives should be able to utilize their Business Policy training to some extent; they need not wait until they achieve much higher rank before putting their knowledge and acquired skills to work.

TOP MANAGEMENT IN FIRMS OF DIFFERENT SIZE

Business Policy is concerned with top management, and top management, of course, varies widely in firms of different size. Variations may be found in such important aspects as make-up, staff support, procedures, ultimate responsibility, and, most especially, in functions or activities performed. Despite these differences, however, underlying similarities exist which make the study of any firm in depth a meaningful experience to executives or potential executives in other companies regardless of size.

In the small firm, one man may function as the entire management. Staff support is rarely available, and procedures that seem desirable may not be economical. The single chief executive is frequently an owner-manager and, as such, is legally responsible only to himself. At the other end of the scale, in the very large corporations top management is always a group. It may comprise a board chairman, a president, one or more executive vice-presidents, group vice-presidents, and senior vice-presidents or divisional managers. Staff support is available, and the company is large enough to absorb the overhead of elaborate procedures to enhance efficiency. Corporate executives, unlike the owner-manager, are responsible to an outside ownership of stockholders, whose interests are guarded by a board of directors.

In respect to functions or activities, the single manager of a small company not only determines strategy, plans, and policies; he also acts as chief operating officer. He holds virtually every supervisory position and issues direct orders for the activities to be carried out by his employees. As firms grow in size, however, and work is divided among more top-management people and among more echelons of management, top management tends to pull out of operating details and to perform largely as an agency for setting major guidelines and for reviewing the performance of others.

In our judgment, the minimum role reserved for top management even in the largest firm involves the following responsibilities: (1) the formulation or approval of objectives and strategy; (2) approval of major general policies framed in support of the strategy adopted; (3) review and approval of capital commitments; (4) review of master plans, programs, and budgets; (5) selection and development of key executives; and (6) review and appraisal of results. It is perhaps a moot point whether direct participation in forward planning ought to be included in this list. Certainly top management is responsible for seeing that forward planning is done, for initiating and assigning the task, and for appraising and approving proposals. In many large companies, however, top management itself does not and need not function as the active agency in forward planning.

Although the top-management role in small and large firms differs widely, there are basic similarities. The same functions or activities need to be performed in either case; what differs is mainly the division of labor, reflecting differences in resources and in help available for the top man. This being the case, present or prospective executives in small firms can learn from case studies of large ones—or from consultation with friends or fellow students working in large enterprises. Similarly, executives from large firms can achieve a better grasp of their over-all problems by studying the problem-complex of small firms. From the pedagogical point of view, there is much to be said for thus approaching the macrocosm through the microcosm. Perhaps more important, the effective small-firm manager has something to teach large-firm personnel about the value of speed and flexibility and about the need for breaking down the total managerial load into segments of manageable proportions so that each general management job falls within the scope of what one individual can be expected to administer.

Accordingly, this book contains cases from firms of different size: small, medium, and large. It does not contain as many cases from small firms as we wish it did, for the simple reason that managers of small businesses are so busy carrying on their activities that they lack time to give to case preparation. The book does, however, feature the growth stories of several companies that started with little more than an idea and subsequently built quite substantial businesses. These cases vividly reveal some of the problems created for managers by the growth and change of their firms.

UNDERLYING ASSUMPTIONS ABOUT THE GENERAL MANAGER'S ROLE

In selecting companies for study and in writing about the policymaking function of general management, the authors have given weight to certain underlying assumptions. First, it is assumed that the only viable policy is one that recognizes that a business must behave as a socially responsible institution. Top management should recognize its obligation to make a contribution through the enterprise not only to the owners or stockholders but also to the employees, the customers, the general public, and thus to the national economy. (Perhaps the world economy can already in some cases be added to this list.) All these contributions have a direct or indirect effect on the ultimate right of the firm to continue in business. We cannot forget, as Drucker so aptly stated in his interesting article, "Business Objectives and Survival Needs," that the business enterprise is a creature of society and economy: "If there is one thing we do know, it is that society and/or economy can put any business out of existence overnight— nothing is simpler. The enterprise exists on sufferance and exists only as long as society and economy believe that it does a job, and a necessary, useful, and productive one."[2] Because we wish to observe how top management goes about making a socially useful contribution, we have chosen firms for inclusion in this book only if they were expected to stay in business for a considerable period of time.

A second basic assumption is that the general manager is exposed to and must reckon with a wide variety of systems, both inside and outside the company.[3] A system in its simplest terms is a set of interrelated parts.

---

[2] *Journal of Business* (University of Chicago), April, 1958, p. 85.

[3] Ever since Dr. Walter B. Cannon speculated in the Epilogue to *The Wisdom of the Body* (New York: W. W. Norton & Co., Inc., 1939), p. 306, about whether "it might be useful to examine other forms of organization in the light of the organization of the body," psychologists, sociologists, anthropologists, economists, political scientists, and human relations and personnel experts have been developing systems approaches and systems models. See also F. J. Roethlisberger and W. J. Dickson, *Management and the Worker* (Cambridge: Harvard University Press, 1946), chap. xxiv; L. J. Henderson, *Pareto's General Sociology* (Cambridge: Harvard University Press, 1935).

A social system, whether it is the family or a small group inside a business or some other organization, involves two or more people who interact and share common goals and beliefs. To make an effective business organization, these small groups must somehow be integrated into a department, and departments into the larger system of a major function or division, and these in turn into the system of the company as a whole. Furthermore, when the company looks out to its external world, it encounters additional systems, of which it may be a part but which it cannot entirely control. These environmental systems include other firms in the industry, other industries and institutions, the national system, and even the international system. Any one of these may impose restraints upon, or offer opportunities to, the firm.

A third very basic assumption is that the general manager must cultivate a sense of history, for the history and tradition of the company, the community, and the state or nation affect the policies that can be successfully adopted by the firm. All these histories impose temporary, or perhaps permanent, constraints on the direction of future development. That national as well as individual company history puts breaks on change is hardly a proposition of which European businessmen need to be reminded. It has been repeatedly demonstrated by recent events, particularly in early 1963 when efforts were being made to bring Great Britain into the Common Market. Yet Europe also has a strong tradition of making social, political, and economic changes, to which its businessmen ultimately have adapted. That they do adapt is evident to an observer who looks at the long run. In the short run, however, whether in Europe or America, most members of the business community appear to hold back in making socially useful adaptations. They do not lead but follow. Conceiving of themselves as "conservatives," they forget that their mission is orderly transition to the future rather than mere preservation of the past. In view of the universal human tendency to resist change, to hang on to what one has, the majority's behavior is understandable. But such behavior, even if not obstructive, is too passive to be effective. Business, along with other sections of the community, has an opportunity—or rather an obligation—to make a positive contribution to change. In his own self-interest as well as in the interest of the community as a whole, the business manager should share in the process of determining the pace and direction of change. Thus, for the businessman, whether as a manager or as a citizen, a sense of history includes the capacity to recognize when and where the winds of change are blowing, and perhaps how fast. The time dimension affecting management is one that cannot be overlooked. It is also one for which younger management tends too frequently to have but little feeling.

A fourth important assumption is that management must consider the implications of the fact that the firm is, among other things, an aggregation of individual human beings. Inside the organization, people are subjected to both stimuli and pressures which have an impact on their personal development. It is not the function of this brief introduction to summarize the findings of either the behavioral sciences or administrative experience on the problems which management confronts in those aspects of its task which involve understanding and leading people. The cases in this book, however, do contain much data related to these problems.[4] It is important to recognize, moreover, that skill in human relations is just as important to managers at the executive level in dealing with each other as to operating managers in dealing with workers or the lower ranks of salaried personnel.

As suggested by the foregoing assumptions, the role of the general manager is probably as difficult as it is important. The rise of the specialist, the growing importance of the scientist in business, the development of new tools for decision making as an outgrowth of applied mathematics and data processing—these are trends that divert the limelight from the general manager's job but do not make that job either easier or less important. The key decisions in a business are not ground out by any of these special staffs or special tools. Rather they are aids which the top manager must learn to use. In this sense, they only complicate his job. As a result, the general manager of the future must be an even more competent generalist than he ever was before.

SEQUENCE OF STUDY TOPICS IN POLICY

For studying the wide spectrum of topics of particular interest to the generalist top manager, a particular order or sequence must be chosen. While a variety of outlines might serve, the one preferred by the authors of the present casebook is as follows:

1. Introduction: Previewing Business Policy
2. Determining Objectives and Strategies
3. Developing Coordinated Policies
4. Making Forward Plans
5. Building an Organization
6. Mergers and Joint Ventures
7. Developing Standards of Executive Performance and Appraisal
8. Executive Motivation and Incentives
9. Perceiving and Creating Styles of Leadership
10. The Total Management Process

---

[4] Casebooks on administrative practices or human relations are more exclusively focused on these problems, but usually deal with their appearance at levels well below general management.

As the reader can observe, this favored outline is substantially the one we have followed in setting up the Table of Contents for this book. The only significant difference is that some of the concepts listed separately above have been combined in our Table of Contents into more comprehensive sections. This combination reflects two factors: first, that all cases are broader in scope than any single slot into which they might be fitted; second, that the number of European cases that lent themselves particularly well to listing under some of our concepts proved to be relatively limited.

In connection with this latter point, one important observation must be made. It is not really significant that some topics in our outline appear to be much more fully "fleshed out" with case material than others, for most of the concepts in our Table of Contents are to some extent illumined by many cases in the book, not just by the ones listed as falling under any particular topic. Put another way, the listing of a case at one point in the outline rather than another by no means implies that the case is important only in that single connection. This being so, the cases in this book provide an adequate foundation for a comprehensive survey of Business Policy.

For teachers and students who nonetheless desire to go more deeply into certain section of the course or who feel the need for additional material on any concept, the companion casebook by Professors Learned, Christensen, and Andrews, *Problems of General Management,*[5] is suggested as a supplementary source. This volume contains five series of cases: some on a single company; some on several companies in a single industry—for example, the world wrist watch industry, with special emphasis on Swiss and American companies. Taken together, these two companion casebooks provide an opportunity for both extensive and intensive study of the entire field of Business Policy. They also provide even more of an international flavor than either casebook taken alone.

In the following remarks, which briefly explain key concepts in the field, reference will occasionally be made to cases in *Problems of General Management* as well as to the cases in the present book.

Introduction: Previewing Business Policy. In our preferred outline of topics, as the reader will observe, both the first and final sections are designed to provide an over-all look at the entire field. Such a broad-gauged survey is, we believe, best achieved through a *case series* rather than through a single case, and a series, of course, implies considerable length. Within the confines of the present book, it was not feasible to supply two series that the authors felt were particularly well adapted to these begin-

[5] E. P. Learned, C. R. Christensen, and K. R. Andrews, *Problems of General Management: Business Policy—A Series Casebook* (Homewood, Ill.: Richard D. Irwin, Inc., 1961).

ning and ending needs. We do include, however, a series of cases (The Galvor Company and associated industry notes) that could be used in either position—either at the start or at the end of a course.[6] Our first preference would be to use Galvor at the end and the Midway Foods Corporation series from *Problems of General Management* in the opening position.[7] This recommendation assumes that the course is built around both suggested texts rather than just this one. For a course designed around the present book alone, we would be inclined to sacrifice an opening case series; to rely instead on some introductory explanatory texts;[8] to move the Galvor series up into the section of the course dealing with the three major concepts of objectives, strategy, and policy;[9] and then perhaps to use Galvor again at the end as a means of summary and recapitulation, through which students could test out what they had learned not only from this course but from others in their training curriculum. The idea of teaching the same case twice may appear to some to be a pedagogic novelty, but it has been tried successfully at Harvard from time to time. What students will see in a case at the end of the course should be and will be substantially more than what they will find in it at the beginning.

This is not to say that even a relatively complex case cannot be rewarding if introduced early. The purpose of an introductory case or series is to provide perspective by introducing many of the problems, areas, or issues contained in the broad field of Business Policy. In a classroom situation, such a series provides a useful learning experience for students and professors alike. Students are exposed to the type of complex problems and situations they will be studying for the remainder of the year. On the very first day they have an opportunity to bring their own knowledge, imagination, and experience to bear on the content of the case. They are promptly placed in a dynamic relationship with fellow participants from whom they will be able to learn and to whom they may contribute. It is possible for the professor to encourage group effort in interpreting the case and to exercise his role as a discussion leader by helping class members stay with a point that has been raised and address themselves to each other's remarks. He can also start the class on the process of learning to think in terms of goals, strategies, policies, etc.; learning to diagnose risks and opportunities and relate them to company resources; and learning to make choices or decisions as to action.

Experienced businessmen and beginning students bring quite different

---

[6] The Galvor series was successfully used in the starting position in the Advanced Management course on Business Policy at Harvard in 1963.

[7] This arrangement was successful when employed in the IMEDE course, 1961–62.

[8] Part I of the Table of Contents for this book.

[9] Part II of the Table of Contents.

capacities to bear on an initial learning situation. The former come from many companies, many specialties, many different industries, and sometimes even (as at IMEDE) from many different nations. Such students are generally found only in middle management or advanced management programs. It can be predicted that they will bring to the initial case much depth of understanding. It can also quite confidently be predicted that they will advance many divergent interpretations of the meaning of particular facts in the case. Younger men, in contrast, often bring with them little or no business experience, and generally none at the executive level. On entering graduate business programs, they may have at their disposal little more than fertile imagination, zeal, and past academic training. But they use these assets to define problems and issues quickly. These men are less handicapped by lack of experience than one might expect.

Of course, neither the experienced businessmen nor the young trainees will get as much out of the first or preview cases on Business Policy as they will get out of the final or summary cases. As beginners, they get less in part because they are only starting the process of becoming a group; in part because they will learn a great deal about the nature of Business Policy and general management before they reach the end of the course.

Determining Objectives and Strategy. This section of the course relates to the role of general management in choosing suitable opportunities and adapting the firm to pursue them. It is concerned with such basic questions as the following: What should be the objectives, purposes, or goals of the company? What present and future opportunities can be identified within the industry or other industries for this particular firm? What actual or potential resources exist within the company for seizing this opportunity? What limitations might hold it back? What risks are inherent in the situation that might help to determine what can reasonably be attempted? In short, what course of action best fits in with the opportunities seen in the environment and with the company's essential competence, actual and potential?

Objectives can be defined as the essential purpose or mission of a company. (Sometimes the word "corporate image" is used to refer to a very broad statement of a firm's basic objective or raison d'être.) *Strategy* can be conceived of as the pattern of major policies and plans for achieving these major objectives, purposes, or goals. The definition of objectives and the development of strategy presuppose a careful study of a company's environment. In some respects the development of objectives, strategy, and plans for a business may be compared with military planning. In this analogy, objectives correspond with military mission, and strategy with the grand design for achieving the mission. Both the statement of the mission and the strategy involve careful assessment of "intelligence" with respect to the plans of a potential enemy (competitors). The battle analogy should not, however, be carried too far in connection with business, because there are many areas of agreement and even of legitimate cooperation between competing enterprises, especially with respect to industry positions on public questions.

In the paragraphs that follow, we shall propose a conceptual scheme for determining objectives and strategy. It is fully recognized that all companies do not follow every step in this pattern, for the theory of strategy formulation is only in its beginning stages, and there is a paucity of literature on the subject. Nevertheless, the following outline does represent a working model drawn from the experience of different firms, and it is one that could be used to advantage by any company without a great deal of elaboration or modification.

Let the student or practitioner of business begin by placing himself in the role of a general manager trying to induce his organization, under his guidance, to formulate objectives and a strategy that will ensure the survival of the firm. As a starting step, he certainly should analyze trends and endeavor to perceive his company's actual and potential relationship to its competitive, industrial, national, and international environments. For purposes of analysis, the major trends at which he should look may be classified as technical, economic, political, and social.

The term "technical trends" is used here in a very broad sense; it would include any trend inside or outside the business affecting product offerings, marketing, or production methods, financial and accounting techniques, and research developments and new technologies. Change is almost continuous in all these functional areas of business, but nowhere more rapid than in technology. For example, one has only to mention the implications for the chemical industry of the shift from coal to petroleum as the raw material for many old and new organic chemicals, or the implications for the airlines industry of the shift toward larger, faster, more expensive jet planes.

The term "economic trends" is also used here to cover a wide variety of meanings. Inside the business, economic trends are those related to a changing structure of revenues and costs for particular products or methods of doing business. The study of economic trends would also include analysis of the effect of public policy on the firm and the effect, in turn, of private economic policy on gross national product and public policy.

The importance of political trends need hardly be argued. The classical free-enterprise system has not been free for quite some time. Wars, revolutions, and gradual social evolution have all led to a closer connection between government and business than ever before, especially in Europe and America. As examples, one could mention the importance to business of changing national stances in relation to free trade or protection; to membership in international trading blocs; to policies in regard to promoting or limiting competition, regulating private business, or operating state-owned enterprises; to the cooperation of government with industry and labor in national economic planning; or to the interest of government in improving the growth pattern of the national economy.

Social trends are also important because they are pertinent to understanding how a business currently fits into its environment, how it can develop new opportunities in that environment, and how it may contribute to change in that environment. Social trends express themselves in the views of influential people or groups both inside and outside the business. They express themselves, too, in the views of management about the way to organize and run a business. The American student of business who wants to understand how European social and cultural traditions have moulded the European businessman may find a new book by Professor David Granick on *The European Executive*[10] a useful source. Among other things, this book reveals that there is no single pattern for European culture or for European businessmen. We believe, furthermore, that whatever past patterns have been, they are changing. While we would not be so bold as to generalize about the future businessmen of Europe on the basis of our limited acquaintance, nevertheless we saw many signs that the younger generation holds views that differ substantially from those of their elders. To some extent the new ideas are indigenous products that evolved out of the need for imaginative thinking to rebuild European industry after the destruction of World War II; to some extent they probably evolved from the trend toward international exchange of ideas, particularly between Europe and the New World's industrial nations. Each continent can learn from the other; neither has a monopoly on concepts useful for business administration. European nations have, in our opinion, led the way in creative adaptation of ideas brought in from each other or from overseas.

The whole purpose of analyzing these varied environmental trends is to make possible a better assessment of opportunities and risks for the firm and thus a sounder definition of its objectives and purposes. But looking at outside trends and, of course, at outside competition is only part of the task that must be done by managers prior to the final formulation of objectives. An equally important part is assessing the internal resources of the firm.

In working out objectives and strategy, a firm cannot avoid analyzing

10 Garden City, N.Y.: Doubleday & Co., Inc., 1962.

its existing physical, financial, and human resources so as to determine whether they are adequate, when properly allocated, to achieve the goals tentatively set. In the case of a small firm especially, an owner-manager will also wish to look at his own personal values (perhaps even at his own personal whims) before deciding his objectives. In all cases, the magnitude and type of a firm's resources help to determine what risks it must avoid, what opportunities it may pursue.

Among a company's internal resources, none is more critical than management talent. As indicated by several cases in this book, serious problems often result from a shortage of personnel competent to deal with the type and range of problems introduced by changing technology and other fast-moving environmental trends.

If management talent or other resources currently in hand appear inadequate to pursue favored goals, either the goals should be modified, or management should pause to make forward plans for adding to existing resources if it can. Potential resources as well as present ones are, of course, factors to consider in setting goals.

Developing Coordinated Policies. Once general management has formulated its objectives and strategy, it should ask what major company or departmental policies would be appropriate in guiding action toward these goals. Policy is a general set of guidelines (preferably, but not necessarily, explicit) that help to guide the employees of a firm in their day-to-day activities toward the company's objectives. Without policies, theoretically every decision would have to be either made each time on its own merits or referred to top management. There would be always the further possibility that both high and low levels of management might make *ad hoc* decisions that contradicted decisions by others, invalidated previous decisions, or undermined corporate goals. Once policies are set, management can concentrate on recognizing legitimate exceptions. Some of the broad functional areas in which policies are needed include product line selection; marketing, production, finance; accounting and control; personnel and industrial relations; procurement; public and governmental relations; and internal communications. Some of these areas are, of course, more important in a given situation than in others. Which ones are most important depends on a variety of factors. For example, a firm in a critical financial position may need to pay more attention to cost control and money management than a competitor with a healthy operating statement. A small firm competing on a basis of style and special service to customers may need to put more effort on the marketing area than a large competitor competing on the basis of cost.

Top management itself may wish to set not only company-wide policies but also those for important functional areas. In many instances, however, once a broad general policy has been determined, detailed policy is worked out by departmental personnel who have the delegated power to decide. Since policies in all functional areas need to be consistent not only with objectives but also with each other, men in charge of policy formulation within departments need ever to be alert to the cross-departmental implications of their policy determination. To the extent that they are alert, it may not be necessary to refer most of their policy decisions to higher echelons for ultimate general coordination. Companies included in this book used a wide range of means for coordinating policies. Observing the differences among the various approaches while studying the cases will prepare participants in the course for the types of situations which they may confront in their subsequent business careers. Partly because of the size of European firms (many of small or medium size) and partly because of long-established tradition, there is probably a greater tendency in Europe than in the United States for company policies to be decided at the top. That is, departmental policies as well as general company policies are made at the top initially, or are referred to the top for decision.

Because both external and internal factors are important in determining objectives, strategy, and policy, it is necessary to present in this section of the course some cases that contain well-developed data on industry trends or that are accompanied by industry notes. Examples of the latter included in this book are the Galvor series (the use of which has been discussed above) and the chemical industry notes and cases.[11] The latter series is especially strong on external data.

Making Forward Plans. Making forward plans has been singled out for special emphasis in our course design. In its broadest sense, planning is a part of a process of formulating objectives and strategy. In its narrower sense, which is what we have in mind here, planning consists of mapping a predetermined series of steps to implement the strategy previously adopted. Long-term planning should be distinguished from both forecasting and budgeting, although it depends on forecasts or estimates of future demand for products or services under consideration, and involves the preparation of capital budgets. What is essential in planning is programming a sequence of actions related to goals over some stated period of time.

The length of the planning period depends on the particular industry, product, or service being considered. The minimum time period must cover the longest lead time necessary for research, production, marketing, procurement of capital assets, and development of needed personnel. The

---

11 Part III of the Table of Contents.

maximum period is much harder to define. The conservative businessman limits definitive planning to a period no further into the future than that for which it is possible to attain accurate data and to set concrete, preferably numerical, goals. Other businessmen extend the period beyond this point and attempt an analysis of future opportunities that approaches "dreaming" about the future.

Once objectives, strategies, policies, and long-range plans have been set, the remaining major functions of general management are concerned more with the operating aspects or implementation of plans and policies than with the making of policy per se. These remaining tasks are described below.

Building an Organization.   General management has a major responsibility for building an organization to accomplish its objectives and strategy. The work of the firm must be analyzed so that it can be broken down into activities which then must be assigned to different people, performed in some logical sequence, and coordinated. Thus the organizational design must reflect the flow of work and need for cooperative effort between individuals, groups, and departments or functions. Analyzing the job to be done is thus the key to designing—or understanding—organization.[12]

The job of designing the organization can easily be broken into many subtasks, such as determining needs, structuring organizational units, assigning and developing personnel, fixing responsibility, delegating authority, and establishing accountability. An astute manager will also recognize that, besides the formal organization, there is a so-called informal organization in every company, and that the relationship between the two is something he must consider in his actions. Also he must consider what is the optimum pattern of relationships between staff and line units and between headquarters and the field. American companies have typically carried staff developments much further than European companies. They have also delegated more decision making down the line.

Implicit in the task of assigning and developing personnel are the problems of recruitment and the age-old problem of adapting or restructuring the ideal organization, based upon a logical determination of corporate needs, to the strengths and weaknesses of the individuals available or procurable for assignment to managerial jobs. These persons seldom have the personal characteristics and business capacity required to match the precise job descriptions in an ideally structured organization. The practical businessman has to utilize the people he has, and he has to utilize

---

[12] See, in this connection, Wilfred Brown, *Exploration in Management* (New York: John Wiley & Sons and London: W. H. Heinemann, 1960).

their strengths as well as make allowances for their limitations. It is a commonplace that few "ideal" organizations exist because of people, i.e., manning problems.

To argue that the organization must be adapted to the people available is not to deny that the optimum organization must be derived from an analysis of the work to be done, or to assert that the ideal structure is a function of the particular personalities involved. We believe that top management can go too far in adapting structure to personalities. When requirements imposed by the work to be done are given insufficient weight, not only inefficiency but interpersonal friction develops. Thus going too far in giving recognition to personalities is self-defeating. It can generate more strains and problems than it solves.

Mergers and Joint Ventures. Partly because mergers and joint ventures are so often used to hasten and (hopefully) to simplify implementation of basic company objectives (for example, diversification), they are worth lifting up for special study in a casebook on Business Policy. Indeed, these devices merit special attention anyway in a book on European business, for their use in Europe is even more widespread than in the United States. Moreover, they raise a wide range of interesting internal problems for the participating firms and an equally wide range of external or socio-economic problems involving the relationship of the business enterprise to its environment.[13]

For all these reasons, mergers and joint ventures have been given a special section of their own in this text.[14] Actually, references to mergers and joint ventures frequently appear in other sections, too, reflecting their widespread use in Western Europe. For example, numerous joint ventures are referred to in the notes on the European chemical industry,[15] and the factors that have led to joint ventures in this segment of the economy have been operative also in other segments. The natural concern of European businessmen with merger problems caused the 1961–62 students at IMEDE to be especially responsive to these cases.

Reasons for merger may be numerous and varied. As listed in a recent study of the related phenomenon of acquisition,[16] they include achieving

---

[13] In the United States especially, owing to well-publicized activities of a few individuals and firms, mergers are too much associated in the public mind with "wheeling and dealing." As a study of the cases in this text and in Learned, Christensen, and Andrews makes clear, mergers can be and are often used by responsible businessmen as a logical and legitimate means of perceiving carefully chosen corporate goals. See especially the Merck & Co., Inc., series in *Problems of General Management.*

[14] Part VI.

[15] Part III.

[16] Myles L. Mace and George G. Montgomery, Jr., *Problems of Corporate Acquisitions* (Boston: Division of Research, Harvard Business School, 1962).

a company's general plan for growth, serving a market need, buying time, acquiring technical know-how, achieving product diversification, and finding outlets for investment funds.

In this same source the reader may find an illuminating discussion of some important problems of integrating two or more firms, especially the impact on personnel, interorganizational relationships, management controls, and dealing with key people. Some of these problems are well illustrated by merger cases in the present book.

Developing Standards of Executive Performance. The need for standards and judgment is implicit in any situation where the management task is divided among two or more persons or is delegated in part to lower echelons. Except in owner-operated companies, the top manager expects to be judged by his board of directors. He, in turn, is likely to make either intuitive or formal judgments of his key subordinates—be they vice-presidents of marketing, production, research, finance, etc., or product or geographical division managers in more highly decentralized organizations. His subordinates likewise in turn judge other lower-ranking executives. These in turn judge supervisors and so on down the line. Even staff personnel, whose output is often less tangible than that of a manufacturing or sales executive, are subject to appraisal.

The standard of appraisal for top-ranking executives may range from a seemingly mechanical one based on the return earned on investment committed to the executive's care,[17] to an elaborate breakdown of general and specific objectives to be achieved in measurable terms in the next fiscal year.[18] Setting standards for appraising executives is a relatively undeveloped subject compared with devising ways of measuring output for factory and office workers or salesmen. Complicating the task of creating an effective executive plan is the fact that psychological factors must be taken into account.[19] Most executives are willing to judge their peers and their subordinates but are neither very willing to be judged themselves nor able to understand and allow for a similar reluctance on the part of others.

In view of a trend toward more explicit and more highly developed standards for judging executives, we think it is important to state a philosophy of control that gives meaning to these standards and considers their human aspects. From a top-executive viewpoint, at least, an organization as a whole can be considered under control when (*a*) key people at execu-

---

[17] For a discussion of this approach, see the two articles by Professor John Dearden, reproduced in Part VII of the text.

[18] The case on Phelps Company, ICH 3G 15, which is listed in the Intercollegiate Bibliography, illustrates the latter type of approach in its early stages of implementation. See also Virgil K. Rowland, *Managerial Performance Standards* (New York: American Management Association, 1960); Edward C. Schleh, *Management by Results: The Dynamics of Profitable Management* (New York: McGraw-Hill Book Co., Inc., 1961).

[19] See the article by Professor Likert, reproduced below in Part VII.

tive and supervisory levels have high standards of performance as a norm for judging ongoing operations or activities, (*b*) these standards are generally accepted at levels where operations are performed and funds spent, and (*c*) everyone with responsibility makes a personal effort to correct deviations from these standards.

Under this philosophy, control is widespread throughout a company; it occurs, if at all, in the here and now. In contrast, so-called accounting or budgetary controls merely record long after the event that the company's activities were or were not up to standard.

It is not our purpose here—nor, indeed, is it the job of Business Policy —to describe and evaluate all the available methods for controlling operations, individual supervisors, or executives. Such specialized know-how can best be obtained through other disciplines. We do wish to stress, however, that, whatever control system is used, it is important that both the person judging and the person being judged should understand and agree to the standard being employed. Such agreement and understanding may determine the real commitment of both parties to a desired standard. Deep and voluntary commitment is important, since good and efficient operation involves a substantial amount of self-control by subordinates rather than directives from superiors. Top management's approach to this problem and its behavior pattern in setting the style of review of performance against standards is very likely to have a significant effect on the results achieved.

Executive Motivation and Incentives. The topic of executive motivation and incentives has been placed after the topic of standards and appraisals for logical reasons. Executives first have a need to understand their responsibility and authority, a need to know for what and to whom they are accountable, a need to know what the standards of acceptable performance are, and a need to know what results or successes they have achieved. Finally, but most importantly, they expect to be rewarded or possibly punished accordingly.

In gathering European cases for this book, we did not set out to gather material bearing especially on executive motivation, partly because we lacked the time and partly because we doubted that we were adequately steeped in the culture of European countries to appreciate fully the various important nonmonetary aspects of an executive incentive program. Nevertheless, several of our cases[20] do contain data on the needs of executives,

---

[20] See especially Part V on Building an Organization, Part VII on Executive Control and Executive Leadership, and Part VIII on The Total Management Process as illustrated in the many cases on The Galvor Company.

In the companion volume, *Problems of General Management*, the cases on Midway Foods Corporation, the National Finance Company, and Merck & Co., Inc., also contain data on this important subject.

their personal motivations, and the rewards that appeal to them. Much light is also shed by the same cases on the nature of executive development and executive controls.

Executive Leadership. The importance of the top-executive role has already been stressed in our earlier discussion of the "generalist" or overall manager and his contribution to both business and society. Here we are mostly concerned with discussing patterns of executive leadership as exemplified in all sections of this book and, of course, by all real-life situations. Readers are urged to classify and compare these patterns and to bring to bear knowledge and experience from other disciplines, including human relations.

We know by experience that the cases in this book will raise questions about the nature of executive authority. There is likely to be much argument about authoritative versus democratic management without enough realization that no leader is likely to satisfy all followers. The task role, which is such a large part of an executive's role, will be contrasted to the social role performed by many informal leaders. To what extent an executive can function as both a task leader and a social leader is a question that intrigues many persons.

The role of the leader in the communication process is another factor that always comes up for discussion. Student participants early show a great capacity to criticize the communication failures of the persons in the case. The differences between what is being said by the "transmitting" person and what is being heard by the "receiving" person are often spotted. How to improve two-way communication is not so easy to discern. As a result, we advocate that students be assigned specific roles in the case—be it as superiors or as subordinates—in order to sharpen their skills in the course of group discussion with each other.

We believe that the foregoing discussion is enough to demonstrate the significance of the leadership issue. The rewards of intensive study are limited only by the interests of students and the time available for analysis and collateral reading. One question which each participant must answer for himself is what ideas he wishes to make a part of his own evolving philosophy of management and leadership. The answer is a highly personal one. Uniform answers are out of the question because people are too different.

In the following passages we offer some statements that suggest our own views as to the characteristics or attributes that we would prefer to see in company leaders of the future.[21] This list should by no means be regarded as definitive or authoritative. Rather, readers should hold it in mind and attempt to test its validity in appraising leadership as observed both in case material and in personal experiences. According to our view, the most effective business leaders of the next two decades will be those of whom the following characterization will hold true:

1. These managers will realize that the ultimate success of most businesses depends on the effective and efficient performance of services or the production of products that are or will be in demand.

2. They will realize that they are managers of resources of men, materials, and funds and have some responsibility to use these in socially productive ways.

3. They will view profits as one criterion of success rather than the beginning and end of all their efforts. They will recognize that other values have to be taken into account in adapting the enterprise to its total environment and they will seek to understand what the optimum balance is. This is not an easy job, as the criteria for judgment are not too well established.

4. Within the context of the foregoing, these managers will be profit seekers themselves and also will develop profit-seeking subordinates. They will be:

a) Looking for opportunities for profits in supplying new products, new services, and improvements in old products or services;

b) Measuring the revenue effect of every dollar they spend on products or services;

c) Stopping profit leaks by dropping lines, customers, or markets that cannot be made to pay within a reasonable time;

d) Seeking less expensive ways of producing the same products or services;

e) Endeavoring to exercise revenue control by finding ways to upgrade products and services so as to give consumers or industrial users more useful and often higher-valued products.

5. These men will look for ways to use capital effectively. They will try to reduce the required capital investment in order to utilize this resource economically and to increase the return on investment. They will behave as if company funds were personal funds.

6. To borrow a phrase from a former colleague, Mr. R. S. McNamara, former president of the Ford Motor Company and now Secretary of Defense of the United States, the managers of the future should be "take-charge guys." They should be willing to accept responsibility individually and to make decisions within the range delegated to them. They should seek out the principal resources within or without the company that can

---

21 The senior author presented this list in his final course summary at IMEDE in 1962.

contribute to the solution of the task assigned, and integrate these contributions into their decision or recommended action so far as possible.

7. Managers should provide for the development of other take-charge guys through the subdelegation of leadership opportunities.

8. The wise manager will feel a special obligation to protect minority ideas in his organization, for he will realize that most forward advances have originated with persons who thought differently and/or made original proposals that implied change and criticism of the established ways of doing things. A manager must somehow encourage change while at the same time he endeavors to maintain a moving equilibrium or balance.

9. Managers of the future should be experts in encouraging human involvement and developing human satisfactions in the required work of business institutions. They should go out of their way to get people involved in responsibility and decision making appropriate to their task. Since so many men learn by doing, it is important to give them meaningful tasks to do. Men have to be allowed to make some mistakes, but they should be expected to learn from their mistakes. Above all else, a manager must display faith in his working colleagues and subordinates. The climate set is very important.

A large part of the fun of management is in organizing in such a way as to release the creativity of your subordinates and your peers. Not all men will want responsibility. One of the jobs of management is to provide opportunity for those who want it and to spot those who don't and won't take it. It is foolish to push the latter too far, and wise to give the former more and more to do.

We have an opportunity to show our faith in men by our deeds and words. Put another way, this point implies the following concept of the leader.

In a very broad and much more real sense than is generally supposed, the administrative leader is trying to integrate the needs of the organization with the requirements of the individual for growth and personal development. Unless he understands people as individuals and realizes their expectations, as well as those of the group as a whole, he will not have defined the limits or the opportunities of his work. . . . The concept of the leader as one who helps the organization to do is in fact vastly broader in scope than the concept of the leader as one who holds the helm alone.[22]

The Total Management Process. While, for the alert executive, the study of Business Policy never ends, the ending section of our course or

---

[22] E. P. Learned, D. N. Ulrich, and D. R. Booz, *Executive Action* (Boston: Division of Research, Harvard Business School, 1951), pp. 211, 208.

book is, like the beginning section, designed to provide an opportunity for looking at the field as a whole. Not only Business Policy concepts, but techniques and tools, and learning and experience gained elsewhere should be brought to bear on the analysis of a final series of cases that present all the multifaceted aspects of a total company situation: environmental trends; company resources; objectives, strategy, and policies; patterns of leadership, control, and organization.

For purposes of making such a review, the authors suggest The Galvor Company series, presented in the final section of this book. Of particular interest in this series is the role of top management in leading the organization to make productive and satisfying adaptations to growth and change.

LEARNING EXPERIENCE AND THE CASE METHOD

Under the so-called case method of instruction, there are three important elements in the classroom experience. There is the case itself, the student participants, and the professor. In addition, the objectives of the course as previously stated on page 000 should be kept in mind.

The Case.   What is a case? As defined by a former colleague, Professor Charles I. Gragg,

> A case typically is a record of a business issue which *actually* has been faced by business executives, together with surrounding facts, opinions, and prejudices upon which executive decisions had to depend. These real and particularized cases are presented to students for considered analysis, open discussion, and final decision as to the type of action which should be taken. . . . In other words, students are not given general theories or hypotheses to criticize. Rather, they are given specific facts, the raw materials, out of which decisions have to be reached. . . .[23]

It should be stated, too, that no case is specifically designed to present an illustration of either effective or ineffective handling of problems. Rather, the purpose is to make the case as faithful to the facts of real life—be they "good" or "bad"—as space permits.

At the beginning of a course based on case material, the first case assigned often seems to multiply into as many different cases as there are students in the class! Each member of the group tends to perceive the facts of a case or business situation in accordance with his own particular background and experience. It takes time for men to achieve a reasonable degree of agreement about the meaning of the facts or opinions expressed in a case. This initial diversity and the reasons giving rise to it provide

---

[23] Charles I. Gragg, "Because Wisdom Can't Be Told," *Harvard Alumni Bulletin*, October 19, 1940.

one of the best lessons in the complex character of the communications process that students are likely to get. Insights grow, however, during a discussion, and eventually the real problems to be solved will be isolated, the possible solutions will be clarified, the criteria for making choices will be determined, and conclusions will be revised in the light of close reasoning about the facts and the people in the case. Unfortunately, we cannot promise unanimous agreement on any one conclusion. Few classes ever reach a single answer on all discussion issues or recommendations. It is an important learning experience, however, for each student to know why his answers differ from those of others.

The Student Participant. The student has already dominated our discussion of the case, and we have emphasized the complications caused by the diversity of student background and experience, which in turn reflects itself in a diversity of case interpretations. Although such disagreement may delay case analysis and recommendations, it has its advantages too. Once students realize how much they differ, they begin to understand the behavior and thought processes of others; they learn to predict the behavior of their classmates in the classroom organization; and they start to gain experience in seeking to change other people's beliefs or behavior. In this process, students also become more self-aware, especially if the professor from time to time invites the class to interpret its own experience in problem solving. A well-conducted class should result in the creation of a great debt due from each participant to his fellows.

The Professor. The professor's role in a case discussion is to assist in student-centered learning. As Professor Gragg has put it, the case method offers a real stimulus as well as a real challenge to students to make an independent contribution:

> By the same token the stage is so set as to simplify the teacher's task of encouraging students to participate actively in the process of learning. The students are given the raw materials and are expected to use them. The teacher, for his part, has every opportunity and reason to demonstrate an encouraging receptivity as well as to inform and guide.[24]

Under student-centered learning, the professor must avoid trying to share his wisdom and learning by lecturing or otherwise taking over in the class. Professor Gragg has put this point as follows:

> It would be easy to accept the unanalyzed assumption that by passing on, by lectures and readings, to young men of intelligence the accumulated experience and wisdom of those who have made business their study, the desired results could be achieved. . . .

---

[24] *Ibid.*

This assumption, however, rests on another, decidedly questionable one: namely, the assumption that it is possible by a simple process of telling to pass on knowledge in a useful form. This is the great delusion of the ages. If the learning process is to be effective, something dynamic must take place in the learner. The truth of this statement becomes more and more apparent as the learner approaches the inevitable time when he must go into action.[25]

Even at the end of a class discussion the professor will rarely, if at all, expound his own interpretation or solution. Such action not only would tend to inhibit free, creative student discussion over time but would generate a belief—usually false—that there is one and only one "right" answer to each case and that the teacher knows just what it is. Professor Gragg has eloquently warned against this view:

The case plan of instruction may be described as democratic in distinction to the telling method, which is in effect dictatorial or patriarchal. With the case method, all members of the academic group, teacher *and* students, are in possession of the same basic materials in the light of which analyses are to be made and decisions arrived at. Each, therefore, has an identical opportunity to make a contribution to the body of principles governing business practice and policy. Business is not, at least not yet, an exact science. There is no single, demonstrably right answer to a business problem. For the student or business-man it cannot be a matter of peeking in the back of a book to see if he has arrived at the right solution. In every business situation, there is always a reasonable possibility that the best answer has not yet been found—even by teachers.[26]

All this is not to imply that the teacher plays a purely passive role. One thing he can do is to provide a conceptual scheme—a framework of terms and ideas that should help the student to think constructively about material in the cases.[27] This may be done in summaries, lecturettes, definitions, and in assignments of outside reading not necessarily connected with any particular case, but rather with each section of the course.

Another thing the professor can do is to limit the amount of time spent on analysis and criticism of behavior or decisions made by persons described in the case. It is easy for students to carry diagnosis of a case situation beyond the point of optimum return, thereby subtracting too much from the time available for propounding and discussing solutions. Such misallocation of time is one thing the professor can endeavor to avoid by the way he handles the class.

Still another thing the professor can do is to summarize discussion, holding up points of agreement or dispute. Summaries at the end of a

---

25 *Ibid.*

26 *Ibid.*

27 In effect, this introductory section of our book is an effort to provide such a conceptual framework or scheme to facilitate the study of the Policy cases that follow.

class are especially likely to be welcomed. The professor can also interject leading questions from time to time that will help the students to penetrate deeper into some aspect of the case, to open up new aspects, or to make meaningful comparisons among companies. Confining himself to these rather limited contributions will be very frustrating to the professor, but only by restricting his own role can he fulfill his objective of converting students from "passive absorbers" of knowledge into "partners in the joint process of learning and further learning."[28]

At this point, let us turn to look in more detail at what it is the student *can* learn from the case method and the student-centered learning process that we have been describing above.

Knowledge and Skills That May Be Learned. It is impossible to summarize briefly the knowledge to which learners are exposed in Business Policy. Some of it is only old knowledge that becomes more meaningful when viewed in a new perspective or applied to the solution of a policy problem. Some of it is new knowledge. Within the latter category, special mention must be made of the opportunity provided in Business Policy to learn more about the ways in which organizations work. For example, who is responsible for setting objectives, making policies, and solving problems of various kinds? What human resources are available within the firm for providing suggestions and information, and what pattern of leadership most effectively develops and uses these resources? How do the people at the top motivate and control subordinates? What channels should exist for communication among levels of executives and among functional departments or areas?

As to the skills that might be sharpened or acquired through exposure to Business Policy, these may be roughly divided into two gross categories: those that are useful in analyzing any type of material and those that are especially useful in thinking about Business Policy, although their application would not necessarily be limited to this one field.

In the first category, we might include the skills to do the following:

1. Distinguish between facts and assumptions (his own and other peoples').

2. Take a point of view and marshall evidence in support of it.

3. Address oneself to the arguments of others instead of going off on a tangent.

4. Recognize the extent to which people's diagnoses and interpretations of the same situation will vary, based on their own backgrounds, values, and experiences.

---

[28] Gragg, *op. cit.*

5. Reason logically about data and, where data are missing, define what else is needed.

In the second category, we might list abilities or skills to do the following kinds of things:

1. Look for the presence or absence of objectives that are precise enough to provide meaningful guides to action.

2. Identify implicit as well as explicit objectives of a firm.

3. Assess the risks and opportunities provided by the environment.

4. Assess the resources of the firm, especially its human resources, in relation to actual or possible objectives.

5. Distinguish which functional activities must be performed especially well to meet the needs of the market or markets the company has chosen to serve.

6. Translate general objectives and policies into specific actions.

7. Make choices in such a way as to utilize strengths and to minimize the impact of weaknesses and risks.

8. Discern inconsistencies—as between objectives and resources, objectives and policies, and between policies in one area and those in another.

9. Recognize nascent, as well as fully developed, problems; forecast future problems by projecting current trends.

10. Distinguish among problems as to relative seriousness and urgency.

11. Devise actions to meet and overcome problems and risks in ways that are consistent with company resources and, if necessary, with industry trends.

12. Plan actions in a logical and related sequence over a specified future period.

13. Predict the consequences of proposals and actions; think in terms of long-range, as well as short-range, effects.

14. Consider the organizational implications of proposed strategies and actions as well as the human or personal implications.

We are confident that men who really understand what Business Policy is about will grow in personal ability and will be useful not only to their companies but also to their national economies. As young executives, they will have a better understanding of problems confronting the heads of their companies. In more responsible positions, they will earn an ever increasing satisfaction from the important roles they play in providing product, services, and/or human satisfactions for their customers and fellow workers. If men are allowed to pursue their social goals and are supported by their colleagues, their companies should be able to command the capital required and should succeed in earning a return on stockholders' investment.

PART II

Business Objectives, Strategy, and Policy

ALFRED HERBERT LTD. (A)

JAQUIER S.A.

PROCESS MACHINERY EUROPE, INC.

BERLINER-APOTHEKER A.G.

FOR INSTITUTIONS using only cases in this book for the teaching of Business Policy, Alfred Herbert Ltd. makes a good beginning. Because the objectives of the firm are clear, students gain a feel for the meaning of the words "objectives" and "strategy." Because major policies are clearly delineated, students gain a better understanding of what a major policy is. Alfred Herbert is an interesting firm because of its manifold expansion from little more than an idea to one of the largest machine tool companies in the world. It is interesting to ponder the possible connection between this growth and the marketing concept, which were at the basis of its strategy in its very early years. Particular attention is directed to the firm's definition of its purpose and also to the founder's personal values, which have been successfully incorporated into the purposes of the firm. Finally, Alfred Herbert is interesting because, unlike many Continental firms, it is a company in which men can enter at the bottom and rise to the board-of-director level.

The second case, Jaquier S.A., permits evaluation of the competitive strategy employed by one Swiss watch company and discussion of associated problems. This case was released too late to be included in the studies of the world wrist watch industry published in Learned, Christensen, and Andrews *Problems of General Management.* Students using the latter book will find its "Note on the World Wrist Watch Industry" very helpful background for the discussion of the Jaquier case. Students will also find some interesting points of contrast among the strategies of the several watch companies described in the two books.

In both the foregoing cases, it is wise to discuss the basic question of what is or should be the basic strategy of the firm. Is this strategy related to the distinctive competence of the company and to world-wide industry trends? In addition, both cases permit identification and evaluation of the policies that each company has developed in each major functional area of the business in order to carry out its basic strategy. In Alfred Herbert policies are explicitly stated, while in Jaquier they must to some extent be inferred. Both cases have international dimensions, particularly Jaquier, because of a current crisis recorded in the case regarding its relationships with customers in the United States.

As we stated earlier, these two cases could well be followed by the Galvor series (Part VIII of our Table of Contents) if this is the only textbook being used. While Galvor makes an excellent ending case, it is even more important to make an early presentation of a fairly complex series in which all aspects of Business Policy can be brought to the student's attention.

The last two cases—Process Machinery Europe, Inc., and Berliner-Apotheker A.G.—are limited to narrower aspects of Business Policy. The management of Process Machinery Europe, Inc., was concerned about rationalizing its plants in several European countries. Students should evaluate the arguments for and against the rationalization presented in the case, decide which are economically and technically valid and which represent mostly human rationalizations of questionable validity. Whether valid or not, however, the opinions are offered by men of status and competence and are therefore stubborn realities which must be understood and given weight. To bring the problem of this company beyond the realm of mere analysis to that of action, the student should ask, "If I were Mr. Bruyère, what would I do?" There is also a major question implicit in this case as to what methodology the company should use to come up with rational facts that bear on the question of where the 80,000 components of its machines should be produced.

The Berliner-Apotheker case highlights political and economic questions. What should the manager of this West Berlin company do in response to these outside environmental pressures?

ALFRED HERBERT LTD. (A)

INTRODUCTION

In 1962 Alfred Herbert Ltd., of Coventry, England, was described by company officials as "the largest British manufacturer of machine tools and the largest machine tool organization in the world." Sir Alfred Herbert, who founded the company in the late nineteenth century, largely dominated its management until his death in 1957. He and his top executives had developed a group of policies which they used as guide lines in their direction of the company's progress. This case describes the development of, and rationale for, these policies.

COMPANY BACKGROUND

EARLY HISTORY OF THE COMPANY

In his memoirs, Sir Alfred Herbert wrote:

It was intended that I should go to a university with the idea of becoming a parson, but having seen an old school-fellow, William Hubbard, (a farmer's son like myself) at work on a small lathe, whilst apprenticed to a firm of engineers, Joseph Jessop & Sons in Leicester, I persuaded my father to let me follow his example.

At the end of my apprenticeship I was offered a job of managing a small and not very flourishing general engineering shop, owned by Coles & Matthews in The Butts, Coventry. After a year or so my old school-fellow and fellow apprentice, William Hubbard, joined me in partnership and we bought the Coles & Matthews business and carried on as Herbert & Hubbard.

Our respective fathers gave us £2,000 each by way of capital. A small workshop was built which cost £232.

Having a comparatively small turnover and the low prices at which we were selling, we were not making much of a living. We were then fortunate in finding a sideline which was largely responsible for a marked improvement in our finances. We secured the agency for Great Britain to sell weld-less steel tubes made by a French Company.

Owing to our close contact with the cycle industry, we developed a good turnover with satisfactory profit. We even exported a quantity to America.

After some years of partnership, I bought Hubbard's share of the business and carried on under my own name, until a small private company of which I was Chairman and Governing Director, was formed in 1894.

At the turn of the century, we imported machines—lathes, planers, shapers and drills—from Lodge and Davies of America. These were installed in our own plant both for use and demonstration. We soon began to sell these machines very freely throughout the country and this was the beginning of our importing business.

COMPANY GROWTH

One measure of the company's expansion, the total number employed, is found in Table 1.

Table 1

TOTAL EMPLOYEES OF ALFRED HERBERT LTD., SELECTED YEARS

Year	Employees*	Year	Employees
1899	12	1935	3,700
1910	1,600	1938	4,500
1921	2,700	1960	5,900
		1962	7,350

* Employment figures do not include foreign employees nor, except for the 1962 figure, do they include employees of United Kingdom subsidiaries.
Source: Company officials.

Table 2 gives financial indications of the company's growth in recent years. Table 3 contains certain financial ratios of the Herbert Group in recent years. Table 4 contains balance sheets and income statements for Alfred Herbert Ltd. and the Herbert Group for the year ending October 31, 1961.

COMPANY OPERATIONS

In 1962 the company operated nine manufacturing plants in the United Kingdom: four under its own name and five belonging to subsidiaries. These plants had total floor space of almost 1,500,000 square feet, employed about 7,500 employees, and used some 3,500 machine tools. Each plant specialized in a product or group of products.

The company's selling organization was spread throughout all the machine tool consuming countries of the world except Iron Curtain countries and China. Sales have been made into Iron Curtain countries through their official importing agencies. Subsidiary companies operated in Australia, India, France, and Italy, and selling agents had been appointed in 57 other countries. This network of selling agencies was not only broad, but deep: in the United States, for example, there were 11 Herbert agents strategically spread throughout the country. Foreign sales formed a con-

Table 2

SELECTED FINANCIAL STATISTICS, 1945–61, FOR ALFRED HERBERT LTD.
AND THE HERBERT GROUP (£000's)

Year	Net Profit of AH Ltd.	Net Profit of Group*	Group Net Worth	Group Assets	Common Dividends Paid†
1961	1,746	1,800	19,864	27,833	928
1960	1,601	1,737	19,272	25,399	983
1959	1,335	1,366	18,520	24,069	765
1958	1,418	1,560	17,969	24,255	655
1957	1,821	1,882	17,129	23,854	655
1956	1,798	1,913	15,375	22,043	410
1955	1,771	1,872	13,855	19,629	346
1954	1,483	1,601	12,302	17,394	328
1953	1,348	1,445	11,064	17,249	228
1952	1,186	1,250	9,819	16,980	196
1951	926	972	8,777	14,818	152
1950	756	888	7,739	10,871	121
1949	711	797	6,971	9,800	121
1948	833	864	6,307	9,253	134
1947	533	567	5,680	8,225	121
1946	363	363	5,205	6,944	121
1945	461	471	4,694	6,543	121

* After deducting net profits attributable to outside shareholders.
† In 1945, 1948, 1952, 1955, and 1960 minor capital distributions were made (the largest one was £54,619 in 1960) to the common shareholders, and these distributions have been included in the above dividend figures.
Source: Published financial statements of company.

Table 3

FINANCIAL RATIOS FOR THE HERBERT GROUP

Year	Group Net Profit as Per Cent of Equity*	Group Net Profit as Per Cent of Assets	Increase or (Decrease) in Group Profit from Previous Year	Dividend Payout Ratio†	Equity as a Per Cent of Total Assets
1961	9.1	6.5	3.6%	51.6%	71.4
1960	9.0	6.8	27.2	56.6	75.9
1959	7.4	5.7	(12.4)	56.0	76.9
1958	8.7	6.4	(17.1)	42.0	74.1
1957	11.0	7.9	(1.6)	34.8	71.8
1955	13.5	9.5	16.9	18.5	70.6
1950	11.5	8.2	11.4	13.6	71.2
1945	10.0	7.2	(21.8)	25.7	71.7

* The true net worth of the company was actually somewhat higher than as shown in Table 2; the company treated as a liability (in conformity with British law) estimated income tax which would be owed on profits not yet earned; in 1961 this liability for future income tax amounted to £1,205,000 (see Table 4).
† This ratio was calculated by taking total common dividends as a per cent of total group net profit. A modest amount of preferred dividends had, in reality, first to be deducted from the group net profit, but such preferred dividends, which averaged about £10,000 annually from 1947 to 1961, were relatively unimportant to this calculation.
Source: Computed from Table 2 statistics by IMEDE staff.

Table 4

FINANCIAL DATA FOR ALFRED HERBERT, 1961 (FIGURES ROUNDED TO £000's)
BALANCE SHEET, OCTOBER 31, 1961

Assets	AH Ltd.	Group	Liabilities	AH Ltd.	Group
Current:			**Current:**		
Cash	367	512	Payables	3,236	4,004
Investments*	5,814	6,050	Overdraft	.....	325
Receivables	6,758	7,087	Accrued dividends ...	655	655
			Owed to subsidiaries..	306	.....
Inventories	8,005	10,216	Accrued taxes	1,573	1,622
TOTAL CURRENT	20,944	23,865	TOTAL CURRENT	5,770	6,606
Investment in Subsidiaries	1,898	.....	*Estimated future* tax liability	1,205	1,226
Fixed (net of depreciation)			Minority interests in subsidiaries	.....	137
Land and buildings ...	1,174	1,731	**Equity:**		
Plant	1,318	1,655	Share capital	11,200	11,200
Other fixed	459	582	General reserve	692	838
			Retain profit	6,927	7,744
TOTAL FIXED	2,951	3,968	Other reserves	.....	82
TOTAL ASSETS	25,794	27,833			
			TOTAL EQUITY	18,819	19,864
			TOTAL LIABILITIES ...	25,794	27,833

* Includes investments in various gilt-edged securities and government obligations.

INCOME STATEMENT—YEAR ENDING OCTOBER 31, 1961

	AH Ltd.	Group
Trading profit	3,169	3,304
Interest and dividends on investments	252	263
Dividends from subsidiaries	73	.....
Profit from sale of assets	4	16
PROFIT BEFORE TAXES	3,498	3,583
LESS: Income taxes	−1,752	−1,768
PROFIT AFTER TAXES	1,746	1,815
LESS: Profits attributable to outside shareholders	.....	− 15
FINAL NET PROFIT	1,746	1,800
LESS: Preferred dividends	− 10	− 10
Common dividends	− 928	− 928
TRANSFERRED TO RETAINED EARNINGS	808	862

Source: Published financial statements of company.

siderable portion of Herbert's business: in 1961 over one-third of the company's production was exported.

Herbert began to trade abroad early in its history. The Paris agency was opened in 1903, and in 1907 it was changed to a subsidiary corporation, Société Anonyme Alfred Herbert. Herbert S.A. not only imported machines from the parent company but also subcontracted a considerable number of Herbert designs to French manufacturers under license. The Indian company, which was founded in 1909, was the largest of the four subsidiaries. It had branches in six Indian cities; the main office, in Calcutta, employed over 300 people in 1962.

The Italian subsidiary, established in 1917, did no subcontracting but imported all its machines from the United Kingdom. The Australian company, which had opened in 1919, was also confined to warehousing and marketing operations; no subcontracting was done there.

Herbert's foreign subsidiaries and agencies handled the lines of other machine tool manufacturers in addition to the standard Herbert line. Each of these factoring arrangements was individually drawn up, and it sometimes happened that Herbert would act as agent in the United Kingdom for one manufacturer of, say, milling machines, and in Australia as agent for another United Kingdom manufacturer of similar machines. The only policy restricting such factoring arrangements throughout the world was this: an individual Herbert company, or agency, could not, within its own region, sell machines which competed with one another.

As distinct from arrangements made by subsidiary companies with their own principals, the United Kingdom company's selling arrangements with its principals varied among: (*a*) the company's sales organisation handling the sales of all of a principal's output both in the United Kingdom and overseas; (*b*) selling in the United Kingdom and certain designated countries overseas; and (*c*) for the United Kingdom only.

Company records maintained a definite distinction between Alfred Herbert Ltd. and the Herbert Group. The Group embraced not only the parent company, with its four plants in the United Kingdom, but also the five British and four foreign subsidiaries.

KEY HERBERT POLICIES

PRODUCT POLICY

Herbert and Hubbard began manufacturing machine tools in 1886, at which time Alfred Herbert was 20 years old. The earliest machines produced were small drilling machines and hand-operated lathes. By 1894, when the company became Alfred Herbert Ltd., it was well established as a manufacturer of lathes. Herbert was the first British machine tool firm to sell not only the machines themselves but also all the tooling and accessories needed for their operation.

From the beginning, the company accepted the important principle that no one firm had or could hope to acquire the technical "know-how" to make successfully all the known types of machine tools. This was a recognition of the advantages of specialisation long before it was generally recognised by industry. As a result of specialisation, certain firms throughout the world had evolved and developed machine tools that had established themselves as outstanding for the purposes for which they were designed.

The company therefore decided, as a matter of policy, to specialise in its own line of production and, in order to fulfill a customer's request for types outside its own range, to sell the products of other leading machine tool makers. In this way the company rationalised the selling of its own products and those of other manufacturers of complementary types of machines far in advance of the commercial thinking of the first quarter of this century.

Subsequently the company decided, by arrangement with leading makers of machine tools, to make, under licence, machine tools of outstanding design and merit. In this way Herbert either built thmselves or sold for other makers virtually every important type of machine tool used by the metalworking industries.

It is interesting to note that in its own manufacturing plants the company "took its own medicine" by using, in addition to machines of its own manufacture, mostly machine tools purchased from other machine tool builders for whom they acted as agents.

Mr. B. C. Harrison, Director of Design and Deputy Managing Director, remarked:

People sometimes ask us why, with our considerable resources and experience, we don't branch out and make other types of machine tools, rather than using so many factoring arrangements. Our answer is simply that creating a fine machine tool design is largely a matter of long experience. A revolutionary new design is not developed overnight, nor can it be done without vast experience in the particular field of engineering in which it is to be used. Even with our long familiarity in lathes, it takes us about five years to develop a distinctly new type of lathe from an idea to a saleable product.

In lathes especially we have a very strong background; after all, we've been making them for over 70 years, and we have developed many of the major innovations in lathes, such as the single pulley headstock and the covered vee-bed. If we had spread our effort in an attempt to make all sorts of machine tools, we would not have been able to develop our lathes to anything like their present excellence.

Mr. K. W. Norman, Director of the Factored Division, said:

The factoring side of our business, that is, selling machines on behalf of other manufacturers, began around 1900 and really became important after the First World War. Some of our principals have been with us for 30 or 40 years, or even longer, and in many instances we have grown up together.

Obviously, the process of selecting principals is a crucial affair, both for us and for them. We must be certain that the prospective principal makes machines of the highest quality and that the factoring arrangement will work out to our mutual advantage. We can obviously never have two principals who make competing products, and this has made it difficult to set up our agency for a complete line of machine tools without getting into competitive situations, but we have always managed to avoid doing so. One strong point of our factoring organisation is that our principals are among the leaders in their respective fields; as a result, they keep up with the latest developments and provide us with first-class products to sell. Obviously, these factoring arrangements make our business a complicated one, and problems inevitably arise, but in the main we have worked things out to everybody's satisfaction.

Mr. W. Core, Sales Director, observed:

The advantages of factoring for us and our principals are obvious. First of all, it makes fuller use of the company's widespread selling organisation and so increases the profit Herbert can make without increasing its manufacturing facilities. Second, there is a clear commercial advantage in being able to offer our customers the entire range of machine tools and accessories. The benefit to our principals is equally obvious; they get the advantages of our huge sales force of highly trained specialists, a sales force which no machine tool firm in the world could otherwise afford. In addition, every one of our factored lines gets individual attention from sales engineers who specialise in that line.

In summary, the position as at the date of writing of this report was that Herbert manufactured the range of machines given in Part A of Exhibit 1 and sold on behalf of other machine tool makers the products set out in Part B.

One executive remarked that sales of Herbert and factored products were roughly equal, although the exact ratio fluctuated. He added that the factoring idea was not used to any significant extent elsewhere in the industry and that no other machine tool maker in the world carried nearly so complete a line as did Herbert.

RESEARCH AND DESIGN POLICIES

Mr. Harrison, Director of Design, commented on Research and Development as follows:

We do not perform "pure" or basic research here; our research efforts are all applied to the task of putting a better machine in the customer's shop. There are several institutions doing the sort of basic research into metals and other activities, which interests us, and there is no point in our duplicating this work. We keep abreast of current technology, and if some new development appears likely to be important to us in the future, we suggest to the appropriate people the types of research and approaches which might be fruitful.

To avoid unnecessary duplication and yet, at the same time, to ensure that no possible field of enquiry is overlooked, the company has objectively developed close collaboration with leading engineering industries (outside the sphere of machine tool makers) and with learned institutions. Problems arising from the use of new materials and information relating to new techniques are kept under constant review.

In the main, we are interested in basic research only when it uncovers a new idea which we can translate into a more effective machine tool. This is why we keep up to date on what's being done in pure research.

Mr. Harrison remarked:

One of our major design policies is to ensure that the design of our new machines is production-oriented. We don't bring out a new design just for the sake of newness. When we introduce a new type of machine, that machine has been thoroughly tested in our laboratories and in the field; we can be certain that it provides a definite and valuable improvement over its predecessor. We try to be sure that a new design is theoretically advanced, that it is the best machine of its kind on the market. When we sell this machine to a customer, we want to be able to show that it has real productive advantages over previous types. We test each new design with extreme thoroughness, to be certain that the machine performs as well as promised.

MANUFACTURING POLICIES

Herbert specialised in the manufacture of products set out in Part A of Exhibit 1. All these machines were made in the plants referred to earlier; in addition, limited manufacture of Herbert machines was carried on, under license, in France, India, and Spain.

In 1962 the company's only activity outside the field of machine tools was the manufacture and selling of equipment for pulverising and drying a wide range of materials, such as coal, limestone, fertilisers, chemicals, etc., which were marketed under the name of "Atritor." Atritor was administered by a special department under a director but within the general framework of the company.

The company's most important manufacturing policy, said several executives, was that product quality was considered far more important than selling price in producing a machine. Mr. Allen, Home Sales Director, observed, "Herbert's never build to a price. Quality always comes first. I doubt that we are the cheapest on the market for anything we make, but you don't sell machine tools simply on price."

Another major manufacturing policy, and one of recent origin, was described by Mr. Harrison, who said:

As you know, the machine tool industry is subject to considerable cyclical fluctuations, and in the past we and other manufacturers have adjusted our manufacturing activities to follow these fluctuations. When business slumped, we would cut back production and, if necessary, lay off some of our workers. But when the 1958 recession hit us, we decided at the outset to maintain level employment insofar as possible. This meant that we would have to produce substantial quantities of machines for stock, until the recession ended and demand returned. We had the financial resources to absorb the expected inventory increases, and so we determined that we would go to great lengths to avoid layoffs, especially of our skilled manpower. Once you lay off a skilled worker during a recession, you may not be able to get him back when business starts up again. For some time we have experienced difficulties in getting enough skilled workers, so holding onto the ones we had was especially important to us. Then, too, we felt that this new policy would raise the morale of our work force. Workers generally give to a company about as much loyalty as the company shows them.

So we went ahead and built machines for stock and maintained our work force intact. Our inventories climbed greatly, of course, since our 1958 sales fell 40 per cent from 1957 levels, but when business did pick up, we had the machines on hand to make rapid delivery, which was good for our business. Furthermore, we engaged in a vigorous plant-replacement effort during this slow period, so that at the start of the subsequent boom we were completely tooled up for production and efficiency and did not need to use any productive effort to equip our own plant.

Although Herbert never built machines to compete primarily on a price basis, the company nevertheless recognised that, in some cases, machines of only ordinary quality and precision were best suited to the customer's needs. Accordingly, two lines of lathes were produced. Lathes manufactured under the Herbert brand were of the highest quality, but the company also manufactured a line of lower-priced lathes, under the brand name of "Edgwick," which were less precise than the Herbert machines. As one company official said:

This practice of having two lines is not at all inconsistent with our policy of emphasising quality. It is simply a recognition of the fact that one doesn't always want to drive around in a Rolls-Royce. Oftentimes a less luxurious car, or machine, is good enough for the job. Our Edgwick lathe is just as good value for its price as the Herbert lathe.

One problem we face in a cyclical industry such as ours is in expanding our manufacturing facilities. If we expand rapidly enough to be able to meet peak demand, when business slows down we find ourselves with a lot of idle plant and equipment. We have solved this problem in the short run by subcontracting at times when demand was high, but in the long run we build new plants to handle a permanent increase in demand. Also, in recent years we have taken over some of our former contractors, and this has been a way of expanding our plant. Even more valuable, when we take over a company we also obtain a team of skilled labor and an operating staff to run the company, which are important considerations in expansion. We do find that, over the long run, subcontracting is not an ideal solution to increasing our production, but it is useful to get us over short-term peaks.

In addition to its manufacture of new machines, Herbert also conducted extensive machine-rebuilding operations. The company would rebuild not only machine tools of its own manufacture but also those of any other maker, including competitors. "Herbert-rebuilt machines," one executive pointed out, "are just as good as new and carry the same guarantee as a brand-new machine. We really became interested in rebuilding machines after the Second World War, although this activity was started much earlier, because our industry could not meet the demand for new machines and there was consequently a strong demand for rebuilt machines. Rebuilding helps us to dispose of machines which we get as trade-ins for new machines; it also broadens our product line by giving us a range of machines for customers who don't want, or don't need, the latest machines of a given type."

MARKETING POLICIES

Mr. Core, Sales Director, said:

One of our major marketing policies is reflected in the attention we give to our sales effort. Every one of our salesmen has a minimum of 10 years' experience with machine tools, because we believe that only a machine tool engineer can do an effective job of selling our equipment. We divide our machine tool salesmen into two types: general salesmen and specialist salesmen. As the names imply, the general man is capable of selling the whole line of Herbert and factored machines, while the specialist devotes his attention to a relatively small group of machines. A generalist often sells a machine for which we have specialists; the specialist is usually called in when his intimate knowledge of a particular type is needed.

Mr. Core continued:

In addition to our sales staff centred in Conventry, we have eight branch offices in the United Kingdom located in the principal engineering centres, i.e., London, Birmingham, Bristol, Glasgow, Leeds, Manchester, Newcastle, and Sheffield. Each of these branch offices has a very adequate staff of general salesmen and specialists for the major lines we carry. In addition to the sales force operating from branch offices, we employ a large group of travelling specialists to sell highly specialised lines which cannot be expected to produce a sufficient sales volume in individual branch areas to warrant the expense of a full-time specialist being attached to each individual branch.

Another of the purposes of these branch offices, located as they are in the centres of the principal engineering areas of the United Kingdom is to make readily accessible to our customers a stock of consumable tools, etc., and to provide a place from where customers can obtain the services of our service engineers with a minimum of delay. These branch offices also provide accommodation for the display and demonstration of the company's machines and machines made by its principals.

By way of illustration it would perhaps be well to describe the staff of our London branch office. This office has over 70 employees, including 3 general and 6 specialist machine tool salesmen and 13 accessory and consumable stores salesmen. There are also 5 service engineers available to help our customers with service problems. Finally, we receive about 80 hours' time per week from the various travelling specialists.

Another aspect of our attention to sales is our "Customer Engineering Service." We do not content ourselves merely with describing the machine to the customer— machines are demonstrated in the branch office, or in Conventry, or in another customer's works, performing the particular job he wants done. Our salesmen like to find out what job or jobs the customer wants to perform, so as to enable them to recommend a machine or group of machines, plus the necessary tooling which will best do the job. Our salesman can give a shrewd estimate as to what a particular machine and tooling set-up will cost and the rate at which it will produce. These figures are carefully checked before our actual quotation is made to the customer.

On many occasions the customer will request, or we will suggest, a thorough engineering study of the job to be done and the machines and tooling to do it. This very often involves the design of special tooling and other accessories, and determining exact production rates by means of time-and-motion studies. We have a large group of engineers here in Coventry who work full-time on developing these elaborate production engineering studies; we produce about 280 such studies per month. The result of such a study is normally a set of blueprints for any special tooling, a list of the machines and accessories required, and a guaranteed rate of production and product quality. These studies, I hardly need say, are expensive and therefore are not lightly undertaken but only in response to what is considered to be a serious enquiry. We do not charge the customer for such studies.

Our Director of Engineering and his staff work up these analyses; in doing so, they often follow the general approach suggested by the salesman. This gives us a check on whether the salesman is proposing the right package of machines and tooling to the customer. The Director of Engineering has final authority on whether we shall propose a certain package of equipment; if he sees fit, he can veto the equipment the salesman has proposed and suggest a better way. We want to make sure that we always propose machines which are best for the customer.

I also maintain a file listing every study which we have recently done, or are doing; this file also indicates whether the study resulted in a sale, so that I can quickly see whether our studies are producing good results.

The Factored Division has its own engineering staff available for this type of study; this group, of course, works closely with our principals' engineers but is under the control of the same Director of Engineering.

As you can see, the same principle runs through all of our design, manufacturing, and sales policies: to provide the customer with competent and thorough advice on any engineering problem which involves machine tools.

We are just beginning to extend this policy of customer service even further, with a new service which we call "consultancy." We have only done this so far with a few of our oldest customers, but it is likely that this practice will grow. Briefly, consultancy involves our appraising the entire manufacturing effectiveness of a customer's existing plant and equipment. We will examine the production processes he wants to perform and his current plant and equipment. Then we will recommend the ideal plant for the job, stating which machines should be rebuilt, which can remain as they are, which should be replaced by newer models of the same type, and which should be replaced by different types of machines. This is obviously an expensive service for us to render, but it is clearly in our tradition of keeping the customer's interest uppermost in our minds.

Our policy of selling world-wide, through subsidiaries and agents, is another important feature of the company. Not only does it earn valuable foreign exchange for Great Britain, but it also protects us to a great degree against the cyclical nature of the machine tool business. Unless there is a major world-wide depression, a recession in one country is offset by a boom in another. This has a stabilising effect on our business. Further, the fact that virtually every major industry is a potential customer also helps to cushion us against the worst cyclical effects we would experience if we sold most of our output in a narrower field.

Our Hire-Purchase and Hire schemes are also an important sales tool. We hate to lose a sale simply because the customer doesn't have any cash at the time he needs a machine. To overcome this situation, we have, for 40 years, had our own Hire Purchase Scheme and after World War II we introduced our own Hire (Leasing) Scheme.

The Hire Purchase Scheme provides for hiring terms of from 12 to 36 months. A deposit is payable on or before the machine is delivered, the amount of which varies in accordance with the term of the hiring, i.e., for a term of up to 12 months, 10 per cent is payable; up to 24 months, 20 per cent; and for a hiring period longer than 24 months, a 25 per cent deposit is called for. Interest is charged on the balance of the purchase price after deducting the deposit—this interest charge made by the company is probably lower than is obtainable elsewhere. The amount of calculated interest is added to the capital balance payable, i.e., the purchase price less the deposit, and this total divided by the number of months for which the hiring is taken. On completion of all these monthly payments the machine becomes the property of the Hirer.

The Hiring Scheme is for a fixed period of 5 years. During the Hiring the Hirer pays reducing annual amounts by quarterly payments, which, at the end of the 5-year term, equal the cost price of the machine. The Hirer is given an option of continuing the hiring for a further 5-year period by continuing to pay by equal quarterly payments 7.5 per cent per annum calculated on the machine price. The machine never becomes the property of the Hirer.

One of our "hidden" and important exports is the engineers who are trained here and who then accept positions with other engineering firms overseas. We assist suitable young men to find jobs elsewhere if they feel they can get ahead faster in another company. We feel that, once a man has worked in our plant and knows how our machines are made, he'll always want to buy Herbert machines from then on.

Mr. Allen remarked:

Our entire sales philosophy is built on customer service, on giving the customer the very best machine and engineering service for his particular job. We find that you only sell a customer one wrong machine; he'll remember it for the rest of his life, so we make sure that our machines will fulfill the promises our salesmen make about them. In this regard, we treat a small order for one or two machines with just as much care and attention as an order for 50 machines. Our business has been largely built up on the repeat orders of satisfied customers.

In speaking of the company's publicity and advertising, Mr. Brailsford, as a newcomer to the company, said:

I feel, that, in the past, the company has devoted itself perhaps too exclusively to publicising itself only to its potential customers, the engineering industries. Certainly, the company has done an excellent job in this way, but the layman still doesn't know very much about the company and its products.

The image I would like to project to the general public is the great part the company plays in the industrial scene. This could have many beneficial effects, not least of all being the attraction of the best people to its employment and the removal of the mistaken ideas some people appear to have about the machine tool industry.

FINANCIAL POLICIES

Until the late 1950's, when Sir Alfred Herbert died, the company's growth had been financed primarily out of retained earnings. Mr. Harrison commented:

In Sir Alfred's day we used to cover our dividend 6–8 times in an average year. Sir Alfred, who owned a large portion of the common stock himself, didn't need considerable amounts of dividend income, and he enthusiastically liked to plough profits back into the company to make it grow rapidly. Only in recent years have we started to pay out a substantial portion of profits as dividends; today, we cover our dividends only about twice. Another factor which undoubtedly had influenced this policy change has been the fact that, since 1944, we have been a publicly owned firm. Before that time there was no pressure from outside stockholders for generous dividends.

Another policy change has been in our attitude toward borrowing. In the old days under Sir Alfred, we didn't borrow at all. Today we don't have such a rigid attitude towards debt; we borrow on a short-term basis from our banks, although I must admit that the past lingers on in this regard. One of the figures I check frequently is the cash at bank position. [As of October 31, 1961, Alfred Herbert Ltd. had bank overdrafts totalling £190,548; total overdrafts of the Herbert Group were £325,252.]

Another of our interesting aspects is the large portfolio of gilt-edged securities which we maintain.

Mr. Harrison continued:

We now have about £5,000,000 worth of such investments on hand which earned just about £200,000 in the year ended October 31, 1961. Whilst it may be argued that a high return could have been earned on these funds had they been invested in plant and equipment, we should examine this point more closely. It must be remembered that our industry has proved historically to be highly cyclical and that we operate on a narrow profit margin. In consequence, we require large reserves to provide us with the means to weather our cyclical "troughs." In 1958 our sales, together with those in the machine tool industry generally, fell something like 4 per cent, but we continued to manufacture—clearly this demanded large reserves. However, in consequence of our decision and ability to continue manufacture, we were, when business recovered, able to offer machines from our accumulated stocks and so secure substantial orders. Few other makers had been able to match our manufacturing programme due to lack of financial resources to take the strain of making machines for stock. The company not only enjoyed the advantage of increased sales, but it kept together its highly skilled personnel. It could take advantage of buying raw materials at cheaper prices, which are likely in a period of trade recession. Therefore, whilst the actual interest received on these reserves only showed 4 per cent return, their availability made possible much higher earnings and gave other advantages than would otherwise have been possible.

ORGANIZATIONAL POLICIES

The Herbert organization had been built up in accordance with several major policies. First of all, the company's Board of Directors consisted, with one exception, of members of Herbert's top management. The practice of relying on so-called "internal" directors had been established by Sir Alfred Herbert in the company's early days. "Sir Alfred," commented one executive, "believed that directors were useful only insofar as they were intimately familiar with, and experienced in, our business. This became something of a tradition here, and we have generally continued the practice of our directors being solely engaged in the business of the company. The one director not otherwise engaged in the management of the company is Sir Halford Reddish, Chairman and Managing Director of Rugby Portland Cement Limited, a large cement manufacturer located near Coventry."

A second major policy was to promote from within company ranks as much as possible. Only rarely did the company bring in an outsider to an important position, although this had been done on occasion.

Third, as a man moved upwards within the firm's organisation, he was promoted in a zigzag fashion from one department to another, rather than remaining in one functional area during most of his career. Company officials cited two benefits from this policy: first, it broadened the individual to a far greater degree than would be possible if he remained in one department; second, men advanced by this method did not develop parochial departmental loyalties and could, as a result, act on the basis of the company's over-all welfare. Company officials made great efforts to foster a team spirit within the firm. One executive said:

Obviously, a major asset of any business is its people, and we fully realise that our people will treat us about as well as we treat them. As a result, we do everything possible to be certain that our employees receive fair treatment. For example, there is no limit to a man's opportunity for getting ahead here, provided that he is capable and willing to work hard. We try to point out to our young men the great opportunities they have here. We are genuinely interested in developing people.

Mr. K. W. Norman, Director of the Factored Division, remarked:

My father was a stoker in the boiler room here, and I was made a director of the company when I was 35. Anybody can work his way up here if he has got what it takes to do it.

The company maintained very elaborate training programmes for young employees; these programmes typically involved both formal education in engineering at Coventry Technical College and on-the-job experience. After a five years' apprenticeship in one of these programmes, the trainee was well qualified as an engineer. Some of the programmes lead to degrees in production or mechanical engineering. The company had a number of university graduates on its staff, but such graduates did not receive special preference. They were expected to learn the business as thoroughly as men who had been trained in one of the company's apprentice programmes. Commented one executive:

Although it is not a formal policy, I think that one of our real strengths is that we have an unusual degree of organisational flexibility here. For example, we generally do not like to talk about an organisation chart for the whole company. We expect one of our top men to wear a variety of different hats, and, since he will have experience in each department, he should be able to work smoothly with several different departments. I think it remarkable that, in an organisation as large as this one, our top managers work so smoothly together. Nobody gets worried about having his domain invaded by another executive, because everybody is concerned only with the over-all good of the company. I think that another of our organisational strengths is that we are rather self-critical in appraising our performance. We do not automatically believe that we do everything in the best way.

Long terms of service were a tradition at Herbert. In 1960 Colonel C. W. Clark, Chairman and Joint Managing Director, made a presentation of clocks to employees with long periods of service. Of the approximately 5,900 employees at that time, 851 had more than 25 years of continuous service, 95 more than 40 years, and 12 had 50 or more years. Table 5 gives some background about each of the company's directors as of early 1962.

"It might interest you," commented one executive, "to know that five of our present directors began their Herbert careers as apprentices: Colonel Clark, Mr. Allen, Mr. Harrison, Mr. Norman, and Mr. Muirhead.

Table 5

THE HERBERT BOARD OF DIRECTORS, 1962

Name	*Position*
Colonel C. W. Clark	Chairman and Joint Managing Director
J. C. Blair	Deputy Chairman and Joint Managing Director
D. W. A. H. Allen	Director of Home Sales
T. H. Badnadge	Secretary
V. N. Brailsford	Commercial Director
W. Core	Sales Director
D. M. Gimson	Director of Finance
B. C. Harrison	Director of Design
L. J. Hugo	Technical Director
J. H. Mahler	Combustion Engineering Director
S. A. B. Muirhead	Works Director
K. W. Norman	Director of Factored Division
Sir Halford Reddish	Nonexecutive Director
A. E. Smith	Deputy Financial Director

Source: Company officials.

Mr. Harrison commented on the company's top management as follows:

As you know, Colonel Clark is chairman, and Mr. Blair is deputy chairman. They are also joint managing directors. In broad terms, Colonel Clark looks after Herbert's own manufactures and our export activities, while Mr. Blair is in over-all charge of our Factored Division. I would stress, however, that we try to avoid fitting men too tightly into compartments, and that our top men have overlapping areas of responsibility where appropriate.

Mr. Blair leaves much of the operating detail of the Factored Division to Mr. Norman, who is director of the Factored Division. From the point of view of our principals, they like to feel that they have a strong voice speaking on their behalf at the very top of our company, and Mr. Blair is this voice. Our principals know that anything they want discussed will be handled at our highest level. In addition, Mr. Blair can remain in general charge of policy for the factoring side of the business, while leaving operations to Mr. Norman.

*   *   *   *   *

In summing up the company's position and prospects as of 1962 Mr. Brailsford remarked: "To maintain our current prominence in the industry, we have strong research, design, and manufacturing groups and a powerful marketing organization. With the start we've got, I don't think there's any doubt that 25 years from now we'll still be relatively as strong as we are today."

Exhibit 1

THE PRODUCT LINE

A. *Herbert Manufacturers*

Capatan lathes ....Eleven types, six sizes for bar work up to 2½" and chuck work up 15½" swing

Combination turret lathes ....Seven types, six sizes: 16", 20", 22½", 30", 32", and 36" swing

Cross-sliding turret lathe ....32" swing

Hexagon turret lathes ....2" and 3" dia. bar capacity

Copy-turning lathe ....3¼" dia. × 22½"

Auto-lathes ....Six types, four sizes: 8½", 12½", 16½", and 25" swing

Precision toolroom lathes ....Seven models, fifteen sizes

Vertical milling machines ....Three sizes: 48" × 16" × 23", 62" × 29" × 28½" and 62" × 29" × 30½"

All-electric drilling M/cs. with 1, 2, 3, 4, and 6 spindles ....   For holes up to 1¼" diameter; bench or column types

Planing machines ....Five types, twenty-two sizes

Jigmil (Devlieg, built under license) .....Two sizes, 2½" and 3" dia. spindle

Automatic toolroom machine (Keller, built under license)................. Two sizes, 60" × 30" and 72" × 48"

Atritor dryer pulveriser ....Seven sizes with capacities from 850 to 1,500 lb. per hour

Also Coventry Dieheads, Ground-thread Rolling Dies and Taps, Coventry Chucks, Air and Electric Chucks, Turret lathe tools, Hypercut and Ardoloy-tipped Tools.

Exhibit 1—*Continued*

B. *Factored Products*

SOLE AGENTS *in Great Britain for*

Archdale* .... Milling, drilling, and special-purpose machines
Bechler .... Swiss-type automatics
Brown & Ward .... High-speed automatics
Burrows & Smith .... Gear deburring machines
Chambersburg .... Forging equipment
Cri-Dan .... High-speed treading machines
Cumliffe & Croom* .... Vertical & horizontal milling machines
Daniels .... Plastic & diecasting machines
Daniels/Latymer .... Vacuum forming machines
D.C.M.T. .... Diecasting equipment
Devlieg .... Precision milling and boring machines
Edgwick* .... Range of machines which are designed and engineered in collaboration with reputable British firms
Fellows .... Gear shapers and gear inspection machines
Flexibox .... Lapping machines
Fokker-Eckold .... Sheet-metal working machines
Heald .... Internal and surface grinders and borematics (British-made)
Herbert/Hybco .... Tap sharpening machines
Herbert/Reed-Prentice .... Injection moulding and diecasting machines
Herbert/Smallpeice* .... Multi-cut production lathes
Hilger & Watts .... Projectors and other measuring equipment
Holbrook* .... Precision toolroom lathes
Kellenberger .... Tool and cutter and universal grinding machines
Landis .... Threading machines centreless thread grinders
Lumsdan* .... Surface and tool-grinding machines
Mills* .... "Oilaulic" presses
Planers* .... Planing machines
Pratt & Whitney .... Keller automatic toolroom machines
Pullmax .... Plate and sheet-metal working machines
Richards* .... Vertical boring mills and horizontal boring, crank-pin turning, planing and keyway cutting machines
Sigma .... Multi-dimension inspection machines and miscellaneous measuring equipment
Tatar .... Twist drill grinding machines
Thielicks .... Tool-grinding machines
Waldrick-Siegen .... Heavy lathes, planers, combined planing and heavy milling machines and roll grinders

* Agents throughout the world.
Source: *Machine-Tool Review*, March–April, 1962.

JAQUIER S.A.

At the end of 1958 M. Jean Jaquier, age sixty-five, and his son Paul, age thirty-two, were reviewing recent developments in their small, integrated watch company, Jaquier S.A., in Geneva, Switzerland. For more than 15 years the company had sold over 70 per cent of its production to a major United States watch company, but this business had declined after 1950 and collapsed altogether in 1957. Sensing this possibility, the Jaquiers had started as early as 1949 to find new customers, and in 1954 they had decided to introduce a luxury line under the Jaquier name, hoping the company's regular business would sustain it until it became profitable. By 1958, however, this hope had not been realized. As M. Paul Jaquier put it:

> The failure of our major customer caught us too soon. We needed a few more years to develop other customers and to put the Jaquier line on a paying basis. As it is, however, I think it is surprising that we have survived. What other company in the position of having a single customer account for a large part of its business up to 1952 would still be in business with that customer falling to 10 per cent in only six years?

The Jaquiers believed that their immediate problems were to increase sales of the Jaquier line, retain the company's high-volume customers, and cut operating costs, in order to avoid another year of serious financial loss in 1959.

EARLY HISTORY

The Jaquier family started making watches in Geneva early in the eighteenth century. In 1815 the company was among the first to use master dies to produce standardized movements rather than to custom-build each watch by hand. Later, as wholesalers sprang up in the watch trade, Jaquier sold large quantities under the wholesalers' names.

From 1900 until his death in 1932, M. Albert Jaquier owned and managed the company. In 1915 his nephew, Jean Jaquier, joined the firm; he later became his uncle's assistant, and in 1928 his partner. M. Jean Jaquier described his uncle as a brilliant technician and businessman, under whose leadership the company had made many advances and was very profitable. In 1926 and again in 1930 Albert Jaquier attempted to produce and promote two automatic watch designs developed by independent inventors. He was particularly enthusiastic about the second and spent large sums on advertising and on establishing sales and promotional agencies in Europe and America. A series of difficulties accompanied this venture, and in 1932 M. Albert Jaquier died, saddened and exhausted by these failures. M. Jean Jaquier said that his uncle's automatic watches had been 10 years ahead of their time and that the market showed no real interest in any automatic watch until World War II.

When M. Jean Jaquier succeeded his uncle as owner-manager, the effects of the depression and of the costly failure in automatic watches had left the company in critical condition. Profitable sales averaging 90,000 pieces annually from 1915 to 1930 had fallen to 15,000 annually between 1931 and 1934; large stocks of Jaquier-designed and -produced movements had accumulated; and equipment was depleted from lack of reinvestment during the years spent in promoting automatic watches.

ASSOCIATION WITH CENTURY WATCH COMPANY

Years 1937–49. Total failure of Jaquier S.A. was avoided by finding a new major customer, Century Watch Company, a major name in watches in the United States. Experiencing its own depression crisis, Century had appointed a new president, who, allegedly displeased with Century's Swiss subsidiary factory, placed small orders with Jaquier S.A. in 1935–36. In 1937, Century gave the company ébauche dies for two calibres and orders for 157,000 pieces; thus started a relationship which accounted for at least 70 per cent or more of Jaquier's business for 15 years. In many of these years Jaquier manufactured over 100,000 movements for Century (Table 1).

Of the period before 1949, M. Jean Jaquier stated:

Our association with Century saved us during the depression and carried us through the war with a profitable business. Relations with the president were friendly—he is still a close friend—but he was a tough bargainer in price matters. However, because we had modernized the plant from initial receipts and because production runs were often many months long, we were able to make money despite the low margin prices negotiated by Century.

In 1949 after M. Jean Jaquier became seriously ill, he asked his son Paul to join the company so it would not be left without a family member to carry on. Paul, age twenty-three, agreed reluctantly; he had neither

Table 1

Year	Pieces Ordered by Century (000)	Pieces* Shipped by Jaquier to Century (000)	Franc* Value of Shipments to Century (000)	Century Sales* as a Per Cent of Total Jaquier Sales (in Francs)
1935	33	...	.....	....
1936	71	57	n.a.	....
1937	157	116	1,370	89.4
1938	31	68	814	83.3
1939	135	83	959	86.0
1940	80	119	1,525	85.3
1941	121	131	1,792	89.4
1942	92	110	1,692	78.1
1943	102	92	1,490	83.4
1944	97	77	1,342	79.2
1945	124	107	1,924	81.2
1946	118	110	2,215	78.6
1947	118	112	2,180	82.3
1948	176	105	2,160	74.2
1949	50	95	2,025	76.5
1950	22	71	1,545	72.5
1951	160	83	1,780	66.8
1952	84	94	2,320	70.0
1953	62	95	2,335	52.5
1954	0	46	1,190	38.2
1955	24	29	785	22.6
1956	148	72	1,808	36.3
1957	21	49	1,300	34.4
1958	0	13	351†	10.0

* Excluding terminage work (assembly only) done the last few years.
† In 1958 the value of the Swiss franc was 23 cents; there were 4.28 francs to a dollar.

technical nor commercial training and, having just received a liberal arts degree, had intended to pursue an academic career. Later the elder Jaquier recovered, and he and his son managed Jaquier S.A. together (see Exhibit 1 for an organization chart).

Crisis of 1949–50. The slight pre-Korean War recession in the United States resulted in Century's cutting orders with Jaquier S.A. from a high of 176,000 pieces in 1948 to 50,000 in 1949 and 22,000 in 1950. Although deliveries reacted less sharply, production in 1950 was off 25 per cent. The Jaquiers virtually closed the plant for five months, paying only a skeleton work force and the staff. Thus a Century order for 160,000 pieces in 1951 came as a great relief. This and subsequent orders, along with the growth of other business, brought sales from 2.1 million francs in 1950 to a record high of 4.4 million in 1953.

Second Crisis, 1954. Hopes that the company might be in a less vulnerable position with Century were shattered in 1954 and 1955 when Century's order dropped to zero, causing Jaquier's 1954 sales to drop to 3.1

Exhibit 1

ORGANIZATION CHART, JANUARY, 1959

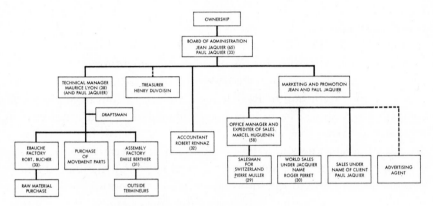

NOTES: 1. After new capital was added in 1958, the ownership was as follows:
           Jean Jaquier, 300 shares (A) at 100 francs each
                        280 shares (B) at 1000 francs each
           Paul Jaquier, 400 shares (A) at 100 francs each
           Equal voting rights were held by each type share.
     2. Men's ages shown in parentheses.
     3. As explained in the case, M. Duvoisin was not a member of the company, merely a public
        accountant and financial adviser.

Source: Prepared by case writer on the basis of interviews with MM. Jaquier and other personnel.

million francs, with a loss of 179,000 for the year. The effect was less severe than in 1950, owing to other large customers. The factory was not closed, but a few workers were released, and the rest spent part of their time in special training courses.

Final Collapse, 1957–58. The second crisis passed suddenly in 1956, when Century placed a near-record order of 148,000 pieces with Jaquier S.A. The latter reacted quickly, delivering 72,000 pieces in 1956 and starting 1957 with a planned production rate of 11,000 Century movements per month. Major purchase commitments were made with parts suppliers, and the factory work force was increased to its former level. "Then," said Paul Jaquier, "it happened again. From deliveries of 11,000 in January and February, requests for deliveries fell to less than 1,000 per month by April."

In view of the rapid recovery following the first two crises with Century, the Jaquiers decided not to react immediately but to continue high production for a few months, in hopes that Century would resume requesting shipments at the contracted rate. Recovery never came, however, and Century continued to accept delivery of less than 1,000 pieces per month through the remainder of 1957 and 1958.

The Jaquiers attributed the collapse of the company's Century business to the dismissal of their friend, Century's president, on charges of mismanagement late in 1956. In recalling this event, Paul Jaquier said: "Here is an example of the mentality and insecurity of American business: firing a man overnight who had served as head of the company for 20 years." In any case, the immediate consequences were severe for Century, which found itself with a serious working-capital shortage after fulfilling a contractual obligation to buy back company stock from the ousted official at prices well above the market. With Century's creditors in danger, the banks, to which the company owed several million dollars, named another president and, according to Paul Jaquier, instructed him to improve the company's liquidity. The new president immediately sold a number of nonwatch activities into which the company had drifted; he also ordered the sale of inventories and a drastic reduction of movements from all except Century's own Swiss subsidiary. According to Paul Jaquier, the new president responded to questions about Jaquier's position and the outstanding orders by stating that, under the circumstances, the fact that Jaquier had been a supplier of Century for 20 years was of no more importance than if it had been a month.

ATTEMPTS TO FIND OTHER BUSINESS

The only non-Century business between 1935 and 1942 came from a few old customers, who, surviving the depression, continued to buy small quantities of Jaquier calibres. The death of the company's sales manager in 1938, together with the beginning of the war, resulted in the loss of all these customers except two in the United States.

From 1942 to 1949 the company had only a few non-Century customers, the largest being Marcel S.A., another Swiss watch firm which purchased about 7 per cent of Jaquier's volume.

With the cutback of Century orders in 1949, M. Jean Jaquier realized that the company had drifted into a vulnerable and overdependent position. During slight recession periods like 1949 and 1954, Century favored its own subsidiary, from which its average annual purchases were about 600,000 movements, and forced its several independent suppliers, of whom Rennaz & Cie and Jaquier S.A. were the largest, to absorb the entire cutback. M. Jean Jaquier was unsuccessful in several attempts from 1946 to 1956 to obtain a guaranteed proportion of Century's total Swiss purchases. "It is against the American business mentality to give us equal standing with their own subsidiary," he said.

Rennaz & Cie and Jaquier reacted differently to their problem. The former arranged to supply a large Swiss manufacturer, reduced its sales to Century over several years, and finally dropped Century altogether and merged with the Swiss firm in 1956. Jaquier S.A., however, chose to preserve its identity and thus in 1949 began seeking other customers to lessen its dependence on Century. These efforts produced several American customers (jewelry-store chains and watch companies) during subsequent years, and, by 1953, some 46 per cent of the year's record sales went to non-Century customers (see Exhibits 2 and 3 for sales analyses).

In 1948 the company developed and started producing J-481, its first Jaquier calibre in 25 years. Although enough units were sold in five years to cover development costs, the company found that its new United States customers were primarily interested in Ebauches S.A. calibres,[1] since they wanted standard movements and spare parts which they could purchase from several assemblers.

Another aspect of the new business, particularly with jewelry-store chains, was the pressure on Jaquier for discounts. M. Jaquier consistently refused to grant illicit discounts, and, as a result, the company felt it lost one major customer in 1953 and another in 1955.

Decision to Sell under the Jaquier Name.   In 1954 Jean and Paul Jaquier made a policy decision which the latter said was "something that had been vaguely in the back of our minds since 1948, but which took the second shock from Century to crystallize." The decision was to develop a number of new calibres and enter the market under its own brand. The Jaquiers decided to use their own name because it was an old and well-known name among members of the Swiss watch industry and because, for years, it had been the name under which a portion of the company's watches had been sold in the United States.

The company could choose among three general quality ranges in which it might introduce the "Jaquier" line: (*a*) medium to high medium (similar to, or slightly above, the Century calibres); (*b*) inexpensive; and (*c*) exclusive. The Jaquiers decided against the first because it would have meant immediate competition with large, fully integrated companies like Omega and Longines, and Jaquier was not big enough, they believed, to undertake the huge advertising program and volume business that they considered necessary to compete in that area. The Jaquiers decided against the second because competing in inexpensive watches involved fierce price competition and thus required high volume to be profitable.

The Jaquiers felt that the third area offered more promise. First, there was less competition in this field, with only three or four top-quality, exclusive names, and no new names for many years. Second, Jaquier was to a degree known in the United States as an exclusive watch because the company's agent there had been selling Jaquier watches in expensive gold

---

[1] These calibres were designed by Ebauches S.A. incorporating its ébauche (plate and bridges).

Exhibit 2

ANALYSIS OF SALES BY TYPE AND CUSTOMER
(In 1,000 Swiss francs)

	1945	1946	1947	1948	1949	1950	1951	1952	1953	1954	1955	1956	1957	1958
I. Century Watch Company, U.S.A.	1,924	2,212	2,185	2,160	2,023	1,547	1,784	2,320	2,335	1,190	785	1,809	1,301	351
Terminage only							257	160	50	21	24	9	24	28
Percentage	81	79	82	74	76	73	77	75	54	39	23	36	35	11
II. Sold under Jacquier name														
U.S.A. (to importer)	210	237	174	309	97	164	130	113	45	8	45	88	67	113
Switzerland (to retailers)												52	56	145
Germany (several importers)												18	29	53
Blanc S.A. (France)												57	83	116
Other (Jacquier wholesalers in over 30 countries by 1958)	9	8	7	11	4	8	5	3	1	nil	1	20	43	78
Percentage												5	7	14
III. Other U.S.A. sales														
Sanders (Jewelry store chain, own name)				41	66	53	122	80	48	31		57		
Norris (Jewelry store chain, own name)							48	120						
Johns (Jewelry store chain, own name)				39	127	148	188	53	190	88	73	116		
Nivens (Jewelry maker, own name)					227	129	83	80	364	406	377	734	536	1,146
United Watch Company (Major U.S. watch company)								73	546	298				
Parker Watch Company (Major U.S. watch company)								302	798	930	1,525	1,057	689	450
Other U.S. miscellaneous												84	84	155
Percentage	0	0	0	3	16	15	16	21	44	57	57	41	35	50
IV. Sold to other Swiss watch companies														
Marcel S.A.	227	363	269	350	122	91								
Cordey S.A.													66	
Henry S.A.									10	14	132	140	280	32
Cervin S.A.										55	94	520	45	189
Terminage for Cervin													105	188
Auberson S.A.														
Percentage	10	13	10	12	4	4	0	0	nil	2	7	13	13	12
V. Other miscellaneous	8	6	28	13		3	52	22	57	66	420	230	367	443
Percentage	nil	nil	1	nil	0	nil	2	1	1	2	12	5	10	13
Grand total	2,369	2,818	2,656	2,912	2,661	2,135	2,664	3,324	4,442	3,107	3,475	4,991	3,773	3,496

Notes:

1. Sales to Swiss retailers consisted of completed watches with cases and wrist bands. Sales in all other categories shown above consisted of watch movements only, with exception of a few cased watches in 1957 and 1958.
2. Jaquier changed its U.S. importer at the end of 1952.

Source: Company records.

Exhibit 3

ANALYSIS OF SALES BY CALIBRE
(In number of movements per calibre)

	1950	1951	1952	1953	1954	1955	1956	1957	1958
I. Movements containing ébauches made by Jaquier (other parts purchased)									
A. Calibres designed by Jaquier									
J-481................	3,702	5,950	560			1,264	482	377	154
J-491................	8	1,718	5,817	22,260	10,360	9,134	8,632	2,790	218
J-553................	....	....	....	....	....	811	4,773	3,539	2,482
J-591................	....	....	....	....	....	....	....	....	97
B. Calibres designed by Century Watch Company									
A....................	16,800	770	31,094	25,800	1,694	....	....	....	....
B....................	9,640	4,844	8,650	7,420	85	....	....	....	....
C....................	....	....	17,556	17,766	21,686	35,490	34,690	8,190	
D....................	19,418	30,940	1,300	....	....	....	....	....	....
E....................	25,590	46,186	48,030	43,760	26,194	7,448	36,834	11,380	5,300
F....................	....	....	....	....	....	....	....	2,800	....
G....................	....	....	500	....	....	....	....	....	....
Total number of movements containing Jaquier-made ébauches	75,158	90,408	95,951	116,796	56,100	40,343	86,211	55,576	16,441
Percentage........	85	65	73	77	57	42	62	49	21
II. Movements containing (purchased ébauches purchased from Ebauches S.A. factories)									
3¾ HF.......	6,301	70	....	34	34	....	169	157	100
4 FL.......	....	....	....	....	151	....	28	138	454
5 A.......	5,782	4,724	1,400	1,400	3,500	1,120	283	....	....
5½ A.......	....	1,120	....	....	....	....	360	550	590
5¾ FL.......	....	....	....	....	526	....	....	....	....
6 FL.......	....	....	....	224	949	1,702	609	181	524
6 HF.......	....	1,680	2,660	5,110	5,706	9,940	12,850	6,168	2,108
6 WT.......	....	....	840	620	....	1,925	....	....	....
6 A.......	....	....	....	....	1,071	....	420	....	....
Listed by 7 A.......	....	....	....	280	420	....	3,310	6,180	1,392
7¾ E.......	....	....	....	....	....	....	77	3	11
Ebauche 8¾ A.......	1,260	2,660	....	700	560	1,400	6,565	1,376	848
8¾ E.......	....	....	....	....	....	....	45	....	202
Size 9¼ A.......	102	1,022	6,650	15,890	22,610	29,540	13,875	7,790	3,305
9¼ E.......	....	....	....	....	....	....	770	....	....
& 9¾ P.......	....	....	....	....	....	....	15	21	22
10½ P.......	....	....	....	....	....	....	45	223	3
Factory 10½ WT.....	....	....	....	420	....	....	66	8	60
10½ A.......	....	....	....	....	....	....	230	72	263
11½ E.......	....	....	....	....	....	2,000	4,252	2,162	2,309
11½ A.......	....	....	....	3,248	1,652	3,529	8,106	12,628	23,282
11½ HF.......	....	....	....	....	....	....	....	....	1,750
11½ P.......	....	....	....	....	....	....	234	57	....
11½ C.......	....	....	....	1,491	651	....	....	....	....
Others (about 15)........	....	29	703	224	71	364	410	168	8
J-611-9...............	....	....	....	....	....	....	....	73	67
Total number of movements containing non-Jaquier ébauches	13,445	11,305	12,253	29,641	37,900	51,520	52,110	37,964	37,238
Percentage........	15	8	10	19	39	54	37	33	40
III. Terminage									
Century watch movements (4 calibres).............	....	36,940	22,758	6,128	4,157	3,556	1,176	5,306	1,554
Cervin watch movements (1 calibres).............	....	....	....	....	....	....	....	5,222	15,960
Others (3 calibres)........	....	....	....	....	....	....	....	10,360	5,082
Total..............	....	36,940	22,758	6,128	4,157	3,556	1,176	20,888	22,596
Percentage.........	0	27	17	4	4	4	1	18	30
Grand total.........	88,603	138,653	130,962	152,565	98,157	95,519	139,497	114,428	76,275

Notes:

1. In Group I, Jaquier made the ébauches (plate and bridges), bought remaining parts, and did the assembly and specified regulation. In Group II, Jaquier bought all parts, then performed assembly and regulation. In Group III, "Terminage," Jaquier merely assembled parts supplied by the buyer. Usually, a "Termineur" is merely a subcontractor who receives the parts, assembles them, and returns the movement to the first party who inspects, cases, and sells the movement under its own name.
2. J-611-S was the extra-thin calibre made exclusively for Jaquier by another manufacturer (not Ebauches S.A., however).
3. There was no correlation between calibres designed by Jaquier (Group I-A) and sales under the Jaquier name (Group II, Exhibit 2). Many of the models under the Jaquier name incorporated Ebauches S.A. ébauches. Conversely, Jaquier sold several thousand J-553 movements to Cervin S.A., as mentioned in the case, and J-481 and J-491 were sold in large quantities to importers and watch companies.
4. All Century movements (Group I-B) were, of course, made by Jaquier exclusively for Century. In these cases, Century designed the calibre and supplied Jaquier with the ébauche dies.

Source: Company records.

and jeweled bracelets. Finally, as M. Paul Jaquier explained, "We hope to turn the apparent disadvantage of the Jaquier name being unknown among retailers and consumers into an advantage of exclusiveness. It would be impossible for one of the major medium-high-quality watchmakers to go into exclusive watches; they are just too well known."

The Jaquiers' ultimate objective was an annual volume of 7,000–10,000 supreme-quality, luxury watches with high enough unit margins to support the operation. They realized that many years would be necessary to build brand recognition, develop special calibres, create a marketing organization, and reorient manufacturing facilities. In the meantime, they were aware that the company's other business would have to be maintained to supply capital during the transition years.

Attempts to Form a "Community of Interest." The 1954 crisis with Century caused the Jaquiers to make a second major decision, e.g., to seek a "community of interest" with another Swiss watch company. They aimed (1) to assure work for the company's production facilities in case the Century business declined further and (2) to find an additional outlet for sales of new specialty calibres that Jaquier S.A. hoped to develop, in order to cover development and tooling costs.

In 1955 the Jaquiers approached Cervin S.A., a large, fully integrated producer and seller of quality watches recognized throughout the world. At that time, Jaquier was developing the J-553, the world's smallest baguette movement.[2] This calibre, expected to be the highlight of the new Jaquier line, was to attract considerable attention throughout the industry when introduced a few months later. The Jaquiers realized that sales potential under the Jaquier name would be insufficient to cover the unusually high development costs. They therefore offered to supply several thousand movements to Cervin on an exclusive basis, and Cervin accepted the offer. Paul Jaquier said the arrangement represented a major policy change for Cervin, for it had never before sold other than its own calibres. By the end of 1958 Jaquier had sold enough of these baguette movements on its own and through Cervin to cover the entire development and tooling costs. During 1957 and 1958, however, Cervin found it could not sell all the watches it had promised to buy from Jaquier. It therefore authorized the latter to sell its unfilled quota to Auberson S.A., another quality firm, which sold them under its own name.

Using the agreement on the J-553 as an example of cooperation, M. Jean Jaquier proposed to Cervin in 1957 that the two firms take definite steps which could lead to eventual merger. In recalling this move, he said:

---

[2] A baguette movement is a long, thin, rectangular movement used in small watches for women.

I have been in the watch business for many years, and I am convinced that things which were true 20 years ago are not true today. Then, I felt that a watch company should be small and within the control and workability of one person. Now I am convinced that there must be a reduction in the number of firms in the industry. Volume production, manufacturer's brand names, and widespread promotion and distribution are becoming much more important.

He supported his proposal to Cervin with two arguments: first, that demand for Cervin watches at that time outstripped capacity, whereas Jaquier had excess capacity; and, second, that Cervin, since it made a line of 10 basic calibres for its annual volume of 400,000 units, was forced to produce several calibres to use in fewer than 30,000 pieces annually; these were uneconomical for its production facilities. Jaquier, on the other hand, could make these small-volume calibres more cheaply because of its smaller factories. M. Jaquier also suggested that if certain calibres could be used jointly by the two companies, economies of higher production would result.

Cervin's management agreed in principle but suggested that a third company, Nervina S.A., with which they had been conducting similar talks, be brought into the agreement, Nervina sold about 400,000 medium-price watches annually. Although its brand name was not as well known as Cervin's, it had a firmly established sales organization. Its manufacturing facilities included assembly, ébauche, and wheel and pinion factories, and it had the right (not at the time exercised) to produce parts like escapements and balance wheels which Jaquier and Cervin were prohibited from making. (Nervina had made these parts prior to 1934, the year that industry regulation first forbade manufacturers to produce components that they had not previously made.) Eventual merger of the three companies might result in volumes high enough to justify Nervina's supplying these parts, which were currently purchased from UBAH[3] companies. Talks between the three firms led to a written agreement calling for a two-year "engagement period," during which they would work toward achieving a more rational distribution of production according to the needs and facilities of each. Specifically, Cervin promised to give to Jaquier orders to manufacture one or two of its low-volume calibres, and Jaquier S.A. agreed to develop and produce a new, small lady's movement (J-591) on the promise of the other two firms to buy certain quantities. In 1958 the two other companies even advanced Jaquier S.A. funds to cover a major part of the development and tooling costs of this new calibre.

The agreement was scheduled to expire in late 1959, at which time

---

[3] L'Union des branches annexes de l'horlogerie, Swiss association of parts manufacturers.

each party would decide whether it wanted to join a complete financial and organizational merger, each retaining its own brand name. Paul Jaquier envisioned a product pyramid, with Nervina as the base, having highest volume and lowest price; above Nervina, Cervin, having high quality and somewhat lower volume; and, at the apex, Jaquier, having very low volume but supreme quality and featuring luxurious specialty designs and expensive gold and jeweled cases and bracelets.

Paul Jaquier said, however, that, by late 1958, many of Cervin's promises to Jaquier had failed to materialize. Claiming that its 1958 business was seriously off, Cervin had delayed supplying Jaquier with ébauche dies, finally giving it dies for only a few bridges. Cervin had, however, given Jaquier over 15,000 pieces for assembly, but this order resulted in a serious loss. Further inquiry by Paul Jaquier disclosed that Cervin's business had dropped 11 per cent from 1957 but that most of the decrease had been taken from work promised to Jaquier S.A. Also, Cervin and Nervina deferred acceptance of deliveries of the new J-591, which Jaquier had started to produce late in 1958. These developments in conjunction with the Jaquiers' opinion that the managements of these companies were very conservative—"hard to move"—raised serious doubts about the significance of the agreement signed with Cervin and Nervina and about the wisdom of a possible merger.

In speaking about mergers and the watch industry in general, the elder Jaquier said:

Large watch companies need a strong central figure to prevent the major sections from going in separate directions. At present, none of the big companies has strong leaders, and, as a result, the industry is suffering. Maybe things are better in German-speaking Switzerland because they have stronger family tradition and are better businessmen. But in the French-speaking part, the watch industry certainly lacks leaders.

CURRENT OPERATIONS

Organization. Paul Jaquier said that he and his father jointly made policy and major operating decisions. "We often argue over the minor questions," he said, "but we are in complete accord on major policy. Although we occasionally solicit the financial advice of M. Duvoisin [treasurer] and draw upon the technical experience of M. Lyon [technical manager], the important decisions within the company are taken completely by my father and me, for we feel ownership responsibility. In our decision-making, the two of us try to seek what is 'right' rather than persist in our individual opinions."

Paul Jaquier and several subordinate members in the company expressed their profound respect for the elder Jaquier through such comments as the following: "He has remarkable intuition—he makes the right decision without having clear-cut reasoning behind it." "He has amazing capacity for new ideas."

M. Jean Jaquier said that during the preceding five years he had been shifting responsibility to his son. "I am still around for advice when Paul wants it, but the company is pretty much what he can make of it now. I am tired and hope to retire completely in a year or two." Paul Jaquier agreed with this statement in principle but added that his father was still active in decision-making. "Besides," he said, "I think I would be lost without the experience and judgment of my father to fall back on."

Paul Jaquier spent much of his time on commercial matters, reading all incoming and outgoing mail and personally dictating much of the latter. By working closely with M. Lyon, he had become familiar with the technical problems of design and manufacturing. He said that many companies had difficulties because their commercially trained management had little appreciation for the design and manufacturing aspects of the watch business.

Directly subordinate to the Jaquiers were MM. Lyon and Huguenin (office manager and expediter of sales), who jointly had the power to "sign"[4] for the company in the absence of the Jaquiers. M. Huguenin had been in the firm over 35 years and, until the arrival of Paul Jaquier, was the "right-hand man" to the elder Jaquier. He still handled a multitude of details for the Jaquiers. M. Lyon had joined the company in 1946 as technical manager, after graduating from the five-year watch technician's school. He divided his time equally between design, ébauche shop, and assembly.

M. Duvoisin, a well-known lawyer and public accountant, had served as auditor and financial adviser to Jaquier S.A. for more than 20 years. He and his staff served in a similar capacity with a number of Swiss watch and other manufacturing firms.

Paul Jaquier said that the company felt a great responsibility to its workers. "One reason why drops in the demand for watches hit the Swiss industry so hard is that, unlike most business in the States, the Swiss are unwilling to cut the labor force at the first sign of a turndown. On our staff, for instance, there are many people who have been with us for years, and I would rather pay them out of my own pocket than lay them off." The elder Jaquier added that one of the real blocks against mergers within the Swiss industry was that every firm wanted to keep its staff.

Product Line. Until 1948, Jaquier S.A. worked with fewer than 10

---

[4] This authority gave the men the title of *fondé de pouvoir*.

calibres annually: from 1 to 3 Century calibres in large quantities, and a small number of Ebauches S.A. calibres which Jaquier assembled and sold to its United States importer. During the next 10 years, with the acquisition of new customers and the move to create a complete "Jaquier" line, the number of basic calibres used rose to over 40 (see Exhibit 3). Many of these had several variations, depending on the customer and market. Within a single calibre, the finish of the ébauche, the quality of parts, and the number and quality of jewels would be different if the movements were to be put in Jaquier brand watches or merely sold to a jewelry-store chain for resale under its own name. In the latter case, price rather than quality determined whether Jaquier S.A. would get the business.

In recent years, sales in terms of calibres comprised five groups:

1. *Century calibres.* The design and dies for these were supplied by Century. Average annual movement price received by Jaquier S.A. rose from 12 francs before the war to 27 francs in 1955–57.
2. *Cervin calibres.* Thus far, the company had not received ébauche dies from Cervin and therefore had merely assembled certain Cervin movements in a typical "terminage" operation. Full manufactured cost for these movements averaged 35 francs.
3. *Ebauches S.A. calibres for non-Jaquier sales.* These were medium-quality movements with manufactured cost varying from 15 to 30 francs.
4. *Ebauches S.A. calibres for the Jaquier line.* Many of the Jaquier line watches incorporated Ebauches S.A. ébauches with special finishes and using highest-quality UBAH parts. Paul Jaquier said the company used certain Ebauches S.A. calibres for three reasons: (*a*) low volume, which did not justify a full line of self-designed calibres; (*b*) lower costs, since Ebauches S.A. and UBAH had priced parts for certain standard calibres very low, to enable Swiss assemblers to compete more favorably with French and German factories, and since parts prices on most automatic calibres were lower than most manufacturers' costs; (*c*) guidance in maintaining standards for Jaquier's own production, since many manufacturers who never used Ebauches S.A. failed to keep abreast of it on design, quality, or cost.
5. *Specially designed Jaquier calibres.* This group comprised four calibres designed by the company and containing its own ébauches, plus the "Golden Line," an exclusive Jaquier calibre whose ébauche, however, was made elsewhere.

By 1958 the following calibres made up the Jaquier line (Groups 4 and 5 above):

J-481: Size 6 × 8, developed 1948.
J-491: Size 5, a small rectangular lady's movement, developed 1950. J-481 and J-491 were initially developed for sale to large United States importers and watch companies.
J-553: World's smallest baguette movement, developed 1955; sold only to Cervin and Auberson besides Jaquier's own sales.

J-591: Size 6, a small, round, lady's calibre, developed 1958, to be used exclusively by Jaquier, Cervin, and Nervina. An important reason for developing this calibre was that the Ebauches S.A. calibre of this size was highly priced.

J-611-S: The Golden Line for men, using the thinnest ébauche in the world. In 1955 and 1956 Jaquier bought this standard superthin ébauche from a maker considered an expert in its manufacture. In 1957, however, the Jaquiers decided that they wanted their superthin calibre different from that of other firms. Working with the ébauche maker, M. Lyon made a few changes involving a few new dies for which Jaquier S.A. paid, and the J-611-S was evolved, different enough from the other superthin ébauche that the company considered it a unique calibre.

39-T: Size 8¾, Ebauches S. A., man's thin calibre.

40-T: Size 10½, Ebauches S.A., man's standard.

42-T: Size 11½, Ebauches S.A., man's with sweep second.

44-T: Size 9¼, Ebauches S.A., man's automatic. Besides using this calibre in several expensive Jaquier models, the company used it in its "Jaquier All-Sport," a specialty watch which was automatic, super-waterproof, super-antimagnetic, and shockproof. It had special features which made it especially useful for pilots, clocking sporting events, and skin diving.

47-T-J: Size 11½ automatic. Using an Ebauches S.A. ébauche as a base and adding a specially designed and self-manufactured jewel-bearing, automatic winding rotor, the company had developed its "Jewel-O-Matic" with 39 jewels. Paul Jaquier said that, besides being an important promotional asset, the jeweled rotor (which accounted for half of the jewels) was a major improvement over ordinary automatic rotors.

Paul Jaquier said that all watches sold under the Jaquier name were given 3-day extended time tests. Maximum allowed deviation during 24 hours was: +15 seconds for the automatics; +30 seconds for the other men's watches, including the Golden Line; +45 seconds for the lady's 6 × 8 calibre; and +60 seconds for J-553. He added that he felt people bought the expensive Jaquier watches for elegance and exclusiveness of the models, not for their timekeeping quality. "It is impossible," he said, "for anyone to know a watch's timekeeping ability until he has bought and worn it. This being the case, people normally take the word of the retailer that the watch will keep excellent time."

Because of the importance of styling, both M. Jean Jaquier and his son spent a great deal of time in selecting cases, dials, and bracelets. The latter frequently assisted the company's bracelet supplier in creating the expensive unique bracelets. Within the preceding two years, the company had assembled a wide selection of jeweled bracelets for women's models and elegant gold bands for men's.

Paul Jaquier believed that the "presentation" was a vital element in selling an exclusive watch. He therefore devoted some of his time to designing unusual and expensive boxes for Jaquier watches and original ways of stating and presenting the guarantee. He said that Jaquier's newly acquired Italian wholesaler, who had visited them a few weeks earlier, had been most impressed with the company's ideas on presentation. The wholesaler remarked that Jaquier S.A. was the first company he had seen which was doing something original along these lines. Paul Jaquier summarized as follows:

> In short, our product policy is to create unique specialty watches, of which the smallest baguette movement, the thinnest man's watches, the Jaquier All-Sport, and the Jewel-O-Matic are examples. We put our watches, when appropriate, into very expensive cases and bracelets, which, together with special effort on presentation, are aimed at creating a snob appeal for our watches which is enjoyed by only two or three other watchmakers in the world.

Marketing the Jaquier Line. Except for the single importer in the United States, nothing was sold under the Jaquier name until 1956. By 1958 the Jaquier line accounted for 14 per cent of the company's business. Switzerland, the United States, France, and Germany were the most important of its more than 30 markets.

In Switzerland the company started distributing through a wholesaler but changed to direct selling in late 1957 and hired as its Swiss salesman M. Muller, a young man having sales experience with a small assembler. By the end of 1958 the company had 30 definite Swiss retail customers and 20 more on a trial basis. Paul Jaquier said that the company tried to get into two or three first-rate stores in each major city. If unsuccessful at first, it tried again later but would not approach second-rate outlets.

When retailers resisted accepting a new expensive line of watches, the company countered with the argument that the retailer should be careful of over-dependence on "presold" brands. Since companies with high consumer advertising must have large sales volumes, Paul Jaquier contended that "the big companies seek many outlets in the same area and slowly impose increasing quotas upon their retailers. As sales of a single brand become a large part of a retailer's volume, he becomes more dependent on that brand and more susceptible to pressure from the company to increase sales of its brand. Soon the retailer finds he cannot afford to be dropped by the particular company." Jaquier also argued that there is always demand for high-class watches and that selling them makes the retailer's outlet a high-class store.

Jaquier S.A. changed its United States agent in 1952, and the current agent sold noncompeting watch brands in addition to Jaquier watches. Paul Jaquier said:

We don't think he is doing as much as he could, but we understand his problems. In the first place, he is selling a brand name known to the watchmakers and retailers but not to the public. This feature is becoming more disadvantageous with the shift toward brand-name watch selling in the States. Secondly, he is short on funds, and therefore he can neither advertise nor grant credit to jewelers as his competitors can.

Paul Jaquier felt that, next to Switzerland, France was the most promising immediate market for the company. Blanc S.A., a leading name in quality watches in France, had bought increasing quantities of movements from Jaquier since 1956, which it sold in several hundred top-quality jewelry stores under the combined Blanc-Jaquier name. He said that Blanc was pleased with Jaquier's product and was expected to place larger orders in the future.

In Germany the company sold to several wholesalers. Paul Jaquier felt that the fact that the wholesalers were competitors resulted in better coverage of the German market.

Jaquier S.A. also had some wholesalers in most other European countries, 12 in Latin America, and a few in Africa and Asia. The company was making concerted efforts to obtain outlets abroad. Watch importers carrying a complementary medium-quality brand were first investigated in several markets, financial strength and scope of operations being the most important criteria for selection. Letters were then written to the several firms best satisfying these requirements in each market, in the hope of interesting one of them. Recently Jaquier S.A. had acquired importing wholesalers in Italy and Portugal.

In 1958 Jaquier S.A. spent 135,000 francs on advertising: 90,000 on publicity, 32,000 on customer reception and gifts, and 13,000 on the Swiss watch fairs. Publicity was primarily in Swiss watch-trade journals. Paul Jaquier hoped to have money in the future to advertise occasionally in what he termed a "snob" magazine like the *New Yorker*.

Marketing to Non-Jaquier Customers. Besides Century and the two Swiss companies buying from Jaquier in 1958, two large United States customers accounted for the bulk of sales outside the Jaquier line. Of these, the Nivens Jewelry Company had been a major customer since 1949. Paul Jaquier expected this business to continue, particularly since Nivens was interested in buying large quantities of the Jewel-O-Matic for sale under its own name. One problem had arisen at the end of 1958, however, to require a major decision from the Jaquiers. In order to retain its license —originally granted in 1954—to sell under the name of a well-known United States company (formerly a watch manufacturer), Nivens allegedly had to buy the stock of the company's controlling stockholder and president. Since Nivens lacked the necessary capital, it had asked its Swiss suppliers to purchase the stock and assign voting rights to Nivens, which would then merge with the United States company, in order to eliminate license fees. Each Swiss company was asked to put up capital in proportion to its share of Nivens' past orders; in turn, Nivens said it would guarantee future business to the participants in proportion to their stock purchase. Paul Jaquier felt he would have to join this move, since he could not afford to lose the Nivens business during Jaquier's present crisis.

Parker Watch Company, another recognized watch name in the United States, was Jaquier's other principal United States customer in 1958. Parker had bought Ebauches S.A. calibres assembled by Jaquier for seven years. After a peak of 1.5 million francs in 1955, its business with Jaquier had steadily decreased and threatened to disappear altogether in 1959. Paul Jaquier said that the difficulty concerned price and that Parker was shifting to other Swiss companies who were willing to shade below Jaquier's prices. He was determined not to lose this major customer, and he hoped that pending changes in the industry pricing regulations[5] would enable him to retain the account, even though he also felt these changes would produce additional troubles throughout the watch industries.

Manufacturing. Jaquier's manufacturing facilities comprised the ébauche shop, normally employing about 50 workers, and the assembly factory, with a normal work force of 170, plus about 40 outside *termineurs* to whom the company subcontracted assembly work during peak years. By late 1958, staffs in the two factories had been cut to 30 and 85 people.

M. Jean Jaquier was proud of his ébauche shop and felt that possessing ébauche facilities made the company one of 60 integrated watchmakers rather than one of 500 companies that were only assemblers. "You cannot expect to sell in the exclusive watch field if you're using Ebauches S.A. calibres which the retailer sees every day."

In both company factories, new superintendents had recently been hired. In the ébauche factory, Paul Jaquier said, the former incumbent was an older man who could not adapt scheduling and control techniques to meet the increased complexity in manufacturing caused by the development of Jaquier calibres and the addition of more calibres purchased from Ebauches S.A. In the assembly plant, two superintendents had proved un-

---

[5] In early 1959 it became evident that the industry regulation on pricing would be relaxed in March. In particular, the price calculation for each company would (1) allow an assembler to use the association's (FH) allowance for assembly labor, even if it were lower than the company's own assembly labor costs; and (2) authorize a reduction in the 25 per cent gross margin on movements sold to major customers on the basis that for such business the supplier has little or no promotion costs.

able to relieve the Jaquiers of additional detailed tasks brought about by the change in company objectives. However, Paul Jaquier indicated that the present incumbents, MM. Bucher and Berthier—the latter hired in 1958—were as good as factory supervisors in any of the larger firms.

Diversification in the product mix necessitated a marked change in the organization and conduct of assembly operations. To the relatively inexpensive Century movements, to which the assemblers were accustomed, were added several high-quality calibres, the extremes of which were the J-553 (baguette) and the J-611-S (the superthin). These respectively required 10 and 30 times more assembly time than the Century calibres. Up to 1954, assembly facilities had consisted of several small rooms, each with groups of workers performing one job. As people in one room completed their task, the movements went to the store room, where they were inspected and reissued to another room for the following task at some later date. Paul Jaquier and M. Lyon found that this scheme not only became very confused with the diversification, but the increased quality control necessary could not be effected.

By experiment, the company arrived at an organization comprising three "assembly lines." Grouping the assemblers according to ability, the company formed one line for the J-553, J-591, and the J-611-S calibres, these requiring the highest skills; it organized a second line for assembly of Cervin movements during 1957 and 1958; and the third and largest assembly line handled all other Jaquier, Century, and Ebauches S.A. calibres. Paul Jaquier listed three advantages of the separate assembly lines: (1) more efficient worker utilization by grouping workers of equal abilities to match the quality demands of one of the three groups of calibres; (2) less work-in-process, since the assembly operation almost approached continuous flow; and (3) more effective quality control. The third advantage was achieved because the worker tended to be more careful when he knew that the pieces were passed directly to the man sitting next to him. The company avoided, when possible, shifting assemblers from one line to another.

Paul Jaquier said it had been necessary to spend much time and money hiring or training skilled workers who could assemble the difficult calibres.

Paul Jaquier estimated that the company had lost more than 100,000 francs in 1957–58 doing terminage work for Cervin S.A. "Not only were its calibres old and more difficult to assemble," he said, "but Cervin manufactures with methods and ideas which prevailed 20 years ago." Differences arose over the concept of quality. Cervin, he felt, considered that the difference between a fine-quality and a regular movement consisted primarily in the fitting and hand adjustments done by a skilled assembler.

"Our philosophy," he said, "is that a quality movement should be as easy to assemble as any other, through the use of expert design and superior quality parts produced by precision manufacturing and utmost inspection control. Time lost before assembly is cheaper than time lost during assembly. However, we must know how to do it as Cervin wants it if we expect to manufacture and assemble for them some day. But we cannot continue to sustain these losses, and we will stop if we are not able to improve the situation."

Paul Jaquier said that he supplied M. Lyon with the ébauche production schedule according to firm and forecast orders. Scheduling of case and dial purchases, movement parts, and final assembly was dictated by the receipt of firm orders.

Finance. Exhibits 4 and 5 summarize the balance sheets and operating statements of Jaquier S.A. from 1945 to 1958. These reports and interim quarterly statements were submitted by M. Duvoisin. Prior to hiring M. Rennaz as accountant in 1957, the company employed only a bookkeeper, who made original entries in the books and sent them each quarter to M. Duvoisin, who closed the ledger, made adjustments, and drew up the financial statements. Since 1957 M. Rennaz had kept all factory and general overhead expense accounts which he closed each quarter, sending the balances to M. Duvoisin. The latter combined this information with the general asset and liability accounting and prepared the financial reports for top management. Although M. Duvoisin commented on results indicated by the reports, the Jaquiers did not consider him an "inside" member of management, for he was not fully familiar with all the company's operations and problems.

Paul Jaquier said that many years were more profitable than reflected by the balance sheet because of a comfortable salary drawn by his father.

In 1958 M. Jean Jaquier decided to increase the capital from 70,000 to 350,000 francs through a personal purchase of new stock. He had given his son most of the original shares, and the voting power of the new shares was adjusted so that the son still held a 40 per cent control. M. Jean Jaquier had also lent the company 430,000 francs in 1958. He said that the new funds had been required to meet working-capital needs during unprofitable operations. The increase in equity capital was considered necessary to secure additional bank credits during 1958 and to improve the balance sheet in case of merger ventures.

Paul Jaquier said that final collapse of the Century business had left Jaquier S.A. with serious financial obligations. The backlog of orders placed but not taken by Century stood at 65,000 pieces, representing 1,800,000 francs, at the end of 1958. At that time, Jaquier S.A. had nearly

300,000 francs invested in partially completed movements and parts, 150,000 in ébauches, and open orders to parts suppliers for 550,000 francs. These represented a liability to the company, according to industry regulation, even if Century went bankrupt and could never take another piece. "The outcome of our current financial difficulties is directly connected with the recovery of the Century situation," Paul Jaquier said. He was hopeful that some firm in the United States would buy out Century before it declared bankruptcy. The prospect of using the company as a tax-loss benefit, plus the use of a name still recognized as a major watch name in America, had interested several companies in 1957–58, but no agreement had been reached, and, to Paul Jaquier's knowledge, no new moves were under way in January, 1959. He believed that if Century went bankrupt, Jaquier would have a preferred position over general creditors, since its claims were against Century's Swiss subsidiary through whom the orders had been placed. Thus the industry regulation specifying that a company must accept all orders it places gave Paul Jaquier reason to believe that the company's claim against Century would be fulfilled to a large extent.

In discussing other sources of capital, Paul Jaquier said that further bank loans would probably not be possible. Additional capital from his father would depend on what his father decided in light of the situation when the need arose. He added that one of his immediate objectives was to conduct the current year's operations without requesting new funds from any source.

Accounting. M. Rennaz joined the company in May, 1957, at age thirty. He had a university arts degree, was certified in economics and tax accounting, and had apprenticed in a stock exchange and two accounting positions. The Jaquiers considered him a very capable and intelligent addition to their staff.

During the remainder of 1957 Rennaz acquainted himself with Jaquier's accounts and worked slowly toward introducing some changes. He said that he did not wish to make an issue of the matter but that he disagreed with M. Duvoisin's accounting conventions in many aspects. In particular, he said that Duvoisin's practice of including in general expenses a great many costs that were associated with the ébauche and assembly shops made true appraisal of factory costs and general overheads impossible. Splitting labor costs between factory and general costs was especially misleading. (According to M. Duvoisin's accounts, only "basic productive wages," e.g., the basic piece-rate wages for workers on incentive, were considered direct factory labor. All additions to these "basic" wages—for example, general wage increases, social security, and family allowances—were included in "general factory and commercial expenses"

Exhibit 4

Year-End Balance Sheets, 1945–58

(In 1,000 Swiss francs)

Assets	1945	1946	1947	1948	1949	1950	1951	1952	1953	1954	1955	1956	1957	1958
Cash & post cheque	7	5	1	13	5	1	11	6	7	8	149	21	30	22
Bank deposits	408	533	358	234	401	420	116	65	43	11	1	172	11	25
Securities	....	....	....	....	....	....	....	....	17	42	42	42	42	36
Accounts receivable	334	213	335	143	77	58	244	85	92	33	151	611	125	309
Notes receivable	....	....	....	....	....	....	....	....	....	....	8	....	6	349
Advances to M. Jean Jaquier	248	97	....	....	....	169	152	152	140	67	140	....	....	....
Inventories	230	157	200	206	188	85	179	351	485	253	255	673	1,017	1,056
Miscellaneous prepaid expenses	....	....	....	....	....	....	....	....	....	....	6	2	32	8
Loans to employees	....	....	....	....	....	1	....	....	....	....	12	7	3	....
Total current assets	1,227	1,005	894	596	671	734	702	659	784	414	764	1,528	1,266	1,805
Buildings & land (net)	55	54	54	24	53	52	164	205	282	280	272	286	244	244
Machines & equipment (net)	57	74	106	123	107	83	99	113	99	76	66	85	104	103
Autos (net)	2	10	12	21	35	24	15	27	11	22	28	21	24	28
Furniture (net)	31	69	74	70	67	59	68	55	42	35	29	24	44	67
New calibre	....	....	....	....	....	....	....	....	....	....	....	....	....	152
Total assets	1,372	1,212	1,140	834	933	952	1,048	1,059	1,218	827	1,159	1,944	1,682	2,399

Liabilities & Net Worth	1945	1946	1947	1948	1949	1950	1951	1952	1953	1954	1955	1956	1957	1958
Accounts payable	589	347	197	137	165	124	202	195	227	83	160	511	274	211
Notes payable	....	....	....	....	84	42	105	84	5	....	....	....	....	....
Insurance premiums payable	....	....	....	....	....	....	....	....	....	....	....	....	28	20
Prepaid income	....	....	....	....	....	22	....	....	50	15	32	14	14	62
Salaries payable	....	....	....	....	....	....	....	....	....	....	....	....	....	16
Loan from workers' welfare fund	90	90	79	89	83	77	52	57	96	71	83	113	89	71

Loan from Cervin SA. & Nervina S.A. for calibre development .... and balance-sheet table follows.

Loan from Cervin SA. & Nervina S.A. for calibre development	....	....	....	....	....	....	....	....	....	....	....	....	....	112
Bank loans	131	230	447	100	34	30	29	111	110	108	257	667	615	737
Mortgage loan	....	....	....	....	....	....	....	....	42	41	41	41	40	40
Loan from M. Jean Jaquier	....	....	....	....	....	....	....	....	....	....	....	....	....	430
Total liabilities	810	667	723	326	366	295	388	447	530	318	573	1,346	1,060	1,698
Capital stock	70	70	70	70	70	70	70	70	70	70	70	70	70	350
Crisis reserve	....	....	....	....	....	....	....	28	70	70	98	70	70	70
Provision for litigation	....	....	....	....	....	....	....	....	....	....	....	....	17	....
Provision for doubtful debtors caused by currency blockage	103	103	81	....	....	....	....	....	....	....	....	....	....	....
Reserve & retained earnings	389	372	266	438	497	587	590	514	548	369	418	458	465	281
Total capital & reserves	562	545	417	508	567	657	660	612	688	509	586	598	622	701
Total liabilities & net worth	1,372	1,212	1,140	834	933	952	1,048	1,059	1,218	827	1,159	1,944	1,682	2,399

Notes:

1. The government required 60% of the *Crisis reserve* to be funded with special bonds. This accounts for the *Securities*.

2. *Accounts receivable* at the end of 1958 contained 177,000 francs from Century Watch Company. The figure was 15,000 in 1957.

3. *Inventories* were valued as follows: Physical count of all material, parts, pieces in process, parts, and finished pieces was made at the close of each year. The pieces were then given a value by M. Paul Jaquier according to their cost minus deductions which represented the risk of selling each particular group of pieces. For example, the 1958 inventory contained about 300,000 francs of parts and undelivered pieces for Century Watch Company. Since ultimate delivery of these was considered doubtful, these items were listed as only 60,000 francs in the inventory. On the other hand, pieces which were completed and scheduled for firm shipment early in the year would be valued at full cost plus allocation percentage for overhead. The inventory value, having been computed as described, was given to M. Duvoisin, the Treasurer, who usually wrote the value down as much as 35% as allowed by tax laws of the Canton of Berne. Any such deduction, of course, created a "hidden reserve" not shown in the balance sheet. From 1945 through 1955, inventories were written down 35% below the figure supplied by the company. In 1956, it was down 20%, and in 1957 and 1958, M. Duvoisin did not write them down at all.

4. M. Paul Jaquier said that the "considered" value (between the insured value and tax value) of the buildings and land was 700,000 francs. He estimated that the 1958 liquidation value of the machinery and furniture was at least double their book value. High depreciation expenses taken the past 15 years accounted for the low book value of these items.

5. *The workers' welfare fund* was a fund to which both workers and the company contributed. The company's contributions (see Operating Statement) were considered expenses. This fund supplied sickness and accident benefits to the workers. Ordinarily, such a fund was completely separate from the company and was in the form of a savings bank deposit. In Jaquier S.A., however, the fund was on deposit in the company. Thus the company was borrowing the money of the fund and paying interest for it.

6. In 1958, the company, for the first time, capitalized expenses of developing a new calibre (J-591). Since movements of this calibre would be sold to Cervin S.A. and Nervina S.A., Jaquier was able to get a loan from them to help cover the development costs. As these two firms purchased the movements which they promised to do, the loan would be paid back and the asset written off.

Source: Company records.

Exhibit 5

OPERATING STATEMENTS, 1945–58
(In 1,000 Swiss francs)

	1945		1946		1947		1948		1949		1950		1951		1952		1953		1954		1955		1956		1957		1958	
		%		%		%		%		%		%		%		%		%		%		%		%		%		%
Sales	2,369	100	2,818	100	2,656	100	2,912	100	2,661	100	2,135	100	2,664	100	3,324	100	4,442	100	3,107	100	3,475	100	4,991	100	3,773	100	3,496	100
Cost of goods sold	1,299	55	1,569	56	1,496	56	1,567	54	1,448	54	914	43	1,417	53	1,841	55	2,770	62	1,783	57	1,837	53	2,941	59	1,851	49	1,652	47
Gross profit	1,070	45	1,249	44	1,170	44	1,345	46	1,213	46	1,221	57	1,247	47	1,483	45	1,672	38	1,324	43	1,638	47	2,050	41	1,922	51	1,844	53
General factory & commercial expenses	1,168	49	1,288	46	1,290	49	1,265	43	1,160	44	1,108	52	1,257	47	1,486	45	1,568	35	1,598	51	1,582	46	2,142	43	2,043	54	2,072	59
Depreciation of plant, equipment, furniture & autos	20		29		3		37		36		51		14		100		77		43		63		44		0		3	
Operating profit or loss	(118)	(5)	(69)	(2)	(123)	(5)	43	2	17	1	62	3	(24)	(1)	(103)	(3)	27	1	(317)	(10)	(7)	nil	(136)	(3)	(121)	(3)	(230)	(7)
Plus: Purchase discounts	56		59		62		60		49		39		57		76		111		68		77		120		53		44	
Purchase rebates	..		..		..		..		..		17		3		18		28		45		28		41		64		27	
Rental income	1		1		1		1		3		..		3		8		14		17		15		15		17		15	
Miscellaneous income	143		..		..		27		..		27		10		..		..		42		41		64		53		63	
Total other income	200	9	60	2	63	2	88	3	52	2	83	4	73	3	102	3	153	3	172	6	161	5	240	5	187	5	149	4
Less: Sales discounts	56		..		39		1		6		29		28		25		33		29		34		29		28		62	
Bad debt loss	..		8		..		3		..		..		..		..		3		..		..		4		..		3	
Interest	6		..		7		14		..		..		13		1		6		4		6		29		13		55	
Miscellaneous expenses	..		..		..		11		..		..		..		..		..		..		..		..		..		..	
Total other expenses	62	2	8	nil	46	2	29	1	6	nil	29	1	42	2	26	1	42	1	33	1	40	1	62	1	41	1	120	3
Contribution to workers' welfare fund	..		..		..		14		..		..		..		21		56		..		35		28		25		..	
Net profit or loss	18	1	(17)	(1)	(106)	(4)	88	3	63	2	116	5	7	nil	(48)	(1)	80	2	(179)	(6)	79	2	17	nil	41	1	(201)	(6)
Profit distribution:																												
Dividend	..		..		..		4		4		4		4		..		4		..		4		4		..		..	
Crisis reserve	..		..		..		..		..		..		..		28		42		..		28		(28)		..		..	
Provision for litigation	..		..		..		..		..		..		..		..		..		..		..		..		17		(17)	
Reserve & retained earnings	143		(17)		(106)		84		59		90		3		(76)		34		(179)		47		41		8		(184)	

Notes:

1. *Cost of goods sold* included all direct material and parts purchased plus piece-work labor in the ébauche and assembly factories.
2. *General factory & commercial expenses* included not only all administrative, clerical, and promotional expenses but also all factory labor and staff on hourly wages or monthly salaries. It also included factory overhead.
3. *Purchase discounts* were given by Ebauches S.A. and UBAH for prompt payment for parts purchased. *Purchase rebates* were given at the end of the year according to the quantity of purchases during the year.

Source: Company records.

until 1958. The general account also included all hourly wages and salaries of factory personnel.)

At the request of the Jaquiers, M. Duvoisin had prepared a supplementary report in 1952, which redistributed expenses in such a manner that the true costs of the ébauche and assembly activities were shown (see Exhibit 6). M. Jaquier had asked that the analysis be carried far enough to allow a valid comparison between the cost of the company-manufactured ébauches and similar ébauches from Ebauches S.A. (see Exhibit 7). The difference, in favor of Jaquier, was found to be 2,394 francs on 114,657 ébauches in 1952.

M. Rennaz began in 1958 to extend the list of factory and commercial expense accounts, and he was working toward isolating ébauche, assembly, and commercial costs; however, M. Duvoisin still grouped expenses according to his convention for his reports to the Jaquiers. M. Rennaz said: "I don't feel it is my business to try to force through a new accounting system, but for my own purposes I am now prepared to give a more complete factory cost analysis. I have been requested to present such analyses on certain questions during the past year. The first time, I had to explain why my total factory expenses were higher than Duvoisin's, and my general costs lower. Now I believe that M. Jean Jaquier understands and sympathizes with what I am doing."

(Exhibit 8, prepared by the case writer, is a comparison of major cost elements in 1952 and 1958, with no attempt to distribute them between major activities.)

Costs and Pricing. For purposes of inventory evaluation and pricing, the company had standard cost calculations for each of its own calibres and those of Ebauches S.A. which it used (see Exhibit 9). A calibre cost card grouped cost elements under three headings: material and purchased parts cost, "basic labor costs," and other labor costs on an allocated basis. Factory overheads supposedly were covered by a 4 per cent margin permitted by the industry association price-calculation formula. M. Rennaz explained these cost-card elements as follows:

Material and Parts Cost. Theoretically, this element consisted of the current prices for all material and parts purchased by Jaquier for the movement.

"Basic Labor Costs." This element was the sum of standard piece-rate labor costs for all operations. Labor cost for each operation was derived from the operation sheet for the calibre, on which M. Lyon and his factory managers had specified the wage classification and time for each operation. M. Rennaz believed that Lyon set standard operational times on the basis of familiarity with each job, knowledge of times used by others in the industry, and general judgment of what they should be at Jaquier.

Other Labor Costs. These allocations were intended to account for the hourly

Exhibit 6

SUMMARY OF 1952 COST ANALYSIS—SUBMITTED BY M. DUVOISIN
(Swiss francs)

Sales		3,323,310
Cost of goods sold		
I. Ebauche factory		
Raw-material purchased*	419,012	
Basic productive wages*	86,719	
Other direct expenses*	13,166	
Deduct: correction for ébauche inventory* increase during year	(76,695)	
Additions to basic productive wages (includes general wage increases, insurance, allowances, vacations)†	48,371	
Direct and indirect hourly and salaried labor (including additions)†	91,829	
Other overhead (includes utilities, insurance, maintenance, supervision)†	125,860	
Depreciation	14,700	
Interest on capital invested	7,035	
Total ébauche factory cost		729,995
(Average cost for 114,657 ébauches made and delivered to Assembly = 6.37 francs)		
II. Assembly factory		
Ebauches delivered	729,995	
Parts purchased*	1,168,489	
Basic productive wages*	259,295	
Other direct expenses*	30,480	
Deduct: correction for assembly inventory increase during year*	(177,000)	
Additions to basic wages†	82,376	
Direct and indirect hourly and salaried labor (including additions)†	395,013	
Other overhead†	125,566	
Depreciation	6,720	
Interest on capital invested	4,375	
Total manufactured cost of goods sold		2,625,309
Gross profit		698,001
Commercial and admin. expenses†	618,125	
Depreciation of office furniture and equipment	12,345	
Interest on capital invested	5,005	
Total		635,475
Operating profit		62,526
Plus: Purchase discounts	77,686	
Rental income	8,158	
Purchase rebates	19,103	
		104,947
Less: Sales discounts		− 25,773
Less: Contribution to workers' welfare fund†		− 21,000
Net income		120,700

Exhibit 6—Continued

Reconciliation with net profit & loss figure shown on Operating Statement (Exhibit 5):

1. Extra depreciation taken:
   Depreciation taken on operating statement .... = 100,115
   Depreciation taken on above analysis .... = 33,765

   Difference is a deduction from above profit .... — 66,350
2. Write-off of inventory increase:*
   Actual inventory increase (above analysis) .... = 253,694
   Increase shown on balance sheet .... = 172,358

   Difference is a deduction from above profit .... — 81,336
3. Other materials and a doubtful debitor written-off on the
   Operating Statement, but not on the above analysis* .... — 35,913
4. Imputed interest included above
   Total interest on invested capital (shown above) 16,415
   Interest expense shown on Operating Statement 1,250

   Difference is an addition to above profit 15,165

   Sum of four corrections .... —168,434
   Apply this sum to net income shown above: 120,700
                                                          —168,434

   Net Loss shown on 1952 Operating Statement .... — 47,734

* The sum of these accounts (and reconciliation corrections) equaled the "Cost of Goods Sold" as computed on the Annual Operating Statement.
† These accounts were lumped together under "General Factory and Commercial Overhead" on the Annual Operating Statement.
Source: Company records.

Exhibit 7

1952 COST ANALYSIS
COMPARISON OF JAQUIER ÉBAUCHE COSTS WITH EBAUCHE S.A. PRICES—
SUBMITTED BY M. DUVOISIN

I. Total cost of Jaquier S.A. ébauche factory (from Exhibit 6) 729,995

II. Purchase price if Jaquier S.A. had purchased the 114,657 ébauches from Ebauche S.A. (calculated by quality and price of each of four calibres made by Jaquier during 1952) 832,691

Must deduct rebates and purchase discounts available if ébauches purchased from Trust
Rebate .... 3% = 25,100
                                   4% = 33,468
Discount .... 5% = 41,834
   Total deduction 100,302
Net price if purchased from Ebauche S.A. 732,389
Difference in favor of Jaquier S.A. 2,394

Source: Company records; company figures derived from cost analysis shown in Exhibit 6.

Exhibit 8

ANALYSIS OF LABOR AND OVERHEAD EXPENSES FOR YEARS 1952 AND 1958
(Swiss francs)

Item	1952	1958
Productive basic wages		
Ebauche	86,719	16,855
Assembly	259,294	87,004
Additions to productive basic wages		
Ebauche	48,371	8,235
Assembly	82,376	31,207
Hourly paid and salaried labor (including additions)		
Ebauche	91,829	255,009
Assembly	395,013	722,589
Factory supervision, office and administrative salaries	243,496	310,334
Social Security and worker insurance costs..	33,534	47,650
Bonuses and year-end gifts	64,722	4,112
Utilities	37,597	57,604
Maintenance, tooling, and auto expenses...	46,560	11,823
Major building repair and modernization..	148,728	105,277
Office supplies	11,673	11,904
Shipping and transportation expenses	9,223	44,292
Entertainment of customers	53,176	32,038
Traveling and salesman's expenses	42,501	60,444
Advertising and promotion	......	103,551
Support to sales agencies	......	53,557
Fees, royalties, commissions, and federation tax on movements	58,290	65,747
Charity donations	21,119	1,855
Taxes	51,926	51,365
All other overheads	47,005	132,461
Total general factory and commercial expenses (below line A-A)	1,487,140	2,072,011
Total	1,833,153	2,215,312

Only items below line A-A composed the General Factory and Commercial Expenses. Those above were included in the direct "cost of goods sold" figure on the Operating Statement.

Source: Prepared by the case writer from company records.

and salaried labor in the manufacture of the movement and were based on Duvoisin's 1952 cost analysis, with increases based on differences in calibre. For example, a certain calibre might be judged to require twice as much hourly and salaried labor in the ébauche shop as the J-481 calibre, for which the exact 1952 cost had been computed.

M. Rennaz felt that in many cases the calibre-cost calculations were not precise and could have led to incorrect unit pricing. In his opinion, errors might be traced to the following causes: (1) operational times for basic labor costs were incorrect, either because the standards were not right or the workers were not working at their expected rate; and (2) allocation of other labor costs—a major cost element—was very crude and was based

Exhibit 9

UNIT COST CALCULATION ON SEVERAL CALIBRES

	CALIBRE DESCRIPTION					
	Century Calibre C	J-491 Supreme Quality	J-553 Smallest Baguette	J-591 6″ Lady's	11½ A Ebauches S.A. Calibre Automatic	9¼ A Ebauches S.A. Calibre (Jaquier Quality)
Barrage calculation:						
Basic barrage price (barrage parts + barrage assembly + 25% gross profit)......	....	25.30	No barrage calcula- tion, since it is a unique calibre	59.30	33.50	36.50
Additions for all parts whose costs exceed that of barrage price (+ 25% gross profit).	....	3.90		9.13	5.34	10.40
Tax......................	....	0.50		0.50	0.50	0.50
Total barrage + Jaquier extras................	....	29.70	....	68.93	39.34	47.40
Jaquier costs:						
Total cost of all parts.......	....	16.44	24.60	22.10	21.15	27.05
Direct labor-assembly.......	....	2.80	27.00	8.65	5.10	2.79
Allocation of salaried & hourly paid factory workers................	....	13.00	10.20	14.80	8.37	11.05
Allowance for factory overhead—4%...........	....	1.21	2.48	1.83	1.38	1.63
Gross profit—25%.........	....	7.88	16.10	11.82	9.00	10.65
Tax.....................	....	0.50	0.50	0.50	0.50	0.50
Total Jaquier costs........	29.80	41.83	80.88	59.70	45.50	53.67
Approximate selling price (movement).............	30.00	43.00	144.00	69.00	48.00	54.00

Note:

1. The Federation of Swiss Watchmakers' pricing regulation, effective until spring, 1959, specified that all manufacturers and assemblers must price their watches equal or above the higher of the barrage calculation or their own cost calculation for each particular calibre. The *barrage calculation* is computed in the following manner: The basic barrage price consists of the Ebauches S.A. and UBAH price for standard quality parts composing the watch; plus an allowance for a "minimum" assembly and regulation; plus 25% gross profit margin, which supposedly covers supervision, testing, commercial costs, and profit. If the company makes or buys any parts whose cost exceeds the cost of standard quality parts, the difference between these part costs and the cost of the standard parts must be added to the basic barrage price. (The converse, however, is not permitted. If, for instance, a manufacturer can make his own ébauches for less cost than he can buy them from Ebauches S.A., he is not allowed to reduce the basic barrage price by the difference.)

   Jaquier's own cost calculation was computed as the sum of the firm's actual parts costs (either purchased or manufactured), actual assembly costs, a 4% allowance for factory overhead, and the 25% gross margin. The 4% and 25% allowances were used regardless of the actual overheads.

2. Due to M. Duvoisin's convention of putting hourly paid and salaried factory personnel into general overhead rather than direct factory costs, the direct cost of company-made ébauches and the direct cost of all assembly contained only piece-work labor and thus were understated. To correct these factory costs, the above cost calculation includes an allocation of salaried and hourly paid factory workers. (See the description in the case dealing with the calculation of these costs.)

Source: Company records.

on an analysis that was becoming less valid as changes occurred between the ratio of piece-work labor and hourly or salaried labor in the factory.

He hoped that the last source of error in the cost calculation could be corrected, since he now had information based on 1958 operations which would allow him to improve the nonpiece-work labor and other factory overhead-cost calculation for each calibre.

Paul Jaquier felt that, in certain aspects, M. Rennaz had exaggerated the company's weaknesses in accounting. He said that in the years when Century was the company's major customer, his father had full knowledge of the factory costs and the unit cost of each calibre. "Otherwise," he said, "my father would have been in no position to bargain with Century over price and still retain a profit margin."

PROCESS MACHINERY EUROPE, INC.*

Late in 1961, the President of Process Machinery Europe, Inc. (PMEI), Mr. J. C. Bruyère, was attempting to determine whether the company should radically change its manufacturing policy. "At the moment," remarked Mr. Bruyère, "we are making most of the items in our product line in half-a-dozen different European countries. My manufacturing executives have been urging me to rationalize our production, that is, to make each product in only one country. But the general managers of my European subsidiaries, and their sales managers, tell me that this won't work, that we must continue to duplicate our manufacturing facilities as we have in the past. A decision really ought to be reached within the next couple of months, because we are about to introduce a major new product into the European market, and we had better decide soon whether it will be made in one place, or in several."

COMPANY BACKGROUND

THE PARENT COMPANY

PMEI was a subsidiary of Process Machinery, Incorporated (PMI), a long-established American corporation. Its basic product line of about 30 items consisted chiefly of complex process machinery for industry. The company had enjoyed outstanding success in the United States, and it had entered the European market with its products around 1930. Subsequently, PMI had opened up subsidiaries in different parts of the world and, by 1961, was selling its products in over 50 countries. The company's basic product line had been developed well before World War II, but in the years following the war PMI, through intensive research and development efforts, created an entire new line of highly complex products which had been very successful. In 1961, the company was one of the leaders of its industry, with, however, some formidable competitors who manufactured products identical in purpose to PMI's. Most observers characterized the industry as a very dynamic one, and PMI's growth record had been for many years a matter of considerable pride to company officials.

The company's products ranged in cost from less than $1,000 for simple, single-purpose items, to several million dollars for highly complex and versatile systems designed to handle many types of processes. The product line was characterized by intricacy of the equipment and a necessity for precision in manufacturing. PMI was constantly searching to improve its basic products and to create new ones. Since competition was intense and since the typical PMI customer's purchase was usually a very sizeable one, product quality was of great importance to the customer and thus to PMI. The company's basic product line required a total of more than 80,000 different parts, most of them of high precision, many of them made from specially ordered raw materials. A PMEI executive remarked that, in recent years, the rate of introduction of new products had increased rather sharply from former levels and that these new products tended to be more complex and expensive than the traditional industry line.

THE EUROPEAN ORGANIZATION

PMI had first entered the European market by setting up sales subsidiaries in the major countries of Europe. As sales grew, the company began to build manufacturing plants in key European locations, and, by the early 1950's, virtually all the company's products were manufactured in one or more European plants. In 1961, there was a PMEI sales subsidiary in every European country (with the exception of such small nations as Andorra, Liechtenstein, etc.). In addition, the company had manufacturing facilities in nine European countries. Immediately after World War II, PMI's top management, foreseeing the rapid growth of its international organization, had established a subsidiary, called "Process Machinery Europe, Incorporated," with full responsibility for the company's operations in Europe. PMEI in turn owned the subsidiary companies in the individual countries, which were generally referred to as the "local" companies. Each local company had a general manager who was responsible to his area manager for that country's sales activities and, if they existed, manufacturing operations. Exhibit 1 shows PMEI's organization.

By 1961, PMEI's sales had attained an annual level of several hundred million dollars. The company employed about 15,000 workers in its 15 European manufacturing plants, which had a total floor space of slightly over 2,000,000 square feet.

EUROPEAN MANUFACTURING OPERATIONS

Of the approximately 30 basic PMI products, all of which were, by 1961, manufactured in European plants, only three simple products were made in all nine manufacturing countries. An additional four products were made in only one country; these four were new products just being introduced to the European market. The rest of the company's products were manufactured in from two to eight plants. A typical product in this group might be manufactured in four or five different countries. In those five countries having more than one PMEI plant (Exhibit 1), a given product was manufactured in only one of the country's plants.

Parts-manufacturing operations were equally complex. Many of the 80,000 parts required were subcontracted to local manufacturers. As a company executive remarked, "If the part is basically a simple one, we often find that a small subcontractor, with his low overhead, can make the part cheaper than we can. Ours is a big organization with high fixed charges. However, we generally manufacture ourselves those parts that are extremely complicated or that require unusually high precision. I would guess that about 40,000 of our parts are subcontracted, either completely or to some extent." In some instances, a given part was made only at one manufacturing plant, which supplied all the requirements of the various European plants. More frequently, however, a part was made (or subcontracted) at several locations. "This situation has developed," remarked the same executive, "because of the freedom we have given the managers of our local companies. If they have the necessary means to expand their manufacturing facilities and if they can make the part themselves at lower cost than by buying it from a sister company, they are pretty free to do so. Because of the duties which are usually imposed on precision-made parts, a local country often finds it can make the part cheaper than paying freight and duty to a sister company. I suppose you could say that the same is true of our assembled machines. In general, duties on assembled machines are higher than on parts, and so a country manager may well decide, if he has the available capital, to assemble the machine himself, rather than importing it."

Sales of PMEI had grown at an average annual rate of nearly 20 per cent since World War II. As a result of this rapid expansion, the local companies tended to have little surplus capital. They could obtain capital, in general, from three sources: first, and most important, from their profits, most of which they had been allowed by the United States corporation to retain in order to finance their growth; second, from occasional grants of new capital from the United States company; third, by borrowing on local financial markets. Each local company was treated as an independent profit center, and the local manager had considerable operating freedom within the limits of basic PMI policies. However, the local manager was responsible to his area manager, and the three area managers reported directly to Mr. Bruyère.

"The situation today is this," remarked a manufacturing executive of the company. "One of our typical machines, costing perhaps $25,000 and containing 5,000 parts, will be assembled in, say, Sweden, with parts from Sweden and five other countries. Total annual sales of this machine in Europe today may be about 400 units, and this machine is probably manufactured not only in Sweden, but in half-a-dozen other countries as well. The system works, but it can get pretty chaotic at times."

ARGUMENTS AGAINST RATIONALIZATION

As has been mentioned, the local general managers and their sales managers were generally convinced that the current manufacturing system was the best one under the circumstances. The arguments against rationalization were well known by company executives; these arguments were grouped into two broad categories: (1) the external complications of rationalization and (2) the internal complications.

EXTERNAL COMPLICATIONS OF RATIONALIZATION

As many company officials pointed out, the most compelling argument against rationalization was the difficulty of importing machines from one European country to another. This difficulty was manifested in three ways. First, there were usually high tariffs on imported goods, especially on the type of precision machinery manufactured by PMI. Although the creation of the Common Market had to some degree resulted in lower tariffs among the six member countries, even in 1961 there were substantial tariffs among the six in the PMI product categories. Also, tariffs among non-Common Market countries tended to be quite high. A second objection in this area was that some countries, in addition to import duties, maintained import restrictions on certain types of products, including some of PMI's machines. This step, which was generally taken to maintain a country's foreign-exchange reserves, meant that occasionally certain products could not be imported at all, regardless of duties paid, unless the importing company could export goods in a certain ratio. For example, in France in the late 1950's, certain types of equipment under import restrictions could be imported only by a company which exported 3 francs' worth of goods for every 1 franc of material imported. Third, certain countries maintained import taxes on goods, so that, even when the duties were not severe, these taxes could often add appreciably to the cost of importing.[1]

Another argument against rationalization, one often made by the sales

---

[1] There is little effective difference, in general, between import duties and import taxes. The distinction is largely semantic. But, because of the existence of import taxes, in some cases an apparently low duty may be accompanied by a high import tax.

and general managers of the local companies, was that there was great prestige and sales value in the fact that PMEI equipment sold in a given country was made in that country. It was argued that this was an important sales tool and that, in fact, certain government agencies, when ordering PMEI equipment, could do so only if the equipment was made in that country. On the other hand, some of PMEI's manufacturing executives suggested that this argument was advanced only because the local managers liked to make all the products in PMEI's line, especially the new and more glamorous ones, and that the managers were unwilling to rationalize because it might limit their future expansion.

A third argument against rationalization was that it might be impossible to rationalize as far as the United Kingdom was concerned. There was, late in 1961, some fear that, if the United Kingdom did not join the Common Market, she would raise her tariffs and import restrictions even higher and thus make it virtually impossible to import PMEI equipment into the United Kingdom. Since the United Kingdom was a major market for the company, this was a matter for some concern.

A final external argument against rationalization was the feeling of many company executives that, in general, the governments of the various companies in which PMEI did business were definitely in favor of having all the company's products made in the country, rather than imported. It was argued that it would be politically unwise for the local companies to disturb their excellent relations with their respective governments by dropping the manufacture of most of the product line from each country. Some PMEI executives, however, dismissed this idea. They pointed out that, since PMEI's management in each local company was almost exclusively composed of nationals of that country, that argument was merely an expression of the patriotism of the local managers involved.

INTERNAL COMPLICATIONS OF RATIONALIZATION

Most of the internal problems which PMEI would face if it rationalized were essentially manufacturing problems, which included the following:

First, it was pointed out that retooling 15 factories would be an immense job. In late 1961, most plants were assembling many types of machines and making relatively few parts for each machine. If complete rationalization were decided upon, each factory would be called upon to produce, for the machines allotted to it, all necessary parts, which would involve the transfer of huge numbers of machine tools from one plant to another, retraining of many workers, changing assembly lines, and other similar tasks. The enormity of such an operation was evident to all company executives.

Second, rationalization might have drastic effects on the work load of some plants, depending on the allocation of products that was made. Since it was the company's policy not to lay off employees if this could be avoided in an economic manner, it was evident that rationalization would require the most elaborate scheduling and coordination if the work force were to be kept fully occupied in all plants.

Third, many of PMEI's machine parts were made from raw materials with unusual specifications, such as steel of special sizes, shapes, and quality. The company had exerted great effort in establishing relationships with its suppliers of such materials in the past. If special material for part X, for example, was now to be used in Milan rather than in Brussels, two problems arose: (1) the difficulty of establishing a reliable new source of adequate material in Milan and (2) fair treatment of the former Brussels supplier. Many of PMEI's suppliers depended on the company for a large share of their sales, and there was some danger that, under complete rationalization, certain suppliers would find themselves losing one of their largest accounts. PMEI did not want to injure its good name for fair treatment of suppliers.

Fourth, if machines and parts manufacturing were to be transferred from one plant to another, an inventory would have to be built up to fill orders during the transition period. PMEI executives feared that it would be difficult to estimate these transition times closely, because of limited experience in this area. Since sales of most PMEI products were increasing steadily, the problem was aggravated.

Fifth, some of PMI's newest products, consisting of entire process systems, were enormously complicated and very expensive, often costing upwards of a million dollars. If production of these products were given to only one country, it was feared that the demand for new capital on the local company might be too great and also that the local company might not be able to expand quickly enough to meet demand for such new equipment. It was also feared that, even if these objections could be overcome, it might be difficult to allocate such big new products to individual countries on a basis that would satisfy everybody concerned.

Sixth, if, under rationalization, only one local company was to make a given machine and if demand for this machine suddenly rose quickly, it was feared that the company might not be able to expand its operations rapidly enough to meet the demand, whereas, with perhaps four manufacturing locations for a given machine, such demand increases could be more easily absorbed. Certain local companies were in areas facing a shortage of skilled labor, the sort of labor required in almost all jobs in the company's plants; such labor shortages might well prevent sufficiently rapid expansion of a local company.

*   *   *   *   *

Two other problems, not strictly of the manufacturing variety, were implicit in any decision to rationalize. First, if one of the smaller manufacturing plants were given only one or two products on which to concentrate and if demand for these products suddenly dropped sharply (perhaps as a result of a new technological advance), that plant might suddenly find its work force idled, and moving in new products to fill the vacuum would clearly take considerable time. A second problem was this: if rationalization proceeded, a local company would, for those products which it stopped manufacturing, find itself suddenly burdened with a much higher cost in many instances. This cost increase would be due to freight charges, duties, import taxes, and perhaps other hidden charges as well. Since it was PMI's policy to sell its machines at nearly identical prices all over the world, a sudden cost increase would reduce a local company's profits, at least temporarily.

*   *   *   *   *

The company's proponents of rationalization, who were mostly manufacturing executives, agreed that many of the above arguments raised valid issues but that these objections were problems which could be nonetheless overcome. These executives pointed out that, although the typical PMEI worker was paid about 30 per cent as much as his American counterpart, every PMI product cost more to make in Europe than in the United States. This fact, they claimed, revealed the high cost of manufacturing in Europe with non-rationalization. They advanced the following arguments in favor of rationalization.

ARGUMENTS IN FAVOR OF RATIONALIZATION

The most compelling reason offered for rationalization was that it was clearly more economical to produce under this policy than by duplicating manufacture at many spots. Production runs could be lengthened substantially for most parts and products. Costly duplication of tooling would be avoided. Under the present policy, it was argued, the difficulties of production scheduling and control were enormous: maintaining uniform tolerances on parts from six countries for one machine was extremely difficult, and assuring arrival of the right number of parts at the right time was equally a problem. It was pointed out that, on occasions, expensive machines had been considerably delayed in manufacture because of the late arrival of one or several crucial parts from another country. If rationalization were adopted, inventories could be lower, since the demand from the entire Europe area would be met from one stockpile, rather than meeting many small demands from many small stockpiles.

Second, it was further maintained that, under the present policy, it took too much time to get a new product into manufacture, simply because of the coordination required to prepare for the new product. The new machines were becoming more and more complex, and this would undoubtedly aggravate an already bad situation.

Third, since PMI's machines did not have to be rigidly designed to customer specifications, it was argued that a machine made in France, for example, would be easily accepted in any other European country. A problem related to this was that, in the past, certain local managements had made minor modifications of a non-functional nature in some of the products, usually in order to adapt a manufacturing operation to local methods or equipment. A top manufacturing executive of PMEI remarked that such modifications were generally not absolutely necessary and had sometimes caused complications.

Finally, it was argued that, in general, tariff barriers and import restrictions were becoming less severe in Europe and that not only was the Common Market removing some of these barriers, but also tariffs would probably become lower throughout Europe in coming years.

In summarizing, the adherents of rationalization pointed out that, even under the present policy, there was already some rationalization. Not all plants made all PMEI products and parts. "Why not," they asked in effect, "go all the way toward rationalization?" They were confident that the technical problems inherent in such a policy change could be overcome, especially if the program were phased in over several years. They were equally certain that the savings in lower manufacturing costs through rationalization would more than cover the increased duties and taxes that would, admittedly, exist at the outset.

*   *   *   *   *

Mr. Bruyère concluded: "As you can see, there are strong arguments on both sides of the fence. I have to decide, first of all, whether any rationalization at all is indicated. If some is, I have to determine how much, whether we rationalize all parts and all assembly operations, or only some of them. Then there is the touchy problem of how to distribute the products among the various plants. Another issue if we rationalize is how long we should plan to complete the job and in what manner we should proceed. Either way we decide, there are certainly going to be problems and expenses, and, unfortunately, we have not been able to form a very good idea of the costs of one approach versus the other. Our business has been growing so rapidly, and we have introduced so many new products, that it has been impossible to make a neat mathematical analysis of the various possibilities. I rather think that this decision will have to be made largely on intuition, because of the lack of economic analysis. Especially because of the large number of totally new products which we plan to introduce in the next few years, the problem appears to us too big for economic analysis at the present stage of that art's development."

Exhibit 1

EUROPEAN ORGANIZATION

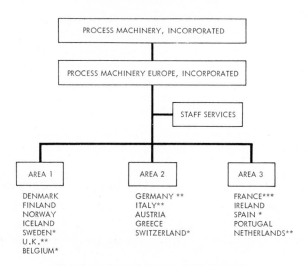

	PROCESS MACHINERY, INCORPORATED	

| | PROCESS MACHINERY EUROPE, INCORPORATED | |

STAFF SERVICES

AREA 1	AREA 2	AREA 3
DENMARK	GERMANY **	FRANCE***
FINLAND	ITALY**	IRELAND
NORWAY	AUSTRIA	SPAIN *
ICELAND	GREECE	PORTUGAL
SWEDEN*	SWITZERLAND*	NETHERLANDS**
U.K.**		
BELGIUM*		

    *   ONE MANUFACTURING PLANT IN THESE COUNTRIES
  **   TWO MANUFACTURING PLANTS IN THESE COUNTRIES
*** THREE MANUFACTURING PLANTS IN FRANCE

BERLINER-APOTHEKER A.G.*

"A business can not be run as if it were on an island; management must be aware of outside forces which will or can affect the company's fortunes and must act accordingly," stated Dr. Franz Seidler, one of the two members of the Berliner-Apotheker A.G.'s Vorstand ("executive committee"). "We must always ask ourselves: what effect could the latest political or governmental action—be it that of the West Germans, East Germans, Russians, or Western Allies—have on our plans or operations. I will grant that we are more dramatically affected by political affairs in West Berlin than business would be in most other places, but I think that the principles involved are fundamental.

"On August 13, 1961, the day the Communists began to erect the wall dividing Berlin, the rules of the game changed, and we had to change with them."

THE COMPANY

Berliner-Apotheker A.G., was a medium-sized pharmaceutical manufacturer located in the Frohnau district of Berlin. (Exhibit 1 shows a city plan of West Berlin.) The company manufactured and sold a limited variety of basic and specialty pharmaceutical products. About 75 per cent of sales were made in West Germany, and the remaining 25 per cent were exported, mostly to the Far East. In 1961, Berliner-Apotheker A.G., had sales of 30 million Deutsche Mark (DM) (about $7.5 million) and employed about 800 workers.

The management of Berliner-Apotheker mentioned shortage of labor as one problem they had had ever since the company's reorganization after World War II. Dr. Seidler explained: "Most firms in West Berlin have had the problem of scarce labor to some degree: however, we have been significantly more affected because we have been separated from our natural source of labor supply by the border. Consequently, we have had to find most of our workers in distant neighborhoods, such as Wedding and Charlottenburg. This was a difficult enough situation before the cutoff of workers from East Berlin.

* All names have been disguised.
Copyright 1962 by l'Institut pour l'Etude des Méthodes de Direction de l'Entreprise (IMEDE), Lausanne, Switzerland. Reprinted by permission.

84

"The immediate impact of the August partitioning of the city on our labor force was not very serious; we lost about 40 workers. But the loss of some 50,000 Eastern workers has made the labor problem generally much more acute, and we are now suffering from severe competition for our labor. Positions have opened in more favorable locations—that is, locations closer to the workers' homes—and we are losing our staff and work force to these firms. What we are facing is an evacuation of workers to town.

"The problem is even more serious for us now because we are trying to build up our work force to 1,100 people by the end of the year. To give you some idea of the magnitude of the problem, we have hired 275 workers and lost 195 workers during the first four months of 1962. That is quite some turnover.

"When you consider that any new man must receive at least 4 hours of attention from a foreman, even for the simplest position, you see that we are losing the time of more than one foreman each month in terms of wasted training. You must then add to that the losses of inefficient production during the indoctrination period of each new man and also the administrative costs of entering and striking a man from the company's rolls.

"Three years ago I used to know every face in the plant and could call most of the men by name. Now I am lucky if I recognize one in three people, let alone know their names or what they are doing."

SPECIALTY PILL MANUFACTURING

"One area where the labor shortage has particularly affected us," added Dr. Seidler, "is in the specialty pill manufacturing department, which employs about 40 girls. We find that there are plenty of women who are willing to go to work if they only have to cross the street to get there, but they lose interest as soon as it involves a 45-minute trip to work, as it does to get to our plant. As a consequence, we had been considering for some time the establishment of a separate specialty pill plant near a ready source of female labor.

"The alternative of trying to attract women to Frohnau for this work by means of high salaries was not feasible because it would have disrupted our whole salary structure. High incentive salaries for this small group of women might give the unions a basis for a general upward adjustment of salaries for the whole plant.

"We could set up the new plant either in West Berlin or somewhere in West Germany. We finally decided, about a year ago, in favor of setting up the plant near Cologne. We based this decision on three reasons.

First and most important at the time, the necessary female labor could be more easily obtained. Second, the proposed site could be enlarged to include storage, which would ensure better distribution of our products. We cannot use public storage facilities for some of our special drugs which must be kept in a climatized atmosphere for extended storage. Third, we thought that it might be advisable to place some of the company's investments outside West Berlin.[1]

"When the wall was put up by the Communists, all three of these reasons became weightier than ever. As I have already mentioned, the labor situation became much tighter. Then, too, since we might have had to face another blockade as we did in 1948, outside storage became more desirable in view of possible interrupted shipments. And the advantage of moving investment out of Berlin during this crisis speaks for itself.

"But when the wall was put up, the decision had to be reversed. Outweighing all other considerations, we believed that it would be politically unwise to try to move any investment into West Germany at a time when the German government was so anxious that West Berlin not fold under the pressure. There was the additional fear that if we set up facilities in West Germany, many of our workers would ask to be transferred to the new location. Many West Berlin companies encountered serious employee problems in this respect. With operations limited to Berlin, at least we did not have this problem.

"Now, nine months later, we are finding the economics of the decision to be changing in support of our move. This is because of the "Berlin Privileges" (tax and legal advantages given to businesses in West Berlin over those in West Germany). Of course, these privileges have existed since the early 1950's, but the advantage given to businesses in West Berlin is becoming greater and greater. And while the economics are only marginally in favor of setting up a plant in West Berlin at this time, the trend is such as to make this advantage greater as time goes on.

"To give you some idea of how significant these privileges are, I should first mention that we are completely free of the 4 per cent federal turnover tax on all manufactured goods sold to customers in the Federal Republic. This exemption is not granted for sales inside West Berlin. Then, too, West German firms receive a 4 per cent rebate of turnover tax on all purchases of West Berlin products. For example, a company is entitled to a 400 DM tax rebate for a 10,000 DM purchase of West Berlin products. Another advantage is that the federal corporation income tax has

---

[1] Many firms operating or headquartered in Berlin have opened facilities and offices in Western Germany for purposes of security. These latter were referred to by the Germans as a *Zweites Bein* ("second leg").

been reduced from 51 to 37.6 per cent for income received from operations in West Berlin.

"Another important privilege concerns special treatment for depreciation allowances. Whereas West German companies can depreciate chattels and buildings only at what is essentially a straight-line rate, West Berlin firms can depreciate up to 75 per cent of either type of property within the first three years. The remaining 25 per cent must be depreciated linearly over the life of the chattel or building. The chattel must remain in West Berlin for at least three years to qualify. This means that the West German firm can choose to depreciate the whole 75 per cent in the first year; the straight-line depreciation for the remaining 25 per cent can then begin in the second year. And, even now, a motion is on the floor in the Bundestag to permit a 100 per cent depreciation in the first year.

"The Berlin privileges introduce complications for companies which add part of the value of a given product in Berlin and part of the value in West Germany. This would have been our position had we located the pill plant near Cologne, since we would have produced the pharmaceutical chemicals here in Berlin and packaged them in pill ampoules there. The difficulty is to determine just how much tax exemption we are entitled to and just how much rebate our customers would be entitled to.

"Locating part of our operations in West Germany would require additional staff personnel and management effort to handle the tax and legal complications existing now. These complications are likely to grow as additional privileges are introduced and the two systems become still more divergent."

TRADE WITH EAST BERLIN

"Our reversal of decision concerning the location of the pill plant was clearly based on political considerations," continued Dr. Seidler. "But one does not always bend to these pressures. A case in point is the action we took with respect to trade in East Berlin.

"For many years we have been maintaining a small but significant trade with East Berlin, as have most, if not all, companies in West Berlin. The West German government, of course, had been aware of this trade. In part, we have maintained trade with the East in order to sell part of our products. In part, we have conducted this trade in order to stay in favor with the East German and Russian authorities. Legally, our products are entitled to pass through the Eastern Sector when being transported by truck to West Germany. However, it is a very simple thing for the Eastern authorities to hinder our shipments by making 'thorough' inspections of our goods and papers. They could easily delay our shipments at the fron-

Exhibit 1

MAP OF WEST BERLIN SHOWING SELECTED DISTRICTS*

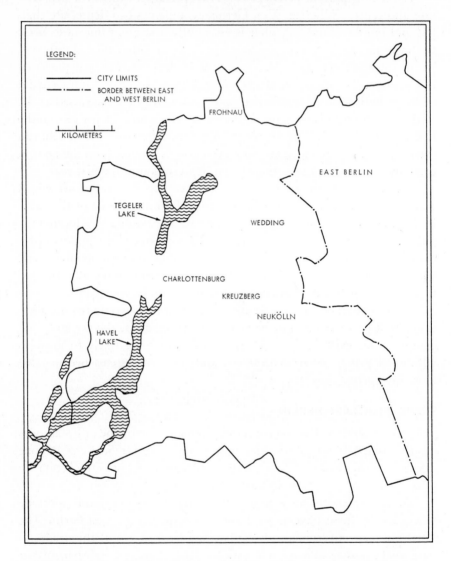

* The Charlottenburg, Kreuzberg, Neuköln, and Wedding districts are worker's residential areas.

tier for a day or two because of the 'pressing load of other inspections' and then have it denied passage because of some technical flaw in our papers. If our shipments were not ruined by the long lay-over in trucks, certainly the inconvenience of having the drugs moved back to Berlin on numerous occasions could cripple our business.

"This last factor—that of holding hands with the Eastern authorities— lost much of its significance during the period immediately following the erection of the wall, because much bigger issues came to dominate the scene. Official and public pressure then arose for such trading with the East to be discontinued as a retaliation for the construction of the wall.

"We decided to ignore this pressure and continue, albeit at a reduced level, our trade with the East. The main reason for this decision was our assessment that the pressures put on us were of a relatively temporary nature. We felt that the unusual severity of the situation would subside within six to nine months. Furthermore, we felt that, once we removed our products from the East German markets it would be very difficult to re-establish them. The reason that we were able to enter so effectively originally was that we did it before there were East German companies that could produce the same goods. This is no longer the case.

"Please understand, I am not a sentimentalist who believes that Germany will be reunited soon and consequently plans for the full reopening of old markets. Nor do I picture myself as an avaricious businessman, who will trade with the devil himself for the almighty profit. I do, however, believe that we in West Berlin must continue to recognize that we are on an island surrounded by Communists who are in a good position to make things as difficult or easy for us as they wish. Well, while the West German government is not officially encouraging resumption of trade ties with East Germany, I am beginning to sense an easing of the government's opposition and a turn towards the former status quo."

PART III

Objectives, Strategy, and Policy in the European Chemical Industry

IN THE PRECEDING section, readers have been looking primarily at objectives, strategy, and policy as these are affected by such internal factors as company resources or top management's personal values. This section has been designed to focus intensively on factors external to the company itself. The purpose is, of course, to permit an assessment of the forces at work in the technical, economic, social, and political environments of the individual firms and its competitors within the industry. Traditionally, there has been a predilection for managements, both in Europe and in the United States, to orient their planning around internal considerations. The more efficient firms, however, have also given great weight to the external environment of which they are a part. The notes and cases in this section should contribute to restoring a better balance between internal and external considerations. If, as the authors have suggested, the student has already been introduced to the Galvor,[1] Midway, or world wrist watch series,[2] then he will already have encountered many of the environmental factors that will be the center of attention here.

In a section focused on external or environmental factors, we believed it better to confine ourselves to one industry only, since otherwise our study would not permit sufficient breadth or depth, or adequate indication of the variety to be found in different industry segments even within a single nation and to a still greater extent when one nation is compared with another. The chemical industry was the one selected for intensive study for a variety of reasons. This industry is a large and important one in many European countries. It is also dynamic and changing. It is complex, and thus by itself encompasses many characteristics that could otherwise be illustrated only by a cluster of less complicated industries. Moreover, it is an industry on which a fair amount of statistical data is available and one in which the authors were able to establish many useful international contacts. Finally, this industry is an interesting one to include in an international casebook because it is internationally oriented, depending either on foreign trade or foreign operations for part of its success.

The European chemical industry, like the world chemical industry, is faced with many new developments, both internal and external. Among these have been a technological revolution occurring at great speed in recent years; the development of the European Common Market and a world trend toward freer trade; a mobility of corporate interest; and a postwar trend against cartels and other "stabilizing arrangements" formerly characteristic of the European environment.

The first note on "General Characteristics of the Chemical Industry" contains information that applies generally throughout the world. The notes on the several European countries contain economic data relating to the industry and to its environment in the top four chemical-producing nations of Western Europe (West Germany, United Kingdom, France, and Italy) and in one small producing nation, Sweden. Our reasons for including Sweden should perhaps be made explicit. Just because the chemical industry in this country *is* relatively small and undeveloped, it clearly and simply manifests the shaping influence of environmental forces which, though equally present in larger and more complex situations, are much harder to trace and see. Also, Sweden's industry is still at a stage through which, roughly speaking, the larger and more complex industries have passed. Thus understanding Sweden adds depth and background to our understanding of forces that have been at work in the industry as a whole.

---

[1] Part VIII of this text.
[2] Learned, Christensen, and Andrews, *op. cit.*

The notes on the five national chemical industries typically contain data on size and growth, the boom in petrochemicals, industry structure, any special role played by the government, and facts on labor, investment, and international trade. While detailed reports on current chemical research that might have a bearing on future product possibilities or competitive changes could not be included, the data do clearly demonstrate the impact of past research on the present state of the industry as a whole and on particular companies in it.

These notes can be used as a basis for analyzing opportunities open to and constraints placed upon individual companies in the different countries. The notes also provide useful background data for the two cases on chemical companies included in this section of the book and also for the cases in the section on mergers and joint ventures.

The two application cases in this section are Croydon Chemicals Company Limited and The Arla Chemicals Company. Croydon was a producer of intermediate chemicals in Great Britain, and its management had some doubts about its economic future. The case contains management's analysis of this problem and indicates some of the steps already taken in the development of the firm. Because management had not reached its final conclusions, the most basic question for study is "What action, if any, should the management of this company take with respect to the problems confronting it?"

The case of The Arla Chemicals Company is a particularly good illustration of the way in which so-called technical and economic trends can affect a company. It is an unusual case, in the sense that the researcher was able to obtain the company's statement of its problem long before management had gathered the facts to help it make definite decisions regarding trends or resulting problem areas. It is not often that a case collector is able to capture the dilemma of management at this phase. Students might examine and discuss, in turn, each problem area mentioned in the case, indicate the relative emphasis which management should give to the various problems areas, consider the relative urgency and proper timing for study of these problems, and make any feasible suggestions for action. Students will get really involved in the case if they try to decide what course of action seems most desirable to them and to give appropriate reasons for their choice. In this connection, the important consequences of suggested actions should be delineated, and any risks assumed should be identified.

In this case, as in many others, students may wish to comment on the prevailing attitudes of various members of management, so far as these affect the possibilities for constructive internal action by the company.

Each student is warned that what he might decide to do, on the assumption that he is in charge of the company, might differ from what he would predict the existing top management might do. In choosing his own course of recommended action, a man is advised to assume the continued presence of any constraints which are inherent in the rest of the company's resources and people, excepting only the one individual whose role he has chosen to play.

As teachers, we can predict that the experience outlined in the above approach is both frustrating and rewarding: frustrating because it is difficult to come to grips with such a complicated situation, but rewarding because the hard analytical thinking involved leads to self-confidence and to confidence that the student's plans of action would in fact put the company further along the road toward ultimate solutions than it was as of the time of the case.

GENERAL CHARACTERISTICS OF THE CHEMICAL INDUSTRY

Products of the chemical industry are everywhere: in the soles of our shoes and in the waterproofing of the umbrellas over our heads; in the additives to the prepackaged soup which begins our meal and in the bicarbonate of soda which may end it; in the simple match-head and in the complex air-purification system of a manned satellite. Because chemical products affect almost every phase of modern life, they have become essential to every industrially advanced nation; the more industrialized the nation, the more important the role that chemical products play.

With the possible exceptions of the electronics and nuclear fields, no other industry has been so profoundly affected by the rapidity of scientific development since 1940. This rapidity has made the chemical industry one that is undergoing constant change and one that is becoming increasingly complex technologically. The chemical industry's dynamic nature is shown by the fact that, in many sectors, over 50 per cent of all current products have been introduced since 1940. An extreme case is pharmaceuticals, where many firms attribute more than half their current sales to products introduced within the last five to ten years. The increase of technological complexity is evidenced by the influx of highly sophisticated processes and products, by the tremendous increase in research and development expenditures, and by the greater employment of scientists and engineers with advanced degrees.

Following a short historical review of what has become the chemical industry, a definition and classification of the present-day industry will be given. Later sections discuss the growth, international nature, structure, cartels, customers, raw materials, methods of production, and research activities of the industry.

DEVELOPMENT OF THE CHEMICAL INDUSTRY

The authors of a comprehensive economic survey, titled *World Population and Production Trends and Outlook*, have summarized the early development of the chemical industry up through World War I as follows:

Chemistry has been an art, a science, and an industry. It was practiced as an art thousands of years ago. As a science it dates from the middle of the seventeenth century. Its beginnings as an industry go back to the early years of the nineteenth century, but it did not come of age until the twentieth.

*   *   *   *   *

The ancients made a few medicines, some animal and vegetable colors, glass and some metals. The Tyrians produced their famous purple dye from shellfish around 1500 B.C., and the Chinese made gunpowder. . . .

In the Middle Ages, the chief industrial acid in Europe was vinegar, easily and cheaply obtained but too weak for most chemical reactions. The lactic acid of buttermilk was used in bleaching textiles. Manufacture of alum was introduced into Europe from Arabia and became a monopoly of the popes. Dung was the industrial source of ammonia. Sulphuric acid, blue cobalt pigment and iron pigments were produced in small quantities. These early beginnings of chemical production were empirical in character, stemming from incidental discoveries and based on the rule of thumb. Despite the small scale of production, monopolistic practices were common; knowledge of a process was often jealously guarded and kept for generations within a single family.

Even in the 18th century, chemical production was limited to a few dyes, pigments, drugs, and small quantities of sulphuric acid and gunpowder. Larger-scale production was made possible in 1746 by the discovery in England of means of producing sulphuric acid in lead chambers and, in 1790, by the discovery in France of a method of producing soda ash.

The two products—sulphuric acid and soda ash—spearheaded the growth of the chemical industry in the early nineteenth century and are still the first chemicals to be produced in countries beginning the manufacture of chemicals.

*   *   *   *   *

Production of super-phosphates, stimulated by Liebig's discovery of the importance of fertilizers for the productivity of the soil, began in England in the 1840's. . . . The incidental discovery of a chemical dye . . . in England in 1856 gave origin to an important new branch of the chemical industry, dyestuffs. The following decade saw the commercial production of explosive nitroglycerine (Nobel, 1862) and an essential improvement in the manufacture of soda ash (the Solvay method, Belgium, 1863), which was already a sizeable industry.

In the latter part of the century, inventions in the field of chemistry followed one another rapidly. Methods were found to utilize light oils distilled from coal tar. Pharmaceuticals, perfumes and paints appeared on the market in increasing quantities. . . . The chemical industry branched out in various directions. New processes and products were developed, one line of production supporting another. Machinery and equipment became increasingly elaborate in line with the growing complexity of chemical engineering.

It was reserved to the twentieth century, however, to integrate all these branches of chemical production through systematic research . . . and to strengthen the ties between the chemical and other branches of manufacturing. The two world wars greatly stimulated chemical production. They brought an immense and urgent demand for all kinds of chemicals, from explosives to fertilizers, from drugs to dye-stuffs. . . .[1]

The two wars also caused great shifts in the division of production within the world chemical industry. For example, prior to World War I, Germany held a dominant, if not monopolistic, world position in the field of dyestuffs. When these products were shut off during the war, the dye-stuff industry sprang up in most of the other industrial countries. On the other hand, Germany gained ground in high-pressure techniques associated with the production of synthetic nitrogen. The increased wartime demand for this product in the domestic manufacture of munitions and fertilizers, coupled with the unavailability of Chilean nitrate, forced Germany to expand its domestic capacity. During World War II the Allied countries, again cut off from German chemicals, again had to catch up with Germany, this time in the organic chemical and plastic industries.

Not only did shifts of production emphasis take place, but many new products were discovered in answer to the critical needs of war. The many processes invented not only met the wartime demands, but also proved themselves widely useful in peacetime.

DEFINITION OF THE CHEMICAL INDUSTRY

The development of the chemical industry and of the science of industrial chemistry is a salient feature of our times. Today's range of chemical products is so wide and the variety of chemical processes used by various industries so extensive that it is becoming increasingly difficult to define the scope of the industry.

There is no single definition of the chemical industry as it exists today. A few experts define it as an industry that produces commodities differing in their molecular structures from those of the raw materials from which they were made. Such a definition would be too broad to be useful.

The common practice is to distinguish the chemical industry, which produces chemicals, from the "chemical-process" industries, in which chemical processes play a major role but the products are not themselves chemicals: paper manufacture, petroleum refining, metallurgy. The line between these groups, however, is often difficult to distinguish, with the result that the chemical industry is defined in as many different ways as there are agencies attempting to define it. The United States includes synthetic fibers but excludes photographic chemicals. Germany includes not only the above two categories but also matches, linoleum, office materials

---

[1] W. S. Woytinsky and E. S. Woytinsky (New York: Twentieth Century Fund, 1953), pp. 1176, 1177.

(carbon paper, pencils, ink, etc.), and roofing felt. The Organization for Economic Co-operation and Development (OECD) excludes synthetic fibers. Great Britain, Switzerland, Italy, and France each have their own variations.

The reasons for the differences among working definitions of the chemical industry are manifold. In the case of national statistics, the definition often stems from the historical development of the chemical industry in that particular nation and from its present orientation and activity. International agencies are handicapped by the need to tailor their definition to include those sectors for which the member nations can supply adequate statistics.

The chemical industry can be defined to include the industrial sectors listed below. This listing follows the OECD definition, to which the synthetic fibers sector has been added because of its inclusion in many other important definitions.

Basic chemicals (elements and compounds)[2]
    (*a*) Inorganic
    (*b*) Organic
Dyestuffs
Tanning agents
Paints and varnishes
Medicinal and pharmaceutical products
Essential oils and perfume materials
Toilet, polishing, and cleansing preparations
Insecticides, fungicides, and disinfectants
Manufactured fertilizers
Explosives
Synthetic resin and plastic materials
Synthetic rubber
Synthetic fibers
Photographic and cinematographic supplies
Miscellaneous (casein, starches, and glue)

Classifying Chemical Products.   By its very nature, the listing of industrial sectors to define the scope of the chemical industry has presented one method of classifying chemical products. This method is known as a product group classification and is the one most widely used for official statistical data on production, sales, and trade. Each industrial sector is further subdivided at least into related product groups (e.g., thermosetting or thermoplastic materials) and often into individual products.

One additional product group classification under consideration in

---

[2] An element is a substance which cannot be decomposed by the ordinary types of chemical change or made by chemical union. A compound is a substance of definite composition made up of two or more elements in chemical combination.

1961 by the OECD breaks the total industry down into two main groups: basic chemicals, including fertilizers, and chemical products largely for consumption.[3] The first group contains products that are sold mainly for industrial and, in the case of fertilizers, agricultural consumption, and the second group contains products prepared primarily for household consumption.

Despite the favored position of product group classification for statistical purposes, there are at least two other methods of classifying chemical products which are widely used throughout the industry, classification by uses and by carbon content.

Chemical Classification by Uses. Not far removed from the two product group breakdowns mentioned above is the custom of classifying chemical products as basic, intermediate, and finished chemicals.

A *basic chemical* can be defined as a product that is produced from a natural raw material, such as common salt, petroleum, sulfur, mineral ore, or water, and is used in a large number of chemical processes. Typical basic chemicals are sulfuric acid, soda ash, naphthalene, and benzene. An *intermediate chemical product* is generally one made from one or more basic chemicals, and one used in turn to make other chemical products. Examples of such products are phthalic anhydride, urea, ammonia, and nitric acid. A *finished chemical* is typically sold to the end user, either industrial or consumer. This classification includes such items as polyvinyl chloride plastic, superphosphate fertilizers, and pharmaceuticals.

The method of classification is loosely applied within the industry, and caution must be taken when these terms are encountered. What one sector of the chemical industry may consider and commonly define as a finished chemical may only be an intermediate chemical or even a raw material for another sector. For example, some oil companies typically consider ethylene a "finished" product, whereas it is only a "raw material" for the manufacture of polyethylene.

Chemical Classification by Carbon Content. Chemical products are also grouped on the basis of the presence or absence of the element carbon. Generally, compounds which contain carbon are called *organic;* all other compounds are classified as *inorganic.* The distinction grew up centuries ago.

---

[3] The first group, "basic chemicals, including fertilizers," contains organic and inorganic chemicals, mineral tar and crude chemicals from coal, petroleum and natural gas, dyestuffs, tanning materials, essential oils and perfume materials, fertilizers, explosives, synthetic plastics materials, and synthetic rubber.

The second group, "chemical products largely for consumption," contains pigments, paints, varnishes, pharmaceutical products, perfumery, cosmetics, soaps, cleansing and polishing preparations, insecticides, fungicides, disinfectants, starches, and similar products.

Originally, organic chemistry implied the chemical examination of living matter, or matter which had once been living (e.g., coal and petroleum). Such examination was generally limited to analysis, that is, an attempt to determine the constituents of the organic material. Most organic materials, such as sugar, fat, and protein, are highly complex chemicals which defied synthesis for many years. In ancient days, accordingly, the limited benefit to be derived from organic chemistry made that branch of chemistry relatively minor.

In recent times, researchers observed that all living matter contained carbon, and so this became the new criterion for classifying chemicals as organic or inorganic. As chemical knowledge grew, scientists gradually learned how to synthesize the more common organic chemicals found in nature, and they also began to create carbon-containing compounds which did not exist in nature. The number of carbon compounds now known is estimated at about 20 times as large as the number of inorganic compounds.

One important reason for maintaining the organic-inorganic distinction is that carbon compounds are characterized by peculiar properties not apparent to the same extent in inorganic compounds. Thus research and production techniques in the two fields are significantly different from one another.

GROWTH OF THE INDUSTRY

The growth of chemical industry production has been very dynamic since the turn of the century. The current value of the world output of chemicals has been estimated to have grown as follows:[4]

Year	Dollars in Millions
1900	1,200
1913	2,380
1938	10,400
1950	32,150
1962	86,000

Not all sectors of the chemical industry have shared the rapid growth indicated above. The important inorganic chemicals of 1938 have continued to grow, but at more moderate rates. The strong impetus to over-all growth has stemmed from a number of the new organic sectors, such as synthetic resins and plastics, synthetic rubber, and synthetic fibers. Chart 1 shows the relative value of production and the rate of growth of various chemical sectors for the world's six largest chemical-producing nations combined for 1938 and 1960.

The well-established sectors of dyes, cosmetics, soaps, paints, and ferti-

---

[4] Source: *Chemische Industrie*, office statistics.

Chart 1

PRODUCTION VALUE AND GROWTH RATE OF DIFFERENT CHEMICAL SECTORS
FOR THE WORLD'S SIX LARGEST CHEMICAL-PRODUCING NATIONS COMBINED*
1938–60

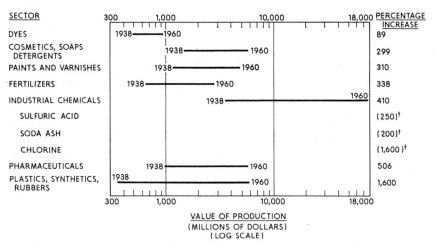

VALUE OF PRODUCTION
(MILLIONS OF DOLLARS)
(LOG SCALE)

* United States, U.S.S.R., Great Britain, Germany, Japan, France.
† Estimated growth of world production from 1929 to 1959.
Source: *Chemische Industrie*, December, 1961; *Chemische Industrie International*, Vol. 2 (1961), p. 54, for sulfuric acid, soda ash, and chlorine.

lizers all grew at a slower pace than the over-all industry. While industrial chemicals as a whole exceeded the industry average growth, it was the organic component, comprising chemicals such as phthalic anhydride for plastics and dodecylbenzene for detergents, that experienced a tremendous gain. Production of most basic inorganic chemicals, such as sulfuric acid and soda ash, grew at rates much below the industry average.

There were some notable exceptions to the growth pattern of inorganic chemicals. In those cases where inorganic chemicals served as supplies for fast-growing organic products, they too experienced rapid growth. Chlorine, a prime example, is used as a raw material for plastics (polyvinyl chloride), chlorinated waxes and solvents, plant protectives, and pesticides. Other examples are nitric acid, used for the production of Nylon and Dacron (Terylene), and calcium carbide, required for acetylene, which in turn is used to produce plastics and other organic materials.

As of the early 1960's the greatest growth is taking place in petrochemicals,[5] which are supplying most of the expanding demands of the various organic chemical sectors, such as plastics and synthetic rubber. Petrochemical production in the member nations of the OECD rose from only .2 million metric tons in terms of carbon content in 1953 to .8 mil-

---

[5] Petrochemicals usually describe chemicals which are derived from petroleum and natural gas and which are one or two chemical transformations from the raw materials.

lion by 1958. Doubling between 1958 and 1960, it reached over 2 million tons in 1961, and is expected to reach 4.3 million tons by 1964 for an increase of over 100 per cent. For the same three-year period, United States production is forecast to go from 11 to 15.4 million tons.[6] The greatest expenditures in plant investment and research are taking place in this sector.

NATIONAL POSITIONS IN THE INDUSTRY

Two indices are often used to rank the importance of the chemical industry of nations: the actual production output and the per capita consumption of chemicals. The former index tends to favor larger nations and the latter to favor smaller industrialized nations.

Of the 1938 world production output, the United States accounted for 29 per cent, Germany for 15 per cent, Japan and the United Kingdom for about 10 per cent each, France for 7 per cent, and the U.S.S.R. for only 6 per cent. By 1960 the relative importance of the various national outputs had changed, as shown in Table 1. It is interesting to note, however, that the top seven chemical-producing nations have together accounted for 80 to 82 per cent of the world's total production with few exceptions since 1913.[7]

Table 1

CHEMICAL PRODUCTION OF THE TEN MOST IMPORTANT COUNTRIES, 1960

Rank	Country	Production (millions)	Per Cent of Total World Production
1	United States	$29,800	40.0
2	U.S.S.R.	8,100	10.9
3	Federal Germany	5,764	7.7
4	United Kingdom	5,700	7.7
5	Japan	5,271	7.1
6	France	4,014	5.4
7	Italy	3,010	4.0
8	Canada	1,350	1.8
9	Holland	820	1.1
10	Belgium	690	0.9
	Total of ten largest	64,519	86.6
	All other countries	10,081	13.4
	World total	74,600	100.0

Source: Production statistics for individual countries, *Chemische Industrie*, April, 1962; world production, office statistics, *Chemische Industrie*.

---

[6] OECD, *The Chemical Industry* (annual), 1960–1961, p. 70; 1961–1962, p. 81.

[7] R. Woller, staff member, *Chemische Industrie*. This calculation considered Germany as it was politically defined before World War II (including East Germany and certain territories now belonging to Poland) but only the West German Republic since the war.

In 1950 the United States had produced about 50 per cent of the world's total output, but the resurgence of the chemical industry in Europe had cut this dominating figure to 40 per cent by 1960 and promises to reduce it even further. Industry observers believe that the ranking in 1965 will be the United States, U.S.S.R., Japan, Federal Germany, and the United Kingdom, with the United States still far out in front. The greatest growth, however, will take place in Japan, which should move well into third place with a production of about $10 billion as compared with Federal Germany's expected production of $7–$8 billion.

The ranking of selected nations by their approximate estimated per capita consumption is shown in Table 2. The per capita consumption was computed after adding imports and subtracting exports from national production. These calculations do not account for inventory changes. This omission is not so serious for the ranking, inasmuch as inventories in most nations would often tend to change in the same direction during a given year.

It is interesting to note that, while Japan and the U.S.S.R. hold the lowest positions with respect to per capita consumption, they rank respectively second and fifth in total production.

Table 2

PER CAPITA CONSUMPTION OF CHEMICAL PRODUCTS FOR SELECTED COUNTRIES
APPROXIMATE ESTIMATE FOR 1938 AND 1960
(Current dollars)

Countries	1938 Per Capita Consumption $ Per Head	1938 Ranking of Group	1960 Per Capita Consumption $ Per Head	1960 Ranking of Group	Per Cent Increase 1938–60
Germany*	31.1	1	94.5	3	...
United States	24.1	2	144.2	1	600
Belgium-Luxembourg	20.6	3	67.3	7	320
Netherlands	17.2	4	62.5	8	360
Great Britain	17.1	5	111.3	2	590
Canada	14.9	6	84.9	5	570
Switzerland	13.5	7	86.8	4	620
France	13.3	8	82.0	6	630
Italy	9.9	9	59.4	9	590
Japan	8.6	10	57.1	10	630
U.S.S.R.	5.2	11	37.9	11	760
Group Average	15.1		82.3		

* The 1938 data are calculated for Germany as defined on December 31, 1937. The 1960 data are calculated for West Germany only.

Source: Office statistics, *Chemische Industrie*.

THE INTERNATIONAL NATURE OF THE INDUSTRY

The chemical industry operates internationally with respect to both its sales and its production. The volume of international trade is high, owing to three factors which, singly or in combination, are present in the case of a great many chemical products: global usability; economies of large-scale production; and scattered sources of raw materials.

Unlike clothing or electronic equipment, for which national tastes or special technical specifications tend to limit the trading area, most chemical products can be used throughout the world, regardless of their source. Production, in turn, tends to become centralized because the chemical industry can greatly benefit, in most cases, from economies of large-scale production and bulk shipment. Finally, suitable supplies of important raw materials are often economically available only in a limited number of geographic areas, frequently in places remote from both manufacturing facilities and markets. These factors have led to the high degree of international trading that exists today in the chemical industry. The role that chemical exports play in the over-all international trade is shown in Table 3.

Table 3

WORLD CHEMICAL AND TOTAL EXPORTS, 1938 AND 1959
(Dollars in millions)

	1938	1959
World chemical exports.	$ 1,200	$ 7,840
Percentage of exports to production for world chemical industry. . . .	10.5	11.8
World exports, total.	$22,400	$115,800
Percentage of chemical to total world exports.	5.4	6.8

Source: *Chemische Industrie*, April, 1961.

While much of the international trade reflects shipments of chemicals from industrialized nations to the nonindustrialized countries, the greater part of the trade takes place among the highly industrialized nations. The reasons that certain countries are dominant international suppliers of certain products are manifold. Certain countries may hold natural economic advantages for certain processes (e.g., Norway's cheap electric power gives it an advantage in electrochemical processes). Other countries may have technological advantages or patent protections. Still other nations may hold a dominant position as a result of having cultivated a market not attractive enough to lure new competitive entries. In any case, no nation can hope to produce economically all the many different chemicals needed throughout its industry.

Table 4 shows the relative importance of exports as a percentage of total chemical production for a number of countries.

INDUSTRY STRUCTURE

The chemical industry is among the most highly concentrated branches of manufacturing, from both a corporate and a geographic point of view.

Table 4

CHEMICAL EXPORTS OF SELECTED COUNTRIES AS A
PERCENTAGE OF TOTAL PRODUCTION, 1950 AND 1960

	1950	1960
Belgium	28	53
Federal Germany	15	26
France	18	18
Holland	26	56
Japan	3	3
Switzerland	67	63
United Kingdom	19	17
United States	5	8
U.S.S.R.	3	2

Source: *Chemische Industrie*, April, 1962.

This concentration has taken place within each of the national industries, and in certain chemical sectors corporate concentration exists on a world-wide basis.

Just before World War II the German dye trust, I.G. Farbenindustrie AG,[8] controlled 85 per cent of the chemical industry in Germany. The firm had virtual monopoly (98 per cent) of German dye production and an equally strong position in the manufacture of nitrogen, explosives, synthetic rubber, and fuels. Moreover, Farben owned or controlled plants in almost every major dye-producing country, including the United States. It produced almost all the raw materials and intermediate products it required within its own organization; each Farben plant was a self-contained manufacturing unit. The company employed 220,000 people. In 1960 Germany's chemical industry was much less concentrated than in 1939, and the three largest firms (BASF, Bayer, and Hoechst) accounted for only 35 per cent of total industry production.

In other important chemical-producing countries, similar concentration exists. Imperial Chemical Industries, Ltd. (ICI), dominates the United Kingdom chemical industry in the same manner, although not to the same extent, as did Farben in prewar Germany. The Italian company, Montecatini S.p.A., produces about 35–45 per cent of all Italy's chemicals. In France it was reported that the 10 leading chemical producers accounted for about 25 per cent of the French chemical output in 1960. Actually, this percentage would be much higher if all the subsidiary companies of these 10 were taken into account as is done in other countries.

In the United States from 50 to 80 per cent of the production of many

---

[8] The Farben trust was broken up into five separate companies by order of the Allied Commanders at the end of World War II: Badische Analine- und Soda-Fabrik AG (BASF), Farbwerke Hoechst AG, Farbenfabriken Bayer AG, Chemische Werke Hüls AG, and Cassella Farbwerke Mainkur AG.

essential chemicals was accounted for by the four largest firms in the product sector, as shown in Table 5. In 1939, at which time 40 major United States chemicals companies had total assets of more than $2 billion, du Pont and Union Carbide together accounted for 52 per cent of this total.

Table 5

SHARE OF U.S. PRODUCT GROUP DELIVERIES ACCOUNTED FOR
BY FOUR LARGEST COMPANIES IN EACH CLASSIFICATION, 1954

	Per Cent
Alkalies and chlorine	63
Plastic materials	45
Synthetic rubber	52
Synthetic fibres	79
Organic chemicals n.c.c.	51
Soap and glycerin	63
Inorganic color pigments	65
Essential oils	62
Carbon black	69
Salt	83

Source: *Economic Almanac* (1960), p. 264.

CARTELS

Like other industries where capital investment is heavy, where ownership or control is concentrated in a few hands, and where the products are globally marketable, the chemical industry has been strongly motivated to organize itself into national and international cartels. A strong inducement exists for the larger firms to protect themselves against unpredictable or excessive obsolescence resulting from the vagaries of technological development; against breaks in the price structure resulting from the use of excess capacity to produce contributions to overhead; and against new competition resulting from the ease of entry into markets for undifferentiated basic and intermediate chemical products. Unlike tariffs or import regulations, which can protect only domestic producers in any one country, cartels can afford effective supra-national protection to members of an international group.

In Europe before World War II, where cartels were not frowned upon by national policy as they were in the United States, the presence of strong chemical cartels was an acknowledged feature of the economies of major producing nations. Since World War II, there has been a significant downward trend in the importance of cartels in the chemical field, but, as we shall see, it is too early to predict with accuracy what the ultimate balance will be.

Two recognized United States critics of cartelization—George W. Stocking and Myron W. Watkins—had this to say of the impact of cartels on international trade in chemicals during the years between the two world wars:

International trade in chemical products is not free. Nor have tariff barriers and arbitrary controls set up by major industrial countries between the two world wars been the sole obstacles to free trade. Within the area circumscribed by government regulation, the world's chemical manufacturers set up their private controls. They divided markets; they marked off industrial fields; they established export quotas; they exploited specified fields and markets cooperatively. Joint control of the market became the general rule; free competition, the exception. [One of the most encyclopedic handbooks of international cartels (L. Ballande, *Essai d'étude monographique et statistique sur les ententes économiques internationales*, Paris, 1936, pp. 40 ff.) states that "international economic agreements, very numerous in the chemical industry, affect every category of product."]

Cartel control arrangements in the chemical field have two aspects. They are not mutually exclusive, but supplement and reinforce each other. First, these controls may be looked at as arrangements governing the marketing of particular chemicals or classes of chemicals. . . .

Or, secondly, these controls may be considered from the standpoint of chemical company relationships. Arrangements for exchange of stocks among major chemical companies in different countries or for exchange of patents, processes, and "know-how" in all or a wide range of chemical manufacturing lines are obviously cartel arrangements. Their express terms and provisions are not always concerned with the marketing of chemical products. Nevertheless, they surely affect the marketing policies of the companies concerned.

In general, the major chemical companies are committed to a policy of collaboration, pacific settlement of disputes, and equitable division of spheres of influence. They endeavor to maintain friendly relations with their rivals. They make non-aggression pacts pledging respect for each other's borders and "sovereign" domains. They enter into permanent or temporary alliance for mutual assistance in defense of vital interests against attacks from any quarter.[9]

Since World War II, however, governmental actions or pressures have greatly reduced cartelization in the non-communist world. Prodded by the United States government, which was acting to promote higher levels of trade by securing removal of restrictive practices, many nations began to police cartels for the first time. Overt evidence of the changing climate of opinion includes the breakup in 1951 of I.G. Farbenindustrie AG, a combine of major German companies originally formed in 1925; the adoption by the United Kingdom in 1956 of a statute against restrictive business practices; Swedish measures canceling hundreds of restrictive agreements; and, most important of all, the adoption of anticartel provisions in the Treaty of Rome (European Common Market) and their incipient enforcement through Regulation 17, passed in 1962. This regula-

---

[9] George W. Stocking and Myron W. Watkins, *Cartels in Action* (New York: Twentieth Century Fund, 1946), pp. 418–20.

tion requires notification to the Commission of a broad category of trade agreements and practices considered apt to affect commerce between the member states.

While the tide of opinion has turned against cartels since World War II and numerous actions to inhibit them have been taken, it must be remembered that the apparent acceptance of this program may be related to the favorable features of the economic environment in which it has been implemented so far. These have been a rapid economic revival, expanding gross national product, and growing domestic and world-wide markets for both old products and new products.

Should the economic climate change for the worse, there is a widely debated possibility that the cartel system in chemicals might be revived. According to our interview material, informed opinions vary widely. One school of thought holds that United States pressures for anticartel legislation have been successful in curtailing cartel activity largely because there has been little need for cartels since World War II. Major companies have had all the business they could digest. Proponents of this view believe that when "hard times" arise, cartels will form again or those in existence will become more active—with or without government sanction. In contrast, another school of thought believes that, once the advantages of free operations are experienced, European governments, if not the businessmen themselves, will successfully press against cartels.

As with most issues of this sort, the predominant prediction falls somewhere in between. It is not expected that Europe will ever swing so far as to adopt the United States view, which holds that cartels and monopolies are bad per se. Traditionally, cartels have not been strongly opposed in European thinking, and the long record of successful and profitable operations under cartels is unlikely to be quickly forgotten or willingly rejected by business leaders for some time. On the other hand, it is not expected that Europe will return to the days of uninhibited cartel operation. Where the balance rests between competition and cartel operation can only be guessed, for the test is yet to come. The future characteristics of the chemical industry will, of course, depend greatly on the ultimate answer.

CUSTOMERS OF THE CHEMICAL INDUSTRY

Practically all industries depend, directly or indirectly, on chemical products and/or processes. The chemical industry itself is one of its own best customers, since products of one branch often serve as raw materials for another. Phenol, for example, is made from benzene and is used, in turn, as a raw material in making lacquers and plastics. The familiar aspirin tablet can be traced from the basic raw material (petroleum distillate) through five different intermediate chemicals, each of which may involve a sale within the chemical industry. The flow is: petroleum distillate—ethylene—ethyl alcohol—acetaldehyde—acetic acid—acetic anhydride—acetylsalicylic acid (aspirin). Aspirin synthesis typifies the chain of chemical processes that is often needed to make a single consumer product.

Table 6 gives some idea of the percentage of chemical products going into various end uses. The textile and clothing category is greatly understated because these statistics are from the OECD, which does not include synthetic fibers within its definition of the chemical industry. Direct consumption includes such items as pharmaceuticals and paints. The export item contains a mixture of all the items listed above it, probably with a greater proportion of agricultural and direct consumption products.

Table 6

USERS OF CHEMICAL PRODUCTS IN WESTERN EUROPE, 1958

User	Estimated Per Cent of Total End Use in Value
Agriculture	11.0
Food	2.5
Coal, electricity, oil gas	3.0
Iron & steel, nonferrous metals	1.0
Timber, pulp, and paper	4.0
Textiles and clothing	4.0
Chemical industry	16.0
Machinery	7.0
Hides and skins	1.0
Cement, industries n.e.s.	8.0
Construction	6.0
Inland & maritime transport, trade, and services	1.0
Direct consumption	24.0
Exports to nonmember countries	11.5
Total	100.0

Source: *The Chemical Industry in Europe, 1959–1960*, OECD, 1959–60.

It can be seen that the chemical industry itself, using about 16 per cent of its own total production, was the second largest consumer of its products. It has been estimated that over 75 per cent of the United States chemical industry's output has been consumed in recent years by the chemical and process industries (paper, petroleum, etc.).

As a consequence of the cross-supply characteristic of the chemical industry, changing demands for one product can reverberate through many other sectors of the industry by causing a change in demand for other basic and intermediate chemicals. One could liken the chemical industry to a maze of interconnected pipelines. Changing a flow valve in one output pipe may require adjustments in all the supplying pipes directly connected.

In turn, adjustments may then have to be made to the pipes feeding the supplying pipes, and so forth, in order to maintain a balanced flow. If the output valve were opened, increased outflow might not result until all the supplying pipes were opened in turn. On the other hand, closing the output valve could cause fluid to back up in the input stations.

The example of Terylene (Dacron) shows how the introduction of a major new organic chemical end product can both affect and be affected by other branches of the chemical industry. Although Terylene was an entirely British invention, its commercial exploitation in the United Kingdom began considerably later than large-scale manufacture of the same product under the name of Dacron by du Pont in the United States. The slowness of British industry to profit from this discovery was not a question of insufficient technological follow-through but rather one of insufficient capabilities of a supplying sector. Whereas in the United States the basic raw materials for Terylene—ethylene glycol and paraxylene—were provided relatively easily by other branches of the American chemical industry, production in the United Kingdom had to wait for the building-up of the new petrochemical industry. The availability of mixed xylenes from coal carbonization was quite inadequate, and there was not enough of this material to provide the requirements of paraxylene by the simple process of freezing out this isomer, as practiced in the United States. In Britain an elaborate process had to be developed to increase the yield of para from the available mixed xylenes.

RAW MATERIALS

While other industries must have specific raw materials—hides and skins to make leather, iron ore and scrap to make iron and steel, textile fibers to make fabrics, and so on—the chemical industry, because of its ability to change the structure of materials, can produce an identical finished commodity from various raw materials and many products from the same raw material.

In woodwork, for example, the same raw material is used throughout the fabricating process, and the by-products—scrap, sawdust, shavings—are also wood. But when a chemical plant subjects the same wood to destructive distillation, it produces charcoal, crude pyroligneous acid, wood tar, and gas. Each of these is used for a variety of products: charcoal in smelting some metals, in the manufacture of some grades of gun powder, in sugar and oil refining, and so on; the acid in making methanol, acetic acid, acetone and many other products; wood tar, apart from its use as fuel or as a binder of briquettes from waste charcoal dust, in the recovery of creosote and other wood preservatives. From the same raw materials the chemist can produce fuels, fertilizers, beverages, drugs, and explosives. Exhibit 1 shows some examples of the variety of raw materials and products for various sectors of the chemical industry.

On the other hand, sulfuric acid, one of the most important inorganic chemicals, can be made from many different raw materials: for example, from native sulfur, from iron pyrites, from zinc blendes, and from sulfur waste in refining petroleum and manufacturing fuel gas.

The chemical industry makes wide use of abundantly available and almost universally cheap raw materials, such as salt, lime, and coal. It has been estimated that about three dozen raw materials are used in making the 150 most important chemicals in the United States, as shown in Table 7.

Table 7

RAW MATERIALS USED TO MAKE THE 150 MOST IMPORTANT CHEMICALS
IN THE UNITED STATES, *circa* 1945

Water	Iron ores
Air	Phosphate rock
Petroleum	Sea water
Coal	Copper ores
Natural gas	Fluorine minerals
Sulfur	Arsenic minerals
Mineral salts	Magnesium minerals
Limestone	Mercury ores
Sulfide ores	Zinc ores
Brines	Antimony minerals
Saltpeter (nitrates)	Barium minerals
Potassium minerals	Boron minerals
Gypsum	Manganese ores
Lead ores	Tin ores
Sand	Bismuth minerals
Aluminum minerals	Silver ores
Chromium ores	Titanium ores

Source: Woytinsky and Woytinsky, *op. cit.*, p. 1179.

Even complex chemical products, such as nylon and vitamins, can be made from such common materials as air, water, and coal. Techniques for producing complex products from simple raw materials are, however, often so intricate that only highly industrialized countries can use them profitably.

Raw materials have been a very important determinant of the character and direction of each nation's chemical industry. The industry will often build around the raw materials that are more economically available. For example, Germany early developed an important organic industry because of her economic coal supplies. Belgium, on the other hand, formerly emphasized inorganic chemistry because of her important metallurgical activities. Switzerland developed an industry, largely pharmaceuticals and dyestuffs, which required a minimum of raw materials and a maximum of research and value added because of her lack of almost all raw materials. A most singular example might be Sweden, which once based her entire organic industry on wood, her one plentiful organic material. In recent times, many of these traditional differences have lessened as oil supplies increased throughout Europe and the world.

With some exceptions, chemical plants are situated for proximity to their industrial outlets rather than for proximity to the raw materials required. Only plants using bulky and cheap raw materials need be situated near their sources of supply. Thus, in this latter case, a caustic soda plant will normally be located near salt deposits or sea water and where limestone is also available at low cost.

METHODS OF PRODUCTION

Since the turn of the century a shift has been taking place, led by the United States, from making chemicals in batch lots to production via continuous processes. The shift to continuous-process production has played much the same role in the chemical industry as the introduction of interchangeable parts played in the metalworking industries. While it requires more complex and expensive equipment, the continuous-process system saves time and labor and assures a more uniform product. No longer need each chemical reaction be carried out separately, here in a kettle, there in a filter, and so on. Instead, the raw material travels from one piece of apparatus to another by means of conveyors or piping, until the finished product emerges at the end of the system.

Another technique that is becoming steadily more common is the automatic control of chemical operations. Such control assures greater precision in all steps of the process, guarding, as it does, against minor differences in pressure, temperature, humidity, etc., throughout the process. Automatic control also effects a marked increase in output per worker: for example, a fair-sized plant for alcohol production can be operated by one man per shift.

These new techniques of continuous process and automatic control not only bring benefits of greater output per man and more product standardization but also increase enormously the cost of capital equipment needed. Furthermore, industrial chemical technology has changed so rapidly in recent years that the risk of rapid obsolescence of capital equipment has far exceeded that found in most other industries.

RESEARCH IN THE CHEMICAL INDUSTRY

There is a saying in the chemical industry that technical brains are the most important raw material. Research is its life blood; its birth, existence, and development have depended on patient work in countless laboratories. From these laboratories a constant stream of new products has flowed: plastics, dyes, nitrogen compounds, synthetic fibers, and synthetic rubber. Discovery of a new product often indicates promising avenues for further research.

The story of Penicillin's creation demonstrates clearly the impact that original research and continued development can have on the chemical industry. Penicillin was discovered by the British scientist, Sir Alexander Fleming, in the 1930's. He extracted the first few grams of this substance, which he discovered in one of the bread molds, with great difficulty and expense. Years later 17 chemical companies invested $25 million for research into ways of mass-producing the drug. The first mass-production involved growing the mold under closely controlled conditions and extracting the drug from it. From a price of $20 per injection in 1943, continued research and development lowered the price to $1 by 1945. Then a method was developed for synthesizing the drug, rather than growing bread mold, and by 1951 the cost of Pencillin was less than that of the bottle containing it. United States government statisticians have calculated that such "wonder drugs" saved at least one million lives in the period 1938–53.

Another recent development—polyethylene—provided the major impetus for the rapid growth of the plastics industry. Polyethylene, the most famous of the post-World War II plastics, is used in flexible pipe, squeeze bottles, household goods, refrigerator trays, containers, and packaging film. Production of this material has soared from an annual rate of under 5 million pounds during World War II to more than 1 billion pounds in 1960. During recent years, increased production has permitted economies of scale to be exploited, and industrial chemical research has developed constantly improved methods of making polyethylene. This combination has caused the cost of this versatile material to drop lower and lower, thereby creating still more new markets.

The crucial importance of research to the chemical industry is illustrated by the fact that a country lacking the raw materials for most chemical products, but having trained personnel, mechanical power, and capital, can readily develop a significant chemical industry. Switzerland, as has been mentioned, has become one of Europe's major producers of dyestuffs and pharmaceuticals, although it has to import the basic raw materials. Brazil, on the other hand, has almost all the raw materials needed in the chemical industry but has, until recently, produced almost no chemicals.

Because of constant changes in production methods, raw materials, and products, the industry is particularly dependent on laboratory experiments, tests, and discoveries. Every chemical manufacturer must be constantly alert to the impact of new procedures, devices, and products. It has been estimated that R&D expenditure as a per cent of sales has more than doubled (from about 1.5 per cent to about 3.5 per cent) in the United States during the 10-year period 1950–60. The average leading United States chemical firm invested in 1959 more than 4 per cent of sales in R&D, and some drug firms invested as much as 10 per cent of sales. According to one reliable source,[10] research costs in Europe were of an order of magnitude in 1960 similar to those in the United States for comparable companies.

THE CHEMICAL INDUSTRY: ITS PRESENT STATE AND FUTURE

The chemical industry is continuing to become more and more important to the world's total economy. Its products help men in all parts of the world to do all types of work: fertilizers for farmers, explosives for miners, and a vast array of chemicals for industry. As Table 2 has shown, the average consumption of chemical products per capita for 11 important industrialized nations rose from about $15.1 per head in 1938 to about $82.3 per head in 1960.

In some cases the output of the chemical industry is directly usable as a final product, such as pharmaceuticals and paints. But in most cases the chemical industry serves other industry, and both its present structure and its future are profoundly affected by other industrial activity. While there is value in generalizing about this industry, as with any other complex entity, it is most important to understand the differences which exist from country to country, from industrial sector to industrial sector, and from product to product. There are great differences between the over-all structure of the chemical industry in Italy and in Sweden, between the synthetic rubber industry and the inorganic fertilizer industry, between thermosetting plastics and thermoplastics.

Because the chemical industry serves other industries, its growth will be coupled with that of other industries, but probably at some multiple factor. For example, since World War II, the industry has grown in most of the important European nations at one and one-half to two times the rate for over-all industry. As the raw-material and process requirements of other industries become more complex, the contribution of the chemical industry will increase as a percentage of the total value added. But the greatest growth potential for the chemical industry lies not with the increasing demands of existing industries but rather with the new industries which will be founded on the yet-unknown products coming from the busy research of the chemical industry itself.

---

10 Dr. Otto Horn, Director of Research, Farbwerke Hoechst AG, pamphlet entitled "Chemical Research in Germany" (undated).

Exhibit 1

The Chemical Industry as Consumer-Producer

Chemical Industry Plants That Make	Consume These Raw Materials	To Produce These End Products
Chemicals (including petrochemicals)	Air, sea water, soil, petroleum, salt, sulfur, natural gas, coal, fluorspar	Chemical intermediates, alcohols, solvents, industrial gases, dyes, organic pigments, hundreds of organic chemicals, rubber chemicals, synthetic resins
Drugs and medicines	Acids, alcohols, molds, sugars, microorganisms, herbs, vegetable and animal extracts, essential oils, coal	Antibiotics (Penicillin, Streptomycin, etc.), antihistamines, hormones, vaccines, serums, vitamins, perfumes, cosmetics
Fertilizers and agricultural chemicals	Ammonia compounds, sodium nitrate, nitric and sulfuric acids, air	Fertilizers, herbicides, insecticides, germicides
Paints and allied products	Oils, petroleum products, chrome, various organic and inorganic compounds	Paints, varnishes, lacquers, enamels, pigments, putty
Plastic materials	Petroleum, lime, salt, coal, water, natural gas	Celluloid, cellophane, acylates, polyvinyls, polystrene, melamines, silicones, polyethylenes, epoxies, phenolics, polyesters
Explosives and fireworks	Ammonium and other nitrates, sulfur, toluene, lead azide, mercury fulminate, nitroglycerine	Blasting powders, explosives, ammunition, flares, rockets, propellants
Soaps and related products	Caustic soda, glyceryl stearate, stearing acid, tallow, fish and olive oils	Detergents, soaps, surface active agents, water repellents

Source: McGraw-Hill Publishing Co., *The Chemical Process Industries*, July, 1961.

THE CHEMICAL INDUSTRY IN WEST GERMANY

By 1960 the West German chemical industry had been rebuilt from the rubble of World War II into the third largest producer in the world, after the United States and the U.S.S.R. It had regained much of its prewar eminence in organic chemicals and plastics. In 1960 Germany's chemical industry accounted for about 9 per cent of her total industrial production and ranked second in size (after mechanical engineering) among all industries. The chemical industry was also an important earner of foreign exchange for West Germany, exporting about $950 million more than it imported in 1961.

The following sections of this note will comment on (1) the size and growth of the West German chemical industry; (2) chemical prices; (3) the boom in petrochemicals; (4) reasons for and extent of the geographical concentration observed in the industry today; (5) the structure of the industry; (6) trends in capital investment; (7) labor; (8) the competitive impact of imports and exports; and (9) possible future trends. An appendix provides additional data on four of the major German chemical companies of today.

SIZE AND GROWTH OF THE WEST GERMAN CHEMICAL INDUSTRY

Total German chemical sales in 1960 were $5.22 billion[1] according to the OECD definition of the chemical industry and about $5.5 billion according to the German definition.[2] In 1961 sales reached $6 billion under the latter definition. Chart 1 shows the growth of sales and exports over the past 10 years.

As might be expected, the rate of growth began to lessen as the industry matured. Sales expanded by only 9.1 per cent in 1961, compared with an average annual growth of 10.4 per cent for the four-year period starting in 1958, and 12.1 per cent for the previous four-year period.

---

[1] The conversion rate used in this paper, unless otherwise noted, in Deutsch Marks (DM) 4.2 = $1 for all years except 1961, for which DM 4.0 = $1 was used.

[2] Some items included in the German definition of the chemical industry and not in the OECD definition are fibers (both from natural polymers and fully synthetic), ferroalloys, linoleum, roofing felt, office materials (carbon paper, stencils, ink, pencils), matches, candles, and wax. Some items included in the OECD definition and not in the German definition are mercury, fermentation alcohol, crude benzin, starches, and raw casein.

All sectors of the chemical industry shared in the prosperous growth, but some individual products grew much faster than others. As in all the other important chemical-producing countries in Western Europe, the greatest advance took place in the organic chemical field and, within this field, in petrochemicals. Table 1 shows the level of output for 1961 and the growth since 1951 and 1959 of selected chemicals and chemical sectors.

PRICES

German chemical prices remained relatively stable following 1953. The over-all chemical price index was 98 in 1960 (1953 = 100), while that for all German industries was 107. The index number for inorganic chemicals was 103, and that for organics was 93.

This low price index for organics reflected strong competition in this sector, which harbored pockets of overcapacity, frequent incidence of dumping, and markedly improved production processes.

RAW MATERIALS FOR ORGANIC CHEMISTRY: THE PETROCHEMICAL BOOM

Just before World War II, 90 per cent of German organic chemical production depended on coal tars and gases (obtained mainly as a by-product in the process of making coke, which was required for the production of steel). These coal-based raw materials were still the source of 82 per cent of all organics as late as 1955. After that time, however, German organic chemical production mushroomed, while the raw materials available from coal did not grow nearly so rapidly. This situation resulted in part from the fact that much less coal was required by 1960 than formerly to produce a ton of steel and in part from the fact that the growing demand for home-cooking gas claimed some of the supply formerly used to produce organic chemicals.

The petroleum industry filled this supply gap, just as it did in France, Italy, the United Kingdom, and, to a lesser extent, the United States. From 1955 through 1960, 80 per cent of the new German organics capacity was supplied by oil and natural gas, which, in the latter year, fed 50 per cent of the entire German organics capacity, compared with only 18 per cent in 1955.

One interesting side effect of the entry of oil and natural gas into the traditionally coal-based German organics industry was the reaction of the coal industry. It decided not to compete against oil and gas but to benefit from them by investing in petroleum-based facilities and by developing licensable processes based on chemicals with which it had long been fa-

Chart 1

SALES AND EXPORTS OF THE
WEST GERMAN CHEMICAL INDUSTRY, 1952–61

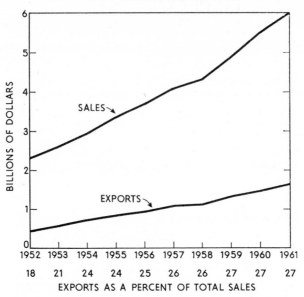

1952	1953	1954	1955	1956	1957	1958	1959	1960	1961
18	21	24	24	25	26	26	27	27	27

EXPORTS AS A PERCENT OF TOTAL SALES

Source: *Chemie Wirtschaft in Zahlen* (Verband der Chemischen Industrie e.V., 1962).

miliar. A prime example of the coal industry's participation in petrochemicals was the 50 per cent participation held by four coal and coal-
product companies in Chemische Werke Hüls AG, a major petrochemical
company.

While coal production was stagnating, oil was flooding into Germany.
Refinery capacity was increased, both by the major international oil companies and by the German independents, to a 1960 figure of over 40 million metric tons (about 880,000 bbl/day). Oil pipelines were rapidly becoming more common. Two pipelines to Cologne, from Wilhelmshaven
(28-inch, 245-mile) and from Rotterdam (22.6-inch, 175-mile), were
completed by 1960. A new pipeline (34-inch, 485-mile) from Marseilles
to Karlsruhe was scheduled to begin operations early in 1963. This line
had the largest diameter in the world at that time, with a top nominal
capacity of 30 million metric tons per year (about 660,000 bbl/day).
Rights-of-way were acquired in 1962 for the construction of a new 26-inch
170-mile Rhine-Danube pipeline extending from Karlsruhe to Ingolstadt,
not far from Munich. In addition, Italy's Ente Nazionale Idrocarburi
(ENI) had plans to lay lines to Ingolstadt from northern Italy. Map 1
shows the locations of these pipelines. It appeared likely that German or-

Table 1

SIZE AND GROWTH OF SELECTED CHEMICALS AND CHEMICAL PRODUCTS

Products	Units	1961 Production	Per Cent Increase 1951/1961	Per Cent Increase 1959/1961
INORGANIC INDUSTRIAL CHEMICALS				
Sulfuric acid	Thousands of tons	2,533	81	5.6
Caustic soda	Thousands of tons	1,063	108	0.6
Soda ash	Thousands of tons	811	27	1.6
Chlorine	Thousands of tons	725	183	22.5
Syn. ammonia	Thousands of tons	1,277	169	16.8
Calcium carbide	Thousands of tons	1,089	67	5.2
ORGANIC INDUSTRIAL CHEMICALS				
Methylalcohol	Thousands of tons	329	236	10.8
Formaldehyde	Thousands of tons	160	341	28.0
Acetic acid	Thousands of tons	110	47	9.0
Naphthylene	Thousands of tons	120	140	20.0
Phenol	Thousands of tons	104	N.A.	37.7
INDUSTRIAL CHEMICAL PRODUCTS				
Nitrogenous fertilizer	Thousands of tons	1,179	164	12.2
Phosphate fertilizer	Thousands of tons	768	110	14.3
Insecticides, herbicides	Thousands of tons	94	61	6.8
Synthetic fibers	Thousands of tons	65	N.A.	69.6
Plastics and synthetic rubber	Thousands of tons	1,160	577	37.4
CONSUMER CHEMICAL SECTORS				
Paints, lacquers, solvents	Thousands of tons	542	161	20.2
Pharmaceuticals	Millions of dollars	577	205	24.3
Cosmetics and perfumes	Millions of dollars	185	296	33.5
Photographic chemicals	Millions of dollars	115	284	16.1

Source: *Chemische Industrie in Zahlen* (Verband der Chemischen Industrie e.V., 1962).

ganic chemical producers would have little difficulty, in coming years, in obtaining adequate supplies of petroleum-based raw materials.

The growth of organic chemicals in Germany and the increased use of petroleum and natural gas as raw materials had important impacts on two major aspects of the chemical industry: its structure and the pattern of investment within it. These aspects will be discussed later in some detail.

GEOGRAPHICAL LOCATION OF THE GERMAN CHEMICAL INDUSTRY

Most of Germany's postwar growth in chemicals followed the prewar pattern of massive concentration in a few relatively small areas along the Rhine. The country had three major chemical centers, near Düsseldorf, Frankfurt, and Mannheim. These locations offered two major advantages: (1) proximity to water for transportation, processing, and cooling uses and (2) proximity to markets—some 60 per cent of the West German population was also in these areas.

Within these three major areas the plants tended to be large, even by chemical industry standards. Farbenfabriken Bayer AG at Leverkusen, for example, covered 1.5 square miles and had 35,000 employees in this one location. Chemische Werke Hüls AG, some 40 miles to the north near Essen, had 16,000 employees there. Farbwerke Hoechst AG and Badische Anilin- und Soda-Fabrik AG (BASF) at Ludwigshafen had complexes of comparable size. Map 1 shows the location of the most important chemical centers.

The industry was becoming more dispersed, however, as expansion of these enormous plants became increasingly difficult and less desirable. Nonetheless, most satellite plants were situated either on the Rhine or on one of its tributaries nearby. The rapid growth of petrochemicals and petroleum refining caused many new plants to be built. The refineries were located on the Rhine, in order to have access to shipments of crude oil. The petrochemical plants, in turn, were located on the Rhine both to be close to their source of raw materials (the refineries) and to be close to markets for their by-products as well as their main product. As the network of oil pipelines penetrates new areas, however, petroleum refining and petrochemical production is expected to become geographically more dispersed.

STRUCTURE OF THE INDUSTRY

In West Germany by 1960 there were at least 5,000 chemical producers of one sort or another. Of these, at least 250 had annual sales volumes exceeding $2 million. The so-called "Big Three"—Bayer, Hoechst, and BASF—accounted for 35 per cent of total sales, and 80 relatively independent firms produced the next 25 per cent.[2]

The Big Three, together with one other large and one smaller chemical company, had emerged—or re-emerged—as independent companies in 1951, following a split-up of the German chemical giant, I.G. Farbenindustrie, AG. Farben, founded in 1925 through a union of Germany's eight largest chemical companies, had been the world's industry leader, its sales peaking at about $750 million in 1943 (at the 1960 rate of exchange). Because of its predominant position, the Western Allies were resolved to split apart the approximately 50 per cent of Farben that remained in West Germany after World War II.[3] One popular plan had envisaged a split into 43 independent firms, but a more moderate course

---

[2] According to a 1961 survey by *Fortune*, Bayer, Hoechst, and BASF ranked, respectively, 13th, 26th, and 30th in a list of the 100 largest non-United States industrial companies (*Fortune Directory*, August, 1962).

[3] About half of Farben's domestic holdings lay in Germany's eastern territories and fell into the hands of the Soviets. Today they form the basis of East Germany's important chemical industry.

Map 1

GEOGRAPHICAL LOCATION OF THE MAJOR GERMAN CHEMICAL PLANTS AND PETROLEUM PIPELINES, 1961

Major chemical centers ▬▬▬Operating pipelines ▬ ▬Proposed pipelines

Source: *Chemical Engineering and News*, June 5, 1961.

was actually chosen when, during hostilities in Korea, it was decided to preserve a strong West German chemical industry. Farben was accordingly split into only five independent units:

	Per Cent Share of Original I.G. Farben Capital Stock
Company	
Farbenfabriken Bayer AG	32
Farbwerke Hoechst AG	27
Badische Anilin–und Soda-Fabrik (BASF)	28
Chemische Werke Hüls AG	10
Cassella Farbwerke Mainkur AG	3

By 1960 relationships among these five companies had undergone additional changes. While the three largest—Hoechst, BASF, and Bayer —remained substantially independent of each other, each of them had bought into the two smaller Farben descendants: into Casella directly and into Hüls through a joint holding company. Relationships among the five Farben companies as of 1960 are depicted in Chart 2.

Chart 2

IMPORTANT INTERRELATIONS AMONG THE FIVE
I.G. FARBEN DESCENDANTS

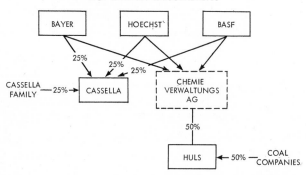

Source: *Wer Gehort zu Wem, 1961*, Commerzbank AG.

Reflecting their common origin, the Big Three chemical companies emerged from the Farben breakup with complementary, rather than competitive, product lines. Traditional lines retained their differences in 1960, but by this time each of the Big Three had also entered the field of petrochemicals, where they subsequently paced the rapid German growth in organics. Reliable industry observers estimate that in the three to five years through 1960, Bayer, Hoechst, and BASF directly or indirectly allocated more than 60 per cent of their capital budgets to research, development, expansion, and modernization in their petrochemical facilities.

In part, the Big Three entered petrochemicals through buying into

Hüls, which had represented Farben in that field prior to the breakup of the company after World War II. In part, their entry was achieved through other joint ventures with suppliers.

Almost all crude oil and natural gas had to be imported into Germany, and the Big Three took various approaches toward forming joint ventures with the companies that imported and sold petroleum. Bayer, moving farthest in this direction, participated in the petrochemical sector through a 50-50 joint venture with B P Benzin und Petroleum AG. BASF, taking a middle approach, had a 50-50 joint venture with Deutsche Shell AG to produce polyolefins, but manufactured other organic chemicals—for which it used mainly coal-based materials—on an independent basis. Hoechst had no joint ventures but in 1961 provided special inducements, mainly in the form of a long-term purchase contract, for the California Texas Oil Corporation (Caltex) to establish a new refinery at Frankfurt. Here Hoechst intended by 1965 to double or even triple its existing 350,000-ton annual capacity for benzine and olefin processing.

In obtaining and developing new petrochemical processes, the Big Three used several approaches, depending on the circumstances involved: developing their own process, licensing from others, and engaging in joint ventures with foreign firms. For example, Hoechst and British Celanese Ltd. joined to produce synthetic fibers; BASF used licenses from Imperial Chemical Industries, Ltd., and Phillips Petroleum Company (U.S.A.) to produce polyethylene via two different processes.

TRENDS IN CAPITAL INVESTMENT

Germany's chemical industry grew steadily and rapidly after 1948, and most of the funds for this expansion, after initial aid from the Marshall Plan, were provided by the German chemical companies themselves. This situation began to change in recent years, however, and foreign firms began to make substantial investments, especially in petroleum refining and petrochemical facilities.

Some $3.1 billion were invested in German chemical plant during 1952–60. The annual average was more recently about $400–$500 million, as seen in Chart 3. Investment as a percentage of total sales remained close to 10 per cent for a number of years.

In recent years capital investments were divided about equally between new plants and modernization. This marked a shift from the early post-war period, when most investment was necessarily made in new plants to replace those destroyed by the war or to replace those which were in East Germany. The heaviest investments were made in petrochemicals, plas-

Chart 3

THE GERMAN CHEMICAL INDUSTRY: INVESTMENTS, 1953–60

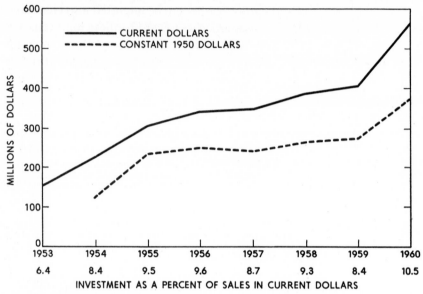

Source: *Chemische Industrie*, November, 1961.

tics, synthetic fibers, and pharmaceuticals. These investments paralleled equally substantial investments in petroleum refining: German refinery capacity doubled in the period 1957–60.

The chemical industry requires unusually high capital investment: comparing Germany's chemical industry with her other industries, chemicals in 1960 ranked fifth in total employment, second in sales, and first in capital investment. There are four major reasons for this high capital requirement: (1) the constant development of new products; (2) the rapidly increasing demand for established products; (3) the quest for new cost-cutting technologies; and (4) the need to save labor by increased use of machines.

LABOR

Germany for some time enjoyed virtually full employment; 1960 unemployment was under 1 per cent. Conditions in the West German labor market continued to be so tight that labor availability could scarcely keep pace with the growth in output. This tightness of the labor market affected the chemical industry adversely in two areas: investment and costs.

The difficulty of obtaining the labor needed to operate new chemical facilities tended to discourage foreign companies wishing to invest in

Germany, and it also discouraged German chemical firms themselves from building new domestic plants. Bayer's recent decision to build a large chemical complex at Antwerp, Belgium, was reported to be largely motivated by the factor of labor supply.[4]

At the same time the pressure for wage increases was becoming steadily greater. In 1961 the Deutschmark was slightly revalued, raising its worth from $0.238 to $0.25 and thus effectively increasing wages by about 5 per cent. This augmentation did not stop labor from demanding a 15 per cent wage increase. Despite pleas for "a restraint in wage demands at this critical time" by government and business leaders, labor's bargaining position was so excellent, because of full employment, that the 15 per cent demand did not have to be lowered. Increasing labor costs directly raised all manufacturing cost structures, including those of the chemical industry.

To some observers it appeared, also, that West Germany might be starting to suffer certain social consequences of prosperity with which the United States was already familiar. According to one publication, managers made the following complaint: "Workers resist demands for overtime, do not work as effectively during their normal hours, no longer take pride in their work, and continually seek both direct and fringe benefits without attendant rises in productivity; costs go up and quality goes down."[5]

Because there were too few workers to staff the new jobs created by the total industrial expansion, Germany imported some 340,000 workers, most of them after 1957. They came mainly from Greece, southern Italy, and Spain. Not only did they create language problems within the companies that hired them but also social problems within the communities which housed them. A goodly percentage of these foreign employees stayed only six to twelve months in Germany and then returned to their homes. Training these workers was thus expensive and continuous, and much of its benefit was lost by high turnover.

Table 2 shows the growth of the German chemical industry's labor force during 1957–60 and also the steady rise in output per worker. Under the German definition of the chemical industry, the labor force was 458,000 in 1960 and 483,000 in 1961.[6] Of the 437,000 employees shown in the OECD figures for 1960, 67 per cent were plant operatives, and the remaining 33 per cent were administrative, technical, and clerical personnel. The chemical industry in Western Europe, excluding Germany, employed about 70 per cent operatives in 1960.

---

[4] *International Management*, October, 1961.
[5] *Chemical and Engineering News* (C&EN), June 5, 1961.
[6] *Chemie Wirtschaft in Zahlen*, Verband der Chemischen Industrie e.V., 1962.

Germany's 1959 figure for value added per worker ($5,560) was significantly larger than the figure for the entire European chemical industry ($5,100) in the same year, but it was still far from the 1960 United States figure of $16,200.[7] The United States figure was much higher primarily because of the much larger percentage of automation found in the United States chemical industry.

Table 2

LABOR FORCE IN THE WEST GERMAN CHEMICAL INDUSTRY

	1957	1958	1959	1960
Employees (thousands of persons)	366	384	396	437
Value added (dollars in millions)	$1,878	$1,988	$2,205	$2,515
Per cent change in work force since the last year		+5	+3	+10
Per cent change in value added since the last year		+6	+11	+14
Value added per employee (dollars)	$5,130	$5,170	$5,560	$5,750

Source: *The Chemical Industry in Europe*, OECD.

INTERNATIONAL TRADE

German chemical international trade resulted in a favorable balance of $950 million in 1961. Exports of $1,621 million were more than double imports of $671 million. As in past years, the chemical industry accounted for approximately 13 and 6 per cent of Germany's total exports and imports, respectively.

Table 3 shows the five most important chemical sectors for Germany's imports and exports. In comparing exports and imports, a greater emphasis can be seen among imports on basic industrial chemicals.

Table 3

FIVE MOST IMPORTANT SECTORS FOR GERMANY'S EXPORT AND
IMPORT CHEMICAL TRADE, 1961

Chemical Sector	Per Cent Share of Total Value	
	Exports	Imports
Industrial organic chemicals	17.5	20.6
Plastic resins, cellulose derivative, celluloid	13.8	9.9
Artificial silk and synthetic thread	*	7.6
Pharmaceutical products	10.4	7.1
Dyestuffs	7.5	*
Industrial inorganic chemicals	7.2	9.3
Total	56.4	54.5

* Not applicable.
Source: *Chemische Industrie*, April, 1962.

[7] The U.S. definition of the chemical industry is slightly different from the European definition, but this fact does not significantly alter the relationship among the figures cited.

Table 4 shows the trading distribution for West Germany's chemical products and the five most important trading partners in 1961. The regional pattern of German trade has been generally stable for some time. In 1961 the European Free Trade Area (EFTA) continued to be the most important export area and the United States the most important supplier, although its percentage was down from the 28 to 30 per cent of the preceding three years.

Table 4

MOST IMPORTANT TRADING PARTNERS FOR GERMAN CHEMICAL INDUSTRY, 1961

	Exports		Imports	
Customer	Per Cent Share of Total Dollars	Supplier		Per Cent Share of Total Dollars
BY NATION (Five Most Important)				
Netherlands	7.1	U.S.A.		26.5
Italy	7.0	France		12.0
France	6.7	Switzerland		9.5
Switzerland	6.1	Netherlands		8.8
Benelux	5.1	Italy		6.9
Total	32.0	Total		63.7
BY REGION				
Europe	63.5	Europe		63.5
(EEC—25.9%)		(EEC—34.1%)		
(EFTA—26.8%)		(EFTA—22.4%)		
Asia	14.2	North & Middle America		28.8
North & Middle America	7.9	Other		7.7
(U.S.A.—4.3%)				
South America	7.4	Total		100.0
Other	7.0			
Total	100.0			

Source: *Chemische Industrie*, April, 1962.

THE FUTURE OF THE GERMAN CHEMICAL INDUSTRY

Two questions regarding the expansion of Germany's chemical industry are most obvious: How long can this expansion continue? What directions will it follow?

According to a special report by *Chemical and Engineering News*,[8] German chemical executives felt that the industry's expansion had been generally sound and would continue for the foreseeable future, although the rate of increase would probably decline. German per capita production of certain basic chemicals (some plastics, synthetic rubber, basic or-

---

[8] June 5, 1961.

ganics and inorganics of certain types) was still well below United States standards. For example, Germany produced only half as much sulfuric acid, chlorine, caustic soda, and chemical fertilizers per capita as did the United States. On this basis, it appeared that the German chemical industry had ample room for growth before it reached market "saturation."

One danger that German companies will have to face, however, is that foreign companies will enter the German market to fill demands which the domestic industry cannot meet. Chemical producers in other Common Market countries will find it increasingly easy to sell in Germany, since, by 1967, tariffs between member countries will have virtually disappeared (Table 5). Companies outside the Common Market either can invest directly in Germany or can invest in chemical plants in other Common Market countries with the same effect. Of course, Germany will also find easier access to its ECM partners and, perhaps more important, a significant tariff advantage in this area over United States chemical exports to Europe.

Table 5

GERMAN TARIFFS ON SELECTED CHEMICALS
(Average percentage ad valorem)

	Before ECM	After ECM Adjustment	
		To ECM Countries	To Non-ECM Countries
Inorganic chemicals	12	0	15
Organic chemicals	15	0	17
Coal-tar dyestuffs	12	0	15
Pigments and paints	12	0	15
Medicinals and pharmaceuticals	15	0	15
Nitrogenous fertilizer	10	0	10

Source: Howard S. Piquet, *The European Common Market*, American Management Association, Management Report No. 18, 1958.

Most German executives conceded that international competition in chemicals was becoming steadily more severe, especially because the United States had excess capacity in many important product areas. Americans were accused of "dumping" their products in Germany and other European countries. Some German chemical experts also eyed with considerable apprehension Italy's ability to produce low-cost organic products, such as man-made fibers, because of a favorable raw-material position.

Recognizing the increasing competitive pressures on both their export and domestic markets, German chemical firms were beginning to make heavy investments in other nations. These have been permitted only since 1952, having previously been forbidden under Allied Occupation decrees.

Total German chemical investment abroad reached over $50 million in the years between 1952 and mid-1958. The heaviest investments were in Europe and the Western Hemisphere, but a significant amount went to Asia, especially India. The geographic pattern of investments followed the export pattern closely, and investment was regarded by many as one more step by the German chemical industry to further its position as a world-wide chemical supplier.

Appendix

THE CHEMICAL INDUSTRY IN WEST GERMANY
Résumés of Important German Chemical Companies

✿✿✿

FARBENFABRIKEN BAYER AG, LEVERKUSEN

In terms of turnover, Farbenfabriken Bayer AG was the largest of the five companies emerging from the breakup of I.G. Farbenindustrie AG and was the largest German chemical company. In 1961 sales were DM 3,051.7 million (about $763 million),[9] and the company employed 61,200 persons.

Founded in 1863 as the partnership, Friedr. Bayer & Comp., the company continued independent operations until 1925, when it merged with seven other leading German coal-tar users to form I.G. Farben. Bayer was re-established as an independent firm by the Allied Powers in 1951.

The growth rate of Bayer outstripped that of the West German chemical industry as a whole. By 1961 Bayer's sales were 3.52 times those of 1952. During the same time period, sales for the German chemical industry grew 2.58 times, and those for all German industries combined grew only 2.35 times. Chart 4 shows the growth of Bayer's sales. By 1961 exports accounted for 46 per cent of the company's total volume.

Bayer manufactured a range of products touching on nearly all fields of chemistry. Its major product lines were dyestuffs, industrial chemicals, pharmaceuticals, synthetic fibers, insecticides and pesticides, and photographic products. Bayer's production was spread over four major factories. The most important of these, located at Leverkusen, was one of the largest facilities in the world, producing a widely diversified line of organic and inorganic chemicals. A plant at Uerdingen produced chiefly inorganic chemicals, and one at Wuppertal-Elberfeld produced pharmaceuticals and insecticides. The fourth plant, located at Dormagen, was largely involved in the production of fibers. It also included the Erdolchemie GmbH facilities, founded in 1957 by Bayer AG and BP Benzin und Petroleum AG in order to exploit the petrochemical sector.

Bayer's interests included holdings in many other chemical companies

---

[9] These figures were for Bayer and its wholly owned subsidiaries. Counting also companies in which Bayer held a 50 per cent interest or more, sales were approximately DM 3,620 million (about $905 million).

Chart 4

BAYER'S SALES, 1952–61

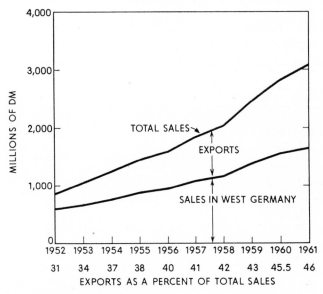

EXPORTS AS A PERCENT OF TOTAL SALES

Source: Bayer's Annual Reports.

throughout the world. Its largest participation was the wholly owned Agfa AG, which supplied about two-thirds of Germany's demand for photographic products and cameras and ranked second in the world to Kodak in this industry. Other important interests, held in conjunction with BASF and Hoechst, were in Cassella Farbwerke Mainkur AG (another of the I.G. Farben splinter companies) and in Bunawerke Hüls, GmbH, the leading synthetic rubber manufacturer in West Germany. Table 6 shows a distribution of Bayer's investments.

Table 6

NUMBER OF BAYER'S HOLDINGS IN OTHER COMPANIES, 1961

Location	No.	Type	No.	Holding	No.
Europe	51	Producing	34	Majorities	
North America	7	Assembly and		(51–100%)	80
Central and South		marketing	14	Minorities	
America	32	Marketing	64	(25–50%)	24
Africa	6	Other	3	(Under 25%)	11
Asia	16		—		—
Australia	3	Total	115	Total	115
Total	115				

Source: Bayer Annual Report, 1961.

FARBWERKE HOECHST AG, VORMALS
MEISTER LUCIUS C. BRUNING, FRANKFURT AM MAIN

After 1959 Farbwerke Hoechst AG ranked second in sales among German chemical companies, replacing BASF. In 1961, sales were DM 2,876 million (about $714 million), and the company had 52,162 employees.

Founded in 1863 to produce synthetic aniline dyestuffs, the company diversified into pharmaceuticals, electrochemistry, and other chemicals. In 1925 it entered the merger which formed I.G. Farbenindustrie. Hoechst was re-established as an independent firm in 1951, and connections of the parent company with its former subsidiaries were renewed.

Over the 10 years between 1952 and 1961 Hoechst attained the greatest increase in sales among the "Big Three,"[10] having expanded 3.77

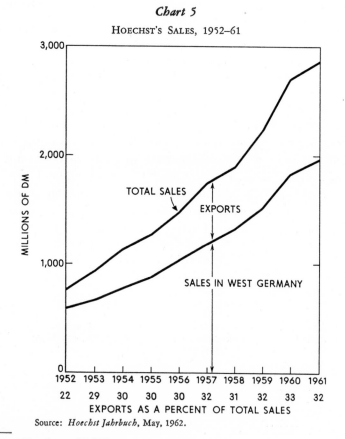

Chart 5

HOECHST'S SALES, 1952–61

Source: *Hoechst Jahrbuch*, May, 1962.

---

[10] Bayer, Hoechst, and BASF.

times. During this period, except for 1952, exports remained relatively stable as a proportion of total sales, accounting for slightly under one-third. Chart 5 shows the growth of Hoechst's sales, both in the home market and abroad.

Keeping pace with this rapid growth of sales was an impressive increase in expenditures for plant investment and research (Table 7). Plant investments were about 4.5 times greater in 1961 than in 1952, and research expenditures were about 3.2 times greater.

Table 7

HOECHST'S INVESTMENTS IN PLANT AND RESEARCH
(In millions of DM)

Year	Plant Investment	Research
1952	92	37
1955	241	69
1958	248	93
1961	446	120

Source: *Hoechst Jahrbuch*, May 1962.

The range of Hoechst's products, like those of BASF and Bayer, has grown wider and wider during recent years. Important product lines included dyestuffs, pharmaceuticals, inorganic chemicals, raw materials for paints and solvents, plastics, synthetic fibers, fertilizers, and herbicides. Among the companies derived from I.G. Farben, Hoechst was the only one to enter the nuclear field by 1961.

Like the other large German chemical firms, Hoechst had large interests in a number of important companies. Some of the most important holdings are listed in Table 8.

Table 8

SOME IMPORTANT HOLDINGS BY HOECHST, 1961

Name of Company	Per Cent Participation by Hoechst
Knapsack-Griesheim AG	100
Kalle AG	100
Behringwerke AG	100
Spinnstofffabrik Zehlendorf AG	60*
Hüttensauerstoff GmbH	50
Wacker-Chemie GmbH	50
Ruhrchemie AG	33*
Cassella Farbwerke Mainkur AG	25*

* Approximate figures.
Source: *Hoechst Jahrbuch*, May 1962.

BADISCHE ANILIN—& SODA-FABRIK AG (BASF), LUDWIGSHAFEN

The third member of Germany's "Big Three" chemical firms, BASF, had sales of DM 2,597 million (about $649 million) and employed 55,900 in 1961. Exports were DM 960 million, or about 37 per cent of total sales.

BASF manufactured a wide range of products (some 5,300 in 1961); a greater emphasis was placed on basic industrial products than was the case with Bayer and Hoechst. The important product lines are shown in Table 9.

Table 9

RELATIVE IMPORTANCE OF BASF PRODUCTS IN 1961

Group of Products	Per Cent of Total 1961 Sales
Plastics and raw chemicals for synthetic fibers	30
Plasticizers and solvents	14
Industrial chemicals, organic and inorganic–glues, binders, and hardening agents	15
Fertilizers, nitrates, and plant-protection chemicals	23
Dyes and tanning agents	18
Total	100

Source: *Chemische Industrie*, May, 1962.

The first of the above-listed groups was by far the most dynamic. In this field BASF dominated the German market but nevertheless limited its activities to production of raw materials. Up to 1962 the company had not attempted to enter the field of finished or semifinished products developed by its own customers.

BASF concentrated its production in one factory at Ludwigshafen, which became the biggest chemical plant in Europe. In an area of 620 hectares (about 1,530 acres) the company operated seven manufacturing departments, one technical section, an applications service section, and several research laboratories.

Some of BASF's important holdings in other companies are listed in Table 10. The company's activity in the petrochemical field was largely carried on through Rheinische Olefinwerke GmbH, which it owned 50-50 with Deutsche Shell AG. Rheinische Olefinwerke was mostly involved in the production of ethylene and polyethylene.

Table 10

SOME IMPORTANT HOLDINGS BY BASF, 1960

	Per Cent Participation by BASF
Name of Company	
Gewerkschaft Auguste—Victoria	100
Rheinische Olefinwerke GmbH	50
Dow Badische Chemical Company (Freeport, Texas)	50
Dispersions Plastiques S.A. (Paris)	50
Chemische Fabrik Holten GmbH	46
Cassella Farbwerke Mainkur AG	25
Bunawerke Hüls GmbH	16⅔

Source: BASF Annual Report, 1960.

CHEMISCHE WERKE HÜLS AG, MARL/KREIS RECKLINGHAUSEN (NEAR ESSEN)

Chemische Werke Hüls AG, another company born from the I.G. Farben group, was far more specialized than the Big Three in its range of products. Its activities were concentrated on the production of synthetic rubber and a wide range of other petrochemical products (including plastics, plasticizers, and solvents), synthetic tannins, chlorinated hydrocarbons, and technical gases (oxygen and hydrogen). Industry observers estimated that the company's activities in plastics accounted for about 45 per cent of its 1961 sales of DM 664.8 million (about $155 million). The company employed about 13,000 in 1961.

Table 11 includes data on Hüls's sales and investments in fixed assets. Lower sales in 1961 were attributed to the general drop in prices for plastics and also to the revaluation of the Deutsch Mark,[11] which placed German chemicals at a disadvantage in the tightly competitive sectors. Exports ranged between 30 and 36 per cent of total sales over the past 10 years.

Table 11

HÜLS'S TOTAL SALES, EXPORTS, AND INVESTMENTS, 1958–61
(In millions of DM)

Year	*Total Sales*	*Exports*	*Investments*
1958	578.4	380.7	87
1959	612.5	405.1	84
1960	709.6	480.6	92
1961	664.8	462.7	122

Source: *Hüls Geschäftsbericht*, 1961.

---

[11] The Deutsch Mark was increased in value by 5 per cent in May, 1961.

Chemische Werke Hüls's participations included the following:

1. Bunawerke Hüls GmbH, which manufactured butadiene, different types of synthetic rubber, and carbon black. The DM 42 million capitalization was shared equally by Hüls and Synthesekautschuk Beteiligungsgesellschaft GmbH (which in turn was equally owned by the Big Three).

2. Faserwerke Hüls GmbH, which manufactured a new polyester fiber. The company was founded at the end of 1960 as a 50-50 joint venture between Hüls and the Tennessee Eastman Company, a member of the Eastman Kodak group.

Hüls, in turn, was equally owned by coal and chemical interests. In 1955, 50 per cent of the company's capital was owned in equal proportions by Hibernia, a German state-controlled mining company, and Kohleverwertungs, representing many private interests. In order to prevent the German coal-mining companies from procuring majority interests in Hüls, the Chemie-Verwaltungs AG was organized by the Big Three to acquire the remaining 50 per cent of Hüls's capital. In 1960, Chemie-Verwaltungs' investments and loans to Hüls represented 96 per cent of its own total assets.

THE CHEMICAL INDUSTRY IN THE UNITED KINGDOM

From a position far behind Germany's in 1938, Britain's chemical industry[1] emerged as the leading producer of Western Europe after World War II. By 1960 it was fourth largest in the world, following the United States, the U.S.S.R., and just an edge behind West Germany. The United Kingdom's chemical production for that year represented about 8 per cent of the nation's total industrial output and about a quarter of Western Europe's chemical production. In recent years per capita use of chemicals was exceeded only in the United States.

The chemical industry has always been an important earner of foreign exchange for the United Kingdom. For a country besieged with balance-of-payment difficulties since World War II, the roughly two-to-one chemical export to import ratio during recent years has been vital. In 1961 chemical exports exceeded imports by almost $500 million.[2]

The following material on the chemical industry in the United Kingdom briefly reviews these topics: size and growth; the boom in petrochemicals; industry structure; employment and investment; international trade; and the future outlook.

SIZE AND GROWTH OF THE CHEMICAL INDUSTRY

In 1960 total sales of the United Kingdom's chemical industry[3] plus man-made fibers reached about $5.37 billion. The increase over 1959 was about 11 per cent for chemical output, as compared with 6 per cent for over-all industrial production. This two-to-one growth relationship was characteristic of the period after World War II; the average annual growth rate between 1950 and 1960 for all chemicals was about 7.1 per cent and that for all manufacturing industries about 3.2 per cent.[4]

---

[1] The definition of the chemical industry used in this survey includes chemicals and man-made fiber yarns, as defined by the Board of Trade, *Accounts Relating to Trade and Navigation of the United Kingdom*, October 1962, Class D, Divisions 1 and 8.

[2] An exchange rate of $2.80 = 1£ is used in this survey.

[3] Based on the definition of the industry used by the Organization for Economic Co-operation and Development (OECD).

[4] OECD, *The Chemical Industry in Europe, 1960–1961*, p. 59; *Chemische Industrie*, February, 1962.

Leading the pace during the period were organic chemicals, with an annual growth rate of about 11 per cent, and, within this sector, petro-chemicals, with an annual growth rate of about 30 per cent. Some of the products responsible for this high growth rate were ethylene and propy-lene for plastics, butadiene for synthetic rubber, synthetic detergents, and synthetic fibers, many of which were not produced at all in commercial quantities before 1950.

As examples of the extraordinary growth rates achieved by some of these products, plastics and synthetic rubber may be cited. Production of plastics rose 280 per cent from 1952 through 1962, the greatest growth occurring in thermoplastics.[5] Production of synthetic rubber did not start until 1958, but output reached 92,000 metric tons by 1960[6] and was ex-pected to reach 180,000 tons by 1965.[7] Large-scale commercial production was expected to include butyl, ethylene, propylene, and polydiene rubbers, in addition to the S-type rubber which dominated 1960 output.

Levels of output and rates of growth for selected chemical products in the United Kingdom are shown in Table 1.

THE PETROCHEMICAL BOOM IN THE UNITED KINGDOM

At the end of World War II the United Kingdom was still dependent for its organic chemical products on coal carbonization as a source of aro-matics; on fermentation (mainly of molasses) for aliphatics; on coke for synthesis gas; and on calcium carbide for acetylene. As late as 1949, pe-troleum accounted for only 9 per cent of the raw materials used in chemi-cals. Serious entry into petroleum chemical production began in that year, when Shell Chemical Co. Ltd. began manufacture of alcohol, Ketone solvents, and butylene. The next major step took place in 1951, when these firms (British Hydrocarbon Chemicals Ltd., Imperial Chemical In-dustries Ltd., or I.C.I., and Petrochemicals Ltd.)[8] completed naphtha-cracking installations. Subsequently petroleum became the prime source of supply for the incremental production of organic chemicals, furnishing almost 50 per cent of total raw-material requirements in 1959 and pos-sibly 63 per cent by 1962, as shown in Table 2.

The expansion of organics was dependent on petroleum for two rea-sons. First, the production of coal tar—being only a by-product of coal

---

[5] Central Statistical Office, *Annual Abstract of Statistics*, No. 98 (1961) (London, 1961); *Chemical & Engineering News*, October 8, 1962.

[6] OECD, *op. cit.*

[7] H. P. Hodge, Manager of Market Research and Development, Chemicals Division, Esso Petroleum Co., Ltd., "The Petroleum Chemicals Industry in the United Kingdom" (unpub-lished paper, August, 1961).

[8] An associate of Shell Chemical Co. Ltd.

Table 1

PRODUCTION OUTPUT AND GROWTH OF SELECTED CHEMICALS
AND CHEMICAL PRODUCTS

Products	Units	1960 Production	Per Cent Increase 1956–1960
INORGANIC INDUSTRIAL CHEMICALS			
Sulfuric acid	1,000 ton	2,745	20
Caustic soda	1,000 ton	813*	2*
Soda ash	1,000 ton	1,533*	6*
Chlorine	1,000 ton	563*	22*
Synthetic ammonia	1,000 ton	569	31
Calcium carbide	1,000 ton	216	60
ORGANIC INDUSTRIAL CHEMICALS			
Ethylene	1,000 ton	300*	200*
Benzene	1,000 ton	195*	80*
Styrene	1,000 ton	50*	N.A.
Naphthylene	1,000 ton	63	28
Phenol (synthetic and natural)	1,000 ton	51	56
INDUSTRIAL CHEMICAL PRODUCTS			
Nitrogenous fertilizers	1,000 ton	449	34
Phosphate fertilizers	1,000 ton	406	12
Synthetic fibers	1,000 ton	61	165
Plastics	1,000 ton	613	78
Polyethylene	1,000 ton	107†	134
Polyvinylchloride	1,000 ton	105†	119†
CONSUMER CHEMICAL PRODUCTS			
Paints, lacquers, solvents	1,000 ton	543*	15*
Pharmaceuticals	$ million	535	67
Cosmetics and perfumes	$ million	170	52*

* Estimated.
† Net sales rather than production figures.
Source: *Chemische Industrie*, February, 1962, pp. 46–52 and 85; H. P. Hodge, *op. cit.*, for estimates
on ethylene, benzene, and styrene.

Table 2

RAW-MATERIAL SOURCES FOR UNITED KINGDOM ORGANIC CHEMICALS
SELECTED YEARS, 1949–62

Raw Material Used	Production of Organic Chemicals (Thousands of metric tons)				
	1949	1953	1955	1959	Estimated 1962
Coal tar	175	230	275	365	540
Acetylene (carbide)	70	80	110	135	150
Synthesis gas (coke)	55	70	80	95	90
Fermentation	160	170	140	80	30
Petroleum	45	195	290	595	1,400
Total	505	745	895	1,270	2,210
Per cent made from petroleum	9	26	32	47	63

Source: *Petroleum*, August, 1961, p. 301.

carbonization for producing metallurgical coke—did not increase nearly as fast as the needs of the organic chemical field. Second, many of the fastest-growing organic products depended on aliphatic compounds—ethylene, acetone, long-chain olefins for detergents, and butadiene for synthetic rubber—which could not be supplied in sufficient quantity by the old fermentation method. Petroleum chemistry and the petroleum supply system were sufficiently developed to favor this product as the solution to the raw-materials problem.

The United Kingdom was the first country to embark deliberately on large-scale cracking of oil feedstocks with the purpose of producing chemical raw materials rather than fuel as main end-products. As the demand for ethylene and propylene increased, oil companies in other countries also resorted to cracking naphtha, which not only gives a gas rich in ethylene but also produces butadiene as a primary product. Table 3 shows the size and expected growth of petrochemical production in the United Kingdom. The production levels cited were the highest for Western Europe.[9]

Table 3

DEVELOPMENT OF PETROCHEMICALS IN THE UNITED KINGDOM
(Production in thousands of tons carbon content)

	1953	1960	Estimated 1963
Petrochemical production	124	567	1,000
Per cent of growth since 1953		360	710
Per cent of Western Europe's total petrochemical production	57	33	27

Source: For 1953, *Chemische Industrie*, December, 1961; for 1960 and 1963, *The Chemical Industry in Europe, 1960–1961* (OECD, 1962).

As in other oil-importing countries in Western Europe, oil refineries in the United Kingdom tended to develop at centers where good deep-water shipping facilities were available for the economical transportation of oil and bulk products. Petrochemical plants were located close to these centers, in order to obtain both economical feedstocks and ready disposal of by-products. Map 1 shows the location of the principal petrochemical plants and oil refinery sites in the United Kingdom. Major producers of selected important petrochemical products are listed in Table 4.

INDUSTRY STRUCTURE

The chemical industry was and remains highly concentrated in the United Kingdom, as elsewhere. A dominant position is held by Imperial

---

[9] See Table 4 of the note entitled "The Chemical Industry in France" for data on other nations.

Map 1

GEOGRAPHICAL LOCATION OF THE MAJOR PETROCHEMICAL PLANTS IN
GREAT BRITAIN AND THEIR PRINCIPAL PRODUCTS, 1961

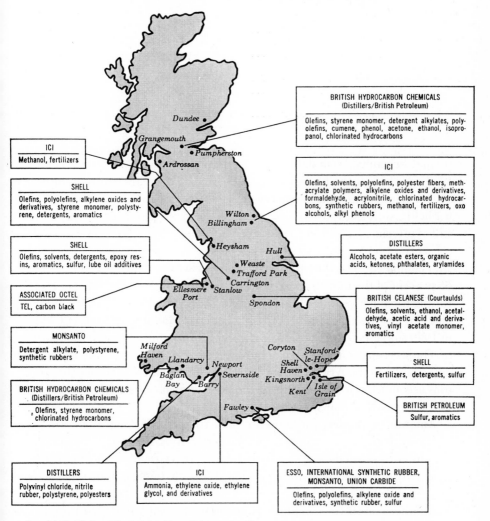

Source: *Chemical and Engineering News*, February 5, 1962.

Chemical Industries Ltd., which has accounted for about 30 per cent of total national sales in recent years. Shell Chemical is second. The circle of giants is completed by five to ten other firms, including such names as Distillers Co. Ltd., Albright & Wilson Ltd., Laporte Chemicals Ltd., Fisons Ltd., and Monsanto Chemicals Ltd. The rest of the industry, running into thousands of companies, comprised many medium- and small-sized firms, mostly specialized.

Some idea of the extent of concentration in the British chemicals indus-

Table 4

MAJOR PRODUCERS, SELECTED PETROCHEMICAL PRODUCTS
IN ORDER OF THEIR 1961 CAPACITIES

Product	Major Producers
Butadiene	Esso, I.C.I., British Hydrocarbon Chemicals
Dodecyl, benzene (detergent alkylate)	Shell, Monsanto, Grange Chemical
Ethylene	I.C.I., British Hydrocarbon Chemicals, Shell, Esso, Courtaulds
Ethylene oxide and glycol	Shell, Union Carbide, I.C.I.
Phenol (synthetic)	I.C.I., British Hydrocarbon Chemicals, Monsanto
Polyethylene	I.C.I., Shell, Union Carbide, Monsanto, British Hydrocarbon Chemicals

Source: H. P. Hodge, *op. cit.*

try may be gained from data on the distribution of the work force (Table 5). Even though the figures in the table do not cover the entire industry (they exclude firms employing fewer than 25 persons and also many product fields, such as explosives, paints, plastics, man-made fibers, etc.), they still represent a significant cross-section.[10] These figures reflect a higher concentration of employment in the chemical industry than in all industries combined. Thus the top 5 per cent of chemical firms accounted for 65 per cent of the industry's work force, as compared with only 47 per cent for the top 6 per cent of all industrial firms. A roughly comparable study made by the Association of British Chemical Manufacturers (ABCM) in 1949 suggests that inclusion of the small firms omitted from the Board of Trade census would have had but little effect on the distribution shown in the table. In the ABCM study, companies employing fewer than 25 persons accounted for 30 per cent of the 268 companies listed, but for only 1 per cent of the total work force.[11]

Among the reasons for concentration, competition from domestic as well as foreign companies played an important role. Thus I.C.I.—through its combined size, efficiency, and high degree of vertical integration—undoubtedly prompted many other chemical firms to engage in mergers and joint ventures.

Another reason for combining was the widely held view that product diversification and corporate growth could be achieved in less time and at less cost through joint companies than through self-development. For example, the only large producer of synthetic rubber in the United Kingdom, the International Synthetic Rubber Co. Ltd., was jointly owned by

---

[10] The Board of Trade census listed a total of 582 firms in the chemical industry, including firms with fewer than 25 employees. Over 2,000 firms were listed for the industry when defined to include the related sectors, such as pharmaceutical preparations, fertilizers, dyestuffs, etc. (see notes to Table 5).

[11] ABCM, *Report on the Chemical Industry, 1949*, p. 71.

Table 5

SIZE DISTRIBUTION OF CHEMICAL FIRMS IN TERMS OF
NUMBER OF EMPLOYEES, 1958*

No. of Employees	Chemical Industry, 1958†			All Industry, 1949	
	No. of Companies	% of Total Firms	No. Employees as % of Total No. Employees	% of Total Firms	No. Employees as % of Total No. Employees
25–99	112	51	5	63	18
100–499	74	34	13	30	35
500–999	14	6	8	4	15
1,000–1,999	8	4	9	1	13
2,000 and over	11	5	65	1	19
Total	219	100	100	99	100

* For firms with 25 or more employees.
† Defined to include organic chemicals (excluding those from coal tar), inorganic chemicals, industrial gases, pigments, fine chemicals (including pharmaceutical chemicals), chemicals for nuclear uses, and others not reported elsewhere. Not included are the following: pharmaceutical *preparations*, dyestuffs, fertilizers, pest-control chemicals, coal-tar products, toilet preparations, explosives, paint and printing ink, soap and detergents, synthetic resins and plastics materials, synthetic rubber, and synthetic fibers.
Source: Board of Trade, *op. cit.;* ABCM, *op. cit.*

a consortium of all the major rubber companies. A widely publicized instance of an attempt to expand through acquisition was the effort by I.C.I. to take over Courtaulds Ltd. in 1961. Had this effort succeeded, I.C.I. would have emerged as the world's second largest chemicals and artificial fibers firm, next to the United States' E. I. du Pont de Nemours & Company. As it was, I.C.I. emerged from the take-over attempt with some 38 per cent of Courtauld's stock, further complicating the structure of the industry.[12]

A third important reason for combination was the hope of obtaining assured sources of raw materials and assured outlets for sales through vertical integration. For example, Monsanto Chemicals Ltd. acquired a large holding in Forth Chemicals Ltd., which supplied styrene monomer for Monsanto's polystyrene. Similarly, I.C.I., a major producer of polyethylene, owned one of the largest polyethylene film producers in Britain, British Visqueen Ltd. Charts 1 and 2 show some of the intercompany relationships which existed in the United Kingdom chemical industry in mid-1961.

By 1961, most of the larger companies were broadly diversified. I.C.I., for example, not only made a very large range of inorganic and organic chemicals but also had companies manufacturing metals, textiles, drugs, paints, veterinary products, explosives, and even zipper fasteners. The

[12] See, "I.C.I.—Courtaulds: A Takeover Attempt That Failed."

Chart 1

SOME INTERCOMPANY OWNERSHIP RELATIONSHIPS IN 1961
I.C.I., COURTAULDS, SHELL

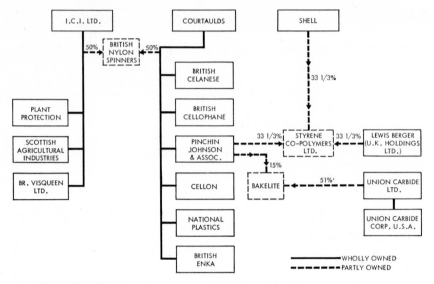

Source: H. P. Hodge, *op. cit.*

Chart 2

SOME INTERCOMPANY OWNERSHIP RELATIONSHIPS IN 1961,
BRITISH PETROLEUM, MONSANTO, DISTILLERS COMPANY, FISONS

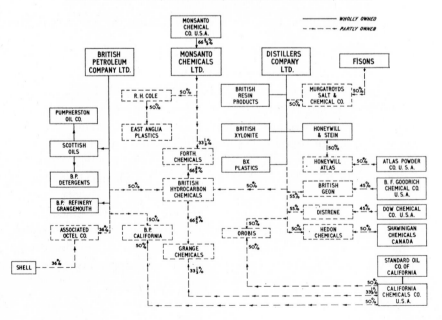

Distillers Co. Ltd. (DCL), though primarily a producer of whiskey and gin, also had large interests in petrochemicals, plastics, biochemicals, foodstuffs, and yeast. Courtaulds, Britain's largest rayon producer, went into petrochemicals when it took over British Celanese Ltd. It also owned half of Britain's largest nylon producer, owned Britain's second largest paint company, produced plastics, and engaged in engineering contracting. Fisons Ltd., with a long history in fertilizer production, was in chemicals, drugs, milk products, prepared foods, and gardening products.

Numbered among the more than 2,000 firms of the broadly defined United Kingdom chemical industry were about 120 companies wholly or partly owned by United States interests. They ranged from large well-established companies such as Monsanto Chemicals Ltd., formed in 1934, to many small and recent entries. While England was long the favorite location for American chemical companies seeking a European base because of the advantages of common language and similar business methods, West Germany was recently reported to have taken the lead.[13] Among the reasons for this shift were the desire of American chemical firms to operate directly in the fast-growing Continental market and also the apprehension that plants located in the United Kingdom might not be able to service the Common Market if the United Kingdom did not enter. Table 6 shows an estimated distribution of United States wholly owned and partly owned chemical producing companies in Europe.

Table 6

EUROPEAN CHEMICAL PRODUCING FIRMS WHOLLY OR PARTLY
UNITED STATES OWNED, 1961

Country	Estimated No. of Firms
West Germany	160
United Kingdom	120
France	75–80
Netherlands	60–65
Italy	50
Belgium	30
Luxembourg	2
Total EEC and United Kingdom	497–507
Total Western Europe	750

Source: *European Chemical News*, February 2, 1962.

LABOR AND INVESTMENTS

Perhaps much of the credit for the chemical industry's ability to stay in the black during Britain's troubled 1950's was due to the high level of capital equipment per employee. While other British industries suf-

---

[13] *European Chemical News*, February 2, 1962.

fered from mounting labor costs and in some cases from low productivities, continued heavy investment in capital equipment caused the average value added per chemical employee to increase significantly each year.

Table 7 shows the size of the labor force, value added, and annual investment per employee in the United Kingdom from 1956 to 1960. The

Table 7

LABOR FORCE, ANNUAL INVESTMENTS IN THE UNITED KINGDOM CHEMICAL INDUSTRY, AND VALUE ADDED PER EMPLOYEE, 1956–60

	1956	1957	1958	1959	1960
Employees (000)	355	357	367	390	403
Annual % change of work force		1	3	6	3
Annual % change of value added		8	16	9	10
Value added ($ million)	1,405	1,520	1,769	1,935	2,130
Value added/employee ($)	3,960	4,250	4,810	4,960	5,280
Annual investments ($ million)	356	358	425	384	358
Investment/employee ($)	1,000	1,000	1,160	985	890

Source: OECD, *op. cit.*, 1959, 1960, 1961; *Chemie Wirtschaft in Zahlen* (Verband der Chemischen Industrie e.V., 1962).

average value added per employee slightly exceeded the average for Western Europe as a whole ($5,280 versus $5,100), but it was less than one-third that of the United States ($16,200 in 1959).

INTERNATIONAL TRADE

Chemical products represented one of the United Kingdom's largest export sectors and were exceeded in value only by exports of machinery (other than electric) and motor vehicles (including aircraft). The 1961 value of chemical exports, including man-made yarns of £21 million, was about £346 million ($970 million); this figure represented about 9 per cent of total United Kingdom exports.[14] In 1960 chemical exports accounted for about 52 per cent of total chemical sales.[15]

Imports, including man-made yarns of £2 million, were only about £169 million ($473 million) for 1961, leaving a favorable balance of trade of about £177 million ($495 million).[16]

Britain, of course, had a traditional market of sizable proportions for her chemicals in the Commonwealth, which purchased about 37 per cent of her chemical exports. Nevertheless, Europe represented the largest regional customer for United Kingdom chemicals, accounting for approximately 30 per cent. Within Europe, the European Common Market

[14] Board of Trade, *op. cit.*
[15] OECD, *op. cit.*
[16] Board of Trade, *op. cit.*

(ECM) purchased 16.6 per cent and the European Free Trade Area (EFTA), of which the United Kingdom was a member, purchased about 9.5 per cent. Table 8 lists the five most important import and export trading partners for the United Kingdom's chemical industry in 1961. Table 9 shows the five most important import and export sectors for her chemical trade during the same year.

Table 8

MOST IMPORTANT TRADING PARTNERS FOR UNITED KINGDOM
CHEMICAL INDUSTRY, 1961

	Exports			*Imports*	
Customer		*Per Cent Share of Total Value*	*Supplier*		*Per Cent Share of Total Value*
Australia		6.4	U.S.A.		26.4
Netherlands		4.7	West Germany		15.6
India		4.2	France		9.4
Republic of South Africa		3.8	Netherlands		8.3
Sweden		3.5	Canada		5.8
Total		22.6	Total		65.5

Source: Board of Trade, *op. cit.*

Table 9

FIVE MOST IMPORTANT IMPORT AND EXPORT SECTORS OF THE
UNITED KINGDOM'S INTERNATIONAL CHEMICAL TRADE, 1961

	Per Cent Share of Total Value	
Chemical Sector	*Exports*	*Imports*
Pharmaceuticals	14.1	*
Plastics	13.9	16.6
Industrial organic chemicals	11.7	23.4
Industrial inorganic chemicals	10.6	13.0
Synthetic fibers	6.1	*
Fertilizers	*	10.2
Essential oils and perfume materials	*	5.6
Total	56.4	68.8

* Not in the top five for column indicated.
Source: Board of Trade, *op. cit.*

THE FUTURE AND THE COMMON MARKET

The future of the United Kingdom chemical industry will depend in great measure on whether or not the nation joins the Common Market. The decision on this issue, which will help to determine the United Kingdom's whole trading pattern, is of special interest to the chemical industry, which depends on exports for a large share of total sales.

There are many arguments against, as well as for, joining EEC. Should the United Kingdom make this move, the chemical industry will have to compete without the protection currently afforded by the high tariff wall which has long sheltered it in the home market. Eventually, tariffs would be completely eliminated on chemical products from competing EEC member nations. In many cases, also, significant reductions would have to be made in tariffs on competitive chemical products from all other nations, that is, wherever the common EEC tariff was lower than the old United Kingdom level. In other cases, where the opposite tariff relation-

Table 10

SELECTED TARIFF RATES*
(Per cent)

	United Kingdom Rates (in force January 1, 1963)			
	General	*EFTA*	*Commonwealth Preference*	*Eventual EEC Common Tariff to Nonmembers*
Sulfuric acid, oleum	10	5	0	4
Ammonia, anhydrous	20	10	0	15
Silicon carbide	0	0	0	9
Borax	16	10	0	12
Other than listed inorganic chemicals†	25–33⅓	25	0	12–15
Methanol, synthetic	27½	16⅔	0	18
Polyketones	33⅓	16⅔	0	12
Phthalic anhydride	33⅓	16⅔	0	18
Other than listed organic chemicals†	33⅓	16⅔	0	16–18
Insulin (hormone)	0	0	0	16
Vitamins, other than natural concentrates	33⅓	16⅔	0	9–18
Penicillin	25	16⅔	0	21
Other antibiotics	25	16⅔	0	9
Fertilizers				
Superphosphates	14	8¾	0	6
Ammonium nitrate	16	10	0	10
Potassium chloride	0	0	0	0
Synthetic organic dyestuffs	20	10	0	17–19
Detergents, general	10	5	0	17
Polymerisation and copolymerisation products‡	10	5	0	19–23
Cellulose acetate, unplasticised	33⅓	16⅔	0	19
Synthetic fibers				
Monofil, strip	(16+	10+	⅚ of	13
Yarn	(7½d/lb	4½d/lb	full rate	15
Synthetic rubber	10	5	0	0

* The rates quoted are subject to qualifications and exceptions.
† Includes most categories listed as "other."
‡ For example, polyethylene, polystyrene, polyvinyl chloride, and polyisobutylene.

Source: *H.M. Customs & Excise Tariff of the United Kingdom of Great Britain and Northern Ireland* (London: Her Majesty's Stationery Office, 1960), chaps. 28, 29, 30, 31, 32, 34, 39, 40, 51; *Customs Tariff of the European Communities* (London: Her Majesty's Stationery Office, 1962), chaps. 28, 29, 30, 31, 32, 34, 39, 40, 51.

ship existed, there would be an increase in tariff rates on needed chemical raw materials—for example, on silicon carbide. Table 10 shows 1961 tariff rates of the United Kingdom and the EEC for selected chemical products.

On the other hand, by joining the EEC, the United Kingdom chemical industry would eventually have a tariff-free access to the home markets of all member nations. Thus it would compete with their home industries on a more favorable basis than formerly. Moreover, should the United Kingdom remain outside the EEC, it would face an effective increase in tariffs on its trade with member nations, which are scheduled to raise tariff rates to outsiders. At the same time, competing products from other member countries will, by 1970, gain tariff-free entry into the EEC, thus giving them a tremendous advantage in hitherto important United Kingdom markets.

The advantages and disadvantages of entering the Common Market would be different for different industries and also for different sectors of a single industry, such as chemicals. However, on balance, it was widely believed that the chemical industry was one that, most likely, would benefit from the nation's entry into the EEC.[17] Industry representatives have pointed to arguments for joining, as follows:

H. W. Vallender, an official of the Association of British Chemical Manufacturers, notes that the European internal consumption of chemicals has doubled in eight years and Britain's exports to the Continent have jumped strongly while shipments to the Commonwealth declined. . . . Mr. Vallender notes, though, that Britain's share of intra-European chemical trade is only 13.5 per cent of the total and that the industry believes it can take a considerably larger slice of the cake competing on even terms inside the Common Market. . . .

*   *   *   *   *

Dr. T. Ward of Imperial Chemical Industries' plastics division sees an extended Common Market as the world's biggest plastic market, representing about half the world's import trade. . . .

*   *   *   *   *

In the field of synthetic fibers, C. F. Kearton, deputy chairman of Courtaulds, notes that Britain's industry is already ahead of many parts of the European industry in the size of its manufacturing units. British Nylon Spinners, 50-50 owned by Courtaulds and I.C.I., is one of the biggest in Europe and should have "the lowest cost of production." I.C.I.'s polyester fiber facilities are also described as the biggest in Europe, and in acrylics Courtaulds sees its own British and new French facilities as meeting European competition.[18]

---

[17] Westminister Bank Ltd., *The Common Market and the United Kingdom*, May, 1962.
[18] *Oil, Paint and Drug Reporter*, July 30, 1962.

Mr. S. Paul Chambers, chairman of the board of I.C.I., and others have argued that Britain, choosing between Commonwealth and EEC ties, would be better off with the latter:

> . . . the proportion of U.K. chemicals exports going to the Commonwealth and other under-developed countries is perhaps too high for our own good, while the proportion going to the rapidly expanding markets of Western Europe is too low— a characteristic which chemicals shares with many other sectors of British industry. The danger of having too many eggs in the Commonwealth market is that, since in most cases this is a price market and not a quality one, U.K. sales could be vulnerable to low-cost competition from Japan, Germany or the U.S.—or in the long term from behind the Iron Curtain. Moreover, it is a market with a slow growth rate, and an increasing tendency to develop indigenous protected chemicals industries.[19]

Although it was generally recognized that the removal of the high protective wall would jolt the industry, this result was not considered wholly deleterious. On more than one occasion spokesmen for the United Kingdom chemical industry have pointed out that the ensuing competitive scrap could be beneficial by arousing the lethargic, but healthy, giant.

---

[19] *Financial Times*, October 2, 1961.

THE CHEMICAL INDUSTRY IN FRANCE

One of the most important industries in France, chemicals in 1959 ranked second after textiles and just ahead of steel and automobiles in terms of sales[1] and accounted for 5–6 per cent of gross national industrial output. In 1961, sales of the French chemical industry ranked sixth in the world and third in Western Europe; they were estimated to be about 17 billion New Francs (NF) (about $3.46 billion)[2] under the French definition of the chemical industry and about NF 20 billion ($4.1 billion) under the German definition. Sales for the industry would have been about $3.7 billion under the definition used in the note titled "General Characteristics of the Chemical Industry."[3]

The following material on the chemical industry in France briefly reviews these topics: (1) growth and dimensions; (2) the boom in petrochemicals; (3) industry structure; (4) employment and investment; (5) international trade; and (6) the French system of economic planning. An appendix gives short résumés on selected major French chemical companies.

GROWTH AND DIMENSIONS OF THE CHEMICAL INDUSTRY

Since the mid-1950's the growth of the French chemical industry has been remarkable. Production has grown at an average annual rate of 19 per cent from 1956 to 1961 in current prices, and sales have grown 16.7 per cent annually for the same five-year period. Removing the influence of price changes, production and sales growth were about 15 and 12.7 per cent, respectively, in terms of 1956 values.[4]

---

[1] According to the *Rapport Général de la Commission de la Chimie, 1961, Quatrième Plan de Dévéloppement Economique et Social*, total sales for 1959 were as follows:

[2] Exchange rate of NF 4.9 = $1.

Sector	Millions of NF
Textiles	18,060
Chemicals, excluding perfume	13,118
Steel	13,100
Automobiles and bicycles	12,740

[3] The French definition understates the definition set forth in the note on "General Characteristics of the Chemical Industry" by omitting man-made fibers; the German definition overstates it by including such activities as ferroalloys, matches, linoleum, roofing felt, and office materials (see "The Chemical Industry in West Germany").

[4] *Rapport Général de la Commission de la Chimie*, p. 22.

As in all the more important European chemical-producing countries, it was the high growth rate of the organic sector that advanced the industry to such an extent. According to the French Planning Commission,[5] chemical production of the organic sector has been growing at almost twice the rate of the inorganic sector in recent years. Table 1, which defines the three major branches of the French chemical industry (inorganic, organic, and parachemical), shows the growth rate experienced by each since 1954 and the anticipated rate through 1965.

Table 1

SIZE, RATE OF GROWTH, AND DEFINITION OF THE THREE MAJOR AREAS
OF THE FRENCH CHEMICAL INDUSTRY

	Inorganic Sector	Organic Sector	Parachemical Sector	Total Industry
1961 estimated production value ($ million)	870	1,680	685	3,240
Annual rate of growth, 1959–1961	9.2%	17.5%	9.0%	13.9%
Annual rate of growth, 1961–1965	6.9%	11.2%	6.6%	9.1%
Total growth expected, 1961–1965	30.2%	53.0%	28.8%	41.7%
Principal products defining the major sectors	Inorganic Industrial chemicals Electro-chemistry Industrial gases Fertilizers	Organic Industrial chemicals Detergents (basic raw materials) Dyestuffs Plastics Synthetic rubber Explosives Pharmaceuticals	Abrasives Detergents (excluding basic raw material) Protective coatings Paints and varnishes Perfumes Photographic chemicals Insecticides pesticides	

Source: *Rapport Général de la Commission de la Chimie, 1961.*

Projected figures indicate, however, that the rate of expansion is expected to decline. Whereas the average annual growth was 13.9 per cent for 1959–61, it is expected to be only 9.1 per cent for 1960–65. The reason for the anticipated slowdown is that the spectacular expansion of the organic sector (especially petrochemicals) must lessen as capacities finally approach market demand.

Chemical production levels for 1965 have been set by the Commission at the following levels:

---

[5] See note entitled "Economic Planning in France."

Sector	Value (dollars in millions)
Inorganic	1,140
Organic	2,560
Parachemical	880
Total	4,580

Source: *Rapport Général de la Commission de la Chimie, 1961.*

The relatively faster growth of organic products may be seen in Table 2, which shows growth rates (both past and anticipated) and 1961 production levels for selected products within the industry's three major sectors. The higher output in the organic sector was composed mainly of intermediates required by the plastics and solvents industries, such as methyl alcohol, synthetic phenol, formaldehyde, chlorinated hydrocarbons, and plasticizers. Those inorganic chemicals that showed exception-

Table 2

PRODUCTION OUTPUT AND GROWTH OF SELECTED CHEMICALS AND CHEMICAL PRODUCTS

Product	Estimated 1961 Production (In thousands of tons)	Per Cent Increase 1952–61	Per Cent Increase 1959–61	Expected Per Cent Increase 1961–65
Inorganic Chemical Sector				
Sulfuric acid	2,200	85	16	32
Caustic soda	570	83	14	22
Soda ash	860	35	11	24
Chlorine	380	257	42	58
Organic Chemical Sector				
Methyl alcohol	105	480	128	49
Ethylene	105	*	139	138
Propylene	156	*	46	60
Phenol, synthetic	65	348	56	32
Dyestuffs	16	60	5	34
Plastics	474	915	96	69
Polyvinyl chloride (PVC)	135	1,235	69	85
Synthetic rubber	64	*	975†	169
Parachemical Sector				
Paints and varnishes	506	105	12	25

* No, or negligible, production in 1952.
† Estimated.
Source: *Rapport Général de la Commission de la Chimie, 1961,* Annex I.

	Production (thousands of tons)	Times Growth 1950–60	Per Cent Increase 1958–60
Natural polymer fibers (e.g. rayon)	119	1.4	6
Synthetic fibers (e.g. nylon)	45	18.0	95

Source: *Chemische Industrie,* December, 1961.

ally rapid growth in most cases served as raw materials for booming organic products. For example, the production of both calcium carbide and chlorine began to rise in 1957 with the opening of the first vinyl chloride (plastic resin) plant.

Although many organic chemicals have attained an important place in over-all production, the traditional inorganic sector is still the nation's largest in terms of sales. Table 3 shows the relative importance of various product groups in total French chemical output.[6] (Although man-made fibers are not a part of the chemical industry according to the French definition, they have been included in the table because of their importance in France and their high growth rate.)

Table 3

RELATIVE IMPORTANCE OF CERTAIN CHEMICAL SECTORS IN FRANCE,
1938 COMPARED WITH 1960

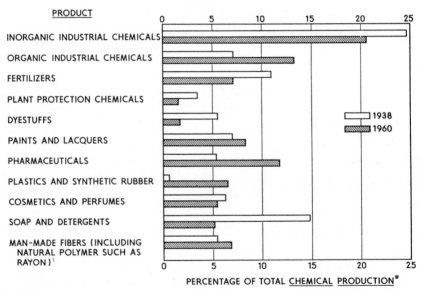

PERCENTAGE OF TOTAL CHEMICAL PRODUCTION*

* Based on the German definition of the chemical industry which includes ferroalloys, matches, office materials, linoleum, and roofing felt.
† Excluded from the French definition of the chemical industry, but included in the German definition.
Source: *Chemische Industrie*, December, 1961.

THE PETROCHEMICAL BOOM IN FRANCE

While it is true that the organic sector sparked the growth of the over-all French chemical industry, the great underlying driving force was the

---

[6] The statistics of Table 3 are based on the German definition of the chemical industry, and so the percentages will be a little lower than if computed on the basis of the narrower French definition. The relationship among the different sectors, however, is not essentially affected.

striking progress of petrochemicals. Whereas European petrochemical production (in thousands of tons of carbon content) rose almost eightfold between 1953 and 1960, the French multiplier was more than 14. Table 4 shows the size and expected growth of petrochemicals in France. By 1963 France is expected to produce one-fifth of Europe's total output.

Table 4

DEVELOPMENT OF PETROCHEMICALS IN WESTERN EUROPE
(Production in thousands of tons carbon content)

	1953		1960		Estimated 1963	
	Production	Per Cent of European Total	Production	Per Cent of European Total	Production	Per Cent of European Total
France	16	7	230	14	700	19
Germany	55	25	504	30	900	24
Italy	12	5	243	14	750	20
United Kingdom	124	57	567	33	1,000	27
Other	12	5	153*	9	370*	10
Total Western Europe...	219	—	1,697*	—	3,720*	—

* Estimated.
Source: For 1953, *Chemische Industrie*, December, 1961; for 1960 and 1963, *The Chemical Industry in Europe, 1960–1961* (OECD, 1962).

The extraordinary petrochemical growth rate reflected the greatly increased dependence of the French chemical industry on petroleum as a raw material for organic chemicals. Since coal production has remained close to 60 million tons ever since 1962, practically all additional raw material requirements for organics had to be met elsewhere—namely, from petroleum and natural gas. This achievement was made possible by the increase of refinery capacity by 1960 to 40 million metric tons per annum (880,000 bbl/day), the successful prospecting and development of the Lacq natural-gas field, and the emerging exploitation of Sahara oil and gas. By 1959, petrochemicals already accounted for 50 per cent of total organic production, and this share was expected to increase to 70 per cent by 1962. For comparison, petrochemicals contributed 70 per cent to total United States organic chemical production in 1960. Gross petrochemical production in France was 449,200 tons in 1960 and was expected to reach 1,900,000 tons by 1962.

As in most oil-importing countries, the more important refineries were located in the lower reaches of the major rivers, where sea transportation was available. In order to utilize the raw materials at source, 18 new plants for the manufacture of petrochemicals were built near these refineries, while another 5 plants underwent major expansions of capacity between 1959 and 1961. Map 1 shows the location of the major petrochemical plants in France.

Map 1

GEOGRAPHICAL LOCATION OF THE MAJOR PETROCHEMICAL CENTERS
IN FRANCE AND THEIR PRINCIPAL PRODUCTS, 1961

Source: *Chemical and Engineering News*, October 9, 1961.

The most important local source of raw material was the Lacq gas field, which had an estimated reserve of 200 billion cubic meters. The development of this huge reserve was under the direction of the Société Nationale des Petroles d'Aquitaine (SNPA), which was 50.6 per cent owned by the French government in 1960. The buildup of this area proceeded very rapidly. Between 1960 and 1961 alone, 7 new petrochemical works were completed and brought on stream. All used methane from the purified gas exclusively; most of this gas was processed to acetylene, and the by-product, hydrogen, was used to make ammonia.

Lacq gases have a very high sulfur content (15.12 per cent hydrogen sulfide by weight), which is extracted by SNPA itself. This production will make France the largest European producer of very pure (99.88 per cent) sulfur, with an output expected to exceed the total future minimum needs of Europe by 50 per cent.

The reserves of the Sahara gas field at Hassi R'Mel are still larger, with estimated reserves of 1,600 billion cu.m. The future utilization of this field, as well as of the two oil fields in the Sahara (Hassi Messaoud and Edjelé), will necessarily depend on the policies followed by the new Algerian government. The French chemical industry is continuing to invest and operate in these areas in view of greatly augmented future requirements.

THE INDUSTRY STRUCTURE

Superficially, one of the most striking features of the French chemical industry is its apparent fragmentation into hundreds of small enterprises, most with a very small share of the market. In 1961 the chemical sales of the seven largest French producers totaled about $800 million, or 23 per cent of the total industry sales. In comparison, the Big Three of Germany (Bayer, BASF, and Hoechst)[7] accounted for about one-third of national chemical sales. In England, I.C.I.[8] alone accounted for about 25–30 per cent of British sales, and in Italy Montecatini[9] accounted for about 35–45 per cent. Table 5 lists sales of the major French chemical companies.

Actually, much of this fragmentation is a matter of accounting. The big French companies do not consolidate the sales of their numerous specialized subsidiaries. It has been estimated that if the leading 7 companies had reported consolidated chemical sales, these would have totaled about $1.6 billion, or 46 per cent of total chemical sales in France.[10] The chairman of the Chemical Commission of the French planning system remarked that if sales figures of the larger companies included those of their subsidiaries, the 15 largest companies would account for more than three-quarters of the total industry sales as compared with reported sales of only about 30 per cent.

One consequence of the fragmentation is that a downward correction of about 10 per cent should be made in sales figures for the French chemical industry when comparing them with sales of other major chemical-producing countries.[11] This is necessary because total sales figures include

---

[7] Farbenfabriken Bayer AG; Badische Anilin—und Soda-Fabrik AG; and Farbwerke Hoechst AG.

[8] Imperial Chemical Industries Ltd.

[9] Montecatini Società Generale per l'Industria Mineraria e Chimica. Anonima.

[10] *Chemische Industrie*, June, 1962, p. 302.

[11] American Embassy, Paris, Foreign Service Dispatch No. 29, *French Chemical Industry, 1960*, July 11, 1961.

Table 5

SALES OF TEN MAJOR FRENCH CHEMICAL COMPANIES, 1961
(Dollars in millions)

Company	1961 Chemical Sales	Other Important Sales	Per Cent Change Total Sales 1960–61
1. Rhône-Poulenc*	$190	$0.9	5.5
2. Kuhlmann (including Matières Colerantes)	198	....	7.5
3. Pechiney†	95	132 (aluminum)	15.7
4. Saint-Gobain	82	163 (glass)	20.8
5. l'Air Liquide	116	....	15.0
6. Ugine	71‡	141‡ (iron & steel)	10.2‡
7. Progil	49‡	....	10.0‡
8. Nobel-Bozel	39	....	6.0
9. ONIA	37	....	11.3
10. Huiles, Goudrons, et Dérivés	34	....	11.8
Next 32 companies	340‡	....	7.3‡

* Sales for Rhône-Poulenc and its controlled subsidiaries would have been $228 million.
† The 1961 chemical sales figure indicated in the annual report was about $66 million. The above figure includes ferroalloys, graphite, and other products.
‡ Estimated.
Source: *Chemische Industrie*, June, 1962.

intraindustry sales; the relatively greater number of intercompany sales in France results in an inflated report.

France's traditionally fragmented chemical industry is becoming steadily more interlocked. While the industry has been creating joint ventures for many years, the pace has quickened over the past five years. One result has been that the pattern of interrelated ownerships and participations of French chemical companies has become highly complex. Another result is that the real size and influence of the various companies has become obscured and difficult to estimate. Chart 1 shows the involved network of interrelationships for only one French company, Progil SA.[12]

While particular relationships are subject to continued re-examination by participating companies, there are a number of reasons which favor continued joint ownership by chemical firms in France. First, joint ownership permits the pooling of financial resources so that raising capital can be done internally. This eliminates the need for borrowing from sources subject to government influence that might in turn transmit this influence to the companies. Second, splitting the investment load permits the companies to enter more fields at the same time. Third, since the size of the domestic French market for a given product is frequently large enough

[12] SA = Société Anonyme.

for only one plant of economic size, a number of companies can join hands to fill that market with one plant and thus avoid disastrous competition. In this way, too, the French can compete on the international market with a plant that is big enough for its costs to be competitive.

One of the most important joint ventures was agreed to late in 1959, when Pechiney[13] and Saint-Gobain,[14] two of the five largest chemical companies in the country, agreed to merge most of their chemical interests, Pechiney, however, retaining its interests in nonferrous metals and Saint-Gobain retaining its interests in glass and caustic soda (an important material in glass production). The new company, Produits Chimiques Pechiney-Saint-Gobain, began effective operation in January, 1962.

Meanwhile, another major company, Etablissements Kuhlmann SA was also adding to its operations. It absorbed Société des Produits Chimiques Coignet, the primary French producer of phosphors. In addition, Kuhlmann reached a dominant position in the French dye industry by absorbing Société des Matières Collorantes de Saint-Denis and by acquiring complete control of Compagnie Française des Matières Collorantes (Francolor), in which it already had a controlling interest.

A third major coalescence was formed during the summer of 1961, when Rhône-Poulenc bought out Celtex, its partner in four synthetic fiber and plastic companies. It also completed its control of a fifth company, Société Normande des Produits Chimiques, and subsequently started the process of reorganizing to improve its profit position. When Rhône-Poulenc[15] digests its new acquisitions, it will be as large as any other European chemical company except I.C.I. and will account for about 16 per cent of France's chemical sales.

In line with this evidence of consolidation in the French chemical industry, one executive in the industry stated:

> I believe that in five years' time there will be only three or four big French interests or groups. As I see it, Rhône-Poulenc and Progil will merge interests. Perhaps Ugine[16] will also join this group. This will form the largest of the groups. A second group will center about Pechiney and Saint-Gobain. The third large group will be that of the Kuhlmann interests. You might add a fourth group centered about Nobel-Bozel SA, but this would be considerably smaller than the other three.

EMPLOYMENT AND INVESTMENT

In 1960 the French Planning Commission reported a chemical labor force of 230,400, while the OECD reported 248,500. Of the latter num-

---

13 Full name, Pechiney Compagnie des Produits Chimiques et Electro-Métallurgiques SA.

14 Full name, Compagnie de Saint-Gobain SA.

15 Full name, Société des Usines Chimiques Rhône-Poulenc.

16 Full name, Société d'Electro-Chimie, d'Electro-Métallurgie et des Aciéries Electriques d'Ugine.

Chart 1
Network of Participations Involving Société Progil, February, 1962

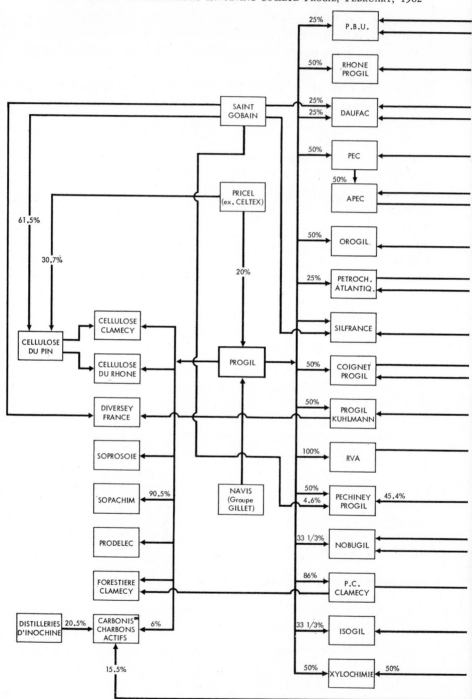

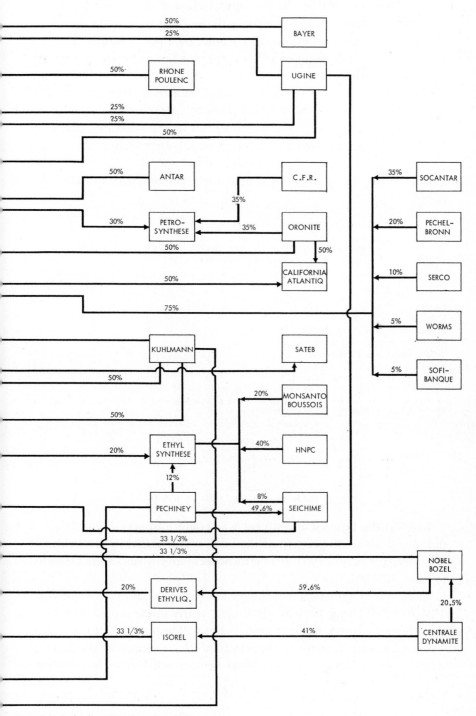

ber, only 68.8 per cent were actual operatives, while the remaining 31.2 per cent were classified as administrative, technical, and clerical personnel. (The breakdown was approximately the same as that obtaining in the work force of Western Europe as a whole: 69.5 per cent operatives and 30.5 per cent other categories.) Except for packaging operations, very few women were employed.

Total manpower of the French chemical industry increased only slightly over the five-year period to 1960. Thus the great production increases of these years were achieved through a great increase of value added per employee. This productivity increase, in turn, was brought about by very high investment in capital equipment. Table 6 shows employment, value added per employee, and annual investment per employee in France for recent years.

Table 6

NUMBER OF EMPLOYEES, VALUE ADDED PER EMPLOYEE, AND
INVESTMENT PER EMPLOYEE, 1957–60

	1957	1958	1959	1960
Employees (000)	234	240	245	249
Value added ($ million)*	N.A.	1,020	1,160	1,385
Percentage change in employees		2.6	2.1	1.6
Percentage change in value added			1.4	1.9
Yearly investment ($ million)	118	161	174	184
Value added per employee ($)		4,250	4,730	5,560
Yearly investment per employee ($)	500	670	710	740

* Exchange rates of 4.9 NF=$1 and 490 Fr. Frs.=$1 have been used for the purpose of comparison. The actual figures reported by OECD were as follows:

Year	Unit	Value Added (Millions)	Yearly Investment (Millions)
1957.............................	Fr. Frs.		58,000
1958.............................	Fr. Frs.	500,000	79,000
1959.............................	NF	5,700	852
1960.............................	NF	6,800	900

Source: *The Chemical Industry in Europe, 1960–1961* (OECD), 1962).

In 1960 the heaviest investment was going into petrochemicals; $72 million, or about 40 per cent of the total, was reported in this field. For the three-year period 1961–63, petrochemical investments were predicted to total $265 million.[17]

Table 7 shows the expected change in total chemical investments from 1959 to 1965. Using 1959 as a base year, yearly investments will be 1.87 times higher in 1965, whereas annual sales will be only 1.78 times higher.

To aid in supplying the investment funds that members of the industry would need, an interesting cooperative venture was formed in the spring

[17] Source: OECD, *The Chemical Industry in Europe, 1960–1961*, (1962).

Table 7

INVESTMENTS IN NEW CHEMICAL PLANT*
ESTIMATED BY FRENCH PLANNING COMMISSION
(Dollars in millions)

	1959	1961	1965
Commission's estimate	171	237	320

* Excluding perfume sector.
Source: *Rapport Général de la Commission de la Chimie, 1961*, p. 126.

of 1960. Called "Groupement de l'Industrie Chimique de Synthèse," it would facilitate long- and medium-term financing of synthetic chemical enterprises. Patterned after the steel industry's "Groupement de l'Industrie Sidérurgique," the chemical "Groupement" was made up of the nine largest chemical companies of France, together with several important banking houses. The first loan of NF 67 million was floated in December, 1960, for the benefit of 13 members in France engaged primarily in the organic field.

INTERNATIONAL TRADE

Depending on the definition used, the French chemical industry in 1961 accounted for a favorable balance of trade of $147 million or $157 million. According to one set of figures, exports were $564 million and imports $417 million;[18] according to another set, $521 million and $364 million.[19]

The six most important chemical sectors of French international trade in 1960 are shown in Table 8, and the most important geographical trading areas for French chemical products are shown in Table 9.[20] As shown in the latter table, the United States continued to be the most important supplier and Algeria the most important customer.

According to the 1961 report of the French Planning Commission, several major factors made it impossible to predict the future of French international trade on the basis of past experience. These factors included the following: (1) possible changes in the relative values of currencies; (2) the unknown effect of the suppression of quantitative restrictions (i.e.,

---

[18] Union des Industries Chimique, *L'Industrie Chimique Française en 1961* (Paris). Using a definition based on nomenclature of the Institut National de la Statistique et des Etudes Economiques (INSEE), the source gives a slightly broader definition of the industry than that of the French Planning Commission. For example, INSEE figures include perfumes, while Commission figures do not.

[19] French Planning Commission.

[20] Tables 8 and 9 are not comparable because they are based on two different definitions of the chemical industry. Under the French definition, the leading customers for French exports in 1960 would have been Algeria, Germany, Great Britain, United States, Italy, Belgium, and Switzerland in order of importance.

Table 8

SIX MOST IMPORTANT SECTORS FOR FRENCH INTERNATIONAL TRADE

Chemical Sector	Percentage Share of Total*	
	Exports	Imports
Industrial organic products	20.6	27.6
Essential oils and perfumes	15.0	7.0
Pharmaceuticals	14.8	
Industrial inorganic products	12.8	10.1
Plastics	10.4	13.2
Fertilizers	4.3	
Synthetic rubber		10.2
Paints, varnishes, tannins, dyestuffs		8.7
Total	77.9	76.8

* Percentage calculations are based on the French definition of the chemical industry. Man-made fibers, which are excluded, had an export value slightly exceeding plastics and an import value slightly exceeding industrial inorganic products, according to the 1960 ranking under the German definition.

Source: *L'Industrie Chimique Française en 1961* (Paris: Union des Industries Chimiques).

Table 9

MOST IMPORTANT TRADING PARTNERS FOR FRENCH CHEMICAL INDUSTRY, 1960

Exports		Imports	
Customer	Per Cent Share of Total Value	Supplier	Per Cent Share of Total Value
BY NATION*			
Algeria	12.2	U.S.A.	26.4
Germany	9.4	Germany	21.1
Great Britain	6.1	Great Britain	7.8
Switzerland	5.6	Switzerland	6.6
U.S.A.	5.4	Italy	6.1
BY REGION			
Europe	49.3	Europe	57.7
(ECM—23.3%)		(ECM—38.7%)	
(EFTA—17.9%)		(EFTA—16.0%)	
Africa	26.8	America	33.5
America	12.3	Other	8.8
Asia	10.4		
Other	1.2		

* Five most important nations.
Source: *Chemische Industrie*, September, 1961.

import quotas) among OECD members; (3) changes connected with the evolution of the Common Market, such as the projected reduction and ultimate disappearance of tariffs, the possible entry of Great Britain and other European countries, and the practice of outsiders' building plants within the boundaries of ECM; (4) the unpredictable course of future trade between Western Europe, Eastern Europe, and Far East countries;

and, finally, (5) the unknown future relationships that will emerge within the Franc Zone, especially between France and Algeria.

In light of these difficulties in projecting past trade patterns, the Planning Commission made forecasts of a global[21] scope, based on a correlation between exports and imports and predicted production and consumption. As shown in Table 10, exports are expected to rise 40 per cent from 1961 to 1965, reaching a level of about $729 million. Imports will rise 46 per cent during the same period, reaching about $533 million. A favorable trade balance of about $200 million will be achieved in 1965 under forecast conditions. Some of the products which are expected to contribute heavily to enlarged exports are basic organic chemicals, with a forecast growth of 83 per cent; plastics, with 92 per cent; and synthetic rubber, with 210 per cent.[22]

Table 10

Exports				Imports		
1961	1965	Per Cent Change '61–'65	Industry Sector	1961	1965	Per Cent Change '61–'65
$105	$132	25.2	Inorganic chemical	$ 52	$ 64	22.6
301	444	47.5	Organic chemical	254	382	50.6
115	153	33.6	Parachemical	58	87	49.1
$521	$729	40.0	Total industry	$364	$533	46.3

Source: *Rapport Général de la Commission de la Chimie, 1961*, pp. 121–24.

THE FRENCH ECONOMIC PLANNING SYSTEM

Nowhere in the postwar chemical industry of Western Europe has the integration between private initiative and governmental direction been more successful than in France. Under its present form of operation, the Plan of Economic and Social Development appears to enjoy wide support from the chemical industry.

French economic planning is an attempt to combine government coordination with industry's profit-determined actions in such a way as to avoid governmental control. Special planning commissions, such as the Commission de la Chimie, develop plans based on extensive discussions with companies in the industry itself and with commissions in related industries. Emphasis is placed on viewing each industry within the over-all

---

[21] Data are subdivided into trade with the Franc Zone and with foreign countries.
[22] In terms of absolute export values (NF millions):

	1961	1965	Expected Increase
Basic industrial chemicals	191	350	159
Plastics	218	419	201
Synthetic rubber	39	122	83

economy, so that production of each will remain in balance with national demands. The program, generally covering a four-year period, is continually reviewed and revised.

While adhesion to a plan is completely voluntary on the part of any company, the French government has several effective means of making sure that industry cooperates with its planning goals. In the first place, as noted earlier, it takes industry deeply into the work of formulating the plans; thus industry's thinking is taken into account. Perhaps the most important technique is that of controlling the money supply and, in some cases, the interest rate for capital needed to make new investments.

Under the four-year plans, the government can offer a favorable economic environment to projects that are part of the plan. This may involve reductions in taxes on real estate and capital gains, as well as the liberal interpretation of antitrust regulations, tax categories, and other rules affecting parent companies and their subsidiaries. Financial inducements, such as tax postponements, can be granted to encourage research. Special agreements can help start new lines of production. The choice of incentive is made after careful study of each individual case.

The government can also participate directly in projects which industry is unable or unwilling to support by itself. One example of sharing the financial burden is the huge Lacq gas-field development, where the principal development company is slightly more than half owned by the government.

Proponents of the French planning system point out that the chemical plan has probably contributed significantly to the high growth rate of the industry in France. They point out that the existence of high target figures has probably, in itself, been a positive influence. The procedure followed in French planning seems calculated to insure that the target rate of growth is a reasonable maximum, not a conscious estimate of what is "probable." In effect, firms are asked, "Can you do as much as x per cent a year?" Another advantage of the plan is that it permits bottlenecks to be foreseen, so that collective action can be taken where necessary. Finally, proponents of planning indicate that the preparation of successive plans has built up a group of people in industry trained to think about the problems of growth.

Appendix

THE CHEMICAL INDUSTRY IN FRANCE
Résumés of Important French Chemical Companies

✿✿

SOCIETE DES USINES CHIMIQUES RHONE-POULENC SA

Rhône-Poulenc was the most important French producer of pharmaceuticals and organic chemicals in 1961 and also ranked first in the sale of chemical products in France. Sales of the company and its two directly owned subsidiaries—Specia and Prolabo—rose 6.2 per cent in 1961, reaching a level of NF 1,118 million ($224 million). Exports accounted for 25.2 per cent of these sales and were at a level of NF 282 million (about $56 million). Like other large French chemical manufacturers, Rhône-Poulenc had a very important network of subsidiaries in France and abroad, whose volume seemed to be greater than that of the parent company and whose sales were not consolidated.

Rhône-Poulenc was formed in 1928 by the merger of Société Chimiques des Usines du Rhône and Etablissements Poulenc Frères. Usines du Rhône, founded in 1801 to manufacture dyestuffs and tanning extracts, was one of the earliest French companies to manufacture synthetic organic products on a commercial scale. In 1910, with the manufacture of cellulose acetate, this company entered the field of plastic materials and soon afterward started manufacturing artificial fibers. Poulenc Frères was active in pharmaceuticals and photographic chemicals. The merged company, Rhône-Poulenc, continued diversifying into new fields, entering the important field of petrochemicals in 1954 with the production of synthetic phenol. In 1961 the company manufactured approximately 3,000 different products that fell into the following principal groups:

Industrial chemicals
Plastic materials
Pharmaceuticals and antibiotics
Plant-protection chemicals
Synthetic products for perfumes
Chemicals for the ceramic, glassware, and enamelware industries

Rhône-Poulenc also had important subsidiaries in the field of synthetic fibers. Société Rhodiaceta, wholly owned since 1961, manufactured all the Tergal and most of the nylon used in France in 1960.

Rhône-Poulenc had six principal factories which employed about 15,000 persons in 1960. Rhodiaceta had an additional seven plants with a work force of about 8,000.

The Rhône-Poulenc group contained many different subsidiaries and interests. The company listed the following participations as of December 31, 1961:

Millions of NF

Participation in France exceeding NF 100,000 (35 companies)	2,229
Participations in France below NF 100,000	1
Foreign participations	868
Participations in real estate companies	19
Total participation	3,117

One of the most important recent moves was the purchase in 1961 of Celtex, with which Rhône-Poulenc shared equal ownership of Rhodiaceta. Rhône-Poulenc had been planning some form of consolidation and incorporation of all its fiber activities within the present group.

Among Rhône-Poulenc's most important participations were the following:

Company	Principal Activity	Per Cent Participation of Rhône-Poulenc
Normande de Produits Chimiques	Inorganic chemicals	95
Acétalacq	Basic petrochemicals	21
Manolène	Polyethylene	33
Daufac	Polyvinyl chloride	25
Rhovyl	Fibers	77.5
Rhodiacete	Fibers	100

ETABLISSEMENTS KUHLMANN SA

In 1825 Professor F. Kuhlmann founded a sulfuric acid plant at Loos-Lez-Lille to supply local industries. By 1960 the Kuhlmann organization owned 26 plants (18 of which belonged to the parent company). It ranked as one of France's largest producers of key inorganic chemicals, fertilizers, and dyes (through a subsidiary), and employed 15,000. Sales reached NF 633 million (about $127 million), not counting the recently absorbed Société des Produits Chimiques Coignet or separately held subsidiaries. Sales growth was as follows in recent years:

Year	Sales (Dollars in millions)
1956..................................	$ 94
1957..................................	89
1958..................................	95
1959..................................	109
1960..................................	127

Exports played a relatively small role in Kuhlmann's activities and it owned only four foreign subsidiaries.

The Kuhlmann organization made its first entry into organic chemistry in 1927, when it absorbed the Compagnie Française des Matières Colorantes. The new acquisition was an important supplier of dyestuffs and intermediary organic products. After World War II, Kuhlmann also moved into fiber production, electrochemical production, and nuclear ore refinement.

In 1960 Kuhlmann's principal products were as follows:

1. Mineral chemicals, principally the following:
   Sulfuric acid
   Electrolytic chlorine, soda, potassium lye
   Sodium sulfates (which give hydrochloric acid)
   Sulfites, hyposulfites
   Ammonia
   Bichromate (the only bichromate works in France)
2. Fertilizers and insecticides
3. Organic chemicals and plastics (largely through subsidiaries)
4. Dyestuffs (of which four-fifths of the total French production came from Kuhlmann's principal subsidiary, the Compagnie Française des Matières Colorantes)
5. Special sectors:
   Nuclear (uranium treatment)
   Ferroalloys

Kuhlmann listed 40 French chemical companies in which it participated as of December 31, 1960. Among the most important were the following:

Company	Principal Activity
Compagnie Française des Matières Colorantes	Dyestuffs
Imphy Kuhlmann	Metals and alloys
Plasco	Resins and plastics
Compagnie Française des Minérals d'Uranium	Uranium treatment
Méthanolacq	Methanol

PROGIL SA

Founded in 1918, Progil developed into one of the larger French chemical groups. By 1961, the parent company's chemical sales had reached about $49 million, of which about 20 per cent were exports. As with other large French chemical companies, even higher sales were made by the nonconsolidated holdings and were not included in the above figure.

In a dozen plants, spread over the periphery of the central highlands in France and particularly along the Rhône valley, Progil manufactured three major product groups:

1. Soda, chlorine, and chlorine by-products
2. Phosphates and sulfides
3. Tannins and cellulose pulp

Chlorine and chlorine by-products experienced remarkable growth in recent years because of their use as a raw material for organic products such as polyvinyl chloride.

These industrial activities of the parent company were rounded off by a very large variety of products manufactured by its subsidiaries. Among Progil's important holdings were the following:

Company	Principal Activity	Per Cent Progil's Participation
Résins et Vernis Artificiels	Polystyrene and plasticizer	100
Produits Chimiques de Clamecy	Wood carbonization and detinning	100
Coignet-Progil	Detergents	50
Ethyl-synthèse	Styrene monomers	20
Progil-Electrochimie	Acetone, phenol	50
Progil-Kuhlmann	Carbon disulfide	50

Chart 1 of the main text shows the known interrelations of Progil with other companies in detail.

PECHINEY COMPAGNIE DES PRODUITS CHIMIQUES ET ELECTRO-METALLURGIQUES SA

Pechiney was the largest aluminum producer in France, accounting for approximately 80 per cent of the national output. In 1961 it was perhaps the fifth largest chemical firm. Total sales for that year reached NF 1,112 million (about $228 million), comprising 58 per cent aluminum, 29 per cent chemicals (about $66 million), and 13 per cent other products (largely ferroalloys and graphites).[23]

The first factory of the company was founded in 1855 to produce caustic soda, potash, chlorine, and sulfuric acid. Four years later the company, then Henri Merle et Cie., began its first activities with aluminum.

Throughout its long history, the company has been known by different names, the name Pechiney having been assumed in 1950. In 1960, Pechiney merged its major chemical interests with those of Saint-Gobain in a new company, Pechiney-Saint-Gobain, which began sales operations in 1961 and took over management of the chemical works on January 2, 1962.

---

[23] Pechiney, *Rapport d'Assemblée Générale Ordinaire* (1962).

Other important chemical participations were listed by the company as follows:

Company	Per Cent Participation Direct or through Seichime*	Principal Products
Compagnie Salinière de la Camargue (Salicam)	30†	Sea salts for electre chemicals
Organico	67†	Plastic (monomer and polyamide) called "Rilsan"
Naphtachimie	53.6	Petrochemicals
Ethyl-synthèse	20	Styrene monomer
Ethylène-plastique	25	Low-density polyethylene
Ethylène-plastique-Normandie	20	Low-density polyethylene
Aquitaine-Chimie	21	Acetylene
Acétalacq	21	Acetaldehyde
Vinylacq	45	Vinyl chloride
Usines de Mette	40	Alcohol, ethers, acetone
Plastichimie	51	Polystyrene, Saran
Pechiney-Progil	45.4	Plant protectives
Xylochimie	49.9	Pentachlorophenol specialties

* Full name, Société d'Exploitation et d'Intérêts Chimiques et Métallurgiques.
† Estimated. Further participation in some of the subsidiaries listed was obtained through investment by other subsidiaries.
Source: Pechiney, *Informations Générales*, 1962; participation shares were obtained from the private records of a chemical company, dated January, 1962.

Pechiney has also entered all phases of the atomic energy industry, including exploitation of uranium deposits, preparation of nuclear fuels, production of nuclear graphite, construction of atomic piles, and the application of radioactive chemicals.

COMPAGNIE DE SAINT-GOBAIN SA

Saint-Gobain was the largest glass manufacturer in Europe, accounting for approximately 50 per cent of the European output and 15 per cent of world output. In 1961 it was the fourth largest chemical firm in France. Total sales for 1961 reached NF 1,214 million ($248 million), comprising 64.8 per cent glass products and 35.2 per cent chemical products (about $87 million), including paper, oil, and nuclear activities.[24] The company had in 1961 about 5,000 products, 28,500 employees, 32 plants (an additional 60 through subsidiaries), and 120,000 shareholders.

Dean of French industry, Saint-Gobain was founded in 1665 to produce mirrors and glass. Starting around 1807, the company began making heavy industrial chemicals. Since 1945 it has strongly entered the organic chemical, petrochemical, and nuclear energy fields.

Saint-Gobain merged its major chemical interests with Pechiney in

---

[24] Saint-Gobain *Annual Report* (1961).

1960 to form a new company, Pechiney-Saint-Gobain, which began sales operations in 1961 and took over management of the chemical works on January 2, 1962. Other important chemical participations were listed by the company as follows:

Company	Per Cent Direct Participation*	Principal Products
Société Shell-Saint-Gobain	40	Petrochemicals
Aquitaine-Chimie	21	Acetylene
Vinylacq	45	Vinyl chloride
Acétalacq	21	Acetaldehyde
Rhovyl	22.5	Synthetic fibers
Thann et Mulhouse	14	Titanium oxide
Société des Produits Chimiques et de Synthèse à Bezone (SPCS)	20.4	Plasticizers, compounds, stabilizers

* Further participation in some of the subsidiaries listed takes place through other subsidiaries.
Source: Saint-Gobain *Annual Report* (1961); participation shares were obtained from the private records of a chemical company dated January, 1962.

PRODUITS CHIMIQUES PECHINEY-SAINT-GOBAIN SA

Pechiney-Saint-Gobain was formed in 1960 to take over the chemical activities of both Pechiney and Saint-Gobain. It handled sales on a commission basis in 1961 and on January 2, 1962, took over complete management of all the chemical facilities. These consisted of 17 plants, 2 research centers, and numerous mineral deposits. The company had about 11,000 employees and annual sales exceeding NF 1 billion ($200 million).[25]

Pechiney-Saint-Gobain represented the largest joint venture in the history of the French chemical industry. As stated in the company's brochure, the move was made to create a large, powerful chemical company that could compete effectively in the Common Market. The parent companies, each holding 50 per cent ownership, stated that such a large company was necessary to meet the heavy investment demands, to keep up with the evolution of many new products, and to support needed research. The conditions for fusion of chemical interests were favorable, in that the two companies were largely engaged in complementary fields.

The principal product groups of this new company included the following:

Chemical products: Chlorine and derivative products (solvents, insecticides, vinyl resins), fluorine, caustic soda, sulfuric and phosphoric acids, phthalic anhydride, etc.

Plastics: Vinyl resins, aqueous dispersion resins, polystyrenes, polyethylene (heavy and light density), polypropylene, polyesters, plasticizers, and stabilizers

Agricultural products: Fertilizers (complex, nitrogen, and superphosphate), fungicides, and ammonia anhydride

[25] Descriptive brochure entitled *Produits Chimiques Pechiney-Saint-Gobain*, printed May 18, 1962.

THE CHEMICAL INDUSTRY IN ITALY

Vying with the French chemical industry for the honor of having Western Europe's fastest-growing production value, the Italian chemical industry in 1960 ranked fourth in Western Europe and seventh in the world, accounting for about 4.2 per cent of the world's chemical production.[1] Within Italy, according to net national production statistics for the private sector, the chemical industry was the fourth largest (after mechanical, construction, and food and beverage industries), contributing more than 8 per cent of the total net national industrial product and about 11 per cent of the total net manufacturing product.[2]

In this report on the Italian chemical industry, the following topics will be discussed: size and growth; development; petrochemicals and the special role of natural gas; industry structure; state competition; investment; labor; international trade; and future prospects.

SIZE AND GROWTH OF THE ITALIAN CHEMICAL INDUSTRY

In 1960 Italian chemical production reached about $2.6 billion,[3] almost three and one-half times that of just a decade earlier.[4] During this same period, world chemical production had grown at only about two-thirds of the Italian rate, so that Italy's share of the total world production rose by 50 per cent (from 2.8 to 4.2 per cent). The average yearly growth rate of 13.1 per cent was also considerably higher than the 8.4 per cent achieved by Italian industry as a whole.[5]

As in other Western European countries, the driving force of the chemical industry's growth stemmed from the organic sector, the greatest growth taking place in petrochemicals.[6] As examples of the rapid growth

---

[1] *Chemische Industrie*, April, 1962, p. 145.

[2] Official statistics from Ministri del Bilancio e del Tesoro reproduced in Montecatini; Società Generale per l'Industria Mineraria e Chimica Anonima, *Dati Statistici 1957–1961* (1962), Vol. 9.

[3] The rate of exchange used was 620 lira = $1 for 1959, 1960, and 1961 and 625 lira = $1 for 1953 through 1958.

[4] Production figures relate to the chemical industry as defined by OECD, plus man-made fibers. This industry definition is similar to the Gorman definition less ferroalloys and "sonstige" (e.g., matches, linoleum, office supplies, etc.); *Chemische Industrie*, April, 1962, p. 155.

[5] Montecatini, *Relazioni e Bilancio, 1960*.

[6] The term "petrochemicals" normally includes products made from natural gas as well as from petroleum fractions and refinery gases.

of organics, Chart 1 shows output of plastic materials and synthetic fibers between 1950 and 1960. Plastic materials, expanding at an annual rate of 38.5 per cent, grew more than 25 times over the 10-year period. Even more sensational was the performance of synthetic fibers; expanding at an annual rate of 48.3 per cent, these multiplied more than 50 times over the same 10 years.

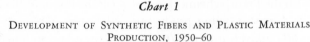

Chart 1

DEVELOPMENT OF SYNTHETIC FIBERS AND PLASTIC MATERIALS
PRODUCTION, 1950–60

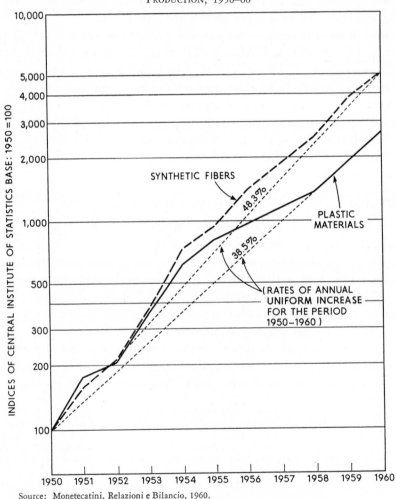

Source: Monetecatini, Relazioni e Bilancio, 1960.

Another striking example of growth in the organic field was that of synthetic rubber. From a negligible figure in 1957, output rose to 88,390 tons in 1961, the largest production in the Common Market (Table 1).

Table 1

PRODUCTION OF SYNTHETIC RUBBER, 1957–61
(Thousands of metric tons)

	1957	1958	1959	1960	1961	Per Cent of Free World Total 1961
France			6	17	41	2.1
Germany	12	23	49	81	87	4.4
Italy		20	48	71	88	4.5
Netherlands	...	...	N.A.	N.A.	N.A.	N.A.
Total EEC*	12	43	103	169	216	11.0
United Kingdom	1	11	58	91	107	5.4
Total Western Europe*..	13	54	161	260	323	16.4
U.S.A.	1,136	1,071	1,402	1,459	1,424	72.6
Canada	134	137	102	162	167	8.5
Japan			1	19	49	2.5
Total Free World*	1,283	1,262	1,666	1,900	1,963	100.0

* Figures for 1959–61 are in error to the extent caused by omission of the Netherlands.
Source: Montecatini, *Dati Statistici, 1957–1961* (1962).

In marked contrast to these examples, sulfuric acid, one of the most fundamental and widely used industrial inorganic chemicals, grew less than 25 per cent over the 22-year period, 1938–60. Table 2 shows Italy's 1960 production levels and recent growth rates for selected chemical products.

Despite the poor showing by several inorganic chemicals, this sector retained first place in terms of output in 1960. As elsewhere, much of the sector's growth came from chemicals (such as chlorine and ammonia) which served as raw materials for organic products.

Table 3 shows the relative importance of the different chemical sectors for selected years. It is interesting to note that heavy industrial chemicals as a whole increased their share of the total from about 28 to 41 per cent. All sectors showed gains in actual production over the 22-year period, though some declined relative to others and to the industry average. The poor over-all showing by man-made fibers was caused by the slow growth of rayon and the cellulose components which heavily outweighed the fast growth of synthetics.

THE DEVELOPMENT OF THE INDUSTRY

The chemical industry is dependent on both raw materials and power. Italy had long seemed poor in both; it was a country that had no important domestic resources of either coal, petroleum, or metallic ores (with the exception of bauxites and iron pyrites). Thus the Italian chemical indus-

Table 2

OUTPUT AND GROWTH OF SELECTED CHEMICAL PRODUCTS

Products	Units	1960 Production	Increase Per Cent 1959–60
INORGANIC INDUSTRIAL CHEMICALS			
Sulfuric acid	Thousands of metric tons	2,298	7
Caustic soda	Thousands of metric tons	426	32
Soda ash	Thousands of metric tons	565	15
Chlorine	Thousands of metric tons	270	37
Ammonia, synthetic	Thousands of metric tons	879	18
Calcium carbide	Thousands of metric tons	292	−3
ORGANIC INDUSTRIAL CHEMICALS			
Methanol	Thousands of metric tons	80	31
Phenol, synthetic	Thousands of metric tons	16	33
Phthalic anhydride	Thousands of metric tons	35	21
INDUSTRIAL CHEMICAL PRODUCTS			
Fertilizers			
Nitrogenous	Thousands of metric tons	560	14
Complex	Thousands of metric tons	353	29
Plastic materials	Thousands of metric tons	329	38
Polyethylene resin	Thousands of metric tons	34	163
Vinyl resin	Thousands of metric tons	131	30
Polystyrol resin	Thousands of metric tons	34	54
Man-made fibers	Thousands of metric tons	200	8
Synthetic fibers	Thousands of metric tons	31	37
CONSUMER CHEMICAL SECTORS			
Paints, lacquers, and solvents	Dollars in millions	103	7
Pharmaceuticals	Dollars in millions	390	8
Cosmetics and essential oils	Dollars in millions	51	24
Soaps and detergents	Dollars in millions	155	12

Source: *Annuario Statistico Italiano 1961,* 1962, Table 227, and *Compendio Statistico Italiano 1962,* Istituto Centrale di Statistica; *Chemische Industrie,* April, 1962.

try started with products using air, water, salt, and pyrites as raw materials.

In a country with high population and limited tillable soil, it was natural for the chemical industry to begin its major development with fertilizers. It was this product group, particularly nitrogenous fertilizers, which accounted for the industry's growth from 1925 to 1935.

From this beginning, the next step involved more complex products, such as pharmaceuticals and dyestuffs. At the same time, the development of man-made fibers was fostered to the point where Italy became one of Europe's leading exporters. In the years immediately preceding World War II, the Italian chemical industry had begun activities in petrochemicals and synthetic rubber.

The war wreaked havoc on the Italian chemical industrial plant, and chemical production did not regain its 1938 level until 1948. But by that

Table 3

RELATIVE VALUE OF PRODUCTION FOR THE DIFFERENT CHEMICAL SECTORS
SELECTED YEARS
(In percentages)

	1938	1956	1960	Change of Position 1938–60
Inorganic industrial chemicals	18.9	24.4	22.1	3.2
Organic industrial chemicals	9.0	16.4	18.8	9.8
Fertilizers	7.2	6.3	6.3	−0.9
Pesticides	6.0	2.1	1.6	−4.4
Plastics	0.5	5.0	8.4	7.9
Synthetic rubber			1.3	1.3
Man-made fibers	22.6	12.8	11.4	11.2
Mineral colors and pigments	1.8	1.2	1.0	−0.8
Paints, varnishes, and lacquers	2.9	5.0	3.9	1.0
Dyestuffs	2.5	1.0	1.0	−1.5
Pharmaceuticals	9.3	14.6	15.0	5.7
Soaps aand detergents	11.6	6.9	6.0	−5.6
Cosmetics	1.7	1.3	1.3	−0.4
Essential oils	1.2	0.7	0.6	−0.6
Tanning agents	4.8	2.2	1.4	−3.4
Total	100.0	99.9	100.1	0.0

Source: *Chemische Industrie*, April, 1962, p. 155.

time, one very important change had taken place—raw materials for organic chemicals had become available to the Italian chemical industry. A combination of several factors accounted for this change: the advance of olefin[7] chemistry, which permitted the switch from coal to petroleum and gas as the major raw materials for organic chemical products; the discovery and development of gas fields in northern Italy; the increase of oil production in the Near East; and the improved oil distribution system. For the first time, Italy was not at a great disadvantage to her coal-producing neighbors to the north.

THE PETROCHEMICAL BOOM AND THE SPECIAL ROLE
OF NATURAL GAS

During the years after World War II, petrochemical production in Italy advanced in two principal directions: the development of chemical derivatives of natural gas and the development of olefins obtained from petroleum. By 1960, Italy had the third largest petrochemical production in Western Europe, with about one-half the output of the United King-

---

[7] Olefins are largely derived from petroleum and natural gas. Included in this hydrocarbon group are ethylene and propylene, neither of which is easily derived from coal. Technically, olefins are unsaturated aliphatics (straight-chain or noncyclic hydrocarbons).

dom or West Germany. Table 4 shows the growth of the Italian petro-chemical output in recent years.[8]

Table 4

DEVELOPMENT OF PETROCHEMICALS IN ITALY
(Production in thousands of tons carbon content)

	1953	1960	Estimated 1963
Production 12		243	750
Percentage growth since 1953		1,925	6,150
Percentage of total petrochemical production of Western Europe 5		14	20

Source: *Chemische Industrie*, December, 1961; OECD, *op. cit.*

Ever since the discovery and development of natural gas (a practically pure sulfur-free methane) in the Po Valley region, this raw material has played an important role in Italian petrochemical production. First, ammonia was produced, followed by methanol, acetylene, hydrocyanic acid, and some chlorinated solvents.

By 1960, natural gas represented a high 36 per cent of the total Italian petrochemical feed stocks, and the production (in terms of carbon content) of petroleum chemicals based on natural gas amounted to 40 per cent of the total.[9] By way of comparison, natural gas constituted about 2 per cent of the total tonnage of petrochemical feed stock in West Germany and about 3 per cent in France. In the latter country, however, this proportion was expected to climb to 8 per cent by 1963, as a result of developing gas fields in France and the Sahara.

Chart 2 shows the extraordinary growth of the Italian consumption of methane to produce synthetic organic chemicals. The popularity of methane as a raw material for producing organic chemicals reportedly did not seem to stem from any significant cost advantage over petroleum, but rather from convenience. Its price apparently has been pegged by the dominant supplier, government-owned Ente Nazionale Idrocarburi (ENI), to that of an equivalent energy value of fuel oil.[10]

It was reported in 1959 that 12 per cent of the natural gas produced was used as a raw material for manufacturing chemicals in Italy. On the other hand, natural gas met only about 10 per cent of the national power need.[11]

---

[8] See Table 4 of *The Chemical Industry in France* for a full comparison of petrochemical production in Europe.

[9] *The Chemical Industry in Europe, 1960–1961* (OECD, 1962).

[10] *Chemical Week*, October 27, 1962.

[11] Dr. Giulio Ballabio, *Italian Chemical Industry Today*, September 2, 1960, unpublished. Dr. Ballabio was a member of the Hydrocarbon Division in Soc. Montecatini.

Chart 2

THE GROWING USE OF METHANE FOR OR-
GANIC CHEMICAL SYNTHESIS IN
ITALY, 1955–60

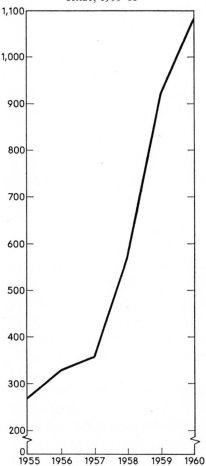

Source: *Relazione del Consiglio Direttivo
all'Assembles delle Associate, Esercizio 1960,*
Associazione Nazionale dell'Industria Chimica
(Aschimici).

A major corollary of Italy's natural-gas supply and of her dependence upon this resource has been
increased research in petrochemis-
try. Outstanding among the many
contributions resulting from this
work was the discovery of polypropylene, a plastic material similar to
polyethylene, but with several physical property advantages.[12]

INDUSTRY STRUCTURE

Most of the drive behind the
growth of the Italian chemical industry can be attributed to the four
or five industry giants. Within this
group, Montecatini has been recognized as king, though inroads have
been made into its dominant position. According to one report, un-
official estimates indicated that
Montecatini's share of total Italian
chemical output fell to about 35
per cent by 1961 from an estimated
45–55 per cent only 10 years earlier.[13]

Possibly making the deepest single dent in Montecatini's share of
the industry was Società Edison.
Long an electric and gas utility,
this company diversified into chemicals in the expectation that the
government would nationalize elec-
tric energy—as was done late in 1962.[14] One anticipated result was that
Edison would receive considerable cash for new investment. Up to 1962,
Edison grew largely through joint ventures and the purchase of chemical operations. The company had done little in the way of chemical

---

[12] Polypropylene was discovered by Professor Giulio Natta, Institute di Chimica In-
dustriale del Politecnico, under the sponsorship of Montecatini, which has all commercial
rights.

[13] *Chemical & Engineering News,* July 10, 1961.

[14] The government measure to nationalize electric-power production and distribution
passed on November 27, 1962. See *The New York Times,* November 28, 1962, p. 12.

research and development and had rather relied to date on its partners' know-how.

A second strong contender was Azienda Nazionale Idrogenerazione Combustibili S.p.A., more commonly known as ANIC (pronounced Anish). This powerful chemical-producing subsidiary of the state-owned gas and petroleum company, ENI, will be discussed in the next section.

Another growing power in the industry has been Snia Viscosa S.p.A.[15] Long associated with the manufacture of rayon, this company moved heavily into the new polymers in the textile and plastics sectors. As a result of intensifying research since the close of World War II, Snia Viscosa came up with a caprolactam[16] process which it licensed to Allied Chemical Corporation in the United States, Courtaulds Ltd. in Great Britain, and Teikoku Rayon Co.[17] in Japan. Snia Viscosa's research and development organization was credited in one report as being possibly the only one capable of challenging Montecatini's domination of Italian chemical discoveries.[18]

Completing the circle at the top of the industry in 1961 were a number of companies with smaller but nonetheless important chemical interests. Among these were both Italian and foreign-owned companies. The former included Rumianca S.p.A., very active in the production of plastic materials and numerous industrial chemicals; Asfalti Bitumi Cemanti e Derivati S.p.A. (ABCD), an affiliate of the large Bombrini Parodi-Delfino S.p.A. explosive group, polyethylene producers; Pirelli Lastex S.p.A., a subsidiary of the giant Pirelli tire company, in polyurethanes; and Società Italiana Resine in industrial chemicals and plastics. Foreign interests included Shell Italiana S.p.A., Dow Chimica Italiana S.p.A., Mobil Chimica Italiana S.p.A., Esso Standard Italiana S.p.A., Cyanamid Italia S.p.A., and Société Ugine[19] from France. Map 1 shows the locations of the major Italian chemical complexes.

In contrast to the situation obtaining in Britain and France, there were very few joint ventures among the larger Italian firms. The tendency was rather to join efforts with foreign chemical companies, leaving the big chemical groups insular in Italy.

The Italian chemical industry in total comprised more than 5,500 enterprises in 1961, most of which were small and specialized.[20] One interest-

[15] Full name, Società Nazionale Industria Applicazione Viscosa.
[16] Caprolactam is the monomer for Nylon 6.
[17] Full name, Teikoku Jinzo Kenshi Kabushiki Kaisha.
[18] *Chemical & Engineering News*, July 10, 1962.
[19] Full name, Société d'Electro-Chimie, d'Electro-Métallurgie et des Acieries Electriques d'Ugine.
[20] *Annuario Statistico Italiano 1961, op. cit.*

Map 1

GEOGRAPHICAL LOCATION OF THE MAJOR CHEMICAL PLANTS IN ITALY, 1961

Most of Italy's Chemical Plants Are in the North; Interest in Sicily Is Growing

Corsica, a French island north of Sardinia, is not shown on the map.
Source: *Chemical & Engineering News*, July 10, 1961.

ing fact was that Italy had more pharmaceutical companies than any other country in the world—over 1,000. The reason was that a rash of small firms had evolved to take advantage of the absence of any drug patent law in Italy. These firms served the domestic market with drugs that were copied outright; they supported no research other than that needed to find drugs for imitation. A consensus of Italian drug makers and political leaders, however, foresaw passage of a drug patent law in the near future. Such a move would greatly reduce the number of Italian pharmaceutical companies, bringing it in line with that of other nations.

STATE COMPETITION: ENI-ANIC

Any study of the Italian chemical industry must include special attention to ENI, the state-controlled company that competed with the private chemical companies through its subsidiary ANIC. ENI was reported in 1961 to have produced 94 per cent of the country's natural gas and 20 per cent of its crude oil and to have controlled 20 per cent of its refinery capacity,[21] while ANIC occupied third place in chemicals, after Montecatini and Edison.

One of the major clashes with the private chemical companies came in fertilizers, where Montecatini held a near-monopoly until ANIC entered the field in 1959. Prices were soon lowered 15–30 per cent, with accusations being made that ANIC enjoyed an unfair cost advantage over private companies buying gas from ENI for use in the manufacture of competing products.

A more recent controversy revolved around the new $1.92 million ANIC refinery and petrochemical complex at Gela, Sicily, which was scheduled to begin operations in 1963. Industry charged that the project was politically inspired and uneconomical, that it would only add to existing overcapacities, and that it would do little to solve Sicily's unemployment problem. ENI, devoted to expanding industrial activity in southern Italy, countered that the project was calculated to be economical and that it would also benefit the Sicilian economy.

Other controversial features of ENI's operation included its policy of buying oil from the Soviet Union and its plan to construct pipelines through Europe. It was reported that Italy had imported Soviet oil in 1961 at a rate of 126,000 barrels a day, representing about 15 per cent of total Italian oil imports. Chemical and allied production facilities, including complete plants, were part of the reciprocating trade. The Black Sea oil was reportedly purchased at $1.08 per barrel, about $1 per barrel lower than the delivered price of comparable Arabian crude, based on posted prices.[22]

Arguing in favor of state participation in the petroleum and chemical fields, Enrico Mattei, the late president of ENI, spoke as follows:

---

[21] *Chemical & Engineering News*, July 10, 1961.

[22] *Hearings before the Subcommittee to Investigate the Administration of the Internal Security Act and Other Internal Security Laws of the Senate Committee on the Judiciary, Soviet Oil in East-West Trade* (87th Cong., 2d Sess. [Washington, 1962]), pp. 13, 14.

. . . One more example of a public enterprise breaking a monopoly is provided by the experience with ANIC, the company in the ENI Group which has built the large petrochemical works at Ravenna and which is now about to build a colossal new petrochemical plant on the south coast of Sicily.

. . . It is a well-known fact that Italian agriculture is still, unfortunately, even today among the most backward in Europe, in spite of the advances in the last 10 years. One of the chief reasons for this is the very limited use of chemical fertilizers per unit of cultivated land. In the 1958–1959 agricultural year the consumption of nitrogen was 17.6 kgs. per hectare in Italy while in France it was 18.1, in England 26.7, and in Germany 42.1.

. . . The discovery of a big natural gas field near Ravenna in 1952 enabled ANIC to start up large-scale production of nitrogenous fertilizers and of other products, such as synthetic rubber, which before Italy had to import. . . .

. . . The nitrogenous fertilizers have been offered by ANIC at one price over the whole country, a price which is much lower than the average price prevailing before in a market dominated by large private industrial combines. The unification of retail prices at a level which is one of the lowest in the world has enabled the disparity of prices which was to the detriment of the south of Italy to disappear. The southern areas had before to pay higher prices because they were further from production centres and thus transport charges were higher.

. . . The bogey of public enterprise as a squanderer of wealth has too long served to cover up well-protected and fenced-in hunting preserves. Now the most tenacious opponents of public enterprise prefer to raise a shout against its dynamic action and aggressive competition. I must confess that these reactions provide us with the best proof of the efficiency with which public enterprise is responding to the tasks for which it was created, achieving maximum efficiency in running business in the national interest.[23]

Concerning the battle with ENI, one high official of a large private firm observed: "So far, the initiative has all come from Enrico Mattei; the private companies have only been reacting to his moves." After Mattei's untimely death in an airplane crash on October 27, 1962, speculation arose that ENI would become less "revolutionary" in its dealings with private industry.[24]

INVESTMENT

Investment in the Italian chemical industry amounted to almost $1.3 billion between 1955 and 1960. As shown in Table 5, investment in petrochemical facilities was an increasingly important factor, accounting for 24.5 per cent of total chemical investments for 1958–60 inclusive as compared to only 8.9 per cent for 1955–57. Over the same period, the chemical industry's share of Italy's total industrial investment rose from 11.3 to 14 per cent.

---

[23] Enrico Mattei, "Public Enterprise in the Energy Sector," a lecture given at the Catholic University of Milan, March 30, 1960.

[24] New York Times, October 30, 1962, p. 45.

Table 5

INVESTMENT IN THE CHEMICAL INDUSTRY
(Millions of dollars)

	Total Industry	Chemical Industry	Chemicals as a Percentage of Total Industry	Petrochemical Sector	Petrochemicals as a Percentage of Total Chemicals
1955	$1,365	$168	$12.3	$19	$11.3
1956	1,525	145	9.5	7	4.8
1957	1,720	206	12.0	22	10.7
1958	1,655	208	12.6	45	21.6
1959	1,725	258	15.0	55	21.3
1960	2,110	306	14.5	94	30.7

Source: *Compendio Statistico Italiano 1962*, Table 268, and *Annuario Statistico Italiano 1961*, Table 396; OECD, *op. cit.*

In recent years Italy has become an increasingly popular place for foreign chemical investments. Typical of United States investments were United States Rubber Company's participation with Rumianca S.p.A. to build a plastics enterprise near Turin; American Cyanamid Company's three operations in Sicily (insecticides, pharmaceuticals, and antibiotic fermentation); Dow Chemical Company's construction of a polystyrene plant at Leghorn; and the American-controlled international oil companies' new petrochemical plants. Britain and France have also become a large investor in Italian chemical activity. While one of the important attractions for the foreign investor has been to establish a position behind the tariff barriers of the EEC, another important attraction has been the fast-growing industrial and consumer market in Italy itself.

As a result of the huge investments needed to develop a significant chemical industry in Italy, the annual investment per worker has been considerably higher than the average for Western Europe. In 1959 Italy's new investment per employee reached $1,560 compared with the Western European average of $920 and the United States figure of $1,450. Table 6 shows the development of Italian investment per employee.

Table 6

EMPLOYMENT, VALUE ADDED, AND INVESTMENTS PER EMPLOYEE, 1957–60

	1957	1958	1959	1960
Employees (000)	165	165	165	170
Annual per cent change of work force	....	Nil	Nil	3
Value added ($ million)	852	890	990	1,135
Annual per cent change of value added	....	4	11	15
Value added per employee ($)	5,170	5,400	6,000	6,680
Annual investment ($ million)	206	208	258	306
Annual investment per employee ($)	1,250	1,260	1,560	1,800

Source: OECD, *op. cit.*

LABOR

Despite high unemployment in Italy, the domestic chemical industry has faced a tight labor supply, although perhaps not quite to the same extent as the chemical industries of other Western European countries. This paradox is resolved when it is realized that, in effect, there are two different Italys: the unindustrialized Italy of the south with huge reserves of unskilled, largely uneducated, rural labor, and the modern industrialized Italy of the north where skilled labor has been in short supply. Largely located within the second area, the Italian chemical industry faced several obstacles in moving to the south, despite important governmental incentives. For one, the chemical industry requires skilled labor, which was scarce in the south. For another, chemical plants prefer to locate near each other and near other industries because of their interdependence as suppliers and consumers and the high cost of transporting bulky chemical products. Spurred on, however, by the government and by the southward moves of ENI and some of the larger private oil and chemical companies, a balancing-out is beginning to take place.

The Italian chemical work force was reported to be 170,000 in 1960 (see Table 6), representing only about 2.2 per cent of the total industrial work force of about 7.6 million.[25] Heavy investment over the years caused the average value added per employee to increase greatly (15 per cent in 1960). By 1960 this value was well above the average for Western Europe ($6,680 vs. $5,100).

INTERNATIONAL TRADE

Exports played a relatively minor role in the activities of the Italian chemical industry. As a per cent of production, chemical exports were reported to be lower for Italy than for any other nation in EEC and EFTA, only about 12 per cent in 1960.[26] This figure compared with about 17 per cent for the United Kingdom, 18 per cent for France, 25 per cent for West Germany, and over 50 per cent for the Benelux countries. As shown in Table 7, the chemical industry accounted for only about 9 per cent of total manufactured exports.

The reason for the poor showing in exports is clear. The growing demand for products has kept ahead of growing home production, so that there has been relatively little pressure for the Italian chemical industry to develop an export trade. The excess demand for chemical products has caused imports to grow rapidly, despite increased domestic output. Table 7 shows the chemical industry's exports, imports, and negative balance of

---

25 *Annuario Statistico Italiano 1961, op. cit.*
26 *Chemische Industrie*, April, 1962, p. 146.

Table 7

BALANCE OF TRADE
(Dollars in millions)

	1957	1958	1959	1960	1961
Chemical industry*					
Exports	$ 153	$ 177	$ 223	$ 286	$ 353
Imports	194	210	240	344	364
Balance of trade†	−40	−32	−18	−58	−11
Total Italian balance of trade	−880	−441	−385	−893	−931
Total Italian balance of payments‡	286	850	764	522	643
Total Italian manufactured exports	2,150	2,230	2,520	3,240	3,760
Chemical exports as a per cent of total manufactured exports	7.1	7.9	9.2	8.8	9.4

* As defined by the Istituto Centrale di Statistica, *Annuario Statistico Italiano, 1961*, Table 312. This definition differs little from that of the OECD (see "General Characteristics of the Chemical Industry"). Synthetic fibers are not included in either definition, and would not in any case have numbered among the five most important sectors.
† Varies from the difference of exports minus imports because of rounding.
‡ Balance of payments includes the balance of trade as well as invisible trade (tourism, services), net investment, and other fund flows.
Source: Montecatini, *Dati Statistici 1957–1961* (1962), Table 17.

trade in recent years. While the total Italian balance of "visible" trade has approached $1 billion outflow in 1960 and 1961, a huge favorable balance in "invisible" trade, especially income from tourism, has been a major factor in Italy's positive over-all balance of payments.

In the chemical industry, by far the greatest net earner of foreign income has been the fertilizer sector, which in 1961 had a favorable balance of about $55 million (exports $62.5, imports $7.4), the highest on record. The only other important net earner of foreign income was the plastics sector, with a favorable balance of about $20 million (exports $57.8, imports $37.7). Table 8 shows the five most important chemical sectors of Italy's foreign trade. Of other important chemical exports, only pharmaceuticals showed a favorable balance of trade.

Table 8

FIVE MOST IMPORTANT IMPORT AND EXPORT SECTORS OF
ITALIAN CHEMICAL TRADE, 1961

Chemical Sector	Per Cent Share of Total Value	
	Exports	Imports
Organic industrial chemicals	19.5	24.2
Fertilizers	17.7	*
Plastic materials	16.4	10.4
Pharmaceutical products	12.7	10.8
Inorganic industrial chemicals	8.5	8.5
Dyestuffs, paints, varnishes, enamels, and lacquers	*	8.5
Total	74.8	62.4

* Not in the top five for column indicated.
Source: Montecatini, *op. cit.*

In one respect, Italy's foreign trade in chemicals resembles a sprinkler: the input comes in a few conduits, and the output is sprayed. In 1960, as can be seen in Table 9, over 50 per cent of Italy's chemical imports came from only two countries (the United States and West Germany), while almost 80 per cent came from only five countries. On the other hand, the largest customer for Italian exports, West Germany, accounted for only 10 per cent of the total, the largest five customers for only 34 per cent. To reach approximately 80 per cent, one must count the purchases of 25 nations.

Table 9

MOST IMPORTANT TRADING PARTNERS FOR ITALIAN CHEMICAL INDUSTRY, 1960

Exports		Imports	
Customer	Per Cent Share of Total Value	Supplier	Per Cent Share of Total Value
BY NATION			
West Germany	10.0	United States	28.1
China (continent)	7.1	West Germany	26.4
France	5.8	United Kingdom	8.6
United States	5.5	France	8.3
United Kingdom	5.3	Switzerland	7.5
Total	33.7	Total	78.9
BY REGION			
Europe	57.9	Europe	66.3
(EEC—20.1%)		(EEC—41.8%)	
(EFTA—17.0%)		(EFTA—18.4%)	
Asia	18.4	America	30.2
America	13.3	Other	3.5
Africa	6.7		
Other	3.7		

Source: Aschimici, *op. cit.*, Table 12.

As suggested by the export figures to Communist China, Italy has had significant trade dealings with the Eastern Bloc in recent years. In 1960 about 21 per cent of total chemical exports were purchased by Communist nations.[27] About 29 per cent of man-made fiber exports and 28 per cent of fertilizer exports were purchased by these nations (Red China alone accounted for 22 per cent of the fertilizer purchases).[28] Synthetic rubber was another important export to the Eastern Bloc. One report showed the U.S.S.R. and China as receiving over $5.6 million of this product in 1959, or roughly 50 per cent of total synthetic rubber exports.[29]

[27] Aschimici, *op. cit.*
[28] *Annuario Statistico Italiano, 1961, op. cit.*, Table 314.
[29] *Chemische Industrie International*, June, 1961.

A PROMISING OUTLOOK?

Optimism in respect to the future has prevailed in the Italian chemical industry in recent years. Much of this optimism has been based on one or more of the following three reasons: the great potential of the Mediterranean market served by this industry; a favorable competitive position; and the development of the Common Market. On the other hand, the prevailing optimism has not been accepted without challenge.

The primary reason for optimism has been a belief in the great untapped potential of the Italian market. This belief has been based on the fact that the domestic market has been growing by leaps and bounds and on the expectation that a high rate of growth will continue. In support of such a forecast, it has been argued that projected industrialization of the still undeveloped southern half of the nation will greatly increase effective demand. In addition, merely bringing Italian per capita consumption up to the levels obtaining in several other European countries would require a very large expansion, as shown by the comparative statistics cited in Table 10.

Table 10

COMPARATIVE CONSUMPTION RATES FOR SELECTED PRODUCTS, 1960

Country	Total Chemicals ($/person) 1960	Nitrogenous Fertilizer (Kg/hectare)	Phosphatic Fertilizers (Kg/hectare)	Plastic* Materials (Kg/person)
Italy	$ 59.4	22.4	23.6	4.9
West Germany	94.5	45.6	49.1	14.4
France	82.0	N.A.	N.A.	7.5
Belgium-Luxembourg	67.3	N.A.	N.A.	7.4
Netherlands	62.5	97.1	49.6	8.7
United Kingdom	111.3	N.A.	N.A.	9.2
United States	144.2	38.0	36.9	11.3

* Production rather than consumption.

Source: Verband der Chemische Industrie, unpublished statistics; *Chemical Week*, October 27, 1962; Rumianca S.p.A., *Annual Report*, 1961.

Besides looking forward to a fast-paced growth at home, the Italian chemical industry hopes to benefit—although to a lesser extent—from growth in many of its foreign markets as a result of the drive toward industrialization in other countries ringing the Mediterranean. For this trade Italy's historic geographical advantage will become important again, especially when production facilities in Sicily and southern Italy begin to operate.

A second basis for optimism has been Italy's favorable competitive position, which derives from her relatively low production costs. This advantage stems in turn from lower wages, modern plant, and a favorable situation in respect to raw materials for organic chemicals. Domestic supplies of natural gas and low-cost Soviet petroleum (15 per cent of Italy's imports in 1961) have given Italian producers of organic chemicals an edge over their Common Market competitors. Furthermore, a growing emphasis on research has helped to create confidence in Italy's ability to stay ahead.

The third basis for optimism has been the rapidly growing demand for chemicals in the Common Market. Managers of Italian chemical firms have felt confident that they could compete effectively against companies in the other EEC nations. As one observer commented, "Every time I talk Common Market with Italian chemical managers, they start to lick their chops."

There were other observers, however, who did not agree with the optimistic outlook prevalent among Italian chemical industrialists. For example, a London executive of one international oil company took a dimmer view. He stated that some chemical plants in Italy were much too large for the probable size of the Italian home and export markets and that the Italian chemical industry had in his opinion counted on capturing too large a share of ECM demand. He pointed out, further, that lack of information on production plans throughout the European chemical industry had led to a tendency for almost every company to overestimate its own market share, a tendency which will probably lead to more capacity and tighter competition than has generally been foreseen.

THE CHEMICAL INDUSTRY IN SWEDEN

By international standards, Sweden's chemical industry is a small one. Its sales in 1960 were about $340 million,[1] or less than 2 per cent of the Western European total.[2] Moreover, chemical output represented a smaller share of total manufacturing activity in Sweden than in the large Western European countries. In 1959 sales and value added for Sweden's chemical industry constituted roughly 3.4 and 3.7 per cent, respectively, of total manufacturing values as compared with around 8 per cent for the United Kingdom and Germany.[3]

In spite of its small size, the Swedish chemical industry is still of special interest because it shows, perhaps more clearly than any other, the effects of different economic forces which influenced its early development. Somewhat isolated from the crosscurrents of the Continental chemical trade and limited by shortages of raw materials and capital, Sweden's chemical industry still has many promontories and voids in the pattern of its coverage of the broad spectrum of possible modern-day chemical manufacture. In seeking to understand the reasons for the particular combination of chemical products now made in Sweden, one comes also to understand the historical background of most other national chemical industries, before numerous secondary developments and activities were added to round out the skeletal structure.

The following sections include material on basic economic factors in Sweden's chemical industry; on important inorganic and organic products on the advent of petrochemicals; and on the implications for Sweden of a possible realignment affecting membership in Europe's two major trading blocks: the seven-nation European Free Trade Area (EFTA), to which Sweden belongs, and the six-nation European Economic Community (EEC).

SOME BASIC ECONOMIC FACTORS

The small size and late development of the chemical industry in Sweden have often been attributed to the lack of indigenous sources of such

[1] Exchange rate of 5.18 Swedish kronor = $1.

[2] Organization for Economic Co-operation and Development (OECD), *The Chemical Industry in Europe, 1960–1961.*

[3] *Ibid.;* Statistiska Centralbyran, *Statistisk Arsbok for Sverige*, Ang 48, 1961, Table 100.

important raw materials as salt, coal, potash, and oil.[4] Where a favorable raw-material position existed, as in iron ore and wood, a flourishing chemical industry arose.[5] Also, where electricity for processing was an important factor, domestic production of some products grew up to take advantage of the power generated by Sweden's numerous mountain streams. But the range of chemicals that could be produced by use of Sweden's natural resources was relatively small.

As recent commentaries have pointed out, not only limited resources but also limited demand has exerted a strong inhibiting force on the growth of the Swedish chemical industry.[6] First, the Swedish home market has been quite small; the population in 1961 slightly exceeded 7.5 million, and the total value added by manufacturing in 1959 was only about $4 billion. If all Scandinavia[7] is considered, these figures are only about twice as large. Second, tariffs and distance place Sweden in a relatively poor position to compete in other European markets. Third, the limited variety of other industries in Sweden has resulted in a narrow pattern of demand for chemicals, thereby limiting the diversification of the industry.

Secondary deterrents to the development of the Swedish chemical industry have been the relative scarcity of talent and capital in the industry. Faced with an unfavorable position in respect to supply and demand, the chemical industry could attract neither the caliber of men nor the amount of money required. Both were by preference directed to the more important national industries, such as timber and metal ores. Sweden could boast of such internationally renowned chemists in the eighteenth and nineteenth centuries as Schéele, Berzelius, Arrhenius, and Nobel,[8] but, as one report noted, ". . . what was, and still is, missing for building up a

---

4 Coal deposits located near Höganäs in southern Sweden are of inferior grade, and oil resources are limited to low-yield shale deposits in central Sweden.

5 Sweden produces about 10 per cent of the world's requirements of iron ore, and 55 per cent of its land area is covered by forests.

6 Erik Brandt, Assistant Director, Association of Swedish Chemical Manufacturers, "Sweden's Chemical Industry," *British-Swedish Economic Review*, March, 1960; Dr. A. Dahlén, Nobelkrut Division, AB Botors, "The Chemical Industry in Sweden," *Chemistry and Industry*, October 14, 1961.

7 Scandinavia is normally considered to consist of Denmark, Sweden, and Norway. Frequently, Finland is added to this group.

8 Carl Wilhelm Schéele (1742–86) was the independent discoverer of ammonia, hydrogen chloride, and, before 1773, of oxygen. He was also the first to produce an organic compound artificially.

Jöns Jakob Berzelius (1779–1848) determined atomic weights for 43 elements and discovered selenium and thorium.

Svante August Arrhenius (1859–1927) established the important theory of electrolytic dissociation of acids, gases, and salts in solution.

Alfred Bernhard Nobel (1833–96) discovered dynamite and other explosives.

vigorous chemical industry is a simultaneous width and quality in personal abilities."[9]

The lack of capital strength will be seen from the small size of the Swedish companies. Even the giants of the Swedish chemical industry were not very big when compared with their Continental or British sisters. For example, Stockholm's Superfosfat Fabriks Aktiebolag (Fosfatbolaget), one of the largest chemical firms in Sweden, recently had sales of about $20 million and employed around 1,800, whereas Farbenfabriken Bayer AG of Germany had sales of over $750 million and employed around 61,000.[10] Little wonder that no single Swedish company could afford to enter any manufacturing activity where the minimum economic size required a high investment.[11]

INORGANIC AND ORGANIC CHEMICALS

Before World War II Sweden produced a limited range of inorganic and organic chemicals that took advantage of her natural resources, mainly in iron ore, water power, and wood. For example, in the inorganic field, native iron pyrites and other sulfide ores were burned to give off sulfur dioxide, the earliest use of which was to make sulfuric acid for the superphosphate fertilizer industry which became important in the 1870's. Considerable tonnages have also been consumed by the textile (principally rayon) and iron industries, by oil refineries, and in the manufacture of dyestuffs and various sulfate products. Another main use of sulfur dioxide has been in making wood pulp by the sulfite process.

Abundant hydroelectric power has permitted economic production in Sweden of other chemicals through electrolytic or electrothermal processes.[12] In the electrolytic group have been chlorine and caustic soda (produced by electrolysis of common table salt, which must be imported), both used in making pulp. Sweden's chlorine output of 158,000 tons in 1960 represented 2–3 per cent of total world production. Also in the elec-

---

[9] Dr. A. Dahlén, op. cit.

[10] A Brief Guide to Fosfatbolaget, Sweden, 1958; Bayer Annual Report, 1961.

[11] It is occasionally pointed out that Switzerland succeeded in developing a major chemical industry with even less favorable natural resources and a smaller home market than Sweden's. However, as Dr. Dahlén has pointed out, a central geographic position and a highly developed textile industry were probably two of the factors that helped Switzerland to get a good start in dyestuffs and in technically similar pharmaceuticals. Two major setbacks for Germany (the world's leading dyestuff producer), an abundance of capital residing in Switzerland, and a broad base of technical talent were additional factors contributing to Switzerland's ability to entrench herself strongly in the dyestuff and pharmaceutical fields. (See Dr. A. Dahlén, op. cit.)

[12] An electrolytic process involves the decomposition of a compound by an electric current (through electric charge). An electrothermal process depends on the heat produced from electric power.

trolytic group has been synthetic ammonia, used mainly in producing fertilizer, and chlorates and perchlorates, used in making match heads and in bleaching paper pulp. In the electrothermal group of chemicals, calcium carbide has been among the most important. Made with local limestone and imported coke, this chemical has found uses in fertilizers, acetylene, and increasingly since World War II in organic chemical production, including plastics. For example, large quantities of calcium carbide are produced and used by Fosfatbolaget, Sweden's largest plastics manufacturer, in making polyvinyl chloride resin.

Abundant forests have provided the main basis of Sweden's output of organic chemicals. Each of several processes for making paper pulp has yielded by-products used in different industries. For example, users of the sulfite process (prohibited by law from dumping spent sulfite liquor into streams) have found uses for its waste in making ethanol, which in turn has been used in Aqua Vite (the well-know Swedish drink), solvents, additives for motor fuel, and since World War II as a raw material in organic chemicals. The sulfate process of paper-pulp making has yielded turpentine, small amounts of methanol, and tall oil, which has been used as a raw material by the soap, plastics, and paint industries.

Sweden's wood resources have also been the basis of her output of acetic acid and vinegar, both of which were made as by-products resulting from the burning of wood to make charcoal for producing high-quality iron. Skånska Ättikfabriken Aktiebolag,[13] one of Sweden's larger organic chemical manufacturers, made its industry start in this way. Later the company expanded into alcohols, acetate, and many plastic resins.

World War II provided the Swedish chemical companies with conditions conducive to the rapid expansion of organic chemical production: forced isolation and wartime demands. While a number of the new production facilities were able to survive only so long as the blockade and high prices continued, most of the expansion remained as part of the new chemical industry.

To understand the direction in which the organic chemical sector has expanded, one must look beyond the immediate industrial demand to the consumer market. Swedish per capita consumption of paints and plastics has been among the highest in the world in recent years (see table 1). Severe climatic conditions have undoubtedly contributed to the high consumption of paint and perhaps to the high consumption of plastics. With relatively high demand for these products, local supplies of raw materials such as ethanol and methanol have been insufficient, and Sweden has had to import increasing amounts. There has also been a growing demand

---

[13] Ättika is the Swedish word for vinegar.

Table 1

PER CAPITA CONSUMPTION OF PLASTICS AND PAINTS
FOR TEN HIGHEST NATIONS, 1959

Plastics		Paint*	
Country	*Pounds Per Capita*	*Country*	*Pounds Per Capita*
West Germany	26.8	Sweden	24.2
United States	24.4	United Kingdom	20.2
Sweden	21.6	Norway	19.6†
Denmark	18.5	France	18.9
United Kingdom	16.5	Benelux	18.3
Norway	15.6	West Germany	17.2
Netherlands	15.6	Netherlands	16.3
Benelux	15.4	Denmark	15.0†
Switzerland	13.9	Switzerland	12.5†
France	13.0	Austria	11.4

* Only European nations are included.
† Consumption figures for 1958.
Source: *Chemische Industrie International*, No. 3, 1961; OECD, *The Chemical Industry in Europe, 1959–1960.*

to import other organic raw materials in order to produce a wider range of organic plastics, solvents, and related products.

THE ADVENT OF PETROCHEMICALS IN SWEDEN

The growing demand for organic chemical products increased the need for organic raw materials beyond the level that could be supplied from cellulose-derived sources. Imports of many basic petrochemicals began to rise. A great advance was made toward increased domestic output when Svenska Esso AB announced its intention to construct, at a cost of about $40 million, Scandinavia's first petrochemical complex at Stenungsund on Sweden's west coast. This facility, based on a steam-cracking unit[14] was scheduled to go into operation in 1963. Chart 1 shows the range of products which Esso expected to be made from its output.

The history of this monumental addition to Sweden's chemical industry began in the mid-fifties when Esso undertook a comprehensive study of the entire Scandinavian organic chemical market. Detailed projections of production and consumption were made for all the important products through 1965, in order to ascertain whether petrochemical production could be justified, what type of facilities might be warranted, and when actual investment should be made.

Esso was not the only oil company researching this market. Since about

[14] The steam cracker will produce gas, raw materials for petrochemicals, and a liquid fraction from a feed of virgin naphtha, a light petroleum cut similar to gasoline. The principal petrochemical raw materials will be ethylene, propylene, and butadien.

Chart 1

PRODUCTS TO BE PRODUCED FROM THE SVENSKA ESSO AB STEAM CRACKER

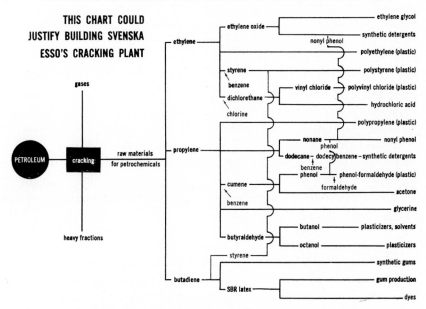

1959, Scandinavia has become a new center of European refinery construction, and a number of these refineries could have been logical bases from which to enter petrochemical production. The market, however, was big enough to support only one facility of this type. Accordingly, when Esso succeeded in signing long-term contracts to supply two of Sweden's largest chemical companies from its projected Stenungsund unit, another interested oil company rescinded its announced intention of producing petrochemicals in Scandinavia. By 1961 Mo och Domsjö AB and Unifos Kemi AB, a joint venture of Fosfatbolaget and Union Carbide Corporation (U.S.A.), planned to build plants adjacent to the Esso cracker to use its ethylene output.

One point on which everyone appeared to agree was that none of the Swedish chemical companies could have undertaken this type of development without the inflow of investment funds from outside sources.

SIXES AND SEVENS

As a part of the seven-nation EFTA,[15] Sweden and her chemical industry have watched with anxiety while EFTA's largest member—the United Kingdom—negotiated for admission into Europe's faster-growing trade

---

[15] The members of EFTA, also known as the Outer Seven, are the United Kingdom, Sweden, Switzerland, Denmark, Austria, Norway, and Portugal.

association, the six-member EEC.[16] Inasmuch as the United Kingdom is Sweden's largest chemical customer (see Table 2), the Swedish chemical industry is eager to retain its United Kingdom ties. Sweden, herself, could apply for EEC membership, but admission might be difficult to obtain, owing to the fact that Sweden is committed to a policy of political neutrality which perhaps is inconsistent with the spirit of the Treaty of Rome. Should Denmark or Norway also enter the EEC (and both have followed Britain's lead in applying for membership), Sweden's problem of being squeezed out of her major markets for both chemicals and other products would be seriously compounded.

If the United Kingdom does not join the Common Market[17] and if EFTA survives, then Sweden may press for a few changes in the EFTA agreement. What she wants most is a speed-up in the time span for reducing tariffs from the present ten-year period to five years. In support of this change, Swedish industrialists stress the high level of British tariffs.

Table 2

MOST IMPORTANT TRADING PARTNERS FOR SWEDISH CHEMICAL INDUSTRY, 1960

Exports		Imports	
Customer	*Per Cent Share of Total Value*	*Supplier*	*Per Cent Share of Total Value*
BY NATION (Five Most Important)			
United Kingdom	15.8	West Germany	25.3
Denmark	9.2	United Kingdom	15.7
West Germany	8.9	United States	15.2
Norway	6.5	Norway	8.1
Finland	6.3	Netherlands	6.9
Total	46.7	Total	71.2
BY REGION			
Europe	72.6	Europe	79.4
(EFTA—36.5%)		(EEC—42.7%)	
(EEC—21.2%)		(EFTA—30.7%)	
America	10.2	America	17.4
(USA—5.3%)		Other	3.2
Asia	0.4		
Africa	5.9	Total	100.0
Other	4.9		
Total	100.0		

Source: *Chemische Industrie*, July, 1962.

[16] The members of the EEC, also known as the Common Market and the Inner Six, are France, Germany, Italy, and the Benelux nations.

[17] The above was written before the rejection of Britain's application early in 1963 (Ed. Note).

For example, they point out that the British tariff on certain organic products is a high 33⅓ per cent and that in five years this will only be reduced to 17 per cent under the terms of the agreement as it stands.[18]

In contrast, Sweden, traditionally a trading nation, has a relatively low tariff structure.[19] For this reason, as Swedish industrialists are quick to point out, domestic companies are exposed to foreign competition in their home market and yet are effectively shut out of potential markets abroad.

---

[18] Erik Brandt, *La Industria Quimica Sueca Ante da Integracion Europea* (a Spanish translation of a speech given in Madrid, February 3, 1961.)

[19] See Table 10, Selected Tariff Rates, of the study titled *The Chemical Industry in the United Kingdom.*

CROYDON CHEMICALS COMPANY LIMITED*

"In light of the trends and problems that we saw, we began to doubt back in 1954 that Croydon had any real long-term future as it stood; so we set a goal of making the company attractive for sale by 1961 as an addition to our major commercial and technical objectives," remarked Mr. G. S. Hartley, Commercial Director of Croydon Chemicals Company Limited, early in 1962. "We have since succeeded in making Croydon a good 'buy,' but now we are not at all sure that we want to sell the company after all.

"The basis for our original feeling of doubt rested on the facts that we were matched against some very powerful competitors, that these companies would take stronger competitive measures against us as we grew, and that we were very vulnerable to attack," continued Mr. Hartley. "Croydon is a converter of heavy organic chemicals, operating in an industry dominated by a small number of giant companies. They have not bothered us in the past, I would guess, for two reasons. First, the markets have been very lucrative, with enough business for everyone. And second, we probably have been just too small. By 1954, both of these conditions were beginning to change. The heavy organic chemical business was becoming more and more competitive, and, as we grew, we were making greater inroads into some of their bread-and-butter lines. Both of these trends, which have continued to the present, have increased the possibility of strong competitive action against us. Our vulnerability to attack stems from the fact that, as an intermediary converter of chemicals, we have to depend on our competitors for our raw materials. It would be an easy matter for a supplier to maintain the price of our raw material while lowering his price of the derivative chemical.

"Coupling our vulnerability to such a squeeze with the generally narrowing margins caused by overcapacity, we simply could not see how Croydon could continue to grow in this industry. And we consider continued growth to be a necessary condition for Croydon's successful survival.

"In 1954, we began our efforts to build a favorable sales and profits record in order to make Croydon an attractive purchase. Thanks to an aggressive program on our part and to some good fortune, we have succeeded in our aims and are now in a good position to sell out. But in the meantime, we have come to realize that we have some very strong personal values and emotionally conditioned reasons which tie us to Croydon. So now we are reluctant to sell the company outright if we do not really have to."

THE HISTORY OF CROYDON

Croydon Chemicals Company Limited, located near London, England, was founded by Dr. W. R. Waldner in 1936 in order to manufacture certain leather finishes for which he had acquired formulations. Formerly employed in his father's chemical plant in Germany, Dr. Waldner left for Sweden in 1936 in order to start business in an area less threatened by war. Not satisfied with the potential market that the Swedish leather-finish industry offered, he moved shortly after to England, where he started Croydon with an original capital of £20,000.

Reviewing the history of Croydon since its founding, Dr. Waldner commented: "By the time of Great Britain's entry into the Second World War, we had gained a very good position in the leather-finish industry, but we saw serious limitations. We recognized that our growth was directly coupled to that of the leather industry, a business which we believe to have scarcely any growth possibilities. There was a clear need to move into other fields if Croydon was really to grow.

"The war certainly opened new dimensions for us. As a result of some leather-chemical research which we had been doing with natural fats and oils, we discovered in 1943 a new process for making a low-temperature plasticizer for use in polyvinyl chloride, a major product of the plastics industry. The government had an immediate use for this item and called on us to produce it. I saw our entry into plasticizers as a way to start our growth outside of the leather industry, and so our diversification began.

"Since World War II we have further diversified into a number of other products. Our growth curve took a decided upswing during the latter part of 1953 when our annual sales were still under £1 million, and we employed about 230. We currently have annual sales of over £6 million and employ over 600 [Exhibits 1, 2, and 3—financial data]. Not only that, but we have also developed a fine management team to continue this progress. Men like Jerry Hartley (Commercial Director), John Swift (Technical Director), Ernst Lang (Production Manager), Ray Ashton

Exhibit 1

SELECTED BALANCE SHEETS, 1958–61

	December 31 1958	December 31 1960	July 31 1961
Current assets:			
Cash	1.0	2.5	8.3
Notes receivable	4.6	....	....
Account receivable	418.4	877.9	1,034.0
Inventory	443.4	841.1	805.0
Fixed assets:			
Fixed assets (cost)	....	1,265.2	1,600.0
Less depreciation	....	397.5	498.9
Net fixed assets	424.5	867.7	1,101.1
Investment	....	8.8	8.8
Prepaid insurance	6.5	8.1	9.1
Total assets	1,298.4	2,606.1	2,966.3
Current liabilities:			
Accounts payable	398.0	1,025.5	1,023.9
Provision for taxes	113.6	108.4	24.0
Overdraft	110.6	489.4	582.8
Other loans	3.2	....	....
Fixed liabilities:			
Mortgage	22.0	22.0	22.0
Bank loan	....	11.0	132.0
Capital and reserves:			
Sinking fund	6.8	8.3	9.1
Fixed-asset investment reserve	270.8	710.3	710.3
Reserve for future taxes	56.0	57.2	148.5
Share capital	77.0	77.0	110.0
Capital reserve	54.6	58.3	28.1
Retained earnings	185.8	38.7	175.6
Total liabilities, capital and reserves	1,298.4	2,606.1	2,966.3

Source: Company records.

(Home Sales Manager), Bob Reddington (Export Sales Manager), and George Bowman (Research and Development Manager) have been responsible for our success in great measure [Exhibit 4—organization chart]. While we are still a small company in the industry, there is no question that we have become an important manufacturer in those product areas in which we compete."

CROYDON'S PRODUCTS

"Croydon has developed a policy of competing in those areas of the organic chemicals industry which promise to become big-volume mar-

Exhibit 2
COMPARATIVE FINANCIAL DATA, 1952–61*

Year	Turnover £ (1)	Net Profit before Tax £ (2)	Taxation £ (3)	Net Profit after Tax £ (4)	Depreciation of Fixed Assets £ (5)	Net Capital Receipts† £ (6)	Total of Columns 4, 5 + 6‡ £ (7)	Capital Expenditure £ (8)	Capital Employed on December 31 £ (9)	Bank Overdraft on December 31 £ (10)
1952.........	711,471	9,116	6,682	2,433	11,529	4,776	18,738	19,605	119,849	60,569
1953.........	998,946	52,925	26,203	26,722	12,540	818	40,081	21,030	165,335	59,570
1954.........	1,498,295	90,311	39,174	51,137	16,749	773	68,659	47,259	229,255	91,912
1955.........	1,923,651	103,016	43,958	59,158	21,350	57,708§	138,217	70,155	341,661	90,512
1956.........	2,178,264	137,222	64,775	72,447	36,441	3,748	112,635	61,047	434,050	91,010
1957.........	2,978,948	234,562	106,459	128,103	49,782	9,204	187,088	125,288	602,978	26,949
1958.........	3,035,437	159,730	66,805	92,925	63,889	5,769	162,583	198,675	651,709	109,958
1959.........	4,207,742	239,722	109,400	130,321	79,917	3,025	213,264	169,000	818,970	228,722
1960.........	5,591,918	232,236	63,624	168,612	108,761	(3,501)‖	273,872	471,326	949,981	489,399
1961.........	6,299,704	374,106	140,791	233,214	158,387	3,309	394,910	479,612	1,234,188	543,407

* All figures have been modified by a constant multiplier.
† Amounts received on realisation of fixed assets and investments less the cost of new investments and the annual sinking fund insurance premium.
‡ Column 7 shows the total of net profit after tax, depreciation, and net capital receipts. This represents the total of additional funds available from within the company. For the 10-year period it is almost equal to the total capital expenditure (col. 8). (£1,610,047 vs. £1,662,997).
§ Includes receipt of £45,000 from the sale of the Platson Investment.
‖ Includes payment of £8,000 for investment in R. C. Carnings Holdings.

Source: Company records.

Exhibit 3

COMPARATIVE RATIOS FOR 10 YEARS, 1952–61 (INCLUSIVE)*

Year	Per Cent Net Profit before Tax on Capital Employed	Per Cent Net Profit after Tax on Capital Employed	Annual Turnover of Capital Employed (times)	Per Cent of Net Profit on Sales	Ratio of Current Assets to Current Liabilities
1952	7.5	2.0	5.8	1.3	1.05
1953	37.1	18.7	7.0	5.3	1.20
1954	45.8	25.9	7.6	6.0	1.23
1955	36.1	20.7	6.7	5.4	1.36
1956	35.4	18.7	5.6	6.5	1.50
1957	45.2	24.7	5.8	7.9	1.62
1958	25.5	14.8	4.8	5.3	1.38
1959	32.6	17.7	5.7	5.7	1.34
1960	26.3	19.1	6.3	4.2	1.05
1961	34.3	21.4	5.1	5.9	1.21

* In calculating ratios involving capital employed the, average of the opening and closing capital employed has been used. Capital employed = issued share capital + capital reserves + revenue reserves + reserves for future taxation.

Source: Company records.

kets," commented Mr. Hartley. "We believe that we can do better in competing with the big fellows in these rapidly growing markets than in trying to find a small niche which would not interest them."

The structure of the heavy organic chemical industry and the rapidly changing pattern of products in which Croydon had become interested resulted in some very unusual and complicated relationships between Croydon and its competitors. In amplifying earlier comments, Mr. Hartley remarked: "The industry in Great Britain is a rather exclusive club of a few big companies, such as Avogadro Chemical Enterprise Ltd. (A.C.E.), Drake International Ltd., Priestly & Sons Ltd., H. Davy Food Product Group Ltd., and Morley Chemicals Ltd. Because of the broad range of chemicals which these companies produce, from the most basic chemicals to consumer products, we find ourselves in the very delicate position of having to compete with companies who may also be our suppliers or even our customers. It is not uncommon to be buying raw material from one division of a large company and be selling our converted products to another division, while a third division is producing the same chemical in competition with us for the external market. But the most amusing case occurred a few years ago, when one division of a company was buying a chemical from us which we ourselves were buying from another division in the same company, since our own production facilities had not yet been completed. Somehow, we did not feel this procedure to be cricket, so after some months we explained to our customer that we

Exhibit 4

ORGANIZATION OF MANAGEMENT

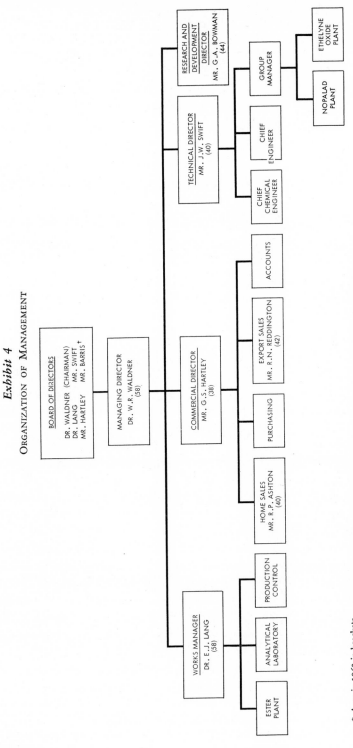

* Ages in 1962 in brackets.
† A Chartered Accountant who has been associated with the company since its founding but is not an employee of Croydon.
Source: Interviews.

Exhibit 5

CROYDON'S PRODUCTS, SUPPLIERS, COMPETITORS, AND CUSTOMERS

Product	Per Cent of Total Sales Revenue	Use of Product	Major Suppliers	Major Competitors	Major Customers
Plasticizers (phthalate)	60	To make polyvinyl chloride	A.C.E., Morley, Drake	Priestly & Sons, Davy Food	J. Hyatt Ltd., A.C.E., major plastic manufacturers
Polyethers	18	To make polyurethane foam	A.C.E., Drake	Bunsen, Urey, A.C.E., Boyle, Curie, Drake, Mendeleieff	Major rubber companies
Surfactants (ethelyne-oxide-based, non-ionic)	14	As a wetting agent in many products	Drake, Acheson	A.C.E., Drake, Acheson	Detergent manufacturers and companies in a wide range of industries
Herbicides (sodium alpha alpha dichloro-propionate)	4	To kill weeds and grasses	Brady Co. Ltd., Davy Food	Kirchhoff, Urey	Drake
Leather chemicals	4	To finish leather	Various	Various	Leather-finishing industry

Source: Interview with Mr. G. S. Hartley.

were simply reselling their own chemical back to them at a profit. Their engineers countered by saying that tests definitely proved that our product was superior to that of their sister division, and they continued buying from us."

Mr. Hartley went on to describe the company's products. He discussed them in the order of their sales value to the company in 1961: plasticizers, polyethers, surfactants, herbicides, and leather finishes. Exhibit 5 contains summary data on the Croydon products, including a list of the major suppliers, competitors, and customers for each product.

PLASTICIZERS

"The plasticizer line accounts for 60 per cent of our current sales. A plasticizer is a chemical which is compounded with a polymer to produce a plastic. The function of a plasticizer is to impart certain characteristics to the final product, such as greater flexibility, heat resistance, or light stability. Although we produce a number of different plasticizers for different applications, the phthalate plasticizer can be used to illustrate this part of our business. The required raw materials, phthalic anhydride and higher alcohols, are sold by A.C.E., Drake, and Morley. We convert these materials into phthalate plasticizer, which is still a basic chemical and sell it to the large plastic manufacturers, such as A.C.E. These firms might, for example, combine the phthalate plasticizer with polyvinyl chloride resin, in a ratio of 40 to 100, to make a plastic compound. The end uses of the plastic vary from leather cloth and thin film to vinyl flooring and cable covering." A diagram of the process relationships, drawn by Mr. Hartley, is shown below.

THE PRODUCTION PROCESS FOR POLYVINYL PLASTIC

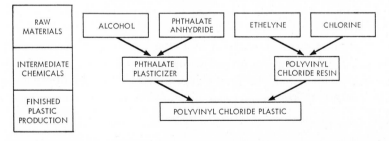

"While there are ten manufacturers of plasticizers in Great Britain, three hold about 75 per cent of the home market. Croydon sells about 16,500 tons of plasticizers in the United Kingdom, which is about 28 per cent of the total current consumption of 60,000 tons per year. Croydon also produces an additional 3,500 tons for export, Croydon being the only substantial exporter of plasticizers in Great Britain. The H. Davy Food Product Group Ltd. holds an equal share of the home market, and Priestly & Sons Ltd. holds about 19 per cent.

"Great Britain is one of the last places in which the plastics raw-material industry has not been fully integrated. In the United States, there are no phthalate converter manufacturers like ourselves. All of the United States manufacturers are at least partly integrated, producing some of the basic raw materials (alcohol, phthalate anhydride, ethelyne, and chlorine), one or both of the intermediate chemicals (phthalate plasticizer and polyvinyl chloride resin), and often the plastic itself. This trend towards integration has also taken hold on the Continent. In Great Britain itself, Davey Food already manufactures all the products on this diagram (shown above) except alcohol, and A.C.E. all but the plasticizer. If Great Britain enters the Common Market and our duty protection is thereby lost, there is little doubt that the other large British companies will also integrate.

POLYETHERS FOR URETHANES

"The polyethers currently account for about 18 per cent of our total sales. This is not bad when you consider that we only entered this market two years ago. Polyether is the principal ingredient of polyurethanes, which in their flexible form are a foam much like latex rubber. The foam itself is made by reacting polyether with an isocyanate. Manufacturers such as Buna Industries Ltd. and Isoprene Ltd. produce the foam and sell it along with other foam and rubber products.

"Of a total polyether consumption in Great Britain of about 8,000 tons per year, Croydon now sells about 5,000 tons. The remaining 3,000 tons are split among our numerous competitors, which include Drake, A.C.E., Bunsen Chemie AG, Urey Chemical Company Ltd., Mendelejeff Ltd., Société Curie, and Robert Boyle Group Ltd. We managed to capture this large share of the British market by helping to introduce the one-shot foaming process in this country. This method produces a better and less expensive product than the prepolymer process which had been in use. Drake and A.C.E. are the main suppliers of the raw materials which we require.

SURFACTANTS—SURFACE ACTIVE CHEMICALS

"Although Croydon entered the detergent business during World War II, our present line of ethylene-oxide-based, non-ionic surfactants was introduced about three years ago," Mr. Hartley continued. "Surfactants now account for about 14 per cent of our total sales. A surfactant is a chemical which reduces the surface tension of a liquid, thereby changing its wetting, emulsifying, and suspending characteristics. It is used in a great number of industries, such as detergents, paints, plastics, pharmaceuticals, textiles, cosmetics, and even road construction. In contrast to the plasticizers and polyethers, surfactants are sold to a wide range of final-stage manufacturers. The largest users are the soap and detergent companies.

Since 1958, we have been able to increase our sales of these products to about 5,000 tons per year in a total British market of approximately 17,000 tons per year. The suppliers of the basic raw material, ethylene oxide, are Drake, A.C.E., and E. Acheson Ltd.; the principal manufacturers of surfactants are also Drake, A.C.E., and Acheson, as well as Priestly & Sons.

HERBICIDES

"We first began to play around with herbicides in 1957 because we thought it advantageous to diversify from our base of industrial chemicals into agricultural chemicals. Our serious entry into the herbicide business took place in 1961 with the production of sodium alpha alpha dichloropropionate, better known as Nopalad.

"We have always realized that, while we could manufacture agricultural chemicals advantageously, we could never market the products with our small, industrially oriented sales force. For this reason we sought a large company, which turned out to be Drake, with which we could work closely in this field. We now have a long-term agreement with Drake, under which they agree to purchase certain amounts of Nopalad at guaranteed prices. Drake markets Nopalad along with a large number of other agricultural products. This first year we have produced about 800 tons of Nopalad, which accounted for slightly less than 4 per cent of our total sales. Our facilities are capable of producing 1,500 tons per year.

"Our primary Nopalad competitors in England are Urey Chemical and Kirchhoff Chemische Werke AG; the latter does not manufacture in England. Since it is still necessary to import propionic acid from the United States, our cost of raw materials is too high to give us any cost advantage over our competitors. Davy Food, however, is scheduled to come on stream with propionic acid in early 1962, and this should place us in a better competitive position."

LEATHER FINISHES

"Despite all of our activity in new markets, we have continued our interest in the leather chemical industry. Nevertheless, sales of these chemicals have shrunk from 100 per cent of total sales in 1939 to approximately 4 per cent of our total current sales.

SALES FORECASTS

Mr. Hartley concluded his comments about the company's products by citing the sales goals that Croydon had set for each of its major products under the assumption of average economic conditions. These estimates are tabulated in Table 1.

Table 1

1961 SALES GOALS BY PRODUCT

Product	1961 Sales Volume (000 Tons)	1966 Sales Volume (000 Tons)	Expected Share of Market
Plasticizers	20	26	Retain the same market share
Urethane	5	15–20	With some loss of market share
Surfactants	5	6–8	Retain the same market share
Nopalad	1	2+	....
Leather finishes	xx	xx	Retain the same market share

Source: Interview with Mr. G. S. Hartley.

FACTORS AFFECTING CROYDON'S SUCCESS

"We have been very successful so far, but I wonder how much of it was due just to luck," Mr. Hartley commented as he spoke about the strengths and weaknesses of Croydon.

CROYDON'S STRENGTHS

"Just being a small company has given us a number of advantages over our competitors. For one thing, we are a lot more flexible in our production and marketing activities and can adjust to changing conditions more readily than any of the others. Closely related to this advantage is the short time we require, relative to the other companies, to make a decision and to act on it. Finally, our small size allows, or requires us, depending on how you look at it, to throw our top talent on the crucial jobs. I would say that, as a consequence, we usually have as high-powered a team of men working on the important product problems as any other company in the field.

"Another advantage that we hold is that our company has always been very customer-oriented. We will only begin producing a product when we know that a need exists for it, and we make sure that our product meets the customer's needs as closely as possible. We work on the principle that the customer knows more about his own processes and products than does Croydon or anyone ele.

"We hold another attraction to many of our customers in that they prefer to deal with an independent supplier. Fortunately for us, the large companies competing with us are, many times, also in competition with our customers. Of course, the reputation that we have built up over the years as a reliable supplier of quality chemicals is a necessary asset for our continuing success."

CROYDON'S WEAKNESSES

Mr. Hartley discussed Croydon's weaknesses as follows: "On the other side of the coin, we are in a very precarious position concerning our raw-material supplies. The cost of our raw material averages about 70 per cent of our total sales volume. This means that we have to cover all of our production and sales expenses, overhead, and profit with 30 per cent of our sales revenue. This is obviously a very narrow margin in which to work, and any changes in the cost of raw materials have a tremendous impact on our financial operations. Since the prices of our raw materials are more stable than those of the semifinished chemicals which we manufacture, we may at any time be squeezed into unprofitable operations. The danger is compounded in our situation where, as we have already discussed, we are buying our raw materials from actual or potential competitors.

"Our second weakness is financial. As a closed corporation, the principal source of new equity has been largely retained earnings, which have not been able to keep pace with our mounting financial needs. Our rapid growth and our entry into new fields have created heavy requirements for capital. Right now, we are extended to the limit of credit that our equity will permit. In approximate figures, our credits are: capital and reserves, 40 per cent; accounts payable, 35 per cent; overdraft,[1] 20 per cent; and long-term bank credits, 5 per cent. This financial constraint has, for one thing, forced us to forgo a number of very promising opportunities. It also leaves us in the disquieting position of having no reserves to cover any mistakes which we might make in a major product move.

"Our third major weakness is the thinness of our management staff. Sales and production simply have grown faster than our management

---

[1] An overdraft is a common form of short-term bank credit in Great Britain. A company is permitted to overdraw its bank account up to a certain limit. The bank then charges interest on the overdraft in the same manner as for any formal short-term loan.

depth. Consequently, we often find that there is a tendency, indeed a necessity, to overdrive our good men for long periods of time. While this problem is not as serious as the others at the present time, it is one that could eventually become crippling if we continue our rapid expansion. One reason we have not built up a larger team is that we feel obliged to ensure a long-term favorable future for any good men to whom we may offer important positions, and we have not felt the necessary security on which to make such commitments."

POSSIBLE COURSES OF ACTION

"In light of Croydon's weaknesses, which we have just discussed and the trend by the large companies in the industry towards complete integration, we have felt that Croydon was too vulnerable to continue operating as it had. As a result, for the past few years, we have been concerned with the major decision of whether to sell Croydon or to try to offset its weaknesses under our own direction. We were more agreed on an answer in 1954 than we are in 1962, now that some move seems imminent."

SELLING CROYDON

"The primary arguments in favor of selling Croydon rest on the serious weaknesses inherent in the company as it now stands. If these problems prove insurmountable for us to solve by ourselves, the consequences may be ruin for the company, or, at the very least, a long, unrewarding battle to survive. On the other hand, if a large company were to buy Croydon, the raw-material, financial, and management problems could be easily taken care of. In evaluating the consequences of whether to sell the company or to take our chances, we must consider our obligations to our employees and their families, as well as top management's welfare. Of the several small independent companies that once existed as converters in the organic chemical industry, we seem to be the only ones in the United Kingdom who have not sold out. Our role as the 'Last of the Mohicans' makes us wonder if we have not overlooked something that all of the others have seen.

"There are two very good reasons which make it particularly favorable to sell Croydon at this time. Most important, the company is now very successful, with a very favorable earnings and profits record [Exhibit 2]. The fact of the matter is that we have already received an extremely good offer for the company, and we suspect that we could solicit other good counteroffers with no difficulty. The second reason is that there is a strong likelihood that a capital gains tax may soon be introduced in Great Britain. By selling the company now, this tax can be completely avoided.

"We must also look at Dr. Waldner's position, since really it is his company and his decision that we are examining.[2] First, there are no pressures on, or inclinations by, Dr. Waldner to keep the company for the sake of the family, since there are no sons. Second, because most of his personal fortune is tied up in the company, the family will require a substantial cash inflow to pay for the considerable estate taxes which must be paid at the time of his death. Finally, Dr. Waldner is at an age where he might seriously consider retiring from active business life to enjoy some of the fruits of his successful career.

"There are, on the other hand, some very strong personal reasons for Dr. Waldner to wish not to sell Croydon. Having founded the company he has naturally developed a tremendous interest and pride in the organization. Despite the fact that he has no family line of succession, I am sure that he strongly desires the company to retain its own identity. If he is not ready to retire, as I suspect the case may be, I am sure that he would much prefer to operate as an owner rather than as a manager. Dr. Waldner is an entrepreneur by nature and would not be happy working for someone else in any regimented manner. Strangely enough, whereas Dr. Waldner considers his loyalty and friendship for us as an important reason to keep Croydon, there is not really as much basis for this conclusion as there is for us to be in favor of keeping Croydon out of loyalty and friendship for him. Actually, there is no real problem for us younger men to continue our work, either with Croydon or with some other company in the industry, especially in light of our successful management of Croydon to date. On the other hand, Dr. Waldner would essentially lose his job as owner-leader of this organization, with no comparable opportunities available to him, if he were to sell Croydon."

KEEPING CROYDON

"Before we can decide to keep Croydon, we must find, a course of action which will successfully counter Croydon's weakness of raw materials, finance and management. Among the countless possibilities for action, we have reduced our scope of consideration to three: (1) to sell stock to the public; (2) to sell stock to one of the big companies in the industry who could act as a 'Big Brother' to us; (3) to sell stock to both the public and a large company in the industry. I shall mention some of the more important arguments which we hold, pro and contra, for each of these courses of action.

Public Sale. "The broad issue of stock could bring in the capital which

---

[2] The common stock of Croydon was owned in early 1962 as follows: 25 per cent by Dr. Waldner, 25 per cent by his wife, 40 per cent by his daughter, and the remaining 10 per cent was split among the key executives of Croydon.

we so badly need. At the same time, we could still remain relatively free from outside influence. A sale of stock to the public would have the additional advantage of establishing a market price for Croydon's stock. Thus Dr. Waldner, or any of us for that matter, would be able to cash in our stocks whenever we should desire.

"The principal disadvantage is that this course of action would in no way solve our weak position concerning our raw materials. Nor would this move assist us with our problem of management depth. Actually, with the mere addition of funds for investment purposes, the strain on our management team is likely to become that much greater. Furthermore, this means of financing the company would release no free funds for Dr. Waldner's estate tax requirements. His family could, of course, sell stock to obtain the necessary funds, but this would require a further dilution of the family's ownership. Finally, market conditions for a small unintegrated company are disadvantageous, because the public is as aware as we are of the precarious position such a company holds.

"Big Brother." "In looking at the second and third choices of action, I should first explain that we are only considering suppliers of our raw materials as likely associates. If we were to sell stock to a nonsupplier company, we would not be much better off than if we sold to the public except that we might obtain a better price for the stock from a company wishing to diversify. We view the ideal 'Big Brother' as a large company, first, capable of supplying at least some of our important raw materials and, second, not involved in the manufacture of our products. This latter criterion should be of importance to the 'Big Brother' because Croydon would become the means of further integration for it.

"We do not expect that selling stock to a 'Big Brother' company would directly alleviate our line management problem, but access to R&D and other staff services of a 'Big Brother' might prove of great use to Croydon.

"A more subtle advantage which 'Big Brother' might afford us would be the latent protection we would gain against unduly tough or unfair competition which might be directed towards us. It is not that we expect to have to call on 'Big Brother' to help us. Just the fact that we were under its protection would tend to discourage other big companies from directing antagonism against us. One other incidental advantage is that the sale can be negotiated so as to provide a certain amount of free funds to Dr. Waldner for the purpose of estate taxes.

"There is one major argument against the sale of a large block of stock to a single company, but I want to emphasize that it is a particularly important one, especially to Dr. Waldner. The 'Big Brother' would be a new important minority stockholder who could exert a tremendous pressure on the management of Croydon. The loss of complete independence is an unwanted but acceptable pill. But this could become a case of the tail wagging the dog. We fear that our minority partner could, and might, assume a command of our operations by using their control of our raw materials as a level whenever a difference of opinion arose. We would have no effective way to counter this pressure.

"It was only about a year ago that a classmate of mine, who works on Wall Street and was in England on business, suggested that we consider combining the sale of stock to both the public and to one of the big suppliers. This suggestion was made in answer to our concern that a large company could exert an undue, and perhaps unhealthy, influence on the management of Croydon. His argument was that we could use the public meetings and announcements as a counterbalance to undue influence by the large company owner, which typically would be very sensitive to public impressions and pressure.

"Of course, the whole idea of selling a minority share of Croydon to a large company, without being forced to give options on the remaining shares, might be a daydream, because very large companies are characteristically not interested in permanent minority positions. Making a decision on what to do is only one step towards effecting a successful conclusion. The truth of the matter, unfortunately, is that attempts to get the best of all worlds often go awry."

MANAGEMENT'S VIEWS

"I have tried to take you through Croydon's problem and the possible courses of action as objectively as possible. I have done much of the talking, but you should not get the impression that there are no other significant voices in Croydon. As you know, there are four or five men who are quite close to Dr. Waldner, and he will wish to consider their feelings and opinions in his decision of whether to sell or keep Croydon. I am just one of the group. I would suggest that you talk with the others in order to learn in which direction they may be thinking. I would just like to add that the views you hear from us today are very likely not the views you would have heard five years ago and may not be our final views. I can remember how strongly in favor of selling Croydon I was, about a year ago, as the only sound business position. I spent many days—evenings and weekends too—arguing my position against Dr. Waldner and Mr. Swift, both of whom were in favor of keeping Croydon. Since then, I have changed my position in favor of keeping Croydon because I think we can do it successfully without hurting the company. It was my ironic task, about two months ago, to have to defend my new position against the same two gentlemen, who had changed their opinions in favor of selling the company. This just shows you how very unsettled this matter is in our minds."

The researcher interviewed each of the six key men to learn their opinions concerning the possible sale of Croydon. The result of these interviews is presented below in the following manner for each man: (1) a brief note on his background, position, and duties; (2) a description of the man, based on a collection of quotes made by his colleagues; (3) and his own views on the possible sale of Croydon.

DR. W. R. WALDNER

Dr. Waldner was founder and president of Croydon. He actively concerned himself with company planning and with major investment and product decisions.

*   *   *   *   *

"Dr. Waldner has been the promoting spirit of this company since its founding. He is rich with new ideas, and our successful diversification over the years owes much to his activities and to the pressures which he has exerted. A born promoter, he relies heavily on his executives to make the day-to-day operating decisions and to follow up his work. Often, he tends to permit details of secondary importance to occupy his time. But he has a gift for enthusing people, and he is a wonderful boon for morale."

*   *   *   *   *

"While you cannot be in this game if you are afraid of competition," Dr. Waldner commented, "I wonder how long we can continue swimming against the stream. If you will permit this analogy, while we were a small body we could manage swimming against the waters. But as we grew larger, the pressure and the drag of the water also grew, but at even a faster rate. While I can accept the proposition that 40 per cent of a good thing is better than 100 per cent of a bad one, I would not care to hold a minority position in my own company. At the same time, I am firmly convinced that a man who endangers his life's work is a fool. Consequently, I am highly concerned with the question of keeping Croydon and my control of the company without submitting the company to ruin. If keeping Croydon involves a high probability of failure, I should rather sell the company for the good of the management and employees, for my own good, and for the sake of the company itself."

DR. E. J. LANG

Dr. Lang, who received his Doctor of Philosophy in Chemical Engineering at the University of Berlin, Germany, joined Croydon in 1938 as Works Chemist. In 1962, he was in charge of the ester plant, the analytical laboratory, and certain personnel functions, such as welfare and labor relations, for the hourly-paid workers.

*   *   *   *   *

"Ernst is probably the best-liked man in the plant. The workers trust him and come to him with their problems, which is a great help to us all. As a consequence, he has been shifting more and more from the technical and production managerial function to that of personnel welfare."

*   *   *   *   *

Dr. Lang remarked: "Until a few years ago, I never saw any real reason to change from our independent status. As we continued to grow, however, we became more pressed financially and more dependent for our raw material. But we could not afford to stop growing. Our rather narrow line of products has always presented us with the prospect of a serious setback, should one of our main products become redundant, a very real danger in these times of rapidly changing technology. We have had to, and still have to, continue growing and diversifying. Nevertheless, I am still not in favor of selling or merging Croydon with a large company for two reasons. The first, and most important, reason is that we would be letting our employees down. They have worked very hard to make Croydon what it is today, and some of them would consider our selling the company out from under them as a stab in the back. I am sure that they would all feel a little less secure if we sold the company, and we must also consider these people who simply would not like to work for a giant company like A.C.E. My other reason is that I should not like to have to change our [the management's] working relations. We operate in an informal manner and are permitted a large degree of discretion in our actions. I am not sure that we would continue this way if we were to become part of a big company."

MR. G. S. HARTLEY

Mr. Hartley, who studied commerce at Manchester College of Technology and later received a Master's degree in Business Administration at Harvard, joined Croydon in 1947 and rose to the position of Commercial Director in 1954. In this position, Mr. Hartley was responsible for the sales and administration of the company.

*   *   *   *   *

"Jerry is a man with exceptional intellect and perception. He can quickly grasp new situations, adapt his thinking, organize to meet the problems, and see a program through. He is also a brilliant negotiator, which is of great value to our type of company. He is, however, still young and professionally growing, and consequently tends to be a bit changeable and emotional in his work."

*   *   *   *   *

"I still think that the business arguments tend to be in favor of selling Croydon," remarked Mr. Hartley. "But, as I mentioned, there are some very strong emotional arguments in favor of keeping Croydon. My opinion is that Dr. Waldner should favor the emotional reasons as long as it does not have to hurt the animal [Croydon] itself."

MR. J. W. SWIFT

Mr. Swift, who received his chemical engineering degree from Manchester College of Technology, joined Croydon's technical staff in 1952, becoming Technical Director in 1957. His responsibilities centered about the technical problems of the plant's design, construction, and operation.

*   *   *   *   *

"John is a chemical engineer of outstanding ability and a genius in his specialty—the planning and design of chemical process equipment and plant. If one could say that one man works harder among this group of hard-working managers, John could merit this compliment. At the same time, he sometimes tends to become too attached to his own people or projects and to overorganize. He can also be moody and changeable on occasion."

*   *   *   *   *

"In general, I have always been against selling Croydon outright to a big company for a number of reasons which I realize are noneconomic. For one thing, Croydon presents a challenge and a task for me as it now operates. I also like the completely independent framework in which I work. In a big company there is a need for infinite consultations and explanations, and one cannot really work as one wishes. Finally, I derive a fundamental satisfaction in knowing that the physical plant that you see out there has been created by my team and me. I believe that if you spoke with some of the other key people in Croydon, such as Ray Ashton, Bob Reddington, or George Bowman, you would find that they are also in favor of keeping the independence of operation which we now enjoy."

*   *   *   *   *

The important role all these men play in the decision by Dr. Waldner was emphasized during the interviews by one executive's comment: "In spite of Dr. Waldner's clear legal ownership, he cannot actually make his decision on a satisfactory basis of whether to sell or keep his company without our approval. He cannot favorably sell Croydon against our desire, because a purchaser will want the management as part of the property. Similarly, he cannot keep the company without our support, because he will need us to see it through with him. So, as you can see, Dr. Waldner is not quite a free agent to deal with this matter as one might first assume. He has to sell us on the decision as well as himself."

THE ARLA CHEMICALS COMPANY*

"If you want to know what our major problems are in 1962, I would say that they all involve some aspect of product planning," commented Mr. Schetty, Commercial Director of The Arla Chemicals Company. "Our business is being squeezed on three sides. For one thing, we are in danger of losing our primary raw material, baurite. Secondly, the market conditions for our most important by-products, the acid group, have been changing, but we are severely hindered by external forces from adapting to this change. Finally, with respect to our other important by-product, ferannal, our customers for this material have been introducing a new process in which no ferannal is required."

Mr. Rybert, President of Arla, commented: "These problems with our suppliers and markets have to be solved. The quickening pace of Europe's economic integration makes the situation more urgent because we expect our competition to increase considerably. I might add that the company must also consider the possibility of diversifying into new fields of the chemical business."

THE COMPANY

The Arla Chemicals Company was a middle-sized chemical firm producing a number of basic inorganic chemicals,[1] all of which were long-established items in industry. The firm had grown with the industry and enjoyed the reputation of being a reliable producer of quality chemicals. Arla was located in one of the European Common Market (ECM) countries and was near the borders of two other ECM nations.

Established shortly after the turn of the century, the company had sales of 76 million Swiss francs in 1960, employed almost 1,300 persons, and

---

Copyright 1962 by l'Institut pour l'Etude des Méthodes de Direction de l'Entreprise (IMEDE), Lausanne, Switzerland. Reprinted by permission.

[1] Chemical products are often subdivided into two broad categories, organic and inorganic. The inclusion of some hydrocarbon in the molecular structure of a chemical product qualifies it as organic. Most of the organic chemicals are derived from petroleum, coal, or natural-gas sources. The better-known basic industrial chemicals, such as soda ash, calcium carbide, ammonia, caustic soda, hydrochloric acid, and sulphuric acid, are inorganic chemicals.

had no significant financial obligations outstanding. Exhibits 1 and 2 show financial data for selected years.

Arla's management had traditionally been proud of the firm's technical

Exhibit 1

BALANCE SHEET BEFORE DISTRIBUTION OF PROFITS, 1958–60
(In thousands of Swiss francs)

	1958	1959	1960
Current assets			
Cash	3,032	4,158	3,317
Notes receivable	1,593	1,933	2,063
Accounts receivable	3,441	7,852	8,313
Government securities	4,220	615	2,521
Investments	7,176	7,117	7,037
Inventory	12,037	10,809	11,626
Total	31,499	32,484	34,877
Fixed assets			
Equipment and buildings	44,646	46,107	51,992
Reserve for depreciation	36,325	39,206	41,652
Net equipment and buildings	8,321	6,901	10,340
Land	260	235	235
Patents and good will	.....	.....	.....
Total	8,581	7,136	10,575
Total debits	40,080	39,620	45,452
Current liabilities			
Accounts payable	7,824	7,543	9,008
Provision for taxes	2,363	1,976	2,766
Matured coupons	57	63	42
Total	10,244	9,587	11,816
Fixed liabilities			
Debenture	164	82	.....
Total	164	82	.....
Capital reserves and profits for distribution			
Common stock	17,000	17,000	17,000
Legal reserve	1,700	1,700	1,700
Capital surplus	300	300	300
Equipment replacement reserve	4,100	4,100	6,200
Reserve for inventory valuation	1,000	1,000	1,000
Employee welfare reserve	3,150	3,430	4,560
Profits for distribution	2,422	2,421	2,876
Total	29,672	29,951	33,636
Total credits	40,080	39,620	45,452

Source: Company records.

Exhibit 2

PROFIT AND LOSS STATEMENT AND DISTRIBUTION OF PROFITS STATEMENT, 1958–60
(In thousands of Swiss francs)

Profit and Loss Statement

	1958	1959	1960
Credit:			
Operating income less operating expenses	2,594	2,434	4,342
Financial revenues from investments and			
accounts receivable*	827	1,020	1,133
Carryover from preceding year	1	2	1
Total	3,422	3,456	5,476
Debit:			
Provision for corporate taxes	750	750	1,600
Charitable funds and grants	250	285	1,000
Profits for current distribution	2,422	2,421	2,876
Total	3,422	3,456	5,476

Distribution of Profits Statement

	1958	1959	1960
Taxes withheld on dividends	750	750	900
Statutory share (directors' compensation)	170	170	200
Cash dividends paid to stockholders	1,500	1,500	1,750
Carried over to following year	2	1	26
Total	2,422	2,421	2,876

* Arla carried accounts receivable for their customers at the bank rates of interest for comparable loans.
Source: Company records.

competence, and they considered their technical staff to be among the foremost in their sector of the chemical industry. The firm's strength was largely due to low-cost and efficient production processes, which allowed it to sell high-quality chemicals at competitive prices.

Arla also sold their patented processes and equipment through a wholly owned subsidiary. This small engineering company often designed complete plants based on Arla operations. Where it did so, this subsidiary would normally assign its own engineers to supervise the construction of the plant, to start the system in operation, to train the customer's personnel, and to assure successful operation of the plant. By 1962, plants and equipment had been sold in most parts of the world.

ARLA'S PRODUCTS AND MARKETS

Arla's principal product was feran. The company used the most common process of making feran, in which two valuable by-products—a sulphurous material and ferannal—were also produced. These by-products had to be profitably sold for the successful operation of the over-all business.

Originally, Arla simply made sulphuric acid from the sulphurous material and sold it and all the unprocessed ferannal to industrial customers. Over the years, however, as the production of feran increased, the company began to introduce new derivative products, in order to market the consequently increasing volume of by-products.

All the company's major products were grouped into three categories: feran; the acid group, which was originally developed to dispose of the sulphurous content of the baurite; and the ferannal group. Of total 1960 sales, feran accounted for about 66 per cent, the acid group of products for about 24 per cent, and the ferannal group of products for about 10 per cent. Exhibit 3 shows the product and product-group sales for 1960 and also shows the product sales volumes for selected years. Exhibit 4 displays the product and process relationships in 1962.

FERAN

Company operations centered about the production of feran. (The process is shown by a double line in Exhibit 4.) All of Arla's other products were originally manufactured in order to sell profitably the by-products, which were produced in a fixed relationship to the production of feran.

Feran was a basic inorganic chemical, about half of which was used by the paint industry and the rest by a wide range of other industries. Most of Arla's feran sales were made within the ECM. Because of the industrial applications for this product, the market for feran was strongly affected by the swings of industrial activity, particularly by those of the paint industry.

Certain of Arla's executives expressed the opinion that the feran industry had not been aggressive enough over the years and had consequently lost ground to other products. They felt that more industry research should have been carried out to improve the product, so that it could be better used in current applications and also introduced for new applications. They stated that, while world sales of feran had increased slightly in absolute terms, feran's share of the total market in which it competed was actually decreasing.

THE ACID GROUP

Until 1937, Arla had disposed of all its by-product sulphurous material simply by producing and selling sulphuric acid. The introduction

Exhibit 3

PRODUCTION AND SALES, SELECTED YEARS, 1926–60

Products	Production (Tons)								Sales in 1960	
	1926	1927	1938	1939	1949	1950	1959	1960	Thousands of Sw. Frs.	% of Total Sales
Main product									65.8	65.8
Feran	21,593	24,397	43,179	40,501	33,408	35,006	44,498	45,722	50,008	65.8
Acid group									24.5	
Sulphuric acid	17,702	17,575	58,007	55,076	57,030	51,489	126,213	159,712	9,691	12.7
Phosphoric acid	....	....	45	56	191	175	724	299	21	....
Simple superphosphate ..	....	....	....	13,701	76,279	32,326	26,198	20,284	1,380	1.8
Triple superphosphate ..	....	....	6,384	3,699	3,307	2,822	15,310	26,098	5,224	6.9
Complex fertilizer	....	....	....	....	....	....	2,083	1,922	769	1.0
Other products (e.g., detergents)	....	....	....	....	....	....	2,526	2,263	1,611	2.1
Ferannal group									9.7	
Ferannal	672	700	5,142	4,891	4,001	3,460	5,158	6,025	2,002	2.6
Food additive	....	....	....	....	19	339	2,774	3,953	5,367	7.1
Total sales	21.8	24.5	50.7	48.8	46.2	44.2	69.6	76.1	76,073	100.0
(Millions of Swiss francs)										

Note:
1. For convenience, local currency has been converted into Swiss francs.
2. All franc values have been adjusted to a 1960 base.

Source: Company records.

Exhibit 4

PRODUCT AND PROCESS RELATIONSHIPS

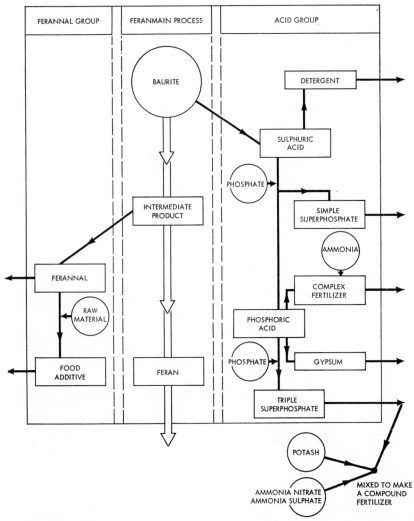

Source: Company records.

of the fertilizer products at this time was made largely because of adverse conditions in the sulphuric acid market. Since sulphuric acid had always been difficult to store or transport, other producers had had repeatedly to dump their output in the local market[2] as supply temporarily exceeded demand. Consequently, the price for sulphuric acid traditionally had fluc-

---

[2] Transportation costs limit the sulphuric acid market to a radius of about 100 to 150 kilometers from the producer.

tuated very much. Furthermore, as the world demand for feran increased substantially in the second half of the 1930's, Arla increased its production of feran and found itself faced with a greater supply of sulphurous material than ever before. At the same time, the general supply of sulphuric acid had outgrown the demand within the marketable area. Under these circumstances, Arla began to process the sulphuric acid into simple superphosphate fertilizer, phosphoric acid, and triple-superphosphate fertilizer. These new products permitted Arla profitably to dispose of its sulphuric acid excess in new markets and also alleviated the problem of storage. Up to 1962, Arla had been the only feran manufacturer in its geographical area that processed sulphuric acid into derivative products —in this case, fertilizers.

After World War II, the local pattern of industrial chemical requirements changed, and the demand for sulphuric acid greatly increased until it far exceeded the supply available from feran by-products in the area. Consequently, by 1962 Arla was producing one-third of its sulphuric acid production from free sulphur to meet these needs.

Although the acid group consisted of ten products by 1960, only four of these were sold in any substantial amounts. Of these, sulphuric acid and triple-superphosphate fertilizer accounted for 80 per cent of the acid-group sales. Simple superphosphate and complex fertilizers represented another 12 per cent, while the other six products accounted for the remaining 8 per cent. Phosphoric acid, one of these six products, actually was produced in great quantities, but it was primarily used as an internal intermediate product because no significant demand existed for it outside the company.

The markets for these products were diverse. The sulphuric acid was sold direct to industrial users within the 100- to 150-kilometer radius mentioned in the footnote below. The fertilizers were sold to farm-supply distributors. Transportation costs limited this market to a radius of 150 kilometers.[3] The other products were normally sold through agents in Europe.

THE FERANNAL GROUP

The one constantly strong market for ferannal was the food-processing industry, where it was used in the production of a certain expensive food additive. Arla had been selling its ferannal to a number of intermediate

---

[3] The 150 kilometers refers to overland transportation. In Arla's case, a seaport lay within this distance, which permitted bulk distribution of fertilizer overseas. Sulphuric acid, on the other hand, was not commonly transported overseas because of the difficulty and expense of handling and storing this chemical on board ocean vessels.

product manufacturers who produced additives for the food-processing industry. No one customer purchased more than 20 per cent of Arla's normal ferannal production.

Starting in 1949, Arla began producing the additive itself and selling it through distributors to food processors. By 1962, the value of the additive sales was about 2.5 times that of ferannal sales.

THE PROBLEMS OF BAURITE SUPPLY

Since 1955, Arla had encountered growing difficulty in obtaining its requirements of baurite at what company executives considered a reasonable price. As a result, Arla had suffered a baurite cost disadvantage vis-à-vis their competitors, while the baurite market had remained a seller's market. An even more serious problem was that world political moves were threatening further to reduce the free supply of baurite. Arla's management was seriously worried about the long-range possibility that free supplies would become permanently reduced, especially since Arla was the only feran manufacturer in its local area wholly dependent on this supply.

Arla's founders located the firm so as to take advantage of nearby baurite deposits. These sources became uneconomical to work shortly before the First World War, and subsequently the company had to import all its baurite from outside sources at the world commodity price. Arla typically purchased baurite from a number of suppliers in normal shipment amounts. The price for baurite was determined on the commodity-exchange market in Paris.

Two unusual conditions caused the baurite world commodity market to be very volatile. First, United States tariffs effectively segregated this large supply and demand sector from the world market. Second, many of the large baurite users outside the United States owned or controlled their own sources; these users came in and out of the baurite market only to meet fluctuations in their requirements. By purchasing baurite when the demand for feran was high[4] and dumping baurite when the over-all demand for feran was low, these firms applied an adverse pressure to the baurite market, which caused wide fluctuations in the price.

Arla was subject to the full swing of these prices for its complete supply of baurite. On the other hand, its large competitors, who met most of their requirements from their own sources, were subject to these swings only for their marginal needs. Up to 1962, Arla had been able to offset

---

[4] The only major use for baurite was for the production of feran.

its baurite cost disadvantage by means of production savings and the profitable sale of its feran by-products.

Arla's management was worried, however, that the recent advantageous position of the baurite sellers in the free market was becoming a permanent condition. If this were so, Arla would find itself at an even greater disadvantage than in the past, since there would no longer be those periods of excess baurite supplies during which Arla could favorably negotiate purchase agreements. A factor which contributed to this pessimism was that a large percentage of the better baurite sources[5] were located in the underdeveloped and politically unstable areas of the world. There was pressure within most of these countries to appropriate the mining operations and to nationalize them. As Mr. Schetty explained: "If they [the inhabitants of these countries] ever seize the source facilities, they will not stop there. Then they will want to produce the chemicals themselves rather than sell the baurite on the world market, more as a matter of prestige than of good economics. What is even more worrisome is that they will damage or destroy the baurite facilities in their ignorance of these facilities' economic value to their nations. In either event, there will be less baurite in the free market."

Arla's top management had not yet attempted to study the economics of this problem. As one member said: "We have a number of major choices. We can continue our present method of purchasing baurite and take our chances. There will always be some baurite available at a price. Or we can invest in baurite facilities, either on our own or with others. However, this is a new business to us, and the source facilities can involve enormous investments. Then there is always the possibility of arranging long-term supply contracts, but it is going to be expensive to interest the suppliers at this time because of the present seller's market. And, of course, with the political situation as it is, we are not certain that we can rely on the performance of such a contract in the future. First, we shall have to select a course of action. Then, if we select any joint ventures, we must also decide what kind of partner we want."

THE PROBLEMS OF THE ACID GROUP

Changing requirements in the fertilizer market had confronted Arla with two major problems. First, there was a technical problem, in that the company's fertilizers no longer met the new specifications. Then there was the business problem of obtaining suppliers for any new raw materials which would be needed. The success or failure with which these

---

[5] Deposits of baurite exist in most parts of the world.

problems were met would clearly affect the whole product balance within this group.

Traditionally, farm-supply distributors had purchased the necessary ingredients for compound fertilizers and mechanically mixed these for the farmer according to his required proportions. One of the most common inorganic compound fertilizers contained potash, superphosphate, ammonia sulphate, and ammonia nitrate. This mixture was referred to as a "three-element" fertilizer, since the latter two chemicals served to provide nitrogen in the two different forms required by plants. In the late 1950's, farmers began increasingly to favor a chemically integrated single-pellet fertilizer because of its technical advantage over the former multipellet mixture.

To meet this new demand pattern, Arla had devised a chemical process to combine phosphoric acid, ammonia nitrate, and ammonia sulphate into a complex fertilizer with two of the major components. The potash would then be mechanically mixed in and the final combination formed into individual pellets. The new complex fertilizer was expected fully to meet the new requirements of the market.

Having solved the technological problem of producing a competitive complex fertilizer, Arla then encountered the problem of obtaining the required ammonia nitrate supply. Both the phosphate- and the nitrogen-product manufacturers were competing for the new complex fertilizer market. The nitrate manufacturers, on the one hand, could either purchase or manufacture the needed phosphates without any trouble. On the other hand, Arla had encountered serious resistance in obtaining the necessary nitrates for a sufficient production of complex fertilizer, and it was unable by itself to manufacture the nitrates economically.

Mr. Schetty summarized the nitrate-purchase problem in these words: "We simply cannot buy the needed ammonia nitrate under reasonable conditions. The only price that they [the nitrogen-product manufacturers] will quote is designed to discourage us from competing with them in the complex fertilizer market. Their terms of sale, which positively exclude us from a large portion of our natural market, pose an even more serious problem. The nitrogen suppliers allege that agreements among the nitrogen-product manufacturers discourage the sale of nitrates to a customer if the resulting end products are to be exported to another West European country. This means that if we want to produce a complex fertilizer containing their ammonia nitrate, we cannot market this fertilizer in our neighboring countries. These countries now purchase over 35 per cent of our fertilizer production and could represent a much higher share in the future. If we should lose our overseas markets as a result of the establishment of fertilizer-producing feran plants in the underdeveloped countries, we would have to turn to our ECM market, in order to offset these sales losses, since the home market within our distribution range is nearly saturated. Under the most severe export losses, we would have to expand our sales in neighboring countries by close to 50 per cent of their current level in order to maintain over-all sales."

In discussing the nitrate-manufacture problem, Mr. Schetty said: "Engineering studies have shown that the smallest economical plant would provide substantially more ammonia nitrate than we could use. And, of course, there is no market in which to sell the excess, since the nitrogen-product manufacturers fully control the nitrate market. Besides, the production of the nitrate is technically difficult, and we are not anxious to contend with these problems."

It appeared to the researcher that two reasons dominated the arguments in favor of actively pursuing the fertilizer market: first, the line of products had been profitable and promised to remain so; and, second, Arla's executives were concerned about an expected deterioration of the general sulphuric acid market over the next ten years[6] and were anxious to maintain a marketing outlet that could absorb the firm's future excess sulphuric acid supply.

Concerning the course of action to be followed, Mr. Schetty stated: "We studied the possibility of fighting the unfair restriction imposed on us by the nitrogen-product manufacturers by requesting relief from our government or from the ECM authorities. Another possible solution would be to try to form a joint operation to manufacture the complex fertilizer with one of the small nitrogen-product manufacturers in this area who is not prepared to enter the complex fertilizer market by himself. Although this type of firm might be a party to any existing agreements, we do have one point of bargaining leverage, namely, that the ECM authorities will probably disallow such agreements on the grounds that they violate the covenants of the Treaty of Rome. The small nitrogen-product firm knows that the eventual breakdown of the industrial agreements will leave him much less protected than ever before, and we are offering him a long-term relation in a profitable business."

THE PROBLEMS OF THE FERANNAL GROUP

The well-established food-additive market for feranal became unsettled in the late 1950's when a new process was discovered which permitted

---

[6] In the past, the manufacture of ammonia sulphate required a large quantity of sulphuric acid. Mr. Schetty estimated that the need would lessen because of technological developments.

the production of the same additive more cheaply without the use of ferannal. Two factors worked against Arla's defensive move of increasing its own production of the food additive: a raw-material problem and a market-saturation problem.

While Arla could recycle ferannal in its main process so as to obtain feran, a much greater marginal profit could be realized by using the ferannal itself to produce the food additive. As for the firm's competitive position, management determined that Arla could produce the additive at the same cost or even at a slightly lower total cost than the manufacturers using the new process. This was possible because Arla would not have to pay for the costly transportation of ferannal.

In order to produce the food additive, Arla required another raw chemical, with the trade name Huzon, which was available from only one manufacturer. Despite a concerted effort to arrange for the favorable supply of Huzon on a long-term basis, the supplier continued to demand a price which Arla executives considered about 30 per cent too high.

In the face of this unacceptable situation, Arla's management investigated the possibility of producing its own Huzon. It was determined that the smallest economic plant would produce about twice the Huzon needed to process the ferannal resulting from Arla's feran production. In the process of making Huzon, a by-product chemical was also produced. According to Mr. Schetty, no market existed for either Huzon or its by-product in the local region because of the tight control held by the aforementioned manufacturer. There was a possibility of selling these chemicals to distant manufacturers, but even there the competition would be very severe. Mr. Schetty finally commented: "If we could find one or two customers who would purchase 80 per cent of our Huzon by-product on a long-range basis, we would go ahead with the plant."

Should Arla solve the Huzon supply problem, a number of officers pointed out, there still remained the problem that the additive market was already tight. In view of the substantial additional facilities Arla would introduce, the industry's production capacity for food additive would far exceed the normal demand.

THE PROBLEMS OF DIVERSIFICATION

A number of the less senior members of top management felt strongly that Arla had to consider diversifying into new areas of the chemical industry in face of the long-term trends. During the course of the field study, however, the researcher noted in this group traces of an opinion that the top executives would be very reluctant to allow Arla to enter fields with which they were not technically acquainted.

Many arguments were advanced in favor of diversification. Diversification was said to be indispensable in order to:

1. Reduce the dangers of an increasing difficulty in obtaining baurite
2. Compensate for the cyclical behavior of the feran market
3. Anticipate the long-term threat of a vanishing market for feran, especially in light of the possible entry of new manufacturers at the sources
4. Move into areas with greater growth prospects than the inorganic chemicals area in which Arla had been active

Organic chemical products, especially the more elaborate organic fertilizers, were of most interest to the Arla management. It was recognized, however, that the company's executives did not have the breadth of technical and business knowledge to ensure, by themselves, the success of diversification into this area. Consideration was, therefore, given to the relative advantages of (1) hiring qualified people to start new operations, (2) setting up a joint operation with a company in the organic chemical field, or (3) merging with such a company.

Discussing the steps taken to diversify, a plant manager remarked that inquires about opportunities were being made by the company's officers through their personal and professional acquaintances and that the company was doing some new-product research. Mr. Parmi, who was in charge of research, mentioned: "New-product research is largely confined to areas related to our present products. Neither I nor my staff are properly qualified to investigate fully the possibilities in organic chemicals." Another executive added that some general exploration into possible joint ventures was being done also by the engineering subsidiary.

If Arla should decide to diversify by means of partnership or merger, it could offer a prospective participant a large plot of excellently located property on which the new operations could be constructed. It could also offer any potential non-European partner its general know-how of operating in Europe. It could not, however, offer a ready marketing organization for the new products, first, because Arla's marketing experience was restricted to a narrow line of inorganic chemicals and, second, because management recognized that it had, to some extent, neglected marketing over the years and that this area would require further development before it could be considered an asset in negotiation.

In recognition of the difficult marketing problems that diversification would entail, one executive remarked: "We must be prepared to merge with or, preferably, to absorb another company which will provide us with an entrée into new fields. Our engineering company has gained us world-wide renown in our industry. We should capitalize on that renown. Any possible merger must take into account the possible extension of our commercial organization in such a way as to replace our now dominant technical orientation with a marketing outlook."

Mr. Klare, Executive Vice-President, summed up his thoughts on the subject with this comment: "Any expansion should be based on our technical strengths, which center about certain inorganic chemical processes. The organic chemical industry, about which we know relatively little, technically or otherwise, is rapidly growing, and changes take place quickly. This means that you have to be very careful in selecting an area to enter, because, by the time you build the plant and start producing, the technologies involved can change so that you no longer have a market."

PART IV

Forward Planning

THE COMPAGNIE ELECTRO-MECANIQUE

KLM—ROYAL DUTCH AIRLINES

A NOTE ON THE INTERNATIONAL AIR TRANSPORT INDUSTRY

PLANNING IN X CORPORATION

ECONOMIC PLANNING IN FRANCE

THIS SECTION consists of cases on forward planning as carried on by a leading French electrical equipment manufacturer and by KLM—Royal Dutch Airlines; a note accompanying the latter case and providing data on the problems of planning in the airlines industry;[1] an internal company memorandum describing a projected planning setup and seeking to identify the qualifications needed by the man selected to run it; and a note on economic planning at the national level in France. In connection with the latter, readers will be interested in reviewing the note on "The Chemical Industry in France,"[2] which depicts the impact of national planning on this major segment of the French economy.

That interest in the idea of national economic planning is growing is attested by various recent events: for example, proponents of the French planning system have suggested its extension to the Common Market; the President of the United States has voiced an interest in the French system; and British business in 1962 made moves toward endorsing more so-called

---

[1] IMEDE has another excellent and much longer set of cases on long-range and operational planning in SWISSAIR. These can be obtained through the Intercollegiate Bibliography. They constitute excellent material for a special seminar discussion of forward planning and can be used for discussion in several different types of courses.

[2] Part III.

planning by industry and government. Because the French system has won considerable industry and public support and has seemingly helped France to achieve her high postwar industrial expansion, the authors believed a note on economic planning in France well deserved inclusion in this book.

The purpose of forward planning is to express major company objectives in terms of specific future actions programmed over a definite number of years and assigned to specific executives or departments. A plan provides a blueprint for coordinated action in all major functional areas: R&D, production, marketing, finance, and so on. To prepare such a blueprint, various activities must be performed, including—to mention just the most important—forecasting, scheduling, and budgeting. In some companies, top management may do this job itself; more frequently, the planning job is assigned to special staff personnel who work closely with the line, or to committees.

Forecasting involves looking at underlying trends affecting demand for a product or service in order to identify profit opportunities. The trends in question are often longer than cyclical trends and involve a reasonable period of time, sometimes as long as five to ten years, or even longer. (The length of time is partly a function of industry conditions.) Complicating the forecasting job in all cases is the question of what competitors may do. Even the best forecasting techniques cannot stave off disappointment or even disaster where all competitors serving the market perceive the same trends, identify similar profit opportunities, and gear to take larger shares of what they believe will be a growing business. The results of such concerted action have recently been seen in the aircraft industry, where, partly for political reasons, airlines in many nations built up tremendously expensive fleets of jets, the combined capacity of which far outstripped air traffic in 1961 and 1962.[3] How long this condition of overcapacity is likely to last is now a matter to be puzzled out by those responsible for the airlines' forecasts of the future.

When, based on its forecasts of profit opportunity, a company decides, for example, to make a new product or enter a new business, the next critical planning job is working out a schedule for coordinated action by all affected departments or areas of the business. Such a schedule must be worked out with reference to lead times. The longest lead-time factor, whether it be completing research, building plant, or some other element, will determine the time when the new product can be introduced initially. Once the target date for introduction has been set, other actions must be

---

[3] In these two years numerous formerly prosperous airlines on both sides of the Atlantic, including the one whose planning setup is outlined in the section that follows, went heavily into the red, with consequent changes in management.

scheduled with reference to it. Some actions must be taken five years or more ahead of time, some a year, some six months, and so forth. It is important to recognize that an action five years in advance of a target date is just as vital to accomplish on time as one three months in advance. Much of the credit for success in advance planning is the result of careful determination of lead times.

Budgeting is still another major phase of forward planning, one that starts with, or soon after, forecasting. Some top managements request that pro forma profit and loss operating budgets be presented at the time a project is brought up for approval, although the necessity for following this practice is a point of disagreement among planners. In all cases, capital budgets are prepared where plant and machinery must be acquired in connection with adoption of a project. Still another aspect of budgeting involves the concept of "strategic funds," i.e., outlays which are often charged to current income and represent expenditures (on R&D, prototype development, market research, and testing, etc.) in support of long plans or product strategy.

With this background, it is hoped that the reader will be in a better position to understand the planning systems and budgetary set-ups of companies described in the following cases.

THE COMPAGNIE ELECTRO-MÉCANIQUE

"We know very well that planning for the next five years is difficult," remarked Mr. Bougé, a member of the Plans and Budgets Staff of the Compagnie Electro-Mécanique (CEM) of France, "but we believe that we must try to plan for this period, whatever the problems we may encounter."[1] This case gives a brief history of CEM, describes the development of its planning system, and outlines the planning process being used late in 1961.

THE HISTORY OF CEM

CEM was founded in 1885; at the outset, it was chiefly a manufacturer of heavy electrical equipment for industry. From that time until the end of World War II, the company expanded the number and types of electrical equipment it manufactured but remained solely a supplier of industry. Shortly after the Second World War, the firm further expanded its line of industrial products and also moved into the manufacture of household electrical appliances. In 1961, CEM consisted of three *filiales;* these *filiales* were individual *sociétés anonymes*, or legal corporations, which in practice formed the three operating groups of the corporation. These groups were differentiated by the types of products each manufactured: Group I, unofficially called MEGACEM, had the legal title of Cie. de Construction de Gros Matériel Eelctro-Mécanique and manufactured heavy industrial electrical equipment. Group II, known legally and also unofficially as NORMACEM, manufactured medium and small electrical industrial goods. Group III, named CONORD, manufactured electrical household appliances. Exhibit 1 shows the organizational structure of CEM in 1961.

THE DEVELOPMENT OF PLANNING AT CEM

The first formal planning system was introduced at CEM in 1950. Planning activities of various sorts had been carried on by the firm prior

---

Copyright 1962 by l'Institut pour l'Etude des Méthodes de Direction de l'Entreprise (IMEDE), Lausanne, Switzerland. Reprinted by permission.

[1] All the quoted passages in this case were, unless otherwise noted, taken from case research interviews with Mr. Bougé in October, 1961. These interviews were conducted entirely in French and translated by the researcher. Mr. Bougé approved the translation.

Exhibit 1

ORGANIZATION OF CEM

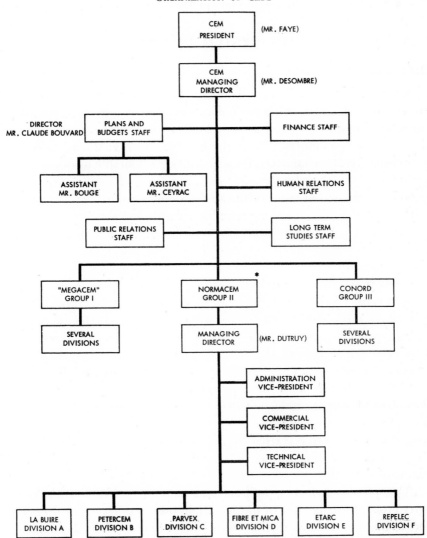

* The organization structure of the NORMACEM Group is given in detail as illustrative of the manner in which each group was organized.

to this time, but it was only in 1950 that these activities were organized into a definite framework. This first system was used to plan corporate budgets for the coming twelve months, and these forecasts were updated every four months. By 1955 it appeared to management that forecasting for one year ahead did not give sufficient information about the future to make investment decisions. Beginning in 1956, the planning period was extended to cover three years into the future. By 1957 it was evident that a three-year forecast was still not sufficient for company purposes; the beginning of 1958 saw the installation of a five-year planning period, which was the system still in use late in 1961.

THE SYSTEM IN 1961

DEFINING THE FUTURE

Mr. Bougé began: "Perhaps I should start by describing the method we use to analyze the future. We divide the future into three periods: shore-term, middle-term, and long-term, thus essentially creating three different types of 'futures.' We do this because, in our view, each of these periods has certain characteristics which make it desirable to isolate that period from the others for the purposes of analyzing what to expect. These periods are defined in terms of the business cycle and, to some extent, in terms of product life. The long-term begins at the moment when, as seen from today, the cyclical influences on our sales will be very small in comparison with the cumulative effect of long-term factors in that product line.

"Long-term considerations end at the point where we can no longer hope to predict anything useful about the technology of the product. Alternatively, the long-term ends where we cannot be certain that there will be any further demand for the product. For example, we sell turbines which are used to generate electrical energy. We cannot predict the major sources of energy much more than 25 years ahead. It may be that, after that time, nuclear, solar, or other energy sources will become vastly more important in energy production than conventional turbines, so that the long-term view for turbines must end about 25 years from now. Of course, we do not pretend to be extremely precise in establishing these points in the future, but they do serve as useful guides in our attempts to define the nature of the future.

"One problem which complicates our planning activities is that the three groups have, because of the definitions used to differentiate between short-, middle-, and long-term views, three different long-term spans. Group I's long-term span ranges from 8 or 10 years to 25 years. For Group II, the long-term is from 5 to 10 years; for Group III, from 2 to 5 years.

"We define the short-term as that period during which cyclical effects on our sales will be much more important than the effects of long-term trends. This is the reverse of our definition of the long-term. For Group I, the short-term covers from 0 to 2 years; this group manufactures its massive and complex industrial goods only to specific order, and the lead time from order to delivery is about 2 years. Group II also manufactures only to order, but its lead time from order to delivery is only about 2 weeks; this group's short-term span is from 0 to 6–12 months, depending on the specific product within the group's line. The short-term view for Group III is from 0 to about 3 weeks because of the wildly fluctuating sales of consumer appliances." The researcher pointed out that apparently the short-term was also the period during which it was possible to predict sales of a given product with near-certainty. Mr. Bougé replied that, although this was generally true, it was not the basis of the definition for the short-term view.

"Thus," Mr. Bougé continued, "we have used the foregoing criteria to define the long- and short-term for each group. Admittedly, these criteria are somewhat arbitrary, but they represent our best judgment about the manner in which to view the future. The middle-term is the gap between these periods. Thus, for Group I, it is from 2 to 8–10 years; for Group II, from about 1 to 5 years; and for Group III, from 1 to 12 months. Because of the way in which the middle-term has been derived, it is in this period that both cyclical and long-term effects on sales are very important. Another problem is that the middle-term is different for each division, and this factor also increases the complexity of planning, especially in our attempts to develop an over-all plan for CEM. Notice that so far I have not described any planning system; this introduction is merely to show the way in which, before attempting to make plans, we analyze the future."

TYPES OF PLANNING

"Now perhaps I can describe the different types of planning which we carry on. 'Short-term' planning consists simply of the routine scheduling and planning carried on by each division in its management of current operations. We do not do 'middle-term' planning as such; rather, we annually produce a unified plan and budget for CEM which covers the next five years in great detail, and it is this system which I shall presently describe. As for 'long-term' planning, this function is not performed for CEM as a whole. Rather, there is a special corporate staff for long-term studies (see Exhibit 1) which studies the long-term prospects for individual products and markets."

NEW INVESTMENTS

"Before describing our five-year planning system, I might say a few words about the process we use to make major capital investments because it is useful to have this process in mind when analyzing the planning system. We have determined that the history of a typical major CEM investment is something like this:

1. The investment possibility is conceived, either by CEM's top management, the management of one of the groups, or the management of some division.
2. For the next 12–14 months, the investment is carefully studied and, if approved, initial plans are made, in these stages:
    a) An initial decision as to whether the investment appears worthy of future study, based on rough cost and revenue estimates.
    b) If the investment appears sound, detailed studies will be made to ascertain—for example, in the case of a new factory—the cost of land, machines, plant, and starting up.
    c) The final stage of the study includes the procurement of the land, drawing up plans for the plant, and placing orders for the needed tools.
3. The investment is made. In the case of a new plant, this would involve construction of a new factory building, installation of machines, and starting up the entire process to make certain that it is working as designed. This phase of a major investment at CEM typically requires about 3 years.
4. Now, 4 years after the investment was first conceived, it begins to pay back its cost.

It takes, then, four years to implement an idea for a major investment. We have found this four-year figure to be quite accurate, whether the investment is the launching of a new product line, building a new plant, or something else. We define a 'major' investment as one requiring an outlay of perhaps 5,000,000 new francs. It is worth noting that our old, three-year planning system did not give us sufficient information about the future to deal with the four-year lead time for major investments."

THE FIVE-YEAR PLAN

"I would say that our five-year planning process has these purposes:

1. To develop, for each division and group of CEM, detailed monthly cost and revenue budgets for the coming year
2. To give yearly cost and revenue budgets for each of the subsequent four years
3. To determine which proposed investments should be made during the coming year
4. To establish effective communication between the three chief layers of management: CEM's top management, group managements, and divisional managements
5. To force the management of each division to work as a team in developing its forecasts, plans, and budgets

The planning process begins in January and ends on December 1, when Mr. Desombre, CEM's General Director, issues to all groups and divisions a document which lists:

1. Cost and revenue budgets for each group and division for the next year, broken down into four-month periods

2. Approval or rejection of all proposed investments for the coming year
3. General agreement with each division's estimated performance for each of the subsequent four years, as outlined in yearly cost and revenue budgets.

The easiest way to describe this process is as a series of steps.

Step One. From January to April, the Economics Section of the Plans and Budgets Staff, under Mr. Ceyrac, develops information on the expected economic performance of those countries which are important to CEM's sales. Ceyrac proceeds in two stages. First, he studies the economic outlook in the three major areas which concern us: the United States, the Common Market countries, and the European countries not in the Common Market. He concludes with a detailed forecast of the economy in each of these areas for the next year and also with forecasts for each of the subsequent four years. Second, in collaboration with economists from some other major French corporations, he makes the same type of forecast for the French economy."

The economic forecast produced in 1960 (for the 1961–65 plan) contained such qualitative observations as the following:

> In conclusion [for the French economy], 1961 appears to be a year of average expansion; after two mediocre years, exports, as in 1959, will be the chief growth factor, with slight assistance from private investment and consumption.[2]

> * * * * *

> The forecast expansion in the European economy for the next five years is based on current positive factors, as well as on our judgment about the tendencies of the economic policies of each country examined. This forecast is supported, to a not inconsiderable degree, by the pressures to be exercised in coming years on Western policy by the progress of the Soviet economy, because the West's position in the world is linked to the maintenance of its economic advantage over the communist countries.[2]

Step Two. "Mr. Ceyrac then does specialized studies on each industrial sector[3] which directly affects CEM's sales. This information will later be used by specialists to forecast CEM's sales in each of its product lines." Some of the quantitative data which emerged from this study included: forecast expansion or contraction of each sector, in percentages, for each of the next five years; French price and wage indices; interest rates; and such traditional economic indicators as forecast consumption and private investment.

Step Three. "In June all of this background economic information has been developed, and it is then discussed by the Plans and Budgets Staff

---

2 Translated from original document, in French, by the researcher.

3 These sectors included energy, steel, chemistry, mining and smelting, automobiles, electrical construction, textiles, buildings and public works, and transportation.

with Mr. Desombre. Mr. Desombre pays particular attention to the effects which these predicted economic trends should have on CEM policies.

Step Four. "As a result of this discussion with Mr. Desombre, he issues the 'basic document' to each group around July 15. This document contains the economic data previously developed, and it also includes a letter from Mr. Desombre which discusses the following areas:

1. General corporate policies for the next year and expected corporate policies for the four following years. Such policies might, for example, be something like: 'Because our forecast shows that interest rates will be very high for the next five years, no major investments will be undertaken until the outlook changes.'
2. Certain changes in corporate policies which, although not linked to the economic forecast, are included here.
3. Any changes in the existing corporate rules, such as how the divisions and groups are to transfer funds.
4. Detailed instructions as to the manner in which the divisions are to furnish the data called for in the following steps.

This document is sent to each division shortly after the groups have received their copies, with the exception that each division receives only that economic information pertinent to its own products. It is on this basic policy document that the cost and revenue budgets for the five-year plan are established.

Step Five. "When this document arrives at the divisions, the various experts in the technical, commercial, administrative, and other areas analyze it from their respective viewpoints. Each division's management group then estimates its monthly revenues, costs, and profits for the coming year and, on a yearly basis, for the four subsequent years. Any investment opportunities which appear worthwhile are also examined at this level and, if they appear sufficiently profitable, are formally proposed. Sometime between October 15 and 20, each division sends to its group these budgets, proposed investments, and plans, in a three-page document organized as follows:

Page 1: Sales, costs, and resulting profits forecast for each of the next five years. (Monthly for first year, yearly for the next four years.)

Proposed investments for the next year.

Number of employees expected in each of the next five years, analyzed by engineers, salaried staff, and hourly workers.

Page 2: Investments in each of the next three years, analyzed from two viewpoints:
  a) Objectives of each investment
  b) Cost of each investment, broken down into appropriate expense categories

Page 3: Financial data for the next three years:
    a) Pro forma balance sheets
    b) Pro forma cash-flow statements
    c) Projected outside financial needs

These documents form the basis for the eventual corporate budgets.

Step Six. "By November 1, each group must unify its subsidiaries' plans into an over-all plan for the group, which contains the same sort of information as in the three-page document mentioned above. In this step, the groups' managements may reject any proposed investments which they consider unsatisfactory from some viewpoint, but this is done only after discussing the investment with the division proposing it. Furthermore, if group management does not approve of an individual division's costs, revenues, or projected profits, there will be conferences between the two levels until both agree that the plan as finally submitted is the best one obtainable. This process helps to ensure that the group and its divisions understand fully the implications of their plans and budgets.

Step Seven. "On November 1, each group sends to the Plans and Budgets Staff its divisions' plans and a unified group plan. These are again examined, with the cooperation of the Finance Staff, to see whether the proposed investments are satisfactory. Then a unified plan and budget for CEM is drawn up, with projections on a four-month basis for the coming year and yearly for the subsequent four years.

Step Eight. "Finally, Mr. Desombre receives the over-all CEM plan and budget, as well as details for each group and its divisions. He will determine whether the proposed budgets for the next five years are acceptable from an over-all company standpoint. If in the course of this examination he finds proposed budgets or plans which appear unsatisfactory, he will discuss the matter with the group concerned, so that agreement can be reached that the final proposals are the best ones. Exceptionally, he may confer directly with a division if it is one of the large ones.[4] And, of course, Mr. Desombre makes the final decision as to which proposed investments should be made. He will also indicate, in a general manner, whether the plans and budgets for the last four years of the plan satisfy him. This approval is in the form of something like: 'The general tone of what you propose pleases me; later, when we know more about what to expect, we shall be able to agree on a firm plan.' His specific approval is only given for the coming year.

Step Nine. "In order to be sure that either (*a*) the plan is proceeding as expected, or (*b*) the reasons for the deviation of the plan from expecta-

---

[4] A large division, Mr. Bougé suggested, was probably one with annual sales of around 20,000,000 new francs or more.

tion are known, there is a final step taken in the process. When the plan goes into effect for a given year, each division begins to observe its adherence to, or deviation from, its projected budgets. By June of the first year, six months after the plan has begun, each division makes another set of budgets. These budgets cover the next 18 months, which is to say the last half of Year 1 and all of Year 2. The Year 2 budgets are done on a four-month basis. These budgets are sent to the groups' managements and then to Mr. Desombre, who again passes on their acceptability. Thus it is possible to keep abreast of recent developments and to modify the plan accordingly, so that it remains a useful document."

*   *   *   *   *

PROBLEMS WITH THE FIVE-YEAR PLANNING SYSTEM

"Forecasting of this sort is never easy, and, as I mentioned, we tend to find that in our five-year plan it is difficult to weigh the effects of cyclical and long-term factors on sales of our products. A second problem is that occasionally there are time lags, when the schedule to be followed in developing the various stages of the plan is not met. However, this problem is generally not a serious one and receives attention as soon as it occurs.

"Our most difficult problem is this: we have to estimate our future prices in order to estimate our revenues, but it is difficult to estimate these prices because of our dependence on our suppliers, whose prices tend to fluctuate quite unpredictably. Our suppliers generally do not do any forward planning, and so they cannot easily tell us what their prices will be, say, three years hence. Furthermore, 10 per cent of our total corporate expenses are for copper, and the price of copper notoriously fluctuates in a wildly unpredictable fashion. Nor can we forecast when the government may intervene and drastically alter the price of something we need. Steel purchases also account for 10 per cent of our total outlays, and steel prices are subject to sudden and unexpected increases. Finally, we have had the problem of some loss in the value of the French franc. The result of these difficulties is that we do not have one price-forecasting policy for all our divisions. Some divisions are expected to have nearly fixed prices for the coming five years, whereas other divisions are not.

"Prices and resulting profit margins are especially important to us in the area of financial planning. For example, if an investment will require 20,000,000 new francs, we may have to have as much as two years' advance notice to obtain this amount if outside financing is to be used.

"One problem we do not have is that of communication between the levels of management. Largely as a result of this planning system, discussions between all three levels of management are frequent and open, and thus there is excellent communication up and down the line."

*   *   *   *   *

Mr. Bougé concluded his discussion of CEM's planning system by observing that management still was not confident that it had a perfect system.

KLM—ROYAL DUTCH AIRLINES
Planning at KLM

In January, 1961, KLM was the third largest international airline in terms of "production offered" (ton-kilometers available) on international flights and the eighth largest airline in the world in terms of total production offered. Since 1955, KLM's production had increased almost 50 per cent to a level of 540 million ton-km. available in 1959. During 1960, the company operated a flight network of over 268,000 km., regularly served 108 airports in 77 countries and carried 3,000 passengers, 8,700 kg. of mail, and over 85,000 kg. of freight each day. Comparative operating statistics for the period 1955–59 are presented in Exhibit 1 and financial data are presented in Exhibits 2 and 3.

COMPANY HISTORY

KLM was founded in The Hague on October 7, 1919, by the late Dr. Albert Plesman, a 30-year-old lieutenant in the Dutch Air Force. Seven months later, the first regularly scheduled air service in the world was inaugurated between Amsterdam and London. This service was operated with open-cabin, single-engine De Havilland DH-9 biplanes, which had been chartered from Aircraft Transport & Travel Ltd. of London. The two passengers on each flight were provided with leather coats, flying goggles, and flying helmets. The travel time varied from 4 to 40 hours, depending on the amount of engine trouble encountered. By October 31, 1920, KLM had carried 345 passengers, 3 tons of mail, and 22 tons of freight.

KLM developed rapidly in the following years. As aircraft were developed with greater dependability, speed, range, and passenger capacity, it was possible to establish air routes over longer distances. By 1939, KLM's 12,960-km. European network included 36 cities.

From the beginning, flights to countries outside Europe were contemplated, and special thought was given to a possible air connection with Indonesia. A fortnightly experimental service between Amsterdam and

This case was prepared by Mr. John Archer under the supervision of Professor Ralph M. Hower.

Copyright 1961 by l'Institut pour l'Etude des Méthodes de Direction de l'Entreprise (IMEDE), Lausanne, Switzerland. Reprinted by permission.

Exhibit 1

COMPARATIVE OPERATING STATISTICS, 1955-59

	1955	1956	1957	1958	1959
Production:					
Ton kms. available.................	364,900,000	406,700,000	460,800,000	475,000,000	540,000,000
Km. flown.........................	58,600,000	63,400,000	70,000,000	69,500,000	77,500,000
Hours flown.......................	169,000	181,000	196,000	188,000	207,000
Average distance per aircraft hour (in km.)........	348	351	357	369	374
Average available load capacity per aircraft (in kg.).	6,220	6,420	6,590	6,840	6,970
Average daily utilization:					
Long-haul aircraft.................	7 hrs. 40 min.	7 hrs. 50 min.	7 hrs. 50 min.	7 hrs. 20 min.	8 hrs.
Convair and Viscount aircraft......	5 hrs.	5 hrs. 10 min.	4 hrs. 50 min.	3 hrs. 50 min.	4 hrs. 20 min.
Traffic (total):					
Number of passengers carried......	725,000	822,000	913,000	941,000	1,104,000
Weight of freight carried (in kg.)...	20,372,000	23,739,000	24,992,000	26,014,000	31,178,000
Weight of mail carried (in kg.).....	2,294,000	2,630,000	2,919,000	2,838,000	3,192,000
Average distance flown (in km.)					
Passengers......................	2,330	2,310	2,320	2,260	2,220
Freight (each package)...........	2,670	2,720	2,790	2,750	2,800
Mail (each bag).................	3,950	3,750	3,570	3,360	3,850
Traffic (on scheduled services):					
Passenger km....................	1,479,500,000	1,737,000,000	1,996,300,000	2,012,100,000	2,255,900,000
Passenger load factor (per cent)...	59.7	61.5	59.5	53.1	54.1
Passenger/Baggage ton-km........	138,800,000	161,700,000	184,700,000	185,400,000	208,300,000
Freight ton-km..................	52,700,000	63,100,000	69,000,000	71,100,000	87,000,000
Mail ton-km....................	9,100,000	9,900,000	10,400,000	9,600,000	12,300,000
Total traffic in ton-km...........	200,600,000	234,700,000	264,100,000	266,100,000	307,600,000
Load factor (per cent)...........	58.5	60.5	59.6	57.6	59.3
Traffic Revenue (guilders)					
Passengers and baggage..........	257,466,000	304,075,000	356,208,000	353,024,000	381,523,000
Freight.........................	52,053,000	61,522,000	69,757,000	71,324,000	81,672,000
Mail............................	24,059,000	26,267,000	27,925,000	25,285,000	28,842,000
Special flights..................	14,509,000	13,783,000	13,472,000	12,361,000	16,692,000
Total..........................	348,087,000	405,647,000	467,362,000	461,994,000	508,729,000

Jakarta was started in 1929. The experimental flights became a scheduled service on September 25, 1930. By this time, the duration of the journey had been reduced to 12 days or 89 flying hours; the first flight in 1924 required 55 days because of engine trouble. Until 1940, KLM's Amsterdam-Jakarta line was the longest scheduled air route in the world—over 14,000 km.

The air service between Amsterdam and Jakarta provided KLM with a sound basis for expanding its network. In view of the need for air transportation in the West Indies, a plane was flown to Curaçao, and in early 1935 flights were inaugurated between Curaçao and Aruba. Until then, that journey took 8 hours by boat; the aircraft reduced this to 45 minutes. In the following years, additional services were started, and by 1939 the company's West Indies division had a route network of 2,700 km.

The Second World War halted the development of KLM in Europe; the only European route operating throughout the war was from Bristol

Exhibit 2

BALANCE SHEET, DECEMBER 31, 1959, AND DECEMBER 31, 1958
(After appropriation of profit)

ASSETS	December 31, 1959 Guilders (in 000's)		December 31, 1958 Guilders (in 000's)	
Flight equipment:				
Cost of aircraft, engines and spare parts	539,861		508,904	
Depreciation	306,205		263,623	
	233,656		245,281	
Advance payments on aircraft on order	117,756		69,260	
		351,412		314,541
Maintenance supplies		24,308		23,309
Other fixed assets:				
Buildings, inventories, etc.	137,107		129,003	
Depreciation	55,857		53,161	
		81,250		75,842
Miscellaneous supplies		7,840		7,452
Investments in and advances to affiliated and				
subsidiary companies		9,428		10,182
Employers' Liability Act deposit		1,765		1,866
Receivables:				
Accounts receivable	81,520		63,496	
Prepaid expenses	31,926		28,217	
		113,446		91,713
Other current assets:				
Investments	16,808		39,894	
Cash and bank balances	80,828		57,078	
		97,636		96,972
		687,085		621,877

Exhibit 2—Continued

CAPITAL AND LIABILITIES	December 31, 1958 Guilders (in 000's)		December 31, 1959 Guilders (in 000's)	
Capital stock and reserves:				
Common stock	147,919		147,919	
Less: Reacquired common stock	2,500		5,000	
	145,419		142,919	
Priority shares	35		35	
		145,454		142,954
Reserves		113,882		113,026
Unappropriated profit		117		73
Provisions for taxes and sundry risks		69,898		78,487
Convertible subordinated debentures		70,300		......
Loans:				
Long-term loans	106,000		51,800	
Other loans	46,750		130,442	
		152,750		182,242
Current liabilities:				
Accounts payable and accrued liabilities	69,329		58,490	
Unearned revenue	59,537		40,887	
		128,866		99,377
Dividend declared	10,181		10,006	
Less: Interim dividend paid	4,363		4,288	
		5,818		5,718
		687,085		621,877
Note: Commitments in respect of current orders and guarantees		342,000		317,000

to Lisbon and Gibraltar. The company's home base at Amsterdam's Schiphol Airport was closed for commercial aviation and was heavily damaged during the German occupation. The activities in the West Indies were not hampered, and, in fact, the network there was extended during the war.

In May, 1945, a new start was made in Europe with the reconstruction of Schiphol Airport, and four months later KLM reopened its first services in Europe. These were domestic flights which were to be maintained until normal surface transportation was available. In December, 1945, KLM resumed its first international service to Copenhagen, and during 1946 it resumed operations to Brussels, Basel, London, Oslo, Paris, Prague, Stockholm, and Zurich, and opened new services to Geneva, Glasgow, and Madrid.

Outside Europe, the old connections with the Near East and the Far East were quickly restored. On May 27, 1946, KLM became the first European airline to open a service to New York after the war. Since that time, Rio de Janeiro, Buenos Aires, Tokyo, Sydney, Moscow, and many other cities have been added to KLM's network.

The company's postwar reconstruction also included modernization of

Exhibit 3

PROFIT AND LOSS ACCOUNT FOR THE YEAR ENDED DECEMBER 31, 1959

	Guilders (in 000's)	
	1959	1958
Operating revenue:		
Transportation revenue	508,729	461,994
Other revenue*	36,652	34,200
	545,381	496,194
Operating expenses:		
Salaries, wages and social expenses	182,549	171,404
Materials, services rendered by third parties and sundries	209,461	179,286
Fuel and oil	75,182	70,248
	467,192	420,938
	78,189	75,256
Depreciation on flight equipment	58,256	62,247
Depreciation on other fixed assets	10,565	11,119
Balance operating revenue and expenses	9,368	1,890
Profit on sales of obsolete aircraft, etc.	5,532	5,321
Balance other income and (deductions)	(2,813)	(1,835)
Profit before taxes and initial costs in respect of new fleet	12,087	5,376
Initial costs in respect of new fleet	8,994	3,018
Released from the provision for taxes on profits	12,330	10,740
Net earnings	15,423	13,098

* Under mutual service agreements concluded with other airlines, at a number of stations the handling and maintenance work for the aircraft of these companies is conducted at cost. In previous years, revenue derived from this source was deducted from operating expenses. It is now included in "Other revenue" and the figures for 1958 have been regrouped in the same manner.

the fleet. The operational core of the KLM fleet in early 1961 consisted of seven Douglas DC-8's, and another five were scheduled for delivery during the course of the year. In total, the company operated about 80 aircraft, including 12 Lockheed Electras, 15 DC-7's, and 9 Vickers Viscounts.

CORPORATE ORGANIZATION

In 1961, KLM's organization consisted of a top-management group which included its president, deputy president, five executive vice-presidents, and eight functional divisions headed by senior vice-presidents (see Exhibit 4). The executive vice-presidents did not have operational responsibility for particular divisions but performed such specialized functions as aircraft procurement and the negotiation of KLM's international traffic agreements. As a group, they were responsible for over-all supervision of

Exhibit 4

GENERAL ORGANIZATION CHART

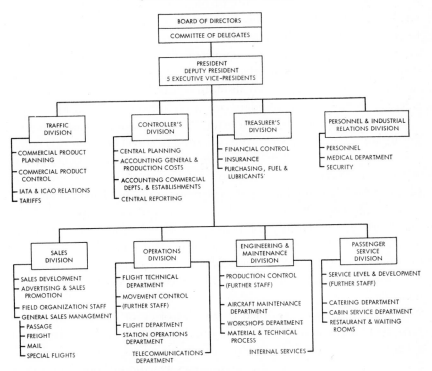

the company and for the determination of broad company policies. In addition, the top-management group approved all plans and budgets submitted by the functional divisions.

KLM'S PLANNING ORGANIZATION

Planning at KLM was viewed primarily as a way of helping the company achieve its objectives. These objectives were identified by one executive as follows: continuity of activity, corporate growth combined with the ability to provide workers with steady employment, and a continued capacity to operate as a nonsubsidized, profit-making organization.

The planning function at KLM was performed at several points within the organization. The commercial product planning department within the traffic division was responsible for the short-range planning which resulted in the company's published schedule. Long-range and medium-range planning was coordinated and administered by the central planning department within the controller's division. In addition, each of the operating divisions maintained its own planning organization.

The Commercial Product Planning Department. Mr. van Leuven, the director of commercial product planning, stated that the final product offered to the market in the form of the company's timetable was the net result of an eternal compromise between three factors: the public demand for service as seen by the sales managers abroad, the capacity of the fleet after allowing for maintenance requirements, and the availability of qualified crews. He pointed out that he excluded safety from this list because safety was considered to be an absolute at KLM; no action would be considered if it violated the standards of safety adhered to by KLM.

The public demand for service could be expressed in terms of the time during the day when most travelers desired to travel between two points. For instance, the peak demand for flights between Amsterdam and London occurred between 9 A.M. and 6 P.M. Therefore, it would not be sensible to schedule a flight at 3 A.M., when no significant demand existed.

Although fleet capacity could be varied in the long-term, the number of aircraft was practically completely fixed in the short-term. A certain flexibility for planning purposes, however, still could be found in the distribution of the different types of aircraft over the routes and in the adaptation of maintenance systems to the demands of the most saleable schedules.

The availability of qualified crews was often of critical importance. First, there was a serious shortage of qualified flying personnel, and it was a lengthy process to hire and train crew members. And, second, once trained and assigned to a route, flight crews were limited both in the number of total hours they could fly within a given period and in the rest time required between flights. On the route between Amsterdam and Sydney, for example, these requirements resulted in the use of three different crews "slipping" at en route stations.

"Our job, therefore," Mr. van Leuven said, "is to find the optimum balance between these three factors, and this optimum is expressed by our schedules. Of course, this process is a continuous one we can never start from scratch in our planning activities because we already have a fleet, a route pattern, crews, and a sales organization in operation.

"Although finding this balance is a problem that can be solved by compromise, we try to find the 'sharpest' compromises. Therefore, close contact with the responsible managers of the operating divisions is required because they have to stick their necks out and each of them has to guarantee that his part of the compromise can be realized. This contact is made possible by bringing these responsible managers together in the exploitation committee. This committee is composed of the executive vice-president with major experience in operations; the senior vice-presidents of the sales, operations, maintenance, and passenger services divisions; the controller; and the head of the commercial product planning department. It serves as the major link between plans and the day-to-day operations of the company. At its Wednesday morning meetings the committee makes all decisions about changes in planned fleet operations during the following 12 months. The committee works with a written agenda, and decisions are usually made on the basis of staff studies of the particular problem under consideration. The above-mentioned optimum which is aimed at in every decision should be interpreted as: what is best from a profitability viewpoint. The handling of this 'tuning-fork' [yardstick] is the specific duty of the controller in this committee."

On Wednesday afternoons the heads of the planning organizations within the operating divisions usually met with Mr. van Leuven to discuss topics related to the problems brought up at the exploitation committee meeting.

Mr. van Leuven described a simple problem as representative of those often discussed by the exploitation committee: "A few weeks ago, the sales division wanted to increase the frequency of flights on a particular route from 14 to 15 per week. The representative of the maintenance division was asked to determine the effect of this change on its schedule, and the operations division was consulted about the effect on crews. When the committee met the following Wednesday, these problems had been studied, and the committee was able to agree to change the plan and grant the sales division's request. Because of the advance notice and investigation of the change, the operating divisions were not surprised when the decision was announced and were able to implement it smoothly.

"I think it would be incorrect to think that the planning at KLM is done by the people designated as planners on the organization chart," Mr. van Leuven said. "While a formal description of our planning process might give this impression, there is really a very complete integration between our planning and operating activities. The exploitation committee provides a good illustration of this integration. As a committee it plans and changes established plans, but as individuals its members are almost all operating people—the only people who have both the knowledge and the experience required to plan and implement plans.

"I should add," he continued, "that about 85 per cent of the problems brought to the exploitation committee are initiated by the sales and traffic divisions. This is not surprising when you realize that these are the divisions which are primarily concerned with reacting to changes in the external environment, where almost all need for adjustments in operations originates. We are not flying to fly but to earn money by serving the public demand. So we should start with finding out what the market wants us to do."

The Commercial Product Control Department. The commercial product control department within the traffic division, although not a planning organization in the strictest sense of the word, performed a function closely related to planning. It may be called micro-planning, or very short-range planning. This department was responsible for coordinating the daily activities of the fleet when it became necessary to depart from the published timetable. A central communications center located at Schiphol Airport was in continuous contact with each of KLM's operations centers throughout the world, and all decisions concerning changes in the planned flying schedule were made at this center. For instance, if a KLM flight destined for Tokyo was delayed at Karachi because of engine trouble, the commercial product control department would decide whether to delay the flight until the engine was repaired, send a relief aircraft to continue the flight, or cancel the rest of the flight and try to transfer the passengers to other lines.

These short-range adaptations of the fixed schedules occurred regularly, and large sums were at stake when making these decisions, which, in fact, were being taken at a relatively low level. Therefore, attempts had been made to develop certain rules for making these decisions. For instance, air-freight flights between New York and Europe could now and then be cancelled and the freight shifted to other flights if the loss of revenue was less than the out-of-pocket expenses of the flight. Mr. van Leuven added, however, that a balance had to be made between the use of these decision guides and the desirability of allowing the people in the center to use their best judgment, even when it violated the established guides. "We do not want to freeze out the spirit of improvisation," he remarked. "These people, who are facing these incidents every day, get a lot of know-how themselves. Moreover, they can always rely on and in practice often do rely heavily on the opinions of the people in the operating divisions which are also located at Schiphol. When the need for a change occurs, the control personnel can immediately contact the people in the operating divisions concerned and ask their advice in the matter."

The Central Planning Department. The central planning department was part of KLM's controller's division. The controller, Mr. van Erp, had previously been the director of central planning, and at that time his organization had functioned as a staff reporting directly to the top-management group. He retained over-all responsibility for central planning when he assumed his present position.

In January, 1961, the central planning department consisted of Mr. van Putten, the head of the department, two technicians, two economic specialists, and four assistants. Most of the staff had come to the department from the line organization and were thus familiar with operating problems and considerations. The others had been trained within the department. In discussing his organization, Mr. van Putten remarked: "You have to have experience in order to convince others that your ideas are sound, and selling planning to our colleagues is our most important activity." Mr. van Putten had been with KLM for 12 years and was 35 years old. After graduating from high school, he attended night classes at the University of Rotterdam. He was currently completing his dissertation for his doctorate in the area of company planning.

Mr. van Putten said that the name "central planning" was somewhat misleading because "here at KLM the central planning department does not do the planning. Our planning process is really built around two basic objectives: first, we try to keep the decision power about planning in the hands of those people responsible for carrying out the plans—in the line organizations of the sales, operations, and maintenance divisions. And, second, we try to put as much thinking as possible into our plans and the planning process. To fulfill these objectives, we help coordinate the planning activities of the line organizations, and we try to teach them how to plan. We get the operating divisions to do the actual planning, and we are ready to help them when it is needed. But our planning function is an informal one, and, as long as the planners in the operating divisions are doing their jobs correctly, we in central planning will not bother them. I try to maintain a close personal relationship with the divisional planners, and we usually get together for lunch at least twice a week. During the warm summer weather we sometimes all pile in a boat and go fishing on our own time. They are all my personal friends, so this type of informal contact is possible.

"I am personally watching to see that our planning activities do not become too formal. If this were to happen, I'm afraid that the whole planning function would break down and competition rather than cooperation between the different people would develop. At one time we tried to build up a formal planning network extending throughout the company with strictly established planning methods, but it just didn't work out. The result is that today we have formal planning departments only in the key functions, such as operations and sales.

"In addition to working with the divisional planners, we provide a service to top management by translating its expressions of basic objectives into a form that can be used by the line divisions to plan. Thus planning is decentralized to the people who know best how to operate— who know how to execute plans. But, first, we have to obtain basic decisions from top management and convert them into forms useful to operating people. Subsequently, we have to bring the products of decentralized planning into a form suitable for top management. We then pass the completed plans back up to top management for their approval."

Mr. van Putten emphasized the importance of his department's function of translating broad corporate objectives into a form on which plans to fulfill these objectives could be based. "The major problem facing any enterprise is, of course, 'How do we stay profitable?' We have a product which is our airline and its organization. How do we exploit or use this product today so that we can continue to be profitable in the long run? How do we repay the funds that must be paid back, and how do we ensure that we can obtain new funds in the future? In other words, how do we stay alive? The basic objectives should answer these questions. They should also answer the questions of how big we should grow, what we should look like next year and five years from now.

"But these basic objectives are always abstract, and they must be linked in some way to today's business. The most difficult part of planning is to be able to know just what top management wants. Sometimes top management doesn't volunteer this information, and it is necessary for the central planning department to press them a bit. In this sense, central planning acts as the conscience of top management. Moreover, my department also has a responsibility for the coordination of the plans during their development and finally also for the quality of the plans developed. I believe that in this function we should also be able to warn top management when difficulties are approaching."

THE DEVELOPMENT OF THE PLANNING FUNCTION AT KLM

Planning at KLM had its origin in 1945 with the rebirth of the company after the Second World War. There was no organized operational or short-term planning, however, and the central planning department at that time reported only to the top-management group. This department was primarily concerned with developing long-range plans and with policy formulation.

From 1945 to 1948, the company operated with a centralized accounting department. Although this department prepared forecasts of costs and revenue by divisions, these were not considered to be operating budgets. And, while the divisional executives considered these forecasts to be interesting figures, they were not looked upon as a goal to be achieved.

It soon became apparent that this centralized forecasting and accounting system was not effective. The company was operating at a loss, and there were indications that the operating executives did not really understand the cost information and forecasts they were receiving from the accounting department.

In 1949, after the appointment of a new controller, KLM's accounting system was decentralized, with the establishment of 11 separate accounting departments in the divisions. The only accounting functions which continued to be centralized were revenue and payroll accounting. And several months later a budget system was initiated which required the divisions to build up their own estimates of costs and revenue.

KLM executives believed that the subsequent improvement in operating efficiency and the resulting return to profitable operations could be attributed in large part to the introduction of a budget and to the decentralization of accounting. Operating executives appeared to have gained a much better understanding of the cost data generated within their organizations and were thus able to work more effectively with it.

Because of the success of the budget system and its emphasis on short-term planning, the activities of the central planning department were reduced to those of planning policies and objectives, without translating these objectives into operating language. Almost all attention was thus being devoted to short-term goals.

In spite of the improved performance after 1949, KLM's management believed that a continued reliance only on a budgetary planning system was inadequate. The budgets submitted by the operating divisions were usually discussed during the first week of the budgetary period. By this time, however, many expenses during the period had already been fixed as a result of actions taken in the past. Thus, if a review of the proposed budgets indicated that they would result in an unsatisfactory rate of profitability, too few items within them were subject to change.

KLM's management realized, therefore, that, in order to discuss the budgets at a time when useful measures could be taken to change them, it would be necessary to prepare preliminary or provisional budgets six to eight months in advance of the budget period. This objective was achieved by enlarging the functions of the central planning department and by dividing the planning process, described below, into three time periods: (1) a three- to seven-year plan dealing with the objectives and policies of the company; (2) a one- to two-year detailed plan expressed in operational terms; and (3) a six-month budget. This budget was really a further refinement of the first half year of the two-year plan.

Mr. van Erp, the vice-president-accounting, became the vice-president-planning. At that time, 1956, the central planning department submitted plans to the divisions which were prepared in broad terms by a staff of between 15 and 20 people.

Between 1956 and 1961 several organizational changes were also developed, and this brought about some changes which KLM executives in 1961 thought had resulted in a workable setup. In 1958 Mr. van Erp was appointed controller in charge of accounting and central planning. However, the responsibility for KLM's short-term planning was given to the commercial product planning department. At the same time, the exploitation committee was formed in order to coordinate the short-term budgetary and operational planning activities of the line divisions. The commercial product planning department had been established in order to provide the more detailed planning required to determine the services to be flown, the type of aircraft to be used on each route, the scheduling of arrival and departure times, and the planning of connecting services. It consisted mainly of a route planning department (12 employees) and a scheduling department (20 employees).

During the period of 1956–58, as divisional planning departments were established and assumed the responsibility for actually preparing their own plans, the staff of the central planning department was gradually reduced to about five people. A separate budget office was also established which reported to Mr. van Erp.

In 1958 the present organizational structure was achieved when this budget office was combined with the central planning department, and Mr. van Putten, the head of the budget office, was named the department head.

THE PLANNING PROCESS

The first step in long-range planning at KLM, according to Mr. van Putten, was a determination of the demand for air transport within a period of two to eight years in the future. To keep the forecasting effort within manageable limits, demand estimates were limited to 10 to 15 countries in which KLM did about 80 per cent of its business. "In the central planning department we try to discover how international air traffic develops, how it is affected by international business cycles, and what political limitations will be placed on KLM's development," Mr. van Putten said.

"This last factor is particularly important when we try to anticipate the routes that will be available to us in the future. The air is not free like the sea. We trust it will eventually become free; we hope it will be free in 10 or 15 years, but at present the air is politically controlled, with countries granting landing privileges in return for similar privileges in other countries. For example, we would like to participate in the stream of traffic between the West Coast of the United States and South America. But since this traffic stream does not touch the Netherlands, it is not politically feasible for us to do so.

"And, finally, after estimating future demands, we try to determine the size and composition of the fleet required to serve this demand. Each route has its own characteristics in terms of number and types of passengers, distances involved, and competition, and to serve each route precisely we would need at least 15 different types of aircraft. The relatively small volume on the individual route segments, however, necessitates some degree of aircraft standardization."

This external forecast of production was then compared with the company's objectives for growth and route development established by the top-management group. Mr. van Putten met with the executive vice-presidents, both as a group and individually, to discuss the assumptions about the number of planes and route frequencies which had to be made to translate objectives into operating plans. Estimates of demand and the type of fleet required to meet the demand in the period three to seven years in the future represented the company's long-range plan. These data were made available only to the top-management group.

This same information in the period from one to three years in the future formed the basis of KLM's medium-range planning. The assumptions about number of aircraft and route frequencies were given to the line divisions, which were instructed to formulate operational plans based upon them. The plans of the line divisions were then coordinated by the central planning department. Mr. van Putten emphasized that in this process his department acted only as a catalyst. "It does not actually *do* the planning," he said. For instance, the plan of the operations division calling for a particular number of flight hours would be compared with the plan of the maintenance division, and if they were incompatible in any way, the central planning department would work with the two line divisions to arrive at a mutually agreeable adjustment in their plans.

During the period of coordinating the divisional plans, Mr. van Putten said there were frequently times when he was asked to present alternative planning proposals to divisional executives. "During these conferences," he said, "I have to be extremely careful not to indicate my preference for a particular plan. Selecting among the alternatives is a job for the line organization, and people tend to become emotionally attached to a particular point of view. If I ever showed favoritism toward one group over another, it would make it very difficult to get the cooperation of that group in the future."

After the plans of the different divisions were reconciled, the divisions prepared detailed forecasts of costs and revenue based upon them. When combined, these forecasts were presented in the form of a profit and loss projection by area, route, and type of aircraft. The revenue required to cover operating expenses, dividends, and other cash flows was then compared with the estimated revenue to determine the financial effects of the planned operations. This financial projection was then submitted to the top-management group for approval. In some cases the projected profits were not acceptable to the top management, and, when this occurred, the top executives would have to adjust either the company's objectives or the assumptions on which the plan had been based. These changes would then be resubmitted to the line divisions and new plans drawn up.

Mr. van Putten pointed out that sometimes many alternative plans could potentially meet the objectives set by top management. "It is not feasible, however," he said, "to have each of the alternative plans worked out in detail and sent to top management for approval. In the first place, to do such a job would require a large staff utilizing many man-hours or extremely expensive electronic equipment. And, in the second place, top management would have to spend so much time just reading and analyzing the proposals that they wouldn't have sufficient time to reach a sound conclusion. Therefore, the planning people at higher levels, either in the central planning department or the operating divisions, must select two or three of the various alternative plans for submission to top management."

When the financial estimate was approved, it was distributed to the line divisions during December and formed the basis for the last step in the planning process, the formulation of detailed operating budgets. For budgetary purposes, the company divided the year into a summer season, from April 1 to September 30, and a winter season, from October 1 to March 31. During the first quarter of each calendar year, all the departments developed their budgets for the coming summer season and repeated the process for the winter season during the third quarter. Mr. van Putten pointed out that while the two- to three-year plan was distributed only as low in the organization as the intermediate executives in the operating divisions, the budget was sent to the lowest levels of the company where some degree of cost accountability could be established.

In order to have the budgets built up and expressed in such a way that they could later be compared with actual results, the central reporting department of the controller's division consolidated the divisional budgets.

After the detailed budgets and plans were developed and returned to the operating divisions, it was frequently necessary to make changes in them. Adjustments in the plan during a period one or two years in the future were made in a manner similar to the changes made while the plan was being developed, i.e., with the central planning department coordinating the work of the line organization. To make changes in the plan which would have their effect in the immediate future required a more direct form of coordination, which formed one of the tasks of the above-mentioned exploitation committee.

Although the personnel and industrial relations division was not represented on the exploitation committee and did not have a separate planning organization, Mr. van Putten hoped that the division could be brought into the regular planning process. He was dicussing future personnel requirements with the division's management and was attempting to demonstrate the importance of long-range planning.

Another function of the central planning department was to contribute to the company's management development program. During KLM's regularly scheduled management courses, time was provided for Mr. van Putten to explain the basic objectives of the company and the steps which were being taken to meet them.

In addition, frequent meetings were held with KLM's representatives abroad and with people who were not normally in touch with broad company operations, such as the flying personnel. "At these meetings," Mr. van Putten explained, "we tell them of future developments and explain the 'hows,' 'whys,' and 'whens.' "

In general, Mr. van Putten was satisfied with the planning system used at KLM. His main concern was to try to find a better solution to the following problem: "As the planning period for a year draws to an end and the time for operations under the plan approaches, a greater and greater percentage of the plan becomes fixed. By December, for instance, about 70 per cent of the items in the plan for the following summer season are not subject to change; the flying and maintenance schedules and the crew assignments are almost in their final form, and there is only time to make rather minor adjustments. Thus, when the plan goes to the top-management group for their approval, they sometimes feel that they do not have as complete control over the situation as they would like to have. I don't think this means that we should change our system, but it does make it particularly important for those of us connected with planning to make sure that our plans are an accurate reflection of the policies and objectives originally set by top management.

"We also have a potential problem in that we always translate operational proposals into financial terms. For instance, if the sales division wants to put on a special flight, we will tell them how it will affect the division's budget. Executives are naturally disappointed when something they want to do is shown to be very costly and perhaps even unprofitable."

THE MEASUREMENT OF PERFORMANCE

The primary means of measuring actual performance against planned performance at KLM was the "10-Day" report on traffic revenue developed by the controller's division. Three times each month, estimated and actual revenues by route and by the different revenue classifications (passenger, freight, and mail revenue) were compared by means of this report. Year-to-date figures were also compared with like data for the previous year.

The second major measurement of performance was the "Flash Report." This report was a profit and loss statement submitted to management by the 15th of each month covering operations in the previous month. All data in this report were expressed in the form of an index number, with 100 representing last year's performance. Thus quick comparisons could be made, and any significant deviations between the two periods or between budget and actual data could be brought to management's attention.

The Flash Report was replaced by a final monthly profit and loss statement about 30 days after the end of each month. Mr. van Erp noted, however, that the Flash Report was quite accurate and that it was used for KLM's quarterly financial report to the New York Stock Exchange.

The top-management group did not regularly receive the reports mentioned above. Once a month they received a financial review expressed in somewhat broader terms. They did receive, however, even more detailed studies on request.

Comparisons between forecasts and actual performance were usually limited to forecasts made in the immediate past. "We are constantly revising our forecasts as we go along," Mr. van Erp said, "and we are not very interested in knowing in 1960 how we thought 1960 would turn out in 1956."

A NOTE ON THE
INTERNATIONAL AIR TRANSPORT INDUSTRY

This note gives a brief description of the international air transport industry, with particular emphasis on industry development and organization after World War II and on problems affecting long-range planning. Selected comparative statistics for major companies in the industry are also presented.

I. INDUSTRY DEVELOPMENT AND ORGANIZATION

DEVELOPMENT TO 1959

World air traffic increased enormously in the period following the Second World War. This was due not only to such external factors as population growth, higher personal incomes, and increased world trade but also to such internal industry forces as fare reductions, the introduction of economy flights of several sorts, and the introduction of better service in general, as a result of better aircraft, more frequent flights, and increasing attention to passenger comfort. From 1952 to 1959, industry production (measured in ton-kilometers of capacity offered rather than ton-kilometers utilized) increased 115 per cent[1] (Exhibit 1). Comparative financial data on 13 major international carriers and two large United States domestic airlines are presented in Exhibit 2. Selected operating ratios for these same companies are presented in Exhibit 3.

ORGANIZATION OF THE INDUSTRY

The international air transport industry, which included public, semi-public, and private corporations, was itself semipublic in character, since air traffic laws involved questions of national sovereignty. The "public interest" was also involved in questions of safety. Consequently, com-

---

[1] "Industry" here includes those airlines whose countries were represented in the International Civil Air Organization.

This note condenses data contained in SWISSAIR (A-1) and SWISSAIR (A-2) prepared by Mr. L. K. Jonas, Mr. B. R. Scott, and Mr. R. C. K. Valtz under the supervision of Professors A. B. Moss or E. P. Learned.

Copyright 1962 by l'Institut pour l'Etude des Méthodes de Direction de l'Entreprise (IMEDE), Lausanne, Switzerland. Reprinted by permission.

Exhibit 1

PRODUCTION OFFERED—ALL ICAO AIRLINES

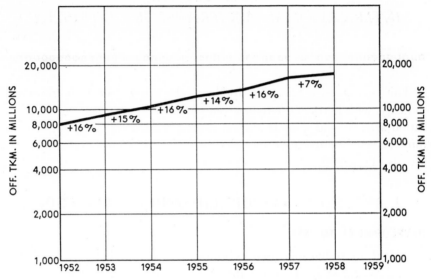

Source: Swissair.

petitors were subject to many governmental restrictions on their operations and on their ability to compete with each other. Also, agreements between various firms tended further to limit competition. Finally, competition was regulated by two international organizations: the International Civil Aviation Organization (ICAO) and the International Air Transport Association (IATA).

ICAO represented about 80 member governments whose countries accounted for almost all international air traffic.[2] Member nations were represented in ICAO by their national air authorities. ICAO's objectives were to establish a framework of rules, regulations, and agreements which would help to create and coordinate international air traffic. This framework formed the basis for bilateral agreements between the member countries for the exchange of "traffic rights." (Traffic rights, which were arrived at by bargaining, permitted air carriers of one nation to fly over and/or land in another country. Some such agreements were made for a specified length of time; most were of indefinite length, with either party having the option to cancel with one year's notice.)

IATA was a voluntary association of 89 international airline companies. Its objectives were to promote safe, regular, and economic international air transport and to provide means for the development of col-

---

[2] Russia was not a member, although Poland and Czechoslovakia were.

Exhibit 2

COMPARISONS OF 13 MAJOR WORLD AIRLINES, 1958
Production in millions of tkm. and Profit & Loss Statements in millions of Swiss francs

ITEM	UAL	TWA	PAA	AF	BOAC	KLM	TCA	SAS	BEA	SAB	SWISSAIR	WAL	DLH
Production in Mil. tkm.													
Offered tkm.	1,551.4	1,299.0	1,243.9	618.2	550.0	475.0	453.2	397.9	264.4	226.2	184.4	180.2	157.3
Utilized tkm.	896.8	750.9	781.1	390.7	313.5	273.6	270.8	203.1	159.7	156.0	111.1	82.8	78.9
Load factor in %	57.8	57.8	62.8	63.0	55.3	57.6	59.8	51.0	60.4	69.0	60.1	45.9	50.8
Income Statement													
Total Revenue	1,405.2	1,259.4	1,387.3	963.8	710.1*	576.4	527.9	487.3	413.2	322.8	248.9	157.7	188.2
Passengers and Surplus Baggage	1,255.9	1,095.9	1,046.9	630.2	518.5	413.0	448.9	384.7	327.2	250.0	186.9	138.5	143.5
Freight	82.9	49.6	145.6	133.2	64.5	83.4	28.6	35.2	25.8	33.5	23.2	5.7	13.7
Mail	47.1	53.2	102.0		123.8	29.6	43.3	29.7	20.9	19.1	17.6	3.2	18.8
Other	19.3	60.7	92.8	200.4	3.3	50.4	7.1	37.7	39.3	20.2	21.2	10.3	12.2
Total Costs	1,342.9	1,267.1	1,365.1	962.1	772.4	561.5	525.5	487.3	411.6	322.8	243.8	151.6	221.6
Operating	384.1	392.9	405.1	--	193.8	--	114.0	--	96.1	--	60.7	44.6	50.8
Maintenance	246.8	245.4	211.8	--	182.6	--	133.0	--	62.2	--	33.1	18.6	35.5
Depreciation	125.8	131.0	136.6	87.1	65.4	70.9	43.2	41.3	31.0	17.8	21.8	18.0	25.3
Ground Handling	193.4	186.9	205.0	--	63.5	--	97.8	--	106.7	--	38.2	21.5	40.7
Passenger Service	101.1	85.7	102.9	--	50.6	--	34.8	--	18.6	--	15.0	11.7	12.9
Selling and Advertising	138.0	157.0	209.2	--	119.5	--	73.6	--	40.6	--	55.5	20.2	41.0
Administrative	58.9	43.6	65.9	57.8	25.8	--	18.2	12.2	35.6	--	12.2	8.9	10.0
Financing Costs and Taxes	94.8	24.6	28.6	67.4	71.2	--	10.9	--	20.8	8.0	7.3	8.1	5.4
Profit or Loss	62.3	-7.7	22.2	1.7	-63.2	14.9	2.4	--	1.6	--	5.1	6.1	-33.4
Dividends as % of Share Capital	4.8	--	93.7	--	--	7.0	--	--	--	--	5.5	78.9	--
Dividends as % of Total Equity	1.3	--	3.7	--	--	3.9	--	--	--	--	5.0	3.9	--
Exchange Rate	4.36	4.36	4.36	103.80	12.21	113.86	4.36	84.21	12.21	8.72	--	4.36	103.83

Income Statement in SFr. per 100 off. tkm.

ITEM	UAL		TWA		PAA		AF		BOAC		KLM		TCA		SAS		BEA		SAB		SWISSAIR		WAL		DLH	
	Fr.	%	Fr.	%	Fr.	%	Fr.	%	Fr.	%	Fr.	%	Fr.	%	Fr.	%	Fr.	%	Fr.	%	Fr.	%	Fr.	%	Fr.	%
Total Revenue	90	100	97	99	112	100	156	100	129	92	121	100	117	100	122	100	156	100	143	100	135	100	87	100	120	85
Passengers and Surplus Baggage	81	90	84	86	84	76	102	65	94	67	86	72	100	86	123	79	111	78	108	91	100	75	76	88	91	65
Freight	5	6	4	4	12	10	22	14	12	8	18	14	6	5	9	7	10	6	15	10	13	9	3	4	9	6
Mail	3	3	4	4	8	7			22	16	6	5	10	8	7	6	8	5	8	6	10	7	2	2	12	8
Other	1	1	5	5	8	7	32	21	1	1	11	9	2	1	9	8	15	10	9	6	11	9	6	6	8	6
Total Costs	86	96	98	100	110	98	156	100	140	100	118	97	116	99	122	100	155	99	143	100	132	98	84	96	141	100
Operating	24	27	31	32	33	29	--	--	35	26	--	--	25	21	--	--	36	23	--	--	32	24	25	28	33	23
Maintenance	16	18	19	19	17	15	--	--	33	24	--	--	30	25	--	--	24	15	--	--	18	13	11	12	23	16
Depreciation	8	9	10	10	11	10	14	9	12	8	15	12	10	8	10	8	12	8	8	6	12	9	10	11	16	11
Ground Handling	12	14	14	15	17	15	--	--	12	8	--	--	22	19	--	--	40	25	--	--	21	15	12	14	26	18
Passenger-Service	7	7	7	7	8	7	--	--	9	7	--	--	7	7	--	--	7	4	--	--	8	6	7	8	7	6
Selling and Advertising	9	10	12	12	17	15	--	--	21	15	--	--	16	14	--	--	15	10	--	--	30	23	11	13	26	19
Administrative	4	4	3	3	5	5	9	6	5	3	--	--	4	3	3	3	13	9	--	--	7	5	5	6	6	5
Financing Costs & Taxes	6	7	2	2	2	2	11	7	13	9	--	--	2	2	--	--	8	5	4	2	4	3	4	5	3	2
Profit or Loss	4	4	-1	-1	2	2	0	0	-11	-8	3	3	1	1	--	--	1	1	--	--	3	2	3	4	-21	-15

* Not including loss of preceding year, research and development costs related to the Comet (jet), and losses incurred on sale of aircraft.

Source: Taken from published company annual reports by Swissair's finance department, statistics section.

laboration among international airlines. At the most important IATA meetings, the annual traffic conferences, the agenda typically considered such topics as (1) the maintenance of a "stable and fair" pattern of fares, (2) types of service to be offered on various routes, and (3) the standardization of documents, ticket contracts, and accounting procedures, so as to permit quick interline bookings and connections.

INDUSTRY COMPETITION

In general, as the above suggests, industry agreements had largely ruled out the possibility of price competition among industry members.[3] As a

[3] The industry also had a minor, but significant, competition from two sources not represented in IATA. Certain strictly national carriers (airlines flying only within the borders of

result, competition tended to center around (1) the *date* of introduction of a new type of aircraft, since all airlines would eventually have much the same type of aircraft; (2) the schedule offered; and (3) the quality of passenger service. An airline's growth tended to depend on the excellence with which it competed in these areas and on its success in advertising and promotion; these internal factors were generally within an airline's control. Other important factors affecting growth were of a type which the individual airline could not control. These included (1) the "home" nation's bargaining power for traffic rights, (2) the economic relationship between the airline and its government, and (3) the size of the home nation's internal market. The home nation's bargaining power for traffic rights depended on such variables as the nation's size, location, and economic and political importance. The airlines could request their respective governments to attempt to secure especially desirable routes, but the success of a government in this regard was outside the airline's control. If an airline were subsidized by its government, it might be a more effective competitor, through the ability to take on routes regardless of profitability. Finally, an airline's growth was obviously affected by the size of its home market and by the number of competitors which it had in this market.

INDUSTRY COOPERATION

The competitive structure of the industry was also affected by certain types of alliances between various airlines:

Pooled Flights were flights between two or more points served by two carriers; revenues from such flights were "pooled" and then divided according to a formula. Pooling was considered advantageous for the customer because it tended to decrease the concentration of flights at peak traffic times, thus ensuring a better spacing of flights; its advantage to the companies was that it eliminated possible severe competition on these routes.

Rationalization of facilities was a practice whereby several airlines serving an airport would agree to share the costs of common facilities, especially for aircraft maintenance, thus eliminating costly duplication of facilities. In 1960, the practice was not yet widespread, although it had been notably successful in some instances.

---

a single country) flew routes which duplicated certain routes of the international carriers. This competition was most common in the United States of America, where, for example, a passenger from Los Angeles to Copenhagen could go from Los Angeles to New York on either a national or an international airline. The second source of competition was from small international airlines not in IATA, such as Icelandic Airlines or the BIATA group of 30 airlines operating throughout the British Commonwealth. The airlines in this latter group had influence far greater than their small traffic volume would indicate, because they could upset the IATA rate structure by rate cutting.

Exhibit 3

SELECTED OPERATING RATIOS OF 13 MAJOR WORLD AIRLINES, 1958

a) Aircraft Utilization

Company	Hours per Day	in %
DLH*	9.8	41
PAA	8.3	35
UAL	7.4	31
TWA	7.0	29
SAS	7.0	29
TCA	6.8	28
SWISSAIR	6.7	28
BOAC	6.7	28
AF	5.4	23
KLM	5.2	22
BEA	4.6	19
SAB	4.3	19

b) Load Factor 1957–1958

Rank 1958	Rank 1957	Company	1958 %	1957 %	% of change
1	1	SAB	69.0	72.1	-3.1
2	2	AF	63.0	67.5	-4.5
3	4	PAA	62.8	63.4	-0.6
4	3	BEA	60.4	63.7	-3.3
5	5	SWISSAIR	60.1	61.6	-1.5
6	8	TCA	59.8	59.5	+0.3
7	9	TWA	57.8	57.2	+0.6
8	10	UAL	57.8	56.6	+1.2
9	7	KLM	57.6	59.6	-2.0
10	6	BOAC	55.3	60.5	-5.2
11	13	SAS	51.0	49.8	+1.2
12	12	DLH	50.8	53.2	-2.4
13	11	WAL	45.9	54.1	-8.2

c)

Rank	Company	Revenue per 100 off.tkm. Fr.	Load Factor %	Passenger Revenue per Passenger–km (Fr./Km. x 100)
1	AF	156	63.0	19.4
2	BEA	156	60.4	20.6
3	SAB	143	69.0	19.4
4	SWISSAIR	135	60.1	20.3
5	BOAC	129	55.3	20.7
6	SAS	122	51.0	20.6
7	KLM	121	57.6	20.5
8	DLH	120	50.8	21.6
9	TCA	117	59.8	17.2
10	PAA	112	62.8	16.7
11	TWA	97	57.8	14.8
12	UAL	90	57.8	15.0
13	WAL	87	45.9	16.1

d)

Company	Off. tkm per Employee	Costs per 100 off. tkm in Fr.
UAL	75,990	86
WAL	67,740	84
TWA	67,490	98
PAA	57,460	100
TCA	45,840	116
SWISSAIR	35,700	132
SAS	34,260	122
AF	31,310	156
DLH	28,650	141
BOAC	28,500	140
KLM	27,950	118
BEA	23,380	155
SAB	21,240	143

e)

Company		Revenue per Employee Fr.
American and Canadian Companies:	UAL	68,828
	TWA	65,430
	PAA	64,079
	WAL	59,286
	TCA	53,404
European Companies:	AF	48,817
	SWISSAIR	48,190
	SAS	41,954
	BOAC	36,791
	BEA	36,537
	DLH	34,281
	KLM	33,916
	SAB	30,316

f)

Company	Profit as a % of Revenue	Revenue to Total Assets Ratio	Profit as a % of Assets
	%		%
SWISSAIR	2.05	1.22	2.50
AF	0.18	1.14	0.21
BEA	0.39	0.75	0.29
BOAC	-8.90	0.43	-3.83
DLH	-17.75	0.76	-13.49
KLM	2.59	0.82	2.12
SAB	0.00	0.60	0.00
SAS	0.00	1.19	0.00
PAA	1.60	0.97	1.55
TCA	0.45	1.16	0.52
TWA	-0.61	1.15	-0.70
UAL	4.43	1.05	4.65
WAL	3.87	0.78	3.02

g) Costs, Revenue and Profit per 100 off. tkm. 1958

Company	Net Profit After Taxes Fr.	Revenue Fr.	Costs Fr.	Net Profit as a % of Share Capital
UAL	4	90	86	13.3
WAL	3	87	84	7.4
KLM	3	121	118	5.1
SWISSAIR	3	135	132	7.4
PAA	2	112	110	3.8
BEA	1	156	155	0.7
TCA	1	117	116	3.1
AF	0	156	156	1.1
SAB	0	143	143	0
SAS	0	122	122	0
TWA	- 1	97	98	- 1.6
BOAC	-11	129	140	- 8.6
DLH	-21	120	141	-26.8

* A Swissair executive explained Lufthansa's high aircraft utilization by saying that the company's fleet was very modern, since it grew big so recently, and that it was still very short of planes. He explained that Lufthansa expanded its long-term routes first and had given cabotage rights to other carriers, e.g., Pan American.

Source: Calculated and tabulated by Swissair from published annual reports (see Exhibit 3).

Technical Assistance in the form of an exchange of information was not a recent development in the industry, particularly where such information related to safety. However, with the initiation of airline services by the developing countries, plus their desire for jet equipment, technical cooperation was assuming a more important role.

Standardization of jet aircraft and equipment had been adopted by some airlines. Under this practice, airlines agreed to buy identical types of jet aircraft, including all systems within the aircraft, such as electronic and kitchen equipment. This practice permitted savings in (1) purchase price, through combining to place larger orders; (2) reduced spare-parts inventories; (3) rationalization of aircraft maintenance; (4) greater flexibility in the use of equipment by making it interchangeable; and (5) sharing of information on operation and maintenance of the new aircraft.

In a more comprehensive agreement, four airlines have proposed forming a consortium, called Air Union, to pool all of their international services; the original participants were Air France, Sabena, Lufthansa, and Alitalia.[4] There was increasing speculation that many other international airlines, especially the smaller ones, might be interested in joining either Air Union or the Swissair-Sas combine, in order to maintain their positions in an industry which was increasingly feeling the strains of competition.

PREDICTIONS OF OVERCAPACITY

Noting that industry capacity was expected to increase by 30 per cent in 1960 and by a like amount in 1961, industry executives foresaw a threat of overcapacity for at least a limited time. Executives of one company believed serious overcapacity could have two important effects on their operation, depending in part upon how various airlines might react to such a problem. Overcapacity itself would tend to reduce load factors for all airlines. If price cutting were to accompany overcapacity, revenues would decline to whatever extent they were not compensated for by an increase in traffic volume. Speaking of a possible breakdown in the price-setting machinery, one executive stated: "This is always a problem that develops when competitors agree on prices but do not establish production quotas."

II. PROBLEMS OF LONG-RANGE PLANNING

There were a number of factors in the international air transport industry not found to the same extent in many other industries that markedly

---

[4] As of December, 1962, the long-planned pool was expected to begin operating within the next two months.

affected the long-term planning function. These were (1) rapid technological change, (2) the nature of the industry's product, (3) the importance of cost control, (4) the necessity for absolute passenger safety, and (5) the effect of industry and governmental agreements.

TECHNOLOGICAL INNOVATION AND ITS EFFECTS

One of the most dramatic forces in the air transport industry was the rapidity of technological change and the resulting rapidity of obsolescence. Exhibit 4 shows some of the important characteristics of the various aircraft used by the industry during the last 25 years. This exhibit indicates the rapidity with which passenger aircraft have been improved from the standpoints of capacity and speed.

Exhibit 4

TYPICAL AIRCRAFT USED BY INTERNATIONAL AIR CARRIERS

	1936	1951	1961
Typical aircraft used by industry	DC-2	Convair 240 DC-6B	Caravelle DC-8 Convair 880
Passenger capacity per aircraft per flight	14	CV-240: 40 DC-6B: 70	Caravelle: 70 DC-8: 121 CV-880: 86
Aircraft speed: km/hr	228	300	760
Average loading capacity per aircraft	1.3 tons	3.3 tons	11.2 tons
Price of aircraft without spare parts (Mill. Swiss francs)	DC-2: 0.25	CV-240: 1.9 DC-6B: 6.0	Caravelle: 11.0 DC-8: 24.5 CV-880: 16.5
Delivery time (from order date to delivery)	6 - 9 months	2 years	2 - 4 years
Typical flying hours per day per aircraft	1 - 2	4 - 5	9 - 10
Cost of equipment and buildings per aircraft (Mill. Swiss francs)	0.5	6.0	25 (approx.)

Source: Swissair.

Some industry observers believed that the pace of technological improvement in the industry was accelerating. One industry executive pointed out that, during its approximately 50 years of development, the piston-engined passenger aircraft attained a maximum speed of about 500 kilometers per hour. Subsonic jets have nearly doubled this speed in a short change-over period. It appeared possible, according to this executive, that within the next 15 years passenger aircraft would attain speeds of 2,200 to 3,500 k.p.h. and that within 50 years jet aircraft would be replaced by passenger-carrying rockets capable of many thousand kilometers per hour.

Airlines were generally forced by competitive conditions to take advantage of this technological improvement as quickly as it occurred because their product could be differentiated only by the quality of service offered. An important feature of this service was the excellence of the aircraft in such respects as speed, comfort, and safety. Competitive pressure, according to industry executives, was usually so intense that all major airlines were forced to acquire a new type of aircraft at about the same time. Some members of the industry feared that failure to offer the latest aircraft might result in a disastrous loss of sales. In short, the pattern was one of accelerating technological change forced upon the industry.

This pattern of rapid change had four important effects on forward planning in the industry:

First, modern passenger aircraft were extremely complicated to manufacture, resulting in a long "lead time" from order date until delivery. As can be seen in Exhibit 4, this lead time might be as much as four years. Considerable lead time was also required to train crews to operate the new aircraft and to erect the facilities needed to service and house the new fleet. Thus careful planning of future aircraft requirements had to be conducted up to four years in advance, lest a competitor gain a distinct advantage by being quicker to offer the newest type of plane.

Second, by any previous industry standard a modern jet aircraft required an enormous investment, especially when the cost of the necessary facilities and equipment was included. As Exhibit 4 shows, in 1951 the latest passenger aircraft, the DC-6B, cost 12 million francs complete with equipment and facilities. In 1961, the total cost of the new DC-8, including equipment and facilities, was about 50 million francs. This huge increase in required capital investment demanded that careful financial plans be prepared for approximately five years in advance, if the funds to pay for new aircraft were to be available.

Third, because of its high initial cost and the threat of its rapid obsolescence, a modern jet aircraft had to be used as much of the time as possible, so that it would pay for itself before becoming outdated. Daily hours of usage per aircraft rose markedly after 1936 (Exhibit 4). Without such heavy usage, a modern jet fleet would be uneconomical. The consequent need for careful planning, if the fleet was to be utilized to the optimum, is evident.

Fourth, the jet aircraft's initial cost tended to make it uneconomical for most airlines to keep a spare DC-8 on hand for emergencies, and this reduced an airline's flexibility to maneuver. Typically, only the few largest airlines could afford to have spare production capacity in the form of expensive jet planes which were allowed to stand idle most of the time.

THE NATURE OF THE PRODUCT

The airlines were also faced with a difficult product or service problem. Their product was the capacity of the aircraft at a given time and over a given route. Such a product could not be stored in inventory to provide protection against variations in customer demand. In order to achieve maximum sales, plans had to be made so that the proper amount of capacity was in the proper place when demand materialized. As a result, careful market estimates had to be made long in advance of production, since routes and schedules were normally fixed for considerable periods of time. Market estimates were also needed to plan future aircraft needs. The difficulty of making such estimates two to five years ahead considerably complicated the airline's planning problems.

IMPORTANCE OF COST CONTROL

The airlines in general could do little over the short run to increase demand for their services, as one executive observed. Advertising, promotional campaigns, and other such sales tools had more a long-run effect than a short-run value. Thus an airline could view its revenues for the coming six months to one year as being essentially fixed, unless the route schedules underwent major alterations. Such major alterations were generally not practicable within less than a year's time. Since revenues were thus fixed, the airlines profitability depended to a great extent on its ability to control its costs very closely. "Cost control is probably our major problem," the executive remarked.

PASSENGER SAFETY

For obvious reasons, the airline industry could never make any plan which compromised passenger and crew safety. This tended to reduce an airline's flexibility. In contrast, a conventional manufacturer could often use an improperly trained worker or an imperfect machine, if he was willing to absorb the resulting higher production costs of inferior labor or equipment. In the airline industry, a poorly trained crew or defective aircraft was a definite threat to safety and therefore could not be considered.

One industry executive pointed out that the cost of absolute safety was becoming enormous. The airlines were forced to buy virtually any device which promised to increase passenger safety, no matter how slightly. "Absolute safety is both necessary and desirable," he said, "but expenditures for new safety devices should be carefully examined to be certain that such outlays will actually contribute to increased safety."

GOVERNMENTAL AND INDUSTRY AGREEMENTS

An international airline operated at the pleasure of foreign governments. These governments granted privileges, such as traffic rights; they imposed restrictions, such as those governing the routes and aircraft types that might be used. If these privileges or restrictions were changed, the airline's revenue and, indeed, its entire pattern of operations might be severely affected.

As of 1959, the members of the IATA, accounting for some 95 per cent of international air traffic, had an established rate structure which aided in estimating future revenues. There was, however, no guarantee that this stable rate pattern would continue; the possibility of an industry rate war was regarded as very real.

The reader will perceive that the dependence of any international airline on the current pattern of traffic rights and fares was considerable. The industry's forward planning was complicated not only by uncertainty as to future fares and traffic rights but also by the possibility that the Russian national airline might be greatly expanded to enter the industry as a formidable competitor. Presumably, the Soviet airline, if it decided to compete aggressively in international air transport, would not be restricted by profit considerations, and Russia would probably have great power in bargaining for traffic rights.

*   *   *   *   *

This note has not attempted to present a comprehensive view of the international air transport industry. The emphasis has rather been on (1) presenting a framework for the industry with which to judge the performance of an individual airline and (2) giving the reader some appreciation for those special features of the industry which made planning so complicated a function.

PLANNING IN X CORPORATION

The X Corporation, after a long discussion on the place of long-range planning in the company, prepared the following summary consisting of three parts: (A) the concept of planning at X Corporation, (B) the job of the planning director or planning coordinator at the X Corporation, and (C) some qualifications needed for the job of planning director or planning coordinator at X Corporation. The company may be considered to have essentially a three-divisional organization, each division representing a separate business. One division produced materials processed by a second division. Originally, the third division used some materials or products produced by the second division, but its opportunity and possible scope permitted it to expand independently of either the first or the second divisions. The three sections, A, B, and C, follow:

A. THE CONCEPT OF PLANNING AT X CORPORATION

1. The chief executive officer is responsible for planning.

2. He needs the guidance and advice of a planning committee or other top-management group to establish the long-range growth and profitability objectives of the company.

3. He needs the direct and full-time help of a planning director or planning coordinator to develop comprehensive plans to achieve those long-range objectives. The planning director should be a man of stature, who participates in the deliberations of the planning committee and who has the ability to coordinate the plans of each of our three businesses into a cohesive, challenging, and acceptable long-range plan for corporate growth and profitability.

4. The top planning man will not do the planning for each of our three businesses. Each business will be obligated to develop its own long-range plans on a basis consistent with the corporate objectives and the over-all corporate plan. The top planning director or planning coordinator will advise, guide, and stimulate the planners within each of the three businesses and will coordinate the results of their efforts.

B. THE JOB OF THE PLANNING DIRECTOR OR PLANNING COORDINATOR AT X CORPORATION

1. On behalf of the president, to stimulate and encourage planning throughout the organization.

2. To coordinate the long-range planning activities of each of our three businesses.

3. To review and assemble the plans made by each of our three businesses.

4. To investigate opportunities for corporate growth and expansion of a type that would not normally be encompassed by the plans of any one of our three businesses. This would include participation, along with other members of top management, in the investigation of acquisition or merger possibilities.

5. To submit to the president, at least annually, a comprehensive plan for corporate growth and profitability for ten years ahead.

6. To evaluate results and trends in relation to the long-range plan. This evaluation would aid the operating departments in keeping their activities "on target" with the plan. It should also facilitate appropriate and timely modifications in plans in order to keep the plans realistic and attainable, as well as challenging.

To fulfill these responsibilities and to provide effective coordination, the planning director will:

a) Provide general information and guidance with respect to economic trends and conditions that appear likely to have a long-term effect on the activities and objectives of the company and on the plans to achieve those objectives.

b) Provide background information for the use of the planning committee in developing and reviewing long-range objectives.

c) Furnish, at least annually, basic economic assumptions and estimates of future economic conditions, to promote consistency in planning work throughout the company.

d) Provide advice, guidance, and liaison services to department managers and to planners within the various departments.

e) Obtain periodically from each of our three businesses comprehensive plans for ten years ahead; suggest appropriate modifications or expansion of the plans of each of the businesses; suggest new possibilities for consideration.

f) Consider opportunities and potentialities of research discoveries in relation to long-range planning.

g) Maintain analytical summaries of companies which appear to be

likely candidates for merger with, or acquisition by, X Corporation.

h) Develop or obtain detailed information for top-management consideration on companies which are immediate candidates for merger with, or acquisition by, X Corporation.

i) Analyze opportunities for corporate growth and expansion through
diversification beyond our present three businesses, whenever such
analysis is approved or requested by the president or the planning
committee.

j) Maintain or obtain reports and charts that compare results and
trends with the long-range plan; suggest improvements and modifications in reports and in control and evaluation techniques; evaluate results and trends in relation to the long-range plan and report
thereon to the president.

C. SOME QUALIFICATIONS NEEDED FOR THE JOB OF PLANNING DIRECTOR OR PLANNING COORDINATOR AT X CORPORATION

Prerequisites

1. *Age.* There is sufficient time before his normal retirement date
to develop effective planning.

2. *Availability.* There is a successor ready for his present job, or he
can be spared from his present job. (An outsider may be considered.)

Qualifications (not necessarily in order of importance)

3. *Demonstrated ability to plan* business activities (inside or outside
X Corporation).

4. Apart from previously demonstrated ability, evident *Business sense*
and *Capacity to plan* comprehensively and realistically.

5. Background in and understanding of *Economics.* (This does not
necessarily imply advanced academic training.)

6. *Ability to analyze and evaluate* performance in relation to the long-
range plan, and to suggest performance measures and explanatory
reports that will provide appropriate, adequate, and timely information.

7. *Imagination.* The capacity to see the shape of things to come as
contrasted with a tendency merely to extrapolate present trends.

8. *Flexibility.* A readiness to change his opinions in the light of new
information and a willingness to accept the judgments, guidance,
and criticism of others.

9. *Drive.* Initiative and disciplined persistence.

10. *Understanding of long-range problems.*
11. *Understanding of the various aspects of X Corporation's business as well as of the industry.*
12. *Acceptability.* The selection of this particular man would make sense to the company generally.
13. Negotiating or *Coordinating ability.* He can influence and convince managers and planners within our three businesses to achieve effective planning results.
14. *Stature in industry.* He is known and accepted in the industry. He has a wide acquaintance with men in other companies and with bankers and leaders or planners in other industries.
15. *Ability to lead and stimulate* subordinates and associates. He can provide leadership to planners within the various departments and effectively chair meetings of management groups.

ECONOMIC PLANNING IN FRANCE

In the following material, data on economic planning in France are discussed under four main headings: historical backgrounds; the planning framework—principles and mechanism; Plans II and III; and Plan IV (1962–65). In addition, some current 1961 comments and opinions on planning—especially French planning—are included as an Appendix.

PART I. HISTORICAL BACKGROUND

The French planning commission, the so-called "Commissariat Général du Plan," was created by a decree of January 3, 1946, to coordinate the preparation of the different parts of a "Modernisation and Equipment Plan" and to report on its execution annually.

The provisional Government of the Republic, then headed by General de Gaulle, was strongly dominated by left-of-centre ministers. This political climate led to nationalizations in industry, banking, and insurance and resulted in demands for a state-planned economy to supplement the market mechanisms which had been inadequate to cope with the social and economic problems created by the depression in the 1930's. The consequences of the war and of the occupation also made it imperative that a concerted effort be made to obtain the maximum national income from the limited resources available. Not only did France have damage to repair, but she also had to catch up on the progress made by the other industrial nations during the 1930–40 decade, when France's economy had remained stagnant.[1] Later, another factor in the establishment of a national planning body was the Marshall Plan, which, since 1948, called on the recipient countries for a more systematic presentation of the economic objectives towards which the allocated funds would be used.

The first "Modernisation and Equipment Plan," for the period 1947–50, later extended to 1953, in order to fit in with the terminal date of the Marshall Plan, was drafted under the leadership of Jean Monnet, who was convinced that the French Plan would be successful only if it was a collective enterprise and if all those who were going to implement it, in

This case was prepared by Mr. Harold Ehrenstrom under the supervision of Professor Pierre Goetschin.

[1] Between 1929 and 1938, industrial production actually fell by 25 per cent.

the private as well as in the public sector, took part in drawing it up.

The First Plan was conceived for immediate economic recovery and reconstruction and its fundamental concept was that most of the investment resources were to be concentrated on six "basic" sectors having a driving influence on the over-all and long-term industrial and agricultural development. The selected sectors were coal, steel, electricity, cement, farm machinery, and transport, to which fuels and fertilizers were soon to be added.

Commissions were created to set up production and investment objectives in each sector. They had to determine, in physical terms, the maximum production that could be reached in the period, taking into consideration the availability of labour, raw materials, energy, and the trend in demand. From these assumptions the commissions formulated proposals for new capacity and investment. The Plan called for a rise in production by 1950 of 25 per cent above the 1929 level.

When the Plan ended in 1953, after a downward revision of some targets, its more modest objectives had been approximately attained. In relation to the year 1946, production had increased by 15 per cent for coal, 75 per cent for electricity, 140 per cent for steel, and 150 per cent for cement.

Jean Monnet left the Plan in 1952 to head the European Coal and Steel Community, and one of his aides, Etienne Hirsch, became "Commissaire Général au Plan" when the elements of the Second Plan were being put together.

The Second Plan, which was to be summitted to Parliament for the first time, covered the four years 1954 to 1957, and was defined as "an instrument for orientating the economy and the framework of investment programmes." It differed from its predecessor in that priority was no longer given only to a few key industries but to over-all growth. The new plan was extended so as to cover a much larger portion of the economy, including agriculture, housing, manufacturing, and the development of overseas territories. Hirsch's main problem, then, was to ensure that Monnet's methods remained effective when embracing the whole economy, without the incentives provided by the Marshall Plan or the restrictions resulting from physical controls which were progressively dropped. The "vertical commissions," organised by sector, were then combined with "horizontal commissions," whose task it was to coordinate the projects with respect to their manpower and financial requirements.

The establishment of a national accounting system gave the planners a more accurate tool to measure the economy, to forecast economic aggregates, and to ensure a greater consistency of the various parts of the plan. The emphasis in the Second Plan was put not only on increased production but also on better quality, lower costs, more competitive prices, as well as on the need to encourage scientific and technical research, to develop specialisation of firms, training facilities, and on the improvement of marketing.

The general goal—expressed for the first time in aggregate terms—was to increase the index of gross national product from 100 to 125, through a 35 per cent increase in industrial production and a 20 per cent increase in agricultural production. By 1957, all goals had been surpassed, although at the cost of severe imbalances. Furthermore, excess demand and a tight labour market had led to inflationary wage increases. As a result of the over-expansion of internal demand, imports went up and exports down, and a serious balance-of-payments crisis soon imperilled the position of the franc.

It was in these circumstances that the Third Plan (1958–61) was drafted. Its aims were again to achieve a significant economic expansion, while the maintenance of stability and of the equilibrium of the balance of payments was to receive greater attention. The national product was to increase by 20 per cent in the four years. At the same time, the Plan aimed at preparing France's economy, which had long remained isolated and protectionist, for entry into the European Common Market. It also had to take into consideration the increasing supply of labour resulting from a higher birth rate in previous years.

The Third Plan ran into trouble as a result of the structural disequilibrium in the economy and of the austerity which had been imposed upon the country in 1958–59, after de Gaulle had returned to power. In those years the GNP increased only by 2½ per cent each year. A decisive turning point for the French economy occurred, however, on December 27, 1958, when a timely 15 per cent devaluation took place. The success of the devaluation signalled a new upturn of the economy, and an *"interim plan"* was published in the spring of 1960, taking into account the consequences of the 1957–58 payments and currency crisis and calling for an 11 per cent growth over the two remaining years of the Third Plan. Most of the goals of the interim plan were achieved at the end of 1961. Though production fell a little behind the original schedule, the French economy was again in equilibrium.

In 1959, under the direction of Pierre Massé, a former electrical utility official who took over from Etienne Hirsch, the long process leading to the elaboration of the Fourth Plan (1962–65) began.

PART II. THE PLANNING FRAMEWORK—PRINCIPLES AND MECHANISM

The French planning system has grown in the past 15 years from an effort to determine in which places growth should take place and to direct public and private resources towards them, to a concerted development programme for the whole economy. This "concerted economy" (*économie concertée*) is about halfway between an economy controlled directly by the state and one in which the various sectors or enterprises operate without concern for where they fit into the over-all picture. It is an attempt to reconcile rapid growth with a general economic equilibrium in an atmosphere of free enterprise. The plan, in its authors' view, is less an option on a definite economic system than an instrument of choice for action.

At its inception, the system has definitely been helped by the fact that France already had a kind of mixed economy in which about one-half of gross investment originates with the public sector or is directly controlled by it. It has a large state-owned industrial sector, including electricity (Electricité de France), railways (Société nationale des chemins de fer français), gas (Gaz de France), coal (Charbonnages de France), etc. Then, too, there are closer links in France between the state administration and industry than in most other countries. Industrialists tend to keep in touch with government departments, and many have worked in both sectors. This is partly because the tradition of government is fairly interventionist, and the government has maintained direct control over the credit system. Through the "Crédit National," for instance, which is a private bank whose operations are controlled by the state, nationalized industries and private companies complying with the objectives of the Plan can get cheaper loans than on the open market.

Similarly, the movement towards economic planning was reinforced by the fact that the "laissez-faire" doctrine had lost most of its appeal and adherents since the depression. Furthermore, in the absence of sufficient private savings, the state had to take over much of the financing of private investment and played an important role in many industries. Officials of the "Commissariat Général du Plan"[2] originally numbered about 40, and they have not increased since then, despite the wide extension of the field they have to cover.[3] This means that the Commissariat has to obtain the cooperation of numerous specialized bodies, both in the government and in the private sector.

Its position in the French administration is quite independent. During the first years it was a branch of the Prime Minister's office; but, since 1954, it has been under the Ministry of Finance and Economic Affairs, although it has not been incorporated into this Ministry and its status has

---

[2] The full name is "Commissariat Général du Plan d'Equipement et de la Productivité."
[3] The total staff, including secretaries and chauffeurs, has increased from 100 to 140, mainly due to the absorption, in 1959, of the former Commissariat for Productivity.

remained extra-departmental. This was essential to enlist the cooperation of industry as a partner.

The planning officials must work with many other governmental or private bodies. The "Economic and Financial Studies Department" of the Finance Ministry helps with the preliminary outlines. The "Investment and Planning Section" of the Economic and Social Council, an assembly of representatives of all the main national interests, is consulted about the general objectives of the Plan. Much of the detailed work involved in the preparation of projections and statistics is undertaken in cooperation with the "National Institute for Economic and Statistical Studies" and the "National Institute for Demographic Studies." The CREDOC (Consumption Research and Documentation Centre) establishes most of the projections of private consumption trends.

The French planning system also includes a nominally top council, the "Conseil Supérieur du Plan," which meets twice a year to "supervise" the elaboration of the Plan. It is composed of ministers, employers' representatives, trade unionists, etc. According to *The Economist*, the secret of the French success is that the Conseil Supérieur has been completely dormant and powerless. It is generally agreed that the Conseil Supérieur is too large (57 members) to be effective and that if, with its balance of divergent interests, it tried to be the real initiator of French planning, the result would be disastrous.

One essential feature of the planning system is that it is a collective effort and that it associates those who are going to implement it, directly or indirectly, with the preparation of the Plan. This explains, for instance, the degree of detail into which discussions of industrial trends have gone, with over 3,000 representatives of different economic sectors and industries, in order to determine the projections of future demand to which capital investments by government and private industry are geared.

M. Pierre Massé, Commissaire Général du Plan, explained the French planning system during a three-day conference organised in London, on April 20–22, 1961, by the National Institute of Economic and Social Research. He stated:

> The Plan is not the citadel of a clan or a group, but a meeting place. The role of the Commissariat Général inside the administrative and governmental machinery is confined to that of proposing, advising and estimating. It takes part in discussions and prepares decisions, but it manages no funds and has itself no powers of intervention. No department or ministry has reason to fear its encroachment on their field; but it provides the administration as a whole with the opportunity of co-ordinating its schemes and solving its conflicts on neutral ground.
>
> The main strength of the Commissariat Général is that it is a permanent meeting place for the exchange of information and discussion of the plans, both of the

administration and of the business world. The main agent for such cooperation has always been the "Modernisation Commissions." These consist of up to 50 people, seldom more, who are not paid for their work in helping to draw up the Plan and who are appointed by the government on the Commissaire Général's recommendations. There are such commissions for each of the main sectors of the economy. The members of all these commissions are of three main types: heads of firms and leaders of employers' associations; workers, all four big unions having representatives on the commissions; and officials of the departments involved. Experts, mostly with academic background, and users' representatives make up the rest of the commissions. No rigorous proportions are required in the composition of the commissions; the spirit counts more than the letter, and the commissions seek agreement and not majority votes.

The aim is not to referee between winners and losers, but to piece together a picture of future economic and social activity in connection with national development. In proposing this organisation, Jean Monnet hoped to achieve a real mobilisation of expertise, all the more necessary since available statistics did not provide sufficient material for a small team of specialists to draw up the Plan. Furthermore, he was convinced that those who worked together on the Plan would automatically attend to its execution, thus greatly reducing the need for governmental intervention. Experience has shown he was right.

The drawing-up of the Plan goes through three distinct phases (Exhibit 1). First, the Commissariat staff, in association with the Department of Economic and Financial Studies of the Finance Ministry, sketches several alternative estimates of what the increases in demand in various sectors are likely to be, according to various assumptions about the rate of growth of the gross national product. Then a preliminary decision is taken by the government regarding the selection of a maximum growth rate which seems possible without endangering the equilibrium of the economy, that is, which is compatible with full employment, equality of investments and savings, and a balance of public finance and foreign trade. Consultations also take place at this stage with the Investment and Planning Section of the Economic and Social Council.

After a target for growth has been selected, a more extensive draft of the Plan is prepared for the second phase, which involves detailed discussions in the Modernisation Commissions.

An important aspect of the system is that the Modernisation Commissions do not draw up the plans or projections of demand themselves. The Commissariat makes the original estimates, and the Commissions merely pass comments on the technical difficulties attached to them. There are now 22 "horizontal" commissions which deal with different industries or branches of special activity[4] and 5 dealing with problems that are common

---

[4] Chemicals, fuels, housing, education, commerce, manufacturing industries, agriculture, etc.

Exhibit 1

PROCEDURE OF ELABORATION OF THE FOURTH PLAN

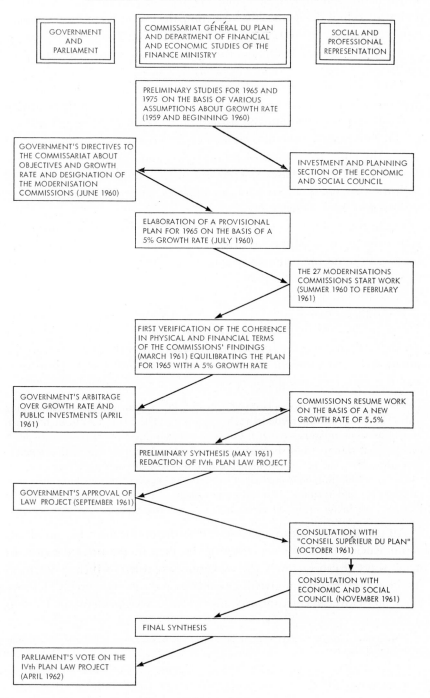

to all sectors.[5] For the Third Plan (1958–61), there were 19 Commissions which had 615 members, of whom 113 represented the Administration, 134 were technical experts, 206 were company executives, 57 were labour-union officials, 25 were farmers, 23 were university professors or judges, 13 were bankers, and 41 represented various groups such as hotel keepers, craftsmen, doctors, and family associations.

The Commissions are usually composed of several specialised subcom-missions and industrial working parties. The dicussions in these groups provide data for checking the assumptions which have been made re-garding the rate of growth, the technological coefficients in input-output tables, the possible progress of productivity, and also regarding each in-dustry's plans for purchases, sales, investments, manpower, etc. Compared with the first phase, the second one appears, therefore, to bring "more realism and less coherence."

In the third phase—the final synthesis of the Plan—which draws to-gether the plans of all the component parts and co-ordinates them while keeping in mind the original assumptions, is prepared and presented to the "Conseil Supérieur du Plan," to the Economic and Social Council, to the government, and, finally, to Parliament for approval.

It is difficult to say how far the system is voluntary, how far coercive. The state obviously has wide powers over its own nationalised sector, for which the Plan is more a directive than a target. For the private sector the situation is quite different. In the last resort, a firm is free to go its own way if it disagrees with the planners.

The logic of "indicative planning" consists in . . . extending to a nationwide scale the market surveys made by each single firm. The Plan gives to each branch of activity some reassurance that it can obtain its supplies and dispose of its prod-ucts without running into shortages or gluts. This only materialises if everybody plays the game. The promise that such conditions will rule acts merely as an incen-tive: it is not binding on everybody. Firms are not relieved from making their own calculations, and forming their own assessment of the risks. But because of the Plan they are better informed when making their own plans.[6]

All this does not mean, of course, that the government has no means of influencing the implementation of the Plan by the private sector. In many ways, it can facilitate the execution of projects which conform to the Plan's targets. It can give tax incentives and can make credit facilities available. Government contracts also provide a very important lever to

---

[5] Manpower, economic and financial balance, regional planning, productivity, scientific and technical research.

[6] From M. Massé's speech, 22nd April, 1961.

affect private investments; in the electronics industry, more than 70 per cent of the turnover depends upon state orders. Both the medium (2–5 years) and long-term (5–20 years) bank loans must now be submitted to the "Commissariat du Plan" by the Crédit National for approval. Bond issues are controlled by the Treasury, and there is a system for the allocation of building licences. Dividends not exceeding 5 per cent of paid-up capital are exempt, for several years, from corporation taxes—provided that they are related to investment deemed desirable by the Plan. Certain price levels, such as those in steel, aluminium, utilities, and cars, can be influenced by the state.

Even in the nationalised sector, however, implementation of the Plan is not always smooth. M. Massé stated:

> By approving the Plan, the government is morally obliged to set the example in its own field as well as in the field of budgetary credit policy and price policy. The government's attitude, however, during the four years over which the Plan extends is often influenced by short-term considerations or by outside economic factors. Day-by-day economic action is, indeed, inevitably a compromise between the short- and the long-term points of view. To overlook the first would be to ignore the demands of life, but shortsighted expediency is also a possible danger. In supervising the execution of the Plan, it is the function of the Commissaire Général to exercise both great understanding and great firmness.

The Plan has been defined by its authors as "a set of coherent objectives"; its success is dependent on its psychological impact, on whether or not it can obtain a general consensus in the economy.

PART III. EVALUATION OF THE SECOND AND THIRD PLANS

The *Second Modernisation and Equipment Plan (1954–57)*, which for the first time covered the whole French economy and provided for a shift in emphasis away from the basic sectors towards a much broader diffusion of investments, set up rather high objectives.[7]

Over the four-year period, the national production was to increase by 25 per cent of its 1952 level, through expansion of its components at a rate of 25–30 per cent for industrial production, 20 per cent for agriculture, and 60 per cent for construction.

Such high rates, which had only exceptionally been achieved in the past, were considered necessary to provide for full employment, adequate investments, and a rise of 4 per cent in the standard of living. Foreign trade was to be balanced by a 40 per cent increase in exports, whereas imports were to rise in proportion with the national product. These goals

---

[7] Parliament authorized the Plan only in May, 1955.

could be attained only through structural reforms, such as reorientation of agricultural production and reorganisation of agricultural markets; specialisation, reconversion, and decentralisation of industrial companies; retraining of manpower; and development of research.

The 1954–57 period saw unprecedented expansion in almost all sectors. In 1957, national production had increased by 29 per cent, industrial production by 46 per cent, and agriculture by 18½ per cent over 1952 (see Table 1). Similarly, the real income per capita had increased by 27 per cent.

Table 1

EVOLUTION OF INDUSTRIAL PRODUCTION IN FRANCE
(Excluding construction)

Year	Index (1952 = 100)	Per Cent Increase over Previous Year
1938	72	...
1949	83	...
1950	88	6
1951	99	12½
1952	100	1
1953	101	1
1954	111	10
1955	121	9
1956	134	11
1957	146	9
1958	152	4
1959	158	4
1960	175	8

Source: Institut National de Statistique et d'Etudes Economiques (INSEE).

Whereas a 6 per cent annual growth rate had been forecast for industrial production, the effective rate during Plan II, as shown above, fluctuated between 9 and 11 per cent. However, distortions between previsions and final results appeared in several groups of industries. The *basic sectors*, for which detailed and rather imperative programmes had been made (Electricité de France, Charbonnages de France, Gaz de France, etc.), were the closest to the objectives (Table 2).

In the *processing industries*, expansion was very marked, especially in farm machinery and consumer goods. For this group, planning was much less imperative and was conceived as a "coordination of forecasts." In most of the sectors the targets planned were exceeded;[8] others were less successful, notably the machine-tool industry (+9 per cent instead of

---

[8] Success in hitting targets can, in some cases, be simply attributed to a selection of objectives which are within an easy range.

Table 2

SECOND PLAN

OBJECTIVES AND REALISATIONS IN BASIC INDUSTRIAL SECTORS FOR 1957

Item	Units	1952	Objectives for 1957	Actual 1957
Coal	Million tons	57.4	61	59.1
Electricity	Billion kwh.	40.6	55	59.5
Gas	Million cu. m.	2.6	3.8	3.6
Fuels	Million tons of crude processed	21.5	30	25.0*
Steel	Million tons	10.9	14.1	14.1
Chemicals	Index (1952 = 100)	100	130†	184†
Cement	Million tons	8.6	...	12.5

* As a consequence of the Suez affair, 26.8 in 1956.
† The two indices are not entirely comparable.

+40 per cent increase between 1952 and 1957). The production of automobiles grew steadily during the four years of the Plan, and the index (1952 = 100), which stood at 97 in 1953, climbed to 119 in 1954, 140 in 1955, 159 in 1956, and reached 176 in 1957 as compared with the Plan's forecast of 120 (Table 3). This was due to a rapid development of car exports, which went up 42 per cent between 1956 and 1957 alone. In this respect it can be pointed out that foreign trade represents the most uncertain sector for the planning authorities; furthermore, the automobile industry has been one of the most difficult in which to predict demand.

The over-all rate of growth for industrial production in France compares favourably with the rates of other Western economies during this period (Table 4).

Table 3

SECOND PLAN

OBJECTIVES AND PRODUCTION IN PROCESSING INDUSTRIES, 1954–57
(Index 1952 = 100)

	1954	1955	1956	1957	Objectives for 1957
Mechanical and electrical industries	111	127	140	155	130
Foundries	94	109	113	124	130
Machine tools	81	84	95	109	140
Farm machinery	152	251	304	355	180
Automobiles	119	140	159	176	120
Textile industries	113	110	119	132	110/115
Clothing industries	105	111	121	126	125/130
Leather industries	101	108	110	116	115
Woodworking industries	108	116	125	132	113
Paper industries	133	146	159	173	135

Table 4

SECOND PLAN

COMPARISON OF GROWTH RATES IN MANUFACTURING INDUSTRIES
BETWEEN VARIOUS COUNTRIES

Country	1957 Index (1956 = 100)	(1938 = 100)	Per Cent Increase 1954–57
Western Germany	106	191	47
Belgium	100	171	23
Denmark	104	180	15
France	109	200	40
Italy	108	222	38
Norway	103	221	36
Netherlands	102	200	26
United Kingdom	103	168	16
Sweden	104	202	19
Canada	100	278	14
U.S.A.	100	298	7

It should be noted that the number of people employed in France did not rise during the period, to the extent that it did in most other countries. France thus recorded the greatest improvement in productivity. From 1952 to 1957, productivity per worker in manufacturing industries increased 45 per cent in France, 43 per cent in Italy, 28 per cent in Western Germany, 22 per cent in Holland, 17 per cent in Sweden, 15 per cent in the United States, and 14 per cent in Great Britain.

The objective of the Second Plan for the *agricultural sector* was a "global" (total French) production rise of 20 per cent over 1952 by the end of 1957. As seen in Table 5, this objective was not quite met, the increase being only 18.5 per cent, although the production of some commodities was above forecasts.

Table 5

SECOND PLAN

OBJECTIVES AND ACTUAL PRODUCTION OF AGRICULTURAL COMMODITIES

Item	Units	1952	Objectives for 1957	Actual 1957
Wheat	Hundred million kgs.	84.2	95.0	110.2
Barley	Hundred million kgs.	17.3	23.4	36.7
Corn	Hundred million kgs.	4.8	10.0	14.2
Potatoes	Hundred million kgs.	110.7	140.0	139.5
Beets	Hundred million kgs.	95.0	120.0	106.3
Fats	Hundred million kgs.	2.5	2.7	1.8
Wine	Million hl.	53.9	45.0	32.5
Meat	Thousand tons	2,065	2,500	2,600
Milk	Million hl.	150	200	200
Sugar	Thousand tons	999	1,500	1,415

GLOBAL INDEX OF AGRICULTURAL PRODUCTION
(1952 = 100)

1954.......... 118.4	1957.......... 118.5 (actual)	
1955.......... 120.2	1957.......... 120.0 (planned)	
1956.......... 118.5		

Despite a more extensive use of agricultural machinery and of chemical fertilizers, agricultural production remained behind schedule between 1954 and 1957. The structure of production was inadequately adapted in quality and quantity to consumption, in domestic as well as in export markets. The distribution system was not improved enough from its very inefficient state, and the spread between production and consumption prices remained very high.

The drop in the production of alcohol followed the recommendations set into the Plan. The production of wheat exceeded the predictions mainly because of the introduction of new species which boosted the yields. Bad atmospheric conditions affected production considerably in 1956 and 1957; export opportunities were missed, and it became necessary to import cereals, fruit, wine, and vegetables. Agriculture did not contribute to the improvement of the balance of trade as had been hoped.

Housing construction was planned at the rate of 240,000 dwellings finished during 1957. The actual figures were:

1952 = 83,900	1956 = 236,000
1954 = 162,000	1957 = 273,700
1955 = 210,100	

However, the investments required to achieve this result were greater than expected. Instead of the forecast figure of 1,896 billion francs (at constant 1954 prices) for the four-year period, they reached a total of 2,435 billion francs. Delays in finishing projects and a low productivity allowed the full impact of rising prices to be reflected in the above figure. The actual and forecast *investment* figures for the sectors covered by the Second Plan are detailed in Table 6.

The inevitable consequence of the higher than expected investment rate in several industries was strong inflationary pressures. The latter were reinforced by labour shortages[9] and by a sharp advance in private consumption. Whereas the gross national product, as shown in Table 7, had

---

[9] One of the main goals of the Second Plan was to obtain full employment; this was realized by 1955, and, as a result of the rapid economic expansion, serious shortages of manpower developed in 1956.

Table 6

SECOND PLAN

OBJECTIVES AND ACTUAL INVESTMENTS, 1954–57
(In billions of Old Francs at 1954 prices)

	Objectives	Actual
Agriculture	1,135	1,170
Energy & mining	1,262	1,315
Steel & iron ore	267	265
Chemicals	165	195
Manufacturing industries	775	730
Transports, communications, tourism	870	805
Housing	1,896	2,435
Schools & hospitals, etc.	352	450
Total	6,722	7,365

Table 7

SECOND PLAN

FRENCH GROSS NATIONAL PRODUCT AND ITS USES, 1952–57
(In billions of Old Francs at 1954 prices)

	1952	1953	1954	1955	1956	1957	1957 Index (1952 = 100)
National production	12,900	13,390	14,030	14,970	15,650	16,670	129
Other GNP elements*	1,700	1,710	1,760	1,770	1,960	2,020	119
GNP	14,600	15,100	15,790	16,740	17,610	18,690	128
Private consumption	9,880	10,330	10,700	11,320	12,040	12,750	129
Public consumption	2,380	2,400	2,370	2,300	2,600	2,710	114
Gross capital formation	2,570	2,480	2,700	3,060	3,360	3,630	141
Net transactions with the rest of the world	−230	−110	20	60	−390	−400	...
Total	14,600	15,100	15,790	16,740	17,610	18,690	128

* Mostly services.

risen by 28 per cent in 1957 over 1952, the corresponding rate for private consumption was 29 per cent, which was considerably more than the 22 per cent forecast by the Plan.

This situation reflected itself in the *balance of payments*. The Plan had provided that at the end of 1957 it would show a small surplus on current account, resulting from a balance of trade in equilibrium and from a surplus in the balance of invisibles. In fact, both showed a deficit by the end of 1957 (Table 8).

The plan had forecast a more favourable balance of tourism. Instead, the amount of money spent by foreigners in France was at the same level in 1957 as in 1952, while the amount spent by French tourists abroad doubled between 1952 and 1957. On the other hand, the deficit of the

Table 8

SECOND PLAN

BALANCE OF PAYMENTS OF THE FRANC ZONE (CURRENT ACCOUNT), 1952–57
(In millions of current dollars)

Balance of trade:	1952	1953	1954	1955	1956	1957
Imports	2,968	2,740	2,971	3,357	4,517	4,842
Exports	2,173	2,288	2,707	3,318	3,464	3,517
Net	−795	−452	−264	−39	−1,053	−1,325
Balance of invisibles:*						
Net	+136	+232	+458	+446	+218	−86
Balance of current payments	−659	−220	+194	+407	−835	−1,411

* *Of which:*

Interest and dividends .... (+)	98	109	115	149	197	209
Interest and dividends .... (−)	45	50	64	78	94	99
Tourism .... (+)	134	122	182	191	153	136
Tourism .... (−)	108	128	121	158	219	216

Franc Zone countries other than France went up three times instead of going down by 50 per cent, as had been hoped.

In total, the deficit on current account reached the sum of $1.650 million for the four-year period, most of which ($1,200 million) was financed through United States loans. To re-establish the equilibrium was one of the main aims of the Third Plan.

The objectives of the *Third Modernisation and Equipment Plan (1958–61)*[10] were established keeping in mind four imperative factors:

a) A surplus of $370 million had to be created by the end of 1961 in the balance of current payments, to maintain equilibrium and reconstitute foreign-exchange reserves

b) A much larger number of young people were to be incorporated into the economy, and considerable additional investments had to be made to create new schools, new housing, and new jobs

c) The maximum possible increase in productivity was not expected to be more than 4 per cent per annum, since the available resources set a limit on the expansion of productive investments

d) The rather isolated French economy had to prepare itself for entry into the European Common Market.

In global terms, the Plan sought to achieve a 27 per cent increase in national production over 1956 (or 20 per cent over 1957), made up of a 20 per cent increase in agricultural production and of a 30–35 per cent increase in industrial production.

To draw up the Third Plan, the scope of several commissions was broadened, and some sectors were studied in much greater depth than

---

[10] Approval of the Third Plan by Parliament took place only in March, 1959.

before; this was particularly true of trade, handicrafts, urban and regional development, radio and television, and foreign trade. The statistical tools were improved within the framework of the national accounting system. In 1954, an input-output table was prepared for the year 1951, and then for 1956, with a view to obtaining a more precise picture of the interdependence between the various sectors of the economy and to enable forecasts to be built on a sounder basis.

Unfortunately, the structural imbalances which had marked the end of the Second Plan also compromised the achievement of the Third Plan. In 1957 and especially at the end of 1958, a series of rigorous measures of restraint had to be taken by the authorities to fight inflation and to prevent a further deterioration of the balance of payments. The devaluation of the franc helped to bring French prices back into line with those of other countries and improved the balance of trade. In the "austerity years" 1958 and 1959, national production grew at a yearly rate of only 2.5 per cent, but by the end of that time the devaluation and other measures were starting to have their effects, and the conditions were more favourable for renewed expansion. However, due to the fact that in 1959 the economy was about one year behind the targets of the Third Plan, an "interim plan" was prepared for the remaining two years of the Plan (1960–61), taking into account the changed conditions and the new possibilities for growth. This led to the revision, up or down, of several forecasts; the level of national production was to increase by 5½ per cent annually, private consumption by 5 per cent, and gross investment by 6½ per cent.

During the four-year period, the GNP did not reach the expected annual growth rate of 4.6 per cent, but increased only at an average rate of 3.8 per cent. The yearly figures were: 1958 = 2.4 per cent; 1959 = 1.9 per cent; 1960 = 6.5 per cent; 1961 = 5 per cent. Table 9 shows the resources of the French economy and their uses during the Third Plan.

Table 10 sets out the actual production figures for 1961, in the *basic industries*, against the amounts forecast in the Third Plan and in the revised "interim plan." It can be seen that the objectives were most closely reached in those sectors where the Plan was most likely to be enforced (primarily because they were nationalized), and where forecasts could be made with the least uncertainty.

Among the *processing industries*, for which objectives had been set only in terms of "coherent predictions," the automobile and farm-machinery industries showed disappointing results. For the automobile industry this was primarily the result of poor export sales in 1960 and 1961, especially to the United States. For farm machinery, it reflected the de-

Table 9

THIRD PLAN

INDEX OF RESOURCES AND THEIR USES IN THE FRENCH ECONOMY
(1956 = 100)

| | | 1961 Forecast | | |
	1960	Original Plan	Interim Plan	1961 Actual
I. Resources				
Gross national production	117.8	127	123.3	123.4
Imports	117.0	110	118.2	123.7
Total	117.7	125	122.7	123.5
II. Uses				
Private consumption	113.0	124	117.6	119.1
Public consumption	105.8	112	117.2	110.8
Capital formation	119.4	128	126.5	128.1
Exports	150.8	135	160.0	156.4
Total	117.7	125	122.7	123.5

Table 10

THIRD PLAN

OBJECTIVES AND REALISATIONS IN BASIC SECTORS

| | | Objectives 1961 | | | Actual | |
Item	Unit	1957	Original	Interim	1960	1961
Coal	Millions tons	59	62	56	58	56
Electricity	Billion kwl.	57.5	76	*	72	76
Gas	Billion therms	27.7	60	*	50	60
Gas (natural)	Billion therms	4.1	36	*	20	36
Fuels	Million tons of crude processed	25	43	*	33	43
Steel	Million tons	14	17.5	*	17.3	18
Aluminium	Thousand tons	160	230	260	235	280
Chemicals	Index (1956 = 100)	113	145	164	160	188
Cement	Million tons	12.5	14.7	14.9	14.2	14.6

* No change from original plan.

creasing purchasing power of the farmers due to several bad crops and to the fact that the 15 per cent discount on the purchase of new machinery was reduced to 10 per cent on 1st January, 1959 (Table 11).

The Third Plan's forecast for the *agricultural sector* was a 20 per cent increase in production, which was met. The detailed predictions and actual index numbers are shown in Table 12.

Rather than emphasizing level of production, the Third Plan had stressed the necessity of seeking a better relationship between supply and demand of *agricultural products* and had suggested basic adaptations of the production situation. Various measures were taken or considered to

Table 11

THIRD PLAN

PRODUCTION INDICES IN PROCESSING INDUSTRIES

(1956 = 100)

	Forecasts for 1961		Actual	
	Original Plan	Interim Plan	1960	1961
Mechanical and electrical industries	142	142	130	136
Machine tools, tools, welding equipment...	150	*	133	150
Other industrial equipment	138	*	130	143
Electrical industries	144	*	138	150
Farm machinery	141	*	97	112
Automobiles, bicycles	146	165	147	140
Electronic apparatus	150	*	160	190
Household appliances	170	*	168	177
Textile industry	131	113	114	121
Leather industry	120	118	118	122
Woodworking industry	119	131	131	138
Paper industry	136	137	144	155
Plastics industry	149	*	170	186
Total manufacturing industries	136	132	126	133

* No change from original plan.

Table 12

THIRD PLAN

OBJECTIVES AND ACTUAL PRODUCTION OF AGRICULTURAL COMMODITIES

				1961	
Item	Unit	1954	1960	Planned	Actual
Wheat	Hundred million kgs.	105.7	110.1	110	93
Barley	Hundred million kgs.	25.2	57.1	50	54
Corn	Hundred million kgs.	9.6	28.1	25	23.7
Fats	Hundred million kgs.	1.0	1.2	25	1.6
Beets	Hundred million kgs.	116.6	190.2	130	118.2
Potatoes	Hundred million kgs.	158.6	148.9	140	139
Wine	Million hl.	60.9	63.1	60	52.9
Beef meat	Thousand tons	1,000	1,100	1,300	1,280
Veal meat	Thousand tons	360	385	450	410
Pork meat	Thousand tons	900	1,160	1,200	1,100
Lamb meat	Thousand tons	110	135	150	130
Milk	Million hl.	215	226	265	236
Eggs	Billion units	8.7	8.5	11	8.9
Sugar	Thousand tons	1,518	2,509	1,550	1,810

raise agricultural revenues, to reorganise the markets with a view towards eliminating some middlemen, and to make possible exports of surplus products, especially beef, so as to adapt a growing production to its internal and external outlets. The purchase of farm tractors was encouraged, with the result that the total number of tractors was 770,000 at the beginning of 1961. The Plan had forecast a figure of 800,000 tractors at the end of 1961, against 425,000 at the end of 1956.

With regard to the *building industry*, the number of dwellings completed grew from 273,700 in 1957 to 290,200 in 1958, 320,400 in 1959, 313,800 in 1960, and 320,000 in 1961. The planned figure for 1961 was 300,000. Expenditures on school construction during the four years were 950 billion old francs, as compared with the 920 billion francs provided for in the Plan. On the other hand, only 97.5 billion old francs were spent on hospitals, asylums, and social welfare equipment, instead of the 120 billion francs which had been planned. This was the first time that the Plan had concerned itself with social overhead investment. The French educational authorities have been faced with an enormous expansion, caused not only by the postwar increase in the numbers of young people but, equally important, by their increased demand for education. The number of school children rose 50 per cent between 1950 and 1960. Educational investment tripled between 1957 and 1961.

In order to allow for the expansion, *investments* were to increase by 28 per cent from 1956 to 1961. As can be seen in Table 9, this figure was reached. The index numbers (1956 = 100) for the various sectors were as follows:

	Planned	Actual
Housing investment	115.4	123
Social overhead investment	134.3	137
Productive investment	131	128.3

In emphasizing the re-establishment of equilibrium in the *balance of payments* of the franc zone, the Third Plan stated that a surplus of $370 million on current account would be necessary at the end of the period. In 1958, the deficit amounted to $98 million, but there was a $1,046 million surplus at the end of 1959 and a $540 million surplus at the end of 1960. Table 13 shows France's exports as a percentage of imports from foreign countries and the evolution of gold and foreign-exchange reserves from 1956 to 1960.

The four years 1958–61 saw several developments which were bound to have a profound effect on France's balance of trade and on its economy in general. Among these were the establishment of the European Common Market, widespread liberalisation of trade, the devaluation and external convertibility of the franc, the transformation of the franc zone, and the necessity to join the other industrialised countries in helping underdeveloped countries.

Table 13
THIRD PLAN

a) EXPORTS (F.O.B.) AS A PERCENTAGE OF IMPORTS (C.I.F.)
(Including the Franc Zone)

Year	Per Cent	Year	Per Cent
1952 =	66	1957 =	71
1953 =	81	1958 =	79
1954 =	87	1959 =	99
1955 =	93	1960 =	99
1956 =	73	1961 =	102*

* January–September, 1961.

b) EVOLUTION OF GOLD AND FOREIGN-EXCHANGE RESERVES, 1956–60
(In millions of dollars)

	1956	1957	1958	1959	1960
Gold and foreign-exchange reserves (at 12/31)	1,180	645	1,050	1,723	2,070

The franc zone, from which came 22.5 per cent of France's imports and to which went 30 per cent of her exports, was undergoing rapid changes. Many ex-colonies became independent and altered their relationships with France in varying degrees; the result was that French exporters met with a greater competition in these markets.

The Third Plan had also indicated the guiding principles of a *policy of regional development*. The country was divided into 21 administrative areas for regional action (see Exhibit 2), in which the various programmes would be coordinated and for which particular objectives would be established in the future. Among the aims of this programme is the decentralisation of the French industry, as well as of educational and administrative institutions, the relief of the congestion in and around Paris, and the development of the role of the provinces.

PART IV. THE FOURTH ECONOMIC AND SOCIAL DEVELOPMENT PLAN (1962–65)

The Fourth Plan defines the objectives for economic growth and social development during the period 1962–65, as well as the various steps to be undertaken in order to reach them.

The first phase (see Exhibit 1) of the elaboration of the Fourth Plan started in 1959, when preliminary outlines were drawn up, corresponding to three alternative yearly growth rates of national production: 3 per cent, 4½ per cent, and 6 per cent. The outlines, prepared by the "Commissariat du Plan" staff, in cooperation with the Department of Economic

Exhibit 2

ADMINISTRATIVE AREAS FOR REGIONAL ACTION, DECREE OF 2ND JUNE, 1960

and Financial Studies of the Finance Ministry,[11] were accompanied by projections up to 1975, in order to pick out important longer-term developments which might otherwise have been missed.

In order to study the implications of the three growth rates on the interdependent parts of the economy (agriculture, industry, services), various sketches were submitted to the government, which then consulted the Investment and Planning Section of the Economic and Social Council before selecting a target rate. In its reports, the Council insisted upon a high rate of growth and emphasised "collective" needs, such as education, research, health, housing, urban and rural equipment, and culture.

Three basic trends were decisive in the selection of a target growth

---

[11] Responsible for national accounting.

rate: (*a*) the better balance between the working and nonworking parts of the population resulting from the higher postwar birthrate; (*b*) the expansion of the Common Market and of the world economy; and (*c*) the transformation of France's relationships with the African countries belonging to the franc area. It was felt that, although a 3 per cent growth rate would have been easy to achieve, it would not have supported full employment or the national effort in the military and social fields. Conversely, the 6 per cent rate was associated with a vulnerable balance of payments and inflation at home.

In June, 1960, the government gave the Commissariat its directives, calling for a yearly compound growth rate of 5 per cent, which would permit the achievement of the "great national tasks," such as adapting to the Common Market, modernising the armed forces, aiding underdeveloped countries, and, in general, meeting the challenge of a scientific and competitive age. The Fourth Plan was to stress national ends, such as the development of France's productive forces, and individual ends, such as the improvement of the population's living conditions. The government further recommended that the Modernisation Commissions study the possibility of moving up the growth rate to 5.5 per cent.

A provisional draft of the Plan was prepared on the basis of these directives. It gave an analysis of the pattern of final demand in the last year of the Plan and assumptions about foreign trade and about the level of investment required. From this an "input-output" table was set up, estimating for each of 28 sectors its sales to, and purchases from, the others.

The second and more detailed phase of the work could then start, at the beginning of July, 1960, with the consultation of the 22 "vertical" and 5 "horizontal" Modernisation Commissions. The Commissions were asked to check the planners' assumptions, notably the rate of technical progress embodied in the "input-output" table; to provide data on sales, divided between personal consumption, exports, sales to government agencies or to other industries; on the materials, manpower, and investment required; and on any special conditions for meeting the objectives, e.g., finance, taxes, or prices.

The Chemical Commission, for instance, started with the planning figure provided by the Commissariat. The over-all growth rate of 5 per cent implied an annual expansion of industrial output of 6.3 per cent, and of chemical output of 8.7 per cent. The task of investigating the consequences of this expansion was entrusted to 35 working groups, 32 of which dealt with separate types of products; 3 were concerned with general problems: research, finance, manpower, and technical education.

When the reports of the Commissions were synthesised centrally in the spring of 1961, to ensure their over-all consistency, it became apparent that most sectors believed they could go beyond the initial 5 per cent rate of growth, and so finally the government decided in favour of a more rapid expansion and adopted a target rate of 5.5 per cent.[12] Such an expansion appeared compatible with the availability of manpower; despite the fact that the Plan was not favourable to any reduction in working hours because of labour shortages, it was expected that the higher rate would involve a small increase in industrial employment, a much larger rise in the number of people employed in housing, transportation, trade, the professions, and education, but a considerable reduction in the agricultural labour force through modernisation. This rate also seemed compatible with the maintenance of economic equilibrium and monetary stability, so long as wages could be kept within the planned improvement in productivity.

With the cooperation of the Modernisation Commissions, all previous assumptions and objectives were geared to the new 5.5 per cent growth rate, and the following compound growth rates were selected for the main sectors:

Section	Per Cent	Section	Per Cent
Electrical construction	10.5	Power	5.5
Automobiles	8.6	Steel	5.5
Plastics	7.5	Paper and cardboard	5.4
Mechanical construction	7.5	Clothing	5.3
Building	7.3	Metal working	5.2
Chemicals	6.5	Transportation	4.3
Fuels	5.7	Food and agriculture	3.8
Telecommunications	5.6	Textiles	3.5

In May, 1961, the Commissions handed their coordinated reports to the Commissariat, which then prepared for the government the draft of the IVth Plan Law Project. After a final debate in the "Council Supérieur du Plan" and in the Economic and Social Council, the Fourth Plan was sent to Parliament on 29th November, 1961. It was expected that the French National Assembly would debate the subject at the April, 1962, session.

According to the Fourth Plan, gross national production should increase by 24 per cent over the four years 1962–65, or about 5.5 annually. Table 14 shows the balance between resources and their uses forecast for the period.

While total investments were expected to increase by 30 per cent, in-

---

[12] Which compares with an average rate of 4.5 per cent for the preceding decade.

Table 14

Fourth Plan
Resources and Their Uses in the French Economy, 1961–65

	1961 1965 (In billions of New Francs at 1961 Prices)		1965 Index (1961 = 100)
I. *Resources*			
Gross national production	271	336	124
Imports	33	40	123
Total	304	376	124
II. *Uses*			
Private consumption ⎱	206	252	⎰ 123
Public consumption ⎰			⎱ 122
Capital formation	59	77	130
Exports	39	47	120
Total	304	376	124

vestments for "collective welfare" (school and university equipment, research, urban development, health, cultural and sport equipment) were scheduled to go up by 50 per cent. Productive investments were planned to increase by 28 per cent, that is, more than the growth of gross national production. On the other hand, public consumption was expected to increase by 22 per cent and private consumption by 23 per cent. It was estimated that real income per capita would progress at an annual rate of 4.5 per cent.

Table 15

Fourth Plan
Investments Planned for 1965, by Category

	1961 1965 (In billions of New Francs at 1961 Prices)		1965 Index (1961 = 100)
Productive investments	35.0	46	128
Administrative investments (collective welfare)	7.3	11	150
Housing investment	12.3	15	125
Other (stock variations, etc.)	5.4	5	...
Capital formation	59.0	77	130

In order to set target figures for the *balance of trade*, always the most difficult sector in which to forecast results, a series of assumptions had to be made. The first was the continued expansion of the Common Market and the adoption of a common agricultural policy in compliance with the Rome Treaty. By 1st January, 1966, tariff protection within the European

Economic Community will be only 20 per cent of the 1957 level; French exports will need to be all the more competitive, since the traditionally preferential markets in overseas territories of the Franc Zone will then be open to foreign goods. Other assumptions made were that the payments between France and the Franc Zone should be balanced in 1965. On this basis, it was finally expected that the balance on current account would show a surplus of $810 million in 1965 ($620 million in 1960) (Table 16).

Table 16

FOURTH PLAN

FRANCE'S BALANCE OF PAYMENTS ON CURRENT ACCOUNT, 1960–65
(In millions of dollars)

	Income		Expenditures		Balance	
	1960	1965	1960	1965	1960	1965
Trade	4,460	6,300	4,420	5,800	40	500
Invisibles	2,100	2,610	1,520	2,300	580	310
Total	6,560	8,910	5,940	8,100	620	810

This surplus would allow France to repay $411 million on its total external debt of $1,256 million, to build up its international monetary reserves, and to take a greater part in the drive to aid developing countries. These hypotheses are, however, subject to a great deal of uncertainty. Inflationary wage increases could rapidly alter the whole picture and threaten the competitiveness of French prices on foreign markets.

Planned increases in production for major sectors were to be as outlined in Table 17.

Because of the oversupply of conventional *sources of power* and, in particular, as a result of developments in the petroleum and gas industry, atomic energy is to be developed only on a relatively modest scale, while the output of coal should be reduced from 58 to 55 million tons annually. Measures have been proposed to retrain the miners and to bring new activities to the regions affected by the abandonment of coal mines. The steel industry is to increase its capacity by one-third, to 24.5 million tons of crude steel annually. The chemical industry will expand rapidly, especially in the area of synthetic fibres. In the chemical industry, as well as in the *processing industries*, specialisation and concentration will be encouraged to improve competitiveness with foreign firms (Table 18). For the textile, automobile, shipbuilding, and aircraft industries, the Plan insists on the necessity for European coordination to prevent overcapacity.

In the *trade sector*, the number of people employed is to increase from

Table 17

FOURTH PLAN

PLANNED PRODUCTION IN MAIN SECTORS

	1961	1965	Per Cent
	(In billions of NF at 1961 prices)		Increase 1961–65
Agriculture	38	45	19
Energy	26	32	24
Metallurgy	14	18	23
Chemicals*	19	24	29
Processing industries	162	200	23
Construction and public works	37	49	32
Transportation & communications	24	29	21
Housing services	9	11	23
Other services	51	64	27
Gross total	380	472	24
Net total†	271	336	24
Net available resources‡	265	329	24

* This figure includes rubber and glass. Partly for this reason, the figures on this table indicate a lower growth rate than those in the Note on the French Chemical Industry, see above, p. 152.
† After adjusting for goods counted twice.
‡ After deduction of excess of exports over imports.

Source: Projet de Loi . . . Plan de development économique et social, no. 1573, November, 1961, p. 11, Ministre des Finances.

Table 18

FOURTH PLAN

PRODUCTION AND INVESTMENT IN PROCESSING INDUSTRIES

	Production	Investments		
	1965 (Index 1959 = 100)	1959 (In billions of NF at 1959 prices)	1965	1965 (Index 1959 = 100)
Foundry and metalworking	139	631	951	151
Mechanical machinery and apparatus	149	667	1,144	172
Electrical machinery and apparatus	185	395	735	186
Automobiles and bicycles	140	555	907	163
Total mechanical and electrical industries	151	2,248	3,737	165
Textiles	130	530	784	148
Clothing and furs	136	91	138	152
Leather	123	61	124	203
Woodworking	141	192	278	145
Paper	150	293	429	146
Other industries	178	311	610	197
Total processing industries	146	3,726	6,100	163

1.75 to 1.85 millions, with 150,000 more employees and 50,000 fewer independent dealers. The creation of supermarkets will be encouraged in an effort to rationalise distribution. Investments in the trade sector are to increase from NF 1 billion in 1961 to NF 3 billion in 1965.

The output in *agriculture* should rise by about 4.5 per cent annually and should exceed the 1961 figures by 19 per cent in 1965. Increases in productivity will more than make up for the fact that the number of people employed in agriculture is expected to decline by about 70,000 each year. As can be seen in Table 19, the forecast production of wheat, barley, corn and milk will be in excess of objectives based on anticipated demand. World surplus in these commodities and the maintenance of some kind of agricultural protection in Europe will prevent an easy disposal of these products in foreign markets. Consequently, an effort will be made to redirect production in favour of products with better sales prospects, such as beef, fruits, etc.

Table 19

FOURTH PLAN
PRODUCTION OF AGRICULTURAL COMMODITIES, 1959 AND 1965

Unit	Output* 1959	Forecast 1965	Index 1965 (1959 = 100)	Objectives 1965
Wheat ....Hundred million kgs.	74.8	91	122	69
Rye ....Hundred million kgs.	0.6	0.3	50	...
Barley ....Hundred million kgs.	21.7	40	184	30
Corn ....Hundred million kgs.	8.9	25	281	18
Oats ....Hundred million kgs.	3.3	2.7	82	...
Rice ....Hundred million kgs.	1.2	1.5	125	...
Total cereals	110.5	160.5	145	...
Sugar ....Hundred million kgs.	9.69	...	...	15.66
Fruit ....Million tons	1,565	2,821	180	...
Wine ....Million hl.	58.3	57	98	57
Fats ....Million tons	157	250	159	250
Wood ....Million cu. m.	25.9	29	112	...
Beef ....Thousand net tons	1,000	1,350	135	1,350
Veal ....Thousand net tons	350	430	123	...
Pork ....Thousand net tons	1,200	1,350	113	1,350
Lamb ....Thousand net tons	123	162	132	162
Horse ....Thousand net tons	76	70	92	...
Poultry ......Thousand net tons	297	435	146	...
Rabbit ....Thousand net tons	222	258	116	...
Eggs ....Billion units	8.1	9.9	122	9.9
Milk ....Million hl.	197	275	140	245

* Commercial production of cereals; total production of other items.

Instead of giving top priority to productive investment as in the previous Plan, the Fourth Plan is much more concerned with the opening of new outlets and the furthering of competitiveness within the farming community. This is to be accomplished through structural reforms, promotion, education, research, and the development of cooperatives. Channels of distribution will have to be shortened in order to reduce costs and provide more rapid adaption of production to demand. The general objective is to bring agricultural incomes closer to parity with other incomes.

Public investment in the agricultural sector is to increase from 2,867 million NF during the period of the Third Plan to 5,500 million NF during the Fourth Plan. The poorer regions of the country are to get preferential treatment in the allocation of these funds. Exports of agricultural products are expected to grow much faster than imports, especially those of beef, cereals, and milk.

One of the major aims of the Fourth Plan is to create 930,000 new nonagricultural jobs by 1965. They will be required because of natural increases in the active population (180,000), immigration (290,000), releases from military service (190,000), and movement away from agriculture (270,000). Most of the new jobs will be created in the building industry (170,000), in teaching (150,000), in mechanical construction (120,000), and in trade (100,000).

A feature distinguishing the Fourth Plan from its predecessors is the importance given to *investments serving social and cultural purposes.* With regard to this matter the philosophy of the Plan is expressed in the Law Project as follows:

> It is apparent that in the long run a society based on mass consumption, as exemplified by certain aspects of American life, and which has found in the U.S. its most penetrating critics, seeks futile satisfactions which themselves generate discontent and uneasiness.

This concern with "collective welfare" extends to housing, urban development, education, and cultural equipment.

Investment in *housing construction* is to increase from 12 billion NF in 1961 to 15 billion in 1965. A yearly rate of 350,000 dwellings completed is planned for 1965.

Urban development projects, benefiting Paris especially, include the building of parking facilities and new subways, the improvement of city transportation and additions to hospital facilities. The Halles (wholesale food market) are to be removed from the centre of Paris, and a new stadium is to be built. In the field of transportation, domestic air routes are to be expanded, railroads are to continue the changeover to electric and diesel traction, harbours and inland waterways are to be further developed, and 1,835 kilometers of new superhighways are to be built by 1975.

Great efforts are to be made in *education:* 20,000 new primary classes will be built by 1965, and the space available to universities should double in 10 years. Expenditures for scientific and technical research is to double during the coming four years, with special emphasis on agronomics and medicine. Budgeted for various health and social facilities are 3.7 million NF (against 1.2 million in the Third Plan).

Exhibit 3

National Income, Gross National Product, and Selected GNP Components*

(In billions of new francs)

	1950	1951	1952	1953	1954	1955	1956	1957	1958	1959
National income	75.2	90.7	106.7	111.6	119.0	129.2	143.3	159.6	180.0	193.4
Gross national product	98.5	121.1	143.7	149.8	158.7	170.0	187.9	209.9	237.7	257.1
Private investment	: : : :	: : : :	23.3	22.1	24.5	27.2	32.9	38.2	43.7	42.0
Private consumption	: : : :	: : : :	97.3	101.7	106.7	114.3	126.7	140.4	157.4	168.5
Exports	: : : :	: : : :	21.0	21.4	25.0	26.7	25.6	28.0	32.3	38.6
Imports	: : : :	: : : :	20.8	22.9	25.0	27.9	31.9	35.0	38.6	41.2

* GNP equals the sum of exports, private investment and consumption, government revenue, and government deficit or surplus, less imports and government transfer payments.

Source: *International Financial Statistics*, IMF.

For the first time, a special commission studied the needs in the area of *cultural equipment*. As a result, the Plan provides that 900 million NF of public funds are to be spent during the Fourth Plan (against only 322 million in 1957–61) for the restoration and maintenance of historical monuments and museums, for the promotion of instruction in the arts, for the construction of new theatres, etc.

The Fourth Plan also stresses the *assistance to the impoverished regions of the country*. It aims at a more balanced growth of the various areas and will direct public investments for social overhead equipment towards regions such as Brittany, the Massif Central, and the North, which lack economic incentives. The Plan also favours decentralisation of public and private enterprises in favour of the less developed areas and away from Paris. The country has been divided into 22 economic regions[13] through regrouping of the 90 administrative departments (Exhibit 2). Each region has its own plan, which is drawn up within the "Commissariat du Plan" with the assistance of regional interests. For the time being, however, the pace at which such plans are being prepared is very slow. A 10-year record of selected national income data is presented for France in Exhibit 3, while comparative growth figures for France and other Western nations are presented in Exhibit 4.

Exhibit 4

GROSS NATIONAL PRODUCT IN SELECTED COUNTRIES
(Volume index at market prices, 1953 = 100)

Country	1954	1955	1956	1957	1958	1959	1960	Yearly Growth Rates 1950–60*
France	105	111	116	123	126	129	136	3.4
Belgium	105	108	112	115	112	117	122	2.3
Luxembourg	99	103	109	114	116	118	...	...
Netherlands	107	116	120	123	124	131	142	3.6
W. Germany	107	120	128	135	139	149	161	6.4
Italy	105	112	117	124	130	140	149	5.3
Total EEC	106	114	120	126	129	136	145	4.6
United Kingdom	105	108	110	112	113	117	122	2.0
Total EFTA	105	109	112	115	117	121	127	2.4
U.S.A.	98	106	108	110	109	116	119	1.5

* At constant prices.
Source: Statistical Office of the European Communities.

13 Including Corsica.

This note was prepared by H. N. Ehrenström, under the direction of Professor P. Goetschin, as a basis for class discussion. Valuable help has been supplied by M. B. Cazes, Chargé de Mission at the Commissariat du Plan; he assumes, however, no responsibility for the accuracy of the note.

Appendix
SOME OPINIONS ON ECONOMIC PLANNING

1. From *Swiss Review of World Affairs*, Salomon Wolff, December, 1961, p. 13.
2. From *The Economist:* "Planning Like the French?" 28th October, 1961.
3. From *The Economist:* "Planning by Whom?" 26th August, 1961.
4. From *The Financial Times:* "France's Plan: Target or Directive?" 19th October, 1961.
5. From *Le Monde:* "The Economic and Social Council Approves of the Objectives of the Fourth Plan," 19th–20th November, 1961.
6. From J. C. R. Dow, "Problems of Economic Planning," *Westminster Bank Review*, November, 1961.

1. Extract from:

Swiss Review of World Affairs
Salomon Wolff
(December, 1961, p. 13)

"The Fourth French development plan is based on an economic philosophy that testifies to a high sense of social and cultural responsibility on the part of its authors. Expansion and acceleration of economic growth, to be sure, are the plan's principal aims. In the view of the planners it is not only the increase of production that counts, however, but also the use that is to be made of that increase. The authors undoubtedly have read J. K. Galbraith's 'The Affluent Society,' and taken to heart the warning it contains against a forced increase of private consumption and simultaneous neglect of investments for the common good. The fourth development plan firmly opposes any artificial inflation of private consumption such as is witnessed in the United States. As a nation with an old civilization France wants to put an increasing share of its growing productive forces to the service of social and cultural tasks."

2. Extracts from:

The Economist
"PLANNING LIKE THE FRENCH?"
(28th October, 1961)

"How far has the mechanism of French planning been *dirigiste*, in the sense of deciding in which places growth should take place and of diverting resources towards them? In the nationalised sector of French industry there was certainly one important early example of this in the first Monnet plan. The first targets for expansion for French electricity production were pitched almost twice as high as anybody had previously expected: the French planners' philosophy here was that "the early stages of instilling a growth mentality are like a bayonet charge, and we chose electricity to lead it."

"In the private sector, one's impression is that French planning today is also much less *dirigiste* than many outsiders suggest. It is made to look *dirigiste* because France has always had a much less efficient capital market than Britain and, to get investment funds on what the British industry would regard as commercial terms, French capital issues generally have to secure official support. But the French authorities have praise-worthily tried to act in the same way as an intelligent private investor would do; they have channelled their funds and support to whichever investment ventures look most profitable, with remarkably little political meandering to help lame dogs over stiles.

"One recent example, which is sometimes quoted as a sign that they are *dirigiste*, shows in reality how little *dirigisme* there now is. Two companies making refrigerators recently applied for permission to make bond issues to increase their production of refrigerators; as the plan suggested that more refrigerators should be bought these were agreed to, but eyebrows were raised when another company came along to join the queue at a time when the future market for refrigerators had begun to look a bit glutted: 'We would not have refused permission for the issue if the company had insisted,' said one French planner, 'but we pointed out the market situation to it, and suggested that it withdraw.' Probably, in that third case, a normal equity issue on the British market would have failed."

3. Extracts from:

The Economist
"PLANNING BY WHOM?"

(26th August, 1961)

"Everybody who has studied the way in which various nations' economic policies have been run since the war knows who these *economic technocrats* are. They are men who think and operate in terms of (sometimes infuriatingly glib) production targets and planned efficiency drives; they play something of the role in some nations' affairs that time-and-motion-study men play in some individual factories; and they have some of the disadvantages and drawbacks of those stopwatch men. Any organisation in which they have too much authority or prestige can become rather soulless; and even at quite an early stage their extreme worship of figures can look more than a little absurd. One should always be ready to grin at such announcements as a recent one from Japan that 'the Government, at a Cabinet conference held in December, 1960, decided to set the 1961 target of the nation's real economic growth at 9.2 per cent.' The planning technocrats can also make big mistakes. Yet the fact remains that several successful countries in Europe—not merely France, which is the case everybody talks about now—have clearly expanded their economies more quickly because men who try to guide governments' policies with both eyes on these statistical production targets are in positions of public influence. . . .

". . . the more that influence is exerted by economic technocrats, and the less by organised industrial groups, the better; it would be a bad mistake to give too much planning power to those who, to some extent, need to be planned against."

4. Extracts from:

The Financial Times
FRANCE'S PLAN: TARGET OR DIRECTIVE?

"What planning had done in France is to create a climate of business confidence, in which the Government underwrites rapid growth and encourages firms to expand on the assumption that it will take place. Planning has also tried to foresee and to forestall the difficulties arising out of rapid growth—balance of payments deficits, inflationary shortages of key products, lack of investment finance and so on.

"But planning in France has been concerned as much to prevent the rate of expansion from becoming so rapid that the difficulties become insurmountable as to make it as rapid as increases in productivity and demand will permit. It has had varying success. It was powerless to prevent inflation during the post-war years of the Fourth Republic, and the balance of payments was only stopped from getting completely out of hand by successive devaluations of the franc. . . .

"Agreed Forecasts

The businessmen give the officials full information about their own plans (on the understanding that it is not passed on to the tax authorities) and the officials give in return information about other sectors of the economy and general prospects. These two sets of data interact until, it is hoped, businessmen and officials more or less agree on demand forecasts for each sector, and on the levels of investment necessary to create the required capacity.

"The fact that some industries—for example, coal—are nationalised, while others—for example, steel—are not, makes less difference than one would think. The nationalised industries have a large degree of independence as a reward for conforming to the broad lines of the plan, while private industries, particularly heavy industries, accept a good deal of State guidance in return for help with finance, raw material supplies, export campaigns, and so on. But it is a fact that each year between one-third and two-fifths of all productive investment is made by nationalised industries, whose key positions were an important factor in getting the plan off the ground after the end of the war.

"The French planners reconcile their methods with economic freedom by arguing that, if both industry and Government are clearly informed about one another and the economy in general, they will agree on a joint programme to be freely carried out by both sides. But, of course, conflicts do arise. The car firms, for example, are far more optimistic about future sales than the planners, and would like to carry out more ambitious investment projects than are allowed for by the Plan."

5. Extract from:

Le Monde
"THE ECONOMIC AND SOCIAL COUNCIL APPROVES OF THE OBJECTIVES OF THE FOURTH PLAN"

"With the exception of the C.G.T.,[1] which rejected the Plan by pointing out that it was orientated towards austerity for the wage-earners and that it would benefit particularly the large capitalistic concentrations, all groups applauded the progress made by planning. Many delegates stressed the advantages of determining objectives on the basis of consumption forecasts rather than from production necessities. Others deplored the absence of any objectives to ameliorate the distribution of incomes which will result from the realisation of the Plan.

"The weakness of the guidelines and objectives will subsist as long as the Plan remains indicative. Only one speaker declared expressly that planning should not

---

[1] Left-wing labour union (Confédération Genérale du Travail).

advance beyond this stage. Most of the others wished, tacitly or explicitly, that the Plan should become more mandatory, particularly to ensure a fairer distribution of incomes.

"Several speakers pointed out the weaknesses and lack of precision of the basic options in the Plan, especially those relating to foreign trade, price disequilibrium and the balance of payments. There were also hopes that planning might be extended to the Common Market so that European countries would not overlap in their industrial efforts.

"On the whole, the idea of planning is well accepted by the members of the Council. A large segment is favourable to State intervention designed to facilitate the realisation of the Plan."

6. Extract from:

Westminster Bank Review
"PROBLEMS OF ECONOMIC PLANNING"
J. C. R. Dow
(November, 1961)

"Conclusion

How far a greater degree of organization in economic planning would contribute to economic growth in Britain can hardly be foretold in advance. Some people find it difficult to see how planning could make a difference, and argue that it is a 'pathetic fallacy' to imagine that, if everybody believed that we could expand at 5% a year, we should in fact do so.

"Nevertheless, the organization of planning might have effects in many places, and the total impact could be important. It is difficult not to believe that a detailed investigation, with the participation of firms, into the possibilities of faster growth, would not have some effects on their ideas and their actions. The investigation could cover at least a large fraction of industry: under a thousand firms must account for a third of industrial production. In the past any one firm's expansion has tended to be related, though not rigidly, to that of its industry. Its plans, therefore, probably stand to be influenced to some extent by its ideas about the rate of expansion of the economy.

"Government economic policy has hitherto been primarily on a short-term basis; and day-to-day preoccupations have prevented officials from spending much time on consideration of longer-term issues. The institution of a new planning body would provide a useful addition of staff free to concentrate on such matters; and its direct contact with industry could hardly fail to improve the empirical basis of government policy.

"The desire for faster economic growth is now widespread and is a new force. A planning organization would be a small addition to our institutional arrangements, but it may be what is needed to let this force express itself."

BIBLIOGRAPHY

"Projet de Loi portant approbation du Plan de développement économique et social," National Assembly, Paris, 29th November, 1961.

"Troisième Plan de Modernisation et d'Equipement," *Journal Officiel de la République Française*, No. 1129, 1959.

"Rapport Annuel sur l'exécution du plan de Modernisation et d'Equipement," Commissariat Général du Plan, 1958, 1959, 1960.

"Les Moyens d'Exécution du Plan," by Gilles de La Perrière, Commissariat Général du Plan, 1961.

"L'Elaboration du Plan de Modernisation et d'Equipement," by Bernard Cazes, Commissariat Général du Plan, 1961.

"Economic Planning in France," *Planning, Political and Economic Planning*, London, 14th August, 1961.

"Planning by Whom?" and "Planning like the French?" *The Economist*, London, 25th August and 28th October, 1961.

PART V

Building an Organization

THE HIGHGATE RUBBER PRODUCTS LTD. series presents a company in the process of reorganizing under the pressure of outside circumstances. The first or (A) case serves as background to the series as a whole. The second or (B) case gives readers an opportunity to evaluate an internal statement to executive personnel by the then managing director, Mr. Davis, regarding the changing pattern of the company's organizational structure, the reasons for the change, and the problems he thought would result from the changes. For focusing discussion of this case at IMEDE, a series of questions was asked, the purpose of some of these being to induce participants to think about the director's statement from the standpoint of its potential audience. These questions were as follows: Had you been in the audience, what questions, if any, would you have liked to have answered that were not answered? What points would you want amplified? What questions, if any, would you have in your mind that you would not articulate to Mr. Davis? The diversity of answers obtained tends to reveal much about the nature of the communication process in the real world. Besides these questions, another of a different order was directed at eliciting an evaluation of certain substantive statements made by the director. We asked, "Do you agree with the principles of organization and the criteria for judgment of executives enunciated in the director's statement?"

For the (C) case in the series, readers should evaluate Mr. Davis' size-up of his management situation.

The (D) and (E) cases pertain to group or headquarters relationships with several product divisions of the company. Again the managing director is heard from, as are several divisional executives, and often headquarters personnel. Their points of view are not identical. Students can quickly be brought to discern the action implications of this case by asking the following two questions: What problems of organization, human relations, and executive leadership are revealed by the interview material on division-group relationships? If you were managing director of the company, what, if anything, would you do about these problems? (We have said several times that asking young or maturing executives what they themselves would do is more rewarding than asking them to predict what the executive described in the case would do. The student is given the executive's problem and his environment, but is forced to take a personal position with respect to the facts he perceives and to devise his own leadership pattern for dealing with any problems presented.)

The two concluding cases in the section, The Solartron Electronic Group Ltd. (A) and (C), are of particular interest because they permit a look at the same company after a considerable lapse of time. The first case describes a young, vigorous, enterprising firm in its early stages. Top management's philosophy of leadership and of organization is made explicit. The reader can be profitably asked to consider how these will fit in with other factors in the situation, such as the company's size, type of business, and long-run objectives for growth. The second case, written about three years later, is based on interviews with various management personnel. It permits discussion of changes made in the company over a period of time and of the reasons for those changes as described by various executives. The authors are particularly indebted to the personnel of this company for the frankness of their appraisals. This case contributes considerable insight into the dynamics of organizational growth and change.

The last case in the section, Compagnie Chillon Electronique, comes from a small research-oriented company in Switzerland. The family and the business were closely intermingled, as they are in numerous European companies. The company had reached a point in its history (as have so many other research- and engineering-oriented companies) when a decision had to be made as to whether or not the firm should expand from its present main specialty of contract research work into production. The owner realized that he was not interested in many aspects of management that might be required for such a venture and contemplated the possibility of sharing control and direction of his company with someone possessed of business skills. The case permits a definition of the various choices open to the owner if he tries to work out the broad design of such a plan. It also permits evaluation of the way in which personal or human factors may limit the range of possible solutions to an organizational problem. From the standpoint of participants in the IMEDE program, this case proved especially successful.

HIGHGATE RUBBER PRODUCTS LTD. (A)*

In 1958 Highgate Rubber Products Ltd. was a leading manufacturer in the British rubber industry. The company's product line included tires, conveyor and power transmission belting, rubber hose, footwear, and a wide variety of industrial rubber products. In recent years, HRP had added plastic and synthetic fibre products to its rubber product line, as these materials were replacing rubber in many applications and their development permitted the company to diversify in associated markets. The company operated 11 factories in various locations in England.

This case consists of a history of the company up to July, 1958, when a conference of HRP executives was held to discuss recent organizational changes recently placed in effect. Selected operating data covering the years 1950 to 1958 are presented in Exhibit 1. Balance-sheet data as of 30th June, 1958, are presented in Exhibit 2.

Highgate Rubber Products Ltd. started operations in 1920 with an original capital of £300,000. The company's original product line consisted primarily of tires, although some industrial rubber products were also produced.

In 1923, the company started production of rubber hose, when the Johnson Rubber Company at Smethwick was acquired. In that year, the capital was increased to £575,000 and before-tax profits reached £22,000. In 1927 the Prince Rubber Company Ltd. was acquired, and a line of rubber footwear was developed at that company's factory at Woolwich.

Highgate Rubber Products really emerged as a corporate group in 1926 by the acquisition of four previously independent English rubber companies.

By 1931 annual earnings had advanced to £147,000, and in 1932 the company's capital was increased to £800,000.

Up to 1937, when earnings reached £254,000, the company showed progressive improvement. In looking at past activities, however, HRP's managing director since 1953, Mr. Frederick C. Stevens, pointed out that "the acquisition of all of these new interests brought us many problems,

---

* Fictitious name.

This case was prepared by Mr. John Archer under the supervision of Professor Ralph M. Hower.

Copyright 1962 by l'Institut pour l'Etude des Méthodes de Direction de l'Entreprise (IMEDE), Lausanne, Switzerland. Reprinted by permission.

Exhibit 1

Profit and Loss Statements, 1950–58
(In thousands of pounds)

	1950	1951	1952	1953	1954	1955	1956	1957	1958
TOTAL TRADING PROFIT	1,668	2,745	2,461	1,969	2,606	2,781	2,353	1,847	1,274
Less:									
Depreciation	182	198	211	214	216	232	257	287	349
Audit fees and expenses	4	5	6	5	5	6	6	7	8
Directors' fees	18	18	13	13	14	32	39	37	41
Total	204	221	230	232	235	270	302	331	398
Profit before taxes	1,464	2,524	2,231	1,737	2,371	2,511	2,051	1,516	876
Less:									
Income taxes	491	985	1,027	808	1,061	1,017	849	633	197
Profits taxes	212	460	233	158	200	200	208	223	118
Excess profits taxes	...	...	104	...	32	...	...	...	...
Total	703	1,445	1,364	996	1,293	1,217	1,057	856	315
Net profit	761	1,079	867	771	1,078	1,294	994	660	561

Exhibit 2

BALANCE SHEET AS OF 30TH JUNE 1958
(In thousands of pounds)

CAPITAL AND RESERVES

Issued capital of HRP 350,000 6½% cumulative preference shares...	350	
Ordinary stock	4,000	4,350
Reserves		7,026

CURRENT LIABILITIES

Accounts payable	1,420
Tax liability	625
Other accrued expenses	222
Total liabilities	13,643

FIXED ASSETS

Plant and equipment	8,142	
Less: depreciation	2,212	5,930

CURRENT ASSETS

Cash	887
Investments	1,325
Tax reserve certificates	530
Accounts receivable	1,602
Inventories	3,369
Total assets	13,643

not the least of which was that, compared with our earlier days, we had a number of widespread factories to run instead of one or two. In most cases these factories were equipped to make the same kind of products. In short, whilst they enabled us to expand our range of products to some extent, they brought us little real diversification."

Other top executives, while agreeing that serious problems had been created by the increased complexity of the company's operations, believed that the serious problems in the past had also resulted from the policies of HRP's previous chairman and managing director, Mr. Phillips Heathecote, who had founded the company.

Mr. Grahem Smythe, company secretary, remarked: "Although Mr. Heathecote never owned many HRP shares, he had an extremely strong personality, and he dominated both the company and its board of directors. On one occasion, I remember him remarking, 'I am the board.'"

An indication of the relative importance of HRP's board of directors prior to 1950 was that, up until that time, the board members received no written reports concerning the company's operations. At board meetings, Mr. Heathecote submitted an oral report to the directors, but they were not expected to formulate policy or to take an active part in the direction of the company. Mr. Heathecote was the only representative of management on the board.

One of Mr. Heathecote's policies was to accumulate as large a reserve of liquid assets as possible. The stated reasoning behind this policy was that large cash balances were necessary to take advantage of all cash discounts and to place the company in a strong bargaining position vis-à-vis its suppliers. Mr. Smythe believed that the policy also stemmed from Mr. Heathecote's desire that the company maintain an ability to withstand depressed economic periods without being forced to reduce its work force, to which Mr. Heathecote felt a strong responsibility. In addition, almost all the companies acquired by HRP had been in serious financial difficulties at the time of their acquisition. While this enabled HRP to purchase these companies on favourable terms, Mr. Smythe thought that Mr. Heathecote had been impressed by their financial weakness and had become determined that HRP should not duplicate their experiences.

As a result of this financial policy, funds for capital expenditures were severely limited. One of HRP's senior plant managers, Mr. John Ellsworth, described Mr. Heathecote's reaction to his request to spend £10,000 on equipment modernization as being "extremely unhappy, and my proposal almost led to my expulsion from his office."

The company was able to continue its growth without large capital expenditures, because it grew largely as the result of purchasing already existing production facilities. In most cases, however, these facilities were old, and HRP was producing with obsolete or, at best, inefficient equipment.

The major effect of World War II on HRP was the heavy bomb damages suffered by one of its largest factories. Major production contracts were carried out in the war effort, and additional production capacity was acquired to replace the destroyed facilities. The war also prevented the company from carrying out a needed modernization program.

With the war over, HRP entered what seemed to many executives to be a new era, as the company began to meet the large built-up demand for its products. Orders flowed in, production was expanded, and plants were worked at capacity. Group profits increased rapidly, reaching £1,079 thousand by 1951. By this time, HRP had become a major force in the rubber industry, particularly in the fields of industrial rubber products and conveyor belting.

In 1958 Mr. Stevens expressed what he considered to be the other side of the coin: "Our factories were crying out for re-equipment and modernization. Obsolescence in many spheres of our activities was rapidly overtaking us, but, instead of putting our money back into the business, we had buried it. We had, in the main, banked it and left it there. Compared with today, those were easy years, when margins were high and demand continued to keep well ahead of supply."

Much of this demand, however, came from one source—the coal mining industry. When the Labour Government assumed power in 1945, the coal mines were nationalized and placed under the administration of the National Coal Board, which consisted of full-time governmental administrators and certain extra part-time directors from outside the industry. Although some of the full-time directors had previously been connected with the industry, either in a governmental or private capacity, others were brought in from outside both the government and the industry. It was then that coming events started to cast their shadows. Up to that time, like others in the rubber and other industries, HRP had enjoyed a rather protected existence. Trade associations were powerful, manufacturers collaborated with their competitors, trading policies and price agreements were important, and efficient manufacturers held an umbrella over the inefficient.

Shortly thereafter, a major event occurred which was to have a far reaching effect on HRP and the rubber industry. The NCB, as a definite policy, stopped buying conveyor equipment complete with belting and started to buy belting from every conveyor-belt manufacturer in the country. HRP had concentrated its belting sales efforts on the conveyor manufacturers and in several cases was the only supplier of belting as original equipment to the manufacturer. Thus, as a result of the NCB decision, HRP's sales of underground belting to mining equipment manufacturers ceased overnight. Although HRP's sales of industrial rubber products and tires were a growing and important part of its business, this event had a serious effect on profits, because HRP's belting activities were its most profitable business.

Soon after assuming its authority over the coal industry, the NCB initiated a major program of mine mechanization, in order to reduce costs. As a result, the demands for belting increased significantly. This increased demand aroused the interest of manufacturers who, previous to nationalization, were either small in the belting business or had never made conveyor belting of any kind. The number of manufacturers increased from seven to fourteen.

In 1952, the NCB decided that, from a given date, all conveyor belting used underground had to be fire-resistant. "HRP was not the first off the mark in meeting this new requirement," Mr. Stevens remarked. "We lost our leadership position and in some ways we have yet to recover it. To do that, we must develop new belts of qualities in advance of those of competitive products.

"And finally," Mr. Stevens continued, "the NCB decided to buy against closed bids, and, as the economic health of the coal industry declined, price became of increasing importance. Today, from a profit point of view, underground belting business is mainly marginal, and further cost reductions are vitally necessary. At the same time, the NCB has reduced its belting purchases, but they still, as a matter of policy, spread the orders over all approved manufacturers. The result is that, in the scramble for the reduced potential, selling prices continue to deteriorate and profits fall. We would, therefore, do well to ponder the NCB's most recent decree that it would apply to hose the same buying methods which have reduced the prices of underground conveyor belting to their present unremunerative levels."

To counteract the reduced profitability of its belting sales and the potential profit reduction in hose sales, HRP began an intensive marketing program designed to increase its tire sales. However, other tire manufacturers also increased their selling efforts, with the result that HRP's position in this area did not show significant improvement.

In 1956 the Restrictive Trade Practices Act, passed in 1955, became law. The most significant provision of the act was that manufacturers were no longer able to determine prices and terms with their competitors. In Mr. Stevens' opinion, "The price structure which previously protected profits has largely been destroyed under the new conditions and the stress of competition. The result of this is that there has developed what is glibly called a 'free-for-all,' which applies not only to underground conveyor belting but to belting of all kinds, to hose, V-belts, fan belts, roller coverings, footwear, flooring—in short, to almost everything we make and sell. Competition today is more rugged than we have ever known it, and I must say frankly that our position is really serious."

During recent years, fluctuations in raw-materials prices also created continuous problems. For instance, the steady rise in the price of natural rubber from a figure of 1s. 9⅜d. per pound in October, 1954, to a peak of 3s. 7¾d. per pound in September, 1955, materially affected costs. In fact, the average price of rubber during 1955 was 68.5 per cent greater than for the previous year.

The net result of the forces affecting the company was a steady reduction in profitability from almost £2,511 thousand before taxes in 1955 to £876 thousand in 1958 (see Exhibit 1). The reduction in profits in 1958 was particularly large due to a general recession in British industry. Coal, iron, steel, and other heavy industries, which represented HRP's most important markets, were strongly affected, and capital expenditures for belting, linings, and other heavy industrial rubber products were among the first to be cancelled or postponed.

Although there was general agreement that the external events mentioned above had weakened the position of the company, some executives believed that internal weaknesses had contributed to HRP's decline in profitability by preventing the company from adjusting quickly enough to the new competitive pressures.

Mr. Heathecote had retired as managing director and chairman in 1953, and Mr. Stevens, who had been marketing manager, was selected as the new managing director. At the same time, the position of chairman was filled by Lord Brinkly, head of a large manufacturing company. Lord Brinkly did not, however, become HRP's chief operating executive but served only in an advisory capacity.

In commenting on the company's internal situation, one executive said: "After the new management of Mr. Stevens came in, I think the company tried to change, but it just did not know how. For one thing, we were extremely short of qualified staff as a result of a policy of not replacing retiring executives. Almost all the executives in the company were advanced in years and were quite overworked. This policy has not changed appreciably in recent years.

"A second characteristic of the company's management that has continued with the present management is the centralization of power in the managing director, with little delegation of authority. Thus it has usually taken a long time to get any decisions. Furthermore, there has been little encouragement for executives to use their own initiative.

"And, finally, I think that one of our most serious problems was that people did not talk about the future. All attention was centered on our day-to-day operating problems. It should be noted, however, that, during most of our past history, there was no apparent need to change. The company was continuing to increase its sales and profits. It was not until the easy money went out of the belting side of our business that the need for change became apparent."

To meet the increased competition, HRP's management did take several steps. Time-and-motion study projects were introduced in the factories in an effort to increase worker efficiency and reduce costs.

Second, increased efforts were made in the export market. In 1957 alone, export sales increased 45 per cent, but were still only 8 per cent of total sales.

Third, a Group Development Department was created, which would be responsible for handling all major products of the Group from laboratory and market research to design. The construction of new experimental facilities was approved to provide the Group with new products and processes.

Fourth, diversification and expansion projects were undertaken. During World War II, HRP had supplied products for the war effort and in several instances had started manufacturing products using rubber substitutes, such as plastics and synthetic fibres. This type of work was continued after the war, and in 1958 the company acquired additional manufacturing facilities for production of plastics. While a large proportion of its sales of plastic products were to the government, there was an increasing volume of business in the commercial field.

And, fifth, several organizational changes were made. Up to 1957, manufacturing activities were under the control of either HRP or the separate subsidiary companies. Selling activities were also carried out by both the parent company or the subsidiaries. With the exception of tires, the products sold through the parent company—mainly belting, hose, and industrial rubber products—were handled by a sales force operating out of three geographical regions. Each salesman sold all the products of the company, and the three regional managers reported to a regional sales manager in the parent company. A separate sales force sold the tire line.

In 1957, however, six divisions were created, headed by division managers, who would be responsible for most of the activities of their divisions. Although the regional sales organization was to remain to perform an administrative function, the members of the general sales force were gradually to be assigned to individual divisions and report to the divisional sales managers.

In his introductory remarks made at the conference held in June, 1958, to discuss the recent "divisionalization" of the company, Mr. Stevens summed up the situation as follows:

"As I see the picture which confronts us, much of the potential profit which the industry previously offered has, for the present, declined. Today supply exceeds demand, there is manufacturing capacity to spare; new competition has arisen and is battling for its share of markets both at home and abroad. And this is true of practically every product made by our Group.

"Those are the conditions with which we now have to contend. The years of plenty have become years of change and, as such, they present us with a challenge. There is much business to be had even under today's conditions. Our immediate task is to secure more of it. To assist cost reduction, we *must* secure a larger share of the available business in all sections of our Group.

"We have in the past done great things, but we can live neither on nor in the past. It is the future of our Group with which we as individuals are all vitally concerned."

HIGHGATE RUBBER PRODUCTS LTD. (B)*

At the end of June, 1958, 55 executives representing all the divisions of Highgate Rubber Products Ltd. assembled for a weekend conference. HRP's Managing Director, Mr. F. C. Stevens, explained the need for the conference as follows:

"The organizational changes which we have already made, I feel sure, have raised questions in the minds of some of us which, so far, have not been answered or resolved. Quite naturally, some are wondering just how their present functions will fit into the new structure and how this will be expected to operate.

"Discussions have been taking place amongst our accountants and also between members of our sales organization and works and production management, but hitherto there has not been an opportunity for all to meet. To facilitate a speedy and well-ordered conversion, it is of the utmost importance that such members of management should have the fullest opportunity to make their individual and collective contributions to the prosecution of these changes.

"With this in mind, it has been decided to hold this conference so that every delegate can offer constructive criticism and suggestions."

The organizational changes referred to by Mr. Stevens concerned the recent creation of six operational divisions, headed by division managers reporting to the managing director. This case consists of a summary of a statement to the conference by Mr. Reginald Davis, HRP's Deputy Managing Director, in which he outlined the changing pattern of HRP's organizational structure, the reasons for changing this pattern, and the problems with which he thought the company would be confronted as a result of these changes. Mr. Davis had joined HRP in 1956 after holding important technical and executive positions in the English engineering industry. He was described by Mr. Stevens as "the architect of the new organizational structure."

"Many of you, I know, feel that this conference is overdue and that we have procrastinated on our organizational changes. This is partly true, but

---

* Fictitious name.

This case was prepared by Mr. John Archer under the supervision of Professor Ralph M. Hower.

Copyright 1962 by l'Institut pour l'Etude des Méthodes de Direction de l'Entreprise (IMEDE), Lausanne, Switzerland. Reprinted by permission.

you will discover as the conference proceeds that our tasks are not easy. We have to change attitudes of mind, find and train the right executives, and, most important, completely reorganize our accounting methods to give you measuring sticks.

"Before outlining the organizational structure we are planning, I would like to talk on the general nature and functions of business with particular applications to our problems.

THE NATURE OF BUSINESS

"Business in the capitalistic world had its origin in the entrepreneur employing labor to make and sell products while attempting to secure the maximum profit for the capital he had invested in his business. The owner-boss and other shareholders were the most important elements of management, while the employees did what they were told. Many businessmen in this and other countries still retain rudiments of the 'boss' complex. The social and political conscience today demands that we recognize a wider business responsibility, with an accountability to consumers, suppliers, employees, local authorities, and government as well as to the boss and the shareholders. Economic conditions and the competition engendered by rapid advances in technology also demand a wider approach to business management, as the problems involved are beyond the wit of the normal individual. Adaptation to those factors has inevitably encouraged the growth of bigness in business.

"Nevertheless, we should accept the 'boss' element, though modified to modern management practices, as essential. With enlightened leadership, we can get what we want in company management, namely, strong and independent individuals as bosses, specialization of product and service activity, and units of management of a size easy to administer. Thereby we might secure the advantages of the small and of the big organization, eliminating the disadvantages of both.

THE FUNCTIONS OF BUSINESS

"When the one-man boss concept is modified, it is usually replaced or supported by the functional concept of organization. There are three prime functions of business, namely—producing, selling, and developing —and the object of business is to undertake these tasks profitably. These functions, for which the boss—that is, the Managing Director or General Manager—is collectively responsible, are supported by the staff functions: Finance and Accounting, Legal and Secretarial, Advertising and Public Relations, Personnel and Training, Organization and Methods, and Purchasing. When a company is small or has few products or factories, this simple organizational structure is most satisfactory, but with many products and with many factories the complexity of problems which arise from a strictly functional structure is such that few men, even of Managing Director status, have the time or intellectual ability to cope with it.

THE HRP ORGANIZATIONAL PROBLEM

"The HRP organization has grown as a result of the acquisition of a number of companies, many undertaking similar activities. With 9 companies and 11 factories, integration has to come but has lagged. A year or two ago the Managing Director had, in theory, 36 people reporting to him and received 120 reports each month. Obviously, such a state of affairs was unworkable, particularly because of the interrelation of problems, as business became tougher. The alternatives were (*a*) to impose a strictly functional structure on the group organization, which becomes an intolerable and unworkable burden for the multiproduct, multifactory organization; (*b*) to reconstitute our many existing companies with a controlling holding company, which would be difficult because of the moribund state of many of these; or (*c*) to divisionalize the activities of the company, making use of the residual goodwill in the names of some of our subsidiaries in so doing.

THE DIVISIONAL ORGANIZATION

"As well as providing a heavy load on top management, the centralized functional organization is defective in the lack of general business training permitted by the system. Even senior executives grow up with just a specialized training in sales or factory matters, without knowledge of each other's problems and often in a perpetual state of war with each other.

"There is usually a wide experience over the company's product range, but this experience always becomes diffuse, as the executive judgment is more important than detailed product knowledge. Switching of personnel between the prime functional tasks is essential for a broad training in any type of organizational structure, but it usually has to be undertaken at an early stage of a man's career and so may not provide the essential business training.

"So let us take a closer look at the possibility of dividing the activities of the company so that we concentrate the load and provide a business training by the creation of little businesses which we can call 'cells of business activity.' A cell of business activity covers the production and sale of a product or service which requires specialized technical, production, or marketing attention. The production, marketing, and technical problems of products such as V-belts, tires, or rubber linings actually have little in common.

"Up to now, rubber has been the common denominator, and our skills have been developed as processors of rubber. Under today's conditions, such a narrow outlook is insufficient to meet the rapidly changing requirements of the highly competitive markets for which we produce. The switch from rubber to PVC[1] conveyor belting was our first shock and the switch to nylon for industrial hoses our most recent; practically every one of our rubber products has now become vulnerable. We are on a tough spot and must be on our toes to attack wherever markets and profits are to be found. This requires concentration of effort on market requirements, using sales engineers to sell service and performance, production engineers to ensure that our products are made soundly and economically, development engineers to study and prepare for new products and processes, and all must work in harmony of thought and action in the business area allotted to them.

"So our plans provide for a division of company activities into cells of business activity in which those composing the cell will be responsible for the operation, development, and profitability of the company's business allotted to the cell-profit centers as they have been described. In each cell the prime business functions will still persist, but the nature of the organization within the cell will depend on the business activity, on the product, and on the personnel available.

"If, of course, we divided the company into too many independent cells of activity, we would be back where we started, with much too great a load on top management. It has been suggested that the maximum number of individuals who should report to one man is seven. However, if the seven men all influence the actions of each other and require continual decisions on the interplay of actions, then the effect is the same as having 7×7 men each reporting on single problems. So, if we can create an organization which minimizes the interplay and entails general managers' just reporting on the development and profitability of their operations, with servicing by expert staff departments, we are moving towards a satisfactory solution.

"The decision to date is to create six operating divisions supported by the usual staff departments (see Exhibit 1). These divisions follow obvious product groupings. The sales turnover of each division is substantial, and the intention is to have each division operated by a general manager as and when appropriate personnel become available from

---

1 PVC is polyvinyl chloride.

within and without the organization. For the time being, we may have to improvise and have one executive undertaking more than one job.

"The top and supporting structure of a division is shown in Exhibit 2. Each general manager must have full executive responsibility but can be

Exhibit 1

CORPORATE ORGANIZATION, 1958

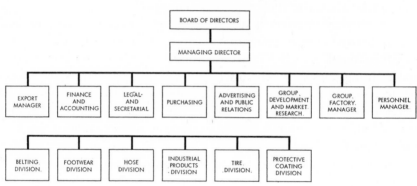

Exhibit 2

DIVISIONAL ORGANIZATION

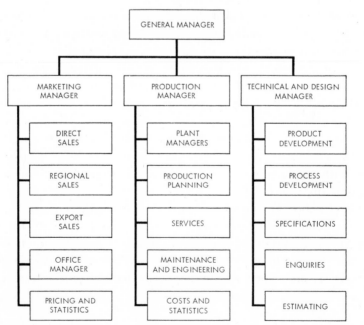

guided in exercising this responsibility through an Executive Committee which, ideally, should have the Managing Director as its chairman, though this function may be delegated. It is never desirable for a man to sit in judgment of his own acts, so the functions of chairmanship and chief executive should be divorced. In this way, we can provide 'Junior Boards' at the head of each division.

THE MARKETING AND SALES ORGANIZATION

"It is of no value to a business to produce goods or have the capacity to produce goods which the market doesn't want. Hence—with due respect to my production friends—the vital emphasis of business must be placed on markets. If we could supply just what the market wants at an acceptable price without any competition, sales would be no problem. For nearly 20 years, selling has been relatively easy, as demand exceeded supply. Today we are faced with a buyer's market, with the buyer, needled by the experience of a seller's market for two decades, developing a keen sense of cost as well as of price to a degree which never existed in the 1930's and which has become vicious in some cases. Suddenly entering an era of overproduction, the buyer has the whip hand and is inclined to use it where it hurts most. Sentiment and service seem to matter little. The young salesman, ill-trained to meet these new conditions, has a tough time ahead, and we must provide him with every possible weapon to go into the attack.

"The first consideration is to know the market and the competition. Statistics are sometimes, but unfortunately not always, available from government sources and trade associations. If not, we must build up our own estimates, in order to have some yardstick of the size and extent of our target. We hope the divisional marketing managers will be developing market information based on customer demand and how much of the customers' business we can expect to get, from nothing to 100 per cent.

"It is recognized that market information is limited by the extent of market coverage. It may not be profitable to seek out every customer, but we must have the means to determine whether the marginal demand is worthwhile. To give an example—assume that we have 25 per cent of the belting market and that we estimate that production capacity is 150 per cent of demand, with at least ten competitors; then are we justified in increasing our representation to attempt to secure an additional 5 per cent? Market studies, with knowledge of our marginal costs, should tell us.

"Divisional marketing managers can also seek help from our Group

Development and Market Research Department, but that department cannot be expected to perform the day-to-day duties of a division; its prime task is to study our long-term problems and interest, and pay particular attention to development projects until they are securely placed on a commercial and economic basis.

"Our salesmen represent the company in the field, and through them our customers judge the company and our ability to serve them. This necessitates a concentration of attention on the sales territory, the customer, and the products. How do we organize to achieve this end?

"For many years we have sold our goods through regional sales offices operated by HRP, with certain subsidiaries playing minor sales roles because of traditional goodwill. Today we have created divisions with their own marketing responsibility which will cut across company and regional operations and procedures. But the new appraisal of our tasks in no way affects the job of the men in the field adversely. Indeed, with a new alignment of duties, the tasks are greater and more responsible.

"The greatest problem confronting us in creating an effective selling organization is the impracticability of organizing the most important element of sales activity, namely, the customer. So we must:

a) Set up an organization which ensures an intimate knowledge of the customer—whether he has personal idiosyncrasies regarding representatives; whether it is right or wrong to handle our contacts only with the buyer, or whether we can approach the engineer, technician, or designer; whether the customer resents seeing several representatives from the same company

b) Arrange our representation and warehousing on a geographic basis to ensure that we are on the spot with our goods and our service, while remembering that geographic representation must always be an economic exercise relating to cost of operating a representative in travelling time, expenses, office and warehouse facilities, relative to the marginal business it produces

c) Ensure that our representation can be of specialist character when we are selling performance and service, so that the customer feels that his requirements have expert handling

d) Organize our representation and distribution to give maximum coverage with economy of manpower and capital.

"Many of the customers of divisions may be important general customers of the company within a region; so knowledge of the customer must be built up for the mutual advantage of the division and the regional sales office. Rivalry must not exist between division and regional sales, and it is hoped that effective teamwork will be forthcoming.

"These specific problems demonstrate that the divisions and our regional and export sales organizations have to work in close accord to ensure that the customer is getting services and that the sales actually mature.

DIVISIONAL MANUFACTURE AND FACTORY OPERATION

"Ideally, a division—or any other cell of business activity—would operate most efficiently if the prime functions were all at one centre, with the factory, the sales office, and the development laboratory under one control.

"Nevertheless, our numerous factories can well be a source of economic strength though providing organizational problems. What we have to ensure is concentration of like manufacturing activities, and this must be one of the prime tasks of the divisions. However, we are faced with some large factories which may always have to be subdivided on a divisional basis. Within the large factory we should be able to secure economy of service, of technical skills, of utility supply, and of rubber-compound processing. Our present location problems and the inevitable consequences of development programs over the next five to ten years render improbable a tidy divisional factory pattern in the sense that the divisions can have control of all our factories.

"Our immediate problem is to develop an organizational structure which permits the division to exercise its full responsibility for ensuring that the products required by the division are manufactured at an economic cost and are of adequate quality. Further, the division must be able to exercise its responsibility to improve and develop the line of products allocated to it. These responsibilities can be exercised through a production manager who controls a plant within the jurisdiction of a Group factory manager. The extent to which the responsibility for operations passes directly from division to production, or from division indirectly to production through factory management, is a matter for determination between divisional heads and factory management. The problem is analogous to that presented by divisional representation and regional sales offices.

"Whatever the organizational structure and line of authority devised, the factory manager must be the disciplinary head responsible for the exercise of the statutory regulations imposed by the Factory Acts, for ensuring that we conform to trade-union agreements, and that the company's policies are properly interpreted in such matters as safety, welfare, suggestions schemes, and cost reduction. He is also there to provide common services to the divisional production line, such as materials and utility supplies, maintenance, engineering services, laboratory testing facilities, warehousing, and shipping. The extent to which these services are supplied from a central factory source or come within the authority of the division will depend on the size and nature of divisional activity and will be determined by economic considerations and the availability of personnel. A divisional production unit may be justified in having under its control a maintenance unit but not an engineering workshop. A division will want to undertake its specification work and maybe its testing, but these functions must not be under production control.

"So you will note that we have a lot to unravel, but the tasks are not insuperable. To solve them will need the closest cooperation between divisional production control and factory management. Many of you have been brought up just to mind your own business, which is a useful characteristic when interpreted as doing an effective task on your own. Unfortunately, the effect has been to discourage a sense of participation in company, factory, or divisional affairs. This attitude of mind has just got to disappear.

THE TECHNICAL AND DEVELOPMENT ORGANIZATION

"It has been traditional in the rubber industry that the mysteries of rubber processing and compounding are locked in the mind of the works chemist. He has become the technical dictator of control and development activity, and the rest of the organization—unable to understand what he was brewing—tended to keep him divorced from other considerations and perhaps narrowed his outlook. He has been the victim of excessive functionalism.

"A revolution in the thinking of the traditional works chemist became necessary with the impact of new raw materials. Inevitably, he found the art of processing rubber was not always the best method of processing the new materials.

"Today we must recognize that we are selling engineering and physical performance and that we are faced with technical problems far removed from the art of the old-type rubber chemist. Our technologists have to understand how the essential character of the materials they now use can be changed.

"To be able to exercise our judgment in the techno-commercial field, we have created a Group Development Department so that it can stand aloof from day-to-day problems and guide us on how and where to concentrate our future activities. This does not mean that the divisions cannot draw upon the Group Development Department. They can, but the case must be justified to Group Development, and then Group Development must justify an addition or substitution in their budget.

"The immediate and urgent problem of technical organization lies between divisional and factory control of technical and laboratory operations. We should attack this problem on the basis of the following principles:

a) On the thesis that no man should sit in judgment on his own acts, finished-products testing, but not necessarily inspection, must be independent of production control but not independent of divisional control, as the final decision to market a product of superior or doubtful quality must rest with divisional management.

b) Raw-material and process control could be under production control, for it is production's inherent responsibility to produce goods as cheaply and efficiently as possible within the specification of the finished product.

c) Product and process changes in specifications to utilize new raw materials, to ensure improved quality or more economic operations, must again be a divisional responsibility, but not within the authority of production control, which can initiate but not authorize.

d) Processing of enquiries for estimating, pricing, and provision of specifications to permit manufacture must again be a divisional responsibility, with the marketing, production, and technical functions determining the justification for pursuing the enquiry by procedures which the division must evolve.

e) Experimental work in the laboratory and in the plant again should be a divisional responsibility, but they may request factory management, group development, or other divisions to assist them or undertake the experimental work for them.

f) If an expense is to be charged against a division, the activity incurring the expense must be a divisional responsibility, though authority to prosecute the activity may have been delegated.

THE MEASUREMENT OF PERFORMANCE

"Divisionalization, with its delegation of authority to perform in a specified area of business activity, cannot work unless those concerned have measuring sticks to control their operations and judge their performance. The essence of the reorganization is to set up profit-earning centers. The company as a whole is not accustomed to be judged in monetary terms, but henceforth every senior executive will be responsible for an expense budget, a production cost, or a profit position. To achieve this has required a complete overhaul, rationalization, and modification of our accounting departments and their procedures. Business is a matter of investing capital for the production of a profit. Those who have been concerned with sales, pricing, and profit margins have tended to be interested only in the profit on the sale. This is fine if you are just a jobbing trader, your fixed assets are negligible, and maybe your stocks and working capital quite small. But in a manufacturing business the capital employed is the important feature, for we have to ensure a return on that capital.

"Divisional profitability will be judged, therefore, not on profits on sales but upon return on investment based on the fixed and working capital used by the division. Some grumblings have already occurred at such an imposition, as the general managers concerned had not personally recommended expending that capital for which they are now responsible. For the first time for many a day, there is surplus capacity to produce within the group, but you can be assured that no capital has been expended without those concerned with sales being consulted. Marketing judgments must now be translated into budgeted sales forecasts, so that our production operations and our future capital programs can be adequately planned.

"The budgetary control system is new to the company, but its importance cannot be overstressed. Nonsense will be made of the budget, however, if it is based on incorrect business premises. Hence the outstanding importance of the sales budgets, backed up by marketing judgment.

"Our cost of production is the prime factor in our ability to continue in business. Our products are so numerous and so varied that it is not easy to impose a standardized cost system. But by introducing standard costs on the basis of a unit, standard to the department concerned, we have succeeded in providing some measuring stick of production performance. Until we know our true costs, it is extremely difficult to be sure whether our pricing policy is correct, and this is of great importance in the tough market of today and as we delegate pricing responsibility to a division.

"The other measuring sticks you need to judge performance are sales against budget or target figures and your expenses of operation. Our accounting team knows the relative importance of time and accuracy in the processing of figures, but they can get nowhere without the data on which to give you figures, and you are the people responsible for supplying the data. If you don't think you are, you had better get moving quick to find out why you have not recognized this responsibility.

"With measuring sticks available to you and to management, you are on the spot, and you will be judged by your performance against a budget you yourselves have compiled. One of our members once suggested that we were bottom-heavy, and this is generally true by the very fact that we have had a complex organization with considerable duplication of effort. All this is being eliminated, and, with the elimination, we may well be faced with redundancy problems. The target of cost reduction at which we are shooting has to be of the order of 3–6 per cent. While trying to achieve this target, we also are aware that we may have to increase our expenses elsewhere, and this must not be regarded as incompatible with cost reduction but rather an inevitable consequence of an expansion program requiring different skills and abilities.

APPRAISAL OF PERSONNEL

"To succeed, we must develop people who have got a little more than other companies have got. Good men are hard to get, and it is true that there are many good men around whom we fail to recognize because we don't put opportunity in their way. Divisionalization will fail if we do not find the right leaders in the first place, and we cannot tolerate the wrong man in the wrong place. This might be management's mistake by placing a man beyond his ability to perform. Recognize your limitations, or else you may well be heading for a very unhappy career. Increased responsibility is tough, but fun, and we want people who are prepared to have a go at it."

HIGHGATE RUBBER PRODUCTS LTD. (C)*

In January, 1960, Mr. Reginald Davis, HRP's Assistant Managing Director, assumed the position of Managing Director. Mr. F. C. Stevens, the previous managing director, became Deputy Chairman of the Board of Directors.

By March, 1961, the organizational changes conceived by Mr. Davis had been largely implemented, although in a somewhat modified manner. First, the number of divisions had been reduced from six to four, as the Protective Coatings Divisions was merged with the Hose Division and the Footwear Division was merged with the Industrial Products Division. Second, the divisions had assumed complete marketing responsibility, and the position of Regional Sales Manager had been eliminated. Third, the factories had been assigned to specific divisions, even though factories producing for more than one division were still operating. And, fourth, a Group Controller of Technical Operations had been appointed, and the functions of the Group Development Department were assumed by this more comprehensive group technical organization.

This case, based upon interviews with Mr. Davis, describes his reactions to the organizational changes and their associated problems. Financial data for 1959 and 1960 are presented in Exhibits 1 and 2.

"As I said at the Executive Conference over two years ago, we were going to try to break the organization up into cells of business activity," Mr. Davis remarked. "We have never shifted from this basic policy since that time, and I am convinced that by so doing we are going in the right direction. I want the responsibility and full authority for operations in the hands of the divisional managers. They are responsible for the profitability and the development of the company's business in those areas allotted to them. I want these people to make decisions by looking at the broad economics of a particular situation, rather than viewing it solely as a marketing or production problem. In other words, they should act only after determining the over-all practicability of a particular job.

"At the same time, however, we have not been able to delegate all functions to the divisions because some are not large enough economically to conduct their own advertising or research and development programs. Therefore, we have centralized certain functions at the Group level, and

Exhibit 1

PROFIT AND LOSS STATEMENTS, 1959–60
(In thousands of pounds)

	1959	1960
Total trading profit	1,223	1,685
Less:		
Depreciation	487	565
Audit fees and expenses	11	16
Directors fees	48	57
Total	546	638
Profit before taxes	677	1,047
Less:		
Income taxes	195	397
Profit taxes	40	97
Total	235	494
Net profit	442	553

Exhibit 2

BALANCE SHEET AS OF 30TH JUNE, 1960
(In thousands of pounds)

CAPITAL AND RESERVES

Issued capital of HRP 350,000 6½ per cent cumulative preference shares	350	
Ordinary stock	4,000	4,350
Reserves		7,816

CURRENT LIABILITIES

Bank overdrafts	1,528
Accounts payable	2,430
Tax liability	461
Other accrued expenses	246
Total liabilities	16,831

FIXED ASSETS

Plant and equipment	9,782	
Less: depreciation	2,540	7,242

CURRENT ASSETS

Cash	137
Investments	693
Tax reserve certificates	....
Accounts receivable	3,204
Inventories	5,555
Total assets	16,831

the divisional managers are expected to look to these Group functions for help. They, of course, pay for these activities by an allocation of Group overhead expenses.

"The difficulty is that as soon as you make a man a division manager, he fights like hell for everything to be under his control and doesn't like to come to the Group for help. One of our biggest problems is that I don't believe any of our division managers have really resolved this problem of the division-Group relationship. For example, one of our divisions is headed by an extremely self-sufficient person who has so much a sense of independence that he has insisted that his organization perform all its secretarial, accounting, and even research activities. His research activities, however, have amounted to over three times his annual net profit.

"We finally told him that we would approve the research but that he would have to come to the Group for support and that the work would be financed out of the central research budget. Even under this arrangement he wants to have complete control over everything that is developed as a result of the research, in spite of the fact that some of the products might be more appropriately controlled by other divisions. I am afraid that, in time, we will have to withdraw the research work from his organization. He just has a tendency to overdo the development function and forget that he has to make a profit in a competitive market.

"To help direct the capital expenditures of the other division managers, we have suggested, as a guide, that they should use all their depreciation funds plus about 25 per cent of their net profits before taxes. We insist, however, that this should not prevent them from making additional requests for capital if they are necessary.

MARKETING

"During the past few years, perhaps the most important changes have occurred in the area of marketing. This is logical, I suppose, since our first major organizational changes took place when we switched from regional selling, using a general sales force, to divisional selling, using specialized salesmen. Perhaps I should explain this decision more fully.

"Up to the time of the Executive Conference, general line salesmen were used for all HRP products, with the exception of tires. Our regional selling organization was headed by a man who was a specialist in the marketing of conveyor belting, and the work of the Belting Division was dominating our marketing effort. I should add, however, that traditionally our belting sales accounted for most of the company's business and provided most of the profits.

"At the same time, because of the influence of the National Coal Board and an increasing trend toward consolidation in British industry, there was a parallel trend toward nation-wide, centralized purchasing. Thus the value of the regional salesmen was decreasing, as purchasing decisions were made at a company's headquarters.

"Although we had been aware of this situation for some time, we had continued to use regional selling for two major reasons. First, we thought that the use of a combined sales force for all divisions was more economical. And, second, we were concerned about the possible adverse reactions of customers when, instead of seeing only one HRP representative, they saw two or three. This would be the result of divisional selling, because many customers purchased the products of several divisions.

"We finally decided that the trend toward centralized purchasing was reducing the economic advantages of regional selling. We also realized that, with our regional selling organization influenced so much by the Belting Division, our other products were not being pushed heavily enough to reach their potential markets. Finally, and most important, we realized that the nature of the selling job was changing to one involving a specialist's knowledge of a customer's needs. Thus, when we asked our customers how they would feel about receiving calls from several HRP salesmen, their reaction was quite favourable. They wanted specialists to call on them, and it was embarrassing for our salesmen when they could not answer their customers' specific questions.

"Because of the rapid changes in technology, it was not even enough to be able to answer specific questions correctly. If we were to increase our sales, we would have to be able to take our technical know-how to the customer and to understand his problems of design. In this way we could answer questions before they were asked. We could suggest uses for our products that customers had never thought of. For instance, we are now investigating the use of synthetic fibres as a reinforcement for concrete and are thinking of using plastics in a broad range of construction applications. No general line salesman could possibly have the technical competence to provide this kind of service.

"Divisional selling, however, is just one of the changes that are taking place in our marketing activities. Another is that the scope of our product line is increasing all the time. And it has to increase if we are to survive. Each time you look at a market for a particular product, you find yourself forced to give an engineering service and not just a product. In hose manufacturing it used to be just a case of extruding rubber over fabric. Now that the use of high-pressure hose systems has become important, the hose fittings are of critical importance, for with improper fittings lives are at stake. Thus the hose manufacturer must understand the problems of manufacturing fittings, even though he doesn't actually make them himself. In fact, we have to understand the character of the whole rubber and allied products systems, including all components, and we are actually supplying some customers with help in designing their products.

"Nor can we continue to think in terms of rubber. For instance, we have made rubber linings and coverings to protect steel against sulfuric acid and other chemicals. We realize now that, with the development of new materials, our whole market could evaporate unless we are able to offer a wide range of protective materials. We now have a corrosive engineering section, and they are only partly concerned with the use of rubber.

"Here is another example of the things that can worry me a great deal: There is a company in Germany that manufactures automobile-lubrication systems. In some parts of the system they were using copper pipes, until they discovered that nylon hose was a more satisfactory material. Having replaced copper with nylon, they looked to see whether they could also substitute nylon for rubber hose, and before long we discovered that they had developed a hose that could take away a large part of our hose market. It is frightening to think that rubber hose, a product that has been used for 130 years, could be replaced so quickly.

"In the conveyor belting field, some people have even suggested that we may eventually get into the business of manufacturing the machines which use belts. As you know, at one time all sales of belting went through the conveyor manufacturers, but the nationalized industries revolted against this system, and at present all big conveyor belting users buy their requirements directly from the belting manufacturers. Since we are now dealing directly with the users and since we are having to pay more attention to the design of the conveyor system, these people argue that we should consider producing conveyors.

"The same type of thing is happening in transmission belting. We are weak in this area because we have never done any pully design work. Now that we are being forced to provide an engineering service, it is essential that we know the type of equipment on which our belts are used, as well as the uses to which they will be put.

"In all our marketing efforts, we have been hampered by a lack of market information. We have to have this information because, with rapid technological change, we have to be able to plan ahead of our markets. We have fairly good information in the Belting Division because of the government interest, but this is an exception. We are encouraging the development of industry data by the trade associations, but at present the only way we can get a feel for a market is to corner a good chunk of it and get a direct flow of information from it.

PRODUCTION

"We have also had serious problems in the area of production. We wanted to create a broad concept of marketing in the divisions, which included the interrelationship between just selling and the activities of production and design. We originally kept the production organization under the direct control of the Group as far as administration and factory operations were concerned. We placed general factory managers in charge who were to operate the factories on a housekeeping basis, renting out space to the divisions. The factory manager would be in charge of the central factory services. We did this because most of our factories were producing for more than one division and did not appear to lend themselves to complete divisional control. Our assumption, of course, was that if the divisions could develop the broad marketing concept, it didn't really matter where the products were actually produced. In other words, we thought that was an internal problem that we could solve without changing the organization.

"We finally realized, however, that, without direct control of production, our divisional managers were not going to understand the important production-marketing relationship. Thus, at the beginning of 1961, we assigned each factory to the division receiving the largest amount of its output. The manager of that division will henceforth be responsible for providing the other divisions with their required output. Any conflicts which the division managers cannot resolve on an informal basis can be brought to the monthly meeting of the Policy Committee, which is composed of the division managers and certain Group executives.

"We have also had to make changes in our costing and pricing systems. We had been pricing on the basis of rules of thumb applicable to broad categories of products. Under this system, the factories supplied cost data to a central estimating department. These data were mainly in the form of material and labor costs plus a percentage figure for the allocation of overhead. The estimating department would then prepare price lists for distribution to the sales force, which was thus not aware of manufacturing costs.

"This procedure worked in the past because margins were very high, and we were able to get by because our average costs were good in relation to those of our competitors. With the Restrictive Practices Act, all this came to an end. I think that the significant reduction in profitability over the past few years is due in large measure to the removal of restrictive practices and a return to tough price competition.

"One of the things we have done, therefore, is to break down profitability in terms of individual products. We are thus able to make better decisions about leaving a product in our line or taking it out. Even when we continue to sell an unprofitable item, we at least know when we are doing it and realize the other reasons which lead us to this decision. For instance, we may continue to distribute an unprofitable product in order to offer a full line or because of its contribution to overhead when other profitable items are not available for substitution. The net result is that we have ended our previous policy of never turning down a customer. We now know where our strengths and weaknesses are and can act accordingly.

"In those cases where we told our customers that we would either have to raise our prices or remove a product from our line, we have often met with a most understanding reaction. I think people respect you more when you are frank and show that you know your business than when they are purchasing your products at unreasonably low prices. We still have a lot of work to do in this area because of our fantastic range of products.

"Another improvement we have made is to look at return on investment data. When I came to HRP, people were looking only at the high margins in existence and did not realize that in some cases our return on investment was quite low because of the large amount of capital investment required in production facilities.

"Something happened recently that was most encouraging to me. When I returned from an extended trip to the Far East, I discovered that the managers of the Belting and Hose Divisions had independently produced graphs which showed the relative profitability of various sizes of hoses and belts. When they saw the tremendous differences between the different sizes, they were shocked to their roots.

TECHNOLOGICAL ORGANIZATION

"We have had some of our biggest problems in the technological area. There was insufficient technological control in the company, and we had not kept our systems or procedures up to date. We were able to operate with a poor technical organization for several years after the war because the shortages created by the war made it easy to sell our products. But, with real competition, we could certainly not continue with an organization in which the people in one factory did not know what the other factories were doing. There were many people who had been with the company for 20 to 30 years and had never met each other.

"We therefore decided to centralize all our technical forces under one man, Mr. George Evans, who had previously only been in charge of research and development. From an organizational point of view this action was entirely wrong because no one man could actually coordinate all the technical activities of the company and continue as head of research and development. We did it, however, because he was the one man in the company with universal respect for his technical competence.

"But even when we centralized the technological program under Mr. Evans, we realized that eventually we would have to move toward getting the major responsibility for technical development back into the division. Furthermore, it would have to be a separate part of the divisions for three cardinal reasons. First, if the technical organization was under the production manager, he would be in a position of being the sole judge of his own acts as they related to the technical aspect of production. Second, marketing and production have to concentrate their attention on what the situation is today. Therefore, we need a separate technical department to look at the future. And, third, much of our development work has to be done near the production process. It is too expensive to perform all development in the laboratories.

"Mr. Evans held this position until two months ago when he was made manager of the Belting Division. Now that he is out of the technical function, we have had to rethink the way technology should be organized in the company. One of our major weaknesses at present is that we still do not have enough technical strength within the divisions.

"At the same time, there are some technical services that have to be supplied from outside the divisions, such as materials research, new-product research, and process research, that are not directly related to a particular division. We now have two experimental labs working on these Group projects in addition to our works labs at the factories, which are controlled by the divisions.

"Three weeks ago we hired a man to be Group Controller of Technical Operations. He will have the responsibility for major engineering projects, process and machine experimentation, and the development of new techniques relative to plant operations, factory layouts, work methods, and instrumentation in the field of production engineering.

"The proper allocation of development and technical resources has been another major problem. Such allocation is easier to handle in the basic industries because you are dealing with fewer product areas. And you also know that if you spend enough money, something profitable can probably be made out of it. This is not the situation in our industry. We may spend a great deal of money in research, only to discover that almost all of it has been completely wasted.

FUTURE OUTLOOK

"As I have indicated, many problems remain. Some people claim, for instance, that, as the process of divisionalization continues, our employees will lose their corporate sense, and, therefore, it is not a good idea to have an organization made up of subsidiary companies. We have tried to solve this problem by transferring people from one division to another and from one functional area to another. We post the job vacancies that exist in all divisions and invite people to apply. A strict divisionalization would not allow us to do this, and we would have no cross-fertilization between different attitudes within the company.

"These people also argue that if you can't integrate the different parts of a business, you shouldn't be in such unrelated fields. I believe, on the contrary, that we have to expand in many new directions because products that were unrelated in the past are becoming closely related today. For instance, a short time ago one could claim that there was no relationship between belting and glass fibres, but today we are putting glass fibres into our belts.

"While there are risks inherent in letting the divisions go on their own, I think, on balance, one has to take these risks. I know of one instance where a customer of one division of a large group was purchasing a product from the division and selling it back to another division at a profit. I think this case is an example of bad selling and bad purchasing and not an indication that the organization is wrong. This is why we have our Policy Committee, where our division managers can see corporate problems as a whole and not just the problems of their divisions. Our goal is to develop the division managers to the point where they are capable of sitting on the company's main board of directors. The Group would then become something like a holding company.

"People who have had experience in very large groups sometimes say that our divisions are too small. But I feel that it might even be logical to go on sectionalizing within our divisions. For example, our high-pressure hose people are really dealing with a much different product than the other hose people, and it may not be logical to keep those two groups in the same division, even though there are certain related technologies between the two products.

"One of our problems stems from the fact that we have tried to make our executives cost and profit-conscious, but this practice has a habit of rebounding on you. Product development and profitability do not always go hand in hand, and it may be that profit consciousness is holding my men in too much. At the moment, however, we are continuing to drive toward increased profitability.

"A continuing problem is the establishment of the proper relationship between the divisional and Group organizations. I do not want to have to exercise a rigid control over the functions of selling, producing, or development. The further you can push these functions down the line, the easier it is for the individual to perform.

"At the same time, however, you have to provide for greater control by the Group when you do not have exactly the right kind of executives in the divisions. I think running a company is somewhat like conducting an orchestra. You have a plan for the composition, but it is necessary to change some parts of the score in order to take advantage of your orchestra's strengths and to minimize its weaknesses.

"For this reason, I haven't really decided on the ultimate relationship between the Group function and the divisions. In some cases I am consciously promoting a pull between the two methods of organization in the hope that the best method will become apparent. To do this, I sometimes wear a Group hat and stress the Group functions, and sometimes I switch hats and emphasize divisional versus Group functions. My current thinking now is to have some people with functional expertise in the Group organization who can advise and guide and help exercise my executive authority when they are dealing with the divisions. But these people will not be able to instruct the divisions to do something unless they are acting on my behalf."

HIGHGATE RUBBER PRODUCTS LTD. (D)*

In March, 1961, Mr. Reginald Davis, Managing Director of Highgate Rubber Products Ltd., stated: "One of our biggest problems is that I don't believe any of our division managers have really resolved this problem of the division-Group relationship." This case is based on discussions with three division managers, in which they were asked to give their views on the relationship they thought should exist between their divisions and the group organization.

THE INDUSTRIAL PRODUCTS DIVISION

The Industrial Products Division of HRP produced a broad range of products, including antivibration mountings, industrial V-belts, rubber and plastic mouldings, extrusions, and prefabricated products. In 1960, the Industrial Products Division had also assumed responsibility of HRP's line of rubber footwear.

The Division Manager, Mr. Arthur Henry, and the Assistant General Manager, Mr. Paul Edwards, were interviewed together. Mr. Henry had been in his position since 1956 and was 44 years old in 1961. Until 1956 he had been the owner-manager of a small rubber-products company. Mr. Edwards, 39 years old in 1961, had also worked for a small company before joining HRP in 1957.

Speaking of these two men, a Group executive remarked: "Mr. Henry is an outstanding salesman with a volatile personality, while Mr. Edwards is the 'commercial man' or 'businessman' of the Division. Because of his commercial abilities, Mr. Edwards is a necessary part of Mr. Henry's equipment, although he tends to want to run things on his own, entirely separate from the Group. Thus there are frequent run-ins between him and his cousins in the Group organization."

"We are new boys here," Mr. Henry said. "We only know our division, and we don't want any unnecessary interference from the Group. In general, we do not accept the Group functions. We believe they lead to frustration and a slowing-down of our operations.

---

* Fictitious name.

This case was prepared by Mr. John Archer under the supervision of Professor Ralph M. Hower.

Copyright 1962 by l'Institut pour l'Etude des Méthodes de Direction de l'Entreprise (IMEDE), Lausanne, Switzerland. Reprinted by permission.

"Of course, we are prejudiced in this matter. We have had so little help and so much trouble from Group that we are sour on the whole concept. I think there are some people within this company who really want to go back to the tight, centralized control we had here at one time. Personally, I'm afraid that the wise efforts to move toward divisionalization have stopped in some cases and we are now going backwards. I think that the old-time managers are disappearing in business, and a cult is developing that believes that a man is no longer responsible to his boss but to the personnel manager or trade union.

"We don't play according to the book in this division. We pay attention mainly to profits. In some of the other divisions I know that the division manager is not really the boss and that they are run by the division's executive committee."

"As for the Group functions," Mr. Edwards remarked, "I think that Group advertising and promotion should be used for developing a corporate image. All other advertising should be done directly by the divisions. After all, advertising is a basic part of the bricks and mortar of selling your products; the whole advertising approach must be keyed to the sales point of view. People at the Group cannot make the advertising decisions of the divisions by themselves; they have to come to us for them. Therefore, we might as well decide on our advertising in the first place.

"The same thing applies to Group exporting. They should do only the paper work and be available to give specialized advice on such things as foreign licensing. Some people say that, by having the Group Export Department, the divisions can carry on exporting activities in places where they could not afford to do it if they were separate companies. I don't accept this argument. I say that a division, like a small company, must earn its keep if it wants to eat. If it can't afford to export by itself, it is not necessarily good to force it to export through the Group."

"As far as purchasing is concerned," Mr. Henry said, "we really do all our own purchasing now. A central purchasing department should operate only as a buyer in the formal sense of placing the orders in order to get volume discounts.

"Market research," he continued, "is one thing we don't do enough of here, but I think it should be strictly a divisional responsibility, except in those cases where the information has nothing to do with a particular division."

"Divisional rather than Group accounting," said Mr. Edwards, "is absolutely necessary. We get data from the Group accountants, and we need an interpreter in order to understand what it means. Sometimes we tell the Group that we don't believe their accounting data. Then they go to our factories for the information, and it is passed back to the Division by the Group. All this is wasted effort and could be handled much more quickly if the divisions did their own accounting.

"Here's what I mean by some of the worthless information we receive from Group." At this point Mr. Edwards left his office and returned a few minutes later with a 20–30-foot length of computer tabulating paper. After throwing it into the air, collecting it in a large pile on the floor, and placing it in a wastepaper basket, he said: "As you can see, there are no words on that paper. There are only numbers because the machine has to work entirely with codes; and it would take me hours to translate the data. Now this is an extreme example, and I don't know why they even sent us that paper, but my point is that when you take the accounting function away from a division, you remove an intimacy with an activity which is essential to business. Unless you have this function within your organization, you are never able to see things realistically.

"The work of the Group legal and secretarial department is also unsatisfactory. Here's an example of what I mean: We wanted to rent a factory in northern England a short time ago. Now, I could have gone north and negotiated the terms of a lease. We could then have employed solicitors, and all arrangements could have been finished in one or two weeks. But no, I couldn't do this. I had to go to the Group secretary, who negotiated the terms. The lease was then passed on to someone in the Group organization who noticed that it contained a clause preventing the building from being used for industrial purposes. When I told him this was ridiculous and that he should get the clause removed immediately, he replied that he didn't think the other party would agree to this change. The case has now been going on for eight or nine weeks, and we still don't have any final action. I had another deal similar to this not long ago, and I didn't tell the Group about it. It was finished in two weeks. What we run into at Group is either a bunch of experienced amateurs or a bunch of amateur specialists, I don't know which.

"Let me give you another example. We wanted to start manufacturing operations in a building here in London, and factory inspection by the authorities is required by law. I wanted the man from Group to call the factory inspector and request an inspection, but he wouldn't use the telephone. He had to write a lengthy letter describing in minute detail what the inspector would see when he went to the building. Then he had to wait for a reply, and, again, the time passed quickly. I would think that this kind of a job should be handled by the divisions."

"Although research and development should primarily be a divisional function," Mr. Henry remarked, "I suppose the Group can do some long-term development. As for the new function of the controller of technical operations, it should not have any line authority. We are willing to accept technical advice if it is offered in the form of a suggestion like we would get from an outside consultant, but we do not want to take any orders from these people.

"Although the factories are more difficult to place within the divisions than the marketing function, I do not think it is impossible. It's mainly a question of accounting chargeability.

"The only time the Group personnel officer has been effective for us is when he has been acting as my own divisional personnel officer. I find it difficult to recognise ways in which he has helped us acting in his formal Group position, except, I suppose, policies formulated for the Group as a whole and for other corporate activities do involve all of us.

"My feelings toward control by Group can be summed up by a small incident that occurred a few weeks ago. The Group would not approve my giving a bonus to the telephone operator for my division on the grounds that her pay classification was too low. Now she can help or hurt our sales directly by the way she answers the phone, and she should be working with an incentive. My feeling is that you should pay big salaries to the top people and pay bonuses to the little people. By making the divisions into autonomous, separate companies, we can help our people relate themselves to their organization, but it is difficult for me to do this when I am not completely free to run the Division the way I want."

THE HOSE DIVISION

Hose Division of HRP manufactured a wide product line, including industrial hose and tubing for all applications, fire-fighting and irrigation hose, corrosion- and abrasion-resistant linings for pipes, chemical- and acid-resisting building materials, and rubber and ebonite roller coverings.

The Hose Division possessed a particularly complex manufacturing organization, receiving its production from five different factories. Only two of these produced exclusively for the Division. On the other hand, the Division was responsible for operating the Slough factory, which produced some products for every other division.

The manager of the Hose Division, Mr. Armstrong Whitney, was a man in his early fifties. He was an engineer by training and had spent most of his career in the rubber industry. At one time he had been co-general manager of a rubber company and general manager of a second. He came to HRP in 1956, and, before assuming his present position, he was the Works Manager at the Slough factory.

In speaking of Mr. Whitney, a Group executive stated: "Of all the division general managers, he has the type of background which would lead one to think that he should be the best equipped to run a division. He is a charming person, but has not the dynamic qualities of Mr. Henry, and I am not sure that he really knows how to implement the divisionalization and other changes that have taken place since the Executive Conference. By this I mean that he still hesitates to run the Division as independently as he should. This is probably because he is a product of the rubber industry, which is an old-fashioned industry. For example, the industry has never paid much attention to developing people in modern management techniques, and we face this problem acutely in the Hose Division.

"There is not yet any obvious number-two man in the Division; this spot is probably shared by the Division's marketing and production managers, neither of whom has yet developed enough drive and knowledge of business management. This is unfortunate, because the future of the Division will depend to a large extent on how hard the men under Mr. Whitney set the pace."

The following statements were made by Mr. Whitney as he explained his attitudes toward the relationship he felt should exist between the divisions and the Group organization:

"I have been with two relatively small organizations during most of my 23 years in the rubber industry. During my career I have become convinced that it is of the greatest importance for people in any organization to know to whom they are responsible at the top. This is sometimes difficult to ensure in larger companies—as was the case when I first joined HRP; thus I fully supported Mr. Davis' idea of divisionalization, which would give the divisional managers their individual organizations (rather like little companies) to look after. It seemed to me to be the right and logical thing to do.

"One of our biggest problems arising from divisionalization continues to be the question of how to operate the Slough factory, which produces for five divisions. The fact that I am still responsible for the over-all operation of the factory, and only production for the Hose Division, sometimes puts me in a difficult position. When, as divisional manager, I may want to transfer some of the Division's production out of Slough, I have to consider the move in terms of its over-all effect on the factory economics.

"Although Slough has been formally designated a Hose Divisional factory, it is run by a Works Superintendent who is responsible only for the administration, discipline, and services, etc., whereas the production for the Hose Division is the responsibility of a Divisional Departmental Production Manager. Services would include production planning, cost accounting, estimating, purchasing, etc. These services must be centralized because we have only one processing department at the factory.

"The trouble with our operations there is that the divisions are sometimes inclined to forget that there are other divisions around. We get divisional people coming down to the factory and talking too much about what they are going to do. The result is that people at the factory sometimes become concerned about the effect of such moves on them personally. For example, one divisional manager said that his division was going to do its own production planning. I told Mr. Davis about this, for I considered this as the kind of case involving a change in policy which should first be discussed at a Policy Committee meeting. An announcement at the factory level should be made only after an agreement is reached at the policy level.

"On balance, I think the divisions are fairly self-contained units. Each division has its own executive committee, where the work of the different divisional departments can be coordinated. Because they are self-contained, the Divisional Manager is fully responsible for efficient control, profitability, etc. For instance, now that the Division has its own selling representatives, I have to be sure that their number and expense are fully justified.

"I believe the formation of the Group Policy Committee was a very wise step because it provides the opportunity for the divisional managers to work together as company men. Before the existence of the Policy Committee, for example, when a division applied for additional capital, the request went to the managing director, who presented it to the Board of Directors for approval. If the request was turned down, the divisional manager was naturally disappointed—not always knowing the reason why the project had not been approved, he was in a very difficult position.

"Now, however, we discuss each other's projects in the Policy Committee, and we have to present our projects on economic grounds. Therefore, each divisional manager now knows exactly why he does not get something he wants. He also knows that the whole matter was discussed and agreed upon among the divisional managers at this committee."

In the discussion on Group versus divisional functions, Mr. Whitney made the following remarks:

"As far as export activities are concerned, I want to be quite clear. The marketing managers of the divisions are responsible for exports, and the Group export people are responsible for exports, and the Group export people are there to advise and assist them. If each division had complete charge of all its exporting activities, it would, in my view, be far too expensive.

"The divisions have their own foreign representatives, and it is important that these representatives should work very closely with the Group export organization. I have informed the head of the Export Department that any technical help or other information I can give him is always available. The only problem I can envisage in this area would be if the Group export manager wanted to run his show entirely separately from the divisions. This is not the case at HRP.

"I have not experienced any difficulty in working with the Group Purchasing Department, and I think enough purchasing responsibility has been delegated to the local people at the factories. For instance, they have recently received permission to write directly to suppliers, as long as they send copies of their correspondence to the Group office. We have a new man in charge of Group purchasing, and I have found him most anxious to cooperate. He says that he will fix the prices of our contracts and that the local buyers can place orders directly against them. Thus we will be able to take advantage of the bulk savings.

"Group advertising and promotion constitute something I would hesitate to take over at division level because it could increase costs. Some Group activities could cost almost as much for each division as they now do in total at the Group level.

"The extent of service that we receive from Group advertising is to some extent a function of how much pressure we in the divisions bring to bear. I am in favour of this function staying where it is, as long as we can say what we want to say in our advertising and can advertise in the journals we select. This is now the case. Eventually, it may be necessary for each division to have at least one man on its staff to look after the division's interests in this field. At present, Group advertising cooperates with us and suggests ways in which we might improve our advertising programs.

"In the area of personnel and training, this must be a Group responsibility, to avoid one factory being able to offer better facilities than another. The important thing as far as personnel activities are concerned is that the divisional manager and factory superintendents must never overlook the fact that they and not the Personnel Department are responsible for those who work under them.

"In the area of finance and accounting, I have no doubt that it should be a Group rather than a divisional responsibility. Of course, the divisions have never tried to run their own accounting, but I do not think it would be in the interest of the company if they did. You have to remember that, since the accountants in the divisional factories are responsible for reporting on the results of the divisions, they are unbiased in giving factual reports to top management.

"We receive a great deal of accounting information from Group, but we have not yet reached the stage where we know the real value of these data. Perhaps we are getting a little too much detail. The main things I want to know as a divisional manager are whether I am meeting my budgets, how much profit I am making, and, if I am not making as much as I should, where I am falling down.

"The development of the proper accounting data is being worked on all the time, and I think we are getting closer to what we want each year. At present we get reams of paper with everything expressed in codes, and it is difficult to check many figures. All I can say is that we are working closely with the Group Accounting Department, and from time to time we have differences of opinion. I know they come in for criticism, but we try to be fair because they still have a lot of work to do.

"The legal and secretarial function is obviously a Group responsibility. These people are the right-hand men of the managing director in terms of patents and other legal affairs, and thus this function has to be right where it is.

"The day-to-day technical problems are the responsibility of the divisions, as is divisional long-term development. At the same time, however, we have to get support from the Group. One thing that strengthens the need for a Group Technical Department is that there are so many current technical problems within the divisions that the future very seldom receives enough attention. Another reason is that we are short of process and design engineers in the divisions. The Group Technical Controller will have under him a team of such engineers who can provide services and advice. I do not mean to say that the divisions are not responsible. For instance, in my division we have just hired our own process engineer. But here again we find a case where we can be helped by having people at Group ready to supplement our own work.

"As far as the Group organization in general is concerned, I could sum up my opinion by saying that we have got so much work to do in the divisions that we are going to need all the help we can get if we are going to accomplish it within a reasonable time."

THE BELTING DIVISION

The Belting Division manufactured conveyor belting for all industrial applications, elevator belting, and flat transmission belts. Although the Division sold to most industries, its major customer was the National Coal Board in charge of the nationalized British coal industry.

The Manager of the Belting Division, Mr. George Evans, had assumed this position in late 1960. Up to 1956 he had been a works chemist at one of the HRP factories and had started his career in one of the company's laboratories as a rubber technologist. From 1957 to 1960, Mr. Evans had held the dual position of Manager of the Group Research and Development and Group Technical Controller. In 1961 he was in his middle forties.

Mr. Evans was described by Mr. Davis as an excellent rubber technologist but with no general experience in business. "He has had no sales experience, and his only line experience was years ago when he was in charge of a small workshop. Nevertheless, I am taking the risk that he has what it takes to become a manager. He has had no opportunity to understand accounting data, but I have hired an accounting assistant for him, who can become the commercial manager of the Division."

In commenting on the Group-Division relationship, Mr. Evans made the following comments. He prefaced his remarks by saying that, since he had been division manager for less than two months, his opinions were still tentative.

"In considering the function of the Group Exporting Department, I think the primary question is how much you do in this area as a division. I know that my division is going to have to take an increasingly active part in the export market, because the potential market of our domestic business is just not expanding very quickly.

"In exporting, just as in any other kind of selling, the division has the responsibility for getting rid of its products. Fundamentally, you give the division marketing managers the responsibility for creating export policies, and we use the experience of the Group Export Department to help you carry out these policies. There's no use crying to these people if you don't make out.

"Market research must be a Group function in its basic sense, although we should have some man in the division to serve as a link with the Group in this area.

"Advertising and promotion are a divisional responsibility, but we have to use the services of the Group.

"While I agree that accounting should be primarily a Group function, I am not completely happy with some of the methods used. For instance, I suspect that they are dividing up the overhead costs allocated to divisions, using the same factor on the basis of the sales of the divisions. However, this does not give an accurate picture of where the overhead costs were created.

"I also have some misgivings about the collection of accounting data for use in our budgetary control system. I see a variance in the red, but, since the man who produced the budget is not in my division, he is not close enough to the production problems really to explain why it is in the red. Nor can he always ensure that the figures on which he bases the budget are close enough to reality. I think that the actual collection of data should be a divisional responsibility up to a certain point, in order to get better reliability in the data.

"And I also believe that we should have divisional invoicing. If you are going to ship something, you might as well invoice it.

"In purchasing, the Group people are able to get bulk contracts, and therefore the divisions should utilize Group purchasing to take advantage of the reduced prices. Factory supplies and other local purchases must be decentralized, and we have done this in the last six months.

"As far as personnel and training are concerned, in some locations we are experiencing some slowness in getting information. I also wonder to what extent we should divisionalize our personnel administration. For example, when we have two factories in two different divisions just a mile apart, are we justified in having separate maintenance departments just because the factories are being operated by different divisions?

"In the technical area, the Group should carry out most of the long-term research, although we will also need long-term research associated with the divisions. The development of products is really a joint responsibility of both the divisional and Group technical people. We should put products in the Group development laboratory until they reach the stage when they can be placed in the divisions. The general pattern of development, however, must come from divisional thinking.

"It is also important to have someone in the Group technical organization to help the Group purchasing people select the proper materials. This was not so important a few years ago when we were just using natural rubber. But today, when there are three or four hundred types of synthetic rubber, it is very important to have someone with technical competence coordinating these purchases.

"In general, my only complaint about our divisionalization program is that sometimes we get so excited about it that we forget that the factories even exist. One man in the Group organization made the remark that he thought that in HRP the tail was wagging the dog, and by "tail" he meant the factories. In my opinion, the factories are the dog and the Group is the tail."

HIGHGATE RUBBER PRODUCTS LTD. (E)*

In Highgate Rubber Products Ltd. (D), three division managers expressed their opinions regarding the appropriate relationship they believed should exist between their divisions and the Group organization. The opinions of two Group executives are presented below.

MR. ADAMS LOWRY, GROUP FINANCIAL CONTROLLER

"I would classify the divisions as being subautonomous. They are reasonably self-contained and have a responsibility for profits. The division managers are free to operate within specified target limits.

"I look upon the accountants in the division as people who are under the line authority of the divisional managers. I can say that these people are my accountants, but they are not my men. I see the Group accounting function as something that can serve as a guide, but improvements should be made by working through the line organization. In my opinion, the relationship between the accounting people in the divisions and the Group organization should not be a simple line relationship wherein a man has no route of appeal except through the line organization. In the area of accounting, a man has a functional responsibility, and he has the right of appeal to the managing director through the Group accounting function.

"You have to realize that this is not a holding company and that the managing director has operating responsibility. If I were going to decide whether to give the accounting function to the divisions, I would consider the economics of this move, and I would look at their accounting methods, to see whether they were the ones required by the managing director. If all these points were satisfied, I would be happy to let the divisions handle their own accounting.

"When people in the divisions complain about Group accounting, I ask them what they would do without this central service. It is our function to draw information from the divisions, process it, and then send it back to the line organization, both downward to the divisions and upward to the managing director.

"In deciding what information to send to the divisional managers, we use a process of give and take and try to find the best answer. After satisfying the requirements of the Group, we are perfectly willing to let a man have his own type of information. We send a total of 15 reports to the divisions. Once in a while we will also give them an IBM run with some detailed figures on it, but we never give this information in this much detail unless it is requested.

"A few years ago the divisional managers were given almost no information at all. Mr. Davis told me that we should give them every piece of information we had until they were overflowing with it. Then, he thought, they would not be able to say they did not have enough information.

"You should also realize that there are wide differences between the divisions in the extent to which they are able to use the information we give them and in the extent to which they accept the central accounting data. The important thing is to get the recipients of the information to the point where they can appreciate what it means. I think the system is working fairly well now, but this is something that takes a very long time. When you introduce a system like this, in the first year it seems theoretically possible; in the second year it is somewhat interesting; in the third year it is of some practical value; and in the fourth year it is getting to be pretty good. What I am finding now is an increasing sphere of inquiry, criticism, and disbelief about the information we give to the divisions. That's fine as far as I'm concerned because it shows that the people in the divisions are beginning to think in this area."

MR. HAROLD MATTHEWS, GROUP CONTROLLER OF TECHNICAL OPERATIONS

In November, 1960, Mr. Harold Matthews was appointed Group Controller of Technical Operations of Highgate Rubber Products Ltd. In this position he would have the responsibility for major engineering projects, process and machine experimentation, and the development of new techniques relative to plant operations, factory layouts, work methods, and instrumentation in the field of production engineering. Mr. Matthews stated:

"I have joined a company that is still weak in the area of engineering technology. First of all, the company does not employ many graduate engineers. Furthermore, the technical side of the business is dominated by the rubber compounders, who are really witch doctors and not engineers. Therefore, one of the first things I want to do is to debunk the theory that the rubber compounder is the key man in the technology of the company, when, in fact, he represents only one-third of the required technological team. The other two are the process engineer and the machinery engineer.

"Though a much younger industry, the plastics industry was until recently just like the rubber industry today, in that it was dominated by one group of specialists—the chemists. The subsequent division of technical responsibility between chemists and engineers, who have much more to contribute to process engineering and machinery engineering, is what has made the plastics industry what it is today.

"What I am saying, in other words, is not that HRP is behind its industry, but that the entire rubber industry is in many ways 30 years out of date because it is dominated by the rubber chemist who accepts the established processes that were developed many years ago. It is not the kind of industry that excites me with its performance. At one time during the war I was a liaison officer between the British and Russian navies, and since that time I have continued to study the Russian economy, including factory management. The Russian rubber industry is in some ways several years ahead of the West, and I think it is somewhat ironic that a great deal of my technical information comes from Russian publications.

"In addition to inadequate technology, the commercial knowledge of the company as it relates to forward thinking about product development has left something to be desired. There were not enough people in the company with business judgment. In the past, I think that the top management tended to confuse short-term profitability with technical efficiency; because the company was profitable, they seemed to assume that it was also technically efficient.

"As in other companies in the rubber industry, our people apparently did not understand that the company was vulnerable when it was selling a product to only one customer. Yet this is the case with the Belting Division, which used to sell almost entirely to the National Coal Board, though it is now diversifying its markets.

"One of the reasons, of course, that the company had been able to stay in business was that the National Coal Board, as a matter of policy, split its business, and we got a good share of that business. We were really cashing in on something that was taking place outside our control.

"When you took a detailed look at the profitability of the company, it was somewhat alarming. This was partly due to people asking only if a particular task was commercially feasible and not asking if it was technologically feasible or searching out the best way of making an article. Yet technological efficiency is a prerequisite of profitability. For example, the industry produces a tremendous variety of rubber moldings which require mathematical study if presses are to be profitably utilized. To continue to be profitable, it is necessary to take steps to optimize the use of production resources, but this is an area that has received litttle study throughout the whole industry.

"One of the things that we must now do is to take a hard look at our present processes to determine their technical efficiency. At every level in the production process, this company may need more process control. For instance, when rubber is calendared, one can expect to get certain variations in the thickness of the rubber, and some of these variations will result in a thickness greater than that required. It will be part of our job to point such things out to divisional management and show them that if they can further minimize this amount of extra rubber, they will maximize the process efficiency.

"I wonder how many colleagues have systematically observed the facts. Do they always know what quality is required in a product in order for it to perform satisfactorily? Some of our production may still be inefficient. How many people in the divisions realize this? The accountants have done a fine job, and the information is available, but there are not enough people in the divisions who know how to use it. One of our greatest difficulties will be in developing the top-caliber people we will require, and we will need a training program at all levels of the company. Although this will be expensive, we cannot afford not to do it.

"I am with Mr. Davis 100 per cent in his plan to divisionalize the organization of the company. However, I do not think HRP Ltd. can go far toward establishing autonomous divisions such as those in some very large companies. First, the company cannot afford to do this because the divisions are not large enough to operate all their own services. And, second, there are not yet enough capable people in the divisions to permit them to be completely autonomous.

"The relationeship between the divisions and the Group should be one of plural loyalty, such as you find in the military. The people in the divisions will have their primary loyalty to their division manager. At the same time, however, they will have a loyalty to the functional heads at the Group level, where policy will be set.

"Another thing that makes divisionalization difficult from a technical point of view is that the company presently operates such an amorphous group of factories. Because the factories are so spread out, it raises the question of whether the company can afford to put the required high-grade technical people in each unit. Therefore, I expect to take a hard look at factory rationalization.

"The Group technological structure that should be created will include the following elements. First, there will be a Group methods study manager, who will create, stimulate, and help carry out the activities of methods study completely lacking at present.

"Second, there will be an engineering design department, which will create capital projects designed to improve existing processes. For instance, at present there is no continuous extrusion of hose in the rubber industry, even though this is certainly technologically possible. The reason we don't do it is because of the domination of the industry by the rubber compounders. Therefore, we need this department to investigate projects like this.

"Third, there will be a research and development department. I do not like to use the phrase 'long-term research' as a means of distinguishing between Group and divisional research activity, for there is certainly some long-term research that can be appropriately handled by the divisions and some short-term research that should be performed by the Group labs. I look at Group research and development as a place where we will perform research and development of a detached nature, having no immediate applicability to a particular division. We will probably need such a Group function for many years to do research and development which require a degree of technical knowledge that the company cannot afford for each division. We have to try to get the maximum utilization out of our highly skilled people.

"Fourth, there will be a unit which will invent, develop, and evolve machinery. We cannot rely on the machinery manufacturers, who are primarily concerned with selling their standard models. If we want to increase the efficiency of our processes, we will have to develop our own machinery engineers. Actually, the user of equipment usually knows more about what he wants than the equipment manufacturers because he knows the processes he wants to use. The machinery that is developed merely carries out a certain process, and thus, the development of the process has to come first.

"And, fifth, we will have to have some people at the Group level keeping up with the technology of our raw materials. This unit will also develop some criteria for the testing of materials and products and will give us the ability to simulate field tests. At present we can determine the physical characteristics of different materials, but no one has come up with a way of comparing the performance of two different materials.

"Each of the divisions now has its own technical managers, but, in my opinion, none of the technical managers has yet acquired the experience or fully developed the ability that the job demands. I have not been brought up with the theory that in business you just fire people who don't meet the requirements of their job, and I also realize that we cannot achieve a monopoly in high-quality people. On the other hand, we will probably be forced to shift some people to jobs they can more adequately perform. We will also probably have to go outside the rubber industry to get the men we need, since they may not be in the industry now. But I do not think it is necessary to get people experienced in rubber. A man with the basic knowledge of technology can apply it quickly enough in this industry.

"In working with the divisions, my job will be primarily an educational one. I will try to ensure that the technological structure is right at the factory level, and, once I have done this, I will delegate control to it. My organization will then support the divisions with professional advice. I will shortly propose a divisional technical structure to the division managers. In the beginning I want to have considerable influence over these divisional technical organizations and who goes into them. For at present there are not enough people in the divisions who are really in a position to judge a person's technological ability.

"I plan to get the cooperation of the division managers by showing them that I shall recruit people with technical competence and that we can help them increase their profits. Some of the division managers have little or no technical knowledge, and these will be the easiest to work with. The hardest will be those who consider themselves to be technologists. Of course, I will also have the opportunity to argue my case with top management and get their support for the implementation of my recommendations."

THE SOLARTRON ELECTRONIC GROUP LTD. (A)

ORGANIZATION, OBJECTIVES, AND PRODUCT PLANNING

"I do not think we could have expanded as we have if it had not been for forward planning," said Mr. John Bolton, chairman and managing director of The Solartron Electronic Group Limited, in November, 1958. "Nor would I have the same degree of confidence in our future as I do if we were not continuing to plan ahead."

The Solartron Electronic Group and its subsidiary companies, with headquarters in Thames Ditton, Surrey, England, designed and manufactured two main types of electronic equipment: (1) A range of approximately 80 laboratory and other precision test instruments ranging in price from £50 to £700, such as oscilloscopes, power supplies, amplifiers, and servo test equipment. In the year ending June 30, 1958, such instruments comprised 66 per cent of total company sales and 69.9 per cent of total company deliveries. (2) A variety of "systems engineered" products with higher unit prices, which were broadly defined as electronic systems designed to perform a series of operations comprising a definable task. In a majority of cases these systems were designed, constructed, installed, and serviced by Solartron for customers relatively unfamiliar with electronic equipment. They comprised single products or families of products, each one of which was so chosen that it could constitute an important field of activity for companies in the Solartron group. They included:

(*a*) *An electronic reading machine* designed to read digits 0 to 9, eight alphabetical letters, and four accounting symbols at speeds up to 300 characters per second. The first production model of this machine had been sold to Boots Chemists (a chain of pharmacies) at a price of £223,000 and was scheduled for delivery in November, 1959. It was to be used in connection with a digital computer to analyse daily the sales registered on tapes from approximately 2,000 cash registers. During the 1958/1959 year, six additional orders from large firms were expected to bring total sales to seven.

(*b*) *Radar simulator devices* designed to produce the radar image of aircraft or missiles, operating singly or in formation, for defense planning and training

---

This case was prepared by Mr. Peter Brengel under the supervision of Professor Kenneth R. Andrews.

purposes. By November, 1958, £400,000 of orders, varying from £60,000 to £180,000 per system, had been received from defense and military authorities of various NATO and other European countries including Germany, Italy, and Sweden.

(*c*) *High-speed electronic check-weighers* designed to check-weigh packaged products at an accuracy of ±0.2 per cent as the filled packages moved on a production line at a speed of up to 120 per minute; to deflect and count underweight and overweight packages; and to signal continuously to the packing mechanism any correction required to keep the delivered weight constantly correct. Thirty-two production units at £1,500 each were planned for 1958/1959, for sale largely to food and other consumer-goods manufacturers.

(*d*) *An X-ray spectrometer* designed to provide an automatic, nondestructive method for the quantitative analysis of crystalline materials, such as metals and chemicals. Six units at approximately £10,000 each were planned for 1958/1959, for sale to scientific and engineering organizations.

(*e*) *Cybernetic teaching machines* designed to teach punch-card operators the manual skills needed for punch-card preparation by giving a series of exercises, evaluating progress and mistakes, and automatically varying the speed of the exercise while concentrating on those parts in which errors were made. This machine was the first of a planned series of inductive logic computing devices. Ten to 12 units at £500 each were planned for 1958/1959, for sale to companies employing punch-card equipment.

(*f*) *A range of analogue computer "building blocks"* from which a custom-built analogue computer could be assembled, designed chiefly for use in solving complex mathematical problems.

Solartron also performed precision engineering and design and development work on a contract basis, and sold electronic equipment made by other firms through its domestic and foreign sales organizations.

Exhibit 1 shows actual and forecast sales by product group and company. Exhibit 2 shows the companies of the Solartron group, their dates of incorporation, deliveries in the fiscal year ending June 30, 1958, and principal products or functions. Exhibits 3 and 4 present the Group's consolidated balance sheets and profit and loss statements for recent years, with forecasts through June 1963. Exhibit 5 shows operating profits of the various subsidiary companies for the nine months ended March 31, 1958. The table on page 365 indicates the rate of Solartron's growth from 1950 through mid-1958.

ORGANIZATION

In November, 1958, Solartron included The Solartron Electronic Group Ltd. (the parent company), eight domestic, and three overseas subsidiaries. The parent company was owned largely by members of management and their families. A number of employees were also shareholders. From 1951 to 1958 a majority of the common shares had been held

Exhibit 1

SCHEDULE OF DELIVERIES 1954/1955 TO 1957/1958 AND TARGETS THROUGH 1962/1963*

(In £000's)

Product Group	Actual				Possible Targets for Next 5 Years				
	1954/1955	1955/1956	1956/1957	1957/1958	1958/1959	1959/1960	1960/1961	1961/1962	1962/1963
Solartron Laboratory Instruments Ltd.									
Standard instruments	£300	£589	£741	£945	£1,400	£2,000	£2,750	£3,500	£4,500
Government & outside contracts	42	63	37	57	60	100	150	250	250
Solartron Engineering Ltd.									
Government & outside contracts	35	87	115	96	60	100	125	150	200
Solartron Research & Development Ltd.									
Government & outside contracts	5	10	44	75	100	100	125	125	150
Data processing	...	...	...	32	130	250	300	400	500
Radar Simulators Ltd.	...	...	6	111	250	400	500	600	750
Solartron Industrial Controls Ltd.	...	...	6	12	60	150	250	300	350
Solartron Electronic Business Machines Ltd.	...	...	2	10	50	200	300	400	500
Solartron Electronic Group Ltd.									
Merchanting & sundries	16	9	54	96	140	200	250	275	300
Total deliveries	398	758	1,005	1,434	2,250	3,500	4,750	6,000	7,500
Export content included in above figures	20	80	186	335	600	1,000	1,500	2,250	3,500
Total orders	400	800	1,250	1,900	2,750	4,000	5,500	7,000	8,500
Total personnel at year end	400	550	600	830	1,250	1,750	2,250	2,750	3,500

* It was apparent in March, 1959, that it would probably be necessary to extend the 1962/1963 targets to 1963/1964, that is, to spread the five-year program over six years. Figures for 1959/1960 through 1962/1963 are "maximum" targets.

Source: Company records.

STATISTICS INDICATIVE OF SOLARTRON GROWTH
(Years ending June 30)

	1950	1951	1952	1953	1954	1955	1956	1957	1958
Personnel	18	22	66	110	240	400	550	600	830
Floor space (sq. ft. 000)...	4	4	6	8	30	35	65	70	85
Assets (£000)	8	12	34	74	226	420	654	902	1,344
Deliveries (£000) of which	13	20	34	90	152	399	758	1,005	1,434
Exports (£000)					10	20	80	186	335
Development write-off (£000) (specific products)	n.a.	n.a.	n.a.	n.a.	n.a.	24	38	76	72
Net profits after taxes and development write-off (£000)*		1	1	3	5	4	12	6	23
Nonspecific development expenditure (£000)†						10	25	50	75	120

* Includes retained profit plus sundry appropriations (see Exhibit 3).
† Written off in overheads—e.g., market research, planning new factories, etc.

by Mr. Bolton. After December, 1958, holdings were distributed as follows:

	Per Cent
Mr. Bolton	40
Other managers, employees, and families	40
Outside shareholders	20

Solartron's senior executive group was the eight-man Group board of directors which met monthly and included two men for each of the following major functions: general management (including personnel administration), production, and finance, and one each for marketing and research and development. The average age of these men in November, 1958, was 38 years. As indicated in the company letterhead, they held the degrees shown below, and most of them held executive positions in Solartron's subsidiary companies:

J. E. Bolton, D.S.C.,[1] M.A. (Cantab.), M.B.A. (Harvard), Member British Institute of Management (M.B.I.M.), chairman and group managing director, and temporarily chairman of Solartron Industrial Controls Ltd. and Solartron Radar Simulators Ltd.

L. B. Copestick, Associate Member Institute of Electronics (A.M. Inst. E.), Associate Member British Institute of Radio Engineers (A.M. Brit. I.R.E.), chairman and managing director, Solartron Research and Development Ltd.

J. E. Crosse, chairman and managing director, Solartron Engineering Ltd.

R. A. Henderson, director of Robert Benson Lonsdale, Merchant Bankers.[2]

Eric E. Jones, Member Sales Managers Association (M.S.M.A.), Group marketing director, managing director of Solartron-Rheem Ltd.

[1] Distinguished Service Cross (war decoration).
[2] An investment banking firm.

Exhibit 2

COMPANIES OF THE SOLARTRON ELECTRONIC GROUP LTD.

(Subsidiaries wholly owned except where otherwise indicated)

Companies in United Kingdom	Date of Incorporation	Personnel Strength in Nov., 1958	External Deliveries in Year Ending June 30, 1958 (000)	1957/1958 Deliveries as a Per Cent. of Total	Functions
Solartron Laboratory Instruments Ltd. (SLI)	1948	375	£1,002	69.9	Manufactured approximately 80 standard laboratory and precision instruments at Thames Ditton plant in production lots of batch size (0–50 per month); sales were made largely to scientific and engineering organizations in the U.K. through a sales force of approximately 20 technical service representatives
Solartron Engineering Ltd. (SE).............	1951	194	£96	6.7	Supplied the mechanical engineering requirements of the individual companies within the Group; also undertook a selected amount of outside work to ensure competitiveness and to utilize fully its capacity; located at recently built Farnborough plant
Solartron Electronic Group Ltd. (parent company)	1954	280	£96	6.7	General management and staff activities, merchanting, and sundries
Solartron Research and Development Ltd. (SR & D)	1954	144	£107	7.5	Performed outside contract R&D work; all research and development on standard electronic instruments; plus a portion of the work on "systems engineered" products (chiefly data handling and analogue computers); also produced prototypes and initial production runs of instruments and other equipment (such as magnetic data tape recorder); located in Dorking, Surrey

Company	Year				Functions
Solartron Electronic Business Machines Ltd. (SEBM)	1955	20	£10	0.7	One of three "development" companies at the Farnborough plant; responsible for developing, manufacturing, and marketing (in cooperation with Group Commercial department) electronic business machines primarily for office use; principal product in 1958 was the reading machine
Industrial Automation Developments Ltd. (jointly owned with Scribbans-Kemp Ltd.)	1956	...	...	...	Responsible for developing under contract hydraulic programmed actuator for industrial packaging use; work actually being carried out by SIC
Solartron Industrial Controls Ltd. (SIC)	1956	29	£12	0.8	Responsible for developing, manufacturing, and marketing industrial controls* under "quasi-consulting assignments"; principal products check-weigher, X-ray spectrometer, and punch-card teaching machine
Solartron Radar Simulators Ltd. (RS)	1957	58	£111	7.7	Responsible for developing, manufacturing, and marketing radar simulator devices for defense and training purposes; principal product aircraft simulator sold to NATO countries
Solartron Rheem Ltd. (jointly owned with Rheem Co. of New York)	1958	...	...	...	Responsible for developing products of joint interest to Solartron and Rheem
Totals		1,100	£1,434†	100†	
Overseas Subsidiaries:					
Solartron Inc. (Associated Company in U.S.A.)	1956	6			
Solartron SRL (Italy)	1957	3			
Solartron GMBH (West Germany)	1958	12			

Associated companies in India, France, and Sweden, and a subsidiary in Holland were in process of formation.

* An industrial control was broadly defined as a device to improve the quality of an industrial process by sensing some property of the product, processing the data thus obtained, and actuating the controls of the plant or machine involved to achieve a desired end. The variety of sensing effects that might be used ranged from simple weighing to spectroscopic examination by X-ray.

† Includes £335 or 23.4% exports.

Source: Company records.

Exhibit 3

OUTLINE PROFIT AND LOSS ACCOUNTS FOR THE YEARS ENDED JUNE 30, 1955–58 AND TARGETS THROUGH 1962–63
(In £000's)

	Actual				Possible Targets for Next Five Years				
	1954/1955	1955/1956	1956/1957	1957/1958	1958/1959	1959/1960	1960/1961*	1961/1962*	1962/1963*
Deliveries	£398	£758	£1,005	£1,434	£2,250	£3,500	£4,750	£6,000	£7,500
Less: Direct labor	75	119	141	192	270	420	560	720	900
Materials	134	226	289	468	750	1,180	1,590	2,000	2,500
Gross margin on deliveries	189	413	575	774	1,230	1,900	2,600	3,280	4,100
Add: Overheads in development & W.I.P. increase	30	60	60	48	70	100	100	100	100
Gross margin on trading	219	473	635	822	1,300	2,000	2,700	3,380	4,200
Less: Manufacturing overheads	105	214	258	356	480	730	950	1,150	1,400
Administration overheads	20	50	63	66	90	120	160	200	250
Commercial overheads	53	123	197	226	320	480	620	720	900
	178	387	518	648	890	1,330	1,730	2,070	2,550
Net profit before dev. write-off	41	86	117	174	410	670	970	1,310	1,650
Development write-off (specific products)	24	38	76	72	125	175	225	300	400
Net profit before appropriations	17	48	41	102	285	495	745	1,010	1,250
Loan interest	5	6	16	29	30	32	32	32	32
Preferred divs. (gross)	4	15	15	16	18	18	18	18	18
Ordinary divs. (gross)	...	...	...	...	22	44	88	132	220
Sundry appropriations	4	...	...	2	...	...	...	...	...
Taxation	4	15	4	34	120	220	320	433	517
Retained profits	...	12	6	21	95	181	287	395	463

* See note, Exhibit 1.

Source: Company records.

BALANCE SHEETS AS OF JUNE 30
(In £000's)

	Actual					Forecast			
	1955	1956	1957	1958	1959	1960	1961	1962	1963
ASSETS									
Cash at bank	£ 77	£ 1	£ 3	£ 7	£ 5	£ ...	£ ...	£ 175	£ 283
Trade & sundry debtors	99	154	259	400	475	750	1,000	1,200	1,500
Stock-in-hand & materials, etc.	85	89	121	158	200	270	350	450	560
Finished instruments	29	96	105	118	150	180	200	225	250
W.I.P. production	59	62	72	233	270	350	440	540	650
W.I.P. development	40	72	103	90	75	50	25	...	...
Associated companies	...	...	...	...	150	150	175	200	225
Total current assets	389	474	663	1,115	1,325	1,750	2,190	2,790	3,468
Freehold land & buildings	40	74	118	88	96	100	110	120	130
Improvements to leasehold factories	2	3	5	7	75	100	125	150	175
Equipment, plant, & machinery	22	36	35	46	125	175	225	275	325
Furniture, fixtures, & fittings	11	26	31	34	80	110	130	160	200
Motor vehicles	13	23	33	37	17	15	20	20	25
Goodwill	18	18	17	17	17	...	...	...	...
Total fixed assets	106	180	239	229	410	500	610	725	855
Total all assets	495	654	902	1,344	1,735	2,250	2,800	3,515	4,323
LIABILITIES									
Bank overdraft	£ 75	£139	£173	£ 58	£ 118	£ 77	£ 20	£ ...	£ ...
Progress payments	...	...	21	109	75	...	...	...	...
Trade & sundry creditors	104	117	166	410	410	600	700	800	900
Higher purchase commitments	10	18	18	18	40	75	70	65	60
Current taxation	8	18	21	30	20	150	260	375	505
Total current liabilities	197	292	399	625	663	902	1,050	1,240	1,465
Future tax	6	18	20	51	150	260	375	505	625
Unsecured loans	53	85	218	364	365	350	350	350	350
6% pref. shares (£1 each)	97	100	100	100	100	100	100	100	100
7½% pref. shares (£1 each)	95	100	100	100	100	100	100	100	100
Ordinary shares (10/each)	47	47	47	47	220	220	220	220	220
Retained profit & reserves	...	12	18	57	137	318	605	1,000	1,463
Total all liabilities	495	654	902	1,344	1,735	2,250	2,800	3,515	4,323
Note: Monthly sales volume	£ 55	£ 70	£125	£ 200	£ 250	£ 400	£ 500	£ 600	£ 750

Source: Company records.

Exhibit 5

Subsidiaries and Group Abridged Manufacturing, Trading, and Profit and Loss Accounts for the Nine Months Ended March 31, 1958

Subsidiaries	SLI	SE	SR&D	SEBM	SIC	RS	Total
Sales	£365,996	£221,473	£114,389	£ 9,798	£	£15,226	£726,882
Increase/decrease in W.I.P.	64,775	(5,850)	30,589	4,667	30,874	.....	125,055
Net output	430,771	215,623	144,978	14,465	30,874	15,226	851,937
Materials consumed	272,995	75,189	60,977	2,596	16,964	4,069	432,790
Direct wages	47,318	38,507	29,213	5,275	6,182	4,959	131,454
Manufacturing overheads	99,145	79,302	39,028	10,713	13,326	6,157	247,671
Works cost	419,458	192,998	129,218	18,584	36,472	15,185	811,915
Net profit (loss) of subsidiaries	11,313	22,625	15,760	(4,119)	(5,598)	41	40,022

Holding Company

	SEG						
Sales	£917,756						
Cost of sales	636,742						
Gross profit	281,014						
Commercial overheads	157,779						
Admin. overheads	46,412						
Net profit of holding company	76,823						76,823
Combined net profit							116,845
Appropriations							
Interest (gross)							21,734
Pref. dividend (gross)							10,103
Total							31,837
Profit before development write-off, taxation, and participating dividend							85,008

Source: Company records.

E. R. T. Ponsford, chairman and managing director, Solartron Laboratory Instruments Ltd.

Bowman Scott, M.B.E.,[3] M.B.A. (Harvard), B.Sc. (Eng.), Associate City and Guilds Institute (A.C.G.I.), Associate Member Institute of Electrical Engineers (A.M.I.E.E.), Group personnel director, and managing director of Solartron Electronic Business Machines Ltd.

J. L. E. Smith, M.A., director of Coutts & Co., Bankers,[4] and chairman of Solartron Industrial Automation Developments Ltd.

The purpose of board meetings was described as follows in a memorandum written by Mr. Bolton to explain and defend his practice (once criticized by the outside members) of allowing board meetings to "wander away" from a strict interpretation of the agenda:

. . . they are not, in these days, intended for transmission of information because this can be done effectively via detailed management data in the form of monthly reports. . . .

It seems to me that [their] main purpose lies in the area of creative discussion in order to achieve not only a better understanding of each other but also of the human and technical factors which govern the job we are doing. These factors of course change almost continuously. This in my view is how an effective and flexible policy (whether it be at board level or at research level) is rough hewn from the range of opinions which a balanced team should have. As you may have seen, I usually endeavour to bring out something controversial so that at least one member of the board will get hot under the collar about it. If we can each of us do this without fear then I think we are creating a very powerful team relationship which will ensure that we are approaching the various new problems which we shall continuously face in a co-ordinated and constructive way. . . .

In addition to the general management functions performed by the board, the parent company also provided a number of services to the Solartron companies, including purchasing, personnel, commercial activity (such as overseas selling), publicity, secretarial, accounting, and internal consulting (Group productivity services department).

The boards of directors of some of the subsidiary companies did not actually meet; management responsibility rested with the managing directors and other senior executives concerned.

COMPANY OBJECTIVES

A number of Solartron's objectives had been stated explicitly in recent years, either in the firm's *Annual Reports*, in other written documents, or orally by company executives. These statements have been quoted or paraphrased below:

---

[3] Member of Order of British Empire (war decoration).

[4] A commercial bank.

For the Long Run. Expansion into rapidly growing sections of the electronics industry as fast as "balanced attention" to the various factors of production would allow, taking into consideration (1) rate of development of the existing staff; (2) rate of integration of new personnel; (3) rate of development of the company's markets; (4) pace of R&D activity, as influenced by human and financial considerations.

For the Next Five to Ten Years. (1) Achieving more intensive effort in the major fields already chosen, in order to build "strong, viable, subsidiary units in those areas." There were to be fewer radically new products developed than in recent years, and emphasis was to be placed instead on perfecting and increasing the applications of equipment already developed. (2) Increasing export sales of Solartron products in order to broaden the company's customer base and spread development costs over an increased number of production units. (3) Making more effective use of the relatively large organizational structure created for the purpose of preparing for future expansion.

With Respect to People. "Our emergent philosophy of life lays great stress not only on the importance of the individual as a person, but on the essential need to devise a 'permissive' system in which individual initiative is nurtured and encouraged to make its maximum possible contribution to the whole. . . . We recognize that in selecting a team of potentially outstanding young men and women at all levels and in training them to carry increasing responsibility, the natural corollary is that they should want to make a personal contribution to decisions affecting their particular working group or company's future, in an atmosphere which is as free as possible of status barriers and prejudice. Furthermore, that they should want to know that those who demonstrate outstanding qualities of leadership and judgment can progress to Board level." In line with this objective the following policies had been adopted:

(*a*) Whenever possible, promotions to senior positions were made from within the organization. The principal exceptions to this rule were senior specialists such as Mr. Christopher Bailey, designer of the reading machine, and Mr. George Sanders, head of the Group productivity services department.

(*b*) To the extent possible, managers at all levels of the company were given the opportunity to discharge their responsibilities as they thought best within the broad framework of agreed-upon objectives. In this regard, Mr. Gordon Bates, who was leaving Solartron to do management consulting in the consumer marketing field, said that he and many of his colleagues felt themselves to be "part of an experiment in British industry." He contrasted Solartron with a number of older, larger firms that he and his friends had worked for, saying, "The standard form in many of these firms is to treat the younger men like useless appendages during the first 15 years or so, and then gradually let them in on one aspect of operations. Here the form is to give a man a little more than he thinks he can handle as soon as possible."

(*c*) To encourage personnel to increase their potential, fees for suitable training courses and conferences were paid by the company, while "Training within Industry" classes were held during working hours. There was also a library of technical and management books.

(*d*) An attempt was made to keep executives throughout the company informed on current developments. In this regard, Mr. P. B. H. Cuff, Group purchasing director, said that in his early years with the company Mr. Bolton had on several occasions stopped him to tell him of recent events that had no immediate bearing on his work but were of great interest to him in understanding the company's position. By 1958, annual management conferences were being held for all senior and junior executives, at which board members described the current state of affairs and plans for the future in their areas.

(*e*) To avoid unnecessary status barriers, reserved spaces in the parking lot had been eliminated. On most memoranda the names of executives were alphabetized; the use of first names was encouraged; and all personnel, regardless of position and function, were expected to "clock in" at the same time.

(*f*) Since 1954, the personnel selection and training functions had been entrusted to a director, Mr. Bowman Scott.

(*g*) To assure attractive working conditions, a pension scheme had been established, as well as an employee restaurant, a health centre, a sports and cricket club, and a trend toward yearly or longer-term employment contracts.

With Respect to Formal Organization. "Our policy is to develop a number of virtually independent company units within the Group, each concentrating on either a specialized function such as research, or a logically grouped sales and production activity such as test instrumentation. . . . We envisage each individual company unit growing to a size of perhaps 500–700 personnel—a size which we believe will meet, on the one hand, the need to maximise personal satisfactions, and, on the other, to operate near to the optimum unit size for the technical requirements of our particular industry. The dangers of growing apart are apparent, but we are confident that through our group structure and because of the experience our senior executives have gained in working as a very closely knit team, we shall be able to achieve the principal benefits of centralized policy-making and the economics of joint services, without hampering the exercise of individual initiative in the separate companies."

Mr. Bolton was particularly desirous of avoiding what he termed a "peaky" organization, in which management thinking would be dominated by his personal views. In this regard he said he had found that people in an organization tended to create a pinnacle, even when the managing director was anxious not to become an all-powerful father-figure. People had come to him, for example, and suggested that he ought to buy a new car, since his Jaguar was not as new as it might be and therefore not fully appropriate to his position. He said that one of a number of problems that could arise in a peaky organization was the difficulty of hiring "number-two" men who were intimidated by the individual brilliance of their prospective bosses and feared being completely submerged by them.

In contrast with the "peaky" organization, "great-man" approach to management, Mr. Bolton expressed the opinion that managerial needs were, like vacuums, abhorred by nature, and that they would ultimately be filled of their own accord. For example, he indicated that if he and Mr. Eric Jones, Group commercial director, had not pushed product diversification, "two other chaps would have, and the result would have been the same." Similarly, he believed that if Solartron had not developed the reading machine or the radar simulator, some other firm would have done so.

With Respect to Finance. Objectives in finance were (1) to increase borrowed in relation to equity and preference funds on a 2:1 ratio; (2) to use company funds principally for working capital; and to use other sources, such as lease-back arrangements, for plant and fixed assets; (3) starting in 1958/1959, to establish a progressive common-stock dividend record against the possibility that in three to five years there might be opportunities for greater expansion than were visualized in 1958 (although profits had been sacrificed for balanced and rapid growth in the first 10 years, increasing dividend payments were believed to be important ultimately because company executives considered that English companies were judged on a dividend rather than earnings-yield basis); (4) to achieve gross margins[5] on products in full production (beyond the initial progress-payment or pilot-production stage) of 60 per cent or more; (5) to reduce overhead spending progressively, until it declined to approximately 33 per cent of projected gross sales.

With Respect to R&D. (1) ". . . We have established a prime objective of achieving entirely new developments which show substantial improvements in contemporary design practice. As a rough rule of thumb we have endeavoured to produce new designs which will be some three to five years ahead of the existing state of the art in other countries, and in this way we hope to achieve a breathing space in which our new products can become fully established before the pressure of competition might catch up with them." (2) "In contrast with many military organizations, where research funds are all too often taken as a symbol of power, and prevailing sentiment is to get as much as you can and to hell with the whole, we are attempting to build the feeling instead that R&D funds are a means by which a subsidiary or research team can make a contribution to the Group, and that this contribution, rather than the power involved, is the important thing." (3) "Eventually we are aiming

---

[5] Sales price less "bought-out" materials and direct wages.

for more and more new projects at SR&D[6]—tending more toward research and away from development—and we intend to have the development work done by the individual manufacturing subsidiaries."

PRODUCT PLANNING

Early Product History. The initial development of Solartron's product line was described by a company executive as follows:[7]

The start and growth of the enterprise has followed a familiar pattern; at first a handful of men in a shed, and then a leap-frogging into larger and larger premises as the work prospered. In 1947 two young engineers, Mr. E. R. Ponsford and Mr. L. B. Copestick, scraped together a few hundred pounds, hired a disused stable, and set up as makers of electronic test instruments. Both had been apprenticed in the electronic industry and were aware of shortcomings in the available equipment. In 1948 they registered the name Solartron, but eighteen months were to pass before they were in a position to produce an electronic instrument of their own—the first proprietary laboratory amplifier on the British market. The main activity of the two directors and their three employees at first was the development, manufacture, and repair of equipment under government contract. This steady work enabled them to lease a small factory in Kingston, and additions to the Board brought enough working capital to proceed with more ambitious plans. Two years after the introduction of their first instrument the company was invited to exhibit at the Physical Society's Exhibition, and this they regarded as a mark of acceptance in the sphere of electronics.

The early years were hard but rewarding in every sense except the material. Many of the founders' old associates and trainees were anxious to join the company, even at reduced wages, for the sake of opportunities to come.

Ploughing back of all profits was never adequate to finance the rapidly growing production and development, and substantial additional capital was introduced when Mr. John Bolton and Mr. John Crosse joined the company in 1951 and 1952, respectively.

Thus, by the 30th June, 1953, at the end of the first five years of its corporate life, Solartron had become established with 110 personnel, 7,500 square feet of factory space, and a turnover of approximately £100,000 per annum. There were then two companies, Solartron Laboratory Instruments Ltd., with a growing product line of electronic test instruments, and Solartron Engineering Limited, which was responsible for the precision mechanical engineering and metalwork aspects of Solartron products. The stage was set for the broadening of the organizational and products base and substantial increase in sales volume during the second five years, 1953/1958.[8]

Diversification. During its second five years, Solartron diversified into "systems engineered" products. The initial decision to do so was made

---

6 Solartron Research and Development Ltd., a subsidiary.

7 Solatron Research and Development Ltd., a subsidiary.

8 From a paper presented May 27, 1958, before a meeting of the Seminar on Problems in Industrial Administration at the London School of Economics and Political Science.

in 1952/1953 as a result of what were considered to be the limitations of laboratory instruments as a product line on which to base future growth. The reasoning of the company's board, as reported in 1958, was as follows (paraphrased):

On the one hand, delivery periods must be kept short. For, once a customer has ordered an instrument, he expects rapid delivery (a month or less) or will seek an alternative source of supply. On the other hand, inventories must be kept at a minimum, because as a rapidly growing company our finances will be limited. Operations will therefore be continuously balanced between the risk of an inventory buildup if sales decrease and a scramble to increase production if sales increase.

Solartron could safely base its expansion on laboratory instruments only if it specializes intensely in one type of instrument, as certain firms have done in the United States. Because of the size of the United Kingdom market, however, this will not be feasible.

Our wisest move would be to seek additional "systems engineered" products with higher unit prices and longer delivery requirements. Such products would broaden our customer base and reduce the complexity of current operations. Because they would lengthen our order book, it would also be easier to obtain outside finance.

In order that we can make the maximum contribution and utilize our resources to the fullest, these new products should be in rapidly expanding sectors of the electronics industry where it will not be necessary to design somebody else out of the market.

Choosing New-Product Areas. In connection with this analysis, Mr. Bolton prepared a rough evaluation of the industry's future growth along the lines of Exhibit 6. This was based on the assumption that already developed sectors of the industry would remain a constant or decreasing proportion of the total, while undeveloped and as yet unknown sectors would become larger. Over-all, a fivefold increase over 20 years was estimated, with particular segments changing in relative importance roughly as follows:

Market Section	Estimated Per Cent of Sales	
	1953	1973
Domestic radio and TV	25	10
Communications	20	8
Radar and navigational aids	5	5
Military requirements	35	15
Data processing (including business machines)	Negligible	20
Industrial controls	Negligible	15
Scientific education	Negligible	5
Atomic energy	Negligible	5
Miscellaneous	15	17

Exhibit 6

SOLARTRON ESTIMATES OF FUTURE GROWTH OF ELECTRONICS INDUSTRY

Market Sector	Solartron Rough Estimates of Sales of Sector as a Per Cent of the Total Electronics Industry	
	1953	1973
1) *Domestic Radio and TV* Comments: Few export sales; domestic market will probably reach a plateau as in the U.S. Would have to compete with large, well established firms. Not for us.	25	10
2) *Communications* Comments: Major European networks already installed. Sales will be for improvement and replacement purposes. Industry cartelized; suppliers often affiliated with communications firms. Not our cup of tea.	20	8
3) *Radar and Navigational Aids* Comments: A growing field which should have possibilities for us. Assume market percentage will remain the same. Total increase will thus be fivefold.	5	5
4) *Military Requirements* Comments: Assume total static even though electronic share will increase, therefore ultimate percentage of the market down. Not so interesting as some other sectors.	35	15
5) *Data Processing* (Including business machines & industrial data processing equipment) Comments: Increasing use for computation as well as to reduce paper work. Digital computers have already been extensively developed by several large firms but analogue techniques and a number of other problems remain. An interesting field for us.	*	20
6) *Industrial Controls* Comments: Ultimately will be larger than data processing. Since automation of production operations will come after the automation of paper work, however, this sector will develop more slowly. This deserves our attention.	*	15
7) *Scientific Education* Comments: May never loom too large but relatively untouched. Has possibilities.	*	5
8) *Atomic Energy* Comments: Insignificant at present but will grow.	*	5
9) *Miscellaneous*	15	17

* Negligible.
Source: Company records.

Entering New Fields.   As a consequence of this analysis, Solartron began slowly to diversify during its second five years. Impetus to enter new fields came from various sources: In 1953/1954 a study was made of the business machine field, and it was concluded that the most important undeveloped requirements were (1) fast input devices for computers; (2) memories with large storage capacity and quick access; (3) equipment for sorting information. Of these, the first was selected for development and work was started on the reading machine (see Exhibit 7). In 1954 a decision to develop the check-weigher was made, based on the belief that accurate control of weight was a fundamental future need in automated processes—especially where packaged articles such as food were concerned, since such items are sold by weight. The choice of this field was also related to development and engineering skills already possessed by Solartron. With this product, work was started in the field of industrial controls. In 1955 evidence of strong interest by the Swedish Air Ministry touched off development of the company's radar simulator device. In 1957 "Anglicization" (adaptation to British components) of an American-designed "data-tape" recording machine was begun under license from the Consolidated Electrodynamics Corporation. During this same period Group sponsored research and development in the field of data processing (chiefly analogue computers).

Exhibit 7

COMPUTERS OR CLERKS*

The electronic computer is ten years old, a teenager among industrial machinery with a teenager's problems of adjustment to society. During its first decade, when it was being used largely as a research tool for resolving equations beyond the capacity of mathematicians, the decision to buy a computer or not depended on the straight-forward point whether a company or a Government research department had enough work of this kind to justify the investment of upwards of £150,000 in a single computer. There was no question of doing the work by other means. Such abstruse scientific, aerodynamic and even economic calculations were either done on a computer or not done at all. But now computers are being offered to a wider market as machines that will mechanise clerical work and control production processes, and they are being judged by different standards. Here a company does have a choice between two alternatives—it can choose between electronic computers and human clerks, or labourers.

The saving of labour by a computer can be exaggerated. The real gift it brings to management is the opportunity to cut through the red tape and the paper work that assumes alarming proportions once a company's operations reach a certain size. Much of this routine could now be transferred to computers, inside which it would be promptly assimilated, sorted, added to, substracted from, pigeonholed, filed for future reference, while a neat printed record appeared at the other end. But is this worth doing?

The answer varies from company to company, depending on how vital it is to the sound management of the business to have quick access to day-to-day information. Boots, which is making a big change-over to electronic accounting, obviously sets great store by prompt reports on the changing level of sales and stocks for the 60,000 different items sold by the company's retail shops. Bibby's, manufacturing

---

* From *The Economist*, December 6, 1958, pp. 915–16. Reproduced by permission.

Exhibit 7—Continued

animal feeding stuffs, uses a computer to keep watch on rapidly changing raw material prices, so that the feeding-stuff formula can be varied to make allowance for them—a job that requires an unexpectedly large number of weekly calculations. Tube Investments, selling products that vary from order to order, uses a computer to sort the orders, stipulate the most economical raw material, give manufacturing instructions and prepare cost figures, spending 30 seconds on planning and printing instructions about each order, against 35 minutes by ordinary methods. The Banco di Roma has just installed a computer to handle all the accounts of its 200–300 branches. Many other examples can be found among the 100-odd computers now in use in this country where resort to a fast-thinking computer has probably improved a company's efficiency. But users are noticeably reluctant to quote any estimate of the amount of money saved by electronic accounting. Boots calculate that the company's change to electronic book-keeping will stop the annual 10 per cent rise in clerical staff that has gone on now for several years. But even this type of saving is difficult to assess.

Computers still have obvious limitations; skillful handling is needed to make them earn their keep. Initial cost is the biggest single factor. At the first exhibition in the world devoted entirely to electronic computers, which has been open in London during the past ten days, the price of the 27 different models on sale ranged all the way from £20,000 to £800,000, the cheapest being made by Elliott and the dearest by IBM. A computer consists of two basic parts; one which does the arithmetic and is relatively cheap to make, and the other which acts as a "memory" and stores all the relevant data and instructions upon which the computer operates. There are several ways of building a "memory"; some of them are cheaper than others but unfortunately they are also slower-working. If the "memory" is slow, this tends to hold up the rate at which the computer works.

As a rough rule of thumb, the cheaper computers have small "memories"; the more expensive the machine, the bigger its memory and the faster it can get at the facts. In scientific calculations, calculating ability is frequently more important than capacious memory, so the small computers, many of which are only just on the market, are ideally suited for research purposes, providing the maximum computing ability for the minimum cost. For business accounting, however, a big "memory" is more important than calculating ability; the machine is required to hold data about stocks, or invoices, or temperature levels, or railway schedules, or insurance policies, and carry out one or two simple calculations on them when the need arises. The ideal computer for business accounting therefore tends to come in the £100,000 to £300,000 range.

It would be unfair, however, to blame the high cost of computers entirely on the electronics engineer. The computer itself frequently costs less than the mechanical equipment that goes with it. The second big limitation on the use of computers is in the design of this equipment. A computer cannot read—yet. Data have to be fed into it in a form it can understand, from punched cards, punched tape or magnetic tape, and fed out again in a form that the operator can understand. This requires tape readers, mechanical feeds and printing equipment, all of which operates at unnaturally high speeds. The purely mechanical difficulties created by these high speeds make all this ancillary equipment extremely expensive, considering the basic simplicity of its design. Some steps have been taken towards the development of electronic "readers" that could read type faces and transmit the results

Exhibit 7—Continued

direct to the computer; the specification put out by the banks for a machine that would "read" magnetic characters printed on cheques has given a marked fillip to this type of research.

The first two "reading" machines of their kind were exhibited at the computer exhibition, one of them being Solartron's complex reader, which is now said to be able to decipher not only carbon copies but even handwritten characters. The cost is £25,000 for a machine "reading" three reasonably similar type faces; the much simpler apparatus developed by Electric and Musical Industries solely for "reading" a specially designed type printed in magnetic ink, and intended primarily for cheque sorting, might cost one-tenth of this amount when in production. These figures give some indication of the cost of the trimmings that go with a computer. Ferranti, the first company to make computers in this country, designing machines used mainly by laboratories for vast calculations, sells one basic computer for £50,000, but the full installation costs £160,000.

The third big limitation on the use of computers lies with the customer rather than the machine. Production engineering must be fairly well understood in industry by now, but the application of the same technique to office work is not. In most cases, wholesale changes in routine are needed to fit the job to the computer and it is doubtful whether this is always appreciated by the buyer. Commercial computers have a vast appetite for work, but they are not the "thinking machines" that scientists were discussing at the National Physical Laboratory a week ago. They cannot plan the way a job ought to be done; they can act only on data and instructions fed to them by human operators and if the work is badly planned, the computer can do nothing to correct it.

Some experts have a shrewd suspicion that managements have found it more difficult to adjust their methods to computers than they had expected, rather in the way of those housewives whose pressure cookers sit unused on the top shelf. Their evidence is the large number of commercial computers used—on the admission of the owners—mainly for calculating wage packets. To put a computer to this work is like taking a steam-roller to crack a nut—a useful way of filling odd moments but a sad under-employment of the machine's great capabilities. But wage calculations happens to be one of the easiest jobs to tailor for a computer—this is why manufacturers frequently use it for demonstrations purposes—and it gives both computer operators and management a breathing space to learn how to use their new toy.

Although manufacturers can supply computers with a plan of work built into them, this is essentially a job that can be carried out only by men who know and have worked in the company buying the machine and who understand its business. The planning of work for a computer goes far beyond the mere mathematics of working out a code of instructions telling the machine how to do the job. It calls for a certain amount of imaginataion to grasp the computer's potentialities for helping the company, and although the manufacturer's staff can give advice on what is or is not technically possible they cannot be expected to understand how each business works or the best way that it should be run. Management must be prepared to spend some time learning to do the job itself. It may take months, or even years, to learn how to get maximum value from a computer. In some cases, it is still going to be cheaper and less troublesome to do the job with clerks.

In speaking of the company's diversification, Mr. Eric Jones, Group commercial director, said: "Not everyone was agreed that we should go into systems, perhaps partly because, when you look two or three years ahead in a new field, it looks more like science fiction than commercial reality. I think even J. B. [Mr. Bolton] thought that diversification might be premature. But I pushed radar simulators, he pushed business machines, we got agreement to develop the check-weigher, and here we are today."

Allocating R&D Funds. "We are compromising between forward research and spending on present products," said Mr. Bolton, "and we are doing it by eye." Mr. Bolton stated that this compromise involved making choices between "picking up basic principles at an early stage, or applying more intensive effort to remaining problems in already developed areas—such as increasing the reliability of a particular kind of oscilloscope." He explained that in the most recent operating year (1957/1958) this choice had been made by allocating Group R&D funds to the various product groups in proportion to their estimated growth in sales over the subsequent five-year period. Mr. Bolton added: "To some extent we are still a little paternalistic in this regard, in that I am still doling the money out as from a family kitty, basing individual allocations on the individual family members' estimates of their needs, scaled down to fit the total budget."

Picking Individual Projects. According to Mr. James Rothman, administrative assistant for SR&D, the principal sources of ideas for new projects were as follows: (1) Company staff, which was the principal source of ideas involving logical extensions of existing products, either by simple adaptation (such as redesigning a machine to read in polar as well as X and Y coordinates), or by using new principles or components. These were the source of the largest number of new projects. (2) Outsiders who joined Solartron and brought new ideas with them. This was the main source of radically new developments. (3) Outside requests of the "we need help badly" variety. In this respect, senior engineers were encouraged to visit with and discuss customer problems. The company's technical service engineers also turned in as many as 2,000 visit reports each month, in which they reported on unresolved difficulties they had encountered in the field.

Over 100 possibilities for new projects were generated by these various sources in the course of a year. Of these, approximately 10 per cent were chosen to be worked on, and the remainder were either rejected or held in abeyance. In the case of SR&D, decisions were made by Mr. L. Copestick, managing director, and Mr. R. Catherall, research director,

In the case of SEBM, SIC, and Radar Simulators, decisions were made by the senior executives involved. Decisions were made on a basis of these criteria: the estimated sales and gross profits that would result from making a given investment, and the interest of the engineers involved in carrying out the project.

Although formal calculations were not always prepared in selecting projects, a work order stating the estimated completion date and cost was issued at the time a project was begun. During the course of the project, monthly comparisons of work-in-progress (labor, materials, and overhead) were made with the budgeted cost by the senior executives and project engineers involved.

In late 1957 Mr. Rothman had been asked to devise a formula so that the decision whether a proposed project should be financed with Group funds could be made by a representative committee on the basis of the project's profitability ratio (the ratio of present value of profits over three years to the initial investment). Efforts to formalize the research and development program had been under way for over five years. This formula was enthusiastically received by Mr. Bolton, but it had not been implemented because it had been viewed more coolly by senior SR&D executives, on the grounds that the present system worked well and that the estimates needed to calculate the profitability ratio would be too sketchy to be of real value. Excerpts from the summary of Mr. Rothman's proposal follow:

NEW PRODUCTS ASSESSMENT SUMMARY

It is suggested that the decision whether a proposed development project should be financed by Group should be based very largely on its profitability ratio. . . .

In order to obtain a fair assessment of the profitability ratios, a representative committee would be formed to collate and agree upon the individual forecasts from which the profitability ratios would be calculated. . . . This committee would also draw attention to other intangible factors that might affect a decision on a particular product.

The Managing Directors of the development companies concerned could start development on any project approved by the Committee. However, in order to ensure that the Group's financial resources are not overstrained at any one time, a subcommittee of the Group Board will decide at three-monthly intervals the amount to be spent on development by each company in the next but two three-monthly period. This decision would be based on a consideration of projects under way and of projects approved by the New Products Committee.

It would then be the responsibility of the Managing Directors concerned to ensure that they did not overspend their budgeted allocation.

The aim has been to provide an agreed selection process and while providing short-term stability in development budgets, it is designed to give long-term flexibility in allocation of funds for SEG sponsored development.

THE SOLARTRON ELECTRONIC GROUP LTD. (C)

"I think that you will find it very interesting," remarked Mr. John Bolton, Managing Director of The Solartron Electronic Group Ltd., "to see all the changes that have taken place since IMEDE studied the company in 1959. In some respects, especially concerning our organization, we appear to have made a complete reversal from our former policies and approach, but I suppose that it is all a part of the process of organic growth. It appears to me that a period of several years of decentralization of initiative and authority is necessarily followed by a period of centralization, and perhaps some years later the cycle is continued with a trend towards decentralization again. Each phase brings its benefits and its counteracting problems."

By the close of 1958, Solartron had developed into a multiple corporate structure, consisting of six wholly owned corporations and a number of partly owned companies. [See case (A) for details of these separate companies and a corporate organization chart on page 384 of this case.] Solartron's underlying organizational policy had been to develop a number of independent company units within the group, each concentrating on either a specialized function such as research, or a logically grouped sales and production activity such as test instrumentation. The goal had been to allow each individual company unit to grow to a size of about 500–700 persons.

Solartron's management gave the following four reasons for the formation of such a multiple corporate structure:

(i) To maintain an atmosphere of work where men would be able to grow with their jobs and the benefits of close teamwork would be maximized

(ii) To permit a flexibility of operation where each activity could progress at its own best rate

(iii) To attract key men to the company when entering new areas of activity by offering directorship posts

(iv) To segregate the new system-oriented activities from the instrument company's dominant influence and at the same time to ensure that the instrument company, the "cornerstone" of Solartron's growth plans, should not be hampered.

ORGANIZATION OF SOLARTRON'S COMPANIES, JULY, 1959

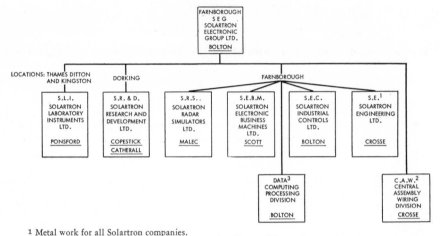

[1] Metal work for all Solartron companies.
[2] Assembly and wiring for all Solartron companies. Responsible to S.E.G. under administrative direction of S.E.
[3] Development and sale of computors. Created July, 1959.
Source: Company interviews.

The Solartron Electronic Group Ltd. (A) case was written in order to permit a broad appraisal and analysis of the company. In contrast to this general approach, The Solartron Electronic Group Ltd. (C) case focuses almost exclusively on the organizational aspects of the changes which took place from 1959 to 1962. The following major topics are discussed: a brief history of the changes which took place in Solartron, forces leading to the organizational changes, the new organization, problems presented by the reorganization, and some evaluations of the reorganization by Solartron's management.

SOLARTRON, 1959–62

"The period 1959–62 has been one of great change," remarked Mr. Bolton. "It has been a period of rapid growth; deliveries and personnel have more than doubled. Moreover, our product emphasis has changed, we have physically moved a number of our plants, and we have reorganized by centralizing all of our systems operations. By 1961 our rapid growth had resulted in our having six locations within a twenty-mile radius. By the middle of 1962 we were centralized in two first-rate new plants—Instruments at Chessington and Systems at Farnborough (25 miles from Chessington). Exhibit 1 gives some general statistics showing Solartron's growth; it contains data provided in case A. Exhibits 2 and 3 present the Group's consolidated balance sheets and profit and loss statements since 1958.

Exhibit 1
COMPANY STATISTICS[1]

	1955 June 30	1958 June 30	1959 July 4	1960 July 2	1961 Dec. 31
Personnel	400	830	1,330	1,550	1,953
Floor space (sq. ft. 000)	35	85	118	150	250
Assets (£000)	420	1,344	2,155	2,811	3,143
Deliveries (£000)	398	1,430	2,107	2,633	4,891[2]
of which					
Exports (£000)	20	335	560	800	1,100[2]
Total orders received (£000)...	400	1,900	2,145	2,980	5,638[2]
Development writeoff (£000) .	49	200	206	180	974[2,3]
Net profits after taxes (£000)..	4	31	5	8	(984)[2]

[1] Differences in the figures for 1955 and 1958 from those in The Solartron Electronic Group Ltd. (A) have come as a result of revisions by the company subsequent to the (A) case's publication.
[2] For a period of 18 months.
[3] All previous development expenditures which had been capitalized were written off in 18 months ended 31 December 1961.
Source: Company's annual reports.

A description of the product mix in 1962 is presented in Appendix A. Also included are some observations by Mr. Bowman Scott (Group Director of Personnel and Managing Director of Solartron Business Machines Ltd.) as to changes and trends in product sales.

"One of the first events in the series leading to the ultimate change in our organization took place early in 1956," continued Mr. Bolton, "when S.R. & D. was moved 14 miles from our Thames Ditton location to Dorking as a result of overcrowding. Soon after, the small systems companies were also moved to Dorking, because they were primarily involved in development engineering rather than manufacturing and were obliged to work closely with S.R. & D. In early 1958 our new facilities at Farnborough were ready, and we moved the systems companies there. In 1961, S.R. & D. was also moved to Farnborough when the second phase of building was complete. By then we had finally decided that we would have to integrate our Farnborough operations; S.R. & D. and all of the system companies, with the exception of the S.E.B.M., were combined into one company—Solartron (Farnborough) Ltd. In the meantime, the instrument company had outgrown the Thames Ditton plant and in 1961–62 was moved to new facilities at Chessington. The decisions governing our various moves were circumscribed (*a*) by the need to move only short distances in order to keep our key personnel and (*b*) by the difficulties of obtaining government planning permission

Exhibit 2
BALANCE SHEETS, ACTUAL 1959–61 AND PRO FORMA 1962
(In £000's)

	ACTUAL			PRO FORMA
	July 4, 1959	July 2, 1960	Dec. 31, 1961	Dec. 31, 1962
Assets				
Cash......................	16	28	33	37
Trade and sundry debtors....	638	562	884	900
Income tax recoverable......	....	44	231	500
Stocks and W.I.P...........	810	1175	1400	1500
Associated companies.......	106	58	48	70
Total current assets.......	1569*	1866*	2596	3007
Freehold land and buildings..	96	95		
Expenditure on leasehold factories................	68	34	530	500
Plant, machinery, furniture...	164	242		
Motor vehicles.............	33	29		
Capitalized R&D...........	208	529	....	....
Goodwill.................	17	17	17	17
Total fixed assets........	586	946	547	517
Total assets............	2155	2811*	3143	3524
Liabilities				
Bank overdraft.............	200	204	34	800
Progress payments..........	31	159	1187	1050
Trade and sundry creditors...	795	717		
Hire purchase commitments..	48	29	59	55
Current taxation...........	6	2	3	....
Total current liabilities.....	1080	1110*	1283	1905
Unsecured loans............	543	450	1343	1343
6% pfd. shares (£1 each).....	100	100	100	100
7½% pfd. shares (£1 each)...	100	100	100	100
Ordinary shares (10/-each)...	220	400	1200	1200
Reserves..................	90	630	90	90
Retained earnings..........	22	21	(973)	(1214)
Total liabilities and capitalization.......	2155	2811	3143	3524

* Due to rounding of figures.
Source: Company records.

to build new plants. We now have three main corporations: Solartron Laboratory Instruments, Solartron (Farnborough) Ltd., and The Solartron Electronic Group Ltd. (the holding company). There is also S.E.B.M. which was kept as a separate corporation in order to facilitate the outright sale or setting up of a joint venture in this area of activity with another firm.

Exhibit 3

PROFIT AND LOSS STATEMENTS, ACTUAL 1959–61 AND PRO FORMA 1962–64
(In £000 and % of net deliveries)

	ACTUAL							PRO FORMA			
	Year Ending July 4, 1959	Year Ending July 2, 1960	6 Mos. Ending Dec. 31, 1960	Year Ending December 31, 1961	(%)	Year Ending December 31, 1962	(%)	Year Ending December 31, 1963	(%)	Year Ending December 31, 1964	(%)
Gross deliveries	2107	2633	1565	3326	...	...	...	...	...	...	...
Net deliveries	...	...	...	3215	100	3560	100	3900	100	4400	100
Cost of goods sold	...	...	...	2742	85	2680	75	2730	70	2890	66
General expenses											
Administrative Overhead	...	...	...	725	23	860	24	770	19	820	19
Commercial Overhead	...	...	...	836	26	380	11	275	7	325	7
R & D	...	...	...	40	1	30	1	25	1	25	1
Royalty payment	...	...	...	...	...	...	...	...	...	...	...
Total operating expenses	2036	2556	1621	4343	135	3950	111	3800	97	4060	93
Operating income/loss before taxes	71	77	(56)	(1128)	(35)	(390)	(11)	100	3	340	7
Other income/loss before taxes	(62)	(69)	n.a.	(109)	(3)	(120)	(3)	(155)	(4)	(150)	(3)
Net income/loss before taxes	9	8	n.a.	(1237)	(38)	(510)	(14)	(55)	(1)	190	4
Taxes	4	...	n.a.	(309)	(9)	...	...	...	...	...	...
Income/loss after taxes	5	8	(56)	(928)	(29)	(510)	(14)	(55)	(1)	190	4
Dividends[1]	13	8	...	10	...	...	...	...	...	...	...
Retained profits	(8)	...	...	(938)	...	...	...	...	...	...	...

n.a. Not available.

[1] Dividends were only distributed for Preferred Stock.

Source: Company records.

FORCES LEADING TO THE ORGANIZATIONAL CHANGES

During an interview with Mr. Bolton and Mr. Scott, the former gentleman said that the main reason for the centralization of the systems companies between 1959 and 1961 was the desire to make the operations more profitable and to develop a maximum return on effort. "I think it is fair to say," interrupted Mr. Bowman Scott, "that the trigger which started off the move towards centralization was the general desire just to get the orders out and to avoid the many bottlenecks that we had.

"It was a combination of operating conflicts and substandard performance and small units which brought the matter of company organization to a head," continued Mr. Scott. "Most noticeable was the fact that sales deliveries of new products were falling considerably behind projections. The causes of this poor performance could be traced back to development and production inadequacies. Another manifestation of the problem was that development costs were considerably higher than budgeted.

"Why was the company not getting better results? We assessed our management team as being more than fully competent to do the job. Our engineers and production people were certainly good enough to handle the Solartron operations of that day. We concluded that much of the blame for the development and production tie-ups was due to a lack of management coordination and control, which in turn was largely attributable to the unwieldy organization under which we were operating during a stage when emphasis changed from development of products and markets to production."

During this discussion Mr. Scott listed the following as major forces which led to the reassessment of the company's organization and to the eventual changes: the problem of coordinating research and development, the difficulties of resolving priorities in the centralized production centers, and the difficulty of providing common staff services while trying to maintain independent companies. Other members of management added to this list of factors the personalities and desires of the top executives involved, the duplications of activity such as sales and accounting, and the geographical placement of the various activities.

In the remainder of this section, the influences of many of the above factors are considered insofar as they affected research and development, production, and organization.

RESEARCH AND DEVELOPMENT

In the opinion of many executives, research and development played a particularly important part in the reassessment of the company's organization because of its vital and costly role in the activity of Solartron. A chronological description of the research and development activity was given by Mr. Reg Catherall, who was in charge of research and development for Solartron (Farnborough) Ltd. and Board Director of all three major Solartron companies. Also given below is another executive's description of some of the problems in allocating research and development funds under the multiple-corporate system.

"To pick up the story at the time when S.E.G. was formed from the original company S.L.I.," remarked Mr. Catherall, "it should be noted that S.R. & D. comprised the design group under Les Copestick which had been responsible for all instrument design. Moving S.R. & D. to Dorking did not overnight change the interests or abilities of the people concerned, and as a group we were still 100 per cent devoted to creating instrument-type products for S.L.I.

"The first pressure for change came from John Bolton, who was concerned with the short-order book situation associated with the sale of electronic laboratory instruments and the certainty of tough competition in future years from American instrument companies having much larger production runs than we could hope to achieve. Furthermore, he did not feel confident that a company producing only laboratory instruments could attract necessary capital investment or provide a sufficiently broad base upon which he could build the size and caliber of organization that he had in mind. John believed that our efforts in the electronics industry should be enlarged into the systems business, directed towards applied measurements for industry as a whole. I think we can now all see that the potential for sound growth for Solartron is, in fact, greatest in the systems business.

"During the early Dorking period starting in 1956, instrument development continued whilst radar simulators, reading machines, and industrial control equipment grew in parallel. These new activities were located in the same premises at Dorking, prior to erection of the new factory at Farnborough, but were not an integral part of the S.R. & D. company.

"If we now take stock of the forces at play we see John's skill in debate, superb as ever, in favor of more emphasis in systems; the need to provide products for the new systems companies; the company's annual review highlighting radar simulators, reading machines, and other new fields; our close working proximity with the systems companies and our physical separation from the instrument company which resulted in a significant difference in the frequency and ease of our communication with the two activities (systems and instruments). Reinforcing these pressures, in time, was the broadening of interest of S.R. & D.'s senior technical personnel into systems engineering.

"The next phase of S.R. & D., covering some four years (1957–61), sees the introduction of magnetic tape machines and transducers under license from the United States, the growth from DC amplifiers to an analogue computer range, the digital voltmeter leading to digital data-handling systems and the inevitable emergence of digital computers. By mid-1960, S.R. & D. was just about equally active in instruments and systems.

"During this time a strong production engineering development force had evolved at S.L.I. and nothing beyond 'normal' difficulties was encountered in getting S.R. & D. prototype instruments to the S.L.I. production floor.

"At Farnborough, following a period during which S.E., S.E.B.M., S.R.S., and S.I.C. led separate lives, a unification of these companies' activities was put into effect in 1959–60. The outcome from a development viewpoint was that Brian Maudsley, originally engaged as Chief Engineer and a Director of S.E., became responsible for all development at Farnborough. His total force, although greater in number than the development groups of S.R. & D. and S.L.I. combined, did not have an electronic production engineering development team comparable with that at S.L.I. Further, it was not possible to identify a man around whom such a team would grow.

"The production at Farnborough of analogue computers and subsequently data-logging systems gave rise to increasing difficulties in view of the above factor. This, I feel, although far from the whole reason, was the trigger resulting in the move of S.R. & D. from Dorking.

"As time went on, we at S.R. & D. were becoming more and more involved in short-term action to help with the Farnborough analogue computer and data-logging production. We saw that it was only a matter of time before these development groups of S.R. & D. would have to come here [Farnborough] in order to bring these efforts to a successful completion. The decision that Les Copestick faced was whether to send part of S.R. & D. to Farnborough or to move the whole company. Not wanting to split up our research and development team, he decided that the whole company should move to Farnborough, a decision with which I completely agreed. John was also interested in the £50,000 per annum saving in overheads which it was calculated the move would achieve.

"We thought at that time that S.R. & D. would operate on the Farnborough premises as a separate company and intended that Brian Maudsley should join S.R. & D. under Les Copestick as a third working director, along with Leighton Davies and myself. But things never turned out that way. After we were here a while, we realized that strong feelings in the Group's Board existed for a full centralization of the Farnborough activities. When Les Copestick agreed to integrate S.R. & D., the centralization was put into effect."

In commenting on this decision to merge S.R. & D. with the systems companies, Mr. Les Copestick, former Managing Director of S.R. & D. said: "I could see that it was absolutely necessary to merge the research and development activities at Farnborough because a rivalry was bound to grow between the two research and development groups [S.R. & D. and the Farnborough systems development unit under Mr. Maudsley] if they continued under separate leadership; their ways of doing things were far too different. Research and development was already costing far more than it should have been, and I could see the need for streamlining this part of the organization."

In discussing the problem of controlling the research and development efforts of the company before the reorganization, one executive revealed his own dissatisfaction with the allocation of funds for development, remarking: "Under the multicompany system, there was real difficulty in planning or allocating funds for research and development activities. It was obvious that people had very strong commitments to their own specific areas of operation, and the over-all company interest took second place in the minds of many.

"The allocation of funds would normally take place at a general meeting of the company's directors during which each man would state his proposals and needs. I can remember one meeting where only one man remained quiet, that was Mr. Bolton himself. Finally, he got up, looked at his watch, said that they had talked long enough about the funding, and then simply allocated funds to each company based upon the estimated growth of sales in each of them over the next four years. That was the end of the meeting and also an end of the research and development funds allocation procedure for that year. Under that system of allocation it was more important that the general manager be an aggressive salesman of his development plans than that he be technically competent."

He felt that the people who shouted the loudest tended to be the people who got the most funds.

PRODUCTION

Mr. George Sanders, Solartron (Farnborough) Production Manager, credited by Mr. Bolton as one of the prime factors in the move towards centralization on the Farnborough site, said: "Production was just not doing the job of getting the goods out on time at a low cost. One of the major disadvantages of the old system was that the various managing directors of the small systems companies were unable to control their own production costs. It was so bad that the production centers themselves, such as the Central Assembling and Wiring Division (CAW), were not able to maintain effective control of shop costs, because each of the three companies supplying work used its own system for progressing and administering its work-in-process.

"Another major disadvantage was that no one person was responsible for the full manufacturing process of a product. A production planner was the only person who knew the complete state of affairs for a product. Consequently, he became the focal point of all communications about production, but he was not a line supervisor and so did not hold authority, nor could he be held responsible, with regard to actual production. The result of this situation was that no way existed to ensure a complete follow-through in the production cycle."

THE NEW PLANTS

By 1958, the first phase (50,000 sq. ft.) of building a modern plant had been completed on a 15-acre site at Farnborough, some 25 miles away from the Thames Ditton/Kingston area. These facilities were of high standard compared with the old converted buildings in use by S.L.I. at Thames Ditton and Kingston.

The second phase of building about 115,000 square feet of factory, laboratory, and office space at Farnborough was then completed in the spring of 1961, including a modern five-story block, to house R&D, Accounts, and Administration.

At S.L.I. moves were also made to provide more and better factory facilities, and during 1959 a 5-acre site was acquired at Chessington, about 3 miles away from Thames Ditton and Kingston, as a center on which to consolidate all S.L.I. activities. Existing modern buildings providing 20,000 square feet of laboratory and office accommodation were increased by building a 50,000-square-foot factory, which was occupied in October, 1961. The new location was convenient for most of the existing personnel and at a better center for further recruiting of production personnel.

ORGANIZATION

"You might be interested," remarked Mr. Bowman Scott, "to hear some comments which I noted verbatim at a director's meeting in September 1959. "The directors spend too much time on coordinating activities and not enough time on leading their company.' 'The directors spend too much time consulting with other people.'

"About that time we had begun to take a close look at our organization. What soon became obvious, as you can see from this chart [Exhibit 4], was that the organization's lines of command were structured along product lines, while day-to-day operations and communications followed functional lines. Decisions were cutting across the separate corporate structures. It appeared to us at that time [1959] more sensible to re-orient the chain of command so as to permit easy and coordinated functional communication and to rely on coordinating meetings for the long-range product decisions."

Exhibit 4

A Schematic Diagram of Lines of Communication and Command, September, 1961

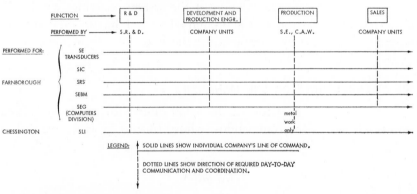

Source: Notes of Mr. Bowman Scott.

"One thing to consider," remarked Mr. Stan Golding, Group Personnel Office (reporting to Mr. Bowman Scott), "was that Solartron's needs have been changing. For example, our need to attract outside experts became significantly lessened as the company grew to a size where it generated many of its own technical innovations. In the case of analogue computers and data-logging and recording equipment, Solartron had within the organization the necessary talent to enter the data-handling field. There was no need to set up a separate company in order to have the managing director's position as bait in attracting an expert from outside. Consequently, the data-computing and processing activity was set up as a division under Mr. Wilfred Fry [formerly a director and Development Manager of S.R. & D.] instead of as an independent company.

"The original intention was that this division would coordinate production and development, and promote sales. It was also intended that this division would, in time, become another company in the group. It was around this time, however, that second thoughts were arising about the advisability of having a decentralized organization, and the intention of spinning off another company was held in abeyance."

An organization memorandum published July, 1959, established the Data Computing and Processing Division. One executive pointed out that this memorandum, by setting up responsibilities across company lines, introduced the germ of the centralization idea. Exhibit 5 contains this memorandum.

THE NEW ORGANIZATION

An organization memorandum, dated November 25, 1959, contains the first formal statement of the intention to centralize the operations of the systems companies. An organization memorandum of October 9, 1961, announced the consolidation of the systems activities within the newly formed Solartron (Farnborough) Ltd. Exhibits 6 and 7 contain excerpts from these two memoranda, the latter of which contains the revised organization chart.

THE CHANGED ROLE OF THE MANAGER

"The Managing Directors of the small units with whom we started can be likened to the commandos, whose function was to establish a bridgehead," remarked Mr. John Crosse, Managing Director of Solartron

Exhibit 5

EXCERPTS FROM A COMPANY MEMORANDUM, DATED 6 JULY, 1959

From: Bowman Scott
To: Directors and Departmental Heads

As from 1st July, 1959, Mr. W. J. Fry, as well as being a Director of S.R. & D., will take over the duties of General Manager of a newly created Division of S.E.G. (F), known as the Data Computing and Processing Division. Mr. Fry will continue to use his office at Dorking for several months until accommodation is available for him at Farnborough.

The new Division will be responsible to the S.E.G. Board through:[1]

> Mr. L. B. Copestick on Research matters
> Mr. J. E. Crosse on Administrative matters
> Mr. E. E. Jones on Sales matters

for the development and manufacture of Computers, computer units, data processing and data recording equipment.

To clarify the position, a chart is included explaining the responsibility of the Directors concerned in Farnborough activities for each main class of product.

---

[1] Messrs. Copestick, Crosse, and Jones were all members of the S.E.G. Board of Directors.

Exhibit 5—Continued

RESPONSIBILITY FOR[1]

Product Classes	Market Research & Forecasting Volume	Budgets	Research	Development	Manufacture by S.E.	Assembly & Wiring	Sales	Coordination of all activities
Radar Simulators	S.R.S. (Malec)	S.R.S. (Malec)	S.R.S. (Malec)	S.R.S. (Malec)	S.E. (Burton)	S.E.G. (Maudsley)	S.R.S. (Malec)	S.R.S. (Malec)
Business Machines	S.E.B.M. (Scott)	S.E.B.M. (Scott)	S.E.B.M. (Scott)	S.E.B.M. (Scott)	S.E. (Burton)	S.E.G. (Maudsley)	S.E.B.M. (Scott)	S.E.B.M. (Scott)
Industrial Controls	S.I.C. (Nutting)	S.I.C. (Crosse)	S.I.C. (Bailey)	S.I.C. (Maudsley)	S.E. (Burton)	S.E.G. (Maudsley)	S.I.C. (Nutting)	S.I.C. (Crosse)
Computers	S.E.G. (Jones)	S.E.G. (Fry)	S.R.& D.	S.E.G. (Fry)	S.E. (Burton)	S.E.G. (Maudsley)	S.E.G. (Jones)	S.E.G. (Fry)
Data Recording & Processing (including data amplifiers)	S.E.G. (Jones)	S.E.G. (Fry)	S.R.& D.	S.E.G. (Fry)	S.E. (Burton)	S.E.G. (Maudsley)	S.E.G. (Jones)	S.E.G. (Fry)
Transducers	S.E.G. (Jones)	S.E.G. (Crosse)	S.R.& D.	S.R.& D.	S.E. (Burton)	S.E. (Crosse)	S.E.G. (Jones)	S.E. (Jones)

[1] Other areas of responsibility listed on the actual memorandum included: Drawing Office, Purchase of Materials, Storage of Materials, Inspection and Modular Test, System Test and Calibration, Finished Goods Stock, Despatch.

Exhibit 6

EXCERPTS FROM A COMPANY MEMORANDUM, DATED 25 NOVEMBER, 1959

From: J. E. Crosse   *To:* All departmental heads at Farnborough.
                                    All directors for information.

At the Solartron Electronic Group Main Board Meeting on the 17th of November, it was decided that in order to accelerate the rate of growth and ensure success of all the units operating at Farnborough, a complete unification should take place over the next few months.

The present structure in which all personnel are divided amongst five separate companies (S.R.S., S.E.B.M., S.I.C., S.E., and the divisions of S.E.G., now known as S.E.G. (F.), and S.E.G. (D.C. & P.), will eventually be replaced by an organization in which all these same people will be united within S.E.G. (Farnborough).

The present subsidiary companies will cease to operate executively, but will continue in existence, and the present nominated directors will remain registered in these companies. This is being done in order to keep alive companies which, we believe, will ultimately be able to operate as independent subsidiaries. The time when these subsidiaries resume their independence is governed by many factors which must be weighed by the Main Board—as a rough guide, however, we now believe that volume of sales must reach a substantial and steady figure at which it is possible to support the required services within the subsidiary.

Until these subsidiaries are in a position to resume independence, there will remain in existence a Product Group Committee associated with each of them. These committees will ensure continuity in the interim phase of unified operation and will concern themselves with medium to long term direction and co-ordination within their product groups.

The first step, namely that concerning Production and Provisioning, will take effect from Monday, 30th November, 1959. The following appointments are made:—

D. W. Burton as Works Director who will be responsible for all production in the Engineering part of the factory.

G. S. Sanders as Production Director who will be responsible for all production in Wiring and Assembly, Test, Final Assembly, and for Stores and Stock Control.

Exhibit 7

EXCERPTS FROM A COMPANY MEMORANDUM, DATED 9 OCTOBER, 1961

From: J. E. Bolton   *To:* All Internal Directors
                                               All Departmental Heads

*ORGANIZATION—SOLARTRON GROUP—
AND FARNBOROUGH*

1. *THE SOLARTRON ELECTRONIC GROUP:*

We are now fortunate in having the U.K. side of Solartron concentrated into two locations, namely at Chessington and Farnborough, with ultra modern factories and adequate room for expansion. It is the intention that these two units will each be fully responsible for its own operating results. At the same time it is

Exhibit 7—Continued

still obviously essential to achieve the best possible results from the Group as a whole by continuing co-operation between the two units, particularly in the sales and development areas.

Increasingly, my own function, and that of other Group personnel who do not have specific locational duties, will be concerned with overall policy and co-ordination, as well as formulating Solartron's longer range plans.

Section 3 of this memorandum is an organization chart showing the major functions in the Group and the Directors who have direct responsibility to me for those functions.

2. FARNBOROUGH

During the past three years an excellent job has been done at Farnborough in building the foundations of an important and expanding unit in the "Systems" field. It is clear that this area of activities has a major role to play in Solartron's future. Starting with 50,000 sq. ft. of factory space and 200 people in August 1958, the Farnborough factory has grown to some 175,000 sq. ft. with 1,100 people and incoming orders running at the rate of £2½ million per annum.

We are certain that our growth will continue at a substantial rate, but our major emphasis for the next few years must be directed towards the achievement of maximum efficiency and productivity in our organization, coupled with outstanding quality and reliability in our products.

During recent months there has been a growing recognition of the need to simplify our organization structure at Farnborough by the establishment of clear lines of responsibility and authority. Thus at the S.E.G. Executive Board Meeting on the 14th September 1961, it was decided to unify activities at Farnborough into a single effective company unit, by welding together the present co-operative structure existing between the personnel who are operating the Farnborough location. The new company will be known as Solartron (Farnborough) Limited. It will not be able to commence trading under its own name until 1st January 1962, at which date the public announcement will be made.

However, the first step, namely the appointment of the Solartron (Farnborough) Ltd., Board, will take effect from Monday, 9th October, 1961. In order to speed up the process of decision making, it has been decided to keep the Board as functional, and as small, as possible, and the following appointments are made forthwith:—

SOLARTRON (FARNBOROUGH) LTD.

J. E. Crosse—Chairman and Managing Director
R. Catherall—Director of Research and Development
L. Malec—Sales Director
G. S. Sanders—Production Director

In addition the following appointments to Executive Directorships of Solartron (Farnborough) Ltd., are made:—

C. E. G. Bailey
D. W. Burton
D. Leighton Davies
R. D. Haxby
B. G. Maudsley

Exhibit 7—Continued

The exception to the broad plan of integration mentioned above will be the Reading Machine activity, which will continue to report directly to Mr. Bowman Scott in his capacity as Chairman and Managing Director, S.E.B.M. Needless to say, it is essential that the existing co-operation between the S.E.B.M. team and other personnel at Farnborough should continue.

Mr. L. B. Copestick will continue to have as his prime responsibility the co-ordination of Group Research and Development policy on a world-wide basis, and he will report directly to me. He will hold meetings of the Group R&D Committee, as necessary, to achieve this co-ordination, and will be responsible for preparing the long range new product framework for the future Solartron as a whole. This is an undertaking of vital importance to us in the years ahead and Mr. Copestick will require the continuing co-operation and advice of the other members of the Solartron team.

3. *ORGANIZATION CHART—SOLARTRON GROUP—MAJOR FUNCTIONS*

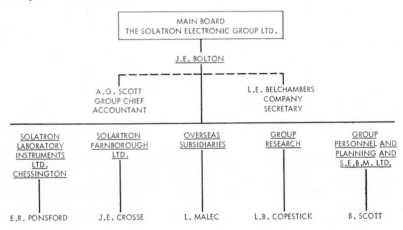

(Farnborough) Ltd. "The company had a need for this type of man during the initial stage of its formation, and the creation of a small, independent company, with its lure of power and prestige, was a good way to attract such a man.

"As the organization grew, obvious needs arose for cross-fertilization of ideas and technology, greater integration of operations, and definition of a united purpose. You might say that Solartron's need for entrepreneurs was giving way to a need for professional managers who could ensure follow-through in the long run.

"To my mind, a manager should be a man who has commercial instinct, is technically capable, and has an appreciation for accounting and business. Our managers had very good technical ability, since this was the basis upon which most were selected, and they also had good commercial ability. What they lacked was a sense of business and accounting, or financial responsibility.

"Solartron now needs men who can think in terms of the company as a whole. The day of pushing only for the analogue computer, or the radar simulator, to the exclusion of all other products, are gone, and we do not want that kind of thinking any more. Unfortunately, the type of men whom we had under the old system did not, in many cases, fit into the new organization, and a number of these men subsequently left the company. A man who is a commando-type cannot really work under a central system; he will buck it."

S.L.I.'S INCREASED AUTONOMY

"With all the talk about centralization," remarked one executive, "people overlook the fact that a significant decentralization has also taken place during our reorganization. The Chessington (instruments) and Farnborough (systems) operations are approaching a fair degree of independence as S.L.I. and S.(F.)—Solartron (Farnborough)—are filling in their own organizations where staff formerly existed in common.

"There are at least three good reasons for this development. First, the two operations differ in a number of ways: product concept, engineering, manufacturing, and selling techniques, just to name a few. We often think of the S.L.I. product as a single box in isolation and the S.(F.) product as a group of quite different boxes in a system. This simple distinction involves a considerably different approach in engineering. Manufacturing techniques are also affected, inasmuch as systems are much less adaptable to mass-production techniques than are standard instruments. Finally, the selling of instruments involves small-lot sales over a wide distribution network, and selling systems involves individually high-valued transactions on a less frequent basis to a much smaller group of customers. Systems also involve a much more engineering-oriented sales effort and more extensive service follow-up than do instruments.

"The second reason is that the two companies are physically located sufficiently apart (25 miles) to make a close joint operation difficult. Certainly one can maintain communications by telephone, but this can never satisfactorily replace face-to-face discussion. What has happened is that the people at the two locations have tended to work more and more independently on their own problems.

"The third reason, and perhaps the most important, is the feelings of the two managing directors, John Crosse and Ed Ponsford. I am sure that they much prefer to run and to control completely their own operations rather than to have to work with common service and line activities which would be only partly under their control."

"For more than a year," commented Mr. Ed Ponsford, Managing Director of Solartron Laboratory Instruments Ltd., "we have been integrating our instrument operation so that it can stand on its own feet. Incidentally, in my opinion, this year [1962] will be the first one in which S.L.I. can properly determine its own profit and loss.

"I have always believed that close coordination must exist between engineering, production, and sales. To get this coordination meant that I had to have these activities here where they could work together. We started to build this organization on two key men, Hugh Binyon (Sales Manager) and Terry Daly (Production Manager). Since then, we have added Don Richards to head our development engineering team. The only key position still left open is that of Research Director. He will have to organize and lead a small forward-thinking team of four or five men who will be concerned with instrument concepts five or more years from now.

"I do not see that there will be any significant duplication between S.(F.) and ourselves in research and development. We have different interests, and, more important, we stay informed on each other's work. Les Copestick will play a valuable role in seeing that neither group crosses into the other fellow's territory.

"This same attitude of not entering the other fellow's domain prevails in all other areas of activity. For example, an agreement has already been made between the two companies to prevent any possible poaching of personnel. A person cannot switch to the other company without the approval of his superiors."

GOALS AND OBJECTIVES

"While most of the goals and objectives mentioned in 1958 are still valid," stated Mr. Bolton, "some significant changes, at least in emphasis, have taken place. For example, Solartron has definitely jelled on its line of products and is now concerned with stabilizing operations and taking greater advantage of its fully developed product lines."

Commenting on the same point with regard to R&D, Mr. Catherall said: "Previously we had been developing products with the purpose of dominating the United Kingdom market. Now we are developing fewer products but with the intention of dominating on a world-wide scale. After ten years of moving full steam ahead in many directions, it makes good sense to shake out and rationalize research and development in order to select the few good products from the many. Most British electronics firms are doing much the same at the present time."

"Up until now it has always been a question of looking ahead and investing in the future," remarked Mr. John Crosse. "I believe that we have started to realize that it is also important to be making money in the present. I am a very strong proponent of the principle that goods going out of the door are the *only* money-makers. Up to now we have been spending much too much on development relative to our sales."

Other changes in policies and procedures appeared to the researcher to reflect the changed attitudes towards the company organization. Among these changes the most obvious one concerned the former policy of avoiding unnecessary status barriers. For one thing, an executive parking lot has since been located directly in front of the building. There were also a special dining-room and a private lavatory for the top executives of Solartron at both locations. Finally, certain privileges with regard to "clock-in" time were being taken. As one executive remarked, "Now that Solartron has been reorganized in a more conventional manner, operations and attitudes have become somewhat more formal. The officers are expected to be more 'organization'-minded than was the case during the days of spirited confusion."

PROBLEMS PRESENTED BY THE REORGANIZATION

A number of Solartron's executives pointed out that, notwithstanding the over-all merits of the organizational changes, certain new problems arose because of the reorganization itself. Some of the many problems stated are listed below. They are divided into transitional problems, which presented difficulties during the period of reorganization, and long-term problems.

TRANSITIONAL PROBLEMS

"One problem we encountered as a direct result of the centralization of the systems activities," commented Mr. George Sanders (Production Manager, S.F.), "was the loss of some good men who preferred to work under the atmosphere and promise of the former system. They saw their future tied to the future growth of their small sub-company and were not anxious to be engulfed in the much larger joint company, Solartron (Farnborough) Ltd.

"A second problem, closely related to the first, concerned the change of status of the former managing directors and operating directors. In many cases these men had originally come to Solartron because of the attraction of directorships. It is quite a mark of distinction in Great Britain, especially for a young man, to be a director of a company, and these men would not take kindly to the loss of this prestige. Of course, it was obvious that one centralized company could not use all the directors from the five companies.

"Our best men were given directorial posts in the new Solartron (Farnborough) Ltd. and important broad functional duties. For example, Mr. L. Malec, who had been the Managing Director of S.R.S., was made a director of S.(F.) and was also put in charge of all systems sales, a very important responsibility. At the same time, he has continued many of his former duties with the radar simulators. The other directors were given the title of executive director [another executive referred to this position as a 'pride crutch'] and were given positions which were as responsible as possible. Despite our serious effort to overcome this problem, it was not easy to make the necessary changes without hurting some people's feelings, and we found that the loss of prestige of the managing directorship or of a directorship was not easy to offset."

Another transitional problem of the reorganization related to the phenomenon of changing grouping loyalties. As the history of the research and development activity suggests, men's organizational loyalties were shifted from instruments to systems, from their own company S.R. & D. to the new company of S.(F.), and, in the case of the engineers under Mr. Maudsley, from their former superiors to the new ones from S.R. & D. Similar problems arose within the sales and production organizations. One executive commented: "It took time and patience to shuffle people around during the reorganization, and we were not always successful. For example, when Brian Maudsley left, we lost a few other good engineers who went with him. After all, people can develop a very strong attachment for their boss on their job."

LONG-TERM PROBLEMS

The problem most often mentioned in 1962 by management as having serious consequences under the new organization at Farnborough related to the loss of the "product-oriented" men. As one executive explained: "At least under the old system, we used to have men whose job it was to follow a product right through from R&D to the final sales effort. They would push the product through production and sales and make sure that everything was kept in balance. This was possible as long as individuals were responsible for individual products.

"Under the present system, there are men in R&D and sales who are interested in certain products and look after these products within their

department, which partly offsets this loss. Although this type of canaliza-
tion does not currently exist in production, George Sanders is planning
to set up shops along product lines, and I believe this will help take care
of the problem in that area. A serious difficulty remaining is that there is
no one to see that a product passes properly through the transitional
points, such as when it changes hands from R&D to production, or from
production to sales. If R&D tells production to go ahead and production
tells R&D that the item is still not ready for the production line, there
is no one in between who can clear up the differences of opinion. So far,
things have been working out on an 'ad hoc' basis, but I am not sure that
we are getting the desired control."

Another long-term problem concerned the reduced availability of "directorship" titles. On the one hand, several executives pointed out that
the need for attracting highly qualified managers from the outside had
been reduced considerably since Solartron had grown to the size where
it could develop management talent from within. At the same time, Mr.
Bolton mentioned that one of Solartron's problems was the difficulty of
attracting talented young men to Solartron because its top management
was relatively young itself. The multiple-corporate structure had always
allowed the attraction of a directorship to figure importantly in the search
for top talent. The combination of young managers and a relatively stable
management hierarchy had become a liability in this recruiting effort.

MANAGEMENT'S COMMENTS ON THE REORGANIZATION

By early 1962, the formal steps of reorganization at Farnborough had
all been taken, and management considered the forthcoming period as
one of consolidation. Current markets had to be more intensively cultivated, current products more strongly pushed and the current organization developed to an efficient unit. A number of executives referred to
the consolidation of the systems groups as an intermediate step in the
company's development. As Mr. John Crosse put it, "I see the centralization at Farnborough as just one swing of the pendulum. It is a step that
is appropriate at this time, just as I believe it will be appropriate to decentralize the units in the future, when they are capable of operating in
a truly independent fashion."

Other executives appeared concerned because they thought that the
consolidation had not been carried as far as it could have or should have
been. As one executive commented: "The logical thing to have done
would have been to consolidate the whole Solartron operation into one
company. While we cut out a lot of wasted work and duplication of

effort by amalgamating the various systems companies, we still have plenty of duplication remaining because we operate two separate companies on different locations. You can see the problem in sales where Farnborough must, to some extent, duplicate S.L.I.'s efforts in order to sell the products which originate at Farnborough. The basic S.(F.) sales force is organized to sell systems and not products. The problem of duplication is also apparent in many of the service activities, such as accounting, medical, guards and caretaking, and in many plant facilities.

"The other lingering problem which might have been avoided if the merger had been carried through fully is the rival loyalties and the 'we-they' attitudes which exist in the two operating companies. For example, in the sales duplication problem I just mentioned, I believe S.L.I. could well handle S.(F.)'s product sales, permitting S.(F.) to concentrate on what they can do best—systems sales. But S.L.I. believes, and perhaps rightfully so, that their sales force is responsible for S.L.I.'s products and would not do justice to, nor should they be expected to cope with, the technical problems of mastering the whole range of S.(F.) products. It is not an easy thing, if it is in fact possible, to be fully responsible on a profit and loss basis for one activity and to think of the interests of the group at the same time, especially if those interests are in conflict with your direct responsibilities."

One top executive suggested that the amalgamation could not have included both companies because it would have been physically impossible to locate them at the same place. He said that the reason for this was the impossibility of moving S.L.I. labor, which is highly skilled and expensive to train, to the Farnborough location, and he stressed the importance of not having disrupted S.L.I's production. About 85 per cent of S.L.I. labor force are weekly- or hourly-paid, and the majority do not have automobiles, and approximately half of this total are women. Another executive thought that the movement of labor was not nearly as significant a deterrent to a full amalgamation as were the personalities of the top executives themselves. As Mr. Ed Ponsford, Managing Director of S.L.I., said, "Solartron could probably be run as one unit, but not with the individuals involved—*not* with me. I personally wanted these two units separate."

KEY "LESSONS" WHICH WERE RECOGNIZED

Looking back over the period of development from 1959 to 1962, John Bolton summarized the "lessons" which he felt had been recognized, though he felt it more realistic to say that they were still in process of being learned:

1. During this period of growth from a small to a medium-sized organization, we were too nondirective in approach, and a better result could, I believe, have been achieved with more positive direction without swinging too far towards an autocratic organization. Although pursuing a very democratic and "consultative" type of policy speeded development of new teams and their ability to carry responsibility, it resulted in much greater problems of coordination, particularly in modifying the wide range of individual aspirations to fit in with the needs of the group as a whole. People want to feel able to "participate," but they also want to be given clear and positive leadership.

2. Under conditions of growth it is necessary to develop and gain acceptance of routines for decision making. In the early days all members of the management team were well briefed on the whole range of activities, and I felt that they could and should participate in making decisions. However, as the complexity increases, so it becomes necessary for individuals to specialize, and also to develop routines, by which a whole host of minor decisions are automatically made. We recognize the need for a "rule book" to help us simplify the decision-making process.

3. Although decentralization into separate product companies was of value in getting new activities started, it did increase the difficulty of keeping an over-all sense of unity and "Solartron purpose" amongst the separate units.

4. When development of a new product runs behind schedule, the effect on profits is multiplied well beyond the cost of development. In the first place, the sales and production organization for the new class of product which has been built up in phase with the program incurs expense, but with no immediate return from deliveries. Secondly, when new designs take longer than planned to go through the engineering and production system, the departments concerned have to handle an increasing proportion of items "in trouble," and the complexity and cost of engineering and preparing for production are increased. Thus there is a snowball effect from deliveries below budget and expenses above budget on the trading results and capital tied up.

5. After working out one's capital requirements in great detail, one should really multiply the "guesstimate" by a factor of three, not by a factor of two as was misleadingly suggested in the New Enterprises Course when I was at H.B.S.!!

Our over-all task during the next few years is clearly to simplify our organizational structure, to concentrate on those expanding product areas in which we have shown we can lead the field, and to re-create a real sense of day-to-day achievement in beating our targets.

Appendix A

✿✿

Exhibit A-1

THE COMPANY'S PRODUCTS, 1962

"We have essentially the same line of products that we did in 1958," remarked Mr. Bowman Scott, "but the relative importance of the various products has significantly changed since then [Exhibit A-1]. Some of the products for which we had great hopes, such as business machines, just did not turn out well. Computors, on the other hand, which were just a development item when you were last here, have become one of the most promising areas in our systems work.

"In 1958 when we were talking about 'building blocks' of an analogue computor, we were primarily concerned with the computor's amplifiers, which are really the heart of the system. Since then we have gradually added other parts until we now are able to manufacture complete medium sized analogue computors. In 1962 we expect our sales in this area to reach £450,000. In addition, we are active in data-logging and industrial process-control instrumentation. Our research boys believe that these three products, all part of the data-processing field, hold the greatest promise of future sales among our various systems activities.

"The other product which has assumed importance during these past four years, the tangential fan, is somewhat unusual in that it does not fit in our general product line. It is a simple mechanical unit with no electronics involved, but it does involve precise manufacturing tolerances and is a technical break-through of great importance in the field of fan technology. We became involved in the production of this unit as a licensee simply because we saw there was a tremendous potential for this product and that it would be a good money-maker. We are keeping the tangential fan manufacture completely separate from our other work, although the actual production is done in the Farnborough factory.

"It is interesting to note some of the trends that have taken place in our product sales [see Exhibits A-2 and A-3]. First you will notice a definite sales trend from instruments towards systems. The second significant trend is the increased importance of our proprietary products. This is a healthy situation because we make our profits from our proprietary products. The third trend has been the increased importance played by exports. Whereas exports accounted for only 20 per cent four years ago, they now account for close to 40 per cent and should soon account for 50 per cent of our total sales."

Exhibit A-2

SALES BREAKDOWN BY PRODUCT AND COMPANY, 1957–63
(Percentage of total sales)

Year	55/57 July 1	57/58 July 1	58/59 July 1	1961 Est.	1962 Est.	1963 Est.
Proprietary manufactured products						
Instruments	75	66	59	54	49	45
Systems	..	12	23	28	31	31
Tangential fans	..	..	..	6	11	14
Subtotal: Proprietary products..	75	78	82	88	91	90
Engineering, merchandising, and other non-manufacturing						
Contract engineering	18	14	11	9	7	7
Merchandising	5	7	6	3	2	3
Miscellaneous	2	1	1	..	..	..
Subtotal	25	22	18	12	9	10
Total	100	100	100	100	100	100
S.L.I. (Chessington)						
Standard instruments				45	42	35
Contract engineering				4	3	3
Subtotal				49	45	38
S.F. (Farnborough)						
Standard instruments				2	1	1
Contract engineering				4	3	4
Radar simulators				6	7	8
Business machines				2	1	..
Data logging				6	8	7
Computors				7	7	6
X-ray spectrometers				2	4	5
Transducers				3	3	4
Tangential fans				6	11	14
Miscellaneous				2	1	1
Subtotal				40	46	50
Overseas subsidiaries						
Standard instruments				7	6	9
Merchandising and other				1	1	1
Subtotal				8	7	10
Total: products and service				97	98	98
Merchandising, non-Solartron products				3	2	2

Source: Company records.

Exhibit A-3

GRAPH SHOWING DELIVERIES TO CUSTOMERS

This chart shows that total sales deliveries to Solartron customers increased 17 fold in the six years from 1954 to 1960. At the same time the percentage represented by Solartron proprietary products had steadily increased to a level of 88 per cent, whilst exports had risen from a nominal level in 1954 to 30 per cent of total sales in 1960. The product base was effectively widened by the development of new "systems" of equipment, and the growth in this field can be clearly seen commencing in 1958 and rising to 38 per cent of total sales by 1960. In the next five or six years this broadening of the customer base will continue, and our program looks towards sales of £5.0 million by 1966, with over half of this figure going into the export market.

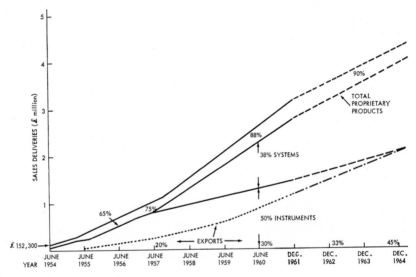

Source: Company records, 1962.

COMPAGNIE CHILLON ELECTRONIQUE*

On January 19, 1962, Professor Harold Stevenson and Research Associate Joseph Wagner first met M. Michel Vallotton, founder and owner of the Compagnie Chillon Electronique. From M. Vallotton's opening remarks, it soon became clear that ChillonEl, as the company was known in trade circles, had experienced remarkable growth during its ten years of existence.

It also soon became apparent to Professor Stevenson and Mr. Wagner that M. Vallotton was facing a serious hurdle in the development of his company. As M. Vallotton remarked, "So far, we have been a development engineering company specializing in electro-mechanical devices. We have traditionally been involved in contract development work, the production of prototype models, and, in recent years, even the manufacture of equipment on a small scale. But I am finding that production problems and odd jobs, such as customer service, are taking up more and more of my time.

"M. Lang, my sales agent in Zürich, tells me that standard production and repeat sales are where the money is to be made. I quite agree, but my heart is not really in this area. My interest lies in solving technical problems and in creating electronic devices.

"I often wonder if there really is a future for a small company like this. I think it is uncommon in Continental Europe to find companies as small as ChillonEl which have been able to succeed in the electronics industry all by themselves."

CASE ORGANIZATION

In discussing their reactions to the meeting which had just taken place, Professor Stevenson and Mr. Wagner both felt that this situation was most interesting and one which might warrant unorthodox treatment.

The situation—the development of a commercial organization from a small technical embryo—was particularly appealing because it was comparable to the emergence of new electronic, and other technically based, companies in the United States since World War II. Both men had been personally involved in the management of small technical companies in the United States, and this former experience contributed to their interest in ChillonEl. As Professor Stevenson remarked, "I see in M. Vallotton a man who has succeeded in building the foundations of a growing company, but who is no longer sure of where to go next. He is a manager who knows that he has a need but cannot define it. In view of his genuine interest in talking with us about his problems, why don't we do what we can to help him?"

For three reasons the researchers decided to deviate from their normal passive role as observers. First, the company faced a problem which was both critical and urgent. Second, M. Vallotton clearly indicated that he would appreciate any objective advice which could be given. Third, the researchers believed that they might be able to offer some constructive suggestions, in view of their interests and experiences.

The format of the case attempts to reflect the unusual situation and case-research approach. First, the data have been organized in chronological order rather than by topical areas, in an effort to capture the evolution of the events. Second, the actions of the researchers are contained in the case, because of the active roles which they played.

A FIRST MEETING WITH M. VALLOTTON, JANUARY 19, 1962

The initial meeting—attended by M. Vallotton, Professor Stevenson, and Mr. Wagner—was held in the company's offices and lasted about one hour. Professor Stevenson started the discussion by describing IMEDE and explaining the purposes and mechanics of case research. To this, M. Vallotton replied: "I find your work very interesting, but I think you will find ChillonEl much too small a company to merit a case study."

Professor Stevenson quickly assured M. Vallotton that big lessons could be learned from small companies and that ChillonEl might well provide valuable case material. M. Vallotton accepted the comment and stated that he and his organization would be completely at the researchers' disposal if they should wish to make such a study. He then continued with a brief sketch of ChillonEl's background.

THE COMPANY AND ITS HISTORY

"I started the company in 1953 with the help of my wife, a small income from royalties, a few contacts in industry, and some ideas which I wanted to explore further," remarked M. Vallotton. "I expect that our sales have reached more than 700,000 Swiss Francs [Sw. Fr.] this past year, and we are receiving more enquiries for our work and services than we can handle. Our major customers are the watchmaking and machine tool industries. We now have about 25 or 30 employees.

"I was educated in physics and mathematics at the College of Geneva and later received a M.Sc. degree in Physics in the United States. My industrial career began in 1946 with the Switch and Signal Union, Pittsburgh. In 1948, I became an engineering consultant for Westinghouse Airbrake Company in Europe. At this time, I also set up a little company to handle royalties received from a number of patents which I held. In 1952, I went to the United States to work in the Westinghouse engineering laboratories. After a year, I returned to Switzerland to start ChillonEl. I might mention that Westinghouse Airbrake was one of my best customers in those early years.

"I have enjoyed these past years because I have had a chance to be creative and to work with interesting technical problems. But lately there has been more and more need to become involved in the manufacturing of some products we have developed, to meet with customers, to service machines in the field, and to deal with many other commercial tasks, all of which are detracting from my engineering work."

"I guess what I need is a man who can help me with manufacturing problems and business details; I am just not a businessman. I think it is more difficult to find a good businessman than a good engineer. Excuse me, but perhaps you would like to see the plant before the employees leave for the day?"

ChillonEl was housed in a modern two-story brick building, located near Villeneuve, Switzerland. The upper floor was all one room, with work benches containing electronic test apparatus and tools conveniently placed. The main floor contained a number of rooms which served for special testing, display purposes, and office space. The total floor space of the plant was about 760 square meters. The plant appeared to the researchers to be exceptionally neat and clean. M. Vallotton's home was located next to the plant, the two buildings being complementary in architectural appearance; they were located on a 9,000-square-meter plot of ground.

At the end of the tour, M. Vallotton added: "I am very sorry that our meeting must be so short, but, as you know, I am just about to leave on a three-week trip around the world. The main reason for this trip is to meet with our new Japanese agents, in order to teach them how to service our equipment. They became our agents as a result of M. Lang's efforts and have already begun to sell our equipment. From there, I will go to the United States to look over my American competitors' products.

"If you should have any questions during my absence or wish to see anything, please get in touch with my wife. She will be in charge of the company while I am gone and will be glad to help you in any way she can."

A SECOND MEETING WITH M. VALLOTTON, FEBRUARY 27, 1962

A second meeting of MM. Vallotton and Wagner was held in the company's offices and lasted about two hours. During this time, M. Vallotton reviewed the functional areas of ChillonEl in detail. He commented on the products, sales, finances, organization, his own job, an important personnel problem, and, finally, the search for a commercial director.

PRODUCTS

M. Vallotton began by giving M. Wagner sales pamphlets for each of the products currently in production. As he explained, "It is no use to give you the catalogue because, although it was printed only last year, it is already out of date. I have not bothered to have it revised, because one can scarcely keep up with the product changes.

"In general, the products can be classified into three groups: (i) products for the watchmaking and small precision machines industries; (ii) products for the machine tool industry; and (iii) miscellaneous products. Here are some sheets which list our complete product line in each group." Exhibit 1 lists the ChillonEl products as of 1962. Exhibit 2 reproduces one page of a product brochure for ultrasonic cleaners.

SALES

"Of the products which you see on those sheets," continued M. Vallotton, "the automatic counters and ultrasonic units have accounted for the major part of the product sales. In addition to product sales, as you know, we do contract engineering and also get some income from our service work. I mentioned last time that I expected our 1961 sales to exceed 700,000 Sw. Fr. Well, they actually totalled 784,000 Sw. Fr. Here is a list of our annual sales figures which I have had prepared for you" (Table 1).

Mr. Wagner asked if he could also have a breakdown of recent sales figures by product groups or by the different sources of revenue activity,

Exhibit 1

THE COMPANY'S PRODUCTS, IN PRODUCTION AND DEVELOPMENT,
FEBRUARY, 1962

GROUP I: Products for the Watchmaking and Small Precision Machines
Industries

a)   Automatic counter–distributor–packager, transistorized (for the counting,
distribution and packaging of small parts)

b)   Automatic counter–distributor, transistorized

c)   Industrial ultrasonic generator, high power (for cleaning small parts)

d)   Ultrasonic generator, high power (for ultrasonic welding)

e)   Ultrasonic generator, low power (for ultrasonic cleaning)

f)   Photo–electric relay

g)   Magnetic field generator (to control clocks)

GROUP II: Products for the Machine Tool Industry

a)   Electronic speed control, transistorized .(to insure the constant speed
of direct current [DC] motors)

b)   A triple–phase variable frequency powersupply, transistorized (for
three–phase motors where the speed must be variable over a
fivefold range)

c)   Command logic circuit, (in development) (electronic control of
machine tools)

d)   Numeric command control of machine tools by magnetic tape
(in development)

GROUP III: Miscellaneous Products

a)   Teaching machine (in development)

b)   Electronic relay

c)   Photo–electric relay

d)   Vibrating distributor

e)   Adjustable variator, transistorized (to control intensity of florescent
bulbs)

f)   Electronic chronometer

g)   Road signals (electronic control mechanism for traffic lighting)

Source: Company product lists.

Table 1

ANNUAL SALES FOR COMPAGNIE CHILLON ELECTRONIQUE
AND PREDECESSOR COMPANY, 1948–61

Year	Annual Sales Sw. Fr.	Year	Annual Sales Sw. Fr.
1948	390	1955	78,831
1949	20,734	1956	120,067
1950	4,304	1957	220,128
1951	17,419	1958	291,540
1952	32,787	1959	280,476
1953	32,236	1960	412,264
1954	87,982	1961	784,687

Source: Company records.

i.e., contract engineering, product sales, and service work. M. Vallotton
replied that the company did not keep any sales statistics other than
monthly aggregate amounts. He added that he would ask his secretary

Exhibit 2

PAGE FROM A PROMOTIONAL BROCHURE FOR ULTRASONIC CLEANERS

Einfache Ultraschall-Reinigungsanlage (in Kombination mit DC 1631).

Installation simple de nettoyage aux ultrasons (en combination avec DC 1631).

Standard ultrasonic cleaning equipment (in combination with DC 1631).

Halbautomatische Ultraschall-Reinigungsanlage (Ausführung auf Wunsch).

Installation semi-automatique de nettoyage aux ultrasons (exécutée sur demande).

Semi-automatic ultrasonic cleaning equipment (manufactured on request).

Die Verwendung in der Uhrenindustrie

Weist ein Uhrwerk **Steinlager** auf, so wird deren Reinigung einer besonderen Behandlung durch Ultraschall unterzogen. In der Tat ist das Spiel zwischen Achse und Lagerstein so gering, dass gar keine Verunreinigung geduldet wird. Ebenso ist der Apparat für das Reinigen von **Platinen mit Sacklöchern** geeignet sowie für die Reinigung von **Uhrzeigerlöchern** von 0,14 mm Durchmesser.

Dasselbe Gerät wird auch in der übrigen Präzisionsindustrie verwendet.

Applications à l'horlogerie

Lorsqu'un mouvement comporte des **pierres** comme coussinets, celles-ci sont l'objet d'un traitement spécial au moyen d'ultrasons pour le nettoyage. En effet, le jeux entre l'axe d'une roue et son coussinet est tellement minime qu'aucune contamination n'est tolérée.
L'appareil se prête aussi bien au nettoyage de **platines comportant des trous borgnes** et des **trous d'aiguilles de montres** de 0,14 mm de diamètre.

Le même appareil est utilisé également dans les autres domaines de l'industrie de précision.

Use in watchmaking

When a movement is equipped with **jewel bearings**, these must be ultrasonic-cleaned. The clearance between staff and bearing is so small that no impurity is tolerated.
The same unit is equally suitable for cleaning **watch plates with dead holes** and **watch hand holes** of 0,14 mm diameter.

The equipment is utilised as well in other branches of precision industry.

to compile these figures from the invoice copies, inasmuch as he himself would be interested in knowing this information. Exhibit 3 contains these data for 1957 and 1961.

Exhibit 3

SALES BREAKDOWN BY MARKET ACTIVITY, 1957 AND 1961
(In Swiss francs)

1957

Machine Activity	Watchmaking Industry	Machine Tool In- dustry	Miscel- laneous	Total	Per cent of Total
Contract Engineering	151,248	--	6,096	157,344	71.5
Products	7,704	--	51,168	58,872	26.7
Service and Repairs	938	--	2,974	3,912	1.8
Total	159,890	--	60,238	220,128	
Per cent of Total	72.6	--	27.4		100.0

1961

Machine Activity	Watchmaking Industry	Machine Tool In- dustry	Miscel- laneous	Total	Per cent of Total
Contract Engineering	109,176	9,600	33,000	151,776	19.3
Products	550,459	--	66,120	616,579	78.6
Service and Repairs	7,848	144	8,340	16,332	2.1
Total	667,483	9,744	107,460	784,687	
Per cent of Total	85.1	1.2	13.7		100.0

Source: Company sales invoices.

FINANCIAL ASPECTS

"Despite the substantial growth of sales and activities over the past few years," continued M. Vallotton, "I cannot say that we have had any financial strain so far. As a matter of fact, I am forever receiving bankers here who want to loan me money. The company has had little or no need for external financing to date. Of course, we are talking about my need to borrow, since the company is a proprietorship and its resources are really my own personal resources. I have actually borrowed quite a bit of money to finance these buildings, but I did this mainly because it is advantageous under Swiss tax laws to use borrowed money for this purpose. You will have to speak to the people at the fiduciary company which handles our account, because they take care of all the tax matters. We just give them the operating figures, and they do the rest.

"You can also get the financial statements that you were asking for from them. They can supply you with the information much better than we can, but you must be careful how you interpret those figures. The accounting has been done so as to assume a most favorable position with regard to taxation." Exhibit 4 contains comparative balance sheets for the company for the period 1955–60. Exhibit 5 contains comparative profit and loss statements for the period 1956–60.

Exhibit 4

BALANCE SHEETS AS OF DECEMBER 31, 1955–60
(In Swiss francs)

	1955	1956	1957	1958	1959	1960
CURRENT ASSETS:						
Cash	9,234	6,222	1,198	77,063	5,588	3,604
Accounts Receivable	11,400	20,542	12,948	4,680	42,012	76,188
Loan, M. Vallotton						8,935
Inventory			8,400	6,000	3,600	2,400
Deposits and Retainers	1,200	1,200	1,200	1,200	1,200	1,200
FIXED ASSETS:						
Vehicles				15,600	10,800	10,800
Furniture and Fixtures	4,800	13,200	9,600	3,840	4,800	3,600
Machines and Equipment			1,800	7,800	16,800	15,600
Buildings and Land			45,827	288,000	435,816	561,600
TOTAL ASSETS:	26,634	41,164	80,973	404,183	520,616	683,927
CURRENT LIABILITIES:						
Accounts Payable	9,415	6,896	10,739	48,883	19,701	21,818
Customer Advances			6,000	3,410	61,200	102,000
Bank Loan			16,762	221,811	172,369	78,986
Loan, M. Vallotton	16,619	33,668	46,872	50,425	58,121	
FIXED LIABILITIES:						
Deferable Payment						
for Construction				79,054	22,721	32,604
Bank Loan					181,104	435,799
RESERVES AND PRO-PRIETORSHIP:						
Reserve for Bad Debt					4,800	6,120
Employee Fund						6,000
Proprietorship						
(legal reserve)	600	600	600	600	600	600
TOTAL CREDITS:	26,634	41,164	80,973	404,183	520,616	683,927

Source: Company records.

"As far as investments are concerned," added M. Vallotton, "I am sorry to say that we have no budget for this purpose. I have no real idea of how much money should or will be spent for tooling and equipment for the following year. I know that I should have some kind of budget for capital expenditure, but we just have not had the time to do this sort of planning."

COMPANY ORGANIZATION AND JOB DESCRIPTIONS

"The company's operating staff is more or less divided into different product-line and supporting groups," explained M. Vallotton, as he sketched an organization plan. "We have an ultrasonic section, a count-

Exhibit 5

PROFIT AND LOSS STATEMENTS, 1955–60
(In Swiss francs)

YEAR	1956	1957	1958	1959	1960
CREDIT					
Sales	120,067	220,128	291,540	280,476	412,264
DEBIT					
Salaries	34,341	54,590	60,760	64,489	106,518
Materials	*	*	130,214	102,700	150,545
Change in Inventory	*	*	· 2,400	2,400	· 1,200
Cost of Goods Sold	n.a.	n.a.	193,374	169,589	258,263
Improvements	61,149	109,915	10,435	13,335	19,544
General Expenses	20,583	38,328	62,453	65,422 [1]	97,590 [2]
Depreciation	3,736	4,781	22,425	29,706	33,531
Total Expenses	116,809	207,614	288,687	278,052	408,928
Net Benefit to Company	3,258	12,514	2,853	2,420	3,336
Total Debit	120,067	220,128	291,540	280,472	412,264

[1] Includes an allocation of Sw. Fr. 4,800 for Reserve for Bad Debt.
[2] Includes allocations of Sw. Fr. 1,320 for Reserve for Bad Debt and Sw. Fr. 6,000 for an Employee Fund.
* Contained in Improvements.
n.a. = not applicable.
Source: Company records.

ing machine section, and a miscellaneous product section. They perform the development and supervise the production of their products. To support these three groups, we have an electronic section, a mechanical section, and a technical section. Every section, except for the technical section, is headed by an engineer." Exhibit 6 shows an organization chart of Compagnie Chillon Electronique for February, 1962.

Exhibit 6

COMPANY ORGANIZATION CHART

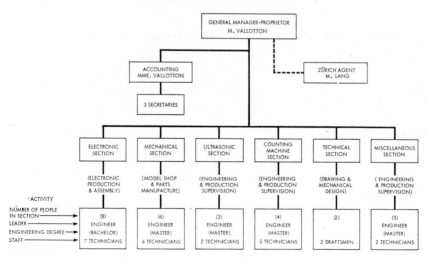

"As I mentioned," continued M. Vallotton, "my wife is in charge of the office force and handles all the bookkeeping and accounting. We might also consider M. Lang, our Zürich sales agent, as part of the organization, since he executes much of ChillonEl's sales efforts.

"As General Manager and sole proprietor of this company, I get involved in a lot of different jobs. I try to limit my activity in the company to a 10-hour day, 5 days per week. The employees work 9 hours and 15 minutes each day, excluding lunch, which comes to a 46¼-hour week. If I were to try to estimate how I spent my time, I would say that I use about 15 minutes of each hour in which I am on the company premises controlling and administering the operations, and 45 minutes studying the new technologies and keeping abreast of the electronics industry.

"I make it a habit to tour the plant quickly every quarter of an hour to see what is going on, to control operations, and to give assistance whenever needed. This task really keeps me a captive in Villeneuve, but I have no doubt that it is one of my most important jobs. You may be interested to know that it cost me more money during my absence because I was not here to control the operations than the expense of the trip itself. It is not really a matter of trying to keep the engineers alert and working, but rather one of providing technical initiative and of helping them over trouble areas.

"Looking at a full week's activity, I would say that on the average my week can be broken down as follows:

(i)	Technical study and development engineering	28 hours
(ii)	Technical and personnel control	10 hours
(iii)	Business administration (e.g. correspondence)	7 hours
(iv)	Selling	5 hours
	Total	50 hours

Mr. Wagner remarked about the relatively small amount of time spent by M. Vallotton in selling ChillonEl's products and services. M. Vallotton responded: "The company is already receiving more orders for products and engineering than it can handle. As a consequence, I do not think that there is any need to spend more time on this function."

PERSONNEL PROBLEMS

"One of the difficult problems that I face," said M. Vallotton, "is trying to get and keep good engineers. This company is in great need of engineers having the equivalent of a Master's Degree in education, about 5 years of experience, and specialization in a knowledge of semiconductors and solid-state circuitry. The problem is that it is almost impossible to compete with American firms for engineers because of the very much higher salaries which they offer, even for work in Europe. An American company might pay three to four times as much in the United States as is normally paid in Switzerland. Just last month I lost one of my better engineers to an American firm in the United States. I had even offered to help this fellow finance a new home and a new boat which he could use on the lake, but the offer from the American firm was just too attractive.

"So far, I have found engineers either through personal contact or through the engineer's own initiative in contacting ChillonEl. After all, one of the main attractions of the company is its location in Villeneuve. Since there are only about ten electronics companies in Switzerland which do any significant amount of development work, those Swiss engineers who are looking for jobs in electronics will probably be aware of this company's existence, and if they are interested in coming to this area, they will probably contact us on their own.

"The company cannot use inexperienced engineers, and so I have not done any recruiting among students. I am planning some day to send a student to the United States for engineering studies with the hope that he will return to the company, but I have not yet made any definite arrangements in this respect."

COMMERCIAL DIRECTOR

Towards the end of the interview, M. Vallotton remarked: "You know, I have been doing a lot of thinking about our previous discussion concerning the need for a commercial man in the company. Since then, the matter has become more urgent than ever.

"If you remember, I mentioned that my wife was in charge of the office force and also took care of the bookkeeping. During my absence, she took full charge of the operations as best she could. Unfortunately, the responsibilities and pressures were much more than should have been thrust upon her, and as a result she became seriously ill and has had to be sent to a hospital. Now not only do I have the pressures of which I spoke to you during our last meeting, but I also have to worry about all those areas which my wife so ably supervised. I do not think she will be able to resume those jobs again.

"Since my return, I have spoken with my brother-in-law about the problem, and he has put me in touch with a woman who might possibly be able to help me with the business. She is managing one of the sanitariums above Montreux and is supposed to be a very good administrator. She was just here this morning to look over the office. Maybe she would be good for the commercial post in the company."

In view of these comments, Mr. Wagner felt that M. Vallotton was failing to distinguish between two different needs of the company. In Mr. Wagner's opinion, the company had a long-term need for a commercial director who could carry the company further into the business of product manufacture and sales, and a short-term need for a special administrative assistant for M. Vallotton to replace his wife.

In order to make this distinction clear to M. Vallotton, Mr. Wagner asked a number of questions. He hoped that the questions would help M. Vallotton think out for himself what it was he was really bargaining for.

Q.1. *"What do you think that the Commercial Director will have to do for the company?"*

A. "I expect that he would start by handling the bookkeeping for the company. From this point, he would assume more and more responsibility until he finally operated as a Commercial Director.

"The Commercial Director would advise me what we should do concerning the commercial aspects of the business. He would make up a budget for capital expenditures and other important expenses. He would control the business while I was away. He would also be able to meet and take care of visiting customers and other visitors whom I did not have to see for any special reason."

Q.2. *"What would be the qualifications that you require of this man?"*

A. "I really do not know!

"I would expect that the man should be about 40 years of age, and he should be able to speak French perfectly, and also English and German well. It is very difficult for me to know exactly what kind of experience a Commercial Director should have. When it comes to engineers and technical people, I know exactly what kind of people we need in this company. I am afraid that my knowledge and experience are not such that I can make any equivalent kind of evaluation of a commercial man."

Q.3. *"What are you doing to locate this man?"*

A. "I have been looking in the newspapers, and this is about all so far."

Q.4. *"What are you willing to offer such a man as regards pay, responsibility, and authority?"*

A. "It is hard for me to think clearly about what salary such a man should earn, because it would not be a productive salary, such as is paid an engineer. Perhaps it would be between Sw.Fr. 1,000 and Sw.Fr. 1,500 per month. A very good engineer, one with 5 years' experience, is paid Sw.Fr. 2,000 per month. This is pretty much the ceiling because the maximum charge that we can invoice for development engineering is approximately this amount."

Mr. Wagner went on to query in general terms what other forms of remuneration might be considered to get a good man. Although it was not possible to determine any definite limits, M. Vallotton expressed a recognition that it might be necessary and even advisable to include a percentage of the company's sales as part of this pay, or even a stake in the ownership of the business.

A THIRD MEETING WITH M. VALLOTTON, MARCH 29, 1962

A third meeting of MM. Vallotton and Wagner was held at the company offices and lasted about two hours. During this time discussions were held about the selection of a Commercial Director, about M. Vallotton's personal values, and also about the contract engineering activity of the company. During the meeting, the researcher accompanied M. Vallotton during one of his normal "control-tours."

COMMERCIAL DIRECTOR

"I have been giving a lot more thought to our conversation concerning a Commercial Director for the company," commented M. Vallotton in opening the meeting, "and I would like to let you know what I have done since we last met. Over the years I have received a number of enquiries and even offers for association or merger from some of my watchmaking customers who were anxious to diversify into other fields. I had never really seriously considered taking such a step before, but under the present circumstances I wonder if such a move might not be a way to solve my problems. What I think would be very good would be to merge with some company that could take over the administrative and commercial operation of ChillonEl, leaving me free to conduct the development engineering part of the business. Perhaps we could form a joint company where I could keep a majority of, let us say, 51 per cent. I would consider such a merger with a British company, an American company, or any other electronics company for that matter.

"With this in mind, I recently paid a visit to the Office Vaudois Pour le Développement de l'Industrie et du Commerce to see if they could help me locate a company which would wish to enter into such arrangements with me. I spoke with M. Breband, the Director of the office, and explained the situation. As soon as I finished telling M. Breband about my thoughts, he began to discourage me from seeking to merge. He said that it would be a shame to let others into the company at this time. He recommended instead that I find a man who could assume the commercial responsibility of the company and then suggested that I contact a M. Durret, who might qualify for the job.

"I first telephoned M. Durret and discussed the possible job opportunity with him. He expressed an interest, and we consequently met here. During our first meeting we agreed that he examine the company closely to see if he would like to take the job. He then spent a period of about 15 days, 4–6 hours each day, examining the company from top to bottom. I think it would be advisable if you would speak with M. Durret, since it might be valuable for you to see the company through someone else's eyes. Furthermore, after his careful examination of our records, he can probably tell you more about the commercial side of the company than I can. I also would like very much to have your opinion about M. Durret's qualifications for the job."

Mr. Wagner agreed to meet with M. Durret as suggested. The only information about the candidate that M. Vallotton could provide was that M. Durret was a 57-year-old Swiss who had been a manager of an oil refinery in Argentina. When Mr. Wagner asked about the woman who had been interviewed for the position, M. Vallotton replied that she had decided against it because she felt the job would be too much for her.

"One example of how the company is suffering from my inability to take on more responsibility," continued M. Vallotton, "can perhaps be seen from the way manufacturing and service activities are stealing men who are better qualified to carry on development work. Just today, two very good engineers are away from the company in order to service some counting machines in Neuchâtel. This is always happening, and the interruptions are hurting our engineering work. I know that I should take on more engineers specifically for the jobs of production and service engineering. But I cannot take this step, because I cannot run a larger organization than I already have. The first step, I believe, is to get this commercial man we have been talking about, and then we can add to the staff as necessary.

PERSONAL VALUES

Following M. Vallotton's comments of his search for a Commercial Director, Mr. Wagner directed the conversation to a discussion of the personal values which M. Vallotton held concerning his interest in ChillonEl.

"I think that I would list my personal business objectives," commented M. Vallotton, "in the following order of importance to myself:

(i) To conduct the business in such a way that it would only place a reasonable workload on me, so that I can also have time for personal interests and my family life

(ii) To be able to devote a large part of my working time to technical exploration and creativity

(iii)   To earn enough money to allow my family and me to live comfortably and to remain free from financial worry

"I might add that I am a little concerned about the possible effects of the workload on my own physical health. Now that I have to deal with the whole operation without my wife's help, I am a little worried that the total workload could be as overwhelming and damaging to my health as it was to my wife's while I was abroad. I find that I am already becoming irritable and nervous and tend to snap at people for little things; this is not good for the people here.

"What I would like to do is get a man in the company who could take care of the commercial problems. Then I would like to get a man in who could be in charge of the technical side of the business. This would allow me to think more about the business as a whole and also permit me to work on those technical problems which really interest me. But it will be some time before this arrangement will be settled."

PRODUCT ACTIVITY

"The fountain of our growth has been and will continue to be our contract development engineering work," commented M. Vallotton. "All of our present products have stemmed from this work, and we will continue to broaden our product line from new developments.

"I would say that, on the average, about 80 per cent of the development work is supported by customer contracts and the remaining 20 per cent is 'in-house' [at company expense]. The rights for patents on all development work sponsored by customers, of course, go to the customers. ChillonEl, however, is fortunate in that most of the customers limit their demands for patent rights to cover their own specific application or field of interest. We are normally free to develop good prospects further for other applications. Most of our 'in-house' development work has originated as an extension of the more promising contract work.

"In those cases where our 'in-house' development work grows too big for us to support alone, we would go to some large company for help or financial support. As an example, we are now looking for someone to support ChillonEl in its development work of a digital position controller for certain machine tools. This position controller had originally been developed under contract for a machine tool company who used the product for lathes. We were permitted to extend the process for other machines at our pleasure, so now we are trying to develop this product for grinders. The project seems promising, but we would like financial backing from a grinder manufacturer to obtain funds for its development and to have a ready customer who will then use and market our controller. I intend to visit the industrial fair at Basel next week to talk with various prospects there, and, as another step, I might write various United States manufacturers to see if they would be interested."

CONTROL TOUR OF PLANT

The researcher accompanied M. Vallotton on one of his normal control tours of the plant. During this walk, M. Vallotton only stopped to speak with two of his engineers concerning some technical point of their projects. The whole tour took about 4 minutes. M. Vallotton said that this tour was typical.

A FOURTH MEETING WITH M. VALLOTTON, APRIL 9, 1962

The fourth meeting of MM. Vallotton and Wagner was held in the company offices and lasted about two hours. The major part of the discussion centered on the problem of selecting a Commercial Director. M. Vallotton also commented on a special project with which he had been concerned during the past week.

COMMERCIAL DIRECTOR

Prior to this meeting Mr. Wagner had prepared a preliminary outline of a job description for the position of a Commercial Director of ChillonEl. A copy of this outline was given to M. Vallotton, and the two reviewed the outline together, Mr. Wagner making explanatory comments as appropriate. During the discussion, M. Vallotton did not ask any questions. At the conclusion, M. Vallotton remarked, "For the first time I am beginning to see what a big job the position of Commercial Director could be. There is really so much to be done."

After the outlines had been reviewed, Mr. Wagner mentioned that he had not yet heard from M. Durret. M. Vallotton answered that he had not been in touch with M. Durret since the last meeting because the latter had been travelling. M. Vallotton then added: "Perhaps M. Durret is not the right man for the job because of his advanced age. You know, M. Durret wants to work only six hours per day and he would like to receive Sw. Fr. 1,500 per month. But don't you think I could hire him for a trial period until December?"

OTHER CONCERNS

M. Vallotton then brought up a new subject. "You might be interested to know that I have just bought a large plot of land next to our present property. I have had my eye on this property for some time and finally took advantage of an option which I held, although it was very expensive. The main reason I bought it was to prevent others from coming in and erecting a tall building which would obstruct the view from my home and the plant. To cover the cost of maintaining it, I shall have a gas station erected on the property. I have been in touch with a number of oil companies, all of whom are anxious to put a gas station on the spot. At least we can keep the profile of a gas station quite low. My only real worry is to clear any zoning regulations which the city authorities may cite."

A FIFTH MEETING WITH M. VALLOTTON, APRIL 25, 1962

The meeting of MM. Vallotton and Wagner was held in the company offices for about 1½ hours. During this time the men discussed engineering personnel and the selection of a Commercial Director.

PERSONNEL PROBLEMS

"I am sorry to keep you waiting, Mr. Wagner," said M. Vallotton as the two men met, "but just 20 minutes ago one of my engineers came into the office to tell me that he would be leaving the company. Fortunately, this man is not one of my better engineers, and he will not be any great loss to the company. However, I will have to find another engineer to replace this man."

When asked as to the reason why this man had resigned, M. Vallotton answered that he had had on many occasions to correct this man's performance and that it was probably these reprimands that had caused this man to seek other employment.

M. Vallotton continued: "You may be interested to know that I have just recently made an offer to my two best engineers of a one per cent share of all sales of their own department's instruments. I think this might give them an incentive to become real leaders of their departments. This is not to say that these men will necessarily become department heads, because I would still like to find a top-notch man who can be placed in charge of both departments. I am not sure, at this time, in which direction I will move. This will depend largely on the results I receive from these two engineers."

The two departments concerned were the counting machines and the ultrasonic equipment departments, and the two engineers were aged 34 and 22, respectively. As a result of questioning, Mr. Wagner learned that there were no titled or responsible heads in the company other than M. Vallotton himself.

COMMERCIAL DIRECTOR

"As for M. Durret," continued M. Vallotton, "I have just about decided that he is not the man for the position. I have spoken with M. Lang [Zürich agent] about M. Durret, and he completely agreed that the man for the position of Commercial Director should be relatively young and certainly dynamic. M. Durret does not seem to meet this need when you consider his desire to work only 30 hours per week.

"Nevertheless, I did ask M. Durret to meet you, but he said he did not care to. He said something about '. . . I know about IMEDE, and I do not wish to see those people.' He did, however, make a tentative appointment to see M. Lang. I think that M. Durret did not wish to meet you because he was afraid that you might tell him that he was not qualified for the job."

M. Vallotton went on to say that he had heard that it was possible to get a good man straight from the University for about Sw. Fr. 20,000 per annum plus some percentage of the company sales. He then asked Mr. Wagner whether he thought such a man might not be good for the job.

After these discussions, Mr. Wagner presented M. Vallotton with a finished set of outlines which described the job of Commercial Director for Compagnie Chillon Electronique and also listed criteria which might be used in evaluating candidates for this position. This set of outlines was slightly changed by Mr. Wagner from the preliminary set as a result of the previous discussion with M. Vallotton and a review with Professor Stevenson. Mr. Wagner suggested that a full discussion of the documents be postponed until M. Vallotton had had an opportunity to review them thoroughly. A copy of the outlines and a covering letter are contained in Exhibit 7.

Exhibit 7

DOCUMENTS RELATING TO THE SELECTION OF A COMMERCIAL DIRECTOR
FOR COMPAGNIE CHILLON ELECTRONIQUE

Monsieur M. Vallotton,
General Manager,
Compagnie Chillon Electronique,
VILLENEUVE
Switzerland

JFW/vT   April 25, 1962

Dear Monsieur Vallotton:

The first of the two attachments under cover of this letter is submitted to you to help you better understand with which managerial functions a new commercial executive may become concerned in Compagnie Chillon Electronique. The second attachment attempts to indicate

Exhibit 7—Continued

some of the abilities and characteristics that you should consider in your evaluation of candidates for this position. Although we have already discussed preliminary versions of these documents for some hours, I should, however, like to elaborate on certain aspects of these present versions.

Basically, the job of Commercial Director has been specified in view of the needs of the company as a whole, and my understanding of your personal objectives and capabilities. I believe that it is important not to limit our thinking to your own currently pressing administrative problem; that is, your urgent need for assistance in bookkeeping and administrative work. This problem, too, is important, but it should not be confused with the broader needs of the company.

I should like to emphasize that not only has the job description been designed specifically for Compagnie Chillon Electronique but that, moreover, it should be considered valid only for this one point of the company's development. It is not to be viewed as a general criterion for a commercial director of an average European company or even for your company at some later stage of organization. The most striking example of the special nature of this job specification is the inclusion of production management within its scope. This inclusion was made, as you may well understand, because of your personal interests and desires. As the organization grows and is better able to support a broader management team, such functions as production supervisor and accounting chief will be placed under the authority of new men.

Attachment I is organized in the following manner. In the left-hand column, the business functional areas in which the Commercial Director will be involved have been listed. These comprise general management, marketing (sales), finance, production, and a limited aspect of personnel. Especially and totally excluded are the important areas of technical research and development, which will remain initially under your direction, as well as legal and other specialist activities. In the right-hand column, the more important duties have been outlined in some detail. Finally, in order to assist in the definition of the many duties listed, the post of Commercial Director has been subdivided in the center column into a number of managerial posts equivalent to those performed in large companies.

Attachment II, listing the most important experiences and characteristics which the new Commercial Director should possess, can only be used as a check-off list. Of course, certain items are much more important than others. We have already discussed this point to some extent. Eventually, we should try to decide which attributes or combination of attributes you would be more willing to overlook, since it is unlikely that any one candidate will meet all the requirements.

I hope that these outlines will help you with the problem we have been considering. Certainly, they are not to be taken as the last or best words on the subject.

Please call me as soon as you are prepared to review these documents.

Very truly yours,
Joseph F. Wagner
Research Associate

ATTACHMENT I

JOB DESCRIPTION OF THE COMMERCIAL DIRECTOR

Business Function	*Equivalent Position*	*Duties*
General Management		1. To help the Managing Director (M. Vallotton) set the general policies, objectives, and goals of the company. This duty involves answering questions such as:
		(*a*) What kind of company do we want in 5, 10, 20 years?
		(*b*) What business activity is most consistent with our personal values, business experience and the company's past accomplishments?
		(*c*) What kind of professional people, work-

Exhibit 7—Continued

		ers, products, services, and so forth, should the growth of the company be based on?
		2. To inform the Managing Director of the impact on the financial, marketing and production activities and resources in the company for courses of action under consideration.
		3. To conduct special studies, as required.
Marketing (Sales)	Marketing Officer	1. To make major marketing decisions, in consultation with the Managing Director, regarding such matters as:
		(*a*) The relative marketing emphasis among various products and market areas;
		(*b*) The proper methods of selling the product (such as agents versus company's salesmen);
		(*c*) The proper channels of distribution, and even the selection of markets for new products;
		(*d*) The extent of employing various marketing activities such as advertising, trade shows, and special promotions.
		2. To execute advanced product planning based on market considerations, pointing out:
		(*a*) New product areas for development;
		(*b*) Desirable revisions of existing products.
		3. To provide the Managing Director with timely records of sales performance and marketing costs.
	Sales Director	1. To conduct sales planning:
		(*a*) Sales estimates;
		(*b*) Sales expenditure budgets.
		2. To supervise the sales force:
		(*a*) Agents;
		(*b*) Company salesmen;
		(*c*) Technical service representatives.
		3. To sell the products:
		(*a*) Calls on customers;
		(*b*) Meetings with customers in Villeneuve;
		(*c*) Attendance at fairs and exhibitions.
		4. To supervise field customers' service activities:
		(*a*) Service and maintenance of equipment by ChillonEl engineers;
		(*b*) Service and maintenance by independent agencies.
		5. To supervise field market research conducted by the sales force.
	Marketing Services Director	1. To conduct and present market research:
		(*a*) Library research;
		(*b*) Special field research;
		(*c*) Research report.
		2. To display products at exhibitions.
		3. To plan and conduct general promotion activities including advertising.
Finance	Financial Officer and Controller	1. To make major financial decisions, in consultation with the Managing Director, regarding such matters as:
		(*a*) Major investments;

Exhibit 7—Continued

(*b*) Borrowing policies and procedures;

(*c*) The capital structure of the company.

2. To conduct financial planning and control, for example:

   (*a*) To devise a capital budget;

   (*b*) To evaluate major capital equipment purchase proposals;

   (*c*) To project fund-flows, and to make up proforma (future) financial statements and statistics.

3. To maintain a contact with financial sources:

   (*a*) To maintain contact and perform negotiations with banks, stock share-holders, debtors, and so forth;

   (*b*) To keep informed on special financial arrangements available for exporters.

4. To maintain control over all corporate funds.

	Chief Accountant	1. To evaluate and design the accounting and control systems—as the company grows and changes form, to introduce the necessary changes in accounting and control. This will involve significant effort when the possible new production center or corporate structure is set up.
		2. To supervise bookkeeping and accounting clerical work—this includes the accounting of billing, purchasing, employees' salaries, and so forth.
		3. To work with the external accountant and to check his work and advice.
	Purchasing Officer	1. To devise purchasing procedures and policies.
		2. To conduct negotiations concerning important purchases, or source relationships.
		3. To supervise the regular purchasing of expendable items.
Production	Production Manager	To advise the Managing Director concerning major decisions on production and capital equipment purchasing.
	Production Supervisor (temporary)	To supervise production work, and to control manufacturing materials.
	Customers' Services Department Head	To supervise service and maintenance of customers' equipment sent in to Villeneuve.
Personnel	This job is an integral part of the jobs listed above.	1. To supervise clerical and commercial personnel in finance, sales, and accounting.
		2. To supervise production personnel (possibly temporarily).
		3. To train personnel for supervisory positions, such as chief accountant and production supervisor.
		4. To recruit clerical and commercial personnel, and initially production laborers (a production supervisor may perform this job in the future; production and service engineers should be recruited by M. Vallotton).

Exhibit 7—Continued

> 5. To advise the Managing Director in regard to salaries, raises, promotions, and disciplinary actions concerning all personnel under his organizance.

ATTACHMENT II

DESIRABLE ATTRIBUTES OF THE COMMERCAL DIRECTOR

A. *Experience and Understanding*
  1. General business experience:
    (*a*) A familiarity with the modern techniques of the various business functions, for example:
      (i) *in finance;* to be familiar with cost accounting, return-on-investment calculations, and capital budgeting;
      (ii) *in marketing;* to be familiar with sales planning, market research, and selling techniques.
  2. Small business experience:
    (*a*) An understanding of the special dangers involved in operating a small business.
    (*b*) An appreciation of the special strengths of a small business.
    (*c*) An awareness of the required versatility of organization and of management in operating a small business.
  3. Experience with a research and development business:
    (*a*) An appreciation of technical problems and the timing involved.
    (*b*) Some experience in conducting a business which has a high proportion of engineers and which is technically oriented.
  4. Familiarity with and contacts in the electronics, machine-tool, and watchmaking industries, especially in Switzerland, the United States, and Continental Europe. (The United States and certain Western Hemisphere countries represent the area of potential growth for this company.)
  5. Experience in conducting, supervising, and analyzing market research for technical products.
  6. An understanding of electronics and of electro-mechanical technology.

B. *Personal Characteristics*
  1. A broad business background and an ability to be flexible in his work.
  2. Ability with languages—French, English, and German.
  3. A fairly young man (30–45 years of age) so as to be able to grow with the company, and to tie in his career for the long-term.
  4. "Self-starter" who can work without supervision or guidance. (This is important since the Managing Director would not be knowledgeable about a number of his activities.)
  5. A man of high integrity and character.
  6. A personable individual who can work well with all people.
  7. A healthy and energetic man.

C. *Educational Qualifications*
  A degree in Commerce and/or Electronics, or equivalent experience.

M. Vallotton finally remarked: "I would guess that I could hold out for about two years, if I had to, in order to find the right man for this job. I do not believe that I could carry the load any longer than that. If I cannot find a good Commercial Director in that time, I will either have to merge with a larger company who could provide the administrative assistance which I need, or sell my company. I have another alternative of just continuing operations at a reduced level, but I do not think this is a good way to do business."

A MEETING WITH M. LANG, APRIL 27, 1962

MM. Lang and Wagner met in the office of Lang S.A. in Zürich for about 2½ hours. During that time, M. Lang described his relations with ChillonEl and commented on various aspects of sales and products. M. Lang also expressed his views concerning a possible Commercial Director for ChillonEl.

Lang S.A. had been organized for the purpose of representing a number of small non-competing manufacturing firms in Switzerland who were dealing or were interested in the export market but were not large enough to exploit it by themselves. In 1962 the company represented more than 10 clients, most of whom manufactured equipment relating to some aspect of the watchmaking and machine tool industries. The company's turnover in 1962 was about Sw. Fr. 6,000,000, of which ChillonEl accounted for Sw. Fr. 300,000 or about 5 per cent. M. Lang himself was a young man of about 38 years of age, who appeared to Mr. Wagner as being very dynamic and competent.

In reviewing the relationship between Lang S.A. and ChillonEl, M. Lang commented: "In 1958 I was looking for electronic counting and packing apparatus because of requests from some of my foreign contacts. As a result of this search, I ran across ChillonEl, which was then only a small laboratory producing a few proto-type models of counting machines which were excellent for my limited purpose.

"After several meetings we agreed that I would handle the full line of ChillonEl products, as a general sales agent. I made an exception and also represented the company in Switzerland because of my many contacts in the watchmaking industry, which would, and did, result in substantial sales within a short time. As part of my service to ChillonEl, I have begun to develop a line of product pamphlets (Exhibit 2) and other sales literature.

SALES

"The contractual agreements between us have always been based on straight commission. The commissions range between 10 and 20 per cent of sales. The spread above 10 per cent is related to any special arrangements and servicing which the agencies have to handle. For example, the commission for products sold in Japan is 20 per cent, because our collaborating agency in Japan handles all service and maintenance. Likewise, a premium above 10 per cent has to be paid for sales in France, because we are obliged to carry accounts for three months on all sales. On the other hand, the charge is normally 10 per cent for sales in Switzerland, because ChillonEl's engineers conduct all service and maintenance.

"I would estimate that the geographical distribution of my company's sales for ChillonEl was as follows:

Switzerland	20%
Germany, France, U.K., Sweden	40%
Japan, U.S.A.	20%
Other areas	20%
Total	100%

Automatic counting machines accounted for 75 per cent of these sales and ultrasonic apparatus accounted for the remaining 25 per cent. The distribution sales breakdown was similar for both machines.

"As far as real growth potential, I believe that the greatest opportunity will be in the four European countries now accounting for 40 per cent. I consider the United States a difficult market, first, because the technology is so advanced in electronics there and, second, because of tariff problems.

PRODUCTS

"There are five products which would be significant in our discussion of the ChillonEl line. This list would include the automatic counting machines, the ultrasonic cleaners, the automatic speed control for D.C. motors, the command logic circuit for machine tools, and a machine tool control by magnetic tape programming.

"The main product of the company is the automatic counting machine. An unfortunate problem is that the market for this product, as it now is, is severely limited. We expect to sell about 20 in 1962, but I would estimate a total market potential, and I do not mean per annum, of only 100 machines. The reason that the market is so restricted is that such an expensive machine is worthwhile only when the parts to be counted are of high value; otherwise, a simple measurement by weight is more practical. Furthermore, this machine will allow only parts which are not too large or which are not intricate to be counted. If the parts are intricate, they might hook or stick together, and then the conglomeration of pieces would be counted as one. These limitations of the machine pretty much restrict its application to the watchmaking industry. It would be wonderful if there were some way to improve the capabilities of the machine. As it now stands, the selling price of this machine is approximately Sw. Fr. 25,000.

"The ultrasonic cleaning apparatus is the other product which we are currently selling. We expect to sell about 15 to 20 of these machines in 1962. This machine, however, has a much greater market potential than that of the counting machine, and I would estimate a future potential of 100 machines per year. The reason for this enlarged sales potential is that these units are not limited to the watchmaking industry. It is a very reliable machine with a high capacity and also a relatively low price. It is probably one of the best machines of its class in Europe. The selling price is about Sw. Fr. 9,000.

"Another product that is of interest is the automatic speed control for D.C. motors.[1] It is now in an advanced stage of development and we are planning to conduct some test sales and market research on this item soon. Such a testing period will last 6 to 12 months and may result in requirements for further product design. When we know that we have a good product, we will then support a full sales effort in Switzerland for one year. We limit our initial efforts to Switzerland, so that we can easily take corrective action, should that be required. I expect that the future market might range between 300 and 1,000 units per year when sales are developed. The selling price might be about Sw. Fr. 1,200 per unit.

"The other two products in development which show promise are the command logic circuit for machine tools and a machine tool control by magnetic tape programming.[2] Both of these products have a high market potential because they will apply to the vast machine tool industry.

"I am very pleased with these new products because they are ChillonEl's first step away from complete dependence on the watchmaking industry, which, after all, is a rather limited market. I think it is important for the company to develop products which will be directed towards markets, such as the general machine tool industry, with much higher potential requirements than are available from the watchmaking industry. It is difficult to say for which markets new products will be developed. There is no telling what new inspirations will result from the laboratory work, and, with electronics, there are really no restrictions."

COMMERCIAL DIRECTOR

As the conversation came around to the subject of the company itself and some of its more general problems, M. Lang remarked: "As I see it, there are two jobs to be done at ChillonEl: the first is to guide the electronic engineers in their work, and this M. Vallotton is well qualified to do; the second is to direct the commercial activity of the company, and

---

1 Item II-a in Exhibit 1.
2 Items II-c and II-d in Exhibit 1.

for this he needs someone else. He simply does not have the time to conduct both the technical and the commercial side of the business, nor is he really interested in the commercial work."

Mr. Wagner then asked M. Lang in what areas of activity he thought the Commercial Director should be involved. M. Lang answered: "It is difficult to pin down all of the many duties such a man will have to do without carefully reviewing the situation. However, I think that the man would be occupied in the following ways: (i) leader of the commercial staff; (ii) supervisor of the sales department; (iii) supervisor of the purchasing department; (iv) head of accounting; and (v) involved with the general administrative work. The man must, of course, be supported in these activities by adequate staff.

"I do think it is very important to add that such a man must be capable of working on his own initiative and not be the type that would go to M. Vallotton for every decision. After all, what M. Vallotton needs is a man who will relieve him of worries, not bring additional ones."

*   *   *   *   *

Having completed the case, Mr. Wagner planned to see M. Vallotton once more. The purpose of this meeting was to answer any questions M. Vallotton might have and to make any suggestions that might be of help.

Mr. Wagner realized that M. Vallotton and he had explored only one problem area to any depth during their past meetings, that of the need for and selection of a commercial director; and, even here, the process of analysis had only been started. Mr. Wagner wondered whether it would not be of greater value to review some of the other problem areas which they had only touched upon in their discussions. He remembered M. Vallotton's concern about the problem of getting and keeping good engineers and whether to set up a manufacturing organization separate from the development company. Mr. Wagner also thought of other possible problem areas which should be brought to M. Vallotton's attention, such as the financial impact of setting up manufacturing facilities and that of advanced product planning.

Mr. Wagner believed that not only would it be appropriate to extend their discussion to these topics, but he also felt that they ought to move beyond general analytical evaluations and begin outlining some specific actions and programs.

PART VI

Mergers and Joint Ventures

THE SOLARTRON ELECTRONIC GROUP LTD. (D)

SELENIA ELETTRONICHE S.P.A.

MOUNT OLYMPUS ENTERPRISES

I.C.I.—COURTAULDS: A TAKEOVER ATTEMPT THAT FAILED

THE CASES in this section on mergers deal with a very timely and important topic in Europe. These cases (and also the Croydon and Arla chemical company cases in an earlier section, and the Merck series in Learned, Christensen, and Andrews, *Problems of General Management*) appealed particularly to European executive trainees, who must envisage facing merger problems during their own business careers. The reasons for mergers, the financial terms of mergers, and some of the human and other kinds of problems which mergers engender are made clear in many of these cases. Additional information on reasons may be found in the chemical industry notes that precede the Croydon and Arla cases.

These cases should be studied not so much with the aim of passing judgment on the actions of participants in attempted mergers or joint ventures as with the aim of learning to foresee pitfalls and to identify factors which tend to make mergers or joint ventures successful. Readers may wish perhaps to ponder the question whether there must always be a dominant partner in a merger or joint venture. In some ways, business undertakings of this sort are like marriage. They involve some form of mutual adjustment and understanding between the partners. Successful mergers and joint ventures need to be continually worked upon by the contracting parties. Recollection of the basic reasons for the venture, adaptive modifications growing out of evolving events, and continued concern about human factors can all be recommended. Our experience in leading discussions of this topic in management training groups indicates that participants bring much valuable experience to bear on the cases and that this provides for rewarding discussion.

THE SOLARTRON ELECTRONIC GROUP LTD. (D)

The first case[1] in a series on The Solartron Electronic Group Ltd. (S.E.G.) described the organization, objectives, and product planning of the Group. The second case (C)[2] focused upon the major changes in organization made between 1959 and the middle of 1962. This case (D) deals primarily with Solartron's solution of finding sources of funds for its expansion and research and development programs.

. The first and major move by S.E.G. in December, 1959, involved the sale of 53.125%, or a majority interest, of its common stock to Firth Cleveland, Ltd., an industrial holding and investment company with its major interests in metals, engineering, radio, television, and electrical appliance retail trades, but with a relatively small electronic subsidiary specializing in liquid flow instrumentation. The second move was made by Firth Cleveland after consultation with the management of S.E.G. It involved the sale of Firth Cleveland's majority interest in S.E.G. to Schlumberger. By October, 1961, Firth Cleveland's interest had been increased to 56.7% of S.E.G.'s common stock. Reactions of S.E.G.'s management to both arrangements are given in this case. The Schlumberger point of view on Solartron is stated by its executive in charge of acquisitions and mergers.

REASONS FOR SEEKING FINANCIAL PARTNER

In the spring of 1961, Mr. John Bolton[3] described to an IMEDE researcher the developments which had led to a decision to sell Firth Cleveland a controlling interest.

"It was already apparent in March 1959 that our original forecasts or 'targets' for the next five years would have to be spread over six years.[4] Since then, we have found ourselves falling behind our schedule of fore-

---

[1] The Solartron Electronic Group Ltd. (A).
[2] The Solartron Electronic Group Ltd. (C).
[3] Mr. Bolton had been chairman of the board of directors and Managing Director of S.E.G. until the sale of stock to Firth Cleveland; thereafter he became deputy chairman and continued as Managing Director.
[4] See Exhibit 2 and 4 of The Solartron Electronic Group Ltd. (A) for these targets.

casted deliveries to an even greater extent. I believe that this turn of events can be largely attributed to two causes. First, the cost and time of developing new equipment far exceeded our estimates on almost every occasion. Second, the time needed to build up markets for new products and equipment turned out to be longer than we had anticipated. For example, it was not unusual for a customer to say that he would order ten units within a month if the original model was successful, and then for us to discover that his additional orders were spread out over a period of two or three years. The effect of these two causes resulted in an increase in overheads which far outstripped increases in deliveries.

"Our consistent underestimation of the penalties of delayed development and the difficulties of creating new markets has had both good and bad results. Not knowing how difficult some of our undertakings would be, we entered areas where the problems were really too tough for us to tackle, and nevertheless we did a pretty good technical job. Had we known the problems which we later encountered, I am certain that we would never have entered some of these areas and would have foregone those opportunities. On the other hand, the lengthened presale period required a much greater investment of funds than we had anticipated and our financial resources were becoming strained.

"When considering our financial requirements in the fall of 1959, we began seriously to analyze our basic financial problems. We realized that we were obliged to make long-term forecasts and long-term plans for research and development, factory construction, establishment of overseas companies, and the development of markets for both new and old products. Yet we had to finance these long-term programs on a year-to-year basis with our investment bankers.

"We explored several ways of bringing our financial capabilities into better balance with our operational commitments. We had had absolutely no luck in trying to interest our investment bankers in underwriting a long-term program of loans or debt-offering, if necessary coupled with equity issues. They explained that the institutions (insurance companies, etc.) with whom they would 'place' our loans operated on an annual financial budget only—our problem was that when they approached these institutions, with our accounts some three or four months after the end of any financial year, we were already fully committed to, and, indeed, incurring expenditure for the current year. If our approach to the institutions coincided with a financial or political crisis, we would probably have found it impossible, at that time, to obtain the finance we required. We saw, however, three other interesting alternatives open to us. First, we could secure additional funds by an offering of common stock in a private or public transaction. Second, we could merge with a larger company in our own industry. Third, we could merge with a larger company in a different type of business.

"The first alternative was discarded because we could not make the necessary forward forecasts with any certainty of accuracy and, in London, failure to meet forecasts involves a disastrous loss of confidence in a company. Our possible need for repeated or unexpected funding was another important reason for rejecting this alternative. Research and market development costs, you know, are absorbing ever larger amounts of cash. Furthermore, in our industry, large and unforeseeable variations in financial requirements can and do occur, owing to the proportion of sales dependent on new designs. On the one hand, we believed that we could rely on a large-company partner for additional funds to meet such needs as they arose. On the other hand, we doubted that financing the company by the sale of additional common stock would be effective, because Solartron's financial statements might look least attractive to an investor when our need was greatest.

"We also decided against merging with a larger electronics company, even though several well-known firms had approached us with this objective in mind. We believed that such a merger would magnify our problem of long-term capital shortage, because other electronics firms would probably be facing the same funding problems. We also believed that a merger with a large, diversified, U.K.-based electronics company could pose a threat to the continued existence of Solartron as an individual organization. If the work performed in the large company's other divisions were similar to ours, top management might very well decide to merge Solartron with some other division and our company would cease to exist in an independent form. This possibility did not coincide with the personal objectives of our management group or with our belief in the ultimate future for Solartron.

"The possibility of joining forces with a large company outside the electronics industry did appeal to us. This type of merger would provide us with new financial resources and would not threaten our corporate existence."

THE MERGER WITH FIRTH CLEVELAND LTD.

During the fall of 1959, Mr. Bolton began talking with Mr. C. W. Hayward, chairman of Firth Cleveland Ltd., about the problems and intentions of Solartron. Mr. Bolton had known Mr. Hayward for many years and considered him to be a valued personal friend. As a result of these discussions, Mr. Hayward became interested in the possibility of Firth Cleveland's purchasing a controlling interest in Solartron, and additional meetings were held during the following weeks. By the end of 1959, the terms of the merger had been developed and the letter shown in Exhibit 1 was sent to the shareholders. A description of Firth Cleveland Ltd., prepared by an investment banking firm on February 26, 1960, is presented in Exhibit 2.

Exhibit 1

LETTER TO SOLARTRON'S SHAREHOLDERS CONCERNING
THE FIRTH CLEVELAND-SOLARTRON TRANSACTION

> Queen's Road,
> Thames Ditton,
> Surrey
> 29th December, 1959

TO THE MEMBERS.

DEAR SIR (OR MADAM),

At the end of my Statement which accompanied the last Report and Accounts of the Company, I referred to the need for substantial additional capital, and the purpose of this letter is to advise Shareholders of financial arrangements that have recently been made, and to explain them.

As you know, Solartron is engaged on a long-term development and expansion program which has required and will continue to require a steadily increasing amount of additional finance each year. In reviewing the forecast of cash requirements for the next five years it became apparent to your Directors that the amounts involved are such that it would be unwise to continue to finance this long-term program on a year-to-year basis. In considering the problem, your Directors were influenced by the fact that during the present stage of your Company's development, it is difficult to make accurate forecasts of profits. In addition, external conditions such as a credit squeeze at home or a serious international situation abroad could have the effect of making it almost impossible to raise the required capital on reasonable terms to a definite timetable. In order to provide for the expected needs of your Company's program over the next five years, and to furnish a reasonable margin for unforeseeable eventualities, your Directors came to the conclusion, after consultation with their financial advisers, that a sum approaching £1 million should be raised immediately and in one operation, whilst economic conditions were particularly favorable.

In order to provide additional finance temporarily, and to enable us to complete the examination of our long-term capital requirements, Robert Benson, Lonsdale & Co. Limited subscribed on 9th November last, at your Directors' request, for the unissued balance of Ordinary Share Capital, namely 60,000 Shares of 10s. each at an issue price of £2 10s. per Share, less a commission of 1s. per Share, so raising £147,000. At the time of the issue, Robert Benson, Lonsdale & Co. Limited agreed that they would offer these Shares to existing Ordinary Shareholders on a pro rata basis and at the same price of £2 10s. per Share, as soon as final proposals for providing additional finance could be put forward.

In view of the size of the overall sum required, your Directors decided that it would be unsatisfactory to attempt to raise this money from existing Ordinary

Exhibit 1—Continued

Shareholders, or from institutional investors or from the general public. They were also of the opinion that the introduction at this stage of an industrial partner who could provide not only the finance but also trading benefits would be in the best interests of the Company.

Your Directors accordingly entered into negotiations with Firth Cleveland Limited, an expanding group which had not only the financial resources, but whose interests included businesses at home and abroad with which an association would be of benefit to Solartron.

I am now pleased to inform you that arrangements have been made with Firth Cleveland, which are detailed below:—

1. Firth Cleveland will subscribe for 300,000 new Ordinary Shares of 10s. each at £3 per Share, to raise £900,000. These Shares will rank pari passu in all respects with the existing Ordinary Shares.

2. Firth Cleveland will acquire 125,000 existing Ordinary Shares of 10s., the consideration per Solartron Share being at the option of the Solartron Shareholders either:—

    a. £3 in cash, or

    b. the allotment, credited as fully paid, of 2 Ordinary Shares of 4s. each of Firth Cleveland.

To effect this acquisition, Firth Cleveland will offer to purchase 50 per cent of the holdings of all Shareholders, other than the Directors. To the extent that the Shares sold by these Shareholders will be less than 125,000 Shares, the Directors will make up on the same terms the balance, which in any event will be not less than 27,800 Shares.

3. Firth Cleveland have undertaken to make a further offer on or before 31st July, 1961, for the Solartron Ordinary Shares not then owned by them, their holding being after the present transaction 53.125 per cent of the issued Ordinary Shares. The terms of this offer will provide that the consideration per Solartron Share will be not less than £3 in cash. If the Directors of Firth Cleveland so decide, Solartron Shareholders may be given the option to exchange their Shares for Firth Cleveland Ordinary Shares, on a basis to be determined at the time by the Directors of Firth Cleveland.

4. Firth Cleveland have agreed that an application for quotation for Solartron Ordinary Shares on The Stock Exchange, London, will be made not later than the end of 1965, unless the holders of a majority of the Ordinary Shares not owned by Firth Cleveland vote to defer such application. Firth Cleveland are not, however, bound to make any Shares available for the purpose of obtaining such quotation.

5. The Directors of Solartron have agreed that until quotation is granted, they will not sell any Solartron Ordinary Shares (other than in connection with obtaining quotation) without first offering such Shares to Firth Cleveland.

It is proposed to appoint Mr. Charles W. Hayward, the Chairman of Firth Cleveland, and Mr. Gordon Harries, A.C.A., the Secretary of Firth Cleveland, to the Board of the Company. My co-Directors and I have asked Mr. Hayward to accept the Chairmanship of the Board of the Company and so give us the direct benefit of his extensive experience. Mr. Hayward has agreed to accept this appointment. It is intended that I shall then become Deputy Chairman.

In entering into this agreement with Firth Cleveland and so making Solartron a subsidiary in a much larger group, it could be thought that the character of Solar-

Exhibit 1—Continued

tron as a company would in future, to some extent, be changed. Throughout the negotiations the Directors of both Companies have agreed on the importance of Solartron retaining its present policy and independent spirit. Nevertheless, both Boards were very mindful of their responsibilities to the Shareholders of Solartron, and the need to protect minority interests. Accordingly, certain of the terms which are detailed above were put forward with the express purpose of safeguarding the interests of existing Shareholders. Thus, whilst the Directors have ensured the transaction with Firth Cleveland by guaranteeing out of their own holdings the availability of 125,000 Ordinary Shares, other Shareholders will be completely free to act as they wish.

Shareholders will shortly receive a Circular Letter from Robert Benson, Lonsdale & Co. Limited making the offer on behalf of Firth Cleveland. At the same time Robert Benson, Lonsdale & Co. Limited will be offering pro rata to Ordinary Shareholders the 60,000 Shares subscribed by them in November, and referred to above.

It was in view of these developments that your Directors decided that it would be inappropriate to propose at the Annual General Meeting to-day the resolution increasing the Company's share capital to £1,000,000; at the date the Notice of Meeting was despatched, the negotiations with Firth Cleveland were only at a preliminary stage.

In the light of the above information and as the first step in the arrangements with Firth Cleveland, your Directors now propose that the authorized capital of your Company be increased to £600,000 by the creation of 300,000 new Ordinary Shares of 10s. each, which will be subscribed by Firth Cleveland. Finalization of the arrangements is, therefore, conditional upon the necessary resolution being passed, but your Directors and other Shareholders controlling between them more than 50 per cent. of the Ordinary Capital intend to vote in favor of the resolution.

Enclosed in the case of Ordinary Shareholders is a Notice of Extraordinary General Meeting to be held on Thursday, 14th January, 1960, at which an Ordinary Resolution increasing the Capital and approving the issue to Firth Cleveland and appointing Mr. Hayward (who is over 65) to the Board of the Company will be proposed. A Form of Proxy is enclosed, as appropriate, in case you are unable to attend the Meeting; in this event it should be lodged at the Registered Office of the Company not less than 48 hours before the time of the Meeting.

None of your Directors has any interest in the Share Capital of Firth Cleveland.

Yours faithfully,
JOHN BOLTON,
Chairman

Source: Company records.

Exhibit 2

EXCERPTS FROM INVESTMENT BROKER'S REPORT ON FIRTH CLEVELAND LTD.

February 26, 1960

FIRTH CLEVELAND AS AT MID-1959

From the prospectus dated July 1959: "The company is an industrial holding and investment company and its main interests in metals, engineering and the re-

Exhibit 2—Continued

tail trade have been built up as a result of a policy of reasoned diversification, intended to give a measure of insurance against fluctuating demand. . . . The acquisition of new subsidiaries has been largely guided by possibilities of integration with existing interests, inter-company trading, and ensuring supplies of raw materials and outlets for finished products. It is the intention of the company to continue the acquisition of suitable companies within the framework of this policy.

"The Group's customers are found in practically every type of industry. Its products range from semifinished raw materials to complicated electronic devices, and they find their outlets in such diverse activities as agriculture and the generation of atomic energy as well as in motor vehicles, shipbuilding, aircraft, domestic appliances, radio, television and many other industries. Group turnover for 14 months to December 1958 was approximately £21 million; direct exports in that period amounted to over £1.8 million."

The Group then comprised some 17 principal U.K. companies in addition to five manufacturing companies in Australia, Brazil, South Africa, and Holland, the whole employing over 5,850 people.

DEVELOPMENTS SINCE MID-1959

The market in the Ordinary Shares opened very quietly in July and it was some time before any significant premium was established. However, by early December the shares had reached 23/6d; a month later they were 47/9d.

The explanation of this remarkable rise lies in the announcement during December of two major acquisitions, the effect of which was to increase the total of Group assets by well over 50%.

BROADMEAD

The first was the acquisition of Broadmead Ltd., retailers of radios, TV sets, and domestic electrical appliances. This business had been founded in 1946 by its Chairman, Mr. John James, in a single shop in Bristol. By 1959, it controlled a chain of more than 300. Adding these to Firth Cleveland's own retail chain (to make a total approaching 500), has had the effect of creating what is the world's largest radio and electrical retail group.

The price paid by Firth Cleveland for Broadmead was £5.8 m. made up as to £2.9 m. in cash and 2,416,667 4/– Ordinary Shares in Firth Cleveland (valued at 24/–) representing 12.9% of the present equity.

SOLARTRON

The second acquisition, announced on the 29th December, related to Solartron Electronic Group Ltd. Ten years ago, Solartron consisted of three men making instruments in a barn behind the Odeon Cinema at Kingson-on-Thames. They were joined by John Bolton (also a Wolverhampton man), who invested £50,000 in the business and took over commercial operations. Since then, the labor force has grown to 1,330 (of whom one-fifth are engaged in research) and the sales turnover from £30,000 to £2.1 m.

Solartron now ranks as a leading unit in the British electronics industry. Defense demands were important in the Group's early development (it is a leading supplier of radar simulators and servo-testing equipment for guided missiles) but in recent years, product development has been increasingly concentrated on non-military fields. The current range of production is thus very broad. It comprises

Exhibit 2—Continued

140 proprietary products including notably, data processing equipment, simulators and industrial control equipment. The Group also manufactures the leading range of measuring instruments for research and development available in the United Kingdom. Altogether, 82% of last year's £2.1 m. deliveries were of Solartron proprietary products.

Capital requirements for research and product development have been heavy even for this capital-hungry industry and Solartron's need for a further £1 m. was one of the prime factors behind the merger with Firth Cleveland. It explains why it mainly took the form of a cash subscription for new Solartron shares rather than a share exchange. The terms of the merger were the acquisition by Firth Cleveland of 300,000 new shares and 212 old shares in Solartron for £3 each and the acquisition of a further 124,788 shares in exchange for 249,576 Firth Cleveland 4/– Ordinary. The latter therefore holds 425,000 (53.125%) of Solartron's total Ordinary issued capital of 800,000 shares. The balance of 46.875% is retained by the original shareholders but Firth Cleveland has undertaken to bid not less than £3 per share in cash for the minority on or before 1st July 1961 or to award an option to exchange into Firth Cleveland Ordinary shares.

It has also been agreed that an application for the quotation of Solartron on the London Stock Exchange will be made not later than December, 1965, unless the holders of a majority of the shares not owned by Firth Cleveland vote to defer the application.

Profit-wise, Solartron brings little of immediate significance to Firth Cleveland. In the year to 4th July 1959, the Group earned a pre-tax profit of only £9,340, a contraction from the highest level of £72,157 in 1958, due mainly to development charges, and the dislocation of production resulting from the move into its new Farnborough works. Current profits for the year to July 1960 are not easily estimated because deliveries will include new products. However, it is forecast that turnover will increase by nearly one-third over the previous year's total of £2.1 m. (the latter being equal to some 10% of Firth Cleveland's turnover for the 14 months to December 1958). The sales target for 1965 is no less than £6½ m.

From the capital aspect, Solartron has brought in net tangible equity assets of £257,000 (as at July 1959 but including £150,000 from a share issue in November). Adding £900,636 cash subscribed by Firth Cleveland gives a total of £1,157,636 of which £615,000 is attributable to Firth Cleveland's 53% shareholding. For this, and a 53% interest in last year's minute profit of £9,340, Firth Cleveland has paid £1.4 m. in cash and shares. However, the figure of net tangibles at £257,000 necessarily excludes all development expenditure which has been absorbing about 15% of sales. Deliveries since 1953/54 have totalled £5 3/4 m. and therefore it seems likely that something in the region of £750,000 may have been written out of the Balance Sheet over the past five years. Taking that figure into account and remembering that its fruits have yet to be seen in profit development, the purchase price looks highly reasonable.

The Solartron deal involves the creation of a fourth division for Firth Cleveland, namely, "Instruments and Electronics." It is clear that its main effect is to provide Firth Cleveland with a major representation in the fast-growing electronics industry, considerably enhancing the existing interests held through Firth Cleveland Instruments.

Exhibit 2—Continued

PROFITS

The position at the moment is that Firth Cleveland's profits for the year to December 1959 have yet to be declared but we have a prospectus forecast of £1.8 m. A circular is also awaited giving more details of Broadmead's profit record and some information on its current earnings (though we know the profits for the year to March 1959). In the case of Solartron, we know the profit for the year to July 1959 (relatively insignificant in amount).

We therefore give below the profit picture as indicated:

(1) For Firth Cleveland *before* the Broadmead and Solartron acquisitions, based on the prospectus forecast:

FIRTH CLEVELAND ONLY	TURNOVER	PRE-TAX PROFITS*	EQUITY EARNINGS*
Year to 31st October 1954......	......	£1,097,305	£322,701
Year to 31st October 1955......	£14¼ m.	1,471,889	627,614
Year to 31st October 1956......	16¼ m.	1,613,349	727,022
Year to 31st October 1957......	17¼ m.	1,846,737	858,734
14 months to 31 December 1958..	21 m.	1,705,787†	902,013
X Forecast 31 December 1959...	......	1,800,000	......

* Including pre-acquisition profits.
† Equal to £1,462 per annum.
"Equity Earnings" are shown after tax.

PRE-TAX PROFITS	DEBENTURE REDUCTION RESERVE	TAX	NET PREFERRED DIVIDEND	AVAILABLE	EARN-INGS	DIVIDEND
£1.8 m.	£51,000	£852,638	£36,750	£859,612	43.8%	24%

(2) For The Group after Broadmead and Solartron, based on the latest known figures:

INCLUDING BROADMEAD AND SOLARTRON	PRE-TAX PROFITS	NET FOR EQUITY	FIRTH CLEVELAND EARNINGS		DIVIDEND FORECAST
			On TOTAL CAPITAL	On RANKING CAPITAL	
Firth Cleveland Year to 31.12.59	£1.8 m.	£0.859 m.			
Broadmead Year to 31.3.59	0.743	0.381	54.4%	139.5%	24% Costing +£214,082
Solartron Year to 4.7.59	0.009	0.005			
	£2.552 m.	£1.245 m.	+ On £1,456,339 ranking for 1959 dividends		

COMMENT

Clearly, 1959 earnings on ranking capital (but including pre-acquisition profits) will show an extremely strong earnings cover for the forecast 24% dividend. This, moreover, allows nothing for the recent forecast that the original estimate of

Exhibit 2—Continued

£1.8 m. for Firth Cleveland will be "comfortably exceeded," nor for the higher profits that Broadmead will doubtless have earned since March.

The element of retained profits (just over £1 million) will itself provide a substantial sum toward the cost of the Broadmead and Solartron acquisitions.

FINANCES

The Group balance sheet as at 31st December 1958, adjusted for subsequent acquisitions appeared as under:

Fixed assets:			
Land and buildings			
(after £100,604 depreciation)			£1.283 m.
Plant, machinery			
(after £1,267,951 depreciation)............			1.631
			£2.914
Quick assets:			
Cash	£0.888 m.		
Loans	0.635		
Security sales	0.516	£2.039 m.	
Less: Short liabilities (including tax			
and overdraft)		1.524	0.515
Other current assets (net)			3.505
			£6.934
Less: Debentures	£0.894 m.		
Minorities	0.407		
Tax reserve	0.721		
Preferred capital	1.075		3.097
Equity assets attributable to £3,200,000 capital (4⁄9d			
per share) (excluding goodwill and patents)			£3.837 m.

Since then, £2.6 m. has been added from Broadmead and £136,000 in respect of the 53% interest in Solartron (both figures based on their latest available accounts) to give an apparent total of £6½ m. attributable to £3,733,248 capital. Group finances were, however, augmented by additional bank borrowings to help finance the £2.9 m. cash portion of the Broadmead acquisition and the £936,000 subscribed to Solartron. The result has been a rise in the "temporary net bank overdraft" of the whole Group of £4 m. A complete picture of attributable net equity assets must therefore await the publication of a pro-forma consolidated balance sheet.

For the moment, it is stated that including these bank facilities, the Group's existing resources will provide adequate working capital "for the time being." The inference is that while an approach to the market for new capital cannot be ruled out, there is no apparent urgency for a funding operation. The need for one at all will presumably depend as much as anything on the rate at which cash funds can be generated internally. On that point, it is probably true that the expansion of hire-purchase business and the greater level of activity all-round will themselves

Exhibit 2—Continued

present a competing demand for cash backing. It therefore seems a fair, even if obvious conclusion, that over the short-term, at least, Firth Cleveland will now be more concerned with consolidation than with any further widening of the Group's base of operations.

Commenting on the arrangements, Mr. Bolton said, "The terms of the merger were very attractive to our executive group, because we were given considerable freedom to determine the type of relationship that would exist between Solartron and the parent company. For instance, we were able to request which of Firth Cleveland's directors would serve on our Board. Furthermore, although Firth Cleveland gained a controlling interest in Solartron, only two of our ten directors were from the parent company. Finally, the knowledge of having the support of Firth Cleveland concerning our financial requirements would relieve one of the great pressures under which we had had to operate, and leave us free to concentrate on our technical and management problems.

The nondirector shareholders of Solartron exchanged 66,871 shares for those of Firth Cleveland and sold 212 shares for cash. The remaining 57,917 shares were provided by the director shareholders to bring Firth Cleveland's holding up to 53%. Just prior to the sale, the directors of Solartron owned approximately 300,000 ordinary shares of a total of 500,000 shares outstanding.

SOLARTRON AND SCHLUMBERGER

The sale of Firth Cleveland's interest in Solartron was announced in the press information bulletin of October 18, 1961 (reproduced in Exhibit 3). The next day the following article appeared in the European edition of *The Christian Science Monitor:*

Britain's fastest-growing electronics company, Solartron, is, with Treasury permission, to be sold to Schlumberger of Texas, the French-American group with substantial interest in the oil industries of the world and a new interest in electronics.

Schlumberger plans to buy the 56.7 per cent controlling interest at present held by the British industrial holding organization, Firth Cleveland.

A bid also is to be made for the rest of the Solartron shares held personally by the directors, the largest shareholder being John Bolton, a graduate of two Cambridges, Cambridge University, England, and Harvard University.

Mr. Bolton and his colleagues may not sell. Not yet. For this is one of the most remarkable companies in the world and has a long way yet to go.

It is a highly profitable company that as yet has produced few profits for its shareholders in the ordinary sense of the term. All the same it has made at least one of them a millionaire, which is the way of things these days.

Solartron was not profitable enough for Firth Cleveland to hold on to, for it plowed most of its trading profits back into development and produced but little income. Last year it showed gross profits of £112,644 ($315,000), but in the end net profits came to only £7,773.

From the sale of its holdings, however, Firth Cleveland makes, as a capital gain, the money it did not make before as income. It bought at 60 shillings and is to sell at 85. Firth Cleveland makes a profit of £567,000.

Exhibit 3

A PRESS INFORMATION BULLETIN, DATED OCTOBER 18, 1961

The Treasury have now given the necessary consent to the sale by Firth Cleveland Limited of its 56.7% holding in The Solartron Electronic Group Limited to Schlumberger Ltd. The transaction is conditional upon a capitalisation of reserves by the allotment of two new Ordinary shares for each Solartron share now held. The purchase consideration which will be paid in cash is £1,927,940.5.0d. or £1.8.4d. for each share including new shares, which is equivalent to the price of £4.5.0d. per existing Ordinary share in Solartron.

S. G. Warburg & Company Limited on behalf of Schlumberger will make an offer to holders of the remainder of the Ordinary capital of Solartron to acquire their shares. Provided that the agreement becomes unconditional, this offer will be made as soon as possible after the proposed capitalisation, and in any event by 1st December 1961, at the same price, i.e. £1.8.4d. per Share on the increased Ordinary capital. An Extraordinary General Meeting of Solartron will be called as soon as possible in order to obtain the shareholders' approval of the proposed capitalisation.

Schlumberger has agreed to assume the undertaking given by Firth Cleveland in December 1959 to permit an application for quotation of Solartron Ordinary shares on The Stock Exchange, London, not later than the end of 1965, unless the holders of a majority of the Ordinary shares not held by Schlumberger vote to defer such application. Schlumberger will not be bound to make any shares available for the purpose of obtaining such quotation.

Firth Cleveland considers this sale to be in the best interests of its shareholders in view of the long-term nature of the investment in Solartron and the further substantial sums that will be required for Solartron's future development and expansion. Schlumberger believes that this new association should be to the benefit of Solartron due to Schlumberger's interests in electronics both in the U.S.A. and Europe, a view with which the Board of Solartron fully agree.

Schlumberger had its origin in the 1920s when two brothers, Conrad and Marcel Schlumberger, developed a revolutionary method of determining basic geophysical characteristics with the use of electrical parameters. This method proved to be indispensable to the oil industry.

Today Schlumberger is a world-wide organisation giving numerous technical services to the oil industry.

Thanks to the experience gained in developing, manufacturing and servicing data handling systems and components in the oil wells, Schlumberger was ready to solve similar problems in both the military and civilian fields.

Affiliated companies are engaged in these activities both in the United States and in Europe. The Board of Schlumberger and the Board of Daystrom Incorporated, a large and diversified US manufacturer of electronic equipment, have recently agreed to a merger whereby Schlumberger will acquire the assets of Daystrom against the issue of Schlumberger shares. In connection with this merger, Schlumberger has announced that it will apply for quotation of its common shares on the New York Stock Exchange.

Schlumberger spends over ten million dollars annually on research and development, employing more than 1,500 scientists and graduate engineers.

Schlumberger's net worth at December 31, 1960, was approximately $140,000,000, and its net income for 1960 after all provisions and taxes was over $16,000,000.

Source: Company records.

SOLARTRON'S VIEWS OF THE SCHLUMBERGER TAKE-OVER

Because the sale of Firth Cleveland's majority interest to Schlumberger occurred during the period of interviewing and data collecting for this case, the IMEDE researcher was able to observe and obtain management's initial reactions to the change of ownership. Mr. John Bolton, Mr. Ed Ponsford, and Mr. A. G. Scott's views are quoted in the following sections. Mr. Bolton discussed several aspects of the former relationship with Firth Cleveland, described Schlumberger's interest in Solartron, gave his opinion of the benefits of association with Schlumberger, and told of relationships at the board level in both instances.

"One of the basic reasons for associating with Firth Cleveland," remarked Mr. Bolton, "was not for short-run financial assistance, but rather so that Solartron could be assured of funds over the long run. It was believed that the Firth Cleveland's cash inflow, which amounted to £2,000,000 per year, could easily cover the Solartron annual cash needs of about £300,000. We reasoned that Firth Cleveland's business would be a stable source of funds and that Firth Cleveland would have no serious strains on its cash.

"What we could not predict was: (1) that our cash needs would exceed £300,000 per annum as the program of long-term development projects to which we had committed ourselves got significantly out of balance with the sales achieved; (2) that an increased rate of investment in Solartron under such conditions would not prove attractive compared with other investments such as a steel mill, increased credit facilities to retail customers, and expansion of their retail chain; and (3) that the credit squeeze would become more pronounced.

"Schlumberger had been interested in acquiring an interest in Solartron even before we became part of the Firth Cleveland group. When Schlumberger learned that, because of the 'credit squeeze' and prevailing high interest rates, Firth Cleveland had delayed a proposed issue of Preference Stock and would obviously be relatively short of liquid funds, they approached the group with the view of purchasing its interest in Solartron. This was attractive to Firth Cleveland in that it supplied a substantial amount of cash which the group needed to finance the expansion of its retail chain of radio and T.V. stores, which offered prospects for an almost immediate return on the extra capital investment. It also removed the not quite compatible electronics company from the group of operations. I feel certain that more than one of the Firth Cleveland directors felt that they had hold, in Solartron, of a tiger's tail.

"In all fairness, I must add that Firth Cleveland discussed the possible change of ownership with us before making any commitments. They assured us that no deal would be made without the mutual concurrence of all three parties involved. Another decent thing that Firth Cleveland did was to recompense all shareholders who had sold Solartron stock for cash to Firth Cleveland in July 1961 by giving them retrospectively the premium that it received on the resale of this stock to Schlumberger.

"I am very pleased with the new merger for a number of reasons. First, Schlumberger is a company with substantial cash inflows and has made a major policy decision to invest these cash inflows in the long-range possibilities of the electronic field. Second, Schlumberger understands the problems which Solartron faces better than Firth Cleveland. Firth Cleveland could justly criticize our operations, but they could not be expected to provide any real assistance in overcoming our technical problems. Not only has Schlumberger dealt for many years with electrical instruments which have many production and marketing characteristics similar to those of our line of products, but it has also recently acquired electronic companies in other parts of Europe and in the United States. We both have a common background when discussing our operations. Third, as part of the world-wide network of electronics companies which Schlumberger is building up, Solartron can benefit from the marketing, research and development and possibly production activities of its sister companies; at the same time Solartron represents their major electronic interest in the U.K.

"We are also pleased to become a part of a European organization which operates relatively independently of its American affiliate. The Schlumberger European electronics activities will be directed from Paris by a group of very capable French managers who will act in the interest of the European members of the Schlumberger group. While the European group will naturally work in cooperation with the American members of the group, an element of competition will actually exist between these two counterparts—if not in products, at least in their records of performance and profitability.

"I have been very favorably impressed with the attitude of the Schlumberger people towards the new association," continued Mr. Bolton. "For example, at the time that Schlumberger bought Firth Cleveland's interest in Solartron, its management also offered to buy all of the free-floating outstanding stock of the 'widows and orphans' at the same price offered to Firth Cleveland. They also made a successful offer for all Solartron Preference shares. They did this for two reasons: First, so that anyone who wanted to withdraw from Solartron as a result of the change in ownership could do so on an equitable basis; and second, so that they would have a free hand in reinvesting all of Solartron's earnings without becoming involved with minority demands for dividends."

Mr. Ed Ponsford, Managing Director of Solartron Laboratory Instruments Ltd., spoke warmly about a recent inspection visit to the S.L.I. plant, made by Mr. Schneersohn, a director of both the Schlumberger European organization and Solartron. "Mr. Schneersohn's visit here was a great morale-builder for us, because he showed a technical interest in our operations which Firth Cleveland could never do. He spent about four days going through our operations from top to bottom. He made observations during this time and was able to offer some very good suggestions. For the most part, he just asked questions, listened and learned what we were doing at Chessington."

"The change of ownership came at a bad time as far as accounting is concerned," said Mr. A. G. Scott, Solartron group accountant, "because we were in the middle of changing our system to conform with the reorganization, and things were still a bit unsettled. (See The Solartron Electronic Group Ltd. [C].) While Schlumberger has not asked us to change our reporting system, they have asked that our reports be made more often and also that they be distributed much more quickly than we had been able to do for many years. We have also changed to the Schlumberger system of budgeting." Table 1 outlines the Schlumberger system of budgeting as explained by Mr. Scott.

BOARD OF DIRECTORS

"I thought that it was very important," said Mr. Bolton, "to take advantage of the experience and ability of our parent company's top men. For this reason I had asked both Mr. C. W. Hayward of Firth Cleveland

Table 1

THE NEW SYSTEM OF BUDGETING

YEAR	INFORMATION	COMMITMENT	PREPARED BY
Coming year	Detail	Firm	All interested parties
Second year	Detail	Tentative	Small group of planners: Directors and accountants
Third year	Outline	Proposed	Messrs. Bolton, Crosse, Ponsford, and A. G. Scott
	Review six monthly		

and subsequently Mr. Jean Riboud of Schlumberger to sit as chairman of the Solartron Board. In both cases our request was accepted, and both have contributed significantly to our operations in their turn. In neither case has my freedom of action as Managing Director of Solartron been impeded by these gentlemen. I feel very fortunate to have someone like Jean Riboud directing our Board now." Exhibit 4 shows the membership of the Solartron board of directors for selected dates.

Exhibit 4

SOLARTRON'S BOARD OF DIRECTORS ON SELECTED DATES

SOLARTRON BEFORE MERGER NOVEMBER, 1959	SOLARTRON UNDER FIRTH CLEVELAND SEPTEMBER, 1961	SOLARTRON UNDER SCHLUMBERGER JANUARY, 1962
	Chairman: C. W. Hayward†	*Chairman:* J. Riboud‡
Chairman: J. E. Bolton	J. E. Bolton H. D. Binyon R. Catherall	J. E. Bolton H. D. Binyon R. Catherall
L. B. Copestick J. E. Crosse	L. B. Copestick J. E. Crosse L. Malec	L. B. Copestick J. E. Crosse L. Malec
E. R. Ponsford B. Scott	E. R. Ponsford B. Scott G. Harries†	E. R. Ponsford B. Scott A. de Saint-Andrieu‡ B. Schneersohn‡
R. A. Henderson* J. L. E. Smith* E. E. Jones	R. A. Henderson* J. L. E. Smith*	

* Bankers.
† Firth Cleveland officers.
‡ Schlumberger officers.
Source: Company records.

FIRTH CLEVELAND'S VIEW

The sale of their interest in Solartron was announced by Firth Cleveland in the press information bulletin reproduced as Exhibit 5.

Exhibit 5

PRESS INFORMATION BULLETIN ON FIRTH CLEVELAND LIMITED

18 October 1961

Firth Cleveland has accepted, as has also been announced in a joint statement issued simultaneously with this one, an offer by Schlumberger Limited to purchase its holding of 453,633 Ordinary Shares (56.7% of the issued Ordinary Share Capital) in The Solartron Electronic Group Limited for the sum of £1,927,940. 5s. 0d. This is equivalent to £4. 5s. 0d. per existing share.

Firth Cleveland acquired almost all its holding in Solartron in January 1960 but it will be recalled that on 31st July 1961 Firth Cleveland, in fulfillment of its undertaking to The Solartron Shareholders in January, 1960, offered to purchase all the Solartron Ordinary Shares not then held by Firth Cleveland at a cash price of £3 per Share. As a result of that offer Firth Cleveland acquired 26,919 Ordinary Shares.

Although Firth Cleveland received the offer from Schlumberger after 31st July 1961, it is intended that sellers of the above-mentioned 26,919 Shares shall receive payment representing the additional £1. 5s. 0d. per existing Share.

After giving effect to this ex gratia payment the cost to Firth Cleveland of its Solatron holding was 249,576 Firth Cleveland Ordinary Shares of 4s. 0d. each issued at 30s. 0d. each plus cash of £1,032,285. The book value of the holding was £1,406,649.

The sale of the Solartron Shares will greatly improve the cash position of the Firth Cleveland Group and increase the consolidated net tangible assets. Cash resources will benefit not only by receipt of the consideration for the shares but also because of the extinction of the Solartron bank overdrafts, a total improvement in Group liquidity of approximately £2,500,000. Net tangible assets will be increased by approximately £1,500,000 and the Firth Cleveland Consolidated Balance Sheet will be further strengthened by the omission from Long Term Liabilities of Solartron's £450,000 Unsecured Loan Stock.

In view of this improvement in liquidity, the Group is now better placed to maintain the expansion that has been and will continue to be one of the central features of the Group's policy and it is not now intended that Firth Cleveland shall raise cash by the issue of shares in the near future.

As a result of the transfer of control to Schlumberger Limited, Solartron should benefit from association with an organisation with worldwide interests in electronics, in a field where size will be of great importance. From the Firth Cleveland viewpoint, while it was always appreciated that the investment in Solartron was, of necessity, a long-term one, it had become increasingly apparent that there was little prospect of dividends commensurate with its total investments being forthcoming for some time.

The Firth Cleveland Board believes strongly that in the circumstances outlined above it was right for them to accept the Schlumberger offer not only because it was in the best interests of the Firth Cleveland shareholders but also because it was in the best interests of the other shareholders of Solartron.

Mr. C. W. Hayward, chairman of Firth Cleveland, amplified the reasons for the sale in the following paragraph quoted from the chairman's statement distributed with the accounts for the year ended 31st December 1961:

> In October, 1961, we sold our 56.7% interest in The Solartron Electronic Group to Schlumberger Limited. I had already advised you that our investment in Solartron involved further heavy expenditure in projects which could not be expected to produce worthwhile profits for some years. As time went on it became apparent that the investment would be greater, and the delay in profits longer, than originally contemplated. Your Board received an offer from Schlumberger. It was obvious that Solartron would benefit from an association with an organization with world-wide interests in electronics, a field where size is of great importance. With the concurrence of the minority shareholders of Solartron, we accepted the offer. Briefly, the effects of the transaction were that your Group's net tangible assets were increased by some £1,500,000, which included a capital profit of £524,556; Long-term Liabilities were reduced by the exclusion of Solartron's £450,000 Unsecured Loan; and our liquidity improved substantially.

SCHLUMBERGER'S VIEWS OF THE TAKE-OVER

"I have been in charge of Schlumberger's diversification into electronics in Europe," remarked Mr. Schneersohn. "We had decided to diversify by purchasing existing organizations rather than building companies from scratch, because the diversification could take place more quickly that way. Our purchase of Firth Cleveland's interest in Solartron was a part of our diversification program.

"We at Schlumberger believe that there are three ingredients necessary for a company to acquire or merge successfully with another company in order to diversify: (1) a good plan of action; (2) money; and (3) something to offer the other companies. In line with this thinking, I believe that we have the following qualifications for merger: (1) Schlumberger understands how to conduct remote management as a result of its experience in running the oil instrument business throughout the world; (2) Schlumberger has experience in the field of electronics; (3) the company knows well how to manufacture quality products; and (4) the company has money.

"I wish to emphasize that the money is the least important qualification that we offer. Many people have money, or access to it. I believe that Schlumberger's most important attraction is their ability to contribute administrative management and technical skill, probably in that order of importance.

"In return, we are looking for a company with a good product—a high quality industrial product produced in relatively small quantities, not mass produced, a good organization and, most important, with one or two really good management people. Solartron seemed to be a company that would fit well into the group structure that I had in mind, and we therefore approached Firth Cleveland as to the possibility of acquiring its subsidiary.

"Looking critically at Solartron," continued Mr. Schneersohn, "I would say that the company had been run a bit loosely in the past and stood in need of more effective management control. I would say that the company has the following weaknesses:

a) Solartron does not have good reporting and control data.
b) The production output per person employed is very poor (of course this seems typical of many British firms).
c) Solartron has too many people for the job they are doing.
d) Solartron has never really set good targets.
e) Solartron is much too diversified.
f) Solartron is placing too much emphasis on systems.

"Solartron has always placed a great deal of importance on growth. This is no longer as important a requirement as in the past, and they now recognize that they should be more selective in their diversification of products than they have been. Concerning their reporting and control data, I might add that they have all the information within the company to follow and control their operations, but this information has never been properly brought together.

"I do not want you to get a wrong impression from the above criticisms. On the over-all picture, we are very pleased to have Solartron as a member of our European electronics group, or we should never have purchased the interest. We intend to let the present management continue directing the operations of the company, because they are the most qualified men in our organization to do the job. If we can be of help to them concerning management or any other aspect of the business, naturally we shall work very closely together."

SELENIA ELETTRONICHE S.p.A.

In June, 1962, Dr. Leone Mustacchi, General Manager of the Italian corporation Selenia, described to an IMEDE researcher the way in which the company had been created, saying: "Selenia is a classic example of effective cooperation between American and European firms. This type of cooperation will become increasingly important as time passes; we must forget our old views and look to see how Europe and America can work together to raise the standard of living in the Western world. Therefore, your students may be interested to see how such cooperation can be developed, and what ingredients are necessary.

"Naturally, the mechanics of joint American-European ventures differ from case to case, but I would say that Selenia's creation illustrates a number of points which are important to most such ventures. Our company is only two years old, but, because we planned carefully before setting it up, it is successful and growing rapidly."

Selenia was established in mid-1960 by fusing two Italian firms, Microlambda and Sindel. Microlambda was begun in 1951 by Finmeccanica, a large (72,000 employees) industrial complex controlled by the Italian government. Microlambda manufactured radar equipment, submarine detection gear, and fire control systems, initially for the United States Navy and subsequently for other European navies. The firm, which was located in Naples, also produced some electronic equipment for merchant fleets.

The Sindel group was established in Rome in 1956 by Società Edison, one of Italy's five largest private corporations. Sindel specialized in fire-control systems, weather radar, commercial radar, and microwave communications systems.

In effect, Microlambda and Sindel had very similar product lines and customers, and so the two groups competed aggressively with each other. Both companies were licensees of Raytheon, Inc., a large (45,000 employees) United States pioneer in sophisticated electronic equipment, especially in radar, communications, and fire control.

In mid-1960, after a year of intensive discussion and negotiation, a new corporation called Selenia was created. Raytheon and Finmeccanica each received 40 per cent, and Edison 20 per cent, of the ownership of Selenia. The former Microlambda plant, in Naples, took on all of Selenia's manufacturing operations; Research and Development (R&D) were installed in Sindel's plant in Rome. At the time of the merger, Microlambda and Sindel had a total of 600 employees. Two years later Selenia had 1,500 employees, and its sales were three times the combined sales of Microlambda and Sindel for the year preceding the merger.

*   *   *   *   *

Dr. Mustacchi continued: "Before going into the mechanics of how Selenia was created, we might consider the philosophy behind this type of venture. The most important requirement is that each of the partners have something to give and something to gain. Without this common need and advantage, this type of joint affair is not very useful.

"Now, speaking broadly, what does an American company have to gain by acquiring an interest in a European firm? Obviously, it gets an entrée into European markets. You might say, 'Why doesn't the American company export to Europe?' but this is becoming increasingly difficult as European firms catch up with the United States. Of course, some United States companies are refusing to get involved in such joint associations, because they are afraid of competing with their own exports, but this position is rapidly becoming less tenable. Europe today imports from the United States, by and large, only those goods not made in Europe or those products which are mass-produced in America and can be sold here at attractive prices.

"The coming of the Common Market (CM) is worrying a lot of American companies, who see themselves being shut out of the CM. In fact, many nations outside the CM are getting worried and are trying to get inside.

"Today, many American companies which have never given Europe a moment's thought are beginning to wonder about how to get into the CM. In short, an American firm has a great deal to gain by making an association which ensures its access to the CM.

"For companies within the CM, the advantages of a link with a United States corporation are mostly in the area of technology, and this is especially true in electronics, namely, to get the benefit of American Research and Development (R&D). America leads the Free World by a huge margin in electronic R&D, and it will continue to do so. Europeans need not be ashamed of their brains, but they should not waste time and money doing research that an American firm has already done.

"Now we have the first condition for successful partnership: mutual need. Americans need European connections to get into the CM, and Europeans need American technology. As to what each partner can bring to an association, clearly the American contribution will be technological. The European's contribution will be his knowledge of doing business in Europe and the fact that he already has a staff of people to do the job, or else knows where to get them. Sometimes the American can also provide some special management skills, but this is not always necessary or possible.

"These, then, are the broad needs and advantages which foster European-American partnerships: an exchange of technological background for familiarity with European business. To carry this argument even further, any proposed partnership must be built on a common interest which is vital to *both* prospective partners. If, as often happens, the American partner is merely looking for some place to make a good investment in Europe, if he doesn't really care where he makes this investment, he will have no emotional commitment to the partnership, and the arrangement will not be successful. Let him buy stock instead.

"It follows that the prospective European partner must have a clear idea of what sort of partnership he wants and what benefit he expects to derive. I mention this because I have seen some European firms enter into ventures with American companies without any good reason. Mutual need is basic to a powerful, successful, durable relationship.

"Now there are some other conditions which must be met if the partnership is to be successful. First, it is generally advantageous to build the joint venture on an existing foundation, starting perhaps with one or more predecessor European firms, as we did with Selenia. We had two plants and a large group of engineers and technicians, plus lots of experience, which gave us a jumping-off point. An American company generally will not find it attractive to start a joint enterprise from nothing. It is too risky; nobody will know anything about the market.

"Second, there must be a real financial commitment on both sides. I have said that Europe doesn't *need* American capital, but, if the partnership is to be effective, both partners must have a real financial commitment to its success. Lots of American companies hope to contribute only their ideas, and they are unhappy about having to put in dollars as well, but if they don't make the investment, they usually end up sitting on the sidelines. If the American company contributes ideas, let it receive special royalties for its ideas.

"Third, the American firm should take an *active* part in the subsidiary's management, if not on the operating level, at least on the Board level.

The whole point is that a partnership cannot possibly work if each partner does not make his fair contribution.

"Fourth, the joint company should be truly independent; it should be free from excessive interference by any of its parents. I would even say that the subsidiary should be free to make other commercial ventures in the United States, insofar as circumstances warrant, although obviously such ventures must not compete with the American parent. If the subsidiary is not reasonably independent, it will not be able to operate in a coherent and unified manner; it will be pulled in several directions at once.

"Fifth, although perhaps somewhat obvious, the prospective partners must be able to trust one another. If they cannot discuss and negotiate in good faith, with mutual confidence, they will never be able to create a workable arrangement.

"Now, having outlined the general arguments in favor of European-American partnerships and having discussed in theoretical terms the conditions necessary for the establishment of successful joint enterprises, let us turn to Selenia's case. I think Selenia shows just how effective a partnership of this type can be if all the necessary conditions are met. I do not propose to go into many details of Selenia's history, because it seems to me that a general discussion will be sufficient to illustrate clearly the philosophy which I have just outlined."

*   *   *   *   *

Dr. Mustacchi began by describing the predecessors of Selenia, Microlambda, and Sindel. "As you know, the two companies were in tough competition with each other. The total market for their products was not enough to keep both of them prosperous. Professor Carlo Calosi, Raytheon's Vice-President—Europe, had been in close touch with both companies throughout their histories, since both were licensing from Raytheon.

"I was the General Manager of Microlambda, and in this capacity I had many conversations with Professor Calosi. Early in 1959, as a result of these discussions, we came to the conclusion that, although the two companies could not profitably exist side-by-side, the market was large enough for one company to live very well. We accordingly decided to propose the idea of a merger between Sindel and Microlambda and to suggest bringing Raytheon into the venture as a full partner. I made the first proposal to Finmeccanica, and Professor Calosi dealt with Raytheon and Sindel, since he knew the Sindel people very well.

"You know, if you're trying to sell an idea, the most important thing is that you be emotionally committed to the idea. Calosi and I were thoroughly convinced of the soundness of our proposal, and this made us into good salesmen.

"Our task was to clarify for all three prospective partners exactly what we had in mind. This is where the real work was. The idea was basically good, but the exact arrangements to be made were obviously a matter for considerable negotiation. A marriage involving two parties is complicated enough, and when three are involved, then the complications really become formidable.

"In theory, everybody had real assets to contribute. Raytheon had been in this field for many years and thus could provide the necessary technological background. They also had real management ability in this area. Microlambda and Sindel had two physical plants, a large staff of engineers with considerable experience in the industry, and good customer contacts. Finmeccanica and Edison had huge financial resources and excellent relations with the Italian government. Finally, Microlambda and Sindel were not making any money. The advantages of a combination were clear.

"In beginning our discussions, we first determined those points on which the three parties agreed, and we eliminated them from further consideration. This narrowed our job to one of deciding the arguable details. In negotiations of this sort, the most important and difficult job is bringing the parties together in an atmosphere of mutual confidence. Now obviously, in the case of these three companies, nobody thought the other fellow was going to cheat him, but each man wanted to know his prospective partners pretty well before agreeing to the wedding. This atmosphere is usually not an easy thing to arrange; it requires lots of talking to build mutual faith.

"I must say that during the year of negotiations Calosi and I worked incredibly hard. It was worth it, but it is difficult to describe the amount of work which these negotiations required, in addition to our regular jobs. In the end, because the idea was basically sound and because all the partners were acting in good faith, the merger was accomplished, but arranging these things is time-consuming. It can be done only if everyone is acting in the right spirit.

"The critical points of negotiation were: how would ownership be apportioned, who would run the company, what would each member contribute, how would major policy decisions be made, and such things. Let me stress that no real problems arose during these discussions. Of course, there were differences of opinion on certain critical points, and we had to resolve these. We also had to consider what should be done if certain contingencies arose, contingencies which we did not expect but for which we had to provide. The main thing was that we were all discussing things in the right spirit, so there were no problems.

"The first point we decided was that all major policy decisions would be made unanimously; this covered such things as increasing capital, commercial relationships, and other topics normally handled at the Board level. We agreed that Selenia's management would be free to make all operating decisions without interference. Incidentally, the name 'Selenia' was chosen to avoid partiality.

"In distributing ownership, our concern was to do so fairly. Finmeccanica had more experience in the field than Edison, and Raytheon was making a major contribution of technical support and capital, so we decided to make Raytheon and Finmeccanica equal partners with 40 per cent each. We felt that it would be unwise to give anybody a majority, and, following this same argument, we decided on the requirement of unanimity for major decisions. Now obviously it took some time to work out this 40-40-20 stock division which was based more on Microlambda's and Sindel's relative experience in the field than on their contribution of fixed assets, but in the end this division was satisfying to all concerned.

"Throughout the negotiations, we worked hard to find *solutions* to areas of discussion, rather than compromises. In a compromise, nobody is really happy, and when things start to go wrong, trouble starts—the partners fall out. In a real solution, everybody is happy, so that when problems arise, everybody wants to help in finding a remedy.

"The next major decision concerned over-all responsibility for management. We felt that one of the three partners should be solely responsible for operating the company. Finmeccanica and Edison had little experience in this area, and Raytheon had been in the field for years, so we decided that Raytheon would have full responsibility for running the company. This did not mean that American executives would take over, but that Raytheon would choose the management team and take responsibility for its successful performance.

"The final area of discussion was what would happen if one of the partners wanted to sell its share of Selenia. This was handled in a standard fashion: we agreed that, should this happen, the other partners would have first option on the stock to be sold, and it would be sold under specific conditions.

"Once we had reached agreement on these major points, the real work was done. The three partners made a 'gentleman's agreement' regarding sale of stock and Raytheon's right to manage the company, an agreement which in this instance was as good as gold.

"There remained only the mechanics of setting up the new company. First of all, Raytheon put Professor Calosi in over-all charge of the operation, and I was chosen as General Manager. Professor Calosi and I then chose our management team from among the staffs of Sindel and Microlambda, taking about half the management from each. Those Sindel and Microlambda employees who were not chosen for Selenia had no problems, they simply returned to the parent companies, Finmeccanica and Edison.

In building Selenia's management team, we tried to leave top management in very few hands and to leave top management free of detailed work. Professor Calosi, who is responsible for all of Raytheon's interests in Europe, naturally does not involve himself in the daily operating routine of Selenia.

"As soon as Selenia started up, we brought over men from Raytheon to help us; these men, who headed the Manufacturing and Engineering Departments, were brought in as temporary managers. They were to help the company start up and to train Italians as their replacements. They all did highly effective jobs; with one exception, they have returned to Raytheon. Each was an expert in his field, and each made an immense contribution.

"For our Board of Directors, we chose Admiral Ruta as President. Admiral Ruta's distinguished record makes him a real asset to Selenia. Each of the parent companies also has one Board member, and each has one man to audit Selenia's books. I would stress, however, that in the company's operating management there are no loyalties to the parent companies. We do not say, 'X is a Finmeccanica man and Y is an Edison man'; anybody in our management is a Selenia man first, last, and always. We could not afford to have men with loyalties elsewhere than to Selenia.

"Selenia's first six months of operation were utter confusion. We had to integrate all the people from Microlambda and Sindel, except for a few management men who returned to Finmeccanica and Edison, and we had to transfer all manufacturing to Naples and all research to Rome. After six months, we were thoroughly organized, and we had acquired orders for the future. We started acquiring a large volume of business, and, as you know, we have been growing very rapidly ever since. All in all, it took almost 24 months to get everything working smoothly.

"Selenia is successful because, from the beginning we have given responsibility to men trusted by all three parents. Indeed, we wonder now why negotiations took a whole year, because today everybody is completely satisfied with the arrangements. The decisions which we sweated over three years ago, now seem to have been almost painfully obvious. I suppose that the critical thing was for each to decide for himself that his potential partners were entering into negotiations in the right spirit and for everyone to agree on how things would be handled under certain circumstances.

"In summary, it took an enormous amount of hard work to create Selenia, and it took a long time, but I think I can accurately say that we have never had a real problem. We have indeed had discussion and negotiation, but, because the partnership idea was basically a good one and because all the partners were acting in good faith, we were able to iron out the difficulties which arose. Selenia today is a powerful and growing element in Italian electronics and a real bond between Europe and America."

MOUNT OLYMPUS ENTERPRISES*

"Mergers are not all happiness, and a naïve manager in the smaller of the two companies can be hurt if he is not careful," commented Dr. Maximus Zeus, General Manager of Mount Olympus Enterprises (MOE). "The take-over of our company has been successful on all major counts, but a lot of annoying and sometimes professionally dangerous interaction still take place between the two managements. For example, I bet that there are 100 men in our mother company who are actively interested in taking over my job."

MOE was a middle-sized firm manufacturing industrial products and was located in Paphos, a well-known city in Western Europe. The company had 1961 sales of $15 million and employed in May, 1962, about 1,200 workers. The major markets for its products were Western Europe and South America.

In 1954, the management of MOE became interested in the possibility of merging with a larger firm in the industry. Two reasons underlay this interest: (1) the advantage of a large selling force and (2) the availability of extensive services for product engineering and for automation of the production line. At that time, the management began a definite search for a possible mother company.

During the course of the search, MOE entered discussions with the Cronus Rhea Company, known as C-R in the trade, concerning a possible take-over. Late in 1959, as a result of these negotiations, C-R purchased 45 per cent of MOE's outstanding stock from private and bank holdings.

As one of the larger companies in Western Europe (1961 sales of $500 million and about 50,000 employees), C-R could well support MOE in both sales and engineering services. On the other hand, C-R was pleased to add the well-reputed MOE products to their own product line.

POST-TAKE-OVER MANAGEMENT INTERRELATIONS

"Looking back over the past two years, I would judge that the take-over of MOE by C-R has benefited both companies," continued Dr. Zeus. "The C-R sales force is selling our products better than we could ever hope to. When we agree on a quota to be sold, their world-wide organiza-

---

* All names have been disguised.

tion sells it every time. Their engineering department deserves the same praise. Whenever we run across a technical problem, we give C-R a call, and the next day a top-grade engineer flies down from Macedonia and clears up the difficulties. In addition, C-R has been very helpful to us concerning complicated patent and tax transactions which we encounter. For their part, C-R's management appears well pleased with our products' sales performance.

"But there are numerous problems and headaches for us too. First, there are the many differences of policy and operations which need reconciliation between any two merging firms. For example, we now face a problem of adjusting the fringe benefits of our workers, inasmuch as they receive much lower benefits than do the workers of C-R. The unresolved disparities could relate to different philosophies of pricing, product styling, employee relations, and so forth. Sometimes these differences can be allowed to remain, often they cannot.

"There are two other problems which I find particularly vexing, because they cause a lot of concern with no apparent benefit. The first of these relates to the many 'busybodies' from the mother company who are forever volunteering their help to us. The second problem relates to the job hunting manoeuvres for my position and those of my colleagues.

BUSYBODIES

"You would be surprised at the number of C-R people, who visit our plant without invitation in order to give us the 'benefit' of their advice. In some cases their intentions are well meant, but I suspect that in most cases the people come here expecting to show off their cleverness to their boss by straightening out our problems. Of course I am not referring to those occasions where we request help for specific problems, such as for taxation or patent proceedings. The advice we receive from these latter discussions has been, almost without exception, very valuable to us.

"As I see it, many of C-R's middle and junior executives see our company as a nice instrument on which to play the tune of their management virtuosity. Large companies normally train their own management from the start. These men, as a consequence, often believe that their company is the best-managed in the world and that other companies, especially smaller ones, could not possibly be run nearly so well. What they do not understand is that many of the differences in policies and practices between their large company and our small one are necessary precisely because of the difference in size. Naturally, we are very happy to receive useful advice and help, but we do not like to be made fools of simply to serve as a ladder to success for the ambitious.

"I suppose that it all started when the president of C-R announced the take-over of MOE and asked the C-R management to cooperate with us if we should need their help. Many of these men naturally expected that they would be called in shortly to help straighten out our affairs. I suppose that when nothing happened and they did not hear any calls for help from us, they thought, 'Why, it is impossible that those people [MOE] do not need help from our department, I had better go down to Paphos and see what is wrong.'

"The usual procedure is that one of these fellows comes down and ties up one or two of my top executives who have to explain our operation to him in great detail. We then go through the often-agonizing period during which he offers his 'much-needed' advice, followed by our explanation of how we have already tried this or why that may not be feasible. Usually the visit ends with a mutual understanding that nothing has been accomplished, and the man goes home in search of other mountains to conquer. The net result is that we are more or less distracted from doing our own work, besides having the bother of taking these men out to dinner and evening entertainment.

"Of course this is not always the case, and there are times when this 'much-needed' advice is really much needed and very worthwhile. When this happens, I always make sure to mention the valuable help that we receive in my reports to the president of C-R. Unfortunately, I would say that we have benefited from such unsolicited assistance in only 5 to 10 per cent of the cases.

"To be sure, we have been making progress with this problem. No one comes here any more to advise us in my area [Finance], unless requested. The frequency of visits to the other departments has also diminished considerably.

"Unsolicited advice can lead to difficult situations when visiting executives make strong recommendations to which we are opposed. In the few cases where this situation has arisen and where it was obvious that neither party would yield, we simply requested that instructions be submitted in writing before we would follow them. Although C-R cannot legally force us to do anything, we would feel obliged to follow their orders. Strangely enough, we have never yet received any instructions in writing.

"Of course, we do not like these situations to arise because we really lose on every occasion. Even when we are proved right, we still make an enemy in C-R. Naturally, we can go against strong recommendations only when we are positive of our position and when the results can be clearly measured soon after the dispute has arisen.

JOB HUNTING

"The other problem which we managers of the smaller company naturally find disquieting is the desire of many of the executives in the larger company to take our places. After all, there are not many jobs in Europe as attractive as the ones we hold in running a company like MOE.

"I myself, am not too worried. First of all, I have a contract which still runs four more years. Also, I have a much better acquaintance with this company than any replacement could possibly have. And, finally, I have the advantage of knowing that these people are trying to steal my job.

"In connection with this problem, I believe that there is one very important step a manager should take before his company enters relations with a larger company as we have done. He should always make sure that he has a full and well-knit organization with no vacant holes. If you have an organization that needs replacement or filling in, a way is left open for others, perhaps people you yourself would not select, to worm their way into the organization.

"When we first discussed our management with the C-R people, I was able to show them that we had qualified people in every necessary spot covering every necessary aspect of our administration. When they now ask me how things are running, I always tell them that everything is well under control and we are doing very nicely, thank you. After all, I do not ever want to give the aspirants for my job the impression that I am being overworked, or they will be joining my office before I finish talking with them.

"In general, there is no better insurance for keeping one's job than doing the job better than anyone else. Nevertheless, no matter how good a person is, he should not provide his competitors with too many opportunities."

I.C.I.—COURTAULDS: A TAKE-OVER ATTEMPT THAT FAILED

INTRODUCTION

Shortly after 10:00 o'clock on the morning of Monday, December 18, 1961, Mr. Paul Chambers, Chairman of Imperial Chemicals Industries Ltd. (I.C.I.), announced in a press statement that I.C.I. planned to take over Courtaulds, Ltd. Mr. Chambers continued by saying that I.C.I. would offer three shares of their common (ordinary) stock for every four shares of Courtaulds' common (ordinary), and he added that this exchange ratio was I.C.I.'s "final, final" offer.

Mr. Chambers' announcement created something like a furor in the British press, perhaps because this takeover bid could best be described in superlatives. I.C.I. was vastly the largest United Kingdom chemical producer, Courtaulds was by far the largest United Kingdom maker of man-made fibres, and the proposed takeover was much the largest ever attempted in the United Kingdom.

Courtaulds' management were mysteriously silent about the I.C.I. offer until January 5, 1962, at which time they recommended that Courtaulds' stockholders reject the three-for-four bid. The largest takeover battle in United Kingdom business history had begun.

In the weeks that followed, each company argued its case vigorously, and with increasing vituperation towards the other. The British government became an unwilling participant in the affair. Mr. Chambers raised his "final, final" terms to Courtaulds' shareholders twice. The two companies spent enormous sums fighting the battle.

Finally, on March 12, 1962, Mr. Chambers announced that I.C.I. had acquired only 37.4 per cent of Courtaulds' common stock and that the offer was being withdrawn. But for Courtaulds it was a Pyrrhic victory: they had as their largest single stockholder a company which they had been vilifying quite publicly for many weeks.

This case, which is based on articles in the British press, describes the development of the I.C.I.–Courtaulds affair. The focus here is not primarily on the merits and conditions of the proposed takeover, but rather on the tactics used by each side.

BACKGROUND FOR THE STRUGGLE

Exhibits 1 and 2 give pertinent financial information showing the relative size and rate of growth of the two companies. Because the personalities of the top managers of both firms were significant factors in the contest, brief descriptions of the key personnel are given below.

Mr. S. Paul Chambers, who is now in his later fifties, became chairman of I.C.I. on January 1, 1960, taking over from Lord Fleck. One writer commented:

> Fleck as chairman was a scientist and a paternalist. Chambers is neither. He is an Inland Revenue man—the creator of P.A.Y.E.*—who joined I.C.I. at the age of forty-three and rose to the top with a steady and rapid thrust. He is not a man of commanding personality, but he is a voluble, almost a compulsive, talker without striking phrases but with a quick mind and considerable powers of persuasion. He is something of an intellectual among businessmen and a businessman among intellectuals.[1]

Sir John Hanbury-Williams was the chairman of Courtaulds, although his designated successor, Sir Alan Wilson, had been elected in July, 1961.

> Hanbury-Williams was born in Windsor Castle, is the son of a general-turned-courtier and went to school at Wellington—the nearest approach to a major public school attended by any important figure on either side in the battle. He is a banker with even less technical training than Chambers.
>
> His status as a gentleman amongst professionals is rather elaborately respected by the other members of the Courtaulds team, and since a severe illness last summer [1961] he is treated by them like a very delicate piece of Meissen china.
>
> Wilson is a short, round man of fifty-six, who started at Wallasey Grammar School and moved via a fellowship at Trinity College, Cambridge, to join the board of Courtaulds in 1954. He is a scientist of real distinction, an F.R.S.† with a good deal of original work to his credit. He was knighted at the beginning of 1961.
>
> Mr. Frank Kearton [is] now widely considered the architect of the Courtaulds victory. . . . Kearton is a fifty-one-year-old chemist, educated at a Potteries grammar school and Oxford, who came to Courtaulds from I.C.I. in 1952.‡ He can talk as long and as fast as Chambers, and is usually interesting, if sometimes discursive. He knows a great deal about fibres and was made an F.R.S. in 1961.

---

* "PAY AS YOU EARN," the system of witholding income tax from wages and salaries.

1 All numbered footnotes refer to sources of quotations used; these sources are cited at the end of the case.

† Fellow of the Royal Society.

‡ In fact, Mr. Kearton went to Courtaulds in 1946 and was elected a director in 1952.

Exhibit 1

FINANCIAL DATA FOR I.C.I.

IMPERIAL CHEMICAL INDUSTRIES (Years to December 31)

	1951	1955	1956	1957	1958	1959	1960†
				(£ Million)			
Sales	262.7	411.0	435.3	462.9	462.7	508.5	558.4
Gross profit	40.1	53.6	50.1	55.1	44.5	73.1	88.0
Net equity	16.6	23.0	18.3	21.2	16.7	32.8	38.6
Ordinary dividend	4.1	8.2	8.2	10.0	10.9	17.4	21.2
Cash flow	23.6	39.1	38.4	40.4	39.4	54.0	60.2
Net equity assets	227.5	309.3	329.5	344.0	439.0†	476.5	521.7
Ordinary capital	60.6	142.0	143.0	144.2	237.0	246.2	251.6
Net liquid assets .....Dr.	6.0	23.5	0.1	14.3	1.8	19.8	14.9
				Percentages			
Equity earnings*	21.1	21.9	18.8	20.8	15.2	25.4	28.6
Ordinary dividend*	4.3	6.7	6.7	8.0	8.0	11.25	13.75
Percentage payout	25.0	35.5	44.9	47.0	65.5	53.2	54.8
Gross profit/net equity	17.6	17.3	15.2	16.0	10.1	15.3	16.9
Net earnings/net equity	7.3	7.4	5.6	6.6	3.8	6.9	7.4

* Adjusted to present capital.
† Fixed assets revalued.

Source: *The Economist*, December 23, 1961.

Exhibit 2

FINANCIAL DATA FOR COURTAULDS

COURTAULDS (Years to March 31)

	1952	1956	1957	1958*	1959	1960	1961†
				(£ Million)			
Sales	...	...	...	...	...	139.9	171.9
Gross profit	19.0	18.2	15.2	13.9	13.5	21.0	18.7
Net equity earnings	8.3	9.8	7.8	5.7	6.1	10.6	9.2
Ordinary dividend	1.4	2.8	2.8	2.5	3.1	4.1	4.8
Cash flow	10.5	10.0	9.6	9.2	9.3	13.5	12.5
Net equity assets	68.4	110.3	115.4	122.7	126.3	143.3	149.9
Ordinary capital	24.0	48.1	48.2	53.3	53.5	58.9	79.0
Net liquid assets	27.3	25.0	19.1	27.1	28.5	32.9	23.0
				Percentages			
Equity earnings‡	24.8	26.5	21.2	14.0	14.3	24.1	19.1
Ordinary dividend‡	4.2	7.5	7.5	6.0	7.25	9.4	10.0
Percentage payout	17.0	28.2	35.4	42.7	51.0	38.8	52.4
Gross profit/net equity	27.8	16.5	13.1	11.3	10.7	14.7	12.5
Net earnings/net equity	12.3	8.9	6.8	4.7	4.8	7.4	6.2

* British Celanese acquired in June, 1957.
† Pinchin Johnson acquired in February, 1960.
‡ Adjusted to present capital.

Source: *The Economist*, December 23, 1961.

Reginald Mathys [is] an aggressive, controversial, fifty-three-year-old patent expert who has been with Courtaulds since 1946 and is now a deputy-chairman.[1]

*   *   *   *   *

One writer described the background of the contest for Courtaulds as follows:

Discussions between the two companies had been going on for years past. Since 1940 they had owned (with some friction) an important joint subsidiary—British Nylon Spinners—the board of which provided an obvious meeting place for the two sets of directors. And their interests touched at numerous other points. I.C.I. had exclusive rights to the manufacture of Terylene, the only fully developed British melt-spun fibre other than nylon, and sold a sizeable proportion of their production to Courtaulds.

BOTH MERGER-MINDED

Courtaulds had themselves developed "Courtelle," the most successful of the British acrylic (i.e. wool-like) fibres, at first upon the basis of a raw material supplied by I.C.I. but more recently obtained for price reasons from America; for several other raw materials, however, Courtaulds remained dependent upon I.C.I. Together the two companies accounted for over 90 per cent of the country's production of man-made fibres, split about 5:1 in Courtaulds' favour on a weight basis but only 2:1 on a price basis, the discrepancy being accounted for by Courtaulds' heavy stake in cheap rayon and the high prices still charged for nylon and Terylene.

In addition there were overlapping interests in packaging materials (I.C.I. producing plastic film and Courtaulds Cellophane), in paint, and even in some chemicals. But the preponderance of Courtaulds existed only in the field of man-made fibres and in packaging. In paint the interests of the two firms were about equal.

Beyond these industrial groups there was not a great deal to Courtaulds. But the I.C.I. iceberg extended deep into the water. Their sales were about three times those of Courtaulds and their profits and capital employed were each about three and a half times; their shareholders were two and a half times and their employees were a little less than twice as numerous.

But both firms were giants. On one basis of reckoning they were respectively the first and fifth among British industrial concerns; on another they were the fourth and thirteenth. On a sales basis, I.C.I. ranked twenty-second among world companies and Courtaulds ninety-fifth.

As well as the affinity that came from the size and scope of their businesses, the two companies also had in common the characteristic of being "merger-minded." I.C.I. were themselves created by one of the most dramatic company amalgamations of the twenties, with Sir Harry McGowan chasing Sir Alfred Mond to New York, and sketching out, on board the Aquitania, a scheme for bringing Brunner, Mond, Nobel Industries, and two major chemical companies together. Subsequently, although they had grown more by direct expansion than by amalgamation, they had taken an occasional gobble to keep themselves in practice.

And Courtaulds, despite their recent pained protests at predatoriness, had for several years lived an almost boa-constrictor-like existence. In 1957 they swallowed British Celanese, who had long been their main rayon competitor. In 1958, they did the same thing with the paint firm of Cellon. In 1959 they took in the Gossard

Corset Company and National Plastics, in 1960 the more important paint concern of Pinchin, Johnson, and as late as November, 1961, they acquired British Enka, another rayon competitor.

Both companies had therefore long had plenty of mutual interests and plenty of contacts through which they could be discussed. Nor is there any reason to think that the words "merger" or "take-over" would have been inherently shocking to the delicate susceptibilities of the Courtaulds directors.

Nevertheless such a far-reaching proposal would probably never have emerged without the rise to supreme power in I.C.I. of a highly ambitious, clear-sighted and schematically-minded man. This rise was completed on January 1, 1960, when Mr. Chambers took over the chairmanship from Lord Fleck.

$$* \quad * \quad * \quad * \quad *$$

DINNER PARTY AT SAVOY

Now, in his later fifties, Chambers has been strongly actuated by a desire to place his own imprint upon I.C.I. Fleck did this by means of the things he understood—new chemical plants upon the ground in industrial areas. Chambers has tried to do it by means of the things he understands—a vast, London-arranged amalgamation scheme. With this end in view, he opened talks with Sir John Hanbury-Williams, the chairman of Courtaulds, and one or two of their directors, in the autumn of 1960.

These 1960 talks were extremely general. Hanbury-Williams visited Chambers at Imperial Chemical House, Chambers went at least once to the Courtaulds office in St. Martins-le-Grand, and there was a dinner party in a private room at the Savoy Hotel at which other directors were present too. The subject of the talks was nominally the future of the man-made fibres industry rather than the relationship between the two companies as a whole. But proposals for complete amalgamation were not excluded. Hanbury-Williams (then aged sixty-eight) is reported to have said on one occasion that a merger would probably come in Chambers' time as Chairman, but not in his own. The talks did not make much progress.

The Economist gave further background as to why I.C.I. proposed a takeover of Courtaulds:

Courtaulds is said to be the largest producer of man-made fibres in the world. ICI already the second largest chemical group in the world after Du Pont (it has substantially higher assets than Union Carbide, though in 1960 it had an only slightly larger turnover and a significantly lower net profit). Together, ICI and Courtaulds would be little smaller than Du Pont in total assets, by book value. Courtaulds (whose name ICI would retain) would presumably take in all the fibres interests of the combined group. Its interests outside fibres—30 per cent of its assets, producing about 50 per cent of its profits in 1960–61, which was a bad year for textiles—would add substantially to ICI's capacity for sulphuric acid, carbon disulphide, and plastics film, and give the new group about a quarter share of the British paint market. But Mr. Chambers made no bones about the motive for the merger: it is to strengthen command of the British manufacture of fibres.

ICI made the first approach to Courtaulds some time in September. What induced it to take such an initiative at that point? It already holds the expiring "Terylene" patent in this country. It has a predominant stake in nylon manufacture. It has introduced "Ulstron" to this country, which should compete in several uses with "Terylene" and nylon. Perhaps 80 per cent of Courtaulds' fibre output now consists of rayon, either acetate or viscose. Its "Courtelle" is one of several acrylic fibres whose production is being rapidly expanded in this country (others are "Orlon" from Du Pont in Ulster and "Acrilan" by US Monsanto). Courtaulds' half share in British Nylon Spinners gives it, on Mr. Chambers' reckoning, less than an eighth of the total capital invested in the production of this material in Britain.

Since 1950, synthetic fibres appear to have expanded at least tenfold throughout the world; expansion in rayon has not been negligible, but not much more than 60 per cent. ICI puts the growth in all man-made fibres at 10 per cent a year and expects within that total an expansion in the already large production of rayon by 5 per cent. The recent facts, as distinct from the forward estimates, are that Courtaulds, with widely spread rayon interests throughout the world, has been caught by a slump in this sector of the trade which it had evidently foreseen but had been unable to avoid.

Courtaulds itself would sooner or later have been compelled to come to grips with ICI along the whole range of man-made fibres, as patents lapsed and new fibres came along. The two groups, sharing nylon production in this country, had not established a principle capable of extension to every new product. The raw material used in making nylon yarn involves greater capital expenditure than its processing; it is ICI that has controlled the production of that material and keeps a half share in its spinning. Both decided to go it alone in introducing nylon 6 to this country (it has slightly different properties from nylon 66); Courtaulds took up an Italian process, but ICI adopted a Swiss patent.

This departure occurred before ICI embarked on its *pourparlers*. At about the same time, a consolidation of the French synthetic fibre industry was being engineered by Rhône-Poulenc, taking over the fibre interests of Celtex and Pechiney. The advantages claimed for this merger have been echoed by Mr. Chambers; he regards Rhône-Poulenc and Du Pont of America as two groups possessing the "tremendous advantage" of producing a whole range of man-made fibres. It might be remembered, however, that Du Pont, unlike the French group or an ICI-Courtaulds group, has several powerful domestic competitors.

Since a merger with Courtaulds would make ICI's interest in fibres larger than those of Rhône-Poulenc, Mr. Chambers hoped that it could hold its own in the European common market. In fact, as he insisted, in an enlarged common market ICI would not be the virtual monopolist in these fibres that it is seeking to become in this country. In rayon, West Germany is a larger producer than Britain, and France will not be far behind. Output of the newer fibres in France and Germany last year was not far short of Britain's. Italy has a substantial production, and has made impressive strides, developing new raw materials and techniques. In a wider field, Japan is a far larger producer of man-made fibres of all types than Britain, and other Asian countries will undoubtedly follow this lead. And over recent years British exports of man-made fibres have not made a good showing against those of other big producers. The stated intention is to concentrate on the expensive end of the textile market, with a particular drive to win back leeway lost in Europe; but at the same time ICI will have to absorb huge rayon interests that are not everywhere holding their own against cheap Asian cottons.

No doubt real economies should be possible in research and development, which now cost about £3½ million a year for the industry. Man-made fibres have always been characterised by over-optimism about demand, and the excitement of being first with a new fibre has brought about too rapid investment. Too many new fibres have been appearing too quickly to allow the textile industries and other users a reasonable chance to assess their potential. As for rayon, it would have been strange if Mr. Chambers had not been able to claim that Courtaulds is among the most efficient producers. The recent wave of closures and redundancies in the rayon industry will not be repeated when Courtaulds joins ICI: it is evidently not on this side that further economies can be expected.[2]

*   *   *   *   *

Courtaulds and I.C.I. then, had been closely acquainted since 1940, and in late 1960 they had begun to explore ways in which they could improve Britain's competitive position in the world's man-made fibre industry. I.C.I.'s position became clearer and clearer as the affair developed: in order for Britain to compete effectively with the huge man-made fibres groups already formed in some other countries, a British group of equivalent size would have to be formed, which could only be accomplished by complete merger. Courtaulds developed a different position: the British industry did indeed need strengthening, but this could not best be done by complete merger, but rather by limited I.C.I.–Courtaulds joint ventures. This basic difference in approach would persist throughout the affair.

On September 2, 1961, the talks, which had been allowed to lapse in late 1960, were resumed. These talks initially included only Mr. Chambers, Sir John Hanbury-Williams, and Sir Alan Wilson; others from each management team would later become involved.

One writer commented on these talks as follows:

This time [Chambers] was much more anxious to push it [the takeover] to a climax. Courtaulds say this was because I.C.I. had in the meantime become more frightened of their competition. They were cutting deeply into I.C.I.'s profits from the sale of paint for house decoration.

They were doing very well out of the booming sales of Courtelle—and no one knew better how rapidly they were booming than I.C.I. . . .

*   *   *   *   *

This picture of I.C.I. being driven against the wall by Courtaulds may be somewhat exaggerated. Courtaulds in the summer of 1961 still looked rather like a decaying old hulk—and the only figures who were then visible on what served for the bridge did little to suggest that the ship already had some extremely modern engines.

The chairman's annual statement, issued in July, was more like a dirge than a challenge. Nevertheless the picture is far from being totally at variance with the truth. Courtaulds at this stage were on the point of emerging from five years of

painful but successful readjustment. I.C.I., on the other hand, after a decade of expansion and high profits, were facing new problems. If they were going to swallow
Courtaulds on favourable terms, the sooner the better.[1]

On October 12th, Hanbury-Williams told the Courtaulds board of the
resumption of talks with I.C.I.; he indicated that the talks were on the
same general lines as those of the year before, and he was not asked for
details. There appears to have been some misunderstanding as to what
was being discussed in these talks:

Wilson [Courtaulds' chairman-elect] says that what was discussed was the
strengthening of the fibres industry, with particular reference to Terylene, *and
nothing else* [italics mine], but Chambers insists that the idea of a full merger was
unquestionably present in the minds of the two Courtaulds' participants.[1]

The existence of this apparent misunderstanding early in discussions
between the two companies is very important in explaining subsequent
events.

On October 14, Hanbury-Williams left for a two-month health visit
to South Africa. On October 25, Kearton, who had been in South Africa
during most of September and October, returned to London. He made
inquiries about the new series of talks with I.C.I. and then suggested a
dinner meeting between a number of directors from each company. This
meeting was arranged for November 15.

Meanwhile, on November 2, Courtaulds' board decided to cut its interim dividend from 10*d.* per share to 9*d.**

Although the profits were down a little the cut was unnecessary on financial
grounds. It was done as a gesture, partly to the company's employees after a year
in which the original rayon factory had been closed down, and partly to the Chan-
cellor of the Exchequer. Hanbury-Williams, cabling and writing from Johannes-
burg, was the chief advocate of the cut—but he was supported by Sir Dallas Bernhard, the "outside" deputy-chairman, by Aubrey Jones, M.P., by the two family
directors, George and W. P. Courtauld and by Sir Alan Wilson.

The cut was opposed, vehemently, by Reginald Mathys. . . . He received some
support from Arthur Knight, the finance director, and one or two others, but was
heavily defeated on a vote. Kearton voted with the majority.

The decision of this meeting was immediately made public.

* * * * *

This affair of the dividend cut is one of the most mysterious episodes in the
whole tangled story. It knocked 1*s.* 10½*d.* off the price of Courtaulds' shares, which
had already fallen by more than 15*s.* over the previous six months. It conflicted
sharply with the image of a dynamic company, which the younger directors say,

---

* United Kingdom currency is divided into pounds (£), shillings (*s.*), and pence (*d.*)
One pound, which is worth about $2.80 U.S., contains 20 shillings (20*s.*); one shilling con-
tains 12 pence (12*d.*).

they were already anxious to project. *If an agreed merger were in prospect it was likely to worsen the terms offered to Courtaulds' shareholders. And it increased the danger of a bid over the head of the Courtaulds' board* [italics mine].

On the face of it this decision of the board is the best evidence for the view that at this stage Courtaulds were not even thinking of a merger or a takeover [italics mine].[1]

Present at the dinner meeting on November 15 were, from I.C.I., Chambers, Ronald Holroyd (a deputy chairman and important scientist), Leslie Williams (another deputy chairman), Eric Bingen (the third deputy chairman), and P. T. Menzies (finance director); from Courtaulds, Wilson, Kearton, Mathys and Knight.

After dinner they returned to the drawing-room for more serious conversation. At first this took the form of a somewhat unproductive exchange between Wilson and Chambers about Terylene and nylon. Then, at about 11:30, Chambers pushed his chair back and said: "Well, as far as I am concerned, the whole thing could be solved by a complete merger."

Mathys immediately exploded into a snort of opposition, but Wilson, Kearton and Knight remained silent. Then Chambers advanced his case saying: "If the price were sufficiently ridiculous you wouldn't be able to stand in our way." And Williams illustrated a "ridiculous price" as two or three I.C.I. shares for one of Courtaulds. As Courtaulds then stood at 30*s.* and I-C.I. at 63*s.* 1½*d.* the point was effectively made.

. . . Chambers said that he did not want the matter left "in the air," and suggested, first, that he should draw up a merger *pro-forma*, and, second, that he should continue discussions with Alan Wilson, with whom he had the advantage of being on Christian-name terms. At least tacitly, the Courtaulds directors agreed to these suggestions. The party broke up at about 12:30.

Henceforward there was no room for doubt about what Chambers wanted. What did the Courtaulds directors want?

They are unanimous in saying that they did not want a complete merger on any terms. Nevertheless, Alan Wilson did not go to ground and become difficult to find. . . . Wilson went to Imperial Chemical House on five occasions between November 15 and December 12, and he went almost as a conspirator, telling his driver to drop him at the Ministry of Power and then going in through the back entrance.[1]

Wilson says that they [the five meetings with Chambers] were not discussions but monologues. A continuous cascade of words, which he tried occasionally to interrupt, poured out from Chambers. Throughout the series, Wilson insists, he was trying to get Chambers to understand that the Courtaulds board were opposed in principle to a merger, but he admits that he never got him to apprehend the point. . . .

Chambers, on the other hand, claims that the talks took the form of a give-and-take discussion of the general arrangements necessary for a merger.

The financial structures of both businesses were gone into, and Wilson prepared a rough paper showing the strength of Courtaulds. It was proposed by Chambers that, for future organisation, Courtaulds should keep their identity and that Terylene, in which I.C.I. had exclusive manufacturing rights, should be transferred to them. Two of the Courtaulds directors—Wilson himself and Frank Kearton—should immediately join the I.C.I. board.

Chambers had also decided that the merger should be announced to the public at a joint Press conference in the first week of January.

In addition there were detailed discussions about terms. As soon as these began all the ridiculous talk of the November 15 dinner party evaporated. There was no more mention of two or three I.C.I. shares for one of Courtaulds. On the contrary, Chambers began by saying that he was authorised by his board to offer only five of I.C.I. for eight of Courtaulds. This offer, however, was quickly amended to the simpler and marginally better one of two for three. This was unsatisfactory to Courtaulds; after the dinner party they had been expecting at least one for one. And Chambers eventually moved to three for four. This change had to be put to the I.C.I. board, all the members of which, he insists, were kept closely informed throughout.

This was done on December 14, and as Wilson was out of London on that day it was arranged that Chambers should send him a code message (as to whether the 3-for-4 offer was acceptable to the I.C.I. board). This message, Wilson says, was never sent.[3]

This, then, was the background of the takeover bid up to December 14th, 1961. The companies had held a number of exploratory talks on the subject of a takeover, but there had been no agreement by Courtaulds' directors, so far as one can determine from public sources, that even the idea of a takeover was acceptable to them, much less any agreement on the terms which might be offered. Up to this time, no information on the discussions had been given to the press.

In the last few days before the affair became public, negotiations and maneuverings became somewhat complex.

DECEMBER 14–18, 1961

On December 14, Kearton had a luncheon meeting with George Courtauld, at which they decided that a special board meeting should be called for the following day. During this meeting, the Courtaulds' board received news that I.C.I.'s board had agreed to a 3-for-4 offer.

Kearton moved, and carried by a majority of ten votes to seven, that they should prepare to pay a second interim dividend, which would more than make up for the cut of November 2, and that it should be announced at an early Press conference that they were doing this to stave off the I.C.I. threat.

It was in these circumstances that [Wilson] paid his agitated . . . visit to Chambers on the morning of Saturday, December 16. He informed him of the decision of the board. In addition, Chambers says, he warned him that there was a danger that the whole story, pegged to the Courtaulds' second interim dividend decision, would be in the Sunday papers on the following morning.

Chambers did not react to these pieces of news as the Courtaulds' board had hoped (and even assumed) that he would. He did not accept that the moves towards a merger must be suspended. Instead he decided, and decided very quickly, to press still more resolutely ahead with them. . . . Chambers ordered the summoning of the full I.C.I. board for an emergency meeting at his house on the following afternoon [Sunday, December 17].

Wilson, in the meantime, again met his board at 4 p.m. on the Saturday. This was clearly an even more difficult meeting for him than the one at the same time the previous day. Instead of being able to give the other directors the news that they were expecting, that Chambers' plans had been halted, he could only report failure and its completeness was underlined by the arrival in the middle of the meeting of twenty copies of the formal bid. . . . It was eventually decided to adjourn until the following Tuesday in order to give everyone time to calm down.

. . . Paul Chambers was not taking time to calm down. On the contrary he was busily preparing to get the approval of his twenty-four fellow-directors for his plan to go ahead in spite of the fact that, as he believed, Courtaulds' board were split on the issue.[3]

In reality the Courtaulds board was divided, so far as it is known, only on the issue of whether to pay another interim dividend. Wilson had strongly opposed this dividend but was outvoted.

Chambers managed to arrange a meeting of the I.C.I. board for Sunday, the 17th. Somehow, word of this meeting was leaked to the press, with the result that when I.C.I. board members arrived at Chambers' house at 3:30 on the afternoon of the 17th for the meeting, they found the driveway full of reporters and television cameras.

The affair became public the next day, Monday the 18th; it was the lead story on the financial pages of London papers, under such headlines as "I.C.I.–Courtaulds Talk." Chambers issued a written statement to the press at 10 o'clock that morning and held a press conference that afternoon. He consulted nobody at Courtaulds before making I.C.I.'s takeover bid public. He subsequently explained that he had been unable to reach Wilson and that he had not wanted to undercut Wilson by discussing the matter with another Courtaulds director.

The only plausible explanation [for Chambers' failure to confer with Courtaulds before bringing in the press] is that Chambers had already decided—Hanbury-Williams apart—that Wilson was the only man he could deal with at Courtaulds, but that he could afford to go direct to the shareholders over the heads of the others.

Chambers conducted his Press conference that afternoon with his usual grasp and skill. . . . He put the case for a merger in terms of producing a vertically integrated British fibres group of approximately the same size as Duponts in America and Rhône-Poulenc/Rhodiaceta in Europe. He referred to "our friends in Courtaulds," and implied that Sir Alan Wilson might well have been present at the Press conference had there not been a danger of this appearing discourteous to Hanbury-Williams (who was still in South Africa).

At the same time he made it clear that Courtaulds had given no answer to his detailed offer, which he described as "final, final terms," although he expressed confidence that the answer would eventually be favourable. When asked whether he would if necessary go over the heads of the Courtaulds' directors he tried to parry the question, but did so in such a way as to give a hint of an iron hand behind the velvet glove. "You are asking me a question which would make it very difficult for the Courtaulds' board to come to a judgment in a calm and collected atmosphere," he said. But he did not suggest that he expected such a judgment to be made in a hurry. . . . He would be happy to wait.[3]

This, then, was the situation on December 18th, when the takeover bid became public: I.C.I. was making a "final, final" offer of 3 of its common shares for 4 of Courtaulds' common shares. I.C.I. expected to acquire enough Courtaulds' common by this offer to make the takeover complete. (Under British law, if 90 per cent of the common stock could be acquired, I.C.I. could force the holders of the remaining 10 per cent to sell their shares to I.C.I.); Courtaulds' management had so far not commented on the bid, but there was no real indication that they would recommend refusal of the bid.

Now that the offer was public, commentaries on it began to appear. *The Economist* observed:

Here is the biggest bid in British industrial history, worth approximately £180 million, disclosed without ceremony or even dignity. All the comings and goings in the last four months—deputy chairmen by the back door—became public knowledge without decent introduction. Out of the confusion the terms at least are clear: three ICI ordinaries* for four Courtaulds and take it or leave it.

Courtaulds' stockholders will presumably take it; at any rate the prospect of ICI being forced higher, by Du Pont or anyone else, looks remote enough, even though ICI's terms will be lying on the table for six weeks until the formal offer can be made. So, in a different sense, ICI stockholders are taking it: their ordinary shares have fallen by 1*s.* 6*d.* to 57*s.* 3*d.*, while Courtaulds have jumped 10*s.* to 40*s.* ICI's bid, which puts a value of 43*s.* on Courtaulds, is generous enough against recent prices, although it is almost £1 below Courtaulds' 1960 peak. After "four months of friendly discussion," Courtaulds' directors can hardly fight for the rejection of ICI's offer and the continued independence of the company. (Having just reduced the interim dividend, they cannot even use the mischievous counter ploy of raising the dividend.)[2]

Clearly, the success of I.C.I.'s offer depended greatly on the relative prices of the two stocks. Courtaulds' common stock, just before the announcement became public, sold at 30*s.* This stock had sold in a price range of 26*s.* 3*d.* to 47*s.* 6*d.* during 1961, although its 1960 high had been about 60*s.* I.C.I. common had, during 1961, sold from 55*s.* 10½*d.* to 81*s.* 6*d.* and was quoted at 58*s.* 9*d.* just before the offer became public.

---

* "Ordinary" is the British term for a share of common stock.

The market immediately raised the price of Courtaulds by 33 per cent (to 40s.) when the offer was made, since the imputed value of a Courtaulds' share, based on a 3-for-4 offer and I.C.I. price of about 58s. was approximately 43s. It appears that the market did not consider it likely that I.C.I. would increase their terms; otherwise, the price of Courtaulds would presumably have been pushed somewhat higher than the 40s. it immediately reached. (Exhibit 3 shows the market prices for I.C.I. and Courtaulds common through February 15, 1962.)

Exhibit 3

MARKET PRICE OF COURTAULDS AND I.C.I. COMMON STOCKS AND IMPUTED VALUE
OF BID 15 DECEMBER, 1961, TO 15 FEBRUARY, 1962

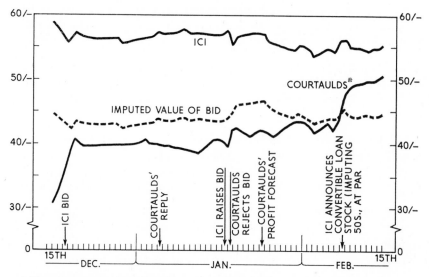

* Of course, as soon as I.C.I. announced the loan stock on February 8, under the loan-stock alternative the imputed value of a Courtaulds share was 50s., assuming the loan stock sold at par. This graph shows the value after February 8 of a 4-for-5 exchange.

Source: *The Economist*, February 17, 1962, p .639.

Courtaulds' directors made no public comment on I.C.I.'s bid during the last days of December. Then, on January 5, they announced that they were advising their shareholders to reject the 3-for-4 offer. The fight had begun.

THE BATTLE FOR COURTAULDS:
JANUARY 3–MARCH 12, 1962

Just when Courtaulds' management decided to oppose the takeover vigorously is unknown, but the decision was probably reached soon after I.C.I.'s announcement on December 18. Courtaulds' directors faced a formidable task: they had to show their shareholders that a common share of Courtaulds was worth significantly more than the 43*s.* imputed price I.C.I. was offering, and that accordingly Courtaulds' shareholders should reject the offer.

The first step was taken on January 3, when Courtaulds suggested to I.C.I. that the two firms create a joint research team to consider the future of British man-made fibres and to report in June. Observers of the struggle commented that this move was presumably made to give Courtaulds more time in which to prepare their defences. Chambers immediately rejected this proposal.

On the next day (January 4), Courtaulds:

> . . . set up a sort of battle group composed of four of the younger executive directors. These four—Frank Kearton, Reginald Mathys, Arthur Knight, and Patrick Koppel—were the most effective fighting material Courtaulds could deploy, and they were all instructed to devote their whole time to the struggle.
> . . . Although Kearton was the leader he was by no means the only talented member of the group. Mathys was tough and resourceful; Knight was highly ingenious; and Keppel was buoyant, patient and personable. Together they were a formidable team.[4]

On January 5, Courtaulds announced publicly that they were recommending that their shareholders reject the I.C.I. offer.

On January 8, while the I.C.I. board was meeting, Courtaulds delivered to them a suggestion that, during the next 7–10 days, two alternative courses of actions be examined. Alternative I proposed that Terylene (the I.C.I. man-made fibre) be given to British Nylon Spinners, the company owned 50-50 by I.C.I. and Courtaulds, and that I.C.I. be given a controlling interest in British Nylon Spinners. Alternative II was that I.C.I. and Courtaulds set up a new joint company, in which Courtaulds would have a majority interest, which would take over all fibres controlled by both parents. One writer commented:

> These were shrewd proposals. They did not go far enough to give Chambers what he wanted—he had already said that only a complete merger would do this —but they went sufficiently far to make it difficult for him to get the I.C.I. board— on which some murmurs of caution were beginning to be heard—to reject them at once. A joint Press statement was therefore issued that afternoon saying that these further talks were to take place.[4]

Observers commented on the fact that these talks were held in an atmosphere far different from the friendly spirit in which the September–December, 1961, talks had been conducted. The talks were broken off on January 17, and the announcement issued to this effect by each company also contained sharp criticisms of the others' policies.

I.C.I. suggested that Courtaulds were essentially producers of cheap old-fashioned rayon, uncomprehending of the need in the case of the modern synthetic fibres for integration back to the raw material stage. Courtaulds accused I.C.I. of seeking a captive market for the primary chemicals in which they [I.C.I.] had made a heavy capital investment.[4]

I.C.I. also announced at this time that they were raising their offer of 3-for-4 to 4-for-5. At the day's market price, this imputed a value of about 46s. 6d. to a share of Courtaulds' common. Courtaulds' directors told Chambers, before he increased his offer, that they would still recommend rejection of the bid, and they did so publicly the next morning, January 18. The time for polite talks and research teams was over.

In the announcement of the increase to 4-for-5, Chambers said:

There is no question in any circumstances of I.C.I. making any alteration in the bid. There is no question of I.C.I. withdrawing from the matter, and we will go straight on on these present terms.[4]

Now that I.C.I. had increased their offer, Courtaulds' task was more difficult than ever: they now had to show that Courtaulds' common was worth more than the offered price of 46s. 6d. per share. They began by having their financial advisers, Baring Brothers & Co., Ltd. (bankers), and Messrs. Binder, Hamlyn and Co. (chartered accountants), prepare a revised estimate of Courtaulds' true net worth and earning power. This financial statement, which was released on January 24 and widely published, is contained in Exhibit 4. Some important excerpts from the statement were:

... [I.C.I.'s 4-for-5 offer] would seriously undervalue the earning capacity of Courtaulds in relation to that of I.C.I.

Total Group profits for 1960/61 and those forecast for future years are as follows:

1960/61 actual	£18.7 million
1961/62 (final 3 mos. estimated)	£17.5 million
1962/63 estimated	£23.0 million
1964/65 estimated	£28.5 million

The substantial increase in profits from Courtaulds' own fibre and associated activities is expected for the following reasons:—

(i) The vigorous and effective action taken to arrest and reverse the decline in profits from viscose yarns and fibres.

(ii) The continued expansion in profits from British Celanese Limited and from Courtelle.

(iii) The recovery already apparent from the short-term market recession in the first part of 1961.

Courtaulds are confident that the cash flow from the increased profits which are foreseen will be adequate both to provide the additional fixed and working capital called for by their future plans, and at the same time to allow for a policy of *consistent and steadily increasing dividend distributions* [italics mine].

Exhibit 4

COURTAULDS' FINANCIAL STATEMENT, JANUARY 24, 1962

This financial review of your Company's present position and future growth prospects has been prepared by the Directors in consultation with their financial advisers, Baring Brothers & Co., Limited, and Messrs. Binder, Hamlyn & Co., Chartered Accountants, in order to provide Stockholders with up-to-date information regarding the Group, its assets and its earnings. As Stockholders will be aware, the Directors have already announced that they must advise Stockholders not to accept an Imperial Chemical Industries Limited offer on the terms disclosed on 17th January, 1962, on the grounds that it would seriously undervalue the earning capacity of Courtaulds in relation to that of I.C.I. They have based this advice on information regarding past and future earnings of I.C.I. disclosed to them in confidence, which has not yet been made available to the public. This review does not contain the Directors' comments on the I.C.I. offer, which will be sent to Stockholders when the offer document is available.

Courtaulds tend to be regarded by investors as primarily a textile company, even though by far the greater part of their capital is employed not in textiles but in man-made fibre production, packaging, pulp, chemicals and paint. In these circumstances, this financial review of your Company's present position and future growth prospects has been divided into two parts, the first dealing with Courtaulds' own fibre and associated activities (including textiles) and the second with their other investments.

The major factors regarding Courtaulds' financial position, as disclosed by this review, are summarised below:—

(*a*) Total Group profits for 1960/61 and those forecast for future years are as follows:—

1960/61 actual	£18.7 mn.
1961/62 (final three months est.)	£17.5 mn.
1962/63 estimated	£23.0 mn.
1964/65 estimated	£28.5 mn.

(*b*) The substantial increase in profits from Courtaulds' own fibre and associated activities is expected for the following reasons:—

  (i) The vigorous and effective action taken to arrest and reverse the decline in profits from viscose yarns and fibres.

  (ii) The continued expansion in profits from British Celanese Limited and from Courtelle.

  (iii) The recovery already apparent from the short-term market recession in the first part of 1961.

Profits before tax from this section of the business in 1962/63 are expected to be some 40–50 per cent higher than the £9.7 millions earned in 1960/61.

(*c*) The current value of Courtaulds' investments outside their own fibre and associated activities is assessed at £120 millions equivalent to more than 30*s*. per £1 Ordinary stock in issue. On the basis of 1960/61 results, the distributable income from these other investments, even after allowing for

Exhibit 4—Continued

substantial retentions of profit by the constituent companies, is equivalent to £5.62 millions, representing 7 per cent. (or 1*s*. 5*d*. per £1 unit) on Courtaulds' issued Ordinary stock.

(*d*) Total profits before tax for the year to March 31, 1963, are now forecast at £23 millions. This compares with an earlier routine forecast of £18.5 millions, completed in September, 1961, which was disclosed to I.C.I. on December 12, 1961, together with a forecast dividend of 11 per cent. for that year. At the same time I.C.I. were told that a rapid increase in profits from 1963 onwards was expected. The increased forecast now given is largely due to the acquisition of British Enka Ltd., in November, 1961, and the recent arrangements to take over the Lustrafil viscose yarn production which have made it possible to accelerate the rationalisation of the U.K. viscose industry.

(*e*) The value to be attributed to Courtaulds' issued capital should take into account both:—

(i) The value of their own fibre and associated activities referred to in (*b*) and

(ii) The value of their other investments referred to in (*c*).

DIVIDENDS

Courtaulds are confident that the cash flow from the increased profits which are foreseen will be adequate both to provide the additional fixed and working capital called for by their future plans, and at the same time to allow for a policy of consistent and steadily increasing dividend distributions.

It is Courtaulds' practice to prepare long-term estimates of future results, and these have been carefully reviewed during the past few weeks in the light of all the information at present available. The figures of future profits used in this statement have been extracted from these forecasts, and are intended to indicate the trends which are expected by the Board to be applicable in the future.

1. FIBRES AND ASSOCIATED ACTIVITIES INCLUDING TEXTILES

Courtaulds' interest in Net Assets at Balance Sheet Values at March 31, 1961— £122 millions.

These can be divided into three main groups:—

(*a*) *Viscose Yarns and Fibres and Related Activities* (including pulp, viscose chemicals and Courtaulds' weaving subsidiary).

Courtaulds' profits from viscose and related activities have suffered heavily in recent years from structural weaknesses within the viscose industry; in the year ending 31st March, 1962, profits are estimated at only £5.1 millions, compared with £12.0 millions in 1955/56. Courtaulds have, over the past few years, taken vigorous and effective steps to deal with this situation. They have shut two of their older factories, absorbed and closed down Harbens Limited, taken over Lustrafil's production, and have acquired British Enka in order to achieve further rationalisation. This radical re-organization of the industry, which caused large non-recurrent expenses, has eliminated idle capacity and duplication of overheads.

Products have been improved and lower raw material prices have been estab-

Exhibit 4—Continued

lished. In pulp the Group's activities have been very successful. In the five years since Courtaulds' pulp producing subsidiary in South Africa was established, to provide part of the Group's requirements, earnings on the equity capital of £6 millions have improved every year, amounting to over 25 per cent. for the year ended 31st December, 1961. At the same time the price of pulp has been reduced by 15 per cent. The economy programme carried out by Courtaulds (Alabama) Inc. has put that company in a strong position to benefit from the better market situation now prevailing in the U.S.A.

These measures have stopped the downward trend in profits from viscose and related operations and the Board are confident that already in the year ending 31st March, 1963, a substantial increase in profits to more than £8 millions will be obtained. This improvement in the viscose situation when taken together with the upward trend in other group activities will result in a major increase in overall Group profits as shown in the table given later.

(*b*) *British Celanese Group* (including acetate yarns and fibres, related chemicals and other activities).

During the years prior to their acquisition in 1957, the profits of British Celanese had been falling sharply. Courtaulds have carried out vigorous rationalisation (including shutting down unprofitable activities), and expansion has been financed from British Celanese's own resources. The profits of British Celanese reached their low point of £680,000 in 1957/58, the year of acquisition; at the end of 1957/58 the small Acetate Division of Courtaulds which earned some £300,000 in that year was purchased by British Celanese. In the year ended 31st March, 1961, profits from the combined operation reached £3,788,000. Profits for the year to March, 1962, will be approximately £4,500,000 and as a result of steps already taken or planned, these should increase substantially in succeeding years.

(*c*) *Courtelle and Other Synthetic Fibres*

Courtelle, the first British acrylic fibre, has had a remarkable success since commercial production started in 1959. Courtaulds' unique process, which was developed in their own laboratories, is believed to be the lowest cost process in the world both as regards capital investment and running costs, and Courtelle is expected to become one of the world's major man-made fibres. United Kingdom production is already providing profitable despite heavy initial promotion and development costs, and profits for the years to 31st March, 1961 and 1962 have been running at the rate of about £700,000 per annum. For a new fibre to be making profits at such an early stage of its development is unprecedented. Continuing heavy promotion and development expenses will limit the increase in profits in the year to 31st March, 1963, but thereafter as production expands both in the U.K. and abroad, the increase in profits should be rapid.

2. OTHER INVESTMENTS

Courtaulds' interest in Net Assets at Balance Sheet values at 31st March, 1961 —£70 millions.

The table below shows Courtaulds' share of the profits of their subsidiaries outside the fibre and textile fields and the income from their trade and other investments for 1960/61 (except where otherwise stated).

Exhibit 4—Continued

	Current Market Value Where Quoted (£ mn.)	Income before Tax Attributable to Courtaulds' Stockholders (£ mn.)
I. *Subsidiaries:* (Companies in which Courtaulds have a majority interest)		
British Cellophane Ltd.		2.64
Pinchin, Johnson & Assoc. Ltd., and Cellon Ltd.		.98
Gossard (Holdings) Ltd.		.22
Engineering Contracts, including receipts for know-how (1960/61—£1.84 mn.) annual average, say		1.00
Others		.07
		4.91
II. *Trade Investments:*		
British Nylon Spinners Ltd.		2.40
Snia Viscosa	18.9	.31
Excess Insurance Company Ltd.	1.3	.02
Other—Quoted	2.3	.10
Unquoted		.21
		3.04
Usutu Pulp Company Ltd. (£2 mn. invested to 31.3.61)		Not operating on 31st March, 1961
III. Government Securities and cash assets available for investment on an assumed average yield basis of 5½% per annum*		1.10
Total		9.05
Deduct: Allocation of Courtaulds' administration expenses to cover management		.20
Net Income before tax attributable to Courtaulds' stockholders		8.85

* The current market value of the Government Securities and cash assets available for investment at March 31, 1961, would be approx. £20 mn. About £5 mn. has, however, been used since that date to purchase further investments the income from which is not included above.

If the above interests are considered as a separate entity, and on the basis of:—

(i) a maintainable annual profit of £8.85 millions as shown above;

(ii) present rates of taxation, including profits tax at 15 per cent;

(iii) subsidiaries distributing only half their profits;

the sum available would be equivalent to a gross distribution of £5.62 millions, representing 7 per cent. (or 1*s*. 5*d*. per £1 unit) on the present issued Ordinary Stock of Courtaulds.

It is emphasised that the above distribution of £5.62 millions is arrived at after allowing for retention of earnings by subsidiaries of 50 per cent. and by British Nylon Spinners of 54 per cent.

In addition there are the normal retentions of the other trade investments.

The Directors, in consultation with their financial advisers, have made an assessment of the present value of the above interests and they believe that, in total,

Exhibit 4—Continued

they represent about £120 millions or 30*s*. per £1 of Ordinary Stock compared with their book value of £70 millions. At this valuation, the distribution referred to above would give a dividend yield of 4.68 per cent.

Comments regarding the future prospects of the principal investments are given below.

(*a*) BRITISH CELLOPHANE LIMITED

Profits of this company rose from £2.42 millions in 1955 to a record £3.53 millions in the year ended March 31, 1961. In spite of a temporary recession a profit of £2.9 millions is expected for the year to March 31, 1962, increasing to over £3 millions in 1962/63, and further expansion of sales and profits are forecast for future years.

(*b*) PINCHIN, JOHNSON AND ASSOCIATES LIMITED, AND CELLON LIMITED

At the time of acquisition, the Pinchin Johnson Group consisted of many semi-autonomous units, some of which were in serious difficulties. Major re-organisation is well advanced, including the merging of Cellon (following the acquisition of the minority interests in this company last year) with Pinchin Johnson. Profits in 1961/62 despite a recession in the automobile and consumer appliance industries, the company's main customers, have been running at the same level as those of 1960/61, namely just over £1 million p.a. and an increase to over £1.5 millions is forecast for 1962/63.

(*c*) GOSSARD (HOLDINGS) LIMITED

This Group was acquired in 1959 for £2,362,000. Appreciable re-organisation was found to be necessary to meet the more competitive conditions of the 1960s. Profits, which in the year of acquisition (1959) were £181,000 increased to £245,000 in 1960, and to just over £400,000 in 1961.

(*d*) ENGINEERING CONTRACTS

In 1958, Courtaulds decided to exploit their extensive engineering facilities and technical know-how by supplying complete factories to overseas countries. Contracts totalling £23 millions have already been obtained and further contracts are being negotiated. Total profits from this source amounted to £1.85 millions in the year to March, 1961. Although such business is by nature spasmodic, an average profit, taking one year with another, of at least £1 million a year is forecast.

(*e*) BRITISH NYLON SPINNERS LIMITED

Dividends received from British Nylon Spinners have increased from £1.2 millions five years ago to £2.4 millions in the year to March, 1961. Although the British Nylon Spinners' management is expecting an increasing sales volume, some decline in profits over the coming years is forecast because of lower selling margins; nevertheless, it is their present intention to continue to pay the same dividend since they consider that it will no longer be necessary to retain such a high proportion of the Company's earnings.

(*f*) SNIA VISCOSA

This company, in which Courtaulds have a substantial minority holding, has a history of continuous expansion since the war and further major growth is planned. Snia Viscosa is well placed to benefit from the resurgence of the Italian economy

Exhibit 4—Continued

and to take advantage of new opportunities presented by the European Economic Community. Like so many important companies in the European Economic Community, its present market value is high in relation to the dividend income actually received.

OVER-ALL GROUP PROSPECTS

Group profit prospects are strongly influenced by the substantial recovery in viscose profitability which is now taking place earlier than previously expected, as a result of the additional steps taken by Courtaulds. The upward trend in profits from British Celanese, Courtelle and other activities is expected to continue. These factors, together with the recovery from the short term market recession in the first part of 1961, are expected to result in an increase in Group profits before tax to the record figure of around £23 millions in the year ending 31st March, 1963.

The profit trend can be illustrated as follows:—

GROUP PROFITS BEFORE TAX AND BEFORE PREFERENCE DIVIDENDS
(Year to 31st March)

	1955/6	1960/1	1961/2 (Est.)	1962/3 (Forecast)	1964/5 (Forecast)
			(in £ millions)		
Viscose yarns and fibres and related activities	12.0	5.6	5.1	8.5	9.1
Other fibres and investments (including subsidiaries)	5.3	13.1	12.4	14.5	19.4
TOTAL GROUP PROFITS	17.3	18.7*	17.5	23.0	28.5
Minority interests	.6	1.3	1.3	1.5	2.0
Courtaulds' interest in Total Group Profits before tax and before Preference Dividends	16.7	17.4	16.2	21.5	26.5

* Reconciliation:

	£ mn.
Total group profits as above	18.7
Additional profits credited direct to capital reserve	.9
	19.6

The 1964/65 forecast of profits results in an increase in the return on capital employed as shown in the Balance Sheet from 9% for the year ended 31st March, 1961, to 12½% for the year ending 31st March 1965, made up as follows:—

	£ mn.
Viscose yarns and fibres and related activities	5.6
British Celanese	3.8
Courtelle	.7
Other Investments—Courtaulds' interest	8.9
	19.0
ADD: Minority interests' share of profits, less consolidating adjustments and minor items	.6
	19.6

Exhibit 4—Continued

EUROPEAN ECONOMIC COMMUNITY

Courtaulds and their principal products are in a strong position to face the increased competition in the home market which will result if the U.K. joins the European Economic Community, and a detailed appraisal suggests that the profits of £28.5 millions forecast for the year to 31st March, 1965, are unlikely to be reduced by even 10% on this account. In contrast, the chemical industry is more vulnerable to European competition.

Courtaulds are particularly well placed to take advantage of the opportunities which would arise from closer European economic integration. They have important manufacturing subsidiaries and associated companies in the principal European markets. They have already set up special marketing offices in France, Germany and Scandinavia. British Celanese are already exporting to Europe where the development of acetate fibres has been slower than in the U.K. and North America; increased expansion of these exports, particularly Tricel, is foreseen. A Courtelle factory has been established in France and the expected rapid growth in demand for this fibre in Europe will require substantial expansion of the present capacity. British Cellophane, with the largest and lowest cost production operations in Europe, are also well placed to compete there. In the long term, Courtaulds look forward with confidence to closer economic ties with Europe.

By Order of the Board,
H. L. Light,
Secretary.

24th January, 1962.

Source: *Investors Chronicle*, January 26, 1962, pp. 294–96.

In this financial statement, then, Courtaulds not only argued that its profits would rise by about 60 per cent over 1961/62 within three years, but also that the company would henceforth be generous with dividends. There was a minor embarrassment for Courtaulds in this financial statement, as they admitted: the future profit estimates were markedly more optimistic than the estimates given to I.C.I. on December 12, 1961. I.C.I. had been told that profits for 1962/63 would be £18.5 million; now they were to be £23.0 million for the same year.* When questioned about this revision, Sir Alan Wilson said that the estimates I.C.I. had received in December were given "solely as an indication of profit trends," and that it had been made in September, 1961. He added that this estimate had shown profits for the year ended September 30, 1963, as £22.5 million, so that the revised estimate "merely advances the original forecast by six months."

Reactions to Courtaulds' new financial statement were generally not encouraging. The price of Courtaulds' common, which had risen to 41s.

---

* The Courtaulds fiscal year, on which the profit estimates in the January 24 financial statement had been based, ended on March 31.

7½*d.* just before the estimate, fell back to 41*s.* I.C.I.'s common stock had also been dropping, among other reasons because it was believed that I.C.I.'s 1961/62 profits, soon to be announced, would be down perhaps as much as 25 per cent from the previous year. The 4-for-5 bid, however, still imputed a value of 44*s.* 6*d.* to a Courtaulds' share, so that the drop of 7½*d.* in that equity must have been discouraging in the Courtaulds' board room.

Mr. Chambers reacted to Courtaulds' revised figures as might have been expected: he suggested that such sudden optimism could hardly be justified.

Outside observers' reactions to the financial statement were mixed, largely because evaluating Courtaulds' new profit estimates was complex and based on speculation at best. As *The Economist* remarked:

> In coming to their decision . . . shareholders will not be swayed by nuances in an economic and technical argument. . . . Their course of action will be determined, first, by the prices that ICI and Courtaulds can command in the stock market, and, secondly, by the impression they have gained in the past and during the present struggle of the quality of the top management of the two concerns. What will happen to the price of ICI shares when its latest profits are published remains to be seen. But Courtaulds' directors are, in effect, asking the shareholders to reject completely the comparative images of ICI and Courtaulds' managements in the past as any guide to the future. They are also asking shareholders to forget and forgive the cut in the interim dividend, which they now openly admit was an absurd mistake. At this late stage in the day, can the Courtaulds' directors, able and fierce as some of them have proved themselves in the latest bout of in-fighting, create a brand new image?[6]

The two weeks following Courtaulds' financial statement were relatively quiet ones in the struggle. They were not marked by any major new announcements on either side. Around February 7, Courtaulds began a series of full-page advertisements in major journals; these advertisements were clearly prompted by the take-over attempt. Each advertisement in the series centred on the theme "Courtaulds ALONE"; the general argument advanced was that Courtaulds would do better operating by itself than if I.C.I. were in control. I.C.I.'s advertisements during this period were purely "institutional" in character and made no reference to the attempted take-over.

Meanwhile, the British government began against its will to get involved. As soon as the first take-over proposal had been made, back in December, cries of "monopoly" had been raised in some quarters. It was, at least, demonstrable that if the take-over occurred, I.C.I. would have something on the order of 90 per cent of all British capacity in man-made fibres and perhaps 25 per cent or more in paint. Furthermore, the proposed combination would produce a huge company. I.C.I. was already much the largest United Kingdom chemical producer, and this take-over would considerably increase its lead over its competitors.

The government, in the person of Mr. Erroll (President of the Board of Trade), decided that it could do nothing. On January 30, Mr. Erroll announced that, under the Monopolies and Restrictive Trade Practices Act of 1948, the government could take no action against a potential monopoly. In short, the government would not forbid the take-over, although it reserved the right to examine the resulting company. Thus the government effectively "washed its hands of the affair," as observers commented.

The next stage in the battle began at a press conference held by Chambers on Thursday, February 8. Essentially three major points were made at this conference and in the formal announcement in the following day's newspapers (the entire announcement is found in Exhibit 5):

1. I.C.I.'s pre-tax profits for 1961/62 were estimated at about £62 million, as against £88 million for the record year of 1960/61. This was a drop of almost 30% justifying Courtaulds' direst predictions.
2. As Chambers had previously stated, Courtaulds' revised profit figures were again held to be unrealistically optimistic.
3. I.C.I. was offering Courtaulds' shareholders an alternative exchange plan, which in effect again raised I.C.I.'s bid.

The 4-for-5 offer still stood, but Courtaulds' shareholders now were offered the alternative of £2½ (50s.) worth of convertible unsecured loan stock in exchange for each share of Courtaulds' common: this loan stock (known in the United States as a "convertible debenture") carried a 6.5 per cent coupon. In effect, if the market valued the loan stock at par, a Courtaulds' shareholder was now being offered 50s. per share, a substantial improvement over the approximately 44s. per share that the 4-for-5 offer was worth.

The loan stock could be converted during the period 1963–65, but the most advantageous ratio, which would obtain only for 1963, was the same 4-for-5 simultaneously being offered on an outright exchange. The conversion rate would decline slightly in 1964 and again in 1965, and the loan stock would be retired during 1972/77. Thus Mr. Chambers was able to claim that he had not really raised his bid a second time, but had merely altered the terms of the offer.

Courtaulds' directors now had to prove that Courtaulds' common was worth more than 50s. per share, since the consensus of London financial opinion was that the convertible loan stock would sell at par or slightly above, once it reached the market. Courtaulds now began to make rather

IMPERIAL CHEMICAL INDUSTRIES LIMITED

A Statement to the Stockholders of I.C.I.

Your Directors wish to place before you certain information about their proposal for a merger with Courtaulds. As an estimate of the Company's profits for the year 1961 must be included in any offer to the stockholders of Courtaulds, it is our duty to give our own stockholders this information before the offer goes out to the Courtaulds stockholders.

1961 PROFITS AND FUTURE PROSPECTS

On the basis of unaudited accounts we expect the group income for 1961 before taxation to be about £62 million compared with £88 million for 1960 which was a record year for I.C.I. We shall recommend a final dividend of 1s. 6d. for 1961 on the present Ordinary capital, thus maintaining the total dividend for the year at 2s. 9d. per £1 stock unit.

This reduction in profits for 1961 can be attributed to three factors:

(i) substantial falls in world prices of certain chemicals —notably in some parts of the plastic field where there were temporary surplus capacities, particularly in the United States, which had a direct impact on prices in Europe;

(ii) the Board's policy to anticipate Britain's possible entry into the Common Market by deliberately adjusting some prices which might not otherwise have remained competitive;

(iii) difficult trading conditions in the United Kingdom and an increased proportion of our business being done in fiercely competitive overseas markets.

In all these circumstances it was inevitable that there should be a fall in profit margins. None the less, the record volume of business achieved in 1960 was more than maintained in 1961 both at home and in exports.

Recently doubts have been expressed about the future prospects of the chemical industry. These are entirely without foundation. Official estimates have been published which show that a continuation of the present growth trend in the standard of living in the free world will demand a doubled output of chemicals during the next ten years and any surplus capacity for individual products will be of brief duration. I.C.I. is well placed to secure an appropriate share of the increased demand. I.C.I.'s own separate estimates, which were made before the negotiations with Courtaulds began, and have since been confirmed, lead to the firm belief that I.C.I.'s sales will increase by at least 80 per cent. in volume during the same period. No weight should be attached to statements that for certain products, such as "Terylene", our patent rights are running out. These products, and "Terylene", in particular, which are very profitable and which have an expanding future, depend more upon the steady build up of know-how and special skills on which

I.C.I. have concentrated their efforts than upon the mere possession of patent rights.

Every year for the last eight years I.C.I. has increased its volume of exports and even during the conditions prevailing in 1961 it achieved an appreciable increase in export volume when the f.o.b. value of its exports reached nearly £100 million. These facts are ample proof of I.C.I.'s ability to match world quality and prices. Moreover, this increase in exports has been achieved in spite of the erection by I.C.I. of additional manufacturing units overseas.

The I.C.I. Board would consider it quite irresponsible to seek to influence stockholders by detailed forecasts of profits two or three years ahead. Industry knows full well that these depend in part on factors outside its control and can be greatly influenced by political events —both at home and abroad—by labour conditions and, above all, by the success or failure of plans to raise living standards throughout the world.

We expect 1962 to be a better trading year than 1961, in which the maximum impact of surplus capacity was felt. The improvement will be mainly in the second half of the year, and our present forecast is that the 1962 profits should be appreciably higher than those of 1961. Beyond 1962 we expect the trend of profits to be upwards and indeed we expect the record profit of 1960 to be exceeded within the next two to three years, with the trend continuing upwards. I.C.I. has now £80 million invested in plants under construction or not yet in commercial production, all of which will in due course contribute to profits, either because they will meet the increased demand referred to earlier or because they will enable I.C.I. to reduce its production costs by the adoption of new processes and cheaper raw materials.

The I.C.I. Board sees no reason why I.C.I. should not maintain the same rate of growth, with a substantial increase in profits, during the present decade as it did during the last. We should draw your attention to the fact that as a result of progressive increases in the I.C.I. dividend, the effective dividend on I.C.I. Ordinary Stock has more than doubled since 1956 and that there has not been a reduction in any I.C.I. dividend, either interim or final, for over a quarter of a century.

I.C.I.'s RESEARCH AND DEVELOPMENT

We cannot leave unanswered the suggestion that I.C.I.'s research and development effort has in recent

Exhibit 5—Continued

years proved inadequate. It is true that neither I.C.I. nor Courtaulds has so far made a major basic discovery in the man-made fibres field. These basic discoveries are to some extent a matter of chance; what is more important is to recognise a significant discovery when it is made and to direct the weight of research and development resources to those discoveries which have the greatest market potential. Only a large business can have an effective and well developed organisation capable of quickly and profitably exploiting on a large scale the new ideas and developments which are constantly coming forward. We claim that I.C.I.'s effort in this field does not suffer by comparison with that of any other large group and the successful expansion in the volume of our business in the competitive markets of the world bears witness to this fact.

I.C.I. AND THE COMMON MARKET

As indicated above we have already taken action to reduce the prices of our products in cases where we had reason to doubt whether they would remain competitive if Britain enters the Common Market. This policy has reached the point where tariff protection is of small account and we are satisfied that the enlarged trading area represented by the Common Market will afford I.C.I. substantially greater opportunities for the profitable expansion of its business.

TERMS OF THE MERGER

(a) **Preference stockholders**

Courtaulds Preference stockholders are offered I.C.I. Preference Stock on a basis which gives the same income in future years, to which is added a small, once and for all, cash payment, which is usual in such cases.

(b) **Ordinary stockholders**

Courtaulds Ordinary stockholders are being given an alternative of exchanging £10 Courtaulds Ordinary Stock for either:

(a) £8 I.C.I. Ordinary Stock or

(b) £25 6½ per cent Convertible Unsecured Loan Stock 1972/77 of I.C.I.

The Convertible Loan Stock will be convertible into Ordinary capital of I.C.I. on a basis which in the first year of conversion, 1963, is equal to £8 of I.C.I. Ordinary Stock for every £10 of Courtaulds Ordinary Stock, i.e. the same terms as the share exchange offer. For subsequent conversion in the years 1964 and 1965 the amount of I.C.I. Stock issuable on conversion is slightly reduced.

So far as estimates can be made, the profits of Courtaulds to be brought into the Group will be sufficient to provide (with a suitable margin) the Ordinary dividend payable on the new Ordinary stock to be issued. This does not take into account the additional profits which are expected to arise as a result of the merger.

The interest payable on the Unsecured Loan Stock is in line with the interest payable on similar loan stocks, but is greater than the current rate of dividend on the corresponding amount of I.C.I. Ordinary Stock. As, however, the interest is allowable for profits tax, the net additional payment on the Convertible Loan Stock, so long as it remains in existence, is comparatively small.

NEGOTIATIONS WITH COURTAULDS

It is common ground between the Boards of I.C.I. and Courtaulds that the man-made fibres industry needs strengthening if Britain is to remain fully competitive in this field. It is therefore a matter of regret to the I.C.I. Board that, despite repeated discussions during several years, complete failure to agree on the necessary steps has led to the present position. In this connection we should make it clear that detailed negotiations for a full merger had been proceeding from early in September last year, i.e., well before the announcement of the reduction

of Courtaulds interim dividend. These negotiations had by mid-December reached a stage at which we had every reason to believe that the only matter remaining for discussion between the two Companies was the terms of the offer to the Courtaulds stockholders. I.C.I. is convinced that only a full merger will meet the situation and has reached this conclusion after full examination of alternatives. In our view the matter is of vital importance to the British textile industry—in which I.C.I. is playing an increasingly large part—so that we have no alternative but to make the present approach directly to the Courtaulds stockholders. In so doing it should be emphasised that we have no desire merely to make I.C.I. still larger or to protect or develop a monopoly position to the detriment of industry or the consuming public.

REASONS FOR THE PROPOSED MERGER

I.C.I.'s basic objective is the establishment in the U.K. of an integrated man-made fibres industry, able to compete in world markets on equal terms with the large and powerful American and European producers.

World consumption of man-made fibres other than rayon is increasing rapidly. It is most important from the point of view of the U.K. economy that U.K. producers should obtain an increasing share in this growing world business.

Our major foreign competitors are fully integrated. Vertically their operations start in the manufacture of the complex chain of chemicals, ending with the polymers and their spinning into fibres. Horizontally they cover the production of all the different types of man-made fibres which are partly competitive with and partly complementary to each other.

The case for vertical integration is made stronger by the fact that the chemical industry has played a dominant part in the history of modern fibres. Both nylon and the so-called acrylic fibres (of which " Courtelle " is only one example) were originally discovered and developed by chemical companies. Although Calico Printers Association Limited, a textile company, discovered " Terylene ", they immediately recognised that it could only be developed and manufactured by a chemical company and accordingly entered into a licence agreement with I.C.I.

The man-made fibres industry in the U.K. is mainly in the hands of I.C.I., Courtaulds and their joint company, British Nylon Spinners. Thus fragmented, the industry is less able to compete successfully for this growing market against fully integrated companies such as the du Pont Company in the U.S.A. (whose output of fibres other than rayon is three or four times that of the total U.K. production) and the newly formed Rhone Poulenc-Rhodiaceta Group in Continental Europe. These competitive disadvantages will be increased if the U.K. joins the Common Market.

A complete merger between I.C.I. and Courtaulds would increase efficiency and reduce costs in a number of ways:

(1) **Research and Development.** Many problems are basically common to the whole range of fibres. Research and development in this field is very costly and can only be conducted effectively on an adequate scale by a large integrated organisation able to spread the cost over a large production volume and a wide field of fibres.

Production of a fibre with the required characteristics involves the use of appropriate spinning and other techniques applied to the most suitable type of polymer. Clearly this combination is most easily achieved in an organisation concerned with both fibre production and polymer manufacture. Further, when a new polymer with possible fibre applications is discovered, the best method of converting it to a fibre cannot be determined in advance. It may best be produced by the technique used in the manufacture of any of the existing fibres, including rayon, or indeed by an entirely new technique.

(2) **Production.** Common ownership of the plants for the manufacture of the polymers and the fibres would lead to substantial reductions in capital and operating costs.

(3) **Marketing.** A common marketing organisation would result in lower selling costs, better advice and technical service to the user. It would also ensure that the broadest technical skill can be applied to meeting a customer's particular needs, even to the extent of modifying an existing fibre to suit his requirements.

(4) **Overseas.** In competing for overseas markets the U.K. industry would be much stronger if it were united and able to present a full range of fibres to the overseas buyer. Where manufacture abroad is involved there is the opportunity to use common sites, services and management.

These factors lead us to believe that the merger would soon increase the profits of the combined group by not less than £2.5 million per annum above what would otherwise be achieved. Within a decade it is believed that this figure should rise to £10 million per annum.

There would be additional economies and increased efficiencies, though on a smaller scale, in non-fibre fields in which I.C.I. and Courtaulds are both engaged.

WHY IS A MERGER THE ONLY SOLUTION ?

Several alternative forms of association, most of them involving some form of joint company, have been examined both recently and in the past. None of them was mutually acceptable. Either they failed to cover the full range of fibres involved or, in so far as they did, the relative contributions of the parent companies were not, in our view, adequately taken into account. None of them offered anything like the full advantages of a complete merger, without which the British man-made fibres industry will continue to operate at a disadvantage opposite its larger foreign competitors.

THE NATIONAL INTEREST

As when I.C.I. was originally formed in 1926 a great deal has been said and written about the national interest in this matter. The comment has been made that the merger will result in diminished competition in the United Kingdom, and more restricted choice for the consumer. We suggest that at this particular moment, when Great Britain is discussing entry into the Common Market, the question of competition in the United Kingdom is much less important than that of competition from very large firms overseas. In our opinion, the consumer here can rely on competition from foreign companies and foreign-owned companies manufacturing or planning to manufacture in the U.K. to ensure that he receives good value. Moreover we suggest that one effect of the merger, even from the domestic point of view, will be substantial economies and the prospect of lower prices. As for our prospects in the Common Market, I.C.I.'s. policy of

reducing prices has reached the point where tariff protection is of small account. We face the future, therefore, with confidence, and the I.C.I. Board are unanimously of the opinion that this merger is in the national interest; it will help to improve British industry by making it more competitive in world markets, and it will make a notable contribution to the problem of Britain's balance of payments.

FUTURE PROSPECTS OF THE MERGED CONCERN

We have given above a full statement of our views on the future prospects of I.C.I. Although we view with reserve the detailed forecasts made by Courtaulds we are convinced of the potentiality of that Company if merged with I.C.I. and have also indicated our view that the benefits of the merger should soon result in very substantial additions to profits above what would otherwise be achieved by the two Companies on their own.

By any standards the amount of Convertible Loan Stock which will be issued if a substantial number of Courtaulds stockholders select this alternative will be very large. The amount has, however, to be judged in the light of the size and profitability of the combined concern. The combined net assets available as cover for the Convertible Loan Stock will be of the order of £800 million and the total profits before tax are now running at about £80 million and should soon rise to over £100 million. We are satisfied, therefore, that the proposals are financially sound.

We are convinced that the proposed merger is in the national interest and that the terms are fair to the stockholders of both Companies whose expectations of earnings and dividends from the merged concern are, in our view, greater than those for either Company if they remain apart. We shall therefore strongly and unanimously recommend the merger proposals to the Stockholders of I.C.I.

EXTRAORDINARY GENERAL MEETING

This Statement will be incorporated in a circular letter to be dispatched within the next two weeks to all Stockholders of I.C.I. With this letter will be a Notice of an Extraordinary General Meeting of I.C.I. to be held on 16th March, 1962, for the purpose of authorising the additional capital necessary to implement the proposed merger.

By Order of the Board,
R. A. LYNEX,.
Secretary.

8th February, 1962.
Imperial Chemical House,
Millbank,
London, S.W.1.

pointed comments in what were, ostensibly, straightforward financial announcements:

I.C.I. have such a high opinion of your Company that they have progressively increased their offers. . . . Your shares are worth more than I.C.I. are offering. All you have to do to reject the I.C.I. offer is to destroy all the paper which you have received.[4]

But this argument by itself was not sufficient to destroy the attractiveness of I.C.I.'s newest offer. The price of Courtaulds' common rose quickly, as soon as the convertible loan stock was announced, to nearly 50s. per share, the imputed value if the loan stock sold at par. Clearly, Courtaulds had to prove that 50s. was still too low a price for a stock which, only two months before, the market had been valuing at about 30s.

On Wednesday, February 14, Courtaulds announced that they were making substantial changes in their dividend and investment policies. The formal notice appeared in the papers on Friday, February 16, and is reproduced as Exhibit 6. Some major points made in this announcement were:

. . . the exploratory discussions which had taken place never contemplated a take-over bid; they had for their object the strengthening of the man-made fibres industry generally. No detailed negotiations for a take-over have ever been conducted.

*   *   *   *   *

I.C.I. have now themselves tacitly admitted the inadequacy of their second proposal by making a further and alternative offer in 6½% Convertible Unsecured Loan Stock.

. . . On all counts—net assets, past and present earnings and future prospects—the I.C.I. offer of 4-for-5 is totally inadequate.[7]

The announcement continued with financial arguments designed to show that a 4-for-5 exchange ratio would mean that Courtaulds' shareholders were receiving less than the book value of their equity and that their share in I.C.I.'s earnings, both in the past and through 1964, would be appreciably less than their share in Courtaulds' past and projected earnings for the same periods. The announcement used, for these comparisons, the same Courtaulds' profit estimates given to I.C.I. in December, rather than the higher estimates announced on January 24. Courtaulds' directors were thus attempting to show that the 4-for-5 offer was still unsound. No detailed attempt was made to analyze the value of the loan stock as a long-term investment; the announcement assumed that the loan stock would, if received, be converted at the most advantageous rate, equal to 4-for-5.

The announcement continued with the details of a proposed new investment trust. The significant features were:

Exhibit 6

To the Ordinary Stockholders and, for information, to the Preference Stockholders of Courtaulds, Limited.

COURTAULDS, LIMITED

Advice to Stockholders

The Board of Courtaulds firmly believe that it is in your best interests to ignore the offers made to you on behalf of Imperial Chemical Industries.

As you will see from reading this letter, we are giving you this advice because we believe that:

(a) your Courtaulds Ordinary Stock is worth more than the corresponding I.C.I. shares or Loan Stock you would receive;

(b) I.C.I.'s proposal to take over and control Courtaulds is unsound both commercially and industrially.

We have received throughout the strongest support from the Courtaulds staff and operatives, from customers both at home and overseas, and from other interested people throughout the world. Numerous stockholders have also written pledging their support.

We profoundly regret that precipitate and wholly unexpected action by I.C.I. has led to a course of events which has been most distasteful, brought uneasiness to employees at all levels and caused the voicing of grave concern in both Houses of Parliament, in the Press and elsewhere.

RELATIONS WITH I.C.I.

Since 1928 Directors of Courtaulds and I.C.I. have met regularly in the normal course of business and until recently had always found sound industrial solutions to their problems. The relations of the two companies have been primarily that of Courtaulds as a user and I.C.I. as a supplier of chemical raw materials.

As was said in the press statement of 9th February, the exploratory discussions which had taken place never contemplated a take-over bid; they had for their object the strengthening of the man-made fibres industry generally. **No detailed negotiations for a take-over have ever been conducted.**

I.C.I. first disclosed that they were contemplating a take-over bid on 15th November, 1961, when they said they might offer a price so attractive as to outweigh Courtaulds' firm objections on industrial grounds.

The first definite proposal in writing was made in I.C.I.'s letter delivered by hand on Saturday, 16th December, 1961. For reasons which are still obscure its main contents were disclosed publicly by I.C.I. on the following Monday, 18th December, 1961, without reference to anyone in Courtaulds.

INDUSTRIAL ARGUMENTS AGAINST THE TAKE-OVER

Courtaulds Board firmly believe that the fields of business of the two companies, their organisations and their industrial philosophies are so different that a take-over would fail to bring benefits to stockholders, or to employees or to customers of Courtaulds.

I.C.I. Directors seem to believe that by control of all the fibres and of all the raw materials they could regulate supplies to the market to suit the I.C.I. investment programme. Courtaulds know from their very much longer and wider experience in fibres that it is imperative to understand the needs of the customer and to meet them on a competitive basis.

The economies which the I.C.I. Directors envisage are trivial in relation to the turnover and profits of the two groups and are principally in research and promotion expenditure in the narrow field of 'Terylene.'

FINANCIAL ARGUMENTS AGAINST I.C.I.'s TERMS

As indicated in the Courtaulds Financial Statement of 24th January, 1962, already sent to you, the year 1962/3 and the following years are expected to show a rapid growth in the profitability of your Company's wide range of activities. This reflects both the effective action taken by the Board in recent years to overcome the industrial problems with which they have been faced and also the development of new activities and fibres.

Your Directors have already informed you that they must advise stockholders to reject the offer of £4 I.C.I. Ordinary Stock for every £5 Courtaulds Ordinary Stock (itself an increase on the original 3 for 4 offer) on the grounds that it seriously undervalues the earning capacity of Courtaulds in relation to that of I.C.I.

I.C.I. have now themselves tacitly admitted the inadequacy of their second proposal by making a further and alternative offer in 6½% Convertible Unsecured Loan Stock.

In his letter dated 14th February, 1962, addressed to Robert Fleming & Co. Limited and Morgan Grenfell & Co. Limited, Mr. S. P. Chambers advises the Courtaulds Stockholders that, in making their choice whether or not to accept the I.C.I. offer, " it is necessary to compare the past performance of the two Companies, their current position and their future prospects ". Nowhere, however, are these comparisons made by Mr. Chambers or his advisers. This is hardly surprising since, as shown by the graph which follows, the comparisons disclose clearly that on **all counts—net assets, past and present earnings and future prospects—the I.C.I. offer of 4 for 5 is totally inadequate.**

The figures from which the graph has been prepared are those included in I.C.I.'s offer, with the following additions:—

(a) Courtaulds estimate of profit for the year ending 31st March, 1962 of £17,500,000.

(b) The forecasts of profits for the next three years. The figures which have been used for this purpose are those exchanged by the two companies in December, 1961.

Proportion attributable to Courtaulds Ordinary Stockholders of combined Net Assets available for Ordinary Capital and combined Equity Earnings of I.C.I. and Courtaulds.

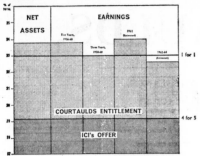

NOTES:

1. I.C.I.'s figures are for calendar years, and the corresponding Courtaulds figures are those for the years ending in each case on the subsequent 31st March.

2. The assets and profits of British Nylon Spinners Ltd. have been consolidated since, if the two groups were to be merged, it would become a wholly-owned subsidiary of I.C.I.

3. The profits of British Celanese Ltd. and of Pinchin, Johnson & Associates Ltd. have been consolidated with those of Courtaulds both before and after acquisition since the Ordinary Capital of both those companies was acquired by issuing fully paid Ordinary Stock of Courtaulds.

Appendix II to the I.C.I. offer gives a misleading impression of I.C.I.'s growth insofar as it only shows Group income and does not disclose the issued capital to which such income relates. During the period I.C.I. has raised some £80,000,000 by the issue of new Ordinary Capital.

A more appropriate method of examining their growth and that of Courtaulds is to express equity earnings as a proportion of issued Ordinary Capital. This is shown in the graph below from which it will be seen that taking into account the bonus and cash issues:—

(a) I.C.I.'s earnings per £ of issued Ordinary Capital were less in 1961 than they were in 1951;

(b) in 1961 and indeed in all but 3 of the last 11 years Courtaulds earnings per £ of issued Ordinary Capital were greater than those of I.C.I.

COURTAULDS AND I.C.I.
EARNINGS PER £ OF ORDINARY STOCK

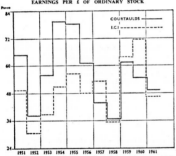

NOTE: The earnings per £1 of issued ordinary stock of each company on which this graph is based have been calculated as follows:—

The gross equivalent (after taking into account income tax at the standard rate applicable to the ensuing fiscal year) of the profit after taxation and after deduction of the net amounts applicable to minority interests and net preference dividends, as shown in the published consolidated accounts, and of half of the retained earnings of British Nylon Spinners. has been expressed as a percentage of the issued ordinary share capital at the end of each year adjusted for subsequent bonus issues.

I.C.I.'s figures are for calendar years and the corresponding Courtaulds figures are those for the years ending in each case on the subsequent 31st March.

The facts set out above show conclusively that an exchange of Courtaulds Ordinary Stock into I.C.I. Ordinary Stock on a 4 for 5 basis would be disadvantageous both now and throughout the period of the options offered by I.C.I. in connection with their proposed Loan Stock.

COURTAULDS PROPOSALS

Your Directors have every confidence in the future of Courtaulds and they have formulated certain plans for its future policy and reorganisation.

Investment Trust

It is recognised that at the present time Courtaulds hold, outside their trading activities, substantial assets on which only a low rate of return is being obtained. In these circumstances the value of these assets has not been fully reflected in the price of the Courtaulds Ordinary Stock. As a first step towards remedying this position, it is intended to transfer to a wholly-owned subsidiary the principal trade investments of Courtaulds, other than that in British Nylon Spinners. It is also intended to transfer to this subsidiary such liquid assets, including Government Securities, as can be regarded as surplus to the requirements of Courtaulds trading activities, as well as a number of properties which are not required for manufacturing operations. Taking the investment in Snia Viscosa at its present market value, it is expected that the current value of the assets to be transferred will be of the magnitude of some £40,000,000.

The subsidiary will be run as an Investment Trust and suitably experienced individuals from outside the Group will be invited to join its Board.

It is believed that under vigorous management, the Investment Trust will have considerable potential and your Board have every intention of making appropriate arrangements in due course for passing on to Stockholders the full benefits expected to arise from its development.

The accounts of the Investment Trust will be published as a separate part of the accounts of the Courtaulds Group.

Dividend Policy.

Your Directors have already stated their belief that the resources of Courtaulds should allow a policy of consistent and steadily increasing dividend distributions. **They have now decided that it will be their policy in the future to recommend for distribution by way of dividend the whole of the income, after expenses, of the Investment Trust, together with all other investment income and not less than 50% of their trading profits.** They have taken the following further detailed decisions:—

(a) **1961/62 Dividend.** Although the current year which ends on 31st March, 1962 began badly and the first half year's profit only amounted to £7,600,000, trading has now improved to the point that, as already indicated, profit for the second half of the financial year is expected to be approximately £10,000,000, i.e. at an annual rate of £20,000,000. Bearing in mind the Company's strong cash position and future profit expectations, the Board are satisfied that they will be able properly to recommend a final dividend which will bring the total dividend for the year to 12½%.

(b) **1962/63 Dividend.** During the year ending 31st March, 1963 the first substantial benefits of the acquisition in November, 1961 of British Enka will be felt, and it is expected that the improvement in trade indicated above will continue. Your Directors have already informed you of their estimate of profit of £23,000,000 in respect of that year. Such profit (after meeting 'interest on the Loan Stock referred to below) would in the light of the policy decision referred to above justify the recommendation of a total dividend for the year of not less than 13%.

(c) **Tax-free Distributions.** The reorganisation of the Group's activities carried out in the last few years, together with the development of new fibres, should result in increasing profits and dividends. In order to supplement the Ordinary dividends during the next few years of growth, it has been decided to recommend out of capital profits a **special cash distribution of 2½% free of tax in each of the three years 1961/62, 1962/63 and 1963/64.**

Unsecured Loan Stock.

Since it will be some years before the full benefits of the above arrangements are felt by Stockholders, it is desired to make an effective distribution to them immediately. Accordingly it has been decided (subject to the consent of H.M. Treasury for which application has already been made) to recommend the capitalisation of some £40,000,000 of reserves (representing capital profits) by the issue to Ordinary Stockholders, credited as fully paid, of 10/- of a 7% Unsecured Loan Stock 1982/87 for each £1 of Ordinary Stock. Application will be made to the Council of the Stock Exchange, London, for permission to deal in and for quotation for this Stock which it is considered will command a price of at least par in the market. Stockholders will thus be in a position to realise for cash a part of their investment without giving up any of their interest in the equity of Courtaulds.

CASH FLOW

Your Directors are satisfied that the cash flow of the Group will be sufficient, after the proposals set out above have been implemented, to finance their present plans for capital expenditure and to provide adequate working capital.

CONCLUSION

It has been pointed out earlier in this letter that I.C.I.'s offer to convert into its Ordinary Stock on a 4 for 5 basis under-values Courtaulds Ordinary Stock both now and during the option period. Under the alternative Loan Stock offer, therefore, a holder of Courtaulds Ordinary Stock is in effect being asked to part with the whole of his equity in Courtaulds for a fixed interest security on terms which your Directors are convinced are quite inadequate.

The following table shows the gross income which a holder of £100 Courtaulds Ordinary Stock could expect to receive under each of the three choices open to him:

	1961/62	1962/63
If I.C.I.'s 4 for 5 offer were to be accepted	£10	£11
If I.C.I.'s offer of Loan Stock were to be accepted	£10	£16 5s. 0d.
If Stockholders support Courtaulds and reject I.C.I's offers:		
Ordinary Dividend	£12 10s. 0d.	£13 minimum
Gross equivalent of 2½% tax free payment	£4	£4
Loan Stock	—	£3 10s. 0d.
	£16 10s. 0d.	£20 10s. 0d.

After consultation with their financial advisers, Baring Brothers & Co., Limited, and Binder, Hamlyn & Co., Chartered Accountants, the Directors of Courtaulds strongly recommend their Stockholders to reject the I.C.I. offers and to place their confidence in the future of Courtaulds as an independent and progressive company.

Notices convening an Extraordinary General Meeting of the Company on the 15th March, 1962, a proxy paper for the Meeting and resolutions and details regarding the proposed Unsecured Loan Stock will be posted to you shortly.

J. C. HANBURY-WILLIAMS,
(Chairman).
A. H. WILSON,
15th February, 1962.　　　　　　　*(Chairman Designate).*

It is recognised that at the present time Courtaulds hold, outside their trading activities, substantial assets on which only a low rate of return is being obtained. In these circumstances the value of these assets has not been fully reflected in the price of the Courtaulds Ordinary Stock. As a first step towards remedying this position, it is intended to transfer to a wholly-owned subsidiary the principal trade investments of Courtaulds, other than that in British Nylon Spinners. It is also intended to transfer to this subsidiary such liquid assets, including Government Securities, as can be regarded as surplus to the requirements of Courtaulds' trading activities, as well as a number of properties which are not required for manufacturing operations. . . . it is expected that the current value of the assets to be transferred will be of the magnitude of some £40,000,000.

The subsidiary will be run as an Investment Trust and suitably experienced individuals from outside the Group will be invited to join its Board.

It is believed that under vigorous management, the Investment Trust will have considerable potential and your Board has every intention of making appropriate arrangements in due course for passing on to Stockholders the full benefits expected to arise from its development.[7]

The next section of the announcement contained details of the promised change in dividend policy:

[Courtaulds' directors] have now decided that it will be their policy in the future to recommend for distribution by way of dividend the whole of the income, after expenses, of the Investment Trust, together with all other investment income and not less than 50% of their trading profits.[7]

The details of this change were as follows. The dividend for the fiscal year 1961/1962 would be 12.5 per cent (a percentage based on the par value of a common share). The dividend for 1962/63 would be "not less than 13%," it was expected. In addition, for each year 1961/62, 1962/63, 1963/64, a special tax-free dividend of 2.5 per cent "out of capital profits" would be paid.

Finally, Courtaulds proposed, subject to Treasury approval, to capitalise £40,000,000 of its reserves and create a new security, the 7 per cent Unsecured Loan Stock. Each Courtaulds' shareholder would receive 10s. of this Loan Stock for every £1 (at par value) of Courtaulds' common.

Thus Courtaulds were (*a*) increasing their regular dividend, (*b*) promising a special extra dividend out of capital profits, and (*c*) giving stockholders a high "dividend" of loan stock as well. It was hardly surprising that, having done all this, Courtaulds ended their announcement by comparing the income Courtaulds' shareholders would receive under the new dividend proposals with the income they would receive as I.C.I. stockholders. Courtaulds came out comfortably ahead on this comparison.

This latest move was, as the *Financial Times* succinctly observed, the "up-ending of the Courtaulds' cornucopia." It was Courtaulds' most powerful weapon, and it was effective. The price of Courtaulds' common rose to 52*s*. Courtaulds' management had finally pushed the price above the 50*s*. level imputed by I.C.I.'s third offer.

The announcement by Courtaulds, together with I.C.I.'s third offer, proved to be the final major attack of each side. I.C.I. did not raise their offer again, nor did Courtaulds further increase their promises of dividend generosity. At this point, all that remained was for Courtaulds' shareholders to decide what to do.

*   *   *   *   *

One rather curious development, which had occurred earlier in February, may have had some influence on the outcome of the take-over attempt. On Sunday, February 11, London papers broke the story of Russia's involvement in the affair. Kearton, it was announced, had spent February 5–7 in Rome in conference with Mr. Vlas Klentsov, head of Russia's Techmashimport, the Soviet state-controlled buying agency.

Mr. Klentsov, it was reported, had told Kearton that Russia was most anxious that I.C.I. not gain control of Courtaulds. To this end, Russia was immediately prepared to place a contract with Courtaulds for a £7,000,000 textile plant in Latvia. Italian and American firms had been competing for this contract.

During the take-over attempt, many of Courtaulds' foreign customers had expressed their support for Courtaulds, and Russia had been one of the leaders in this camp. The U.S.S.R. had, since 1958, placed £20,000,000 worth of orders with Courtaulds and relied heavily on the company's technological skills, it was reported. Courtaulds had maintained very friendly relations with a number of the Communist countries and had been a major supplier of many of them for some time. Just what effect Russia's involvement had on the I.C.I.-Courtaulds affair, if any, cannot be accurately measured.

*   *   *   *   *

All the major barrages had now been fired (ending with Courtaulds' final details on generous dividends announced February 14), but the mechanics of the war continued. Although I.C.I. had announced their terms back in December and subsequently raised the terms twice, it was only on February 14 that they posted to Courtaulds' shareholders their first formal offer. This offer, which had been approved by I.C.I.'s board on February 8, contained the third set of terms (4-for-5 or the loan stock); it announced that both operations would be kept open until March 8, but that I.C.I. reserved the right to discontinue the loan stock offer after that time.

Shortly after their announcement of February 14, Courtaulds announced that they would go ahead with their new dividend and investment trust policies unless I.C.I. acquired over 90 per cent of Courtaulds' common. Courtaulds had already called an Extraordinary General Meeting for March 15, at which time the new dividend and investment trust proposals would be submitted for stockholder approval.

On February 28, I.C.I. made their second formal offer to Courtaulds' shareholders; the terms of the offer were unchanged, but I.C.I. were now making their offer unconditional, regardless of the percentage of Courtaulds' stock they should acquire. This announcement committed I.C.I. to accepting a minority position in Courtaulds if they should not acquire over 50 per cent of the common. I.C.I. also announced that, in order to be equitable, they would not extend the 4-for-5 offer beyond March 8 unless the loan stock offer were also extended. This removed pressure from Courtaulds' stockholders, a pressure which many London financial observers had argued was unfair.

This change [I.C.I.'s willingness to accept a minority position] was on the whole well received, but there were a few shrewd observers who thought it a major error of judgment. It reduced the pressure to accept and it greatly diminished Chambers' own room for manoeuvre. After he had done this he was entirely in the hands of the Courtaulds' shareholders. He had no option but to take whatever result they chose to give him.

But the issue remained in doubt for at least another week [after February 28], although there was a growing feeling of confidence among the Courtaulds' directors. Once they had succeeded in creating a mixed and confused picture so far as relative investment prospects were concerned, they had two powerful forces working on their side amongst their small shareholders. The first was a vague feeling of loyalty to the smaller, more personal and, to them, better-known firm. The second was inertia. It is always easier to do nothing than something, to postpone a decision rather than to take one. And to support I.C.I. positive action had to be taken. To support Courtaulds nothing had to be done.

Among the bigger investors these considerations had little influence, but they were replaced by a belief that Chambers had misplayed his hand; and by a fear that the deal, if it went through, was likely to cause more political and other trouble than it was worth.[4]

The Economist of March 10 tabulated the opinions of the major British financial journals as to what Courtaulds' stockholders should do:

CITY EDITORS' VOTE

Stockholders in Courtaulds have been given plenty of advice—from ICI, Courtaulds, their brokers, their bank managers, their friends, the know-alls in the pub and the financial press. The advice given by leading newspapers in the last few days, tabulated below, cannot show all the qualifications made by the financial journalists. Many listed in the pro-Courtaulds camp, for instance, said: hold on to

Courtaulds if you are in for the long term but sell in the market if you are a short term speculator. And some described as neutralists, including this paper, were prepared to back the new men at Courtaulds a good part of the way.[8]

For Courtaulds	For I.C.I.
The Times	The Guardian
The Financial Times	The Daily Mail
The Daily Telegraph	The Sunday Times
The Daily Express	The Evening Standard
The Birmingham Post	The Statist
The Evening News	*Neutralists*
The Sunday Times	The Scotsman
The Observer	The Glasgow Herald
The Sunday Telegraph	The Yorkshire Post
The Investors Chronicle	The Stock Exchange Gazette
The Investors Guide	The Economist

Finally, on Thursday, March 8, when the offer was due to expire, I.C.I. announced that they were extending the offer until 3:00 p.m. on March 12; they did not indicate what percentage of common stock had so far been pledged to them.

Everything was now done except for tallying up the score. I.C.I.'s terms were finally "final," and Courtaulds had gone as far as they would in promising increased dividend distribution for the future. In the first week of March, informed observers gradually changed their positions: from having thought at the outset that I.C.I. could hardly lose, they now were prepared to admit that I.C.I. would be lucky to acquire a simple majority of the shares and might, even, end up with a large but inconclusive minority.

*   *   *   *   *

END OF THE BATTLE AND AFTERMATH

At noon on March 12, the news tickers read:

The offer for the Ordinary Stock of Courtaulds Limited will close at 3 p.m. today, March 12th, and will not be extended. Acceptances so far received amount, subject to confirmation, to 37.4% of Courtaulds' Ordinary Stock.

It was subsequently learned that, during the extension period from March 8–12, I.C.I. had acquired only 0.7 per cent. Clearly, extending the offer again with the same terms would have produced no significant increase in I.C.I.'s holding.

One analysis of the outcome and its implications was made by *The Economist*:

If ICI, halfway through the struggle, had not made its alternative offer of convertible loan stock, it would have commanded no more than a handful of supporters. The assents it received have come largely from institutions who have taken the loan stock primarily for its good running yield, and only secondarily as an escape from the present uncertainties of the equity market with the option of getting back in if conditions next year or later are more favourable. Some private holders of Courtaulds sold out, but the vast majority decided to stand by their directors.

The complex of reason and emotion that swayed the individual stockholder led many observers astray; but, in the broadest terms, three factors appear to have been especially important. First, many investors resented the aggressive, dogmatic manner in which Mr. Paul Chambers and ICI saw the only possible answer to the problems of the man-made fibre industry in submitting Courtaulds to a total merger. Secondly, in the course of the battle, Courtaulds' directors convinced many stockholders that the stuffy, conservative past was dead and that the new men with their new policies, embodied in a number of far-reaching forecasts and promises, would henceforth keep their interests in the forefront. Thirdly, a week before the closing date, when ICI declared its offer virtually unconditional, it admitted that it was prepared, if need be, to hold a minority interest in Courtaulds and could justify paying about 50s. a share. This tactical error has created a situation that is surely without parallel in British industrial history. What an unsuccessful bidder normally arranges is to slip out; but ICI made this impossible for itself and so remains as holder of a substantial minority interest.

What has been said and done in the last three months by the two sides must profoundly influence their future—how, no one can foretell, for the main personalities must first set themselves on constructive courses. It could be argued that although it now has over a third of the Courtaulds' equity ICI really has no mandate except to hold the shares as a trade investment. But could ICI be expected to "neutralise" its holding in Courtaulds as Imperial Tobacco has done with its 37 per cent in Gallaher? A holding of this sort is more likely to form the base from which either mischief or some form of reconciliation could be attempted. Some of the moves in the closing stages of the struggle suggested hope of conciliation; but there is an equal possibility that unless both sides practise a little accommodation, war could continue with ICI as a militant minority interest.

This week ICI has refused to give any hint about its future course and certainly a breathing space in which emotions and tempers can cool is welcome. Nor has Courtaulds any ready-made solution to offer; it, too, wants time to reflect. One can, presumably, disregard the possibility that ICI might be tempted to buy more Courtaulds' shares to gain control (which would cost about £27½ million) or would try to dispose quickly of the investment it has already made. Courtaulds would certainly consider possible forms of cooperation, but while it is not in the nature of Mr. Chambers to come to Canossa, it is he who has argued for a complete merger. If a hint came that ICI was now prepared to discuss answers to the problems of the man-made fibres industry other than its own decisively rejected solution of an outright merger, a way might be opened.

In the past the two companies have sought remedies in opposed directions; ICI in vertical integration and Courtaulds in greater independence from the suppliers of basic raw materials. After last year's abortive negotiations and the hard words about basic differences in industrial philosophies, is any workable scheme of technical cooperation possible? Negotiations to this end could easily fail, but they would have served some purpose if they created an improved atmosphere and diminished the prospect of perpetual war between two companies that are tied together as suppliers and customers, as partners in British Nylon Spinners, and as stockholders.

But before they can seriously talk to each other about their future, both ICI and Courtaulds have to take an objective look at their own organizations. ICI has come out of the struggle far weaker than it went in. The weaknesses were there already; they have now been exposed to public scrutiny and criticism. ICI's chairman, Mr. Paul Chambers, has suffered a personal rebuff, not merely for the policies he has advocated, but even more for the manner in which he has tried to impose them. It may be that some other ICI directors followed his lead with increasing misgivings; but they did follow him and they must feel bound by the doctrine of collective responsibility in the boardroom to offer no support to suggestions that Mr. Chambers, having so signally failed, should now resign. Yet, for all his outstanding gifts, Mr. Chambers will hardly be able to lead ICI with the same ebullient self confidence in his own ideas and in the "big brother" philosophy of ICI as he did in the past.

The difficulties currently confronting ICI and the chemical industry have been sharply exposed. ICI has also lost goodwill among the investing public and it will go into a conference—with Courtaulds or anyone else—with less prestige and fewer friends than it possessed less than a hundred days ago. One way of regaining favour is to be reasonable and circumspect in its future dealings with Courtaulds. In its turn, Courtaulds would like to get back to "square one"—back to a situation and atmosphere where its representatives and ICI's could examine fresh solutions to their mutual problems. The Courtaulds' directors have not had time to formulate what solutions they would find acceptable. Nor has ICI; though on the day of defeat Mr. Chambers continued to extol the virtues of vertical integration. The proposals put up by Courtaulds at the "truce" conference in January envisaged either the formation of a joint company to deal with all melt-spun (i.e. non-rayon) fibres, in which ICI would have a majority interest, or of a joint company to deal with all fibres, in which Courtaulds would have a majority interest. If these were the absolute limits of conciliation that Courtaulds were prepared to stomach at that time, it must be seriously questioned whether it would be prepared to go so far now. But the possibility of some joint venture with ICI in melt-spun fibres over and above that already established in British Nylon Spinners cannot be ruled out, though any idea that ICI might transfer its interests in polymers and fibres to Courtaulds seems to be a non-starter. The two companies may in the end decide that some rigid scheme for a further joint venture in man-made fibres is impossible; in that case, let them be opposed in competition, but partners against mutual destruction.

Courtaulds has its own real problems to settle. In one sense, it can never get back to "square one" as it existed last September; the new voices have been lavish with promises and they have shifted decisively the balance of power with St. Martin's-le-Grand. The shift is not finished yet, nor has its effectiveness yet been proved. In the rayon division, for instance, senior executives whose experience stems from the palmier days for viscose might create a barrier of change to policies keyed to leaner, more competitive days. At the top level—in the boardroom itself —a real drama is being played. Some of the Courtaulds' directors are on the point of retirement, the present chairman, Sir John Hanbury-Williams, among them. Their retirement presents an opportunity for demonstrating conclusively that mediaeval traditions, epitomised in the discussions that led to the arrogant decision (and gigantic error) to reduce the interim dividend in November, are truly dead and buried. It could also open the way to the most conciliatory gesture—that Courtaulds accepts representation of its biggest stockholder, ICI, on the board.

Sir Alan Wilson has already been designated as Sir John's successor. He figured prominently in last year's discussions with ICI but took no great part in the battle from December onwards; his somewhat aloof, intellectual personality appeared to be smothered by the fire and smoke. Whether he was more attracted to the idea of a merger with ICI than some of his colleagues would be impertinent for an outsider to guess. Should he decide to accept the chairmanship of Courtaulds, he will have the full support of his colleagues. If he does not, an obvious candidate may at first sight appear to be at hand in the person of Mr. Frank Kearton, whose fire, courage and ability, supported by Mr. H. R. Mathys and Mr. A. W. Knight and other Courtaulds' directors, have made a decisive mark. But although there can be no doubt of his ultimate role in the future conduct of Courtaulds' affairs, it may still be true that the task of building bridges may be better undertaken for a few years by someone from outside who can bring independence as well as experience to bear upon Courtaulds' problems. The crucial question of Sir John's successor will have to be settled before Courtaulds can explore any area of agreement between itself and ICI.

Courtaulds has emerged from the struggle both stronger and weaker—stronger because the majority of stockholders have been persuaded to overlook the past (though many of them cannot have forgotten it) and to pin their faith on new men with new policies and promises, and weaker because ICI's minority holding breaches the St. Martin's-le-Grand citadel and could easily bring it down if the directors fail to justify the faith that investors are now putting in them. Their promises about future profits and dividends are halters that they have knotted round their own necks. If the knot tightens, it will be their own fault. Courtaulds' shares, currently standing at 50*s*., will not have to fall much below that level before the growls are heard. The only mandate the Courtaulds board has been given is to do as well as they promise and this prospect could be jeopardised if they failed to reach some sort of concordat with ICI.

Homilies and admonishments are thick in the air. The role that the Government can play in regulating monopolies and the engrossment of a market needs to be re-examined. So, too, does the ill-defined nexus of relations between a company and its directors, and the stockholders and general public. This goes far beyond a public relations image. Courtaulds' decision about the interim dividend has, in the end, provided another demonstration that the interests of stockholders can be ignored only at the directors' peril. The remedy does not lie in creating impressions of remote boardroom benevolence, but in the readiness of directors to treat stockholders responsibly and to justify candidly and publicly the courses they pursue. Equally, what has happened to ICI demonstrates that lasting goodwill is not built on an image of what a company thinks it would like to be, but on what it actually is. A man greater in his faults and virtues than any at Millbank or St. Martin's-le-Grand once asked to be painted, warts and all. ICI, Courtaulds and other companies should have learnt some such humility from this bitter and at times shoddy episode.[9]

And, finally, a briefer analysis also stressed some of the same points made by *The Economist:*

Chambers had bad luck. He could hardly have foreseen the emergence of an unexpected pattern of power relationships within the Courtaulds' board. Once the unexpected had happened, however, he showed an excessive rigidity of approach and an unwise deployment of one bid after another. Had he been generous to begin with, he might well have won. But here again he was perhaps misled by the early talks giving him no full picture of the financial strength of Courtaulds.

Courtaulds themselves emerged from the struggle committed up to the hilt to giving their shareholders every penny that they could reasonably lay their hands on, but also greatly shaken up and improved from a management point of view. Their new look will give them a better prospect as an independent company, but will it make them more able to co-operate with the company which now owns more than a third of their equity? And without this co-operation, will the internal strains not be intolerable?[4]

On July 5, 1962, Courtaulds' common closed at 42s. 7½d.; I.C.I. at 52s. 9d. Courtaulds' shareholders had received, as promised, one 10s. share of loan stock for each common share held, and this loan stock was selling slightly above par.

PUBLISHED QUOTATION: SOURCES USED

SOURCE:

FOOTNOTE
NUMBER:

1.* *The Observer Weekend Review*, London, March 18, 1962, pp. 21 and 24.
2. *The Economist*, London, December 23, 1962, pp. 1227–28.
3.* *The Observer Weekend Review*, London, March 25, 1962, p. 21.
4.* *The Observer Weekend Review*, London, April 1, 1962.
5. "Courtaulds, Limited: Financial Statement." This advertisement appeared in many publications, among others in *The Investors Chronicle*, London, January 26, 1962, pp. 294–96.
6. *The Economist*, London, January 27, 1962, p. 341.
7. "Courtaulds, Limited: Advice to Stockholders." This advertisement appeared in many publications, among others in *The Financial Times*, London, February 16, 1962, p. 17.
8. *The Economist*, London, March 10, 1962, p. 927.
9. *The Economist*, London, March 17, 1962, pp. 1037–39.

---

* These formed a series of three articles in the *Weekend Review;* the articles, written by Roy Jenkins, M.P., were entitled "How I.C.I. Became a Thwarted Giant."

PART VII

Executive Control and Executive Leadership

THE MATERIALS in this section cover a variety of topics. The subject matter can be dealt with in much more expanded form if the companion casebook, *Problems of General Management*, by Learned, Christensen, and Andrews is used. Or it can be expanded by assigning expository reading on these topics, as the professor chooses.

The first article included in this section, "Of What Use Is a Board of Directors," by Dr. Vannevar Bush has stimulated excellent discussion in many classroom situations. If the class is an executive training group, a simple question like "What is the role of the board of directors in your company?" will get discussion off to an excellent start. At IMEDE, where the international nature of the student body is the outstanding element in the situation, raising a question as to the applicability of the views of Dr. Bush "in your country or your nation" actually sparked one of the most interesting discussions of the entire year. An Italian banker, for instance, talked to this point constructively for nearly 45 minutes. Egyptians talked about top-level control in a country which mixes state and modified private enterprise. Germans, Swiss, Japanese, and others were eager to add their special contributions.

The "Note on German Business Organizations" included next in this section of the book is designed to stimulate thinking about the impact which different kinds of corporate structures might have on the pattern or the problems of leadership and control. The note describes a variety of corporate forms; outlines some intercompany relationships that have no counterpart in the United States; and also presents data on organizational arrangements in companies of different size.

The third case, Société des Machines Marveau, reveals arrangements made by a Belgian company for the institution of a junior board of directors. This case permits participants to analyze the conditions under which the idea developed, the objectives of the board, and the varying concepts regarding the role of the junior board held by various members of top management and members of the board.

The Rugby Portland Cement Company is a series raising varied discussion points. The (A) case describes the basic concept of management and leadership held by the chairman, and his use of profit sharing and the "A-share plan" as devices to get personnel to internalize his goals. The (B) case, based on selected interviews at different plants with down-the-line personnel, permits students to diagnose, explain, and evaluate the results achieved. Among these results is an increasingly rare, very tight discipline of the work force. It is interesting to argue whether this result could be achieved by the chairman's methods in other situations.

Next, we have included in this section three articles from the *Harvard Business Review* dealing with some aspects of executive control. The two on decentralized profit responsibility by Professor Dearden present both the good points and the limits of profit-centered control on a decentralized basis. Professor Likert's article on "Motivational Approach to Management Development" has implications for both executive control and executive development.

The final case in this section, Société Normacem, brings to a head the discussion of leadership philosophy and the leadership role of top management. At this point readers are urged to review other patterns of leadership described in the cases in this book or elsewhere. A particularly interesting comparison may be made between this company and the much smaller Galvor Company (next in the text) in respect to the problems of executive development, delegation of responsibility, and leadership confronting the top executive in each case.

OF WHAT USE IS A BOARD OF DIRECTORS?*

The following material was prepared by Dr. Vannevar Bush in connection with his duties as a member of a corporate board of directors. It was privately printed and circulated among directors of a number of corporations. Dr. Bush was a former member of the faculty and chairman of the Massachusetts Institute of Technology Corporation and president of Carnegie Institution of Washington, 1939–55. He has been a director of Metals and Controls Corporation, American Telephone and Telegraph Company, Merck & Co., Inc., Putnam Fund, and Director of the Office of Scientific Research and Development, United States government, 1941–46.

*　　*　　*　　*　　*

Large American companies have evolved into a form quite in contrast with the original pattern. It is true that small companies continue to appear, in which a group of individuals furnish the capital, adding to this by providing for a minority public interest, and borrowing from banks but holding full control themselves. But, sooner or later, great growth, the dying-out of the originators, the effect of estate taxes produce a form in which control becomes diluted and diffused. The trend is accentuated today by a shift in the status of investors in common stocks, under the pressure of high income taxes and an increase in the number of individuals able and willing to make savings in this way. The extent to which large companies have proceeded along this path toward diffusion of control differs greatly, but the trend is general. It is a salutary trend on the whole, but it has its inevitable dangers.

In the fully developed form of organization, control resides in a self-perpetuating management, including a board of directors either made up from management, or in effect largely selected by management. There are wide variations here. The form under which the board is made up of operating personnel only has usually appeared when a strong individual or family in the background exercised its control in that manner, and relations become strained at times, as that family control becomes diluted. An offset, and an interesting one, is then to add a number of so-called public directors, selected by the management, representing no special

---

* Reproduced by special permission of the author, Dr. Vannevar Bush.

financial or business interest, paid a retainer for their part-time services, ordinarily active only on the more general problems of the business, but sometimes forming an exceedingly important court of last resort when there is an internal crisis, such as sudden disability of the operating head. Another common form is one in which, as the original control through concentrated stock ownership becomes spread, the company is in effect taken over by a group of directors representing special interest, financial and otherwise, who maintain their positions by mutual understanding rather than by any explicit stock representation. Laws regarding interlocking directorates have rendered this form much less prevalent.

The soundest form is undoubtedly one in which the board and management together make up a self-perpetuating group, the former part-time and the latter full-time, acting together to choose all replacements, with the external interests of board members so widely spread or remote that the company welfare is paramount in all decisions. This state of affairs is not easy to bring about, but it has been achieved in some instances. Its advent is rendered difficult by a dearth of qualified personnel; there are not enough individuals in the country capable of bringing sound judgment to important boards; those that are qualified are often spread too thin to be of great service; and men of genuine talents for such work but without established reputation are hard to find and present a hazard, in that they may not work out well in novel relationships. It is a notable fact, however, that a few progressive companies which are still in the position where effective stock control resides in an individual or a small group are nevertheless creating boards with extensive independent membership. The combination of independent directors with directors who represent important blocks of stock, or other legitimate interests, seems to work out well. In fact, the trend toward this form seems to be fully as marked in such companies as in the large company where there is no real remaining stock control.

American business seems to be at a crossroads in regard to the problem of independent directors. It does not have the old German system, where outstanding professors in many fields in universities were more or less expected to serve on industrial boards. It has not extensively adopted the British system of creating a group of individuals with special professional qualifications who earn their living by serving as directors. It is justly distrustful of both these schemes. When it seeks independent directors, it does so with the distinct impression that it is trying an experiment. There are some companies of such standing that they can attract outstanding individuals merely because of the prestige of being on the board, or even because of the genuine opportunity for performing a public service.

Just as there is no doubt, in spite of public cynicism, that a significant fraction of government posts are thus filled, sometimes under conditions where there is neither glory nor opportunity for advancement, and some personal hazard is incurred—so there is no doubt that such motives are increasingly operative in large business. There is also a salutary tendency to utilize in boards of directors the services of men who have retired from active business. Fortunately, sound judgment is likely to be retained by an individual long after he should relinquish all direct executive activities. Sometimes, not often, a man retired from the business itself can safely be used thus. More often men from associated professional groups or allied business will be more dependable in times of difficulty. But even these two sources of directors do not fully solve the problem, for there are not enough such individuals to go around, and they again tend to become spread too thin and to fail to understand any one business fully. Moreover, when they are paid a nominal sum rather than being on a retainer, there is an understandable reluctance to call on them for much real service. Thus, in the country as a whole, we approach the problem of the independent director somewhat timidly and without confidence. This is inevitable, and perhaps just as well, for experimentation is desirable until a pattern becomes established. But under present trends the problem needs to be solved.

The management of a company and the directors have a four-way responsibility: to their stockholders, to the public they serve, to their labor force, and to government. Fortunately there is growing in the country a management group with a distinctly professional outlook and a sense of social responsibility of a high order, with pride in resistance to arbitrary pressure, and an esprit de corps which is based on none of the trappings or ritual of the older professions, but which has fully as much coherence and exclusiveness. None is admitted to the circle unless he qualifies, in rather subtle ways, seldom expressed, but nonetheless real. This is not to claim that there are no longer any pirates or buccaneers about in American industry or that the pulling of an interlaced fabric of strings for coarse purposes is obsolete. It is merely to note that there has been increasingly superposed a salutary trend toward something much more solid, which is indeed the hope of large independent business in this country. It is not to claim, either, that competitive business can be operated successfully in an altruistic haze or with an idealist's disregard of hard facts or that, merely because the objectives of the managing group are sound and in the public interest, it will be safe from encroachments of several sorts. But it is to assert that many American business organizations, an increasing number, have created governing groups at the top which are well rewarded, open to any individual having enough brains, perseverance, and ambition as judged generally by his peers, and, it must be admitted, having also good health and a bit of luck; governing groups which are self-perpetuating and which have risen far above the mere crude idea of making a dollar in a turbulent, complex, and often amoral market place. With full recognition of their responsibility to stockholders, they nevertheless take a broader view of their social responsibilities. It is an extraordinary and salutary development. It will be well to examine how such a group operates to best advantage.

The most important function of a board of the sort described is to select the operating head of the company. When that problem arises, the board needs to go into action vigorously as an independent body, open to advice, but exercising full and prompt control. If it does this job well, it will not matter too much if it is largely an ornament in normal times. But it can still be useful, if it will, in normal times. It can then judge programs and plans, but should not undertake their formulation, for it should never enter directly into management. The board and its individual members can suggest, and these suggestions on all phases of the company's activities, coming from a group with highly diverse backgrounds, can be of genuine value. They will be truly valuable only if there is such understanding between board and management that rejection of a suggestion carries with it no embarrassment on the part of anyone concerned.

That a board should judge and not manage is a key point in proper relations. Any executive in any organization, no matter where placed, should be called upon to justify his important plans and programs before some individual or body competent to judge them adequately. The judgment should be sympathetic but nonetheless rigorous. This is desirable not only from the standpoint of the company, in the interest of sound planning, but even more so from the standpoint of the executive himself. The executive who has no review of his plans and programs except by committees of subordinates is in a tough spot. He needs to have a group before which he appears and presents his plans and from which he eventually draws approval; such review does not need to be exceedingly formal, but it needs to be very real. This is not merely a matter of the group's sharing responsibility with him, although that is important. It is a matter of his relations with his own staff and organization. He can lead strongly and at the same time consult freely with his subordinates if he is being supported by them in presenting his plans before a tough tribunal, not if he is being judged by his own subordinates. The worst case of all is when there is no review of his plans, either above or below. The principle of review holds at every level in an organization of course, but especially at the top. There it can be maintained only if the board actually sits in judgment and if it carefully refrains from entering into management and thus vitiating its exercise of its primary function.

This principle is often violated in industry. It is habitually violated in government, and that is government's greatest weakness. Many a government executive finds no sound centralized review of his plans at all, but rather a review spread piecemeal through a dozen bureaus, some of them hostile, all examining into minutiae, together with responsibility to a President so overburdened he hardly knows that particular executive exists, with a Congress in the offing ready to provide an annual ordeal. I can write with feeling on this point. It is not a system peculiar to democracy; in fact it probably takes worse forms under a dictatorship. But in the present state of public understanding, fractionization, confusion, overlapping authority, judgments based on special interests are inevitable in a political system. That is why a government usually manages badly. It is why the socialized state does not operate so well as private enterprise in the conduct of business of any complexity whatever. Confirmed socialists will claim that the same sound system can be created within government as within private enterprise, a pyramidal organization with proper staff cross-connections, provision for review of plans by disinterested groups, and all the rest. It never happens, except in the books. Government bureaus and officials will always interfere in a thousand ways and produce confusion. Military organizations avoid the morass to some extent by rigid chains of command and the indoctrination of the academies, but they get equally confused as soon as they go into business or even into purchasing. The primary difficulty is that there is no concrete effective top command, but a diffusion and confusion of this function. If a private industry is going to avoid the same pitfalls, it needs, above all, to maintain a board that operates effectively. The prime criterion is that the board must retain and exercise the function of final judgment and refrain from any other activity. True, many businesses operate well, at least for a time, with boards that are merely rubber stamps, and so do businesses that have no boards in the proper sense at all, but merely committees of management. Usually when such a business succeeds, it is because there is a really powerful control in the background, or the ghost of an earlier control not yet recognized as a ghost. Inertia, tradition, company loyalty can take even an imperfect system safely a long way. But, under present trends, it is essential that American industry organize soundly for the long pull, emphasizing the essential feature that distinguishes private enterprise from government ownership. The key is an effective board, properly constituted, vigorously retaining its prerogatives, acting as the judge and ultimate authority, the balance wheel for management but not a part of it.

The chief executive should sit on the board. It does not matter much whether he presides or not. With him should sit his executive officer, to be posted and ready to carry on if need be at a moment's notice. The system where there is a chairman, concerned primarily with external affairs, and a president who runs the company internally is workable. In such a case three officers should be present, for the president still needs his principal executive officer ready to carry on as a substitute. Beyond this there is serious question whether any officers of the company should sit as members of the board. If they do, they are in an equivocal position; either they are there merely to back up their chief, in which case their votes are an anomaly, or they are sitting in judgment on their chief's recommendations, which is an absurdity. It is an entirely different matter to invite them to be present when subjects which particularly concern them are under discussion. Under proper relationships many matters will be thrashed out in the board in preliminary fashion before going back to management to become explicit; in such cases, a wise chief can encourage his subordinates to present diverse opinions without embarrassment. The experience of presenting, for his chief, a program on which management is agreed is also excellent for a vice-president, and it usually cheers the board to listen to someone else than the president for a change. But it should always be crystal clear that, except when the president himself desires preliminary board discussion for guidance, nothing goes to the board from the management except the considered conclusions and plans of the president, initiated by him or in response to board initiation. If the board is not satisfied with the chief's performance, its members can reason with him privately, and the board can, if necessary, get a new chief; but it cannot enter into his relations with his staff without creating chaos. By the same token, the president is responsible before the board for the acts and omissions of all his subordinates, and if he tends to forget this, he needs to be reminded of one of the cardinal principles of sound organization.

Departures from the hourglass form of organization, with all internal matters funneling to and from the president, are embarked upon at great risk. A common form of departure in practice involves financial matters. Here the alternative path, from a part of the organization through a finance committee to the board, short-circuiting the president, often makes sense. In a university, for example, control of endowment in this manner is reasonable, particularly if the president's background in finance consisted of a course in economics thirty years before. The danger of a finance committee in which the president plays little or no part is that it will begin to exert management under the guise of financial control. There are then likely to be two managers of the business, and the devil to pay. On the other hand, a finance committee which passes on recommendations of the president regarding internal financial affairs, on their way to the board, and exercises control for the board within limits is all right, provided that it does not in effect relieve the full board of responsibility for important financial decisions. A finance committee can also itself properly initiate in the field of external financial relations, especially under conditions where internal and external responsibility are divided between a president and a chairman. But if a finance committee finds it has to manage internally in order to make the company function, its proper recourse is to convince the board that a new president is needed; and if it indulges in managing activities because it doesn't understand the consequences, the board needs a new chairman of its finance committee. All this, of course, is quite independent of the subject of audit, which is a function of the board and which the latter should exercise independently, usually through a committee of outside directors, and with such service of internal officers as it may need.

An executive committee seldom presents a difficult problem except in one respect. It substitutes for the board between meetings and acts within delegated limits. Its relations with the president are those of the board itself. It is a great time saver, for there are many points on which a president needs action which are not of such moment as to require the time of the full board, and a preliminary shakedown of a tough important question in a small group is a great aid when subtle matters are on the way to the board. The only danger with an executive committee is that it will perform altogether too well. When it does, board meetings become perfunctory, and members not on committees are bored. The offset in the form of a member at large who insists that everything be reargued is not a happy one, and this situation is usually cured by putting him on the committee. In general, it can be said that if every recommendation of the executive committee is always followed exactly by the full board, there is something wrong. For some strange human reason, executive committees shy at passing matters to the full board, even important matters, without expressing formal judgment thereon and thereby putting the subject pretty much on ice. A wise executive committee will avoid even the appearance of omniscience. But very few executive committees are thus wise.

The question of other committees of the board is an intricate one. A committee on technical, scientific, or engineering aspects of the business is sometimes used. Certainly in some sorts of business there are scientific and engineering plans and programs of as great moment, from the standpoint of company progress and prosperity, as the financial, legal, or organizational plans of management which are habitually sifted by committees on the way to the board, or acted upon by committees within limits for the board. The difficulty is, of course, that boards are often made up of men of business, legal, or financial background with little deep grasp of the processes and techniques on which the company is founded. On the other hand, the president is likely to know something about them, and therefore technical programs come to the board through the president or not at all. This is not a universal situation; for example, there are oil companies in which the board understands the full technical complexity of the oil business and where plans are discussed technically in full board. When a company is in a highly technical field, it is unfortunate for the board never to hear of that aspect of its affairs except when it is being mildly educated. The usual explanation of such a situation is that technical matters are too complex for board judgment. They certainly cannot be boiled down into a balance sheet and an operating statement. But they often need judgment on a broad basis as much as anything else, and they are inherently no more complex than many a legal or financial question. When the board includes individuals with adequate background for technical judgment, a technical committee of the board can perform the same sort of service as a finance committee. It also presents the same danger, namely that it may begin to manage; but that danger is avoidable. Another apparent barrier to the use of such a committee is found in cases where the president did not come up through engineering or research and has a natural reluctance to present technical matters to any group except in the broadest generalities. This should not be a barrier. After all, a president cannot himself be a master of every aspect of his business. In fact, from the standpoint of personal mastery he is probably outstanding in one branch only. Unless he is surrounded by staff members who know the intricacies of diverse branches far better than he does, there is something wrong, often very seriously wrong. His function is to have such over-all understanding that he can judge every branch in the light of its interrelations with all others. So it would be no novelty for him to sit with a board committee while a vice-president presents a specialty, with which presentation he has agreed beforehand. If he has no vice-president who can do this, with his full support and confidence, he should

get one. Thus there are no genuine barriers to the procedure of presenting engineering, scientific, or technical matters through a committee to
the board, unless the board lacks individuals who can judge them with
adequate background. This is unfortunate in any business founded on a
specialized, rapidly developing technical base, for the future of the company may well hinge on the skill with which technical trends are judged.

Members of the board should not, however, operate merely in meetings of committees or of the full board. Of course, a man who can do
that only may often be valuable to a board, if he is a wise man who is
very busy elsewhere. But members generally need to be active far beyond
mere attendance at meetings. If they are not, how can they suitably perform their main function when it comes to a change of top command?
And this leads to quite a puzzle, for directors need to have close contacts
inside a company, yet they should not interfere in management. As a general principle, contacts within an organization for purposes of information should be inhibited to the minimum extent consistent with orderly
procedure, while all business continues to be done through channels. This
principle needs to be applied at all levels, but especially in connection
with board relationships. There is no principle of organization with more
necessary shades of subtle qualification. The executive who can talk freely
with an individual two ranks below him, while keeping it clear that he is
issuing no orders and that he expects the individual to apprise his immediate boss of anything pertinent which occurs, is rare. Still rarer is the organization in which discussion and criticism of a policy or procedure
which is in the process of formulation can proceed generally both up and
down, with effective exclusion of personalities throughout and complete
loyalty to policy, once adopted. Even when this is the case, the director
who can wander about an organization and learn something about it beyond the cold statistics, without appearing either officious or foolish, is
usually a director who for some reason knows the company rather intimately at the outset. Yet the director who penetrates no farther than
meetings, conducted tours, and chats with the president can hardly be
expected to understand a vital, breathing organism in such a manner as
to proceed beyond a machine-like judgment of its status and probable
evolution. There are several devices which help to break down the barriers without introducing artificial stress. One is the informal, semisocial
gathering for discussion of broad company policy, spread over a day or
two and preferably remote from the place of business. It is used with
groups of top executives and, when planned with a bit of skill, seems to
work well. It could advantageously be extended to include directors. Another scheme, and a good one, is the *ad hoc* committee of the board, op-

erating on the same pattern as a regular committee, but concerned with a concrete temporary problem of direct interest to the board members engaged. Sometimes this can even be a committee of one, but it needs some formal recognition, for board members need, at all hazards, to avoid being suspected of snooping. It is notable that the one matter on which board members need to be informed most completely—namely, the character and qualifications of individuals near the top of the organization—is the one thing into which they cannot inquire directly except among themselves, and can inquire indirectly only with the greatest of care and circumspection. Still, that is a rather prevalent condition in human relations generally, and somehow men learn to judge other men in nonobvious ways. A great deal could be written on the problem of educating a board. The key, of course, is to get them intensely interested in the business, and that often means primarily interested in the people who are running it. This hardly happens of itself, especially when boards are made up largely of individuals each of whom is on a dozen boards. It is best done when there is a genuine and specific object to be attained.

Much more could be written concerning the internal functioning of boards of directors. Their function of orienting the company in its external relationships is equally important. In particular, if the system they represent is a good one, they should guide and back up the president and chairman in such manner as to ensure as far as possible that that system escapes disaster from without.

If they do this, and if they perform their main task well when it comes to selecting a new president, they can genuinely be of great use to the company.

A NOTE ON GERMAN BUSINESS ORGANIZATIONS

* * * * *

German law recognizes a variety of forms of business enterprise: the individual proprietor, the association of personal partners, corporations, and combinations of these. The first part of this note describes some of the important legal aspects of these organizations. Corporations are emphasized because they are the most important form of enterprise in Germany and also because they are the form of business organization most likely to be selected by foreign businesses establishing operations in Germany. The second part of this note includes some comments by two German businessmen dealing with the modus operandi of corporate top management.

* * * * *

PERSONAL LIABILITY: PROPRIETORSHIP AND PARTNERSHIPS

The simplest form of German business organization is the sole proprietor or individual merchant. There are no restrictions as to who may set up such a business except that the proprietor must be of sound mind and must be of legal age. The proprietor or individual merchant assumes unlimited liability in the operation of his business; he is liable with his personal fortune for any debts which his business may be legally required to pay.

Partnerships. There are two common forms of business association: the general partnership (*Offene Handelsgesellschaft:* OHG), and the limited partnership (*Kommanditgesellschaft:* KG). The OHG is a simple form of partnership in which all the partners are personally liable without limitation for the debts of the business association.

In the KG, one or more active partners (natural persons)[1] are liable without limitations for the debts of the association, while one or more inactive partners (any legal person) are liable only to the extent of their agreed contribution to the partnership. The active partners are called

---

[1] The term "natural person" is used to denote an individual as opposed to a corporation. Both the corporation and an individual are legal people.

Komplementär, and the inactive partners are called *Kommanditist*. It is quite common and legal in KG agreements to give a Kommanditist, or his representative, wide rights of control over the seemingly more important figure of the Komplementär, especially where the financial contribution of the Kommanditist is substantial.

The partnership agreements for the OHG and the KG are not subject to any prescribed form. They are usually in writing and completely subject to the German laws of contract. Court interpretations permit corporations to be partners of both the OHG and the KG. Where, in consequence, a corporation is liable without limitation for the debts of a business association, such liability does not affect the limited liability of the corporation's shareholders.

CORPORATIONS

The two common forms of corporations are the "agreement" corporation. (*Gesellschaft mit beschränkter Haftung:* GmbH) and the stock corporation (*Aktiengesellschaft:* AG). Both are described below in some detail. There is a third corporation, called the *Kommanditgesellschaft auf Aktien*, which is a combination of the Aktiengesellschaft and the KG forms of business organization. The Kommanditgesellschaft auf Aktien is a corporation with two groups of members: one of which is composed of natural persons, who are personally liable for the debts of the business, and the other of which is composed of shareholders without personal liability. The former group of members—those personally liable for the business—represent and manage the Kommanditgesellschaft auf Aktien.

THE GESELLSCHAFT MIT BESCHRÄNKTER HAFTUNG: (GmbH)

The GmbH is based on the agreement of two or more partners on articles of association which are registered in court. The partners may be natural persons, partnerships, or any other legal persons.

The name of the organization must contain the words *Gesellschaft mit beschränkter Haftung*, and also must either contain the full name of at least one partner or else indicate the nature of the GmbH's business. This latter requirement may be waived if the GmbH continues the name of an acquired business. A combination of a partner's name and the business purpose is also permissible. One restriction is that the chosen name must not infringe on any existing firm's name.

The minimum capital required for the formation of a GmbH is DM 20,000. The minimum value for a single share of the business is DM 500.

Share certificates are optional but uncommon, since they are not negotiable. A share is transferred or signed by a notarial record.

Except for special majority rights which may be granted in the articles,
the minority enjoys many statutory rights, among which are included the
right to (i) receive information about the operations and status of the
business; (ii) have a shareholders' meeting; (iii) cause the meeting to
consider motions; (iv) exclude a shareholder for cause, etc. Shareholders
also have a direct statutorial right against the GmbH to dividends in the
amount of the profits shown in the GmbH's annual financial statement.
This provision may be, and often is, replaced in the articles by the right
of the annual shareholders' meeting to decide with simple or qualified
majority whether to pay out such profit or to apply it to the company's
surplus profit account. Generally, the courts give protection against a
misuse of the majority power for objectives which are foreign to the business purpose of the GmbH.

Legal Officers. The GmbH is legally represented and directed by one
or more executives or managers (*Geschäftsführer*). The authority of
the Geschäftsführer is an unlimited statutorial authority with respect
to third parties and cannot be restricted. In other words, the GmbH is
fully liable for any commitments made by the Geschäftsführer. The
Geschäftsführer may be bound by his own contract to procure prior approval from the shareholders for any desired type of transaction or business decision.

A supervisory Board of Directors (*Aufsichtsrat*) is not required for
the GmbH unless the regular number of employees exceeds 500. The
Aufsichtsrat has access to all information in the GmbH and has the right
to control the management. The Aufsichtsrat is a body separate from
the management; no person may serve on both at the same time.

The law stipulates that employees have the right to elect one-third of
the members of a corporation's Aufsichtsrat. The first two labor representatives selected must be employees of the enterprise; further labor
representatives may be outsiders, for example, trade-union officials.

Audit. Except for banks, the law does not require the election or
appointment of independent auditors to approve the GmbH's annual
financial statements. These statements need not be filed in any court or
with any administrative authority, and their publication is not required.
Since a number of rather large enterprises of major economic and social
importance use the GmbH form of business organization, it has been
proposed to subject the "large" GmbH to the mandatory audit and publicity provisions which are applicable to the Aktiengesellschaften.

THE AKTIENGESELLSCHAFT (AG)

The formation of an Aktiengesellschaft requires registration of the articles of association in court by five incorporators. The incorporators may be any legal persons.

The minimum capital investment for the formation of an AG is DM 100,000. The capital investment is divided into capital shares, which must have a nominal money value of at least DM 100; the more common denomination of a share is DM 1,000. The AG's capital share is negotiable and, in practice, is a bearer share. As a rule, shares are bought and sold by the public in Germany through the banks. It is customary to leave the shares on deposit with the bank, which may exercise rights with the consent and upon the instructions of the depositor.

Legal Officers. The AG is legally represented and directed by one or more executives on a Board of Management (*Vorstand*). The Vorstand alone decides all questions of management, and its statutory authority to represent the AG to external parties, both in and out of court, cannot be limited. The Vorstand, however, may be bound to observe limitations required by the Articles of Association, the Shareholders' Meeting, or the Aufsichtsrat.

Members of the Vorstand are appointed by the Aufsichtsrat. This appointment may not exceed five years, although reappointment is common procedure. For the larger Vorstand, it is customary for the Aufsichtsrat to appoint a chairman (*Vorsitzer*) of the Vorstand.

An Aufsichtsrat with labor participation is mandatory for an Aktiengesellschaft, irrespective of the number of employees. Excepted from this law are Aktiengesellschaften with less than 500 employees if the corporation is owned by one natural person or a family. As with the GmbH, the management and the Board of Directors are distinctly separate; membership by one person in both groups is not permissible. For a limited time, a member of the Aufsichtsrat may be delegated to replace a member of the Vorstand, but he may not, during this time, exercise the Aufsichtsrat's function. Members of the Aufsichtsrat representing the shareholders are appointed by the shareholders.

Audit. The annual financial statements (balance sheets and income statements) of each fiscal year must be audited by an independent certified accountant and filed in court, together with the reports of the Vorstand and the Aufsichtsrat. The financial statements must also be published. The certified accountant is elected annually at the shareholders' meeting.

FOREIGN PARTICIPATION

All forms of commercial positions are open to foreigners without discrimination. Individual merchants, business partners, shareholders, members of an Aufsichtsrat, managers or employees of a German enterprise, or of a German branch of a foreign enterprise, may all be foreign nationals. Residence in Germany for business owners or executives is a matter of practicality rather than law. Passport regulations, however, require a residence permit for commercial activity of a foreigner in Germany.

Foreign enterprises wishing to operate in Germany normally prefer the corporate form of business enterprise. One reason for this preference is a significant tax advantage. As a rule, branch operation or the ownership or participation in an enterprise with unlimited liability commits the foreign owner or partner to more German taxes than operation through a German corporation. Many of the Double Taxation Conventions favor the foreign investor in a German corporation. A second reason for the preference for the corporate form is the limited liability of the shareholders for the debts of the corporation. The rule of limited liability applies to a wholly owned corporation.

Of the two available types of limited liability corporations, the AG and GmbH, the GmbH is considered by most businessmen as a preferable form wherever public financing by way of stock issue is not needed—that is, for a closed corporation. The major reason for this preference is to avoid the more restrictive regulations which apply to the Aktiengesellschaft, such as required audit, publishing of financial statements, and formation of an Aufsichtsrat with labor representation.

*   *   *   *   *

The following sections contain comments by two German businessmen about shareholder-Aufsichtsrat-Vorstand relationships. The first set of comments largely relates to middle-sized AG corporations, and the second set relates to large AG corporations.

MIDDLE-SIZED CORPORATIONS

Dr. Werner Engelhardt, a Vorstand member of Bayrische Chemie AG, made the following comments about the top management of his company and also made some general statements about the German Vorstand. The company was a middle-sized firm producing a moderate line of industrial chemicals. Its 1961 sales were approximately DM

60,000,000 (about $15 million), and it employed just over 1,000 people.

"We have an Aufsichtsrat of twelve members of which eight members represent the shareholders and four members represent the workers. Shareholders' members are elected at an annual shareholders' meeting as directed by the company's bylaws; two members are re-elected each year for four-year terms. The procedure for the workers' members is dictated by the labor laws and the workers themselves.

"Our Vorstand consists of three members who are appointed by the Aufsichtsrat for five-year terms. We all hold equal authority, and operate somewhat on a 'troika' principle, making all major decisions jointly. In most cases there is no difficulty in making decisions. Whenever a problem clearly falls within one of our three areas of expertness, we normally go along with the recommendations of the Vorstand member who is responsible for that function of the business. One of my colleagues is directly responsible for sales, and the other is responsible for both production and plant personnel. I am responsible for finance, accounting, control, purchasing and the IBM facilities."

Figure 1 shows the organization of top management for Bayrische Chemie AG, for 1962.

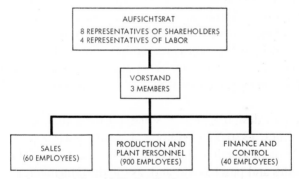

Source: Interview with Dr. Engelhardt.

"Problems often arise when we are discussing general policies or situations which overlap two or three of our areas of interest," continued Dr. Engelhardt. "We do our utmost to come to an agreement by ourselves before taking action. If we cannot agree, we then take the problem before the Aufsichtsrat and ask for their recommendation, even though the Vorstand has the legal power of action in accordance with the majority ruling of its members. Often, we do not take the formal step of presenting our case before the full Board, but only speak privately to the Vorsitzer of the Aufsichtsrat. One example of a problem, which we brought before them, concerned whether we should join a cartel. I am directly opposed to all cartels in our business, and one of my colleagues is in love with cartels. There just was no meeting of the minds; we finally took the problem before the Aufsichtsrat and asked their advice as to which way we should act.

"Of course, we try to keep these arbitration-reviews to a minimum, because it would not do to give the Aufsichtsrat the impression that we members of the Vorstand cannot work together as a team. Once they thought that, they would be sure to bring in a new team to replace us when our contracts expired.

"There are also a number of decisions which the Vorstand must submit to the Aufsichtsrat for approval, in accordance with our company's bylaws. For example, we must have the approval of the Aufsichtsrat for investments of more than DM 100,000. Again, we three Vorstand members try to agree on the presentation and recommendations associated with these decisions before presenting them to the Aufsichtsrat.

"Actually, it is unusual for a company of our size to have three members on the Vorstand. Medium-sized companies, such as ours, normally have two members: a commercial director and a technical director. Smaller companies and closely held family companies tend to have one member on the Vorstand. This latter position, of course, resembles very closely the president's role in an American company. Larger companies naturally have more members on a Vorstand, perhaps ten or fifteen members. When the Board becomes greater than three or four people, it is customary to have a chairman (*Vorsitzer*) appointed by the Aufsichtsrat. He normally has somewhat more authority than the other members of the Vorstand.

"If I were to design a perfect Vorstand for a company with sales of DM 150 million ($30–$40 million), I would select a technical man to be in charge of production and engineering; a commercial man to be in charge of sales and purchasing; and, as the third member, a good lawyer who would be in charge of taxes, real estate, administration of housing, and possibly finance. The real reason for selecting a lawyer is to have a man on the Board who could smooth out the differences among the group, and see that just and workable compromises were introduced and truly accepted by the other two members."

LARGE-SIZED CORPORATIONS

The following remarks were made by Dr. Heinrich Glauren, Vice-Chairman of the Vorstand of Linsel & Schuler AG. Linsel & Shuler was one of the ten largest firms in Germany, with 1961 sales just under DM 2 billion ($500 million) and with about 45,000 employees.

"Our company hierarchy includes a wide base of shareholders, an Aufsichtsrat of 15 members, and a Vorstand of 10 members. Ten of the supervisory board (Aufsichtsrat) represent the shareholders and are elected by the shareholders. The members of the Vorstand are all active executives in the company and are appointed by the Aufsichtsrat.

"In realistic terms, the administration of the Vorstand rules supreme. The reason for this is that most of the shares are voted by the banks and they usually vote with the administration, at least while things are going well. I would guess that as much as 95 per cent of the shares for this company are in the hands of, and voted by, the banks.

"The real power lies in the hands of the Vorsitzer of the Vorstand. If he controls the Vorstand, as he does in our company, then he really controls the destiny of the company. In this respect, he would play a very similar role to that of the president of an American company. The extent of his dominance, however, would depend on the personalities involved much more than is the case with an American company's president.

"Only rarely do the banks actually put pressure on an administration by voting against it. Normally, one bank, called the *Haus-Bank,*[2] is most directly concerned with the company and will have representatives on the Aufsichtsrat. If the bank is dissatisfied with the operation of the company, it puts pressure on the company, first by calling the matter to the Vorstand's attention and then by threatening the company with tighter credit. I believe that a bank, rather than ever voting directly against a Vorstand, would tend first to extract itself from the whole organization by disposing of its shares."

---

[2] *Haus-Bank* is the name given by a company to the bank which has very close financial dealings with the company.

SOCIETE DES MACHINES MARVEAU*

At 5:00 P.M. Saturday, September 10, 1960, M. Henri Saint-Dutain, President (*Administrateur-Délégué*) of the Société (*Sté.*) des Machines Marveau, called a meeting of the top management to announce the formation of a new management committee. This committee, to be comprised of the three junior line executives, was assigned the unprecedented authority of full presidential power in the absence of both the President and the General Manager. M. Saint-Dutain coupled this declaration with the announcement that both he and M. Gallimard, the General Manager (*Administrateur-Directeur*), would be leaving on the following Monday for a three-week trip to the Belgian Congo and that he expected the committee to take full charge of the company's operations.

THE COMPANY AND ITS MANAGEMENT

The Sté. des Machines Marveau, founded in 1872, produced a line of machines and process equipment for the metallurgical industry. By 1962, the company had two large plants, located in the outskirts of Verviers, Belgium, and employed just over 2,000 people. Sales in 1961 slightly exceeded one billion Belgium francs (about 20 million dollars).

Although Marveau was a publicly owned company, a controlling interest had been held by the Saint-Dutain family since the turn of the century. M. Henri Saint-Dutain entered the company in 1926 as secretary to his father, who was the former president of Marveau. From this position, he soon began to exert an important influence on the operations of the company, assuming the positions of General Manager in 1936 and President in 1941. M. Saint-Dutain joined the board of directors in 1936, becoming the Chairman of the Board (President) in 1957. In 1962, two of M. Saint-Dutain's three sons and also two of his nephews were working for the company.

Marveau's management had been organized over the years in a line-staff relationship. The company's organization, prior to the creation of the new management committee, was as shown in Exhibit 1. The senior

---

* Fictitious name.

Exhibit 1

MANAGEMENT ORGANIZATION PRIOR TO SEPTEMBER, 1960

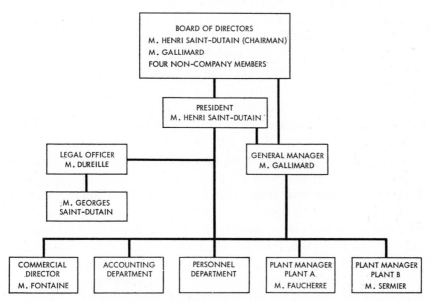

and middle ranks of the line management traditionally included the President and the General Manager in the former group and the two Plant Managers and the Commercial Manager in the latter group. In general, prior to 1960, the two senior executives were the only line personnel who dealt with over-all company operations. The middle manager's responsibilities had been limited to the operation of their own particular departments.

M. Saint-Dutain, as Marveau's President, was actively concerned with all the major business decisions within the company. Although an engineer by education, his training in finance and administration under his father had given him a strong business orientation. He had also been active in a government financial agency and in a metallurgical-equipment industrial organization. Because of this experience, he maintained a formal, direct control of all decisions regarding the company's finances and its relations with stockholders, the Belgian government, and the industry at large. Referred to by one of the executives as ". . . a man endowed with an extraordinary capacity for work and with a superior intelligence," M. Saint-Dutain was a dominant figure in Marveau's management and appeared to the IMEDE researcher to have strongly concentrated the leadership and control of the company within his office. During an extended interview, he revealed a mastery of detailed knowledge about many facets of the company's operation which was unusual for a man of his position.

Second-ranking officer, M. Gallimard, was responsible for the internal operations of Marveau and, in the absence of M. Saint-Dutain, for the over-all direction of the company. An outstanding engineer in the field of metallurgical machines and equipment, M. Gallimard was promoted to Chief Engineer in 1940 and to General Manager in 1952. In this latter capacity, he was occupied, to a large extent, with major technical and personnel problems. M. Gallimard reported directly to the board of directors, of which he became a member in 1952, as well as to the President.

The three members of the middle line-management reported directly to both senior officers. MM. Faucherre and Sermier, both engineers by training and experience, were the managers of the company's two plants. Each man was primarily responsible for the operation and personnel of his plant. Because two completely separate lines of products were manufactured in the two plants, no appreciable interchange of work, personnel, or technology was feasible. The third member of the middle line-management group was M. Fontaine, the company's Commercial Director. In this capacity, he was responsible for the sales of the full line of company products and for the major purchases of materials.

THE JUNIOR BOARD

The management committee, created on the late Saturday meeting mentioned above, was formed on a temporary basis to function during the absence of the senior executives. The minutes of the special meeting in which the management committee was appointed, are contained in Exhibit 2. The committee was not, however, disbanded on the return of the senior executives from the Congo.

On November 10, 1961, a request was made by M. Henri Saint-Dutain and approved by the board of directors that the management committee be transformed into a permanent "Junior Board" to assist in the daily management of the company.

M. Georges Saint-Dutain was made a member of the Junior Board in addition to the three members of the original management committee (MM. Faucherre, Sermier, and Fontaine), and M. Paul Saint-Dutain, who had been acting as secretary for the management committee continued in this position. MM. Georges and Paul Saint-Dutain were both sons of the President. Exhibit 3 contains an extract of the minutes of the Board of Directors' meeting during which the Junior Board was formally created.

Exhibit 2

MINUTES OF THE SPECIAL MEETING APPOINTING THE
MANAGEMENT COMMITTEE

SPECIAL MEETING CALLED BY MONSIEUR SAINT-DUTAIN, PRESIDENT
PRESENT:

M. SAINT-DUTAIN, Chairman
M. GALLIMARD
M. FAUCHERRE
M. SERMIER
M. FONTAINE
M. SAINT-DUTAIN, P., Secretary

*   *   *

The meeting was called to order at 5:00 p.m., Saturday, September 10, 1960. M. Saint-Dutain opened the meeting with a comment stressing the importance of what he had to say. He then remarked that the purpose of the meeting was to inform the persons present of a decision which he had taken, in agreement with M. Gallimard, to provide for the continuous management of the company in the absence of M. Gallimard and himself.

M. Saint-Dutain explained that the complexity of current operations made it important that the company have a management capable of acting at all times. Because both he and M. Gallimard were going to be absent for the remainder of September, the decision was made to confer temporarily the whole of the powers given to the president by Article 15 of the Statutes, without infringing on those decisions requiring approval of the Board of Directors, on a committee of three persons—MM. Faucherre, Sermier, and Fontaine—to begin September 12.

M. Saint-Dutain stressed the fact that in case delegation of power should prove necessary on another occasion, other persons might be chosen. This should not be construed in any way as a disapproval of the current members of the committee.

M. Saint-Dutain requested that the three persons appointed be aware that they are to make all the decisions of management, including those that have become bogged down or those that have been kept in abeyance for a long time. Decisions by the committee must be made unanimously. Requests to M. Saint-Dutain or M. Gallimard for arbitration should be made only in case of prolonged disagreement and as infrequently as possible.

M. Saint-Dutain deemed that the committee should meet three times per week in his absence. He informed the members that they were to inform each other of the events within their area, which were then defined as follows:

—M. Faucherre is to report on the activities of the staff at his plant.
—M. Sermier is to report on the activities of the staff at his plant and the staff listed on the company records as engaged in research or technical studies.
—M. Fontaine is to report on the activities of the sales and administrative staffs.

In answer to a question by M. Fontaine, M. Saint-Dutain stated that minutes would be kept of each meeting and that M. Paul Saint-Dutain would act as secretary of the committee. The minutes were to include the declaration of the problem, the arguments proposed, and the decision taken.

In answer to a question by M. Faucherre, M. Saint-Dutain explained that the minutes will serve as the only official testimony of the activity of the committee at the end of the mission.

The meeting was adjourned at 6:15 p.m.

The Junior Board continued to hold meetings two or three times per week, with either M. Saint-Dutain or M. Gallimard attending. Although M. Faucherre was the titular chairman of the Junior Board, the members all considered themselves to be equal in authority and responsibility regarding the actual execution of the Junior Board's daily operations. Exhibit 4 contains a typical agenda for one of its meetings. During its first

Exhibit 3

EXTRACTS OF THE MINUTES OF THE BOARD OF DIRECTORS' MEETING
CONCERNING THE CREATION OF THE JUNIOR BOARD

". . . The President informed the Board of Directors that, because both M. Gallimard and he had to make several prolonged trips to the Congo during the last months, a management committee had been appointed on the tenth of September, 1960. Provision for such a committee had been made by the Board of Directors in June of 1957. He reported that the committee had already begun to play a useful part in the daily management of the company. During the absence of M. Saint-Dutain, M. Gallimard has been entrusted with the supervision of the decisions taken by the committee, within the limits of article 15 of the Statutes."

A director who had applied a similar management committee in one of his companies remarked that the formula was interesting and requested the reaction of the senior executives. The President replied that they have all found the operation attractive.

The Board decided that this experiment should cover a long period of time if it is to prove conclusive and voted that it be carried on. It was finally decided that:

1) the Junior Board would meet even in the absence of one of its members, and
2) that the Junior Board would hold its first session on Tuesday, 13 December, in the presence of M. Gallimard.

year of operation, the Junior Board had made studies and recommendations on a number of major company problems, among which were the Formation-Information Program and a new plan for the company's organization.

Exhibit 4

AN AGENDA FOR A TYPICAL MEETING OF THE JUNIOR BOARD

AGENDA—NOVEMBER 1961

PROGRAM:

1. PERSONNEL PROBLEMS
    a) Description and movement of personnel (see tables 1, 2, 3)
    b) Current problems

2. ECONOMIC AND TECHNICAL PROBLEMS
    a) General situation of the Business Cycle
    b) Supplies (see table 4)
    c) Marketing
        —sales position of the products (see tables 5, 6, 7)
        —1961 production
        —improvement of marketing methods
    d) Conclusion: forecasting results

3. PARTICULAR PROBLEMS
    a) Presentation by M. Darbre on our new milling line
    b) Publicity film by A.T.L.

*　　*　　*

TABLES

1—Personnel in service on 30 September, 1961.
2—Salary structure of our personnel by nationality
3—Rotation of salaried personnel compared (60–61)
4—Record of metal stocks for Jan.–September 1961
5—Production Statistics for Belgium
6—Protective coatings for machines in shipment
7—Production of small hydraulic presses
8—Sales of divisions

The Formation-Information Program was really two separate programs designed to improve the supervisory staff of Marveau. The Formation Program was a course of supervisory-management training given to 40 selected supervisors under the direction of M. Dureille, the corporate legal officer. M. Dureille performed a variety of staff functions under M. Henri Saint-Dutain, in addition to his legal work, because of his previous training in business administration in the United States.

The purpose of the Information Program was to present timely news and information about the company's operation on a regular basis to all of the company's 90 supervisors. Members of the Junior Board presided at these meetings, during each of which a question-and-answer period was held on any topic of interest to the supervisors. Both Formation and Information programs were designed to continue on a permanent basis.

Another innovation which originated in the Junior Board concerned a basic change in the organization of the management team. Exhibit 5 shows an abridged version of the proposed organization. The Junior Board submitted the proposed organization change in September of 1961, recommending that the change be made progressively, to be completed in 1970. The proposal was approved and returned by M. H. Saint-Dutain within two weeks. The only modification which he made related to the marketing-distribution structure and did not affect the management organization as shown in Exhibit 5. It was later announced by M. Saint-Dutain that the installation of the new organization would start on January 1, 1962, and would proceed in a reasonably accelerated manner.

VIEWS ON THE JUNIOR BOARD

After one year of operation, Marveau's senior and middle management were unanimous in their favorable reaction to the effects and accomplishments of the Junior Board. It can be noted from the comments below, however, that Marveau's President held a different view of the basic function of the Junior Board from that held by its members. In the one case the Junior Board was considered as a body empowered to make decisions, while in the other case it was considered as solely an advisory unit.

THE MEMBERS' VIEWS ON THE JUNIOR BOARD

All the members of the Junior Board appeared to the researcher to hold similar opinions as to the function of the Board and its value to themselves as individuals.

The members considered that the Board served to provide both (1) an

Exhibit 5

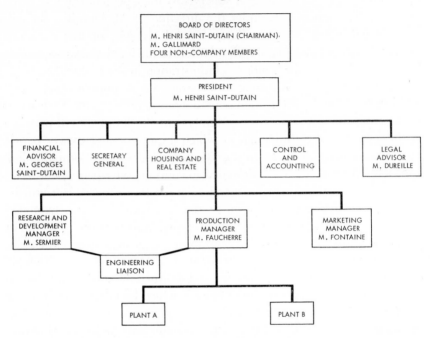

advisory staff for the senior executives and (2) a means of training the members for enlarged responsibilities. One member remarked: "We are organized to study company problems and to submit recommendations to the senior men. These problems can either be brought to our attention by our superiors, or we can initiate a study on our own. In either case, the senior officers are supposed to act on our recommendations through our line organization, which will normally involve one of us.

"On a number of occasions, M. Saint-Dutain (President) has tried to have the Junior Board execute the actions of our recommendations directly, but I do not think that that is our job. As I see it, we, as a Junior Board, are strictly a staff group and should not operate in a line capacity."

Despite the extra work that the Junior Board required, the members were all very enthusiastic and pleased about their experience with it. The benefit of the Junior Board most cited by these men was the opportunity it gave them to become more knowledgeable about the company outside their own line sector. Two of the members added the remark that this broadened outlook had helped them do a better job in their own departments.

The members recognized that they would eventually "graduate" from their positions on the Junior Board. One member commented: "I believe that some of the members of the Junior Board will be elevated to an executive committee which will work directly under M. [Henri] Saint-Dutain. If that should happen, most of us are in favor of continuing the Junior Board by appointing the new middle managers to fill our places. [Exhibit 6 shows the organization as envisaged by the member making this comment.] All in all, we think that we have learned something and also have contributed some valuable work. We naturally want to provide our successors with the same wonderful training opportunity, and we are not at all adverse to tapping their creativity."

Exhibit 6

THE FUTURE TOP MANAGEMENT ORGANIZATION AS DESCRIBED BY ONE
MEMBER OF THE JUNIOR BOARD

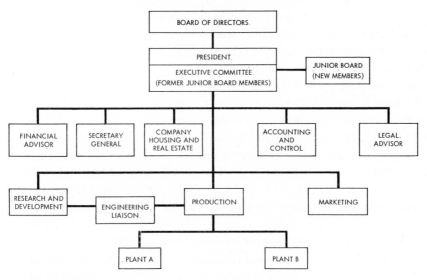

M. GALLIMARD'S VIEWS ON THE JUNIOR BOARD

In discussing the functions of the Junior Board, M. Gallimard remarked: "The Junior Board handles daily problems and is responsible for daily operations under the supervision of M. Saint-Dutain or myself. They have no power to decide on long-term policy but are to make recommendations when asked. For example, the Formation-Information Program was proposed by the Junior Board, but it had to be approved by the President and the Board of Directors before it could be implemented."

Concerning the operation and value of the Junior Board, he went on to say: "All of the men are quite active on the Junior Board, each in his own sphere. Usually that person who is most familiar with, or experienced in, the problem area will carry the most weight, but there is plently of give and take in the discussions. So far, they have usually managed to agree among themselves before passing up recommendations. As to the value of the Junior Board, I believe that both the men and we [senior management] have benefited from it. One of the greatest benefits to the men has been the broadening of their outlook from the partial and immediate picture of the company's operations to an understanding of the whole and long-term situation. The men are now aware of their counterpart's problems, and maybe our problems. They have also become interested and involved in planning. As for our benefit, I would say that the Junior Board has helped us to do our job better and more easily."

M. HENRI SAINT-DUTAIN'S VIEW ON THE JUNIOR BOARD

"The Junior Board has proved to be a valuable help to M. Gallimard and myself, without question," stated M. Saint-Dutain, "but I had one especially important reason for creating this group, and that was to select and train my successor as President. M. Gallimard is scheduled to retire from his position as General Manager in a few years, and I from the Presidency somewhat later. At that time, one man from the Junior Board will assume the senior position of this company and direct its operations. Of course, M. Gallimard and I will continue to retain our positions on the Board of Directors, hopefully until 1975, and so we shall have an opportunity to watch over things. The period during which my successor participates on the Junior Board will afford him an opportunity to exercise a broad authority while still under direct supervision. These years will certainly give me a chance to see, and hopefully the rest of the officers a chance to appreciate, that the best man has been selected.

"There is another very good reason for the Junior Board at this time," he added, "and that relates to the unsettled conditions in Belgium itself.[1] In addition to my business travels, I am also required to be abroad frequently to attend to personal affairs. One never knows what could happen while I am away on a trip, either there or here in Belgium. In any case, it is only prudent to maintain a management at home that can act when necessary. If something should happen to me personally, the person

---

[1] In September, 1960, the Belgian government was beset by difficulties centering about two problems: the loss of the Belgian Congo and the Flemish-Walloon dispute. Tensions continued to mount until the end of the year, when general strikes were called throughout the country in protest against the government's policies. The situation was termed "violent and explosive." The resulting cost of damage and losses was estimated to be about 6–10 billion Belgian francs. Parliament was dissolved in February, 1961, and the general elections of March, 1961, brought about the fall of the cabinet under Premier Gaston Eyskens.

whom M. Gallimard and I consider the most likely qualified at that time
would then succeed me."

When the members' thoughts of continuing the Junior Board as a
permanent committee were mentioned to M. Saint-Dutain during the
case interview, he answered: "Well, that is a decision for my successor
to make in the future. I plan to dissolve the Junior Board because I feel
that the interruption will help establish the authority of the new President. I am convinced that the new man will assume complete independence, once he is given the reins."

Regarding the function of the Junior Board, he stated: "I have vested
the Junior Board with an authority to make all decisions which are permitted the President. The Junior Board is to make the decisions, but I
reserve the right to veto."

When asked if this right to veto did not essentially retain the power
of decision to himself, M. Saint-Dutain emphasized that it did not. He
explained: "The veto has never been used, and, if the need should arise,
I would exercise the veto the very next day so that the matter would remain among ourselves. Any decision publicly made vis-à-vis an outsider
would stand as made, even if I disagreed with it. So far, I have never
wholly contradicted any decision, but have just made suggestions for
modification. For example, when the new organization was proposed, I
saw an error in the distribution system and made corrections before it was
ever released and published."

M. Saint-Dutain concluded: "So far, they have done a fine job, and
we are all pleased with the operation of the Junior Board. I do not believe, however, that they [the members of Junior Board] yet realize that
they have been entrusted with a real executive power. Well, these things
take time."

THE RUGBY PORTLAND CEMENT COMPANY LIMITED (A)

HISTORY, GROWTH, AND ORGANIZATION

The Rugby Company began producing lime in the early nineteenth century at a works near Rugby, England. Cement manufacture, under the company's "Crown" Cement trade mark began at the works in the 1820's and thereafter became its principal product. In 1925 the company, which hitherto had been a partnership, became a private limited company with share capital of £100,000 owned by descendants of the previous partners. In 1929, Mr. (now Sir[1]) Halford Reddish, a young chartered accountant with a consulting practice, joined the board which previously had comprised only representatives of the two descendant branches of the original owners. Four years later, upon the death of the general manager, Mr. Reddish became managing director and, shortly afterwards, chairman.

At that time, the cement industry was in the middle of a deep depression, and prices were at a very unprofitable level. In spite of this crisis, the chairman decided to expand and modernize the company's production facilities. Contrary to previous industry tradition, he also decided to operate the plant 52 weeks per year, thus ensuring steady employment for the workers. Despite the depression and difficulties of selling the increased output, a profit was realized at the end of the first year of the new management. A second manufacturing site was obtained when a nearby company went into receivership. Erection of a new factory at the second site plus the modernization and expansion of the Rugby works required substantial fresh capital. In 1935, the company became a public company with its shares quoted on the London Stock Exchange, and additional capital of £140,000 was introduced. Since that time, additional equity capital had been raised by occasional "rights" issues.

In 1936, Rugby acquired a third site and erected its Rochester works. In 1939, another company was purchased, and its facilities were com-

---

This case was prepared by John Priedeman and Robert C. K. Valtz under the supervision of Professors K. R. Andrews or E. P. Learned.

Copyright 1962, by l'Institut pour l'Etude des Méthodes de Direction de l'Entreprise (IMEDE), Lausanne, Switzerland. Reprinted by permission.

[1] In early 1958, Her Majesty Queen Elizabeth II knighted Mr. Halford Reddish for his public services.

bined with those at Rochester. In 1945, Rugby acquired another company, and, although its production facilities were closed, Rugby used its brand name and distribution organization. Rugby made major additions to its three plants in Great Britain after 1946.

During the immediate postwar years, export trade was very profitable, with unit margins several times those of the home-market sales. The proportion of Rugby's deliveries accounted for by exports reached a maximum in 1951 and 1952 at about 43 per cent. In 1961, however, Sir Halford Reddish said that in recent years export sales had become almost marginal because of the increased competition (much of it subsidized) from non-British manufacturers and the growth of cement industries in areas formerly importing cement. Rugby had itself established overseas subsidiaries and built manufacturing plants in Trinidad and Western Australia. The former started production in 1954, and the latter in 1955. Both units were able to supply cement at substantially lower prices than existing imported cement and made useful contributions to Rugby's consolidated profits.

With a rapidly developing local market plus export trade in the Eastern Caribbean, the Trinidad factory required the doubling of its capacity within less than five years of starting its operation. Management decided in 1961 to expand the Australian plant in the near future.

In highlighting Rugby's growth, Sir Halford said in 1961:

In 1933 we had the one not very modern works at Rugby and total net assets with a book value of £109,250. Today all our works at home and abroad are modern and up-to-date and the total net assets of the company at book values amount to £13,404,369. [The real value is probably in excess of £18,500,000.] Additional capital introduced from 1st January 1933 to 31st December 1960 amounted to £13,295,119. Here's how the money has been found:

	£
Shareholders have subscribed for shares (including premiums and loan stock):	5,890,863
by leaving profits in the company:	5,666,076
And others (by minority interests in, or loans to, subsidiary companies) have found:	1,738,180
	£13,295,119

Net profit before taxes rose from less than £4,000 to almost £1.8 million in the same period. Postwar growth produced 11 years of successively record deliveries from 1945 to 1956 and 16 years of successively record group profits, 1946–61 (see Exhibits 1–3).

Late in 1961, a new kiln, with an annual capacity of 180,000 tons, was

Exhibit 1

Consolidated Balance Sheet Statements 1946 and 1951–61

(In 1,000's of £)

	1946	1951	1952	1953	1954	1955	1956	1957	1958	1959	1960	1961
Assets												
Current Assets	576	1,847	1,982	2,616	3,836	4,211	4,521	4,195	4,692	6,744	7,597	8,226
Fixed Assets (1937 valuation or cost if subsequently acquired)	1,673	3,271	3,591	3,876	6,171	7,861	8,613	9,309	9,487	9,809	10,627	11,258
Less accumulated depreciation	436	987	1,125	1,261	1,562	1,635	1,969	2,306	2,601	3,008	3,456	3,930
Net fixed assets	1,237	2,285	2,466	2,616	4,609	6,226	6,644	7,003	6,886	6,801	7,171	7,328
Investment in subsidiary companies (not consolidated)	209	33	393	793	760	…	…	…	…	…	…	…
Total assets	2,022	4,165	4,841	6,025	9,205	10,437	11,165	11,198	11,578	13,545	14,768	15,554
Liabilities & Net Worth												
Current liabilities	367	1,355	814	776	1,327	1,498	1,759	1,292	1,190	1,191	1,364	1,328
Debt capital:												
4% debenture	420	…	…	…	…	…	…	…	…	…	…	…
Mortgage loans	…	…	…	…	…	400	480	560	640	720	800	768
4½% unsecured loan 1957–62	…	…	1,000	1,500	1,500	1,500	1,500	1,500	1,500	1,500	1,500	1,500
Total debt	420	…	1,000	1,500	1,500	1,900	1,980	2,060	2,140	2,220	2,300	2,268
Share capital:												
4% & 6% preference shares	325	825	825	825	825	825	825	825	825	825	825	825
Ordinary shares 5/ par	325	500	500	750	1,250	1,500	1,500	1,500	1,500	1,750	2,000	2,000
"A" shares 1/ par	…	…	…	…	50	50	50	50	50	50	50	50
Capital reserve	325	610	563	810	1,265	1,300	1,358	1,415	1,275	2,133	1,950	2,002
Revenue reserves:												
General reserve	100	500	500	750	1,125	1,500	1,750	2,000	…†	1,000	1,217	1,373
Reserve for future taxation	…	249	408	504	352*	390	320	303	350	…	…	…
Reserve for ordinary & "A" share dividend payment (Net)	…	52	55	55	115	201	230	230	276	329	383	383
Undistributed profit	161	73	175	56	120	106	275	451	2,947	3,067‡	3,741	4,520
Total capital and reserves	1,236	2,809	3,026	3,750	5,102	5,873	6,308	6,774	7,223	9,154	10,166	11,153
Interest of outside shareholders in a subsidiary company	…	…	…	…	1,277	1,165	1,117	1,072	1,025	980	938	805
Total liabilities and net worth	2,022	4,165	4,841	6,025	9,205	10,437	11,165	11,198	11,578	13,545	14,768	15,554
Net working capital	210	491	1,168	1,841	2,510	2,712	2,762	2,903	3,502	5,553	6,233	6,898
Equity/Debt Ratio	2.9/1	no debt	3.0/1	2.5/1	3.4/1	3.1/1	3.2/1	3.3/1	3.4/1	4.1/1	4.4/1	4.9/1

* During 1954, £125,000 was transferred from Reserve for Taxation into General Reserve. With reductions in profits tax rate, the tax reserve established by the company in the two previous years exceeded its new liability.

† In 1958 the General Reserve was merged with Undistributed Profit.

‡ In 1959, £440,000 was transferred from Undistributed Profit to Capital Reserve for Future Taxation, against the contingency of overseas profits being brought to the U.K. at some future date.

Exhibit 2

CONSOLIDATED PROFIT AND LOSS ACCOUNT 1946 AND 1951–61

(In 1,000's of £)

	1946	%	1951	%	1952	%	1953	%	1954	%	1955	%	1956	%	1957	%	1958	%	1959	%	1960	%	1961	%
Consolidated Trading Profits....	213		522		656		744		904		1,256		1,369		1,397		1,500		1,877		2,183		2,465	
Other Income....	..		19		20		24		27		39		65		51		52		57		99		105	
Less Depreciation....	79		124		142		136		210		270		340		342		381		443		506		550	
Net Profit before Taxes....	134	100	417	100	534	100	633	100	721	100	1,025	100	1,093	100	1,106	100	1,171	100	1,491	100	1,777	100	2,020	100
Taxation— Profits Tax[1]	39		100		102		125		62		115		109		135		60		45		88		174	
Income Tax....			150		255		300		313		325		255		255		260		475		550		602	
Total Taxes....	39	29	250	60	357	67	425	67	375	52	440	43	364	33	370	34	320	27	520	35	638	36	776	38
Net Profit after Taxes....	95		167		177		208		346		585		729		736		851		971		1,139		1,244	
Preference Dividends....	12	9	21	5	21	4	22	3	22	3	23	2	23	2	23	2	23	2	24	2	24	1	24	1
Ordinary Dividends (Net)	22	16	52	12	55	10	55	9	115	16	172	17	194	18	194	18	230	20	268	18	306	17	306	15
"A" Share Dividends (Net)											29	3	36	3	36	3	46	4	61	4	77	4	77	4
Retained in Business....	61	46	94	23	101	19	131	21	209	29	361	35	477	44	484	44	553	47	618	41	732	41	837	42
Ordinary Dividend per share (Gross)	7½d		1/-d		1/-d		1/-d		1/-d		1/-d		1/1½d		1/1½d		1/3d		1/3d		1/3d		1/3d	
Capital Distribution per share (Gross)	3d		3d		3d		3d		....		....													
"A" Share Dividend per share (Gross)					....		....		....		1/-d		1/3d		1/3d		1/6d		2/-d		2/6d		2/6d	
Net Profit before Taxes as return on Total Capital and Reserves.	10.85%		14.87%		17.65%		19.50%*		17.65%†		17.42%		17.30%		16.30%		16.20%		16.29%		17.48%		18.11%	
Gross Ordinary Dividend as return on capital equity employed, i.e. Ordinary Shares plus disclosed reserves (less reserves credited to "A" Shares).	4.36%		5.04%		4.54%		4.12%*		6.20%†		6.09%		6.36%		5.84%		6.06%		5.43%		5.56%		5.06%	

* Excluding the £500,000 of additional capital introduced at end of 1953.
† Excluding the £1,000,000 of additional capital introduced at end of 1954.
1 *Profits Tax* was the estimated liability for the year ending with the statement. *Income Tax* was the estimated liability for the subsequent two year period. This procedure gives rise to the Reserve for Future Income Tax in the Balance Sheet. The estimated income tax for the future period is put into this reserve; and at the end of each year, the actual tax liability for the year is withdrawn from the reserve and put into current liabilities.

Exhibit 3

INDICES OF DELIVERIES, PROFIT, AND NET WORTH, 1946–61
(Base: 1946 = 100)

Year	Deliveries*	Capital†	Profits
1946	100	100	100
1947	105	184‡	140
1948	138	203	195
1949	139	208	214
1950	155	219	262
1951	168	227	311
1952	208	245	398
1953	214	303§	473
1954	238	413‖	538
1955	302	475	765
1956	307	510	816
1957	294	548	825
1958	296	584	874
1959	319	741¶	1,113
1960	357	822	1,326
1961	388	902	1,507

* These are total group deliveries, in tons, used as an index basing point.
† "Capital" here equals total equity capital, including reserves.
‡ In 1947, £1,000,000 of new capital was raised: £500,000 from new preference shares sold, and £500,000 from new ordinary shares. Without this sale of shares, the index would have remained at 100.
§ In 1953, £500,000 of new ordinary shares were sold. Without this sale, the index at the end of 1953 would have been 265.
‖ In 1954, £1,050,000 of new capital was raised, £50,000 by the sale of "A" shares, £1,000,000 by the sale of new ordinary shares. Without this new capital, the index would have been 330 at the end of 1954.
¶ In 1959, £1,075,000 of new capital was raised through sale of ordinary shares. Without this sale, the index would have been 655 at the end of 1959.

installed at the Southam works. After this addition, the five company works and their annual capacities in tons were as follows:

Southam (England)	:	500,000
Rochester "	:	400,000
Rugby "	:	320,000
Trinidad	:	165,000
Australia	:	120,000

The company also maintained a chalk quarry at Totternhoe, some 48 miles from Rugby.

At the end of 1961, the Rugby Cement Company had about 1,600 employees in its three United Kingdom factories, other United Kingdom subsidiaries, overseas operations, and headquarters in Rugby, England. The headquarters was organized into seven functional departments: Accounting, Production, Engineering, Transportation, Domestic Sales, Export Sales, and Legal. There was also a Secretarial Department. Above these departments was a small control and coordination group called the Administration Department. This group, consisting mostly of assistants to top management, directed and coordinated the activities of the functional departments and served as the intermediate link between subsidiary companies, which addressed all inquiries and reports to Sir Halford Reddish, who was the Chairman of each, and to the headquarters staff departments.

The Board of Directors comprised seven members, three of whom were top executives in the company. These three were Sir Halford Reddish, Chairman and Managing Director; Mr. R. L. Evans, Deputy Managing Director; and Mr. M. K. Smith, head of the Legal Department. Sir Halford and Mr. Evans worked closely with one another, attempting to attain an interchangeability of talents. Sir Halford played a leading role in all major policy decisions but was particularly concerned with financial management and public relations. Mr. Evans' background was also in accounting; he was considered the expert on accounting and technical phases of the operations. As second in command, he in effect headed the Administration Department. Mr. Smith generally confined himself to the company's legal matters and did not become involved in routine company operations.

Sir Halford, who served on the boards of three other corporations and on a number of semipublic councils, spent the greater part of each week in London. His days in Rugby included the weekend, and he normally met with Mr. Evans on Sunday morning to discuss current operations and problems and also to do financial planning up to "two or three balance sheets ahead."

REASONS FOR GROWTH

Sir Halford felt that the company's growth and profitability were attributable to several interrelated activities.

1. *Emphasis on operating efficiency* was considered one of the most important of these activities. Sir Halford said that the key to lower unit costs when producing with expensive, continuous-process equipment was keeping the plant operating as close to full capacity as possible and minimizing every element of operating and overhead costs. Therefore, avoiding down-time, improving efficiency of men and machines, and fuel and power economies were all important. To accomplish these ends, Rugby employed an elaborate monthly cost-reporting system which facilitated pinpointing the items of excessive costs. The factory managers were held responsible for costs under their control, and the chief engineer and production manager were continually watching fuel and power costs and working on means of increasing machine efficiency. Excess overtime, costly repairs, stores usage and factory staff costs were other items which attracted the attention of the central cost-control department. One manager said: "We continually work on the weakest point reflected by the cost analyses."

The company's research on improvement of its manufacturing process produced several cost savings. The major outcome of such research was the recent development of a "wetting" agent for the slurry. Without affecting the chemical properties of the finished product, this agent produced the same "liquidity" and thus the same mixing and handling properties in a slurry containing only 35 per cent water contrasted with 41 per cent previously required. The smaller amount of water to vaporize meant appreciable fuel savings.

Worker efficiency was also a matter of continuous attention. Because of the expensive equipment and need to operate without stoppages, misconduct on the job, unexcused absences, and excessive tardiness were considered grounds for release. Such strictness was necessary because, for example, a kiln burner[2] could, through ten minutes' neglect, permit many thousands of pounds' worth of damage to the equipment. Sir Halford said that his insistence that all employees "play the game according to the rules of the organization" not only was necessary for efficiency but was also a matter of loyalty. "But," he added, "I hold firmly to the view that loyalty should be two-way traffic. If the head of a business expects a man to be loyal to him, then I say that man has every right to expect the same loyalty from the head of the business."

Finally, emphasis was placed on clerical and procedural efficiency. Sir Halford said that greater use of mechanized accounting and invoicing and continuous analysis and improvement of office procedures had slightly reduced the head-office staff in the past few years. Periodic evaluation of the forms and paper-work systems was conducted to eliminate unnecessary ones. "We have even had our competitor friends," he said, "come to look over our reporting and accounting systems. They are amazed by the fact that we get our data faster than they do with a proportionately smaller clerical staff."

2. *An effective sales organization* was the second contributing factor to growth and profits. Manufacturing savings effected by maintaining peak production were attainable only as long as the output could be sold. Mr. Yeatman, the General Sales Manager, remarked: "Since the industry sells on a common price arrangement, you don't sell cement by selling cheaper than the next man. You sell on delivery service, goodwill, product quality, and on contact with the customer. We like to think that we rate very high on all these counts. Selling cement is very much of a team effort, and we have a fine organization here, which naturally makes my job much easier." Under Mr. Yeatman were two area Sales Managers, one for Midland Sales and one for Southern and Export Sales. Each man-

---

[2] The kiln burner was the worker in charge of operating one or more kilns.

ager had eight salesmen, most of whom worked from their homes. Three of the Southern salesmen were located in the London office. The salesmen were paid entirely by salary, because, Mr. Yeatman said, "it's very difficult to say who's responsible for an individual sale. Most of our orders are sent in to one of our four offices—London, Birmingham, Rochester, or Rugby—rather than through the salesman. Our salesmen sell the company in general rather than the product; they are chiefly purveyors of goodwill."

Mr. Yeatman added that many customers bought from two or more manufacturers as a matter of policy. "I might mention," he added, "that all the United Kingdom cement manufacturers make cement which is so much higher in quality than standard British specifications that our customers have come to expect such quality from us. Accordingly, all manufacturers are constantly checking one another's product quality. Finally, since most large users have their own expert technical information on cement, we find ourselves giving technical advice only to an occasional small user. It's not an important tool in our sales kit."

3. *Overseas manufacture and other subsidiary activities* accounted for much of the company's growth and its increased profits in the past five years. Rugby was continually conducting site investigations and negotiations in search of new overseas opportunities for expansion.

4. *Transportation* of the United Kingdom cement sales was another reason for RPC's growth and profitability. Rugby's fleet had grown from 52 trucks in 1946 to 196 in 1961 (77 flatbed trucks, 17 bulk tippers, and 102 pressurized bulk wagons)[3] plus extra trucks hired in the peak construction season. Rugby was proud of the efficiency of its fleet, the operating costs of which remained below the transportation allowance in the delivered price. During 1960, the fleet averaged less than 7 per cent delays for repair, less than 10 per cent nonoperating idleness, and 6 per cent on-the-job delays. Company officials believed that their truck fleet was one of the most efficient in the industry. The major reason for this efficiency, the directors believed, was the highly centralized scheduling of truck dispatches. Each day the central transportation department, working with the sales department, prepared schedules of the following day's dispatches of all trucks from each of the three works. Scheduling attempted to maximize the number of deliveries by each truck and to make as uniform as possible the work load at the packing and loading plants.

---

[3] Flat-bed trucks carried cement in bags; pressurized bulk wagons carried loose cement in large tanks which were slightly pressurized to remove the cement at the delivery site; bulk tippers were fully enclosed dump trucks which carried loose cement.

5. *A philosophy of teamwork:* Sir Halford and the other directors of Rugby believed that the most important reason for the company's success was the achievement of company-wide teamwork through the chairman's human relations philosophy and application of profit-sharing and employee-shareholding plans. Rugby had no "personnel" department; development of teamwork was the job of managers at all levels within the firm. The impersonal term "personnel" and the word "welfare," with its connotation of charity, were banned from the Rugby vocabulary.

During the course of his career, Sir Halford had developed a philosophy of business as a team effort. A concrete expression of this philosophy was his introduction at Rugby of employee-shareholding and profit-sharing plans. Commenting on the relationship between his philosophy and these plans, he said:

> I am convinced that no scheme of profit-sharing or employee-shareholding can succeed unless it is built on a firm foundation of confidence within the business and of real esprit de corps, of a strong feeling on the part of all employees of pride in the company and its achievements. The goodwill of those working together in an industrial enterprise cannot be purchased for cash—of that I am sure. A scheme which is put in with the primary object of buying goodwill is almost certainly doomed to failure from the start. It may indeed not only do no good but may even do positive harm by creating suspicion, however ill-founded.[4]

Teamwork, commendable in any organization, was held to be doubly important in the cement industry, where production in large units of continuous-process plant made it impossible to associate individual effort with specific product output. Mutual confidence was felt to be the basic ingredient of teamwork: the board's confidence that all employees would put forth a fair day's work, operate and maintain the plant intelligently, and follow the leadership of the company; the employees' confidence in the capability and integrity of the directors and that discipline "which is as fair as it is firm" will be maintained.

ESPRIT DE CORPS AND COMPANY POLICIES

The following paragraphs summarize the most important company policies which Sir Halford felt had established esprit de corps within Rugby:

1. Personal contact between top executives and operating people all over the world was relatively frequent. Sir Halford visited the Trinidad and Australian plants at least once a year, and someone from the central

---

[4] Quotation from "This Is Industrial Partnership," a pamphlet written by Sir Halford in 1955 explaining his philosophy and the profit-sharing and employee-shareholding schemes of Rugby.

headquarters staff visited them, on an average, every 2 or 3 months. At home, Sir Halford not only delivered his annual "Message to his Fellow-Workers," but he always personally made presentations which were given to men with 25 years' service and again after 50 years' service. Such presentations were made in the presence of the recipients' colleagues, and Sir Halford usually gave a brief review of the recent progress of the company.

2. In his annual messages to the employees, he described recent developments within the company, emphasizing the cooperative roles played by employees and shareholders. He frequently discussed the importance of profits. The following is part of his message following the 1951 operations:

I want now to say something about profits, because a lot of nonsense has been talked about profits in the last few years, often by politicians of all parties who have never been in industry and have no practical knowledge of industry.

You and I know that profits are the reward and the measure of economy and efficiency, and are essential to the maintenance and expansion of a business. They are, in fact, the real and only bulwark behind our wages and salaries, for if this company ceases to make profits, it can be only a comparatively short time before you and I are out.

Let us recognize that it is up to every one of us in this team to go all out all the time, to give of our best, to maintain and increase our production with economy and efficiency, and, in turn, the profits of the company: first—and note that I put this first—because it is the job we are paid to do, and it is only common honesty to our shareholders to do it; and, secondly, in our own interests to safeguard our jobs for the future.

3. Another aspect of the teamwork was the "works committee" at each plant. Composed of the works manager, the works engineer, the safety officer, and five representatives elected from the factory work force, the committee met without exception each month with a senior member of the headquarters staff in attendance. The committee discussed matters of particular interest to the works concerned and suggestions for operational improvements. The head-office staff took this opportunity to clarify and discuss newly announced changes in policy and other company developments, such as the annual financial statements.

Late in 1961, an IMEDE researcher had the opportunity to attend a works committee meeting at the Rochester Works. Mr. R. L. Evans was the representative of top management in attendance. The committee chiefly discussed matters of plant safety and of amenities for the workers, such as a sink and hand towels for workers at a remote plant location. Mr. Halfden Lav, the Rochester Works Manager, said that this meeting was typical, especially insofar as it was primarily concerned with safety and working conditions. The researcher was impressed at the free and easy manner in which the workers entered into the discussions. Mr. Evans explained in great detail some minor points of company policy on tardiness and vacation time. Mr. Lav commented that the worker representatives occasionally brought up very minor points in the committee; "I think," he added, "that some men do this just to show that they are on their toes and doing a good job for their fellow-workers. We let them talk as long as they want to, and the result is that the committee functions very well, and in a very good spirit."

4. Another policy was that no one but Sir Halford had the authority to release people during slack periods. He had, in fact, never authorized a lay-off. For instance, the rail strike in 1955 almost closed the Rochester factory as coal reserves ran low. As the shut-down date approached, Sir Halford announced that no one would be laid-off, but that (a) some men would have to take their vacations during the shut-down; and (b) everyone would have to agree to do any job given him (at his usual pay rate) during the shut-down. (Last-minute settlement of the rail strike saved Rugby Cement from its contemplated shut-down.)

5. Since 1954, the company had offered its weekly-paid employees the option of having their contract of employment determinable not by the usual one week's notice but by one month's notice by either side for employees having ten years' service, two months for those having fifteen years, and three months for those having twenty years. Of those to whom the offer applied, over 85 per cent had accepted one of these options.

In commenting on the fact that 15 per cent of the workers had not chosen to take one of these options, company officials said that some workmen preferred the independence of being able to leave on short notice. "Our employee turnover is, however, quite low," one executive pointed out. "If we set aside employees with less than two years of service, our average worker has been here about 13 years. We do find that some new employees, especially young men, are not prepared for the demanding work in a cement plant, and such men leave, usually within 12 months. Thus new employees should not be fairly included in our average turnover figure. Incidentally, taking total annual wages and bonuses as an indicator, the cement industry ranks in the top half-dozen British industries in terms of earnings."

6. The final key policy of the company was summarized by Sir Halford:[5]

---

[5] Quotation from "This Is Industrial Partnership."

If there is to be a lively interest and pride in the company and its doings, then it is necessary that all employees be kept informed as far as possible about what is going on.

*   *   *   *   *

We try as far as we can to ensure that everyone has an opportunity of reading on the company's notice boards a few hours *before* it appears in the newspapers any release issued to the Press. We do not think it right that a man should learn from the newspapers something which he could quite properly have heard at first hand within the company.

Besides all of the aspects of teamwork within an organization, two other features of any profit-sharing or employee-shareholding plan were felt necessary by Sir Halford. The first was that any such scheme must be tailored to suit the circumstances of the company and the outlook, philosophy, and intention of its leader. The second feature was simplicity.

THE PROFIT-SHARING SCHEME

Sir Halford said that the Rugby profit-sharing scheme, inaugurated in 1935, was designed to emphasize two things:[6]

 a) that the efforts of the employees are the efforts of a team—that we are all working to one end; and
 b) the essential partnership which exists between the ordinary shareholders and the employees.

In speeches both to shareholders and to workers, Sir Halford referred to the partnership between capital and employees. He said that capital was nothing more than the "labour of yesterday—the production of yesterday which was surplus to the consumption of yesterday."

Fundamental to the partnership was the following bargain:[7]

. . . the labour of today is guaranteed payment for its services and the profit is calculated only after the remuneration of that labour has been paid. Capital, therefore, takes the risk and in return takes such profit (or loss) as arises *after* the labour of today has been paid in full.

But to my mind this difference in the basis of their respective remuneration in no way destroys the conception of industrial enterprise as essentially a partnership between the labour of yesterday (capital) and the labour of today. Nor is it destroyed if the "bargain" is varied slightly by guaranteeing the greater part of labour's remuneration irrespective of profit or loss and by making an additional but smaller part of it dependent on the results of the enterprise as a whole.

The employees' profit-sharing scheme provided for an annual bonus in excess of industry-negotiated wages (wage-earners) or contracted

---

[6] Quotation from "This Is Industrial Partnership."
[7] Quotation from same pamphlet.

salary (staff) for all Rugby workers. Basic points of the scheme are summarized below.[8]

1. To qualify for the profit-sharing bonus, an hourly or salaried employee must have completed, on December 31, twelve months' unbroken service to the satisfaction of the Directors.
2. For the purpose of calculating the bonus, each qualified employee is treated as if he held a certain number of Ordinary shares in the company. A staff employee received two "notional shares" for each £1 of annual salary. An hourly worker received shares in proportion to his length of service. For example, a worker with 1 year's service had 250 "notional shares"; a worker with 5 years' service, 375; a worker with 20 years, 750; and a worker with 40 or more years had 1,250.
3. The bonus is calculated at the full rate per share of the gross dividend declared and paid to the ordinary shareholders for the financial year in question and is paid immediately after the Annual General Meeting. For example, in 1960 the Ordinary dividend declared was 1s. 3d. per share. Thus a worker with five years' service, holding 375 notional shares, would receive a bonus of (375 × 1/3d.) or £23/8/9.
4. Certified sickness or compulsory National Service are ignored in calculating the number of years of unbroken service.
5. Any employee who leaves or is under notice to leave prior to the date of payment forfeits his bonus.
6. The scheme confers no rights in respect of any capital distribution, or distributions other than those declared as dividends on the Ordinary shares of the company out of profits.
7. The scheme is subject to modification or withdrawal at any time at the discretion of the Directors.

Sir Halford emphasized that the bonus was not automatic. In a very small number of cases each year, bonuses were withheld completely or in part because service was not "to the satisfaction of the directors." If a man's record for the year was questionable, including several unexplained tardinesses, for instance, it was submitted, without name, to the works committee of the factory. In all cases, the directors had abided by the committee's recommendation. Sir Halford said that withholding the bonus was not so much a penalty to the slack worker, but was necessary in fairness to those who gave 100 per cent service during the year. Summarizing, Sir Halford said:

I believe that this is important: the bonus must be something that is earned—not something which becomes a right. I also feel that the link with the ordinary shareholders' dividend is fundamental: if the dividend per share goes up, so does the bonus; if the dividend is reduced, the bonus falls too—which is as it should be.

---

[8] This explanation of the profit-sharing scheme contains only the major aspects. Full details are available in Sir Halford Reddish's booklet: "This Is Industrial Partnership."

THE "A" SHARE SCHEME

After World War II, Sir Halford saw two factors that made the profit-sharing scheme inadequate in emphasizing the partnership between capital and labor. He felt that the twin virtues of hard work and thrift no longer assured a man of personal savings for his old age—*taxation* restricted savings and inflation *devalued* them. Unlike the ordinary shareholder's income, which flowed from an asset whose market value reflected both the company's prosperity and inflationary pressures, the employee's profit-sharing bonus was not reflected in a realizable capital asset. Thus he did not have a "hedge" against inflation.

To supply this need, Sir Halford presented his "A" share plan, in late 1954, for approval by the ordinary shareholders. He said that the scheme was designed to do three things:[9]

> To give practical form to the unity of interest which I have always held to exist between the ordinary shareholders and the employees; to give a return to the ordinary shareholders on profits "ploughed back" in the past; and to give to every full-time employee the opportunity to have in his hands a capital asset readily realizable on death or retirement. It was received enthusiastically by shareholders and employees alike.

One million "A" shares of 1*s*. each were created with the following conditions attached to them:[10]

1. For any financial year after 31st December 1954 for which (*a*) the net profits before tax are not less than £900,000, and (*b*) the gross amount distributed as dividend to the Ordinary shareholders is not less than £300,000, the holders of the "A" shares shall be entitled to an amount of £70,000 plus 20% of any excess of the said net profits over £900,000 [See Exhibit 4]. However, (i) the amount attributable to the "A" shares shall not exceed 12½% of the net profits; and (ii) in the event of the issue of additional Ordinary share capital by the company after 31st December 1954, otherwise than by way of a capitalization of reserves or undistributed profits, the said figure of £900,000 shall be increased by a sum of equal to 6% of the proceeds or other consideration received by the company.[11]

2. Any amount attributable to the "A" shares as ascertained under (1) above may be distributed as dividend or carried forward in the books of the company to the credit of the "A" shares for subsequent distribution, as the Directors may decide.

3. The holders of "A" shares have no voting rights.

4. In a winding-up, the "A" shares may participate only insofar as the amount

---

[9] Explanation of "A" share plan summarized from "This Is Industrial Partnership."

[10] Explanation of "A" share plan summarized from "This Is Industrial Partnership."

[11] Because additional equity had been introduced since 1954, the "A" shares now began participating at a net profit above £964,500.

of their paid-in capital value and the "A" share credit carried forward on the company books, but no further participation in assets.

5. No further "A" shares shall be created without the sanction of an Extraordinary Resolution passed by the holders of the "A" shares.

Half of the "A" shares were offered to the ordinary shareholders at par and half to the employees.

"*All* full-time employees of the company were included: this was not a get-rich-quick exercise for the favoured few," said Sir Halford.

Allocation to the employees was done by dividing all employees into groups according to remuneration, responsibility, and status within the company (length of service was not a factor). Those in the first group were offered 250 shares, followed by groups of 500, 750, 1,000, 1,500, 2,000, and so on. (Most factory production workers were in the first group, for example.) Over 90 per cent of Rugby's employees had exercised their option and purchased the "A" shares.

Exhibit 4

PROFIT PARTICIPATION OF THE "A" SHARES
Graph of participation "formula" and schedule of gross profits *before* taxes

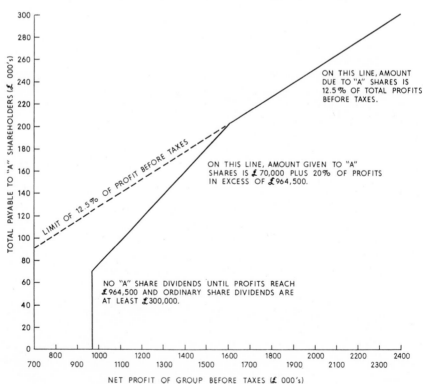

Exhibit 4—Continued

SUMMARY OF EARNINGS AND GROSS DIVIDEND PAYMENTS, 1954–61
(In 000's of £)

Year	1954	1955	1956	1957	1958	1959	1960	1961
Profit before tax	721	1025	1093	1106	1171	1491	1777	2020
Gross ordinary dividend	200	300	338	338	375	437	500	500
Gross payable to "A" shares			95	109	111	124	179	222	252
Actual "A" share dividend			50	63	63	75	100	125	125
Difference carried forward as "A" share credit			45	46	48	49	79	97	127
Cumulative "A" share credit*			45	91	140	189	268	365	493

* The "A" Share credit was contained in the Undistributed Profit account in the balance sheet. The directors considered this credit as a "dividend equalization reserve" to supply "A" dividends if they were not earned according to the formula (i.e., if pre-tax profits were below £964,500.

Sir Halford was particularly concerned about two aspects of the scheme. About the first, he said:[12]

I was anxious that there should be no element of a "gift" from one partner (the holders of the ordinary shares) to the other (the employees); and that the equity owned by the ordinary shares should be unimpaired. I was convinced that the holders of the ordinary shares could have no legitimate cause for complaint if the profits were so substantially increased in the future and some comparatively small part of the increase went to the employees as a reward for their efforts.

The "A" shares should be worth no more than was paid for them when issued, so that the employees could feel that whatever increased value accrued thereafter was due to their teamwork, with, I do not forget, nor do I allow them to forget, the capital provided by their partners in the enterprise.

This reason and tax consideration (discussed later) dictated that the minimum profit level at which the "A" shares would start participating (£900,000) should be well above the profit levels when the "A" shares were issued.

The second aspect was that the main object of the scheme was to insure employees of a capital sum on death or retirement. Sir Halford foresaw that the "A" shares might have some speculative attraction to the general public, and he did not want the employees to be tempted into selling and thus depriving themselves of retirement or death benefits from the plan. He also felt that anyone leaving the firm should be required to sell his shares back at par and thus enable newcomers to participate. To accomplish these ends, Sir Halford designated that the shares allocated to the employees were held in their behalf by Staff Nominees Limited, which was accountable to the employees for dividends declared and authorized to act in their behalf in all matters relating to the "A" shares. The following conditions applied:

---

12 Quotation from "This Is Industrial Partnership."

1. Initially and whenever an employee moves upward to a new group, he is given the opportunity to buy his allocation of shares at par. Failing to do so, he is not given a subsequent opportunity.
2. "A" shares may be sold by the employee at any time *at par* to Staff Nominees Limited and *must* be sold any time he leaves the company.
3. An employee's share may be sold at market value [market price was established by quotation on the London Stock Exchange of the "A" shares allotted originally at par to the Ordinary shareholders] *only* in the event of the employee's death while in the service of the company, or upon his reaching the age of 65 (55 for women).
4. Any dividend declared on the "A" shares is paid immediately to the employee.

Fifty thousand shares remained unallocated to the employees after the initial sale. The Directors felt that this block of shares and those shares which Staff Nominees Limited bought back, at par, from employees who left would be sufficient to offer shares to new and promoted employees for the foreseeable future.

In his message to his fellow-workers in the company following the 1958 operations, Sir Halford said the following about the "A" share plan:

... Quite often a man will say to me: "This 'A' share scheme of yours—tell me, has it increased production?" And I reply: "I haven't the slightest idea, but I shouldn't think so." So he says: "But surely that was the object. It's an incentive scheme, isn't it?" "On the contrary," I tell him, "I have always insisted that it should *not* be called an incentive scheme, because that to my mind would imply that we in Rugby Cement were not already doing our best, were not doing our duty in return for our wages and salaries. And that I will not have."

What our "A" share scheme does is to give to the employees the opportunity to build up capital available on retirement or on earlier death, and to promote the feeling that we are all one team working to the same end in partnership with our shareholders. The value of the "A" shares depends in the long run on the success of our efforts in making profits. And don't overlook the fact that half the "A" shares were issued, also at par, to the holders of our Ordinary shares. They very rightly benefit too, as they have seen these 1s.0d. shares change hands on the Stock Exchange at prices up to 42s.0d.[13]

Apart from the capital aspect, the holding of "A" shares by the employees of the company, and also, of course, our "profit-sharing" schemes, give some reward for successful endeavour—which is surely right.

The Taxation Aspect.   For the company, the profit-sharing bonus was considered a wage bonus and therefore a before-tax expense. The "A" share dividends, however, were similar to ordinary dividends, being paid out of after-tax profits.

---

[13] In 1961, "A" shares were quoted on the Stock Exchange at up to 100 shillings per share.

For the employees, the profit-sharing bonus was taxed as ordinary wage or salary income. Taxation of the employees in connection with "A" share distribution was a most difficult problem and one for which Sir Halford spent many hours in consultation with the Board of Inland Revenue.

The law held that if at the time of issue the value of the shares was greater than the amount the employees paid for them, the difference was taxable as a "benefit" arising from employment. The Rugby "A" share sale to its employees, however, had two characteristics which affected any ruling under this law:

1. "A" shares were not quoted on the market until two months after issue; thus it was a matter of discussion whether at time of issue they were worth more than the par value paid for them.
2. Employees were not free to sell their shares at market price except on retirement or death.

Final agreement with the Inland Revenue was reached which assessed the value of the "A" shares at time of issue slightly above par.

Tax assessment for shares issued subsequently to newcomers or to promoted employees required a different arrangement with the Inland Revenue, since by that time a market value was established. Final agreement resulted in considering a variable fraction of the difference between current market value and par value as taxable income. The fraction varied inversely with the length of time between the recipient's age and 65, when he could realize the market price of the "A" shares. For instance, a 25-year-old newcomer receiving 500 "A" shares would have to consider as income, for income tax purposes, only 10 per cent of the difference between market value and the price paid (1 shilling per share), because he could not realize the market value for 40 years. On the other hand, a 50-year-old man receiving 500 "A" shares would have to consider 60 per cent of the difference as taxable income, because he was much closer to realizing the gain. (The United Kingdom had no "capital gains" tax, but all dividends received by employees on their "A" shares up to retirement age were treated, for tax purposes, as "earned" income and therefore taxed at income tax rates.)

Overseas. An employee profit-sharing plan, similar to that existing for Rugby workers in the United Kingdom, had been established for workers in the Trinidad and Australian plants. "A" shares were offered only to workers in the United Kingdom, including staff assigned temporarily to the overseas operations.

A NOTE ON
THE MANUFACTURE AND DISTRIBUTION OF
PORTLAND CEMENT IN THE UNITED KINGDOM*

CEMENT MANUFACTURE

Portland cement was developed from an invention of a laborer in Leeds, England, in 1824. It was called "portland" cement because the concrete made from it resembled the well-known portland building stone in color and texture. Its manufacture is today a major world industry. World consumption has risen from 81 million tons in 1938 to 315 million in 1960 and is still rising.

Cement itself is manufactured from a closely controlled mixture of calcium carbonate, alumina, and silica. Calcium carbonate is found in various forms of limestone fairly liberally throughout the world. To be suitable for the manufacture of cement, the calcium carbonate content of the limestone must be relatively free from impurity. Soft chalk, which is very high in calcium carbonate, is found uniquely on either side of the English Channel toward the southern part of the North Sea. Chalk is easier to process than hard limestone, and its availability accounts, in part, for the fact that nearly half of British production is located in southeastern England.

Alumina is found in some forms of clay or shale. A relatively small amount of sand supplies the silica requirements.

From 3,000 to 3,600 pounds of raw materials are required to make a ton of cement. These are quarried with large diesel or electric-power shovels and conveyed to the works, which is normally placed nearby. There they are crushed and ground to a fine powder, and—in what is known as the "wet process"—mixed in strictly controlled proportions with water to form cement slurry. (Slurry normally contains about 40 per cent water by weight.) The liquid state of the mixture is necessary

---

* Much of the material included in this description was taken, with permission, from a paper, "The Manufacture and Distribution of Cement," prepared by the Chairman of the Rugby Portland Cement Company Ltd., Rugby, England.

This case was prepared by John Priedeman and Robert C. K. Valtz under the supervision of Professors K. R. Andrews or E. P. Learned.

to facilitate a perfectly homogeneous mixture of the raw materials and to permit rapid adjustment of the proportions by merely adding materials which quickly become uniformly dispersed throughout the liquid.

The slurry, when chemically correct, is fed to the kiln, which in a modern works is a large steel cylinder from 300 to 500 feet in length and 9 to 14 feet in diameter. It rotates at the rate of approximately once every 45 seconds, on a slightly inclined axis. The slurry is fed in at the higher end.

Near the lower end of the kiln is the burning zone, where fuel is injected into the kiln and fired to produce a temperature of about 2,500°F. Pulverized coal is the usual fuel in Britain, but oil and natural gas are used in other countries where these fuels are readily available. The water in the slurry is driven off as steam, together with the carbon dioxide content of the calcium carbonate and minor quantities of other gases. The remaining materials are fluxed in the intense heat and leave the kiln in the form of pea-sized nodules called "cement clinker." The chemical part of the process, completed at this point, is closely controlled throughout by chemists who test the raw materials, the coal, and the slurry every hour, day and night.

Thereafter, the process is largely mechanical. The cement clinker is ground in large water-cooled mills to a predetermined fineness, and a small amount of calcium sulphate, or gypsum, is added, in order to control the "setting time" of the resultant powder, now finished cement.

As it leaves the mills, the cement is weighed automatically and then pumped through pipes by compressed air to the large concrete silos in which it is stored. It remains in storage until it is withdrawn by mechanical means to the packing plant, where it is packed into paper sacks, which are automatically fitted, sealed, weighed and delivered by means of conveyors to the truck, the rail car, or the ship. It may be withdrawn from the silos into special bulk trucks which deliver it unpacked.

THE USES OF CEMENT

Cement is used as the binding agent in concrete and in mortar. Concrete, one of the world's primary construction materials, is composed of cement, sand, aggregate (clean gravel and stones), and water. Cement reacts chemically with the water and hardens, within a few hours after mixing, binding the sand and gravel particles in a solid mass. Concrete can be used without reinforcing (as in highway pavements, which contain only wire matting for temperature stresses), or it can be used with steel reinforcement, as in buildings and bridges.

THE STRUCTURE OF THE INDUSTRY IN THE UNITED KINGDOM, 1960

The cement industry in the United Kingdom consists of nine financially independent groups, all of which have been members of the Cement Makers' Federation since its establishment in 1934.

The three largest interests held, in 1960, about 83 per cent of the home market and have provided much of the leadership within the Federation. Associated Portland Cement Manufacturers Limited is considerably the largest company, with about 62 per cent of the United Kingdom market. The Tunnel Group has about 12.4 per cent, and The Rugby Portland Cement Company Limited 7 per cent of the United Kingdom market. Practically all the United Kingdom export trade is conducted by these three makers, which are also the only companies having manufacturing subsidiaries abroad.

The Federation regulates the internal affairs of the industry and arranges an interchange of technical information and industry-wide statistics. By far its most important function, however, is establishing the basis of selling prices and conditions of sale, in order, it is asserted, that the costs of distribution—which average nearly 20 per cent of delivered cost of cement—can be controlled. Membership is voluntary, and voting power is proportionate, although not directly, to the previous year's home deliveries. Approval of any proposal, however, requires the concurrence of at least four of the nine members. The Federation has no control over the production of any manufacturer, nor is it concerned with the export trade.

The British cement industry also maintains a large research and promotional organization, the Cement and Concrete Association, part of whose function is to increase the use and uses of concrete. Cement itself has no substitute; however, it is used only to form concrete, which is in competition with steel, brick, stone, tile, timber, and many other materials.

The industry also organizes its conduct of labor relations. For more than 35 years it has operated a National Joint Industrial Council at which industry-wide wage rates and working conditions are set. The industry has never had a national strike or lock-out. Holidays with pay and profit-sharing plans were features of the industry for many years before the War.

POSTWAR GROWTH OF THE INDUSTRY

The post-war progress made by the industry is shown in Table 1.

Table 1

U.K. CEMENT DELIVERIES
(000 tons)

	Home	Export	Total
1961 (est.)	13,800	800	14,600
1960	12,463	1,000	13,463
1959	11,683	1,088	12,771
1958	10,675	1,145	11,820
1957	10,709	1,382	12,091
1956	11,275	1,600	12,875
1955	10,759	1,766	12,526
1954	10,079	1,769	11,848
1953	9,335	1,917	11,253
1952	9,147	2,055	11,202
1951	8,144	1,974	10,119
1946	5,479	1,095	6,574
1939	7,587	665	8,252

THE ECONOMICS OF THE INDUSTRY

SITING OF THE PLANT

It is considered a matter of prime importance that cement plants be located as close as possible to raw-material deposits. Adequate water supplies, fuel, and electricity and access to road, rail, and water transport must also be available. Thorough technical investigation is required, since both the physical and chemical properties of the raw materials will influence the design of many of the factory components.

COSTS OF PRODUCTION

The manufacture of cement is a highly mechanized process and employs comparatively little labor. The capital investment is among the highest for any industry; it equals almost £20,000 per man employed, which is over six times what it was before the War. Depreciation is therefore a heavy charge and will become progressively heavier as prewar plants are replaced.

Coal is the largest individual item in the cost of production. It takes approximately 800 pounds of coal, including the coal used to generate electricity, to make a ton of cement.

In general, industry production costs are distributed as follows:

	Per Cent
Coal and power	45–50
Direct labor	10–15
Consumable equipment	9–12
Depreciation (installed cost)	9–12
Indirect factory labor and other overheads (supervision, testing, maintenance, cost accounting, etc.)	15–20
Manufacture cost	100
Average haulage	20–30 of M.C.
Sales expense	5– 8 of M.C.
General administrative overhead	10–15 of M.C.

Profit margins are not disclosed. It has been asserted that current prices allow profits only because the manufacturers are still using, in part, equipment installed in the late 1930's. As greater proportions of new, more expensive plant installations are brought into use, prices may rise to cover increased depreciation charges.

Leaders of the British cement industry have repeatedly stated that manufacture of cement in the United Kingdom has for years been conducted with the highest efficiency and one of the lowest unit costs of any producing country in the world.

DISTRIBUTION

The distribution of cement to the site where it will be used is a more technical and complicated problem than at first sight appears, for it is not the cost of production at the place where the cement is made but the cost at the site where it will be used that is important. The geographical distribution of demand, which in itself varies quite considerably from year to year (and can be materially distorted at different times by large airport programs, road works, reservoirs, and similar forms of construction using large quantities of cement) is not coincident with the geographical distribution of the works.

Most companies in the industry maintain a fleet of trucks for road delivery. Little goes by rail, owing to the costs of double-handling. Delivery in bulk (in special vehicles) has rapidly increased in recent years and now accounts for nearly 50 per cent of the home trade.

PRICING AND THE ROLE OF THE CEMENT MAKERS FEDERATION

The manufacturers feel that a joint policy of distribution and price can avoid the severe price competition which, in the early 1930's, created difficulties for both producers and users. For example, a works near to a large consuming area might be able to supply only one-third of the demand in that area, leaving the remaining two-thirds to come from a much greater distance. If there were not a coordinated price policy, it has been said, a builder taking his supplies from the nearer works would pay one price, while his competitor would have to pay a higher price for cement coming from a more distant works. This would assertedly lead to endless complications in bidding for construction projects.

The Federation's pricing arrangements, therefore, have the following objectives:[1]

1. To sell and distribute cement throughout the country in the most efficient and economical manner commensurate with the interests of the country as a whole, of the users of cement, and of the manufacturers—in particular by:
   (*a*) Encouraging the delivery in any particular area from the nearest works, with the object of avoiding unnecessary and wasteful haulage
   (*b*) Eliminating depots (except where these perform useful functions) and delivering straight from works to construction sites
   (*c*) Providing a stable system of prices which takes into account the high proportion of the cost of transport in the price of cement and avoids disproportionate price differentials which would otherwise arise between various parts of the United Kingdom.
2. To provide a price system giving sufficient stability to enable manufacturers individually and collectively to plan production in advance efficiently and economically, and individually to undertake the heavy expenditure required to meet increasing demand for cement
3. To ensure during any temporary shortage of cement that prices remain at a reasonable level
4. To eliminate unnecessary and expensive advertising
5. To provide for standard forms of packages, bulk delivery, and the like
6. To arrange, for the convenience of both manufacturers and buyers, standard conditions of supply and forms of quotation and contract
7. To facilitate joint research and exchange of information to improve the standard and the potential utility of cement

To achieve these aims, the Federation's present system provides for the same delivered price at the same point of delivery for all brands of cement, irrespective of the works from which the cement may come.

There are 48 cement works in the United Kingdom (Cement works very near one another usually have the same base price.) There are 37 base prices, one for each location where cement is manufactured and one for each cement-importing center on the coast. These base prices are nearly the same at every factory, although there are slight variations made for the type of raw materials used and the delivered price of fuel to the works. For the former, for instance, plants using chalk as their source of calcium carbonate have base prices about 5 per cent lower than those using limestone, since all limestone crushing and grinding expenses are eliminated. In 1961, the base factory price (delivered within 5 miles

---

1 Summarized from a policy statement of the Federation.

of plant) of ordinary portland cement ranged from 111/6*d*. to 127/6*d*. per ton.

Radiating from each works is a series of concentric circles at 4- or 5-mile intervals, the circles from any particular works continuing until they meet the circles radiating from another works. The delivered price within each of these circles increases by 1/6*d*. for each circle (see Exhibit 1).

These price increments do not, in fact, cover actual transportation

Exhibit 1

ILLUSTRATION OF THE FEDERATION'S PRICING AGREEMENT

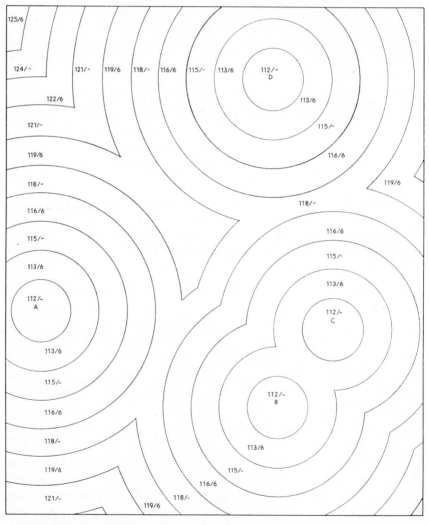

SALES PRICE IN SHILLINGS AND PENCE PER TON SHOWN FOR EACH FOUR- OR FIVE-MILE ZONE.

costs; therefore, manufacturers allow 10–15 per cent of the base price plus the zone price increments for covering haulage costs. As a result, between 20 and 30 miles from a producing unit is considered the "break-even" haulage distance, below which haulage costs are less than the allowance in the base price plus the incremental price increases, and above which the converse is true. The more efficiently a producer can operate his truck fleet, the greater will be his break-even haulage distance.

The pricing scheme means that every buyer at a particular point will pay exactly the same price for his cement. It also means that there is every inducement for a manufacturer to save transport costs by selling as much of his production as possible within the circles controlled by his own works. The further he delivers cement from his own works, the more likely he is to run into the circles controlled by another works, where the price he will receive will begin to decrease. The Federation asserts that the effect of this arrangement is to save as much as possible of the heavy transport costs and so maintain throughout the country, on the average, a lower level of prices than would otherwise be the case.

There exist standard merchant discounts. Retail building material suppliers are entitled to a merchants's discount, but they in turn must sell cement at the same prices, in the particular zones, which apply to the manufacturers. Thus a buyer pays the same price whether he buys from a manufacturer or a merchant. Merchants play a major role in supplying small orders, since the minimum order normally accepted by a manufacturer is 6 tons. A relatively small percentage of industry sales is made directly to merchants for their own accounts, but much more cement is delivered to the customer "on site" at a merchant's order.

THE RESTRICTIVE TRADE PRACTICES ACT

In 1956, England passed the Restrictive Trade Practices Act, which required that all trade agreements be registered with the Registrar of the Restrictive Practices Court. These agreements subsequently had to be justified before the Court, which would decide whether they were contrary to the public interest. On March 16, 1961, the Restrictive Practices Court handed down its decision: it upheld the Federation's price agreements with only minor modifications.

In essence, the Federation argued that, because of its price-fixing agreement, United Kingdom cement manufacturers could operate with more certainty of profit than under free competition. Because of this greater security, they were willing to accept a lower return on investment and thus could sell cement appreciably lower than if prices had not been fixed.

Experts on both sides agreed that, in order to attract new capital into the industry, a net return on investment of at least 15 per cent would have to be available. The Federation proved that, in order to yield such a return, a new cement plant would have to price its cement at least 25 shillings per ton higher than the current average price. It also established that Federation members were earning, on the average, less than 10 per cent return on investment. The court therefore concluded that, had the price-fixing arrangement not existed, the price of cement would have been "significantly" higher, and the public would have suffered accordingly. Thus the court upheld the main price-fixing clause. It found that the industry was efficient and had acted with a sense of responsibility.

The presiding judge was concerned only that the price-fixing agreement should be as honorably administered in the future as had been true in the past. Thus he requested, and the Federation agreed, that if at any future date the Registrar should wish to determine whether prices were still being kept at a fair level, the Federation would cooperate fully by making cost and price data available for inspection.

The Federation's practice of giving quantity discounts based on total annual purchases from *all* Federation members was disallowed by the judge, on the grounds that it did not reflect true economies from volume sales.

The court also scrutinized, and upheld with one exception, minor agreements regarding terms of sale. In summing up his decision, Mr. Justice Diplock remarked:

> In the result, therefore, the Respondents have satisfied us that the main price-fixing conditions, other than those providing for general rebates to large users and large merchants, are not contrary to the public interest, and that the ancillary restrictions, other than that relating to the prohibition upon the quotations and contracts for the supply of cement for periods exceeding twelve months, are also not contrary to the public interest.[2]

In commenting on the Court's decision, Sir Halford Reddish observed:

> I am not being wise after the event if I say that the judgement accorded closely with our expectations, for we were confident throughout that a detailed examination of our arrangements would show conclusively that they were in the public interest. And the cement makers were not alone in their satisfaction with the outcome of the case. Over four thousand buyers of cement sent us replies to a questionnaire before the hearing: something like 97 per cent of them were strongly in favour of a continuation of the present system."[3]

---

[2] *Judgement in the Restrictive Practices Court on an agreement between Members of the Cement Makers' Federation*, printed by the Cement and Concrete Association, 1961.

[3] *Investors Chronicle*, March 24, 1961.

THE RUGBY PORTLAND CEMENT COMPANY LIMITED (B)

Late in 1961, an IMEDE research team decided to attempt to expand the Rugby Portland Cement case by adding information on the ways in which various employees of the company viewed their jobs. To this purpose, an IMEDE researcher toured each of the company's three cement works in England; he also conducted interviews with a number of hourly-paid workers and with a substantial number of middle- and top-management executives. This case includes excerpts from some of these interviews, as well as some of the researcher's impressions of what he saw.

VIEWS OF SOME RUGBY WORKMEN

Rugby's management was very cooperative in helping the researcher to interview some of the workmen. Although in theory it would have been useful to interview a rather large number of workers selected at random, this was not practicable for certain reasons:

1. There were limitations on the research time available for these interviews.
2. There was a chance that some men, if chosen at random, might:
   a) Not be able to articulate their views;
   b) Be less than wholly frank;
   c) Be unable to leave their work posts at the desired time.

Accordingly, Mr. R. L. Evans (Deputy Managing Director) and Mr. Baker (Works Manager of the Rugby works) selected from the Rugby workforce four workers who, they thought, would be articulate, honest, and as representative as possible of the general sentiments of the entire Rugby worker group. The researcher interviewed the four men separately, in an office at the Rugby plant; nobody else was present during the interviews. The names of the four men interviewed have been disguised.

INTERVIEW WITH MR. RYAN

Mr. Evans and Mr. Baker, in arranging the interviews, mentioned that Mr. Ryan should provide a highly entertaining and useful interview, that he was outspoken and highly articulate. Mr. Ryan, who had been working for the company since 1956, was an Irishman; he appeared to be about 40 years old. He worked in the Transport Department of the company as a truck driver and had been a member of the Rugby works committee for some time. The researcher asked each of the four men only one question to begin: What did the man think about working for the company, what were the bad points and the good points? Mr. Ryan began:

Well, I might tell you I'm an old union man, been a sort of union agitator all my working life. Before I came here I never held a job longer than eighteen months. I've been here almost six years now, and I can tell you this, I'm going to stay here the rest of my life. And, mind you, I got a lot less to gain by staying here than most of the men. I have no A-shares, because you know you only get one chance to buy them A-shares, and when I had to buy them, I didn't have the money because my wife just had to have an operation. So now for the rest of my life I got to work here knowing that I'll never have no A-shares, and I think this is unfair, and I keep fighting to get me shares, and maybe I will and maybe I won't, but I'll stay on here no matter what.

And another thing is I'm a very bad timekeeper—sometimes it's my fault, and sometimes it was because I had to take my wife to the doctor and so I'd come in late, and so for three straight years I lost my profit-sharing bonus on account of being late so much. [Mr. Ryan had actually lost his bonus in two nonconsecutive years, management reported.] So you can see what I mean when I tell you that I got much less to gain by working here than the other men.

But even though there's lots of little things could be done, this is a wonderful place to work, and that's the Lord's own truth. I'm not saying anything to you I wouldn't say right to the Chairman's face if he asked me—I'm not a man to say what he doesn't mean.

You got to remember this: it's no good coming down to a cement works if you don't want to work hard. But they pay you good, and the main thing is, you always get treated fair. If you got a complaint, you can take it as high as you want, right up to the Chairman himself, but it's no good complaining unless you give 'em the facts. That's what they want to see: facts.

Another thing you ought to write down is this: in this company, I'm just as good as anybody, as good as the Chairman or Mr. Evans—that's what you won't get anywhere else. We all know this here, and we know you've got to work as a team. And I'll tell you this, I know the Chairman would let me buy my A-shares if he could, but you see he's got to be fair to the other workers too. But I do think that you get punished awful hard for being late. [Mr. Ryan's profit-sharing bonus would have amounted, in those years when he lost it, to about £30. His weekly wages were about £15.]

Over in Coventry, you know [about 15 miles away], in the car and airplane factories a man can make £30 a week, while here he'll only make about £15, but we get the £15 for 52 weeks of the year, plus the profit-sharing, the A-shares, and lots of other benefits. The company buys up lots of clothes for us, so we can get them cheaper. I once compared what I earned in a year with a friend of mine who works in Coventry for £29 a week, and you know what? I came out £48 ahead of him for the year, because those fellows are always getting laid off.

And let me tell you this: you'd never get a better firm to work for, no matter where you went; there isn't another company like this, at least none I've ever heard about.

You know, when I tell you we work hard here, you've got to remember that the Chairman doesn't ask us to do anything he doesn't do himself. You know, he works eighteen hours a day, and when he come down sick recently and had to have that operation, his doctors told him to take it easy, and so he did—he only worked ten hours a day.

[Mr. Ryan then gave the researcher a very detailed description of what was involved in his truck-driving. He stressed that the equipment was the best obtainable, that the company paid much more attention to driver safety than to delivering a maximum daily tonnage of cement, that scrupulous care was taken, at great expense, to be certain that the customer received all the cement he had been billed for.]

You see my truck out there? That truck, it's brand new, and it cost £10,000, and they expect me take care of it like if it was my own, and I do. [The truck in fact cost slightly over £3,500.] And I know I've got 42 hours a week guaranteed, and more hours on weekends if I want to make extra money, and that's a hell of a nice thing for a truck driver. And as soon as I've driven 11 hours in a single day, even if I didn't get home with the truck by the time my 11 hours was up, the company would send out another lorry with two drivers to drive me and my truck home, that's how careful they are about the 11-hour rule. And you see them fine overalls we drivers got, and them jackets? Mr. Reddish, I believe, bought them for us out of his own pocket. That's just the kind of man he is. [In fact he didn't: they are provided by the company.]

I told you I used to be a union man, but I tell you this, if a union came in here now, it would hurt the workers—they'd get less pay, they couldn't touch anything they weren't supposed to. That's the kind of a union man I am today.

In summing up, and this is God's own truth, I think Sir Halford Reddish ought to be England's Prime Minister, and Mr. Evans ought to be the Secretary for Foreign Affairs.

INTERVIEW WITH MR. MASON

Mr. Mason was a foreman in the "raw plant," where the slurry was made. He had been working for the company about 14 years and appeared to be about 50. He began:

Well, wherever I went, I don't think I could better myself, that's what I'd say. The Chairman puts us in the picture about what's going on, he has more of a fatherly concern for us, I think. I've known the Chairman 30 years, and if he says a thing he means it. He's put in some wonderful plans for the men, he has. For example, when my father died, we got about £1,000 for his A-shares, and this was a big help, because I've got a sister who isn't very well, and this money pays for her. From the workman's point of view, if you want it, I find that they're very, very satisfied. I've got 30-odd men working for me, and I get all the points of view, so to speak, and I think I can say that they're all happy to be working here. Now, of course, there's some men as will always find something to complain about, you're going to have that anywhere, but in the main I think that the men like working here very much.

You're an American, so I'll put it in American: damn it all, we're on to a good thing here and we know it.

I've got a brother, a son, and two brothers-in-law working here, and my father before he died. They all came to work here after I did. Now do you think they'd have come if this wasn't a good place to work?

I do believe honestly, and I'm not handing you any bull, that we couldn't better ourselves. And you've got to remember this: Sir Halford will give any of his men a proper hearing anytime. And what's astonishing is that as the firm gets larger, the company seems to give us more attention, when you'd think it'd be the other way around.

Now you take your average Englishman, he's the biggest grumbler in the world, about anything at all. But you won't find much grumbling here. You'd have to kick them out to get the men here to leave.

INTERVIEW WITH MR. TOOT

Mr. Toot, who appeared to be about 50, had been with Rugby about 7 years. The researcher received the distinct impression that Mr. Toot was temperamentally a sort of cynic who only grudgingly would admit that a workingman's life could be decent, although this impression was formed on the basis of very little evidence. Mr. Toot began:

Taken all around, I should say that this is a very good place to work. A workman here knows that he can go as high as he likes, if he has the ability. You get fair treatment here. I suppose that work here is 80 per cent satisfactory. For the other 20 per cent, it's hard to say what the objections might be. But one thing is, when a man first came to work here, he didn't get enough participation in the bonus system [the profit-sharing scheme], but they've changed that now.

If a man's willing to do an honest day's work, he'll generally be satisfied here. I suppose I could say this: the longer a man's been here, the more he wants to stay.

Now, you get some fellows, especially young ones, come in and they can't stick the work; it's too heavy or too hard for them. They usually leave, if they're this type, in 12–18 months. If a man sticks it a year or a year and a half, he'll probably stay here until he's through working.

This is a long-term policy job, so to say. It's good if you're thinking about your old age, because the company really takes care of you after you retire. I don't suppose you know this, but all the company's pensioners [retired workers] get a ton of coal from the company at Christmas. There's a Christmas party for the pensioners. And men like Mr. Evans and Mr. Baker visit the pensioners very regularly. The company doesn't just forget you when you've stopped working for them— they take care of you.

I suppose when I think of it, it's hard to say what kind of objections, you might say, a man could have to working here, if he's not just a casual laborer who doesn't care about doing an honest day's work, if he doesn't care about doing a good job. This is a good place to work.

INTERVIEW WITH MR. FORSTER

Mr. Forster had been working for Rugby for 48 years, and he worked in the quarry. He talked rather little, much less than the previous three men.

Well, I've been working here all my life, and that's a fact. It's hard work, and no doubt about it, but it's a wonderful company to work for. I was here, you know, when Sir Halford took over, and it was wonderful when he did. He promised us steady work, and we've had it ever since. Some of your casual lads, now, who come here looking for an easy day's work and high pay, they don't stay, but a real man, a man who doesn't mind work, he'll be happier here than anywhere else I've ever heard of.

RANDOM IMPRESSIONS OF THE RESEARCHER

In the course of his tour of the three different works, the researcher spent a great deal of time with Mr. R. L. Evans, who toured each plant with him, and with the Works Managers. The researcher was especially struck by two facts. First, Mr. Evans and the Works Managers appeared to know a great deal about the background of every company employee. The researcher was, while walking through the plant, introduced to one worker who had been a chef in Wyoming some years ago. Another worker was pointed out as having been (he was now 72) a good rugby player in his youth. These and similar details were forthcoming quite frequently from Mr. Evans or the Works Managers. Second, the workers all said "Hello" to Mr. Evans as he passed through the plant, and Mr. Evans would chat with them about their families and how things were going.

Another impression, although a difficult one to justify with explicit evidence, was that the various managers were more than superficially concerned with their workers and their lives. Words and phrases which often recurred in the four days of conversation included: "fair treatment," "decent work for a man," "take care of our men," "expect them to work as part of a team." Workers and managers alike constantly referred to themselves as being part of a single team; they did so either implicitly or explicitly.

LIMITS ON DECENTRALIZED PROFIT RESPONSIBILITY[1]

By John Dearden

What limitations exist in most decentralized financial control systems that make it imprudent for top management to delegate profit responsibility completely to the divisional manager?

How can these limitations result in the divisional manager taking actions that are not in the best interests of the company?

How can top management safeguard against such uneconomic actions on the part of divisional management?

In the typical decentralized financial control system, the divisional manager is responsible for earning a satisfactory rate of return on the investment that he manages. To date, this "rate-of-return method" has been the best one available. Unfortunately, the rate-of-return method has four *inherent* limitations that cause a conflict between divisional and company interests—even if investment is calculated in the best possible way. These limitations make it inadvisable for top management to decentralize complete profit responsibility to the division. In fact, specific management action must be taken to safeguard against possible uneconomic actions on the part of the divisional manager.

The purpose of this article is to describe why the rate-of-return method fails to ensure correct divisional action, how such action can affect profits adversely, and what safeguards should be employed to ensure correct divisional action.

DECENTRALIZATION CRAZE

In the past decade, many businesses have adopted some form of decentralized organization because of the growth of their operations in size and complexity. This trend has been so pronounced that some authorities believe that decentralization has become a "fad" in American industry. There is no doubt that, in some cases, decentralization has been carried to extremes. I know of one instance where a company consisting of a single plant, employing less than 50 people, was set up as the B Division

---

[1] *Harvard Business Review*, July–August, 1962, pp. 81–89. Reprinted by permission.

of the X & Y Industries. For the most part, however, decentralization has been undertaken to relieve top management of day-to-day operating decisions so that more time could be spent on long-range planning and strategy.

ORGANIZATION SETUP

A typical decentralized organization consists of a number of independent divisions, with a divisional manager responsible for each. Although in many instances the divisional manager may be held only partially responsible for his operation, in a full-scale decentralized organization he will be delegated complete responsibility for the profitability of the division that he controls. Before this can be delegated safely, however, top management must be sure that the divisional manager will always act, to the extent of his ability, in the best interests of the company. This means (*a*) that the divisional manager must *know* what actions will be to the company's best interest, and (*b*) that he will be *motivated* to take such actions. Furthermore, if decentralized financial control is to be effective, top management must be able to *evaluate* the profit performance of the divisional manager so that effective performance can be rewarded.

These three functions—knowledge, motivation, and evaluation—are most frequently accomplished by using the rate-of-return method. To illustrate:

Knowledge. If all divisions earn a satisfactory return on their investment, the company must automatically earn a satisfactory return. If the divisional manager always tries to maximize the return on his investment, the decisions that he will make will be consistent with the best interests of the company. The divisional manager will *know* what action will be in the best interests of the company because it is the action that will maximize the rate of return of his division. In other words, he does not have to be concerned with company interests because they are consistent with divisional interests.

Motivation. Motivation is obtained by rewarding the divisional manager when he earns a satisfactory profit on the investment that he controls. It is, therefore, to his personal interest to maximize the divisional rate of return. In this way, the interests of the divisional manager are also made consistent with company interests.

Evaluation. The rate of return on investment is also used by top management to evaluate the effectiveness of the divisional manager. In most companies, however, the potential rate of return will be different for different divisions. The reasons for this are numerous: one division may be operating in a depressed industry; another division may have a competitive disadvantage; another division may be benefiting disproportionately from being part of the larger organization; another division may be suffering from a previous period of inept management.

Whatever the reason for the different profit potentials, top management cannot evaluate a division's performance by the absolute rate of return that is earned.

One division may do well to break even; another may be doing poorly if it earns 30% after taxes. In order to evaluate divisional profit performance better, therefore, each division is assigned a profit objective based on the profit potential of the division, and evaluation is accomplished by comparing the actual profits to this objective.

NOT QUITE PERFECT

To my knowledge, the rate-of-return method comes closer to accomplishing these functions than any other method, assuming, of course, that the divisional investment is calculated in such a way as to maintain a consistency of interests between the division and the company.[2] If only the method were perfect, complete profit responsibility could be safely delegated to the divisional manager. In fact, an annual evaluation of performance and review of future plans is all that would be required from top management. However, because of the limitations in the rate-of-return method, each decentralized company must determine the possible impact on its own organization and, where necessary, set up the proper safeguards.

Let us take a close look at what factors limit the effectiveness of the rate-of-return method. Specifically, these limitations result from:

Differences in divisional profit objectives.
The same rate of return being applied to all of the assets in a division.
The high profit objectives in some divisions.
The pressure for short-term profits in some divisions.

DIFFERING OBJECTIVES

In a decentralized company, there may be wide variations in the rate of return expected from the different divisions. It is not uncommon, for example, to find divisional rates of return on investment varying from zero (or even a negative rate) to as much as 30% after taxes. This situation creates a problem because the division with the 30% profit objective will be worse off for undertaking any capital project that earns less than 30%, while any return at all on a project will benefit the division with the zero profit objective.

Accordingly, if the divisional manager is allowed to make his own investment decisions, it will be to his best interests to use his profit objective as the cutoff point. That is, he will invest as long as the proposed capital investment will earn more than his objective. From a company point of view, however, it makes no sense to have an investment in Division A require a 30% return while Division B needs to earn only 5% for the

---

[2] See John Dearden, "Problem in Decentralized Profit Responsibility," *Harvard Business Review*, May–June, 1960, p. 79.

same type of investment. This becomes particularly ludicrous when you consider that the most profitable divisions will be required to earn the highest rates of return.

For example, a company discovered that one of its divisions was replacing its trucks every four years while another division was replacing identical trucks every five years. Investigation revealed that the reason for the difference was that the first division had a lower profit objective than the second. A replacement decision is one of timing. Simple replacement analysis techniques show that the point of replacement occurs when the cost savings for the coming year resulting from investment in new equipment equal the required rate of return on the investment in the new equipment. The higher the return required on the investment, therefore, the slower will be the replacement. (Comparable results will be obtained from more sophisticated analytical techniques such as the well-known MAPI, or Machinery and Allied Products Institute, formula.)[3]

DIVERGING LIMITS

In any event, it is clear that a company must set one limit for replacing comparable equipment and require one rate of return on comparable investments. It was pointed out earlier that so long as the divisional profit objective is different from the return required by the company, the divisional manager will be acting against his own best interest to use the company rate of return. But let's see the implications of this. If the divisional manager's profit objective is higher than the company rate, he will be limiting his ability to attain this objective by using the company return as a criterion for timing the replacement of equipment. If his profit objective is less than the company return, he will be foregoing possible improvements by using the company return as a criterion of replacement.

This problem applies not only to replacement decisions but also to other capital investment decisions. Thus, a divisional manager with a high-profit objective will not want to undertake an expansion project that will lower his rate of return; conversely, if his profit objective is low, he would be willing to undertake an expansion project that might not result in a satisfactory profit from the company's point of view.

UNDESIRABLE METHODS

Although, to my knowledge, there is no completely satisfactory solution to this problem, some practices are worse than others. Let us take them up individually, starting with the least desirable:

1. *Leave investment decisions entirely up to the divisional manager.*

---

[3] See Ross G. Walker, "The Judgment Factor in Investment Decisions," *Harvard Business Review*, March–April, 1961, p. 93.

This is, of course, the poorest of all the methods in that the divisional manager does not even *know* what action he should take to optimize company profits. He will invest in accordance with his profit objective, which will only coincidentally be the company's cost of capital.

2. *Review and approve capital investment proposals centrally.*

Most companies have some centralized system for reviewing and approving divisional capital expenditures. However, while this review makes it possible to eliminate proposed expenditures that are not expected to earn the minimum required by the company, the method does have some limitations. For one thing, it will not prevent a division with a high profit objective from foregoing possible desirable investments— simply because the manager will not allow them to reach the formal proposal stage.

Management should be aware of another danger. There may be a tendency for the divisions with low profit objectives to resolve all questions in favor of replacing or adding new equipment. If a division has a profit objective of 7½% when the company requires 15% for a capital investment, the division may be motivated to try to get authorization if a return of 15% can possibly be rationalized. Even if the actual results turned out to be only 10%, the division will still improve its profit performance compared to its objective.

3. *Equalize the profit potential of all of the divisions.*

In some cases, the profit objective of all divisions can be equalized by adding an intangible asset such as "good will" to the investment base of those divisions with high objectives. This will, of course, make it possible to reduce the objective and, thus, bring these divisions in line with the others.

Assume that a company has four divisions and that their investment and profit objectives are as follows:

	Investment	After-Tax Profit Objective Per Cent	After-Tax Profit Objective Amount
Division A	$1,000,000	15%	$150,000
Division B	1,200,000	20	240,000
Division C	1,400,000	10	140,000
Division D	1,500,000	10	150,000
Total	$5,100,000		$680,000

Assume further that the company's required rate of return for capital investments is 10%. To bring Division A and Division B into line with the other divisions and the 10% rate, add $500,000 good will to the investment in Division A and $1,200,000 good will to the investment in Division B. After this addition, the divisional objectives will be as follows:

	Investment	After-Tax Profit Objective Per Cent	After-Tax Profit Objective Amount
Division A	$1,500,000	10%	$150,000
Division B	2,400,000	10	240,000
Division C	1,400,000	10	140,000
Division D	1,500,000	10	150,000
Total	$6,800,000		$680,000

All the divisions now have the same profit objective which is equal to the company's capital investment rate. However, this method has several disadvantages. For instance:

It is generally limited to a case where, although most divisional objectives are at the company rate, a few divisions are out of line on the high side. For example, it could not be applied if many divisional objectives were far below the company rate. (A negative good will could be used, but the theoretical justification would be difficult to explain to management.)

Adding good will makes it *appear* that all divisions have the same profit potential. This may mislead management as to the direction of future expansion. In fact, since it will always be necessary to calculate the rate of return both with and without good will, management could well find this confusing.

The idea of adding good will to divisional assets is quite abstract and could, at best, be used only to bring down the return of a very few high-profit divisions. Otherwise, neither top management nor divisional management will be likely to understand. And if they do not, the financial control system will be weakened considerably.

4. *Announce company policy to all divisions.*

Inform all divisions what the company policy is with respect to capital investments and state that all divisions will be expected to adhere to this policy when making capital expenditures. At the same time, announce that if any investment results in lowering significantly a division's ability to achieve its profit objective, the profit objective will be adjusted.

Although not completely satisfactory, this is perhaps the best solution. This method does assure that each divisional manager *knows* what the company thinks is best. It also provides for an adjustment if his profit potential is affected by adhering to company policy. But in the case of day-to-day replacement, he may still be expected to act in a way that is not to his best interests, since he could hardly request a change in profit objective for relatively minor investments, even though these investments were at less than his profit objective.

To summarize, where there is a significant range in the profit objectives among the divisions of a company, a danger exists that inconsistent investment policies are being used. Since there must be one optimum investment policy for the company, this means that potential profits are being lost. In any company where divisions have different objectives and no over-all company policy has been formulated, incorrect investment decisions are most likely being made.

STANDARD RATE OF RETURN

Under the rate-of-return method, the same rate applies to all assets. This means that any time an asset is added, it must result in annual earnings equal to the amount of the investment multiplied by the profit objective percentage. This creates a problem because different assets might reasonably be expected to earn different rates of return.

In a previous article, I discussed this problem as it applied to inventories, and pointed out how the use of the divisional profit objective in the equation for economic order quantities could give incorrect decisions.[4] This problem occurs also with respect to other assets. For example, general-purpose equipment does not usually earn as high a rate of return as automatic equipment. Consequently, the divisional manager will not invest in general-purpose equipment when the return is less than his profit objective. (This is all right if it is the company's policy to do this. If, however, money is available for lower return investments, incorrect decisions will be made.)

A good example of the problems created by using the same rate of return for all assets involves warehouse space. In the typical decentralized division, it is almost invariably to the division's benefit to rent or lease warehouse space, rather than to invest in warehouse facilities, because the rate of return from this type of investment is usually considerably less than the divisional profit objective.

A similar situation occurs with long-term leases. Many long-term leases are really nothing more than financing techniques.[5] That is, instead of lending money to a company to buy an asset, the asset is purchased by the lessor, for use by the lessee. The lessee's payments to the lessor represent interest plus return of principal. Contrary to popular opinion, it is the

---

[4] "Problem in Decentralized Financial Control," *Harvard Business Review*, May–June, 1961, p. 72.

[5] See Richard F. Vancil, "Lease or Borrow—New Method of Analysis," *Harvard Business Review*, September–October, 1961, p. 122, and "Lease or Borrow—Steps in Negotiation, *Harvard Business Review*, November–December, 1961, p. 138; also **Donald R. Gant**, "Illusion in Lease Financing," *Harvard Business Review*, March–April, 1959, p. 121.

lessee, not the lessor, who accepts the risk of ownership, because the lessee is responsible for the payments, regardless of the use to which he puts the asset. The effective interest rate, therefore, is more comparable to the bank rate than to the profit objective of a division. Consequently, it will almost always be to the divisional manager's benefit to purchase his assets, where he can, on the basis of a long-term lease. This action, however, may not be to the over-all benefit of the company.

SOLUTION NEEDED

While there is no completely satisfactory solution to this problem, the mere knowledge that it exists at all is a help. The greatest danger occurs when management is not even aware that a problem exists and allows the divisional manager to take independent action without any statement of over-all company policy. In this instance, the divisional manager does not even *know* what the best action is from the company's point of view.

One possible solution is to use different profit objectives for different assets. A division might have one rate of return for land and buildings, another for inventory, and a third for machinery and equipment. In this way, when a division added general-purpose assets, it would be required to earn a smaller return on these assets than would be the case if it had added special-purpose equipment. The difficulty with this method, however, is that it is likely to be too complex and appear too academic.

A more practical method is to establish a company policy which would require lower returns on some types of investments, and to acquaint all the divisional managers with this policy. Here again, if this policy decreases the divisional profit potential, it is well to provide for an adjustment in the divisional profit objectives. In this case, also, it should be recognized that the solution is not perfectly satisfactory. On the one hand, a divisional manager has a profit objective of 15%; yet, on the other, he is told to invest in warehouses that yield only a 5% profit. The apparent inconsistency is sometimes difficult for him to understand and, of course, the less he understands, the less effective the system will be.

HIGH PROFIT OBJECTIVES

In many decentralized companies, certain divisions earn very high rates of return on their investment. When this occurs, several special problems are created. First of all, the problems described in the two preceding sections are accentuated. For such a division can make hardly any investments at all without lowering its return on investment. In addition to this, it is a difficult problem to evaluate the division's performance. For example, criticizing a division that earns 30% after taxes on its investment is not easy—even though 40% might be a reasonable expectation. None of the usual rate-of-return criteria apply in such cases.

Even worse than the inability to judge performance is the possibility that the divisional manager will not try to improve his profit position because the size of the return on his investment makes him believe that it is optimum. In general, the problems that are created by very high divisional rates of return are such that it is usually desirable to try to do something about them.

PRIVILEGED FEW

The first step is to decide why it is possible for the division to earn such a high rate of return. One common reason is that, when the company was decentralized, certain divisions received some special benefits. A typical example occurs when a company decides to set up, say, a merchandising division that has few tangible assets. Profits as a percentage of investment will be large when the merchandising division receives the full benefit of the good will that has been built up by the company over the years. This good will results in extra profits and, since the tangible assets are small, it will have a significant effect on the divisional rate of return. When the effect of the good will is spread out over all of the assets of the company, it may not be large; but, when concentrated in one division, it will make that division's rate of return extremely high.

Take another example. Suppose that a company earns 12% on its investment, even though a 10% return is the competitive rate in this industry. Assume that this 2% premium results from good will which allows the company to sell at higher prices than its competitors. This company now decides to decentralize into several manufacturing divisions and one merchandising division, with the latter buying from the manufacturing divisions at competitive prices. These prices allow only a 10% return on investment. The extra price premium will go, therefore, entirely to the merchandising division. The investment and return are as follows:

	Manufacturing Divisions	Merchandising Division	Total Company
Investment	$9,000,000	$1,000,000	$10,000,000
Profits	$ 900,000	$ 300,000	$ 1,200,000
Rate of return	10%	30%	12%

The effect of the 2% premium has resulted in the merchandising division having a rate of return on investment which is three times as large as that of the manufacturing divisions.

The easiest way of handling this problem is to charge the merchandising division for the good will. This can be done in two ways: (1) add good will as an asset to the investment base of the division; or (2) charge the division a royalty. In the above example, the merchandising division could have been assigned $2,000,000 in good will. The schedule would then look like that in ALTERNATIVE A of EXHIBIT 1.

If the merchandising division were charged a royalty of $200,000, the schedule would look like that in ALTERNATIVE B of EXHIBIT 1.

Although either of these methods is effective in bringing the divisional rate of return in line, two problems associated with using them are:

(1) The use of good will or an interdivisional transfer of royalties is artificial. In some cases, the impression is given to the divisional manager that he is playing a bookkeeping game. This is obviously undesirable because the major strength of a decentralized financial control system comes from providing line management with a feeling of responsibility for the profit performance of the division. Although this disadvantage may appear trivial, in my opinion a company is better off to leave the divisional rate of return alone if it is not possible to convince both top and line management of the rationality of this adjustment.

(2) The second problem lies in calculating the amount of good will or royalty. Obviously, the answer will never be as evident as those indicated in the examples used here. There are many other factors in addition to good will that affect the profit performance of the division. It is often difficult to isolate an amount that can be reasonably imputed as good will. In this case, it may be possible to prove the existence of a minimum amount of good will. Although this amount will not bring the particular division's profits into line with the other divisions', it will lessen the disparity and, consequently, lessen the problems associated with the higher profits.

Exhibit 1

ALTERNATIVE WAYS OF HANDLING HYPOTHETICAL PROBLEM

	Manufacturing Divisions	*Merchandising Division*	*Central Office*	*Total Company*
ALTERNATIVE A				
Investment	$9,000,000	$1,000,000	....	$10,000,000
Good will	....	+2,000,000	−$2,000,000*	0
Total	$9,000,000	$3,000,000	−$2,000,000	$10,000,000
Profits	$ 900,000	$ 300,000	....	$ 1,200,000
Rate of return	10%	10%	....	12%
ALTERNATIVE B				
Investment	$9,000,000	$1,000,000	....	$10,000,000
Profits	900,000	300,000	....	1,200,000
Royalties	....	−200,000	$ 200,000†	....
Total	$ 900,000	$ 100,000	$ 200,000	$ 1,200,000
Rate of return	10%	10%		12%

* An adjusting entry to eliminate the fictitious good will figure from the corporate statements.
† An adjusting entry to balance the charge of royalties to the merchandising division.

CREDIT WHERE DUE

In some cases the higher profits may result because of quite proper reasons; one division may have a very favorable competitive advantage (such as a valuable patent) over its rivals. Then, too, if the general manager's ability is responsible for the high profits, it is usually best not to reduce his rate of return by artificial means, but rather to give him full credit for his accomplishment. If, on the other hand, the high profits result from fortuitous circumstances for which the present divisional manager had no responsibility, there is no reason why the excess profits should not be eliminated from the divisional books (except for the problem of convincing management that this is a logical step).

SOMETHING OLD

A third instance of a high rate of return occurs when the principal assets of a division were purchased prior to World War II. The book value of these assets may be so low that the rate of return of the division will be unduly high. In this instance, the solution is to include these assets in the investment base of the division at an amount more nearly approximating the replacement value.

As with the other limitations to the rate-of-return method, there is no completely satisfactory solution to the problem of the division with the abnormally high profit potential. Whichever action is taken, however, the most important point is for management to be aware of possible problems and to watch constantly for divisional action that might not be to the best interest of the company as a whole.

SHORT-RUN PROFITS

One of the greatest dangers in decentralizing profit responsibility is the motivation that it generates for short-run profit accomplishments. It is nearly impossible to exaggerate the intensity of the motivating force that is induced by most decentralized financial control systems. Line executives have frequently reached their position because of the aggressiveness and determination with which they have pursued their goals. Under a profit center system, the divisional manager is expected to improve the profits of his division. It should not be any surprise if he takes the most direct route toward this accomplishment.

Unfortunately, the most direct route toward profit improvement may *not* be the best route from a long-run point of view. (In fact, it almost always is not.)[6] This problem is particularly intense when a division is earning inadequate profits, although it is not confined only to this situation. There are at least four situations commonly encountered in business where the motivation for short-run improvements can be so strong that serious management errors may result.

The first situation occurs in a company that has decentralized because it has been having trouble earning an adequate profit. The problems of this company are usually not the result of its type of organization. Decentralization, therefore, will not, in itself, solve the problems. When, in addition, the divisional managers' jobs are assigned to people in the organization who have not been trained to accept broad management responsibility, the situation is ripe for some short-run decisions with long-run adverse effects.

The quickest, most direct way to improve profits is to cut costs. And the easiest costs to slash are research and development, administrative staff, advertising, and sales promotions. If these costs are seriously out of line, this may be the best action. In most cases, however, where a company is having serious financial problems, there are other, more difficult problems than high overhead and research costs. In many cases, the correction of the current problems may require increased expenditures in the areas where costs can be most easily reduced. The divisional manager, however, faced with the problem of impressing impatient superiors, can do little but take short-term cost action if he is to make a reasonable showing.

The second situation appears when a divisional manager is replaced because a division is not earning a satisfactory profit. The new manager almost invariably feels compelled to make an immediate improvement in profits. And frequently, before he has any real grasp of the problems of the division, he begins taking action. It takes time to increase production efficiency; method studies and new equipment even cause a temporary increase in cost. The same is true of product design or developing new markets. In other words, most of the basic actions required to improve profits may take several years to become effective. Almost the only immediate direct action that he can take is to begin cutting back on programed costs. It is the unusual divisional manager who will be willing (assuming he is even aware of it) to risk his job by not taking the short-term actions available to him.

The third situation, and perhaps the worst, transpires when a divisional manager believes that he is "on the skids." In this case, he has

---

[6] See Rensis Likert, "Measuring Organizational Performance," *Harvard Business Review*, March–April, 1958, p. 41.

everything to lose and nothing to gain (or so he feels) from deferring profit improvement. In fact, he frequently feels that the most desperate action is justified. If there is one chance in a hundred of an action succeeding, he will be tempted to take it, because he can be no worse off than if he does nothing. Although this action may be clearly uneconomic from the company point of view, the divisional manager may be willing to gamble millions of the company's money to keep his job, if it appears that he will be fired unless "something is done."

The fourth situation occurs when a division has been earning a satisfactory profit, but the new divisional manager wishes to make an immediate name for himself. Here again, the reduction of programed expenses is the answer. I know of one instance where a divisional manager, shortly after taking over a division, reduced the indirect factory labor significantly. In the following year, when the plant was faced with several special production problems, it became evident that the plant was woefully understaffed. The losses that resulted from the lack of trained personnel were far greater than the temporary savings resulting from the reduced overhead.

BUDGET EXAMINATION

As in the other cases, the most important point is that management must be aware that there exist possible strong motivations toward increasing short-term profits at the expense of long-term considerations. The first step is to find out which of the divisions might have the strongest incentive in this direction. It may be a good idea to examine each division to see if any of the four situations just described exists. Once management is apprised of the possibility of inappropriate short-run action, a careful appraisal of the plans of each division should be made. This is usually done in connection with the annual review of the profit budget. At that time, management must decide whether short-term profits are being overemphasized. In my opinion, an annual profit plan or budget is a vital part of any decentralized control system, principally because of the opportunity it gives to top management to guard against incorrect short-term actions.

Evaluating a divisional profit budget is a very difficult job, and I do not wish to give any impression to the contrary. It is at this point, however, that top management has the greatest effect on the coming year's operations. A great deal of judgment is involved; a low projected profit might be good, but, on the other hand, it might not. The fact that divisional profits are being increased because of a decrease in research and development is not necessarily bad, but it may be an indication of shortsighted cost cutting. It is of vital importance to any control system that top management devote enough time to evaluating the divisional profit plans intelligently. In fact, time spent at this point is probably the most valuable of any time spent on divisional problems.[7]

The other thing that top management should do to prevent an over-emphasis on short-term profit is to be very careful about setting arbitrary time limits on the actions of divisional managers. I have known of cases where a manager has been given one or two years to "straighten out" a division. He knows that if he does not succeed, he will be out of a job at the end of that time. Could there be any better invitation to take short-run or even desperate action?

CONCLUSION

A decentralized financial control system has many advantages. It allows top management time for long-term planning and strategy by relieving it of day-to-day operating decisions. At the same time, the operating responsibility is placed in the hands of the people most familiar with the situation. This not only makes for quicker action but for better decisions. Not the least advantage to a decentralized control system is that it helps to develop broad management personnel.

There are, however, limitations to decentralizing profit responsibility. Top management has to be assured that divisional management will make decisions that are in the best interests of the company. In order to be sure of this, divisional management must (1) know what the company's best interests are and (2) be motivated to act accordingly.

The typical decentralized control system provides for this by holding the divisional manager responsible for earning a profit on his investment. Although this technique will provide the necessary knowledge and incentive in most cases, there are, as this article has shown, some important exceptions. And it is vital that management keep these exceptions in mind if the financial control system is to work as effectively as it should. In some cases, the failure to understand these exceptions and provide safeguards against them can result in decisions that have a serious effect on profits.

---

[7] See Bruce Payne, "How to Set Realistic Profit Goals," *Harvard Business Review*, September–October, 1958, p. 87.

MIRAGE OF PROFIT DECENTRALIZATION[1]
By John Dearden

Why does the decentralization of profit responsibility appear to be a panacea for administrative ills?

What are the major obstacles to successful profit decentralization?

What organizational characteristics make successful profit decentralization unlikely?

What are the alternatives to the decentralization of profit responsibility?

Profit decentralization has been embraced by many as the panacea for all administrative ills. It is my belief, however, that profit responsibility should be decentralized only *after* it has been decided that alternative actions will not be effective. For many companies, profit decentralization is the *worst* possible action. In this article, I would like to examine the largely ignored negative aspects of decentralization (*a*) by presenting some practical obstacles to it, (*b*) by describing the kind of organization especially affected by these obstacles, and (*c*) by recommending alternative actions to the decentralization of profit responsibility. But before we discuss these topics, it might be well to consider just why decentralization has appeared so attractive to so many businessmen.

FALSE GLAMOUR

Why does profit decentralization appeal so much to executives in this country? Why does it seem to be such an ideal solution to the problems created by growth and complexity? Although there are additional factors, I believe that this situation has come about principally for the following reasons.

1. IT SOUNDS REASONABLE

The theory of decentralized profit responsibility could not be more reasonable. The company is broken down into manageable units, called profit centers. These profit centers are treated as independent companies. Each one is controlled by a manager who is responsible for earning a satisfactory return on the investment at his disposal. The operating de-

---

[1] *Harvard Business Review*, November–December, 1962, pp. 140–54. Reprinted by permission.

cisions are made by the people closest to the problem. Because these people are held responsible for the effect that their decisions will have on profits, they are motivated to make the decisions that will create the maximum profit. Central management is relieved of responsibility for day-to-day operating decisions. Its time is spent on planning, coordinating, and healing sick profit centers. When divided into relatively small units, a large company is given the advantages of the small company. At the same time, central staff coordination among the profit centers allows the company to retain the advantages of size.

2. CENTRALIZATION IS OLD-FASHIONED

Many people hearing the term "centralized" applied to an organization think of the old-fashioned, bull-of-the-woods-type manager. To some, this type of management is almost un-American because of its lack of democracy. In some cases, it is even worse; it is unsuccessful.

DECENTRALIZATION DEFINED

"Decentralization" has at least two common meanings in business usage: geographic decentralization (referring to the location of factories or offices) or decentralization of authority (referring to the organizational level vested with responsibility for making decisions). In this article, the term will refer only to the decentralization of authority.

But even the term, "decentralization of authority," is a loose one and indicates only approximate degree. For instance, all companies must decentralize authority to some extent because one man simply cannot make all of the decisions required by a going concern. On the other hand, some decisions always will have to be made centrally and, to this extent, there is a degree of centralization in every organization.

It is possible, however, to carry decentralization of authority to the point of dividing a company into a number of profit-making activities and assigning to each of these activities a manager who has the authority to make whatever decisions necessary to return an adequate profit. Only when decentralization of authority has been carried to this point does the term, "decentralized profit responsibility," truly apply.

The annals of business depict numerous cases where companies have failed, or nearly failed, because they were managed by authoritarians who refused to relinquish personal control in the face of increased complexity. One of the most publicized examples of this was the Ford Motor Company during the early 1940's.

Decentralization, on the other hand, is considered modern. If one looks at successful companies—General Motors, Du Pont, Ford, or General Electric, to name a few—it appears that a large proportion of them employ decentralized profit center systems. It is not surprising, therefore, that companies running into administrative problems consider a decentralized profit center system their answer.

3. IF A LITTLE IS GOOD, A COMPLETE JOB IS BETTER

It is evident that some decentralization of authority is called for when companies grow larger and more complex. It is just one step from here to the conclusion that, if some decentralization will mitigate an administrative problem, a lot of decentralization will solve it completely. Hence, the logical decision is to go all the way and decentralize profit responsibility.

4. SUCCESSFUL DECENTRALIZATIONS ARE PUBLICIZED

There has been much publicity given to companies that, in recent years, have successfully decentralized profit responsibility. These articles, together with recurring descriptions of the Du Pont and General Motors control systems (by now these descriptions can be considered almost classics), have been instrumental in creating a definite impression that modern business methods are predicated upon the decentralization of profit responsibility. Although, in every case, these articles point out carefully that this decentralization was only one of several factors that contributed to the renewed success of the company being described, the message comes through loud and clear that success would not have been possible without decentralization of profit responsibility.

5. NO PUBLICITY IS GIVEN TO COMPANIES THAT DO NOT DECENTRALIZE PROFIT RESPONSIBILITY

Companies which solve their administrative problems without decentralizing profit responsibility offer journalists little to write about. These companies, using one or more of the methods described later in the article, handle the problems created by the increasing size and complexity of their businesses in such an unspectacular manner that frequently they, themselves, barely realize they are doing anything worthy of note. This, along with the evolutionary nature of the process (as contrasted to the more revolutionary profit decentralization), makes for unspectacular copy.

6. NO PUBLICITY IS GIVEN TO FAILURES

To my knowledge, an article has never been published with a title such as: "Why Profit Decentralization Failed at the XYZ Company." The reason, of course, is obvious. Yet I know that there are many instances where profit decentralization has created more problems than it has solved. In one instance recently, a major company established a complete decentralized profit center system. Within two years it reverted to centralized profit control, after the cost of the new system and the benefits (or lack thereof) of this system became evident. Naturally, but unfortunately, no publicity has been given to this.

BLOCKS TO DECENTRALIZATION

In my opinion, there are three serious obstacles to successful profit decentralization:

1. The decentralization move is usually accompanied by significant changes in the job performed by top management.
2. A decentralized profit center system is very expensive.
3. It is difficult, if not impossible, to set up a system that will motivate the divisional manager always to act in the best interests of the company.

The impact of these obstacles will, of course, be different in different companies. The decision to decentralize profit responsibility, however, should be made only after the effect of these obstacles has been carefully appraised in the light of the possible advantages that decentralization is expected to bring.

TOP-MANAGEMENT CHANGES

When a company decentralizes profit responsibility, it is usually faced with a significant change in the job performed by top management. The most important change is that top management must stop directing the day-to-day operations of the company and limit its activities to over-all control and coordination. In order to do this, management must rely heavily on budget and accounting reports. This is sometimes difficult, if not impossible, for many operating executives. Executives who for years have made decisions on the basis of personal observations and direct discussions with subordinates find it difficult to make decisions on the basis of pieces of paper covered with figures.

With decentralized profit responsibility, top executives *must* rely on the finance staff for much of the information on which to base their decisions. No individual at the top-management level has, any longer, the intimate knowledge of divisional operations that he had when he personally directed these operations. (If he has, then the decentralization is in name only.) Further, informal information received directly from the profit center manager will almost certainly contain some degree of bias. (As explained later, it is frequently to the advantage of the profit center manager to withhold information.)

The second change in the job of top management is that executives can expect to spend much more time on long-range planning. (This is one of the principal advantages claimed for profit decentralization.) But, in actuality, many managers, successful in the personal direction of a company's operations, have neither the temperament nor the ability to perform the planning job successfully. Under a centralized operation, planning may be delegated to someone else if the chief executive does not have the ability to do the job adequately. With decentralized profit responsibility, such a change is more difficult because the executive has been relieved of operating responsibilities specifically so that he can spend more time on long-range planning.

The change in top-management's job should be recognized *before* the decision to decentralize is made. At that time management should be assured that the new responsibilities can be handled, and, indeed, that this change in management responsibilities is desirable for the solution of the company's administrative problems. If this assurance cannot be given, there is considerable question whether the decentralization of profit responsibility will be successful.

HIGH COST

When a company does decide to decentralize profit responsibility, it should be aware that it may be an expensive proposition to do the job right. On more than one occasion, I have seen top executives refuse to spend the money required to implement adequately the decentralization plan *after* it was put into operation. If the increase in costs had been anticipated, a more workable plan would have been developed from the start. These added expenses come from two major sources: added executive and staff salaries and the costs of a more intricate information system. Let us consider each closely.

Staff Compensation. Decentralization broadens the responsibilities of middle management. It is to be expected, therefore, that those people who are promoted to positions of greater responsibility will expect a corresponding increase in compensation. If they are not given higher salaries, morale problems are almost sure to follow.

Of greater impact than increases in individual compensation, however, is the additional staff which profit decentralization usually entails. There is almost always some duplication in staff activities when each profit center operates as a separate unit. The profit center manager, being held responsible for the profits of his division, will usually insist on having a staff under his personal control.

Although the increase in the number of personnel and their compensation at the profit center level should be partially offset by corresponding decreases in the central office, these decreases rarely, if ever, occur. More typically, the central staff will *increase* in order to compensate for the greater communication problems created by the establishment of the semiautonomous profit centers. So the cost is compounded.

Information Requirements. The decentralization of profit responsibility adversely affects communication in two ways: (1) much of the informal communication between top management and operating personnel is eliminated; (2) the divisions are no longer motivated to cooperate with each other. Therefore, a more intricate, formal communication system is necessary if top management is to be effective in evaluating divisional profit performance and coordinating divisional activities.

The information system adopted is a system of profit budgeting and long-range profit planning. Although procedures differ from company to company, a typical system requires that every profit center manager present each year to central management a profit budget for the coming year and a profit plan for several years following. If management accepts the profit budget and plan, the budget becomes a basis for evaluating profit performance through the year. And as long as the division is at budgeted profit levels, central management does not interfere with profit center operations.

Top management, therefore, exercises control over the profit centers principally at the point where budgets and plans are reviewed. Since these budgets are the basis for evaluating the performance of profit center management, and the profit plans are the principal basis for coordination, they are vital to the effectiveness of the control system. It is imperative, therefore, that the profit budget and planning system be good; and a good budgeting and planning system is *not* inexpensive.

It might be asked why an information system of this type should be more expensive than the cost of a few additional accounting reports. The answer is that the quality of a profit budget system is almost entirely dependent on the ability of the people responsible for the preparation and analysis of the budgets and reports. This means that any company using profit budgets and profit plans must have considerable financial analytical talent, and this talent is not cheap.

As we have already pointed out, the profit budgets and plans are the principal instruments for evaluating and coordinating profit center activities. It is vital to the system that an inadequate budget or plan be recognized as such and, conversely, that an adequate budget or plan be approved. Central management has neither the time nor the background to analyze personally the profit center budgets in detail. This task is the responsibility of the financial analyst. His job is to be sure that top management is aware of the implications of the proposed budgets and plans. He makes sure that all of the pertinent facts are presented to management in a clear and unequivocal manner, and that the proposed budget reflects reasonable financial expectations. This kind of an analysis is indispensable to an effective profit budget system.

In addition, the financial analyst is responsible for making certain that the performance reports reflect the facts as they exist. The profit budget is used as a standard to evaluate the divisional manager. On the basis of the performance reports, management must decide whether or not to interfere in divisional affairs.

In most cases, when a divisional manager runs into trouble, he is interested in keeping top management out of his division until (hopefully) he can clean up the situation. For this reason, a divisional manager may frequently be motivated to understate the seriousness of his situation when explaining his budget variances. The more serious the situation, the stronger will be the motivation to soft-pedal it. This is precisely what top management does not want him to do. Since control is exercised at so few points, it is vital that the communication system at those points be extremely accurate. It is the function of the financial analysts to be sure that it is.

The profit center manager will also require some good analytical talent to assist him. Since the profit budget and plan are a major factor in evaluating his performance (not to mention the real success of his operations), it is imperative to him that these be the best possible. Also, in the explanation of variances, he will want an effective representation of his position to the central staff. (One of the problems in a profit budget system is created by the danger of the central staff and divisional analysts spending a large proportion of their time arguing with each other.)

In summary, in any good profit budget and planning system, a considerable number of financial analysts are needed (depending on the size and complexity of the company) at both the central staff and the divisional level. As companies become larger and more complex, they need more intricate information systems to ensure adequate control. A decentralized profit center system, however, requires a more sophisticated and expensive budgeting and planning system to overcome the problems of communication, coordination, and evaluation that profit decentralization creates.

MOTIVATION DIFFICULTIES

When profit responsibility is decentralized, it is necessary to realize that divisional management may take actions inconsistent with company interests. This occurs in many cases because the division manager does not know what company interests are. In other instances, divisional interests will conflict with company interests and, since he is being evaluated on the performance of his division, the divisional manager will tend to take the action that will be best for his division. For example, a profit center manager has no incentive to give business to other profit centers if he can buy more cheaply (or receive better service) from outside the company. I know of one decentralized company where the divisions always deal with outside firms whenever they can, in spite of the fact that the company has adequate internal capacity. Thus, while the particular division may benefit as a result of lowered purchasing costs, the company as a whole loses the profit margin on interdivisional sales which would otherwise be made.

A good system for the evaluation of profit center performance will motivate the manager to make most decisions consistent with company interests. Such a system of carefully worked out incentives which make profit center and company interests coincidental, however, can be quite sophisticated and expensive. Yet, without such a system, there is considerable danger of motivating the divisional manager in the wrong way. Even with such a system, it is important to recognize that it will not be successful in every instance.

WHO SHOULD DECENTRALIZE?

In view of these rather formidable obstacles to successful decentralization, the logical question is: "Who should decentralize profit responsibility?" A decentralized profit center system will certainly be more expensive than maintaining central control over profit responsibility. Admitting this, we should next ask, "What conditions are necessary before a company should seriously consider decentralization of profit control?" Specifically:

1. A company must be suffering losses in profits from incorrect decisions that cannot be corrected by less expensive methods. This condition usually results when—

(*a*) The company is composed of a number of separate businesses, each more or less independent with respect to product, markets, and production processes.

(*b*) The nature, size, or complexity of these businesses is such that it is not practical for one group of people to make the day-to-day operating decisions.

2. Top management must be willing to delegate the necessary authority; it personally must have the ability to operate under a decentralized profit center system; and it must be willing and able to obtain the people and pay the price to make the system effective.

THE BIG ONES

The giant industrial complexes (General Motors, Du Pont, Ford, General Electric, and the like) certainly qualify as excellent candidates for decentralized profit responsibility. These companies do consist of many complex businesses. Even with the vastly improved communications of today, it would certainly appear unreasonable for these companies to try to control their diversified industrial empires on a centralized basis.

Certainly, also, in these companies, top management is able to make effective use of financial reports in controlling the operating divisions. (In fact, it is no coincidence that many of the top executives have a financial background.) These large companies have been able to obtain or train qualified people. Finally, it has been economic for them to pay the price of establishing and maintaining the type of elaborate information system necessary for adequate control and coordination. (Under any conditions, these companies require an elaborate control system so that the marginal cost of decentralization is relatively less than in smaller companies.)

THE SMALL ONES

The next obvious question then is: "What about other smaller, less diversified, and less complex companies?" It is at this point that my opinions differ from those advanced by others. I believe that many (if not most) of these companies *cannot* economically decentralize profit responsibility. Many of the very large companies have been forced by their size and nature to accept the disadvantages of decentralization. Other companies should follow their example only when they, too, are forced to do so.

One indication that the smaller companies may be making a mistake to follow the pattern established by these large companies is that the large decentralized companies frequently have divisions which dwarf most of the companies currently contemplating profit decentralization. And within these divisions there is centralized profit control (that is, the divisional manager has not decentralized profit responsibility to his subordinates). In other words, many of the companies that have decentralized profit responsibility successfully have generally only gone as far as they *had to* in extending decentralization down the line. For example, although no figures are officially published, I am sure that the Chevrolet Division of the General Motors Corporation would be well up among the top ten largest United States companies if it were an independent corporation. Yet profit responsibility is largely centralized at the divisional level. Thus, it does not follow that what is good for the giant corporation is also good for the smaller, less complex organization. In fact, I believe just the opposite is far more true.

IN BETWEEN

As for the in-between-size companies—the medium to large companies—the question is less clear-cut, and here it is necessary to look closely at the factors which point in the direction of not decentralizing.

UNFAVORABLE CIRCUMSTANCES

What factors would make it unwise for a company to decentralize profit control? My feeling is that the presence of one or more of the following conditions will make it unlikely that profit responsibility can be decentralized successfully.

SHORTAGE OF ABLE PERSONNEL

A decentralized profit center system requires certain types of personnel that may not be found in the typical organization where profit responsibility is centralized. If these people are not available within the organization, they must be trained or hired. If management is unable or unwilling to do this, then the company should not decentralize profit responsibility. There are three needs:

(1) As already mentioned, top management must know how to use accounting and budget reports in controlling and coordinating profit center operations. If the present management cannot do this, profit decentralization should be at least postponed until a change can be made in the top-management echelons.

(2) An effective decentralized profit center system requires capable divisional managers. A company that has always been centralized under a strong top management frequently finds itself with few executives who are broad enough in their outlook to take on the responsibility for an entire division. Not only is breadth of knowledge sometimes lacking, but even the mental attitude required for effective decision making. A man who has spent years carrying out someone else's orders often finds it a traumatic experience to have to make his own decisions and, worse, to accept the responsibility for their outcome.

Generally, the middle-management problem is not as difficult as the one involving top management. Good operating executives are generally available (although not plentiful) both inside and outside the company. Furthermore, it is, of course, possible to train people to accept broader responsibilities. The important point is that a company should not decentralize unless existing personnel are capable of handling new responsibilities or some provision has been made to acquire new talent or train existing personnel.

(3) As previously described, a successful decentralized profit center system requires capable financial and budget analysts at both the central staff and the divisional levels. These people are not easily acquired, either, and it is important that this fact be recognized. In my experience, this is the problem most often

ignored. Management somehow seems to think that a decentralized profit center control system will operate by itself and that accounting personnel can be easily converted to perform the analytical functions. In some cases, of course, it is possible to train present accounting personnel, but this is by no means universally true. Many people who perform well in a routine accounting job have neither the background nor the ability for financial analysis.

ONE MAJOR ACTIVITY

If a company has a single activity on which its success hinges, it is doubtful that decentralization of profit responsibility will be successful. Top management *cannot* delegate responsibility for the success of this activity to a divisional manager. It is too important to the welfare of the company. In this circumstance, an attempt to decentralize profit responsibility merely results in a more expensive and cumbersome control and communications system. For example:

A medium-size company with one major product line and several smaller and relatively unrelated products (acquired for diversification) divided its activities into profit centers, each controlled by a divisional manager. Central management, however, continued to spend most of its time and energy on the major product line, making most of the decisions that normally should be made by the divisional manager. The divisional manager could not be held responsible for the profits of the division, and, consequently, considerable friction resulted. The company was being operated in the same old way except that staff costs had risen and new communications problems had been created.

SIMILAR MAJOR ACTIVITIES

Decentralized profit responsibility seems best adapted to companies that are composed of several *dis*similar businesses. In these companies, management is unable to be intimately acquainted with the relevant details of all of the businesses; therefore, it is necessary to delegate the day-to-day decisions to different people in each activity who are familiar with the various problems.

If, on the other hand, the activities of a company are similar, it may be desirable for one group to make many of the day-to-day decisions for *all* of the activities. For example, a central marketing group might make all of the advertising, sales promotion, and new product decisions for the entire company. When a central group does this, a divisional manager cannot, of course, be held responsible for his profit performance. Hence, there is no real decentralization of profit responsibility.

Any company whose major activities are related closely to one another should carefully consider alternative methods of control before decentralizing profit responsibility. Not only is it more expensive to have each division make its own decisions, but the quality of these decisions is likely to be inferior to those that would be made centrally. Furthermore, coordination among the activities is very important when they are related; this coordination is much more difficult to accomplish properly with a decentralized profit center system.

INDIVISIBLE RESPONSIBILITY

In order to be able to decentralize profit responsibility successfully, a company must find it practicable to divide its operations into logical, profit-determining units. In a typical organization, the principal determinants of profits are marketing, procurement of the product (either by production or purchase, or both), and product design and development. If the control over each of these areas cannot be delegated to a single profit center and a single manager, the control that the manager can exercise over his profits is considerably weakened. For example:

A maker of appliances had a common marketing and product-planning group, but manufactured the appliances in different plants. Although the manufacturing plants were called profit centers, they really were not. The plant managers had responsibility only for manufacturing costs and quality; consequently, they could not be held responsible for anything else.

People are often misled because large, complex companies occasionally treat some purely manufacturing operations as though they were profit centers. This is done because it is not practical, for some reason, to combine the production activities with the marketing and product planning. In these companies, most of the activities actually are true profit centers, and it is simply more convenient to have a few fictional profit centers than to organize in some other way.

The existence of intracompany pricing problems is sometimes indicative of the fact that profit responsibility is not clearly segregated. To the extent that divisions buy and sell to each other, it means that two divisions are sharing in the marketing, production, and product planning. That is, from the company's point of view, the product-planning, marketing, and production activities are spread among two or more profit centers.

Intracompany pricing problems also indicate sometimes that profit centers are not really independent. These problems occur principally when outside competitive prices are unavailable. When this happens, it can mean that there is no effective outside competition. This, in turn, indicates that the concept of the division as an independent company is fictional because, if there is no effective outside competition, the profit centers *must* deal with each other.

ALTERNATIVES TO DECENTRALIZING

Given these organizational characteristics and admitting that in companies where they exist decentralization of profit responsibility will not usually be successful, what then can these companies do when increasing size and complexity of operations create administrative problems? Should they do nothing? Of course not. All-or-nothing thinking is as fallacious in this area as it is in so many others. Companies need not completely decentralize profit responsibility; there are other less drastic and less expensive methods of minimizing their problems. Here are four of them.

1. SPLIT EXECUTIVE RESPONSIBILITY

One way to relieve the pressure on management is to divide the executive responsibilities among the top executives. For example, if long-range planning is a problem, then separate planning from administration. Thus, the chairman of the board can be responsible for planning and the president for the day-to-day management. Or, if the president is an effective planner, he might delegate the responsibility for managing to an executive vice president and do the planning himself. Another alternative is to have a vice president do the long-range planning. The important thing to remember is that it is not necessary to decentralize profit responsibility in order to have effective long-range planning. In fact, a centralized company has more flexibility in handling long-range planning than the company with decentralized profit responsibility.

2. DECENTRALIZE FUNCTIONAL RESPONSIBILITY

Delegation of certain functional responsibilities is an excellent way to relieve pressures on management's time and ability. For such delegation, management can select functional activities that have the most capable staff, or ones to which top management can make the least contribution, or ones that are not vital to the success of the company. For example:

In a company that was largely marketing-oriented, the president delegated the responsibility for manufacturing to a vice president. The president was, thus, able to devote most of his time to marketing and product decisions. Decentralization on this basis can be done with little additional cost, with no disruption to the current organization, and can have every likelihood of success.

3. STRENGTHEN THE STAFF

On several occasions, I have known corporate executives who seriously considered decentralizing profit responsibility when their real problem was lack of adequate staff assistance. Some operating executives regard staff people as a type of parasite and try to keep them at a minimum. On the other hand, they feel that the decentralization of profit responsibility is a good solution to their problems because delegation is being made to operating executives (who are not parasites). As we have seen here, profit decentralization is a very expensive substitute for an adequate central staff.

4. DECENTRALIZE MINOR ACTIVITIES

If a company has several, more-or-less minor activities which are unrelated to its main products, it might sometimes find it useful to set these activities up as profit centers under the control of a central staff executive. This action does not, of course, require the sophisticated control system that full decentralization would require. The responsible executive controls by personal observation, by direct communication with general managers, and by the usual accounting reports. In this way, top management is in a position to devote most of its time to its main business.

CONCLUSION

No single system is all good or all bad for any company; this much is obvious. Yet, every day, executives are faced with the problem of changing their organizational structure. Many times the alternatives end up being expressed in all-or-nothing terms. Since the alternative of decentralization has been so widely and uncritically praised, my intention here has been to play the devil's advocate for centralization of profit responsibility and to point out some of the serious consequences that can result from ill-considered profit decentralization.

In playing this role, I have not intended merely to be critical of decentralization, but rather to offer an objective appraisal of just when decentralization is most likely to prove effective. As you have seen, decentralization offers advantages over a more centralized system only under certain restricted conditions. If these conditions are not met by your company, the answer is not necessarily to do nothing, but rather to consider taking some steps—short of complete decentralization of profit responsibility—that often are overlooked when change is expressed in all-or-nothing terms. By taking whatever steps seem appropriate in your company's situation, you may achieve the desired improvements while at the same time avoiding the high cost, the communications difficulties, and the personnel problems that complete profit decentralization so frequently brings.

MOTIVATIONAL APPROACH TO MANAGEMENT DEVELOPMENT[1]

By Rensis Likert

There seems to be widespread and increasing dissatisfaction with current methods for reviewing the work of managers and assisting them in their development. Not only is the conventional performance review failing to make a positive contribution, but in many executives' opinions it can do irreparable harm. For example, recently a superior in a large company said, after an experience with one of his men in a performance review interview:

"What I would give to have that hour back! That discussion did more harm to my relationship with Joe than I can overcome in a year's time."

The aim of reviewing the subordinate's performance is to increase his effectiveness, not to punish him. But apart from those few employees who receive the highest possible ratings, performance review interviews, as a rule, are seriously deflating to the employee's sense of importance and personal worth. The relationship between the employee and his superior is damaged, which in turn affects adversely the quality and often the quantity of the work. It is virtually impossible to tell an employee either that he is not as good as another employee or that he does not measure up to a desirable level of performance, without having him feel threatened, rejected, and discouraged.

During recent years members of the staff of the Institute for Social Research at the University of Michigan have spent a good deal of time on devising and improving measurements of employee reactions. These measurements indicate to me that when subordinates say they want to know how they stand with their boss, they really are asking for reassurance as to their future in the organization. They want to be encouraged and helped in using more of their untapped potential, but they do not want to be told of their weaknesses and failures. Mark Twain expressed their orientation well in discussing amateur writings:

"From old experience I know that amateur productions, offered ostensibly for one's honest cold judgment, to be followed by an uncompromisingly sincere ver-

---

[1] *Harvard Business Review*, July–August, 1959, pp. 75–82. Reprinted by permission.

dict, are not really offered in that spirit at all. The thing really wanted and expected is compliment and encouragement."[2]

UNWORKABLE PROCESS

The fundamental flaw in current review procedures is that they compel the superior to behave in a threatening, rejecting, and ego-deflating manner with a sizable proportion of his staff. This pattern of relationship between the superior and the subordinate not only affects the subordinate but also seriously impairs the capacity of the *superior* to function effectively.

An incident which occurred not long ago at a workshop of experienced personnel men illustrates well the difficulty with the current performance review process:

This group worked out an ideal performance rating system and agreed unanimously that anyone rated by this process should be informed of the results in order to help him grow and develop. They decided that the review of any rating should be done in such a way as to make the person rated aware of his strong and weak points and to motivate him to take steps to overcome his weaknesses. To illustrate how this should be done, the group decided to role-play a particular case in which poor planning and scheduling had occurred.

A group member volunteered to play the role of the superior in the performance review interview and demonstrate how to tell a person what his weaknesses were in such a way as to cause him to (*a*) appreciate the information, (*b*) accept it as valid, (*c*) motivate him to try to overcome the weaknesses, and (*d*) react favorably to the interview. After 20 minutes the member playing the role of the superior gave up his attempt. He was unable to handle the interview in a manner which did not make the person playing the role of the subordinate feel he was threatened, rejected, and even hostile. Others who played the role of the man being rated also reacted as he did.

Three other members of the group volunteered to play the role of the superior and handle the interview. All were equally unsuccessful in demonstrating how the interview could be conducted so as to meet the conditions specified. No one was able to suggest how the interview could be successful.

Remember, this was a role-playing situation; and the principals in it were intelligent, experienced men of good will. If frustration attended their efforts here, think what most executives are up against in real-life situations! It is no wonder, then, that in the light of this experience the members of the group reversed their previous position and decided unanimously that the results of performance appraisals should not be reported to the person rated.

---

2 Mark Twain, "Mark Twain Speaks Out," *Harper's*, December, 1958, p. 36.

NEW PATTERN

Clearly there is a need to help supervisors and managers to appreciate deficiencies which can and should be corrected. Is there a better method than those now in general use?

I want to outline what I believe to be a new and potentially promising approach to the problem of performance review and managerial development. This approach is based on what I call a "modified theory of management." It has been obtained by integrating into an over-all pattern the principles and methods used by managers who are getting the best performance in industry and in government.[3] These principles clearly indicate the need for a pattern of relationships between the superior and the subordinate that is substantially different from the pattern created by many performance review systems.

Briefly, here are the most important assumptions and features of the new approach:

(1) The quality of superior-subordinate relationships exerts a major influence on the behavior of subordinates and on all aspects of the organization's operation.

(2) The relationship between the superior and his subordinates which results in the best performance is supportive in nature and contributes to the subordinate's sense of personal worth and importance. The superior demonstrates to the subordinate that he is genuinely interested in him and in his career in the organization; believes in his capabilities and is confident that he will perform at a high level; considers him a human being and not a cog in the machine; and is interested in the subordinate's mistakes from the point of view of training and not of punishment.

(3) Subordinates seem to react unfavorably, at least in our society, to negative evaluations by their superior. (Some subordinates are so upset that they actually fail to hear the unfavorable appraisals and report that they do not know how they stand with their boss.)

(4) People seem most willing and emotionally able to accept, and to examine in a nondefensive manner, information about themselves and their behavior, including their inadequacies, when it is in the form of *objective* evidence. (Although new or unusual kinds of evidence may be resisted initially, this resistance disappears as experience in the constructive use of data is obtained.)

(5) People tend to respond positively to information suggesting potential improvements in their behavior when this information is conveyed in the friendly, supportive atmosphere of a small, well-established group in which they feel secure.

---

[3] See, for example, R. L. Kahn, F. C. Mann, and S. E. Seashore, Editors, "Human Relations Research in Large Organizations, Part 2," *Journal of Social Issues*, Vol. XII, No. 2, 1956; D. Katz and R. L. Kahn, "Some Recent Findings in Human Relations Research," *Readings in Social Psychology*, edited by G. E. Swanson, T. M. Newcomb, and E. L. Hartley (New York: Henry Holt & Co., 1952), pp. 650–65; and Rensis Likert, "Motivational Dimensions of Administration," *America's Manpower Crisis* (Chicago: Public Administration Service, 1952), pp. 89–117.

(6) People seek to learn new and more effective ways of behaving only when they, themselves, recognize the inadequacies in their present behavior.

(7) The extent of the individual's desire to learn better ways of behaving depends on how important he feels the situation is to him. The more important he feels the situation is, the greater is his motivation to learn.

(8) When an individual is motivated to improve and modify his behavior, it is essential that he receive prompt, accurate reports on the adequacy of his efforts.

(9) Much of the learning needed for managerial development must occur at the intellectual, emotional, attitudinal, and behavioral levels. Learning acquired at any one level is ineffective unless accompanied by corresponding changes in behavior at the other levels.

(10) Persons in hierarchical organizations generally recognize the power of the hierarchy and try to evoke favorable reactions from superiors who have influence in the hierarchy.

(11) Participation in decisions in the small work group under the leadership of a superior skilled in the process is a particularly powerful method of training and achieving change.

PERFORMANCE VARIABLES

The foregoing approach poses a key problem: Can we measure the human variables affecting organizational performance well enough to satisfy people's needs for objectivity?

Thanks to the achievements of social science researchers, the answer is, I believe, *yes*. Admittedly, we have not reached the millennium; a great deal more needs to be done in the way of refining and improving the present tools. But the measurements we can now make are accurate enough, in my opinion, to enable a meeting of the minds between superior and subordinate on what the health and performance capacity of a human organization are. Here are the kinds of variables that can be measured with objectivity for a corporation as a whole, a division, or a smaller group:

1. Extent of loyalty to the institution and identification with it and its objectives.
2. Extent to which the goals of units and individuals facilitate the achievement of the organization's objectives.
3. Level of motivation among members of the organization with regard to such variables as:
   a) Performance, including both quality and quantity of work done;
   b) Concern for elimination of waste and reduction of costs;
   c) Concern for improving the product;
   d) Concern for improving processes.
4. Degree of confidence and trust among members of the organization in each other and in the different hierarchical levels.
5. Amount and quality of the teamwork in units and between units of the organization.

6. Extent to which people feel that delegation is effective.
7. Extent to which the members feel that their ideas, information, knowledge of processes, and experience are being used in the decision-making processes of the organization.
8. Upward, downward, and sideward efficiency and adequacy of the communication process.
9. Leadership skills and abilities of supervisors and managers, including their basic philosophies of management and orientation toward leadership processes.

If there is any danger in using measurements of the preceding kind, it is not their lack of complete and absolute accuracy. It is that management will *under*estimate the skill required and assume that it is enough if a reasonably intelligent interviewer asks people questions or if a questionnaire is made readily available. Such an attitude leads to costly mistakes and disillusionment with the whole measurement idea. In reality, the measurement of the variables just outlined is a complex process and requires competence in the social science field.

STEPS TO IMPROVEMENT

How can measurements of the performance variables just described be applied? How can they be used to help managers obtain better insights into their strengths and weaknesses and improve their performance?

In examining these questions let us keep in mind that most companies are obtaining satisfactory measurements for such end results as production volume, costs, scrap loss, earnings, and turnover. Moreover, most managers receive regular reports on their performance as measured by these factors. Such indicators of performance are well accepted in management circles. What we want to do now is build the same kind of acceptance for measurements of the impact of a manager's behavior on motivation, loyalty, communication, interaction, and other aspects of the quality of the human organization. Unless we can watch changes in these "intervening" variables, we cannot, as I have pointed out in an earlier HBR article, assess the effects of a manager's action on the *future* capacity of his organization.[4]

To illustrate how the new measurements can be applied, I shall take communication as a case in point.

COMMUNICATION FAILURES

The efficiency of communication is often judged by measuring how well informed lower levels in the organization are with regard to com-

---

[4] Rensis Likert, "Measuring Organizational Performance," *Harvard Business Review*, March–April, 1958, p. 41.

pany goals, earnings, or similar items of information; or by measuring how satisfied the subordinates are with the information made available to them. These are useful yardsticks but are not adequate to measure fully the efficiency of the communication process. For example, measurements should also be obtained of the extent to which the *superior* can estimate correctly:

The production and performance goals of his subordinates.

The problems of concern to his subordinates, and the operating problems of which the subordinates are aware but higher management is not.

The satisfaction of subordinates with the communication and decision-making processes or organization.

In addition, it is helpful for management to know the extent to which *subordinates* estimate correctly the goals of their superiors, and the extent to which they know and accept the objectives of the organization.

In situations where such measurements have been obtained the communication process has turned out to be surprisingly inefficient. The results shown for one organization in Exhibit 1 are typical of the data produced in other studies:

At every hierarchical level subordinates clearly feel that their superiors do not understand subordinates' problems whereas the superiors feel that they do. Similar discrepancies have been found in the superior's capacity to estimate the performance goals which his subordinates feel are reasonable and which guide their productivity level; and subordinates are unable to estimate correctly the performance goals which their superiors expect of them and consider reasonable.

Exhibit 1

SUPERIORS THINK THEY UNDERSTAND SUBORDINATES' PROBLEMS WELL
BUT SUBORDINATES DISAGREE

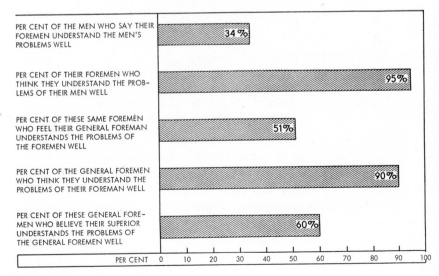

PER CENT OF THE MEN WHO SAY THEIR FOREMEN UNDERSTAND THE MEN'S PROBLEMS WELL	34%
PER CENT OF THEIR FOREMEN WHO THINK THEY UNDERSTAND THE PROBLEMS OF THEIR MEN WELL	95%
PER CENT OF THESE SAME FOREMEN WHO FEEL THEIR GENERAL FOREMAN UNDERSTANDS THE PROBLEMS OF THE FOREMEN WELL	51%
PER CENT OF THE GENERAL FOREMEN WHO THINK THEY UNDERSTAND THE PROBLEMS OF THEIR FOREMAN WELL	90%
PER CENT OF THESE GENERAL FOREMEN WHO BELIEVE THEIR SUPERIOR UNDERSTANDS THE PROBLEMS OF THE GENERAL FOREMEN WELL	60%

PER CENT 0 10 20 30 40 50 60 70 80 90 100

In how many companies is communication no better than in Exhibit 1? Probably quite a few. But the significant fact is that, at least in my experience, neither superiors nor subordinates are likely to realize how inaccurate and inadequate the communication process is. As a consequence, they are very much surprised when measurements such as those shown in the exhibit are obtained and reported to them. Superiors, particularly, are amazed to discover how uninformed or misinformed they are.

FOLLOWING UP

Given an analysis of the kind just described, what does a manager do with it? Where do we go from here?

As measurements of communication, loyalty, and other such variables become available, each manager can see for himself what the data reveal about his strengths and weaknesses. He does not have to depend on the subjective judgment of a superior executive. He can decide for himself, on the basis of the evidence, where he needs to improve and to develop. Moreover, analyses based on the measurements give him information to guide his choice of action. To illustrate, let us go back to our communication example:

When a manager has analyzed the data for his organization and becomes convinced that he can and should improve communication between himself and his subordinates, several alternatives can be considered. Should he seek to use more written and printed material between himself and his organization? Should he hold staff and organizational meetings in order to share information and communicate? Should he issue orders and exhort his subordinates and organization to do more communicating? Or what?

One of the most useful types of information the manager can have is data about the likely results from each possible course of action. This he can get from studies of past performance. Analyses show, for example, that using large volumes of printed material is not likely, in itself, to achieve effective communication—at least, as judged by the kinds of rigorous measurements which have been suggested. But when the data measuring the extent to which superiors can correctly estimate the production goals of their subordinates are examined closely, the results show that the greater the group loyalty and the better the teamwork which exists in a work group, the better the communication and the smaller the errors. Thus, efforts to improve communication should also embrace steps to improve group loyalty and teamwork.

Another illustration of the manner in which the analyses of data can be used to help managers discover the best solutions to the problems appears in Exhibit 2. These data, collected by Floyd C. Mann, indicate that when a superior uses meetings to obtain the ideas and suggestions of his subordinates and honestly tries to do something about these ideas, his subordinates are much more likely to feel that he is good at handling

Exhibit 2

WORKERS' JUDGMENT OF SUPERIOR'S ABILITIES IS MORE FAVORABLE
THE MORE MEETINGS THEY HAVE

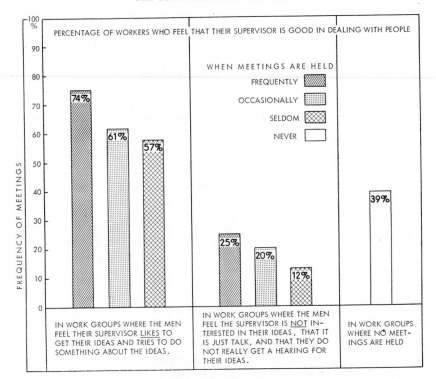

people than in the case of the superior who holds meetings but whose behavior indicates that he is *not* really interested in his subordinates' ideas. In other words, a supervisor is better off never to hold a meeting than to conduct meetings of his work group in such a manner that the men feel he is not interested in their ideas—a finding with an obvious bearing on attempts to improve, say, the amount of teamwork and inter-action among subordinates.

A high level of confidence and trust by the superior in his subordinates is a basic requirement for full and frank discussion of problems. Such attitudes and behavior on the part of the superior are deeply rooted in his personality and are not easily or rapidly changed and improved. But there is ample evidence that they can be changed and improved *if the superior himself wants to change and works hard to do so.*[5]

---

[5] See, for example, Lester Coch and J. R. P. French, Jr., "Overcoming Resistance to Change," *Group Dynamics: Research and Theory*, edited by D. Cartwright and A. Zander (Evanston: Row Peterson & Co., 1953), pp. 257–79; Floyd C. Mann, "Studying and Creating Change: A Means to Understanding Social Organization," *Research in Industrial Human*

The use of measurements as guides to action enables each manager to tap the full experience of his entire company—and other companies—in seeking ways to improve his behavior and his performance. He need not try countless ways of improving an operation on a trial-and-error basis hoping that somehow he will find one that will work.

USING THE TOOLS

Measurements of human variables, together with the traditional data on production volume, costs, waste, earnings, and so on, provide the basic tools needed for a new approach to performance review and managerial development. No doubt there are many ways in which the review process using these measurements can be conducted. The approach I shall outline is only illustrative, and it is worth emphasizing that the exact procedure which should be used in a particular company and with a particular individual must necessarily be tailored to fit the traditions and practices of the organization and the background, expectations, and skills of the individual. Accordingly, I shall concentrate on the basic steps only. These will be much the same from company to company and at low as well as high levels of supervision.

1. *Working with his subordinates as a team, each manager sets objectives for the next period ahead.*

The period I am most concerned with here is the short-term one—three months, nine months, or whatever else is the normal period used by the organization for planning and setting goals.

Of course, the manager might also appropriately set objectives for a longer term. They would be more tentative, and should be examined and readjusted at the end of each shorter period. In any case, the objectives would involve goals expressed as (a) end result variables, such as volume, production, waste and costs, and (b) "intervening variables," such as motivations, attitudes, leadership, and communication.

Measurements of results for previous periods would be used as guides in setting or revising the objectives.

The plans and objectives prepared by each manager and his subordinates would specify:

Relations, IRRA Series, Publication 17 (New York: Harper & Bros., 1959), pp. 146–67; Nancy Morse and Everett Reimer, "The Experimental Change of a Major Organizational Variable," *Journal of Abnormal and Social Psychology*, January, 1956, pp. 120–29; and Stanley E. Seashore, "The Training of Leaders for Effective Human Relations," *Some Applications of Behavioural Research*, edited by Rensis Likert and S. P. Hayes, Jr. (Paris:

UNESCO Publications Division, 1957), pp. 81–123.

Performance objectives for the kinds of variables which have been suggested (e.g., a specified reduction in waste or a specified improvement in upward communication).

Processes or procedures to be used to attain these objectives.

Specifications of measurements needed to ascertain how well each objective is reached, how well each procedure is followed, and what modifications, if any, are desirable to achieve further improvement. Managers would be encouraged to specify the measurements which they feel they need in order to plan, guide, and improve their operation and their own performance.

Earlier in this article I indicated that the system of measurements being proposed was not yet perfect. As a case in point of this statement, managers will probably find that for some of the variables they would like to see measured no satisfactory yardsticks have as yet been developed. An imperfect but workable substitute method in such situations is to obtain systematic judgments from several persons whose objectivity and competence are recognized and accepted.[6] These judgments, while far less satisfactory than actual measurements, are still better than appraisals made by the manager alone or in conjunction with his chief.

Actually, in the developmental stages of the performance review process proposed here, it probably will be desirable to include only those variables for which measurements can be obtained. After the process is well established, variables which can now be handled only by obtaining systematic judgments might be added.

2. *The manager and his superior review the plans and objectives set by the manager and his work group.*

Where the character of the operation permits, this review should be done by the superior and all managers who report to him *as a team.* When appropriate, representatives of staff departments should also be called in. In this way the objectives of related units can be brought in balance and integrated, and the balance and integration achieved will be satisfactory to all concerned. Where necessary the superior should also have personal sessions with the individual managers.

Obviously, it is not wise to set objectives that put managers under severe pressure. But the targets should be such as to *challenge* them.

3. *At the end of each period for which plans and goals have been established, results are reported on all of the variables measured.*

These results should be reported for the entire operation under each manager; where desired they can also be reported separately for the dif-

---

[6] For a fuller explanation of this method see D. C. Pelz, "Motivation of the Engineering and Research Specialist," *Improving Managerial Performance*, General Management Series, No. 186 (New York: American Management Association, 1957), pp. 25–46.

ferent sub-units under a manager. Along with his own results each manager would receive data from comparable operations elsewhere in the company against which to evaluate his own performance. The other units may or may not be individually identified in the data, depending on what top management thinks best.

4. *Each manager studies the results of his operation and evaluates his leadership and performance.*

What implications does he see? What insights can he gain? Which results surprise him? Following his own study, he should proceed to review the data with his subordinates as a team and examine such questions as:

What was done well in relation to the objectives set?

Where did performance fail to measure up?

Which factors contributed to the successes achieved, and which contributed to the shortcomings experienced?

What should be done in the next period to extend the successes and to overcome the past shortcomings?

The manager should meet also with his superior and review the results reported as well as the interpretations that he and his subordinates have placed on them. Most of this review should be done in group sessions with the superior and with the other managers reporting to him so as to gain the benefit of their experience, insights, and suggestions.

5. *At the same time that results of the previous period are being reviewed, objectives and plans are drawn for the period ahead.*

Existing procedures and methods can be improved or modified as called for by the data; new approaches can be devised. The aim, of course, is to exploit all the data in order to bring about desirable improvements. All of this work can go on individually and in groups: by managers working alone, by managers working with their subordinates in work groups, by the superior alone, and by the superior working with the managers.

6. *The complete cycle just described is carried out continuously so that each manager will have a constant flow of information coming to him about his operation and behavior.*

The process of planning, taking action, measuring results, feeding data back to management, and planning again must be a never-ending one if learning also is to go on continuously.[7]

---

[7] The proposed cycle has been suggested by the work of Floyd C. Mann, Don R. Hamann, and Virgil K. Rowland.

IMPORTANT ADVANTAGES

The basic pattern of executive relationships just described is similar in many ways to that which is sought in the new appraisal system developed by General Mills, Incorporated and used also by General Electric Company. The role which that kind of appraisal plan prescribes for superiors and subordinates has been described by Douglas McGregor in the course of his excellent article, "An Uneasy Look at Performance Appraisal."[8] There are, however, two essential differences between that plan and the review process proposed here. The process I propose uses objective measurements. It also emphasizes group procedures. The use of the group (instead of the more private man-to-man relationship described by McGregor) is an attempt to apply the findings of the Institute of Social Research and other organizations making studies in human relations.

The effect of these features is to create entirely different roles for the superior and his managers. The fact that they want the measurements for their *own* information and guidance motivates them positively. They cooperate and assist in securing the information and strive to see that it is accurate.

This is an entirely different situation from what all too often prevails today where measurements in the form of accounting data are used by top management to police and "second guess" the persons directly responsible for operations. When measurements are used in this latter way, the persons who are policed distort the data effectively to show the picture which top management wants to see rather than the true picture. This "doctoring" of the data has been found to be widespread even in companies recognized as being well managed.

INDIVIDUALIZED LEARNING

With continuous measurements to guide him, the manager's learning at all times is focused efficiently on his deficiencies. He does not waste time learning what he already does well by being compelled to participate in a variety of company-wide programs taking a shotgun approach to training (and implying, by virtue of their being company-wide, that all managers have equal need for the same training). He concentrates on his own needs. Some managers need training in methods of interviewing subordinates. Others need coaching in improving communication or su-

---

[8] *Harvard Business Review*, May–June, 1957, p. 89.

pervisory skills. Others need help in coordinating activities. And so on. These *individual* problems are the ones calling for attention.

Note the value of group discussions of the measurement data. These discussions occur in the two work groups of which the executive is a member: the one in which he is the superior, and the other in which he is a subordinate. He has a key role in the interpretation of the data and in the decision on action to be taken. He can pace his learning and change to fit his situation. He gets constant feedback informing him of the success of his efforts to improve. His boss does not evaluate him. He evaluates himself and so grows in competence and self-confidence.

This is not to say that the individual should not ask for assistance and counsel in making his diagnosis and planning a course of action. He should—and will. But when the measurements given him are what he—not his boss—has requested, he is far less likely to be submissive, dependent, or defensive.[9]

The approch outlined in this article is not a finished one. It needs experience, testing, and refinement. Nevertheless, it does appear to represent a significant improvement over the procedures in widespread use at present. Those procedures, I am convinced, are fundamentally inconsistent with the pattern of management used by executives who are achieving the best performance in American industry. When effectively applied, the proposed methods should help a well-managed company achieve substantially better results—both financially and in the development and use of the full potential of its personnel.

---

[9] See Chris Argyris, *Personality and Organization* (New York: Harper & Bros., 1957), pp. 229–39.

SOCIETE NORMACEM

Late in 1961, an IMEDE researcher discussed with the top management of NORMACEM the processes by which its management team operated. As previously described in *La Compagnie Electro-Mécanique,* NORMACEM was one of the three manufacturing groups of France's Compagnie Electro-Mécanique (CEM). The management of CEM had been substantially decentralized in 1956 and remained so in 1961; thus Mr. André Dutruy, NORMACEM's General Director, had great freedom in his management of his group's operations.

This case describes the manner in which the corporation's formal policies on management were translated into effective executive action. The case contains three sections. First, selections from NORMACEM's policies on the role of the manager are presented. Second, M. Dutruy discusses his role as he perceives it. Third, the fulfillment of this role is illustrated by the way in which an idea of M. Dutruy's was implemented. The example chosen was the creation of a research and development center, called CREL, to serve all of NORMACEM's divisions. This third section (a) describes the creation of CREL, and (b) gives remarks by M. Dutruy and two of his divisional managers on the creation of CREL and the problems it involved.[1]

NORMACEM POLICIES ON THE ROLE OF A MANAGER

NORMACEM had issued a number of policy documents which dealt with the role of the general manager. These documents were formulated by NORMACEM's top management and then issued to the divisional managers. Some of these documents precisely defined the responsibilities, authority, and functions of specific positions in the NORMACEM organization, such as the director of a NORMACEM division and his key subordinates. The most recent policy memorandum, issued in February, 1961, was titled *The Role of the Manager;* this memorandum, rather than

Copyright 1962 by l'Institut pour l'Etude des Méthodes de Direction de l'Entreprise (IMEDE), Lausanne, Switzerland. Reprinted by permission.

[1] All the quoted interviews and documents in this case were originally in French. They were translated by the researcher, and the translation was approved by the NORMACEM executives concerned.

specifying details for a definite position in the organization, embodied the precepts by which NORMACEM's management expected all its important executives to be guided. Only portions of this document are reproduced here, those defining the general philosophy which should guide the manager and some statements on a manager's relationships with his superior and subordinates.

THE ROLE OF THE MANAGER[2]

The Manager is responsible for the *management and administration* of the department or enterprise which is entrusted to him.

The accomplishment of his function implies:

—The existence of *valid and adequate policies* which he should, by his *attitude*, make his subordinates follow. (A maximum of policies which are common to all levels should be defined as high up as possible.)

—The establishment of *objectives* and the determination of what are the necessary means. (Personnel, organization, material means.)

—*Effective action* in order to attain these objectives and to use the various means well. For this action the manager must:

- Set up and maintain his team, made up of himself and his direct subordinates.
- Keep in mind at all times that, though he is at the head of one team, he is also a member of another team, and that the particular interests of his department or enterprise are subordinated to the general interests of the whole organization.
- Be the only executive link between his own superior and his direct subordinates.
- Be concerned with accomplishment.

DUTIES AND POWERS OF THE MANAGER

POLICIES

—To CONFORM to the established policies and to PROPOSE, with justifications, the alterations or additions which may seem desirable.

*   *   *   *   *

ORGANIZATION

Structure

—To propose the organizational structure of his unit while respecting the framework adopted by his superior.

—To SUGGEST any modifications to this framework which he may think desirable.

Functions

—To DEFINE the functions of his direct subordinates, with their participation.

—To FOLLOW UP on the application of the definitions and to REVISE them whenever necessary.

---

2 The layout of this text, including italicizing (underlined in the original) and capitalization, is taken from the original document.

—To ENSURE that the definitions made by his direct subordinates follow the guidelines which he has laid out.

Means

—To FORECAST and REQUEST the necessary means.

* * * * *

EXECUTIVE DEVELOPMENT

—To develop his direct subordinates, possibly with aid of specialists.
—To help them train their own subordinates.

* * * * *

DECISION MAKING

—To HAVE DECISIONS MADE at the lowest level at which they can validly be made.
—To DELEGATE progressively, after having developed his subordinates, additional duties, and then the corresponding authority.

* * * * *

In Relation to His Superior

—To REMAIN always and totally RESPONSIBLE, whatever the degree of delegation to subordinates.
—To DARE tell him that he (the superior) is not informed and to see that he IS INFORMED by someone competent.

In Relation to Direct Subordinates

—Not to INTERFERE in matters which have been delegated.
—Not to GIVE ORDERS unnecessarily.
—To RETAIN authority. (In order to carry out the orders of his superior, the subordinate must give orders in his turn and not just transmit an order.)
—To HAVE his subordinates PARTICIPATE in the formulating of directives and orders.
—To ENSURE the comprehension of an order.
—To RECOGNIZE the right to fail.
—To FORCE the subordinate to decide alone, if he seems capable of doing so.
—If the subordinate asks for advice, NOT TO GIVE HIM AN OPINION, but by judicious questions, to MAKE HIM THINK and to get him to find a solution himself.

* * * * *

CONTROL OF DIRECT SUBORDINATES

—To DEVELOP them so that they themselves can control.
—To OBSERVE the differences between the objectives which were assigned to the direct subordinates and the achieved results.
—To DEMAND to be immediately informed of what goes wrong, and to OBLIGE the subordinate to refer to his superior:
  • when his own means are not adequate.
  • whenever a matter can have repercussions in areas outside his own, if the horizontal communication lines did not allow for a joint solution.

* * * * *

INFORMATION

—To CREATE a flow of useful and objective information between his superior and his direct subordinates and vice-versa.

STAFF RELATIONS

—To GET ADVICE from the staff or from the heads of the organic departments and to GET HELP from them each time they can make him better understand a policy or a problem, or furnish him with services or information or advise him with regard to decisions already taken.

—To FURNISH them with the information necessary for them to accomplish their role.

ANDRE DUTRUY'S ROLE

The NORMACEM group, headed by M. Dutruy, had 1960 sales of about 180,000,000 new francs; the group's sales had been growing steadily, as can be seen from the following figures:

NORMACEM Sales (in millions of new francs)

1956	125
1957	153
1958	168
1959	168
1960	183
1961 (projected)	205

NORMACEM consisted of six divisions for which Table 1 gives some pertinent information.[3] M. Dutruy, who had first accepted a position at

---

[3] Source: Company officials.

CEM in 1937, was made General Director of NORMACEM in 1956. In October, 1961, the researcher requested that M. Dutruy describe his role as he perceived it. M. Dutruy asked for several days to reflect on this subject; he then described his function and the problems associated with it.

Table 1

Name of Division	Products Manufactured	Per Cent of Total NORMACEM Sales
La Buire	Electric motors of all sizes; some welding equipment	50
PETERCEM	Switching equipment	25
Parvex	Fractional horsepower electric motors	10
Fibre et Mica	Electric insulators, decorative plastic panels	10
Etarc	Welding equipment	2.5
Repelec	Repair of electrical equipment	2.5

He began, "In attempting to analyze what I do, I would say that my activities can be differentiated on a chronological basis into (*a*) management of current operations and (*b*) management of NORMACEM's future. My first concern is to get my current operations working properly. To do this, I must have standards by which to measure the performance of each of my divisions and of NORMACEM as a whole. I must determine such things as the following: Are our products what people want? Do our products live up to the promises we make about them? Are they well suited to the present market in terms of price and quality? Is our volume of sales adequate, considering our competition and the current state of business? Are our various methods good ones? Can they be improved? These and similar questions help me to measure our present performance. Our budgetary system, which estimates costs and revenues in each division for the next five years, helps to provide precise standards by which performance can be measured. If I observe variations between what is desirable and what we are achieving, I must take measures. My two special problems, then, are (1) to be sure that I know of any variations of performance from the ideal and (2) knowing of such variations, to be able to take corrective measures.

"NORMACEM can be regarded as one of three squadrons in the CEM fleet, and each division as an individual ship. In my job, I must be aware of what is going on within this fleet and how it affects me. One of my major problems is to know all my problems.

"When I observe that corrective measures should be taken in some area of NORMACEM's concern, I have to follow this series of steps. First, I decide exactly what the problem is and what remedy should be used. Second, rather than merely giving an order, I will discuss with the man involved the nature of the problem and the best solution for it. I often find the Socratic method useful; rather than simply telling a subordinate, 'This is bad—fix it,' I will ask him what he think about the problem. In this way, although the process is often slower than giving a direct order, there will be agreement on both sides as to what to do. Only rarely do I give a firm order against the wishes of one of my subordinates. Occasionally, I may have to do so if we are unable to agree, but I do not like to do this.

"This, then, is the first part of my job, but it is not necessarily the major part. I would say that the future is just as important as the present from the viewpoint of the General Manager. There are today certain forces which considerably complicate my activities concerning the future. In general, problems tend to develop very quickly in industry today. It is not always possible to see, five years in advance, a major crisis. Undoubtedly the coming of the Common Market has contributed to this, because it has radically altered traditional European concepts of how, and in what environment, industries function. Furthermore, since the countries involved are voluntarily accelerating the coming of the Common Market, the problem is aggravated. Perhaps the other great problem in this area is the accelerating pace of scientific and technological development. Our knowledge is growing so rapidly that it is difficult to maintain one's self up to date on the latest technical developments. CEM and NORMACEM, of course, depend greatly on technical developments, and so this problem is especially severe for us. Today our company forms a moving element, if you will, in a total industrial stream which is also moving. The rate of movement is rather rapid, and the problem is to see that we move at least as fast as the main stream.

"Now, in order to deal with the future in a useful manner, one has to do several things, I think. First, we must have good information on the developments of the various economies which concern us, as we need this information at least five to ten years ahead. We have to know what pattern the business cycle will follow, what government policies to expect, what changes in population growth and distribution lie ahead. Second, we must have a good idea of what scientific and engineering developments are coming. In this regard, we have to know very well what our competitors are doing and what they plan to do. Have they new products, new methods, new processes in their plans? And, of course, we need to know not only what course the future will take, but what this course means to us.

"When I have some idea of future developments and their significance, I must share these ideas with my subordinates. They may not have exactly the same viewpoint as I, and it is important that we be able to agree on the meaning of the trends which we foresee. Getting information to my divisional managers is one of my special problems; another is the development of their managerial abilities. I have to be certain that, through formal and informal education, they are kept abreast of what is happening. Since my divisions are located at a considerable distance from Paris,[4] this makes the communication problem more severe, especially in the case of informal communication.

"The job of the General Manager involves not only making decisions, but selling these decisions, and this process of selling is one of my constant preoccupations. It goes something like this: I have an idea, or perhaps somebody presents me with an idea. I will take this idea to the Gen-

---

[4] NORMACEM's top management was located at CEM headquarters in Paris; NORMACEM's divisions were in the vicinity of Lyon and Dijon.

eral Director of CEM; we discuss it and reach a decision as to what to do. Then, by the methods I have already suggested, I must convince the divisional managers of the soundness of the decision. I might say that the human problems I encounter are the most difficult. One cannot go too quickly in changing things when men are involved.

"In summary, I would say that there is a sort of equilibrium between the two parts of my job: the present and the future. It is impossible, or perhaps not of great use, to say which is more important. Both are necessary."

THE CREATION OF CREL

1. THE HISTORY OF CREL

In 1958, M. Dutruy and his staff began to consider the possibility of uniting the research efforts of NORMACEM's divisions into one research service for the whole group. Up to this time, each division had maintained its own research and development groups. These groups were often of considerable size; the La Buire division's research and development team numbered more than 35 people, most of them engineers and scientists.

On January 13, M. Dutruy issued an 8-page document entitled *Reflections on the Organization and Establishment of a NORMACEM Center of Research and Development*. This document began with a list of the chief purposes for creating such a center; these purposes can be summarized as follows:

1. To concentrate NORMACEM's research efforts in one location, rather than using the necessarily smaller divisional groups which could not have the same efficiency as one large group.
2. By setting up the center outside the factory atmosphere, to give freedom to do advanced thinking; to lessen our research team's involvement in production problems.
3. To build a team which will think in new product terms, which is not always done sufficiently by the individual factory teams, which cannot take such a viewpoint.
4. This center will be a resource of information and technical help on which the various divisions can call.
5. This team will be large enough that it should be able to develop a backlog of potential new products for NORMACEM.

This document also contained preliminary thoughts on (1) how the center would function and with what areas it would concern itself; (2) how different types of new products would be brought into production, once invented; and (3) how the center would probably be launched.

On September 20, 1960, a 9-page document was issued by NORMA-CEM's top management which discussed a research center much more precisely than the document of 20 months before. This new document was in four parts, from which the following material has been taken:

1) *Purpose of Creating CREL[5]—Its Role*

Purpose: . . . by means of concentrating NORMACEM'S resources, to increase our effectiveness in the areas of research, development, and the use of new production techniques.

Role: . . . CREL is a staff under the direct supervision of NORMACEM's General Director.

It will act as advisor and supplier (of information to the establishments.)

2) *Structure of CREL*

CREL will include:
1. An "applied research" group
2. A "studies" group, made up of:
    a) A calculating group
    b) A design group
    c) A model shop
3. A laboratory
4. A "production techniques" group
5. A "technical publications" group

3) *Operation of CREL*

[This section dealt with CREL's relations with the divisions in developing new products and in providing other services.]

4) *Restrictions on CREL's Sphere of Operations*

The separation between the studies to be done by CREL and those to be done by the divisions is as follows:
1. CREL's role [is] to study the concept and production techniques of
    a) New series of products which are already in NORMACEM's line.
    b) New products,
        whether new to NORMACEM but already made by others, or whether completely new.
2. The divisions' role becomes:
    a) Modifying products (not requiring a new concept) to obtain:
        —improved quality
        —a better factory price, etc.
    b) Adapting products to specific customer needs.

On March 6, 1961, M. Dutruy issued the following memorandum:

CREATION OF A RESEARCH AND STUDY CENTER

A new group, called "Centre de Recherches et d'Etudes Lyonnais" or CREL is hereby established.

---

[5] The name "CREL" was an abbreviation for "Centre de Recherches et d'Etudes Lyonnais."

The purpose is to increase, by concentrating resources, the efficiency of NOR-MACEM's divisions in the areas of research, study, and new production techniques.

This group reports to NORMACEM's top management and will act as a consultant and provider of services to the divisions, in a manner which management will later define.

The group will begin operations on September 1, 1961, in the plant on Rue Seignermartin in Lyon.

Two days later, on March 8th, M. Dutruy issued a second memorandum which gave a more precise definition of CREL's role, along the lines of the memorandum of September 20, 1960.

In October, 1961, CREL consisted only of a management group of less than ten men; it was located in a former NORMACEM plant which had been vacated several years previously. It was expected that, over the coming two years, CREL's team would be built up to full strength, largely by taking over much of each division's research group.

2. M. DUTRUY'S VIEWS ON THE CREATION OF CREL

"My chief problems in establishing CREL were human relations problems, especially with the General Directors of my divisions. They felt that, because CREL was going to take away their research teams, their roles were being diminished. As a result, I had to have many discussions with them to get my ideas across and to explain why CREL would be a good thing for NORMACEM as a whole. This took quite a lot of time because, as I mentioned, you can't go too quickly in trying to change men's opinions.

"My major reasons for wanting to establish CREL were these. First, in the old arrangement with each division doing its own research, the research groups were always being pulled away from their work in order to help with production problems. They weren't doing as much research as they could have done. When a new process was being introduced and some problem developed, the research team had to help. In short, there was too much stress on immediate results. Second, with the old system we were spreading out our research effort instead of concentrating it for maximum effect. We had experts in each division who, if brought together in a team, could work more effectively. Third, and also worth mentioning although less important than the previous two reasons, with the old system it was difficult to determine whether more money could profitably be spent on research.

"The other chief problem in starting CREL was the cost. CREL represented a major investment, both in physical facilities and in the costs of starting it in operation. This problem was overcome, of course, but it did exist."

3. M. CHADENET'S VIEWS ON THE CREATION OF CREL

M. Hubert Chadenet was made Director of NORMACEM's La Buire division on September 15, 1958. During the previous year he had been Marketing Vice-President of NORMACEM. A graduate of France's Ecole Centrale de Paris, M. Chadenet's first job had been with CEM, where he began in 1945. Just before becoming Marketing Vice-President of NORMACEM, M. Chadenet had spent about four months taking a marketing course given by the American Marketing Association in New York.

When asked how he reacted to the idea of CREL, M. Chadenet began: "When M. Dutruy reaches a decision which will affect his subordinates, 90 per cent of the time he can get the support of his subordinates for that decision. The other 10 per cent of the time, he simply has to say 'This is what is to be done.' It's a good question as to whether the issue of CREL was in the 90 per cent or in the 10 per cent. I think that there is a real team spirit in the NORMACEM management, and we think that we work pretty well together. We have many informal meetings, especially between NORMACEM's top management and the divisional managements, to iron out differences of opinion that may exist, and these meetings generally have that effect. Also, the company is quite decentralized, so that the divisional managers have a great deal of freedom in conducting their operations.

"I guess I was probably the hardest to convince about the usefulness of CREL. The managers of the smaller divisions were very happy about the idea because they couldn't afford very elaborate research teams with their small sales. But my division has sales of over 100,000,000 new francs per year, and we have a research staff of about 50 men, 20 of them engineers. I think that we are large enough to do all the research we need, so that naturally I was not especially convinced of the need for CREL in my case. But I admitted, however, that we had some trouble with long-term research, or with developing 'revolutionary' new products. I think that M. Royer, who runs Petercem, our second largest division, also has felt that he could carry on the necessary research with his own group. One objection I had was that it appeared to me that the cost for CREL would probably exceed considerably the total cost of all the divisional research teams, so that there would be no direct saving. Another objection was that CREL would, in practice, be devoting almost all, say 90 per cent, of its effort to research for only three divisions: La Buire, Petercem, and Parvex. A further objection was that CREL was very expensive, and we had already been making major investments in other areas. Last year NORMACEM made a major investment of 20,000,000 new francs in a new, very automated factory for small electric motors. This plant is at Decines, a few miles from Lyon, and is one of the four La Buire plants. As a result of this investment, we had to postpone starting CREL for a year; without Decines, we would have begun CREL a year ago. And because of this financial problem, we decided to minimize the investment in CREL by using a factory building which we already owned. We're refurbishing this building satisfactorily at much less expense than if we had built a whole new structure. Of course, we expect to put CREL into specially designed quarters sometime in the future, but at this time it appeared unwise to do so.

"The idea of CREL was first proposed by M. Dutruy in January, 1959, and I would say that it took about a year to a year and a half to get agreement that we should go ahead with the project. There were many informal meetings to accomplish this. Although CREL is theoretically now in being, it still hasn't its full staff, and I expect it will be probably two years before it is fully staffed and doing all the work which is to be assigned to it. For a while, CREL will use the divisions' laboratories until its own are ready.

"As to how CREL will actually function, once it has been established, I think that undoubtedly there is real value in isolating some 'long-haired' research people away from the factories to do some new basic thinking about our products. The divisions do tend to take a rather narrow view of new product research, which is quite understandable, so they can use some help in this area. I suspect that, if CREL had existed ten years ago, we might be further along in the development of some products than we are today. But it will be important for us to keep clear in our minds where responsibility for product development belongs, and especially responsibility for the success and profitability of new products. CREL can only do research up to the point where it has a new design. Then, at least ideally, there should be close cooperation between CREL and divisional people to be sure that the new product can be produced economically. There will be work on production problems which will be chiefly the division's job. In fact, I think that, at least for the next five or six years and possibly longer, I will have to maintain a small research group to work on some problems which CREL isn't really suited to solve. This will involve such things as special models to fulfill specific customer demands, where speed is important. We can certainly do this kind of think much quicker than CREL will be able to, at least for some time.

"When I say that, at first, I was somewhat resistant to the idea of CREL, perhaps I ought to qualify that. It is no secret that, because I have been in NORMACEM headquarters, I am not only La Buire-oriented, but also NORMACEM-oriented. I would not say that I was difficult to convince of the value of CREL; I only wanted to make sure that we all understood what CREL involved for all of us. In the end, I think that, if CREL works as we hope it will and if there is good cooperation between the division and CREL, it will be a very good thing for NORMACEM. Also, CEM has been for many years the French affiliate of Brown Boveri Company, which is a major Swiss manufacturer of electrical material with affiliates and subsidiaries throughout the world. We think that CREL will be able to work very effectively with the Brown Boveri research group in new product development, and in light of Europe's rapid integration, the value of this is obvious.

"As I mentioned, I think that the only serious reservations about CREL came from Royer and me, and I think we were pretty quickly convinced, once we understood what CREL would and would not do, of the value of CREL to the divisions and to NORMACEM as a whole. I might mention that I have given CREL a couple of problems to begin working on; these are fairly easy problems, but not too easy. If we gave them some fantastically difficult problem, we wouldn't be helping them at all, and it would be no way to start CREL. This way, they can really help us on these problems and, at the same time, build their own confidence."

4. M. ROYER'S VIEWS ON THE CREATION OF CREL

The Petercem division, which manufactured switches and switching systems, had been formed in 1956 by merging Contacem (the former NORMACEM division manufacturing switches) with a competitor. Petercem sales for 1961 were forecast at about 40,000,000 new francs, nearly double their 1956 level. M. Royer, who was made Delegate Director of Petercem in 1956, had previously been at Parvex and La Buire.

"I won't deny," M. Royer began, "that I seriously doubted the need for CREL. I had come from La Buire, where our research team seemed to me generally sufficient to do the necessary research, and so I saw no need to have CREL. It was after going to Parvex that I realized that in this division, one much smaller than La Buire, the kind of research team necessary for progress could not be justified [by the division's sales].

"At Petercem I found a good team to do studies and product development, but this team lacked sufficient potential in the area of applied research.

"In reflecting on the subject, I have sometimes wondered whether the creation of CREL would save money for NORMACEM. Today, I believe that CREL will cost more than the total cost of individual divisional research groups, but that if CREL functions according to certain conditions, it will give us in years to come some definite competitive advantages. These advantages will be in the areas of our present and future basic products.

"The present organization of NORMACEM gives the Delegate Director of a division a set of responsibilities which definitely makes the job an attractive one to hold. My immediate subordinate, the Director, is chiefly concerned with production and related technical problems, as well as with personnel. I concern myself with the technical-commercial service and with the research team. As a result, I am more likely to be concerned with our future operations, while my Director is usually involved with daily problems.

"One danger which CREL must absolutely avoid is that it become involved in solving problems and doing jobs which can be handled by skills which the divisions already possess. (I am thinking especially of the process of getting a new product into manufacture and also of certain activities of our methods department.) If CREL tried to do these jobs, it might be quickly buried under tasks which aren't its own; this would be detrimental to doing research on future products and production techniques. CREL has to do all our research and all our product studies. The product studies must be handed over to the divisions as soon as the latter are ready to take over. There has to be a truly effective dialogue between CREL and the divisions.

"CREL needs men with ideas, with creative imaginations, men who can develop new ideas; but as soon as a new idea has been realized as an actual product, the division must be ready to take over.

"I am genuinely convinced that if CREL operates in the manner I have defined, it will be a real aid to the development of the divisions."

PART VIII

The Total Management Process

IN THIS LAST section of the book, a series of cases giving relatively complete data on a single firm—The Galvor Company—is presented for analysis. This company had started in the 1930's with little more in the way of assets than the founder's idea for a better way to satisfy customer demand. It had grown by the 1960's to occupy an important place in the French electric and electronic measuring-instruments industry.

As previously noted, the series is one that could be used in a starting as well as in an ending position, to acquaint the reader with the wide range of issues or topics that will be encountered again and again in the study of Business Policy. Alternatively, the series could be used when the important concept of strategy is being introduced. Galvor is suggested for an ending role, however, in situations where some other series, such as that on Midway Foods Corporation or the world wrist watch industry,[1] has already been analyzed.

The object of providing so much data on a single company is to permit study in depth. The Galvor series, accordingly, presents material on the company's past as well as present stategy; on industry trends; on policies in such key functional areas as marketing and finance; on a major current problem (as identified by the company) in the area of inventory control; on future anticipated problems of growth; and on adapting the organization to meet future needs in a growing international market. Because the series raises so many varied problems that are common to other rapidly expanding firms, The Galvor Company's experience has proved both exciting and rewarding to groups of executives.

For providing all these data, Galvor's president, M. Latour, and all other personnel named in these cases are deserving of special thanks.[2] M. Latour was generous enough to cooperate not only in the case-collection but also in the teaching stage. For the 1961–62 session at IMEDE, he attended the concluding meetings of the course and listened to a series of reports, prepared by six competing teams of trainees, and focused on recommendations for the company's future course of action.

For students, trainees, or interested executives studying these cases on their own, the difficulty of analysis may be reduced by the following notes and questions that have been designed to accompany the parts of the Galvor series.

The Galvor Company (A) and the Industry Notes. These materials can best be looked at as a single unit.[3] The case provides data on the company's history and strategy; the three industry notes respectively provide background material on electronics, material designed to place Galvor in its industry context, and pertinent material on competing firms.

---

[1] Learned, Christensen, and Andrews, *op. cit.*

[2] M. Latour was at first reluctant to provide the series because he was aware that he had some unsolved problems. He was very modest about the accomplishments of his firm and doubted that it was a model for case instruction. When it was explained to him that the most useful cases are likely to come from firms that know they have problems and, further, that perfection on the part of the firm is not required, he readily agreed to cooperate in the assembly of this material. Professor Learned, who has been gathering case material for 35 years at the Harvard Business School, has never received more wholehearted cooperation than M. Latour and his staff gave the faculty and research staff of IMEDE. M. Latour did not censor anything that anyone said, nor did he make any effort to rebut directly some of the criticisms made of him by his collaborators, as he called them.

[3] The Galvor Company (C-3) could be added to this list, except that such addition results in an exceptionally heavy study load.

Study questions put to participants in the IMEDE program were as follows:

1. To what factors can Galvor's success be attributed? How can Galvor capitalize on these factors in the future?

2. What are the principal problem areas with which Galvor's management should be concerned? What should be done now to resolve these problem areas?

3. How do the characteristics and competitive trends of the industry affect Galvor's future?

4. What objectives and goals for Galvor might be established by top management for the next decade?

The Galvor Company (B). This case introduces—though it does not exhaust—the material about management personnel in Galvor. More data will be found in other cases, particularly in the two that conclude the series. Although Galvor (B) provides only a partial view, it will add richness to all subsequent material.

Experience at IMEDE has shown that opinions will vary widely as to the meaning of the data included in this case. We would emphasize that such differences are to be expected, considering the differing backgrounds of readers and the differing views advanced by members of the company itself. Such differences, we believe, are useful rather than otherwise. They serve to enlarge the horizon of participants regarding such questions as the nature of executive leadership and the character of relationships between the top manager and his immediate subordinates.

The following questions are designed to induce students to take precise positions of a diagnostic and predictive character:

1. What do you make of M. Latour and his management group? What problems do you see? (How do you reconcile, if you can, some of the contradictory opinions voiced by management personnel?)

2. Could you hazard a guess as to the future success of this management group over the next ten years? Particularly how the "succession" issue may be handled?

The Galvor Company (C-1), (C-2), and (C-3). These three cases deal with aspects of marketing, including distribution, pricing, and product-line considerations.

Suggested questions for the (C-1) and (C-2) cases are as follows:

1. What strengths and weaknesses do you see in Galvor's French distribution system?

2. Do you agree with the company's use of sales agents? What criteria should be used in installing direct sales offices?

3. What is your evaluation of Galvor's pricing policy?

4. With whom do you side in the discussion between M. Chambertin and M. Latour regarding research and development and factory overhead?

The (C-3) case on product policy might be treated along with (A) and the industry notes as part of the whole strategy picture. Suggested questions on this case are as follows:

1. Should Galvor proceed with development of the digital voltmeter?
2. What criteria should the company employ in evaluating new product proposals?
3. Do you agree with the composition of the company's present product line? What, if anything, might be done to improve it?

The Galvor Company (D). Suggested questions for Galvor Company (D) on financial policy are as follows:

1. What is your appraisal of Galvor's current financial condition?
2. To what extent could Galvor borrow additional funds?
3. Keeping in mind M. Latour's aversion to selling any equity at all, how fast could Galvor grow? How big might it be in five years? In ten?
4. If M. Chambertin decided to introduce capital budgeting procedures, what types should he plan on using, and how should they be introduced?
5. Make a rough estimate of the value of Galvor, if M. Latour decided to sell.
6. Comment on other aspects of Galvor's financial policies which you find interesting.

The Galvor Company (E). The Galvor management defined inventory control as one of its major operating problems, and a case on this issue was accordingly prepared. Suggested questions for discussion are as follows:

1. What are the principal problem areas in Galvor's inventory-control system?
2. Are these problems peculiar to Galvor, or are they inherent in the industry?
3. Can Galvor improve its inventory-control system?
4. What management actions should be taken to improve their system of inventory control?

The Galvor Company (F). In anticipation of growth of the company on an international scale, this case was prepared around a series of questions raised by the case collectors. Since these questions appear in the text of the case itself, there is no need of repeating them here.

The Galvor Company (G-1) *and* (G-2). These two final cases involve further aspects of Galvor's organizational problems, growth, and management development. The following questions on these cases produced significant discussion at IMEDE:

1. Everybody in the executive group at Galvor talks about "organizational problems." Do you agree with their assessment? What do you see as the major problems?
2. The organization for the future was discussed by several member of the executive group. What do you think of these plans? Will they solve the problems?
3. What do you think of M. Latour's administrative behavior with respect to M. Armagnac?

4. In the short period of time that M. Armagnac has been with Galvor, could you form an opinion of his actions? His future?

In discussing these cases, members of the group have an opportunity to crystallize their own patterns of organizational leadership. In effect, students can mentally place themselves inside the company and indicate the role they would play if they could take the place of M. Latour. It is important to recognize that in playing such a role they may be differentiating themselves from the predictions they would make about how M. Latour himself would or should behave.

THE GALVOR COMPANY (A)*

INTRODUCTION

"In 1936, I borrowed a little money from a friend, made 25 tube checkers working at home, and went out on the road and sold them; that's how Galvor began," commented M. Georges Latour, president and owner of France's Galvor Company. "Today in 1962, Galvor is still here in Bordeaux where it started, but now we make a broad line of electric and electronic measuring and test instruments, and we operate in this large, modern plant. (See Appendix A.) We have just had a record year in every respect: net sales were over 12,000,000 New Francs (NF), profits after taxes were about 1,000,000 NF, and our net worth today is approaching 6,000,000 NF. Twenty-six years ago the firm consisted of my wife and me; today we have about 430 employees and a strong management team to direct our constantly growing affairs. (An organization chart for Galvor is found in Exhibit 1 on page 631.) It has certainly been an exciting and rewarding experience to build the company."

THE FOUNDING OF GALVOR

M. Latour continued: "You might find the detailed story of how the business started rather an interesting one. In 1935, my wife and I had just had our first child, so it was necessary for me to earn a good living. I went to work for a radio manufacturer, selling his radios to retailers. During the summer of 1935, as is traditional in France, most people were away on vacation, so business wasn't too good. In an effort to help my customers and earn their good will, as I made my rounds I would try to fix any broken radios which might have been sent in to the retailers. In those days there wasn't the vast network of radio-repair shops which exists today, and so if a radio required complicated repairs, it had to be sent back to the factory. The retailers usually didn't have much technical knowledge about radios—they just sold them. But when making my rounds I would carry along a stock of extra tubes, and so, when a re-

Exhibit 1

THE GALVOR ORGANIZATION, FEBRUARY, 1962

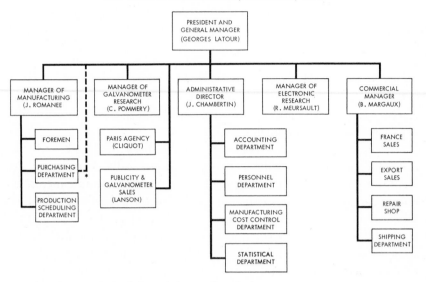

* M. Latour to some extent supervised purchasing activities.

Source: Company officials.

tailer gave me a broken radio to look at, I would first replace the radio's tubes with good ones from my stock. Since most radio failures are due to faulty tubes, this method usually fixed the radio. If that didn't work, I could then inspect the wiring to see if that was O.K., and I could check the resistors and condensers to make sure that they were not obviously defective. But if none of these methods fixed the radio, then it had to be sent back to the factory; it was, however, usually an easy matter for me to fix a radio.

"One day that summer, a customer gave me a broken radio. I quickly located the defective tube, but when I substituted one of my own tubes, the radio still didn't work. I checked the wiring and the other parts carefully, but I could see no reason why the radio shouldn't work. I regretfully admitted that I couldn't fix it and suggested that it be sent to the factory. I thought no more about the incident until, a little later, another customer gave me a broken radio to fix. This radio, I discovered, also had the same type of defective tube as the first one, and when I substituted my own tube, again the radio didn't work. Again a check of the chassis showed that there was apparently nothing else wrong, but still I couldn't fix it. After a while, and quite by accident, I decided to substitute for the defective tube again from my own stock, but this time I used a different, although identical, tube from my selection. Immediately the radio worked. I was horrified; how was I supposed to do a good repair job if I couldn't be sure that my own stock of tubes, which was brand new and supposed to be perfect, contained some defective tubes?

"I had been educated as an engineer, and it quickly occurred to me that I could easily construct a simple device which would test a tube. You have to understand that, in those days, there were only a few tube testers on the market, and all of them were vastly too complicated and expensive for the average radio retailer. About all the retailer could do was to check tubes by substituting new ones (if he had any); if this didn't work, he could not do much else.

"Well, during the fall I constructed a tube checker at home, and when it was finished, I started taking it on my customer calls. This little instrument was very simple: it had only a tube socket and a simple meter, and it only checked the tube's emission.[1] If the meter indicated over 30, the tube was all right, less than 20 the tube was defective, and from 20 to 30 it was questionable. My customers were delighted by this little instrument, because it was simple. They could easily use it themselves to check their customers' radios, and so I got many requests for copies of it.

"It occurred to me that somebody ought to make a simple tube checker for the radio retailer to use. I had no interest in doing so, because my sales had started to increase greatly during the fall of 1935, so I was making a good living as a salesman. My customers appreciated the repair service I gave them, especially since I did not charge for this service. So, by December, I decided to talk to the president of my company; I hoped to persuade him to make the tube checker himself. When I came to the home office in December, there was a fine commission check waiting for me, and a message that the president of the company wanted to see me. That was fine, because I also wanted to see him.

"As soon as I got to his office, he started explaining to me that I was making too much money; I was even earning more than he was! 'When your contract expires next June,' he said, 'we will have to rewrite it to lower your commission rate.' I said nothing to this and proceeded to show him my tube checker. I guaranteed that it would be an instant sales success and that he could easily manufacture it. He would have nothing to do with it; he would hardly discuss it at all. I was very disappointed when I left his office.

"In the spring of 1936, my sales and commissions continued to be

---

[1] Emission is only one of the characteristics of a vacuum tube; a modern tube tester checks many other tube characteristics as well. Checking emission is rather like determining whether an automobile's fuel pump is feeding gasoline into the engine; after such a check, one still does not know whether the engine is running well and efficiently.

high, and radio retailers continued to ask me to get them duplicates of my tube checker. Finally, I made my decision. My contract expired on June 1st, and so, when I got to the head office late in May, I handed the president my resignation. This upset him considerably, because I was one of his most successful salesmen. He admitted that it was possible to make a mistake, and he offered to keep my commission rate at the old level, but my mind was made up. I told him I was going into business for myself to make the tube checker, and I resigned. His parting words were that, within a year, I'd be bankrupt. The very next day, I started Galvor. (I met the president many years later; by then his company had gone bankrupt.)

"In order to start the business, I had borrowed what would today amount to 6000 NF from a friend in Lyon, and with this I immediately ordered enough parts to make 25 tube checkers. Those first days as my own boss were wonderful; maybe they were the happiest days of my life. My wife and I worked long into the evenings assembling those first 25 checkers; when they were finished, I took them out and sold them almost immediately to radio retailers, except for one that I kept as a demonstrator. With the proceeds from this first batch, I was able to make about 40 more checkers, which I sold just as quickly, and I was on my way. We branched out after that into another, more complicated type of tube checker, and subsequently into related types of test equipment. Within a year I was an employer: I hired an assistant, and Galvor grew from there.

"You know, life is dependent to a great degree on luck, and especially on seizing a piece of good luck when it occurs. If I hadn't one day seen the need for a simple, reliable, cheap tube checker, if I hadn't had the technical skill to design one, if it hadn't been so enthusiastically accepted, and, of course, if my boss hadn't refused to manufacture it, well, without any doubt, I wouldn't be sitting in this office today.

"My basic business philosophy is this: first, you should find out what people need; then, if someone isn't meeting this need as well as you can, you have an opportunity. Second, if you can build a better product and sell it cheaper than your competitors, you will be successful. Our company has grown by capitalizing on these two facts."

GALVOR IN 1962

Galvor had grown greatly, since its early days, but in 1962 the firm retained many of the features it had had 26 years before. M. Latour still owned 97 per cent of the company, and the basic operation was still one of buying parts and assembling them into electric and electronic measuring and test equipment. During its growth, Galvor had broadened its product line considerably, but the company still concentrated on electric and electronic measuring instruments. In general, the company's products had become increasingly sophisticated technically; this trend was typical of the electronics industry's development throughout the world. In 1962, however, most of the firm's products were still of only moderate technological complexity, and most sales came from products in the price range of 50–1,000 NF. In comparison, more sophisticated branches of the industry, such as those dealing with electronic computers, often manufactured products of extraordinary complexity which sold for millions of New Francs. In its own sector of the industry (measuring instruments), Galvor was one of the major French firms, but there were many firms in other sectors of the industry which were vastly larger than Galvor.

THE GALVOR SERIES

Galvor (A) is designed to give the reader a basic familiarity with the company and the way in which various aspects of the firm's operations developed. To this end, the case discusses the development of the product line, manufacturing operations, marketing, research and development activities, and the financial and management control of Galvor. Subsequent cases in the series develop in greater detail certain aspects of Galvor's operations in 1962 and its plans for the future.

THE GROWTH OF THE GALVOR PRODUCT LINE

After the favorable reception of his first tube checker, M. Latour expanded Galvor's product line by the addition of a tube analyzer in 1937. Then in 1937–38, Galvor produced its first generators and multimeters. In 1941–43, the company further broadened its operations; during this period, impedance bridges, galvanometers, vacuum-tube voltmeters, and more types of generators were introduced.

After the war, the first order of business was to modernize and upgrade the existing products. When M. Latour felt that his established products were sufficiently improved to meet the demands of the postwar market, he was again ready to expand Galvor's product line. Recalling this period, he said: "In 1946, as soon as it was possible to get a booking, I flew to the United States in order to study the development of electronics there. During the war, we had become very impressed with the high level of U.S. technology; jeeps and bombers were good illustrations, to us, of this level. So I thought I had better go over to see how much progress had been made in measuring instruments. I was very happy to observe that, despite my fears, the design and performance of Galvor's products appeared to be at least as good as that of the comparable U.S. products. This realization encouraged me to continue Galvor after the war and to succeed."

In 1946–47, after the basic products had been satisfactorily improved, Galvor branched out into several new types of multimeters; the company also introduced its first VHF generator, in anticipation of television's requirements. Then, in 1952–53, as television became more and more important, additional TV test equipment was added: wobulators and marker- and pattern-generators. Throughout the postwar period, Galvor's products were steadily improved in terms of performance, reliability, durability, and price. In the late 1950's, as FM radio broadcasting became increasingly important, Galvor introduced its first FM generators. The emergence of transistors at this time also spurred the company to develop a transistor checker. Further development of VHF generators continued as television became increasingly common in France. In 1958, 15 years after Galvor had first started manufacturing galvanometers for use in its own equipment, it began to sell these meters to other instrument manufacturers.

Galvor had traditionally engaged in three different kinds of product development. First, as outlined above, there was the continuous process of adding distinctly new types of products to the catalogue. Second, and of equal importance, each basic product was being updated and improved almost constantly. Thus the original tube checker and tube analyzer were still important Galvor products, but each of these instruments was, in 1962, a vastly more sophisticated and useful device than its ancestor of 20-odd years before. Third, many of Galvor's basic product types had been gradually expanded into a line of similar instruments for varying applications and requirements. For example, the original multimeter of 1938 had, by 1962, grown to a line of about 15 different multimeters.

In addition to its basic line of measuring and test instruments, Galvor had developed a number of other products of lesser importance. These products could be classified in three groups. First, many Galvor instruments could be made more versatile by the addition of accessories, and so the company manufactured (or bought outside for resale) a considerable number of such accessories. Second, starting around 1950, Galvor had begun to manufacture certain products which were essentially unrelated to its traditional product line. One such product was an instrument which, when attached to an oil burner, would shut off the burner when there was a danger of explosion. Third, in late 1957 the company introduced a small line of instruments under the trade name of TRO-NEX. This line contained some of the high-volume products in the Galvor line, but TRONEX products were considerably lower, in both price and quality, than the equivalent Galvor products.

In commenting on Galvor's product line and the philosophy which had created it, M. Latour remarked: "You already know why I built our first product, the tube checker. From there, it was a logical step to make a more complicated instrument, with an analogous function, and with similar but more advanced technology: the tube analyzer. Until the war these tube checkers and analyzers were our most important products. But as we gained more technical experience, it was logical to branch out into other types of electronic measuring instruments.

"We entered the electric instrument business with our multimeter for one simple reason: the multimeter is the basic measuring instrument in both electrical and electronic applications, and so, when we wanted to expand our product line, we naturally chose the easiest things to sell, which were multimeters. During the war, multimeters, generators, and tube checkers and analyzers were our chief products.

"My basic product philosophy has been this: First, to find a product with which we have some technical familiarity and background, because without this technical basis we cannot really compete. Second, having found such a product, to determine whether we can sell it in profitable quantities. This means finding out (a) if the total market is large enough to justify our entry and (b) how much competition there is for this market. Our introduction of the impedance bridge is a good illustration of this philosophy. We knew in 1941 that we had the technical ability to make this bridge. We decided to design and manufacture it because, although the total market for bridges was not very large at the time, there was almost no competition for this market, so we thought we could get most of the market for ourselves, which would justify making the bridge. Most of the products which we introduced after the war were in response to the new demands for television and FM radio equipment, two fields which we had the technical ability to enter.

"I think I should also say something about my philosophy of quality. I am proud to be able to say today that Galvor instruments are sold primarily on the basis of their outstanding quality,[2] but this has not been

---

2 The U.S. Bureau of Standards, in Washington, D.C., used a number of Galvor instruments as reference sources.

an easy thing to achieve. From the very beginning, and after the war especially, we have constantly aimed to raise quality and lower prices. This has been a basic philosophy of mine and one which, I should say, has contributed greatly to our success.

"In the 1950's, as our Galvor products gradually became higher and higher in quality, we found that we were shutting ourselves out of the considerable market for low-price instruments of average quality. The typical radio repairman, for example, doesn't look very far ahead in purchasing his basic test instruments; he wants the cheapest product, no matter what the quality. I decided that we could profitably bring out a line of low-price instruments of good, but not Galvor, quality, to help meet this demand. We did so with our TRONEX product line.

"As for the few products we make which have little relation to our basic product line, such as the oil-burner instruments, we have gone into these when (1) the product in question is essentially a measuring instrument and thus related in theory to our other products and (2) when there already exists a good design for such a product, a design on which we can improve. In these cases, we have never developed the fund of technical knowledge which we have in our own area; we have contented ourselves with merely refining somebody else's design so as to get market acceptance. The trouble with this policy is, of course, that, since we are not expert in the technology of such products, we cannot lead in the market, but must follow others, and so when design changes in some fundamental respect, we lose our market. We have had some success with certain of these products, but they have not been an important factor in our business.

"Finally, I might say that today we are not particularly looking for new fields to enter. We have found that there are plenty of challenges and opportunities remaining in our own speciality of measuring instruments."

Galvor's basic product line was divided into two categories: electric and electronic instruments. The distinction was generally based on whether the instrument contained electronic tubes and/or transistors. Table 1 shows the main groupings in Galvor's product line and gives certain statistics about each group.

MANUFACTURING OPERATIONS AT GALVOR

PHYSICAL FACILITIES

By 1962, Galvor's manufacturing processes bore little superficial resemblance to those of 26 years before, when M. and Mme Latour had

Table 1

THE GALVOR PRODUCT LINE, 1961

Product Group	Number of Models	Price Range (NF)	1961 Sales* (NF 000's)	Percentage of Total 1961 Sales
Electric products				
Multimeters	15	100–550	5,188	36.2
Galvanometers	Over 100	60–150	1,412	9.8
Milliammeters	2	200–230	105	0.7
Special products	....	....	275	1.9
Accessories and spare parts....	....	....	795	5.5
Total electric			7,775	54.1
Electronic products				
Tube and transistor checkers and analyzers	5	250–2,340	881	6.1
Generators				
Wobulator	2	700–1,800	67	
Pattern generator	1	1,100	153	
Audio generator	1	680	156	
Service	1	670	191	
HF	2	1,850–2,250	1,073	15.7
VHF	2	1,665	127	
UHF	1	n.a.†	227	
AM and FM	3	1,200–2,000	245	
Marker	2	800–2,000	11	
Total generators	....	....	....	
Wobuloscopes	2	1,320–2,050	986	6.9
Oscilloscopes	3	1,115–2,200	321	2.3
VTVM's‡	3	365–1,300	781	5.4
Impedance bridges	3	n.a.	417	2.9
Vacuum-tube bridge	1	3,800	126	0.9
Accessories and spare parts....	....	....	344	2.4
Equipment racks	....	....	11	nil
Total electronic	....	....	6,117	42.6
Sales to Tronex	....	....	192	1.3
Equipment repairs	....	....	281	2.0
Total	....	....	14,365	100.0

* Including all taxes.
† n.a. = not available.
‡ Vacuum-tube voltmeters.
Source: Company officials.

worked long evenings to assemble the first products. As shown in Table 2, Galvor's total floor space had increased considerably since 1936.

Galvor had acquired a considerable stock of machine tools in the course of its growth, despite the fact that the company's primary activity was still one of assembling purchased parts into instruments. Late in 1961, company officials estimated the real value of all machine tools as approximately 466,000 NF, and the real value of scientific instruments used in

Table 2

DEVELOPMENT OF GALVOR FLOOR SPACE

Year	Location	Total Floor Area (Square Meters)
1936	Rue de l'Arbre, Bordeaux*	80
1937	Rue Kafka, Bordeaux	120
1941	Avenue de Camus, Bordeaux	400
1948	New factory (Rue Costello, Bordeaux)	1,850
1953	Factory elongated	2,100
1956	Factory partially raised	2,600
1958	Wing added to factory	5,252
1962	Wing extended	8,917

* M. Latour's home.
Source: Company records.

testing and research as 208,000 NF. (No value was assigned to the many Galvor instruments which were used in the laboratories and testing departments.) Although these machine tools and instruments were estimated to have a true value of about 675,000 NF, they were carried on the company's books at about 168,000 NF.

Commenting on the company's machine tools, M. Jacques Romanée (Manager of Manufacturing), remarked: "In my opinion, we should be constantly looking for new machines to replace the ones we have, in order to make our operations more and more efficient. But M. Latour thinks that Galvor already has all the necessary machine tools and that no new ones should be bought until all the present tools are being used 100 per cent. I am not sure that our management is sufficiently production-oriented."

M. Latour, in commenting on this question, said: "We have all the machines we need for our present operations. Most of our machine tools are used for producing molds, tools, and special jigs and fixtures. However, the trend in the industry is towards equipment of higher frequencies. Such instruments involve much more mechanical work than lower-frequency products, and so we will have to manufacture more and more of the components ourselves if we are to make the maximum profit from these products. Obviously, this will require that we considerably expand our machine tool capacity." M. Chambertin (Administration Director), was substantially in agreement with M. Romanée, thinking that Galvor could profitably increase its investment in production equipment.

THE WORK FORCE

In commenting on Galvor's workers, M. Romanée said: "On the whole, I would say that they are rather highly skilled. We have trained all of our workers ourselves, out of necessity, because they have to do precision work of very high quality. In general, by Bordeaux standards we pay our people well, near the top of the range. We would pay men and women the same wages for the same work, but this issue does not arise, because they never do the same jobs. We pay no incentives, only a straight hourly wage. About half of our workers are women, many of them working in the Galvanometer Department." Galvor workers were ranked in five categories, according to their skills. Category I consisted of unskilled workers; category V included the highly skilled toolmakers. Table 3 gives pertinent information on the classification of the male work force early in 1962.

Table 3
DATA ON THE GALVOR MALE WORK FORCE, 1962

Skill Category	Approximate Number of Workers in Category	Pay Rate of Category (NF per Hour)		
		Minimum	Average	Maximum
I.	31	1.90	2.20	2.90
II.	57	2.20	2.75	3.30
III.	35	2.75	3.05	4.00
IV.	12	3.15	3.35	3.65
V.	11	3.50	3.80	4.00

Source: Company records.

Galvor's foremen were paid between 1,110 and 1,500 NF per month, rates which M. Romanée considered extremely high in comparison with other Bordeaux firms. The average male worker at Galvor had been employed by the company for over seven years, M. Romanée estimated, and the average woman at least five years. He pointed out that these figures would have been considerably higher, except that the company was expanding so rapidly that many of the workers had been hired only recently. Table 4 shows the growth of Galvor's work force in recent years, according to the categories used by the company in differentiating among employee groups.

ORGANIZATION OF THE DEPARTMENT

Exhibit 2 shows the structure of Galvor's Manufacturing Department in early 1962. M. Romanée, in commenting on this organization chart, said: "Unfortunately, since I have no line assistant below me, all of the foremen report directly to me, and as a result I have to give them much more authority, and much better pay, than they really should receive. I'd like to find a good assistant, but I haven't the time to train him; besides,

Table 4

GALVOR: AVERAGE NUMBER EMPLOYED BY YEARS

Year	Direct Labor	Indirect Labor	Research	Administrative and Clerical	Total
1953	n.a.*	n.a.	n.a.	n.a.	115
1954	80	26	11	10	127
1955	92	26	24	10	152
1956	108	33	20	11	172
1957	133	50	24	13	220
1958	144	58	22	25	249
1959	162	63	30	37	292
1960	195	68	26	42	331
1961 (end)	242	80	33	68	423

* n.a.: Not available.
Source: Company records.

you can't teach a man everything I've learned about this business in 30 years."

THE MANUFACTURING PROCESS

Starting from its early days as a pure assembly operation, Galvor had gradually begun to manufacture an increasing number of the components in its products. M. Romanée remarked: "If we had not done so, we could never have grown to our present size. It was absolutely necessary for us to make more and more of these parts, but, even today, most of the pieces in our products are bought from suppliers and assembled here." The photographs found in Appendix A show some typical manufacturing operations and work areas at Galvor.

For accounting purposes, Galvor divided its direct labor into two categories: assembly labor and manufacturing labor. Manufacturing labor was chiefly used in the fabrication of parts for instruments, but it also included some toolmaking and jigmaking labor. "Assembly" labor consisted of wages paid to assembly workers. Table 5 shows Galvor's manufacturing cost structure in recent years.

In general terms, Galvor manufactured an instrument's case, the chassis on which it was mounted, the galvanometers used to display the findings of the instrument, the switches and dials used to operate the device, and occasionally certain other important parts as well. As a rule, the electronic components forming the heart of the typical Galvor instrument were purchased from suppliers. These components included electronic tubes, transistors, resistors, condensers, transformers, coils, potentiometers, and wire. Galvor was, as of early 1962, preparing to enter the so-called "component" industry by manufacturing some of its own re-

Exhibit 2

THE GALVOR MANUFACTURING DEPARTMENT, 1962

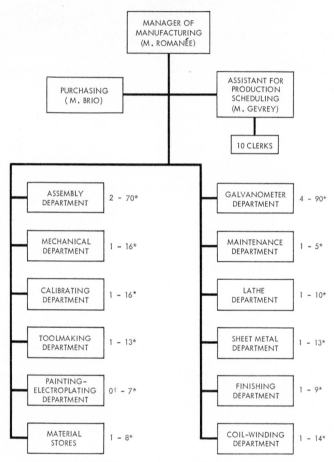

* These pairs of numbers indicate (first) number of foremen in department, and (second) approximate number of workers in department.
† The chief of this joint department was not officially a foreman, but his pay and responsibility approximated those at the foreman level.

Source: Company officials.

sistors.[3] The manufacture of such complicated components as tubes and transistors was a highly sophisticated and specialized operation requiring very large investment and considerable technical background. Since, for example, tube manufacture could be conducted profitably only by mass production and since Galvor generally required a relatively small number of each of a great variety of tubes, management was not, in 1962, contemplating entry into this field.

"We will make, rather than buy a product," said M. Latour, "under

---

[3] Resistor manufacture was scheduled to begin in the new factory as soon as it was completed.

Table 5

PERCENTAGE BREAKDOWN OF GALVOR COSTS IN SELECTED YEARS
(Sales = 100%)

	1961	1960	1959	1958	1955
Parts manufacturing:					
Raw materials*	2.8	3.5	3.0	5.2	8.2
Direct labor†	2.6	2.9	2.7	3.1	3.0
Subcontracting	0.4	0.3	0.5	0.5	1.3
Factory overhead‡	4.5	4.7	5.0	9.0	6.2
Total parts manufacturing cost	10.3	11.4	11.2	17.8	18.7
Purchased parts*	29.2	31.7	27.0	24.5	19.7
Total cost of parts	39.5	43.1	38.2	42.3	38.4
Assembly expenses:					
Direct labor†	6.7	6.8	6.4	6.3	7.8
Factory overhead‡	11.6	11.0	11.7	18.1	16.3
Total manufacturing cost§	57.8	60.9	56.3	66.7	62.5
Net inventory adjustment	1.0	(1.7)	1.6	(4.9)	0.2
Final manufacturing cost	58.8	59.2	57.9	61.8	62.7
Sales expense	11.8	12.0	12.4	11.7	12.2
Research expense‖	5.4	5.6	6.6	. . .	. . .
Administrative expense	5.4	5.7	5.8	8.4	7.0
Other profit and loss#	9.8	9.7	9.5	10.2	7.1
Profit after taxes	8.8	7.7	7.9	7.8	11.0
Total sales**	100.0	99.9	100.1	99.9	100.0

Computed from company records by IMEDE staff.
  * Including purchasing expense.
  † Including social security charges, etc.
  ‡ Apportioned between parts manufacturing and assembly in direct proportion to the amount of direct labor used in each department.
  § Before adjustment for changes in inventory.
  ‖ Before 1959, Research Expense was not treated as a separate expense item.
  # This item consisted chiefly of taxes paid on profits; pre-tax profits were taxed at a 50% rate in France.
  ** Sales here are net sales after sales tax is removed from gross sales figures; percentages do not add to exactly 100% in all cases because of rounding off.

any of these circumstances: (*a*) when the quantity we require is so small that it is difficult, or very expensive, to subcontract; (*b*) when we can make a given part ourselves at a substantial saving over purchase price, if we have the capacity; (*c*) when the part is very crucial to the instrument and we dare not rely on an outside source." Galvor's purchases were of three sorts: (1) wholly finished components, such as electronic tubes, to be mounted directly in the instruments; (2) partially finished products which would undergo further manufacturing operations at Galvor; and (3) raw materials, such as sheet metal, where all manufacturing operations were done by the company. In 1961, of Galvor's total purchases from outside suppliers, 8 per cent were raw materials, 87 per cent were partially and wholly finished products (mostly components), and 5 per cent were products to be resold to Galvor customers, such as leather carrying cases for multimeters. These percentages had not, company officials said, changed very much in recent years.

About 15,000 different parts were used in making the products in the Galvor line. Of this total, about 10,000 were bought in a wholly or semi-finished state. M. Chambertin remarked that, although it was difficult to generalize, the typical Galvor electric product, such as a multimeter, contained from 2 to 3 times as much purchase content as direct labor content. The typical electronic product, he added, contained from 3 to 5 times as much purchase content as direct labor. This was due to the fact that most electronic products contained a considerable number of relatively complicated and expensive components, such as electronic tubes and transistors, while electric products, such as multimeters, contained few sophisticated components.

Production runs varied considerably in length, depending on the type of product involved. The electric instruments, consisting primarily of multimeters and galvanometers, were assembled in batches of from 1 unit (on a special order) to perhaps 2,000 units. The average figure for runs of these instruments was probably, M. Romanée estimated, between 500 and 1,000 units. The electronic instruments were usually assembled in batches of 25–50 units. In general, the more complicated the instrument, the shorter the run. Company officials cited two reasons for this variation in length of production runs. First, the electric instruments were usually simple devices where substantial cost savings could be realized by long production runs, whereas the cost of electronic instruments was not lowered nearly so much by mass production. Second, unit sales volumes were much higher for galvanometers and multimeters than for the more expensive and specialized electronic products.

There was a considerable amount of special-order production done in the electronic instruments category, most of it at the request of various agencies of the French Military. Company officials estimated that such special orders might average as much as 20 per cent or more of total production of electronic products, but most of these special orders required only minor changes in Galvor's standard products. Little special-type manufacture was done for electric instruments. The Galvanometer Department manufactured to specific customer order, but this department usually produced meters listed in the catalogue rather than meters designed especially for a customer.

CONTROLLING THE PRODUCTION SYSTEM

Galvor's production scheduling system was, M. Romanée pointed out, basically a simple one. Every two months, the Statistical Service (under

Mme. Bollinger) produced a production schedule for a two-month period beginning eight months hence. This schedule listed the number of units of each Galvor product which were to be produced in each month of the future two-month period. Mme Bollinger based this schedule on her annual sales forecasts for each product.

When this production schedule was received by M. Gevrey (Assistant to M. Romanée for Production Scheduling), he and his clerks drew up a list of the parts to be purchased outside and the worker-hours called for in each department by the schedule. M. Gevrey was in charge of ensuring that the necessary parts to meet this schedule arrived by the time that it went into effect.

Approximately four months before a given production schedule was to go into effect, Mme. Bollinger again checked that schedule to see if recent developments indicated that it should be changed. There were changes made to every schedule as a result of this reappraisal of sales prospects. These changes were initiated by Mme. Bollinger, who issued an *ordre d'urgence* ("urgent order"), making the appropriate changes in the schedule which was to take effect in four months.

"In general," commented M. Romanée, "the system works pretty well. We have a certain amount of flexibility, because we do have some inventory of most Galvor products on hand, although not very much. We sometimes find that we cannot deliver a product on the planned date, but this problem is usually not severe. Many of our products have, in effect, no direct competition, especially the electronic ones. If a customer wants one of these instruments, he must buy from us; we can make the customer wait for such instruments if necessary. In electrical products there is more direct competition, and so here we are under greater pressure to keep our delivery promises. Accordingly, if we have to postpone making either an electric or an electronic instrument, it is usually the electronic instrument which gets delayed." Early in 1962, Galvor's backlog of orders totalled about 1,900,000 NF.

Inventory control at Galvor had recently been a matter of concern to M. Latour. Table 6 gives selected statistics on the company's inventory levels since 1956.

Commenting on current stock levels, M. Latour said: "I am not happy with our present inventories, especially of raw materials and purchased parts. Every time I ask one of my people why we have so large a stock of such-and-such an item, I get a fine explanation. But this fact remains: I would like to have two months' supply of purchases on hand, not what we have now." M. Romanée remarked that, in general, he had sufficient stocks on hand to ensure a steady manufacturing operation.

Table 6

INVENTORY AT YEAR END AS PERCENTAGE OF NET SALES

Year	Raw Materials and Purchased Parts	Work in Process	Finished Products	Total All Inventory
1956	13.3	4.3	3.4	21.0
1957	9.5	3.8	4.1	17.4
1958	12.0	8.5	7.3	27.8
1959	15.4	9.2	4.2	28.8
1960	10.7	9.5	6.6	26.8
1961	11.5	7.5	8.0	27.0

Computed from company records by IMEDE staff.

Quality control at Galvor had become increasingly important with the passage of time, as the firm had continually upgraded its product line. M. Romanée described the quality control system as based on "auto-control," i.e., on making the workman responsible for the quality of his own work. There was also a calibrating and test department to make final adjustment and checks on finished products. Galvor had very few problems, said company officials, in maintaining the desired quality levels. "Occasionally," said M. Romanée, "we have troubles in the Galvanometer Department, because the assembly work there is very repetitive and yet must be done with extreme care. After a girl has mounted, say, several hundred needles in a day, she begins to slack a little bit, and so we have to keep a sharp eye on the department's output."

M. Latour mentioned that the chief foreman of the Galvanometer Department, who had many years' experience with the company, was a fanatic on the subject of precision, and so the department's products were always of higher specifications than designed. "For this foreman," remarked M. Latour, "precision is like an incurable illness. We could cut our labor costs 15 per cent and still put out galvanos of acceptable quality. We were about to transfer this foreman, when suddenly we discovered that we were making the best galvanos in France, so, for the time being, I'm not changing anything, but eventually we will cure this overprecision."

M. Romanée commented on his method for controlling manufacturing costs as follows: "M. Chambertin takes care of all our costing, but I generally don't use his figures. I just try to make everything at the lowest possible cost, and I don't really need statistics to tell me how to do this; I can sense what needs to be done." Table 7 shows Galvor's total manufacturing costs as a percentage of sales since 1950.

M. Romanée himself established a standard direct labor cost for each product when the final product design was ready. This cost, plus the cost

Table 7

MANUFACTURING COSTS AS A PERCENTAGE OF NET SALES

Year	Per Cent	Year	Per Cent
1950	71.5	1956	63.3
1951	68.5	1957	62.5
1952	64.2	1958	61.8
1953	58.0	1959	57.9
1954	62.5	1960	59.2
1955	62.7	1961	58.8

Computed from company records by IMEDE staff.

of material needed to make the product, formed the basis of Galvor's costing and pricing systems.

GALVOR EMPLOYEE RELATIONS

Galvor's executives believed that the workers were generally content with their jobs. M. Latour said: "The workers who have been with us for many years are generally satisfied, and our pay scale is among the best in Bordeaux. Some of the men we have hired in recent years tend to be a little noisy. Many of them have had bad experiences with other employers and expect the same thing here. Because they are noisy, they tend to be elected as delegates by the workers, and in December [1961] some of them came here to ask me for a pay raise to compensate for increases in the cost of living. I quickly showed them that their recent pay raises had more than covered these increased prices, and so they are silent. I have promised further wage increases based on individual contribution; we're already covering rises in living costs, so now we will pay for human value. We had a meeting on January 15th [1962], and they agreed to this system of raises."

Galvor's workers belonged to a company union unaffiliated with other unions; the chief purpose of this union, remarked M. Romanée, was to "hold conversations with management." Galvor had enjoyed good employee relations throughout its history; there had never been a strike.

In 1962 Bordeaux was still, as for a number of years past, a full-employment area. As a result, Galvor experienced some difficulties in finding workers for its ever-expanding operations. The problem was aggravated because Galvor needed skilled workers, or workers with the aptitude to be trained for precision work; there were many other large firms in Bordeaux requiring such workers, M. Romanée said, and he added that, in an average year, he would expect to lose perhaps 30 workers out of a total of about 300, due to retirement, child-bearing, illness, job-changing, and other causes. A typical new Galvor worker had to be trained for 6–12 months before becoming fully productive, so the company was continually operating in-plant training programs. Workers were also encouraged to add to their skills at appropriate institutes in Bordeaux, and Galvor would typically give a worker one day off per week to attend such courses. M. Romanée summed up by saying that, in the past, he had been able to find enough workers to replace those employees who left and to fill the new jobs created by expansion.

EXPECTED MANUFACTURING DEVELOPMENTS

The new addition to the Galvor plant would be ready, it was hoped, near the end of July, 1962. This addition, amounting to some 3,700 square meters, would increase Galvor's total floor area by about 70 per cent. It was planned to use the new area to expand all manufacturing operations as a whole, rather than only isolated ones. M. Latour expected, however, that the Galvanometer Department, because of its rapid growth of sales, would require a relatively high proportion of this new area.

Galvor's top management had, after lengthy consideration of the issue, decided that the Manufacturing Service's staff should be expanded by the addition of two groups: first, a Manufacturing Bureau and, subsequently, a Methods Analysis Staff. Company executives had generally agreed that a Manufacturing Bureau, by acting as liaison between the Research and Development Services and the Manufacturing Service, would speed the process of getting a new design into production. The Methods Analysis Staff, M. Romanée hoped, would enable him to relieve the foremen of their responsibility for methods study. Tentatively, he hoped to have the Manufacturing Bureau by early 1963, the Methods Staff two years later.

"As I said," M. Romanée concluded, "we found in the past that, in order to keep on growing, we had to do more and more manufacturing ourselves, and this trend will continue as we expand further. It is dangerous for us to be too closely tied to our suppliers. This means that my job will become more and more difficult, and that is why these two new staffs are so important: I am overloaded with work all the time; when these staffs are well established, I will have the time to deal with the long-term aspects of manufacturing."

THE GALVOR MARKETING ORGANIZATION

Early in the company's history, M. Latour had adopted the policy of selling Galvor products in France through a network of manufacturers' representatives. M. Latour himself remained in charge of the Commercial

Service until 1958, at which time he appointed M. Bernard Margaux the Manager of this service. In 1960, by which time Galvor's sales in the Paris area accounted for over 40 per cent of total sales volume, the company established a wholly owned sales subsidiary in Paris to cover that region. In early 1962, however, a large part of Galvor's sales volume still came from the traditional manufacturers' representatives. Exhibit 3 shows the organization of the Commercial Service early in 1962. In discussing his organization, M. Margaux remarked: "M. Crépy is really only a foreman in charge of our repair shop. At the moment I am taking care of exports myself, but I hope soon to find an assistant to do this for me."

Exhibit 3

ORGANIZATION OF THE GALVOR COMMERCIAL SERVICE, 1962

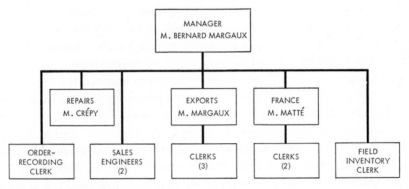

Source: Company officials.

The Paris agency, called Galvor Paris, was moved into new quarters in January, 1961. M. Cliquot, the head of this agency, was assisted by four sales engineers, three of whom prospected in the Parisian region for sales; the fourth remained in the office and assisted M. Cliquot. Galvor Paris was not a part of the Commercial Service, but a separate entity reporting directly to M. Latour.

"Galvor Paris was created," M. Latour said, "when our Paris representative decided to retire. I might add that we were paying this representative far more in commissions than we are now paying to operate Galvor Paris. But we never would have discharged this agent against his will; he had done fine sales work for us for many years. In 1960, when he retired, we paid him 170,000 NF as a bonus. Eventually, we may have our own agencies in the other major French industrial centers, but at the moment the product line is still too narrow to support the expense of such a network."

Export sales were made directly from Bordeaux to two principal outlets: to COMOR S.A. and to importers outside France. Repairs of exported Galvor instruments were made and billed directly from Bordeaux. COMOR S.A. was a French export company, located in Paris, which had an exclusive license to sell Galvor products in 17[4] countries. Virtually all of Galvor's other export sales were made through licensed import agencies throughout the world.

POSITION OF GALVOR IN THE INDUSTRY

Company officials described Galvor as being a producer of high-quality, general-purpose instruments of moderate cost. Certain Galvor competitors sold low-quality measuring instruments; such instruments were usually bought by radio and television repairmen for use in applications where high precision was not necessary and were generally cheaper than the equivalent Galvor product. Other competitors manufactured ultra-precise instruments for specialized applications; such instruments were usually much more expensive than the equivalent Galvor product. Galvor products generally covered the area between these extremes, in terms of quality and cost. As a result, Galvor customers spanned the range from local radio repairmen to highly advanced laboratories. Over 80 per cent of Galvor's sales were made to French customers.

"Our products are sold mainly on the basis of quality," said M. Latour. "Next comes our price, which is usually well below the market for products of equivalent quality, and then our reputation." M. Margaux added that Galvor also won customers by its excellent, low-priced, fast repair service. He said that such good repair service was not always available from Galvor competitors.

ADVERTISING

M. Margaux continued: "Our annual advertising budget of about 50,000 NF is certainly small in comparison with our total sales, but this is typical of our industry. The purpose of our advertising is to keep people aware of our continued existence and, occasionally, to mention some new product. We cannot really sell a product by advertising its specifications. The customer wants to know much more about the product than we can put in an advertisement. As a result, product demonstration and discussion with one of our sales engineers or manufacturers' representatives are very important. Our best publicity is visiting our customers, demonstrating the equipment intelligently, repairing quickly and cheaply, and making a high-quality, low-cost, durable product." Galvor

---

[4] These countries were Austria, Belgium, Bulgaria, Czechoslovakia, Denmark, Finland, Greece, Holland, Hungary, Italy, Norway, Poland, Romania, Spain, Sweden, the U.S.S.R., and Yugoslavia.

usually allowed its customers 90 days from invoice date in which to pay; this was sometimes extended to 12 months for small customers. The company's bad-debt losses were typically about one-tenth of 1 per cent.

GALVOR'S COMPETITION

Most of Galvor's competitors were other French firms which also concentrated in electric and/or electronic measuring instruments. Company officials said that Galvor had 11 significant French competitors, no one of which carried all of Galvor's product types.

There was considerable competition in multimeters and galvanometers, but company officials estimated that Galvor had 80–90 per cent of the total French multimeter market, the rest being shared by about 10 firms. Because of the high quality of its galvanometers, Galvor was, by 1962, a major competitor in this market, and M. Latour hoped that the company would be the leader in galvanos within the near future.

"As for our electronic products," remarked M. Margaux, "competition varies quite a lot. Oscilloscopes are a minor item for us, and we have a small market share. For almost all of our generators, we have only one competitor, and we are not even in direct competition, because he has a different clientele than we have. Our wobulators and wobuloscopes meet little serious competition; we are badly beating our one real competitor in this field. Our impedance bridges are another of our minor products, because the total market is small, and here we have no competition in the same quality range. Our vacuum-tube voltmeters encounter considerable competition, and this is the only Galvor product where we have serious foreign competition in the French market. Our tube checkers and analyzers have no competition in their own class. Our TRONEX products have lots of competition, not only from French firms, but increasingly from Japanese, German, and American imports."

GALVOR'S PRICING SYSTEM

In speaking about the way in which prices were set, M. Latour remarked: "I have been using the same pricing system for many years. M. Chambertin thinks that I should adopt a different method, and perhaps in theory he is right, but at the moment I cannot see any good reason to change. I do admit, however, that our prices may not always reflect our real costs." "GALVOR (C-2)" describes the details of the pricing system.

POSSIBLE MARKETING DEVELOPMENTS

It was M. Margaux's long-term dream, he said, to see Galvor build a network of wholly owned agencies in the major French industrial centers. He added, however, that until Galvor sales in each area climbed considerably, this was not feasible except in the Paris region.

PRODUCT RESEARCH AND DEVELOPMENT

A SHORT HISTORY

Galvor's Research and Development Staff began in 1937 when M. Latour hired a technician to help him develop Galvor's second product, the tube analyzer. Until late 1940, M. Latour himself supervised the development of the company's products. "When the war came to France," M. Latour continued, "many refugees appeared. In late 1940, I heard about a brilliant refugee engineer named Messer. I managed to find the man but discovered that there were two Messer brothers. Since I couldn't find out which was the brilliant one, I took both of them. When they asked me what I wanted, I said 'I want General Radio quality.'[5] Well, the brothers Messer certainly raised the quality and the sophistication of our products. The only complaint ever raised was this: many engineers said that the Messers designed equipment up to the very limits of its capability. All the components in an instrument were pushed very hard. They squeezed the last possible bit out of a given design and the components. But when this was mentioned, the Messers always went into a long, theoretical explanation about how they were actually right. There was one other little problem with the Messers: they were incredibly expensive. They were good, and they charged for their quality.

"By the end of the war, I was paying the better of them about $2,200 per month. As you can imagine, I wasn't paying myself any such salary. Well, the brothers decided that they wanted to move back to Paris now that the war was finished. They said they would stay with Galvor only if I moved the factory to Paris, and they gave me 48 hours to make up my mind. I must admit that I spent a bad night, but in the morning I came in and said that Galvor would stay in Bordeaux. They left, and they took a couple of their assistants with them, including Robert Meursault. I had replaced them within a month.

"Within a year or so, we built our research staff back up to the level it achieved under the Messers. Meursault came back in 1946. We stopped trying to squeeze the last bit of performance out of a design, and this made our customers happier. I again took charge of our R&D for a year or two after the Messers left, and during this period we mostly expanded

---

[5] The General Radio Company, a U.S. corporation, has for many years manufactured a broad line of high-quality measuring and test instruments.

on the basic designs they had developed, but by late 1947 things were again in good shape. Beginning around 1950, we made some excursions into fields different from our own, such as industrial electronics, but, as I said, in these fields we were only improving on somebody else's design, and this didn't work very well. Today we are concentrating on our own specialty. I think that our R&D group now is first-class; Pomméry and Meursault are very effective in creating new products."

THE GALVOR R&D ORGANIZATION, 1962

Exhibit 4 shows the organization of Galvor's R&D groups in early 1962. Describing this organization, M. Pomméry said: "Meursault and I each have our own staff of technicians to develop our respective types of products. We also share the services of the Design and Prototype Services.

"The product development technicians are well-trained, but they are not graduates of the great French technical schools such as Polytechnique. They are not mathematicians and theorists; rather, they are men who can translate ideas into a workable design. These ten men (seven for Meursault and three for Pomméry) do most of Galvor's research. We pay them 1,000–1,600 NF per month. Meursault and I occupy ourselves chiefly with administrative work and with helping to solve problems which may arise."

THE R&D PROCESS

M. Pomméry continued: "The process of product development begins with deciding what products to attempt to design. Generally, market demands indicate what sort of products we will study. We do no pure, or basic, research here; our work is all very much applied research, all designed to produce new Galvor products. Ideas for new products come from our own feeling about what people want or perhaps from seeing what other manufacturers are doing. We try *not* to make *exactly* what other producers are making; we don't want to get into direct competition. Of course, this is easier to do in electronic instruments; in electric instruments, the big differences are in product quality. Most of our research efforts are devoted to products for the Galvor catalogue; however, perhaps 10 per cent of the total research effort in the Galvano Research Service and about 30 per cent in Electronic Research are devoted to studying special products for one customer, usually for the French military.

"The decision on whether to do a full-scale study of a product is usually made at the management conference;[6] of course, M. Latour al-

---

[6] This conference, held every week, included MM. Latour, Chambertin, Romanée, Pomméry, Meursault, and Margaux.

Exhibit 4

STRUCTURE OF THE GALVOR R&D DEPARTMENT, 1962

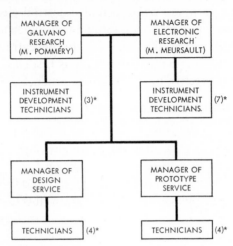

* Indicates number of technicians.
Source: Company officials.

ways has the final decision on whether to do a certain piece of research. We have today, as has been true for some years, a backlog of approved research projects to be undertaken when facilities are available. So, whenever we finish a project and have a man free to begin another job, we only have to decide which backlog project he should study.

"The research process itself follows this pattern. First, the instrument development technician will do the basic study required. For my products, mostly multimeters and galvanometers, this stage takes about 6 months. Meursault's electronic products are more complicated, so that this stage usually requires 1 or 2 years for an electronic product, possibly only 6 months if the job is not complex. This first stage ends with a mock-up of the new product; this mock-up is a highly finished article in every respect, and it will function as designed, but it has not been constructed with any special consideration towards manufacturing it.

"The second stage begins when this mock-up is given to the Design Service. The Design Service studies our mock-up and then redesigns the product in order to make it more easily manufactured. Blueprints are drawn up by the design service, and then the Prototype Service constructs a prototype which is identical with the final product. The prototype is tested electrically and mechanically, and, when we are satisfied, a list of required parts is drawn up, along with the other documents needed to manufacture the product. This second stage takes about 3 months for an electric product, about twice as long for an electronic product.

"Stopping the research process for a given product usually gets done very late, namely, when we have a finished prototype. The usual reason for stopping is that we find that the final price of the product will have to be higher than the market will pay. We haven't found any way around this problem. Our research is always done with the product's final cost in mind, but it is difficult to determine this cost until the process is over.

"In general, I would say that our R&D is quite successful. We do not operate on a tightly fixed budget. If Meursault and I decide that we need an expensive piece of equipment in the lab, we justify it to M. Latour, and then we get it. Our lab is quite well equipped. Of course, if we wanted to try out all the new ideas we have, or even to get rid of the backlog of approved research projects, we'd have to enlarge the research staff. This is gradually being done. We never fully live up to our potential for developing new products, because we have to spend a lot of our time updating the existing products. The Manufacturing Department sometimes requests that we make small modifications in a product's design, and this also takes us away from our main work.

"Another problem is in the process of getting a product from the design stage into manufacture. At the moment, this liaison is being done by the Prototype Service, but when we set up the Manufacturing Bureau, it will be given this responsibility." Table 8 shows Galvor's R&D expense in recent years.

Table 8

GALVOR RESEARCH AND DEVELOPMENT EXPENSE, 1958–61

Year	R&D Expense (000's of NF)	R&D Expense as Percentage of Net Sales
1958	361	5.8
1959	552	6.6
1960	561	5.6
1961	645	5.4

Computed from company records by IMEDE staff.

In commenting on the success of Galvor's R&D efforts, M. Latour said: "Maybe, since it is my company, I should say that our R&D is better than that of our competitors, but this simply isn't true. I think that we are very successful, but our competitors are successful too. I think we do as much research work as we need to. You may remember the old fable about the frog and the bull. The frog saw the huge bull and wanted to become as large, so he puffed himself up, but finally he burst. Well, I think that we shouldn't try to expand our activities too rapidly, but to build on a solid foundation, increasing at a steady pace. It may become harder and harder for us to maintain the real competitive advantages which we have today, but it will always be our goal to provide a bit better quality, at a slightly lower price, than the other fellow."

FINANCIAL HISTORY OF GALVOR

The original loan with which Galvor was begun, amounting to about 6,000 NF in 1961 purchasing power, had evolved into a net worth of about 6,000,000 NF for the company as of December 31, 1961. At the end of World War II, Galvor was a small business; about 50 people were employed by the firm, and sales and profit were at modest levels. The company's period of greatest prosperity and growth began around 1950; in early 1962 there was no indiciation that growth and profitability were decreasing.

Galvor's financial history had largely been shaped by one basic policy of Georges Latour: to maintain complete ownership of the business in his own hands. M. Latour had always believed that only if he had complete ownership of Galvor could he direct its affairs with a free hand. Accordingly, in 1962 he still owned 97 per cent of Galvor's equity; most of the remaining 3 per cent had been given to Jacques Romanée in recognition of his long service to the firm.

Especially after World War II, when Galvor's sales and profits began to grow markedly, M. Latour received a number of offers to buy equity in the company; the offers had been refused. As a result, funds to finance growth had been obtained from three principal sources: retention of earnings, long-term borrowing, and expansion of current liabilities.

With few exceptiones, Galvor had experienced considerable difficulty throughout its history in obtaining substantial amounts of long-term bank credit. When the company had been a small one, it had not been a prime credit risk. During the fifties, the company became successful and, accordingly, a good credit risk. However, through most of this last decade, commercial credit was very tight in France. The government, in an effort to place this credit where it would provide the greatest impetus to the company, had discouraged loans to companies which did not absolutely need credit. This policy was easy to enforce, since the ultimate source of all long-term bank credit was the Banque de France, which put into effect the government's credit policies. Even when expanding rapidly during the fifties, Galvor had still generated sufficient funds to finance its own expansion, and so its occasional requests for credit to finance new construction had been refused. Galvor could borrow for 2–3 years from its local bank, but for longer-term loans the approval of the Banque de France was required.

"In 1948," said M. Latour, "we had our last real financial problem. We were building the new factory, and the price level rose greatly during the course of this construction, so that our initial cost estimates were far too low. I went to the bank for a loan and was, at first, not very encouraged; the bank wanted to buy stock in the company, or for me to raise money by selling stock to others. I was unwilling to do this. Finally, however, I got the loan, and we have had no financial problems since this time. Occasionally we would have liked to borrow to help finance new construction, but lack of long-term credit for such purposes has not affected our plans at all."

M. Chambertin added: "Of course, we could have raised money by selling our own obligations on the open market, and this would not have required very high interest. But M. Latour opposed this idea because he was afraid to let any outsiders get into a position where they might conceivably be able to influence him. Obligations, of course, would not give the bearer as much influence as common stock in Galvor, but M. Latour still preferred not to use this source. Anyway, since 1948 we have been able to finance everything ourselves."

As Galvor grew and broadened its financial base, one major source of funds was an accompanying expansion of current liabilities, mostly in the form of trade credit, accrued expenses, and unpaid tax liability. However, this source of funds was not by itself sufficient to finance rapid growth, and so retention of earnings had been a firm policy of M. Latour. As of early 1962, the company had never paid a dividend, and none was contemplated for the near future.

Late in 1961, in order to help finance the 1,800,000 NF estimated costs for the new addition to the plant, Galvor had requested a loan of 900,000 NF from the Crédit National. A 3-year loan of 600,000 NF had been granted.

Table 9 shows the evolution of Galvor's capital structure since 1950.

As mentioned, it was after World War II that Galvor began to grow most impressively. Table 10 gives selected statistics which illustrate this growth. Because inflation in France has been considerable since World War II, certain of the figures have been adjusted to constant (1961) NF.

Finally, Table 11 shows Galvor's Profit and Loss Statement for 1961 and the Balance Sheet as of 31st December, 1961.

MANAGEMENT CONTROL OF GALVOR

"I am not very happy with our budgetary and accounting control system at the moment," remarked M. Chambertin. "We have our ac-

Table 9

GALVOR: DEVELOPMENT OF CAPITAL STRUCTURE
(Figures in NF 000's)

End of Year	Equity	Long-Term Debt	Current Liabilities	Equity as a Per Cent of Equity Plus Long-Term Debt	Equity as a Per Cent of Total Assets
1950.................	252	83	374	75.2	35.5
1951.................	586	70	376	89.3	56.8
1952.................	734	53	483	93.3	57.8
1953.................	1,161	40	534	96.7	66.9
1954.................	1,453	30	441	98.0	75.5
1955.................	1,788	20	737	98.9	70.3
1956.................	2,213	10	960	99.6	69.5
1957.................	2,714	00	1,178	100.0	69.7
1958.................	3,202	00	1,652	100.0	66.0
1959.................	3,908	270*	2,145	93.5	61.8
1960.................	4,805	190*	2,546	96.2	63.7
1961.................	5,923	147*	2,750	97.6	67.2

* In 1959, 1960, and 1961, Galvor was carrying these amounts under the heading of "Middle-Term Debt"; this loan had been made in December, 1959, and would be fully paid off in December, 1962. The loan had been used to help finance the construction of Galvor Paris.
Computed from company records by IMEDE staff.

Table 10

DEVELOPMENT OF GALVOR SALES AND PROFITS, 1950–61
(Figures in NF 000's)

Year	Net Sales	Profits after Taxes	Total Assets	Net Sales in 1961 (NF)	Profits after Taxes in 1961 (NF)	Profits as a Percentage of Net Sales
1950..........	1,308	71	709	2,210*	120*	5.4
1951..........	1,669	126	1,032	2,203	166	7.5
1952..........	1,568	122	1,270	1,969	153	7.3
1953..........	2,584	434	1,735	3,420	574	16.8
1954..........	2,619	297	1,924	3,530	400	11.3
1955..........	3,205	354	2,545	4,180	477	11.0
1956..........	4,235	425	3,183	5,485	550	10.0
1957..........	5,601	520	3,892	6,835	635	9.3
1958..........	6,197	485	4,854	6,760	529	7.8
1959..........	8,403	666	6,323	8,820	699	7.9
1960..........	10,045	776	7,541	10,200	787	7.7
1961..........	12,030	1,062	8,820	12,030	1,062	8.8

Compiled from company records by IMEDE staff.
* The basis used for these price adjustments is the French Price Index computed monthly by the International Monetary Fund and published in the IMF's publication, *International Financial Statistics.*

Table 11

GALVOR FINANCIAL STATEMENTS, 1961

(Figures in 000's)

INCOME STATEMENT, 1961

Sales (of products and repairs)	14,365
Billing for services performed*	24
Total sales	14,389
LESS: Sales Taxes	−2,359
Net sales	12,030
LESS: Cost of sales (factory cost)	−7,074
GROSS MARGIN	4,956

LESS: Other Expenses:

Sales expense	1,421	
Administrative expense	645	
R&D expense	644	
Other profit and loss†	1,184	−3,894
NET PROFIT AFTER TAXES		1,062

* Charges to TRONEX for services performed by Galvor for TRONEX.
† Mostly comprised of French Corporate Profits Tax, at 50% of pre-tax profits.

BALANCE SHEET

31st DEC. 1961

ASSETS			LIABILITIES			
Current assets			Current liabilities			
Cash	274		Payables	1,110		
Securities	1		Other	1,640		
Receivables	2,796					
Inventories	3,248		Total current			2,750
Other current	222		Depreciation			
			Buildings		430	
Total current		6,541	Equipment		978	
Fixed assets:			Other		57	
Land	265					
Buildings	1,849		Total depreciation			1,465
Equipment	1,438		Mid-term debt			147
Other	192		Net worth			
			Capital stock	2,500		
Total fixed		3,744	Surplus, reserves	3,423		
Total assets		10,285	Total net worth			5,923
			Total liabilities			10,285

Compiled from company records by IMEDE staff.

counting system well organized, and most of the basic data we need are available to us, but we have not gone as far as I should like in the analysis and control of our operations. This is partly because we have grown so fast that, to some extent, it has been difficult to keep tight control over our operations. Perhaps another problem is that responsibility for financial and budgetary control exists only at the highest level of Galvor, namely, in M. Latour's office and in mine.

"We do not have a true budgetary control system. We do not, for example, establish an operating budget for each department at the beginning of the year, and then ask our executives to justify their departmental expenses. When we have to expand a department, say by hiring a new man, we simply add that man's salary to the expected administrative costs for the coming year.

"Moreover, we do not analyze elaborately the economics of our major investments. When we decided, for example, to make this latest addition to the plant, it was simply a case of deciding that we needed more space, that we could finance this addition, and that we could soon sell the output of this additional capacity. We do not make elaborate analyses in determining whether to buy a new machine; either the idea looks good, or it doesn't.

"Perhaps my biggest worry is our cost-price structure. We really do not know what each of our products costs. Until recently, most of our products sold in a relatively narrow price range, say 100–1,500 NF. As long as this was so, it was not too incorrect to say that most products should bear about the same proportion of overhead charges; admittedly, there were differences in the true overhead attributable to different products, but these differences were not too significant with this narrow spread. Now, however, the price range is much greater: we are about to make a product selling for 30,000 NF. The complex electronic products contain far more R&D expense, proportionate to their price, than a multimeter, but our pricing structure does not allow for this."

In commenting on the way in which he controlled Galvor, M. Latour said: "At the month's end, M. Chambertin sends me the following figures for the month: net sales, total purchases, direct and indirect labor, R&D expenses, manufacturing overhead, inventory levels, gross profits, commissions, sales taxes, my personal account, and net profit. I check these figures against previous levels in order to determine whether we are up to standard or should take some corrective measures. Finally, I check our balance sheet, total overhead as a per cent of sales, and our sales to each country. Of all these figures, I am most interested in the net profit figure. Since I sign all our important checks, this gives me another way of keeping an eye on our purchasing."

"I hope," said M. Chambertin, "to push our financial and accounting analyses much further along during 1962; it is the major job I have set for myself. I especially want to learn more about our product costs."

THE STATISTICAL SERVICE

The basic statistical analyses looked at by MM. Latour and Chambertin were compiled by the Statistical Service under Mme. Bollinger. These analyses, consisting of tables and graphs, were contained in four books. In general, these books contained two main types of data: sales and expenses. Sales data alone occupied approximately 70 per cent of the pages in these books. It was possible to find out, for example, exactly how many units of each product type had been sold in each month of every year since 1952, in which countries these units had been sold, and, in the case of France, who had sold them. Galvor's expenses were broken down into minute detail for each department of the firm, and these expenses were available on a monthly basis for recent years.

Finally, these books contained a certain number of tables and graphs which were not strictly connected with sales and expenses: the growth of the unfilled-orders backlog, growth of the work force, total hours worked and wages paid, etc. M. Chambertin also had available, although not contained in these books, standard cost sheets for each product. These sheets were used mainly for pricing purposes.

In addition to supervising the design and compilation of these statistical reports, Mme. Bollinger also produced an annual sales forecast. "I must admit," she said, "that the accuracy of this forecast is much better than the technique used. I make a monthly forecast of unit sales of each product for the next year; this is usually done every January. The main basis for the forecast is historical sales data. These data will usually show clearly any seasonal pattern in the product's sales, plus the over-all trend. I am able to project from this historical information with considerable accuracy. Of course, we have no sales history for a new product, and so it is almost impossible to make a good forecast for such an item. When I have finished my initial forecasts, M. Margaux and I talk them over, because he often has special information or opinions which can improve these forecasts considerably. The final revised forecasts become the basis for the production schedule, which I also draw up." No sales forecasts were made for sales of galvanometers, accessories, spare parts, repairs, sales to TRONEX, or special-order products. Thus the sales forecasts made covered only about 70 per cent of Galvor's total sales volume. Table 12 gives a quantitative measure of the accuracy of these forecasts.

SUBSIDIARY ACTIVITIES OF GALVOR

Galvor had two principal subsidiary operations, the TRONEX Corporation and Indica S.A. The company also had a very small subsidiary

Table 12

ACCURACY OF GALVOR SALES FORECASTS, 1961

Error of Forecast *(Plus or Minus)*	*Percentage of* *Forecasted* Sales* *within Error Class*
0 to 5	37.4
6 to 10	17.3
11 to 15	2.6
16 to 20	20.4
21 to 25	14.7
26 to 30	2.7
Over 30	4.9
	100.0

* As noted, only 70% of total Galvor sales were accounted for by products for which sales were forecast.
Source: Company records.

which owned a number of dwellings, which it rented to Galvor employees.

THE TRONEX CORPORATION

TRONEX was essentially a paper corporation owned entirely by M. Latour; TRONEX's assets and operating results were not consolidated in Galvor's financial statements. Galvor manufactured for TRONEX a small number of low-priced measuring instruments. TRONEX instruments were, M. Chambertin said, of substantially lower quality than the equivalent Galvor products. The TRONEX product line consisted of a multimeter, a vacuum-tube voltmeter, a tube checker, a high-frequency and a pattern generator, and an oscilloscope. TRONEX had no formal organization of its own; M. Margaux to some extent supervised sales of TRONEX products, and one of the development technicians had designed the TRONEX products. As of early 1962, design of new TRONEX products had been suspended but would be resumed at a later time.

TRONEX products were manufactured by Galvor and priced in a manner similar to but not identical with that used for the Galvor products. Galvor then sold these products to the TRONEX corporation at 35 per cent off list price. M. Chambertin said that, at this price, TRONEX was paying about 15–20 per cent over factory cost for the products. TRONEX also paid Galvor a flat sum of about 24,000 NF annually to reimburse Galvor for the overhead incurred by Galvor for TRONEX. TRONEX had begun operations in October, 1957; as of early 1962, its products were sold by three special manufacturers' representatives who did not sell Galvor products, by two of Galvor's own representatives, and by Galvor Paris. TRONEX sales had developed as follows:

NF

1957 (3 mo.)	28,074 (without taxes)
1958	135,453 (without taxes)
1959	197,118 (without taxes)
1960	235,534 (without taxes)
1961	197,524 (without taxes)

TRONEX profits for its fiscal year 1961 (ending 30th September), were approximately 16,500 NF. The corporation's net worth at the same time was approximately 19,000 NF.

INDICA S.A.

Indica was a Parisian corporation engaged in manufactured dials and faces for all sorts of measurement and indicating instruments. The company was entirely separate (except in terms of ownership) from Galvor and had its own work force, plant, and management in Paris. Galvor had bought Indica on April 1st, 1955, at which time the latter had been in bankruptcy; the purchase price was 60,000 NF. Indica's financial figures were in no way consolidated with those of Galvor, except that Galvor carried an asset of 60,000 NF under the heading of "Investments in subsidiaries." Galvor bought many of its meter dials from Indica, but 90 per cent of the latter's sales volume came from customers other than Galvor. M. Chambertin characterized Indica's manager as very aggressive and dynamic. Indica's sales had developed rapidly since 1955, as Table 13 shows.

Table 13

INDICA SALES, 1955–61

Fiscal Year*	Sales (without Taxes) (NF)
1955	388,000
1956	575,000
1957	911,000
1958	1,049,000
1959	1,378,000
1960	1,568,000
1961 (9 mo.)	1,537,000

* Indica's fiscal year ended on March 30th.
Source: Company officials.

M. Chambertin estimated that, for the fiscal year 1961 (which would end 30th March, 1962), Indica's after-tax profit would be about 130,000 NF. He pointed out that the 60,000 NF at which Galvor carried Indica on its books actually represented a true net worth for Indica of about

300,000 NF (as of March 31st, 1961). "As you can see," added M. Chambertin, "Indica is a highly profitable enterprise, and its profits are not added into the Galvor income statement. Moreover, the Galvor balance sheet considerably understates our true equity in Indica."

*   *   *   *   *

In commenting on Galvor's success since its founding, M. Latour said: "The most important reason for my success, I honestly believe, has been in finding men with whom I could share my problems, men who could solve these problems when I alone could not. I am very proud of my executives; every one of them is first-class. Without them, I should not have had any such success." "Galvor (B)" gives further information on M. Latour and the other important executives at Galvor.

Appendix A
EXTERNAL VIEW OF THE GALVOR COMPANY PLANT

Photo Marcel Lombard Lyon.

Photo Marcel Lombard Lyon.

RESEARCH AND
DEVELOPMENT
LABORATORY

Photo Marcel Lombard Lyon.

TESTING AND
CALIBRATING
OF FINISHED
INSTRUMENTS

Photo Marcel Lombard Lyon.

**MAKING AND
INSTALLING COILS
IN GALVANOMETERS**

Photo Marcel Lombard Lyon.

**ASSEMBLY OF
MEASURING
INSTRUMENTS**

Photo Marcel Lombard Lyon.

**TOOL MAKING
AREA**

Photo Marcel Lombard Lyon.

**WINDING SHUNTS
FOR
MULTIMETERS**

ELECTRONICS: A SCIENCE AND AN INDUSTRY

INTRODUCTION

The broad term "electronics," while widely used, has never been fully defined to everyone's satisfaction. Electronics means different things to different people: The scientist views it as a way of controlling some of nature's smallest particles; the engineer as a very flexible tool for accomplishing a wide variety of tasks; the businessman as a dynamic area of enterprise, subject to complex technology and rapid change; and the layman as a somewhat mysterious force which provides radio and TV programs and other, less comprehensible services, such as radar and X-rays. If these viewpoints are markedly different, they are so with considerable justification. Electronics, both as an industry and as a science, is a rather amorphous affair.

This note is designed to be used in conjunction with cases on companies in the electronics industry. It is intended to provide the reader with a conceptual framework for the industry as a whole, so that an individual company may be viewed in light of its relationship to the entire industry. To this end, this note (*a*) gives some definitions of electronics in scientific and industrial terms, (*b*) outlines some general characteristics of the electronics industry in world-wide terms, and (*c*) suggests some trends which are important in this industry in the early 1960's.

I: WAYS OF DEFINING ELECTRONICS

SCIENTIFIC DEFINITIONS

In order to understand electronics and its relationship to electricity, it is necessary to have a basic understanding of the composition of matter. All matter is made up of *atoms*, which consist of *nuclei* and a number of *electrons* in orbit around the nuclei. The nucleus of an atom contains *protons* (positively charged particles) and *neutrons* (particles lacking an electrical charge), as well as other particles. Revolving around the nucleus are from one to more than 100 electrons. (An atom has about as many electrons in orbit around its nucleus as there are protons in the nucleus.) The electron has a negative electrical charge equal in size to the positive charge of a proton. Protons and neutrons are both about *1,840* times larger in terms of mass than electrons.

There are slightly over 100 different *elements* known to exist; these are the building blocks of all matter. Atoms of various elements differ from one another in the number of protons and neutrons contained in their nuclei.

Under certain circumstances, atoms can be made to give up one or more of their electrons; the resulting flow of electrons is called *electricity.*

Electrons can be made to move through vacuums and through all types of matter. The ease with which any type of matter permits the flow of electrons through it determines the classification of that matter as a *conductor, semiconductor,* or *nonconductor.* Electrons move most easily, in general, through metals, and metals are called "conductors." A small group of materials (germanium, silicon oxide, and others) are called semiconductors because, although they are not as conductive as metals, they are not so nonconductive as most other matter. Materials other than metals and semiconductors are called "nonconductors," although all such materials do, in fact, conduct electrons to a limited extent. Only a perfect vacuum conducts no electrons at all.

In general, electricity deals with relatively massive flows of electrons through long metal conductors. Electronics, on the other hand, typically involves much smaller flows of electrons, and in an electronic system the electrons are often not imprisoned within a conductor; they are free to move through vacuums or gas-filled spaces, or through semiconductive material. Electronics is often defined as the science which deals with the *precise control* of electrons and with the use of this control.

Another scientific definition of electronics is based on the type of components which are used in the circuitry of a product. "Circuitry" refers (in electricity and electronics) to the way in which electrons are transferred through a system.

One basic component of electronic circuitry is the electronic tube. The tube creates an environment, either a vacuum or a gas, through which electrons are transmitted and controlled while in transmission.[1]

The semiconductor (of which the transistor is the most famous variety) is another common component of electronic circuits. Semiconductors, like electronic tubes, permit relatively free movement of electrons.

---

[1] As noted, a vacuum does not conduct electrons, but electrons can, by means of high electrical pressure (voltage), be made to move through a vacuum. As a material becomes more conductive, less voltage is required to push a given quantity of electrons through it. The quantity of electricity passing through a given point at any time is termed the *amperage.*

Semiconductors, however, do not generally allow electrons as much freedom of movement as the vacuum or gas environment of a tube.

Thus a second scientific definition of electronics is based on whether a given product contains electronic tubes, semiconductors, or certain other types of electronic circuits. It should be noted, however, that an "electronic" device usually contains not only electronic components but mechanical and electrical parts as well.

ELECTRONICS AS AN INDUSTRY

Until recent years, electronics has generally not been considered a separate industry, but as a sector of the electrical-goods industry. The growing importance of electronics, however, and the increasing divergence of electric and electronic manufacture have finally led to general agreement that electronics should be regarded as an industry in its own right. There are still many types of products which cannot easily be classified as "electric" or "electronic," but which are on the border line between the two industries. This vagueness unfortunately gives rise to occasional confusion and to differences in industrial statistics from different countries.

In broad terms, the electronic industry can be looked at in two ways: the type of products it makes and the use of these products.

WHAT THE INDUSTRY MAKES

One way of analyzing the industry's structure is as follows:

I. *END PRODUCTS*
   A) Consumer Goods (radios, TV sets, home sound and movie equipment)
   B) Capital (or professional) equipment (communications equipment, radar, computers, control systems, etc.)
II. *COMPONENTS FOR THE END PRODUCTS*
   C) Electronic tubes and semiconductors
   D) Other components (condensers, coils, resistors, switches, transformers, antennae, microphones, loud-speakers, chassis parts, vibrators, special crystals, etc.)

As can be seen in the foregoing breakdown, the industry lends itself to an easy division of end-product manufacturers versus component manufacturers. In general, few of the end-product makers are deeply involved in the manufacture of components, and vice-versa. Component manufacture is a highly complex and technical business, especially in the area of tubes and semiconductors. This branch of the industry is usually, therefore, left to firms which specialize in the appropriate technologies. Only the largest electronics firms are extensive producers of both components and end products.

THE USERS OF ELECTRONIC PRODUCTS

When the industry is looked at from the viewpoint of end use of its products, the component sector disappears from sight. It is important to remember, however, that this sector provides the building blocks used by the industry. *British Communication and Electronics* has made a useful analysis of the United Kingdom industry in terms of uses of its products. This analysis, which is reproduced as Exhibit 1, gives a good indication of the many uses made of electronic products. As this table shows, only the consumer products are easy to classify; the rest of the industry's production is extremely diverse and complex. The table also demonstrates clearly the pervasive influence of electronics on modern life.

Exhibit 1

STRUCTURE OF THE U.K. ELECTRONIC-BASED INDUSTRIES
IN TERMS OF APPLICATIONS

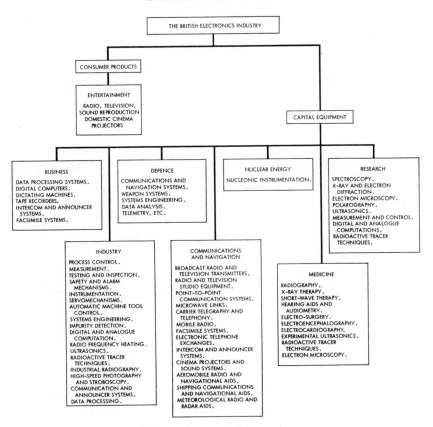

Compiled by "British Communications and Electronics."

II: GENERAL CHARACTERISTICS OF THE WORLD ELECTRONICS INDUSTRY

There are certain salient characteristics of the electronics industry on which many observers agree, and some of these characteristics are useful in obtaining a working understanding of the industry.

First, in every major industrial country, electronics is an important industry. Indeed, it is difficult to imagine the world lacking this industry, so integral is electronics in modern life. Allied to this is the fact that electronics is crucial in the military establishments of all major powers. This involvement of electronics and defense began during the First World War and became vastly greater during the Second World War. It is significant, and remarkable, that half of the cost of a modern combat aircraft may be made up of electronic equipment.

Second, electronics is vitally dependent on advanced scientific technology, and the industry lives in an atmosphere of rapid technological change. This rapidity is due partly to specific demands for more and more sophisticated equipment, notably from military agencies, and partly to the immense amounts of electronic research which are today being conducted. The extent of this research is suggested by the fact that, in 1960, the United States electronic industry spent over one billion dollars (about 10 per cent of total industry sales) on research and development. Massive amounts of R&D expense appear necessary to survival in this industry. Much of this research leads quickly to new electronic products. One consequence of this rapidity of change is a rapidity of obsolescence unmatched by most other industries. Another consequence is the difficulty of securing adequate information about likely developments in electronics. One can only be certain that, for the foreseeable future, electronics will continue to change rapidly; the directions which this change will follow are much less certain.

Third, it is a commonplace to say that electronics is a growth industry. It is probably true that electronics is growing faster than most other major industries in every highly industrialized nation. Until the late 1930's this growth came primarily from consumer demands for radios. Added impetus was given by military requirements before, during, and after the Second World War. Widespread television broadcasting provided additional thrust in the postwar years, and, since the early 1950's, the demands of business and industry for electronic equipment have also spurred this growth. The end of this growth is nowhere in sight at the present time.

Fourth, the "typical" electronic product's cost is mostly composed of technology and labor; raw materials usually account for a small fraction of total cost, perhaps 3–10 per cent for most products. In general, the labor involved is rather highly skilled. Electronic products typically contain many delicate parts which must be manufactured within narrow limits of error and assembled with great care.

Related to the composition of electronic products is the fact that most types of electronic manufacture require a relatively small capital investment. Little heavy machinery is used in electronic manufacturing; most of the manufacturing processes involve delicate operations, carried out by hand, with only the aid of simple tools and jigs. Entry into the end-products sector of the industry may, in many instances, involve nothing more than hiring some engineers and assembly workers and renting a small factory; all the needed parts can be bought from component makers.

Looked at from another viewpoint, it can be seen that the industry has a heavy demand for engineers and workers to design and manufacture its products. The fact that, in recent years, there has been little unemployment in Europe has probably slowed down the growth of European electronics through the difficulty of finding employees in sufficient numbers.

These, then, are some general characteristics which appear to be true, to varying extents, of the electronics industries in the main industrial nations. Table 1 lists and gives pertinent data for the most important electronics industries in the free world.

Table 1

THE MAJOR ELECTRONIC INDUSTRIES OF THE FREE WORLD, 1960

Country	Population (000,000's)	National Income ($MMs)	Electronics Industries		
			Total Employed	Sales ($MM)	Exports ($MM)
U.S.A.	181	400,000	700,000	10,000	500
U.K.	52	53,000	225,000	1,300	170
Japan	94	27,000	160,000	1,100	183
W. Germany	53	53,675	135,000	1,060	400
France	46	40,816	70,000	650	85
Canada	18	26,689	40,000	500	. . .
Italy	49	22,400	40,000	300	14
Holland	11	8,800	30,000	210	. . .
Belgium	9	9,000	20,000	150	. . .
Total	513	641,380	1,420,000	15,270	1,352

Compiled by IMEDE staff from statistics published by the FNIE (Fédération Nationale des Industries Electroniques), the French syndicate which collects data on the electronics industries of France and other nations.

Reliable statistics for the electronics industries of Russia and other Communist countries are not available. Industry observers agree, however, that the U.S.S.R.'s electronics industry is second in terms of total production only to that of the United States. Russia is known to be especially strong in the field of capital equipment, notably for military uses and, to a lesser extent, for industrial applications. In electronic consumer goods, the Soviets still have a long way to go, as shown in Table 2.

Table 2

RADIO AND TV SETS PER CAPITA, SELECTED COUNTRIES, 1960

Country	Radios per Capita	TV Sets per Capita
United States	1.03	0.31
United Kingdom	0.30	0.22
West Germany	0.30	0.09
Japan	0.18	0.07
France	0.27	0.04
Italy	0.18	0.04
U.S.S.R.	0.12	0.02

Source: Computed from FNIE statistics by IMEDE staff.

III: CURRENT TRENDS IN WORLD ELECTRONICS

In a brief note of this sort, it is impossible even to attempt to list and quantify all the trends which are making themselves felt in electronics today. There are, however, certain factors which are often mentioned as being currently important to the industry.

1. The rate of technological innovation in electronics appears today to be accelerating. From the birth of electronics around 1890 until the beginning of the Second World War, the industry devoted itself primarily to communications, notably in the area of radio broadcasting and reception. A glance at Exhibit 1 reveals that communications is only one facet, although an important one, of electronics in the 1960's. The following types of products have been developed[2] since 1940: radar, microwave transmission, digital computers, solid-state electronics, industrial process control, and tape recording, to name only a few. Transistors furnish a particularly striking example of this trend. In 1950, transistors were only a laboratory discovery as yet not transformed into products. In 1952, $20,000,000 worth of transistors and other semiconductors were

---

[2] It is obvious that these products were largely based on scientific discoveries made before 1940; indeed, all of them depend on discoveries of the eighteenth and nineteenth centuries as well as the twentieth. Nonetheless, these products and many other electronic apparati have a commercial existence of only 20 years or less.

produced in the United States; this figure had risen to $425,000,000 by 1960. Transistors and other semiconductor devices have revolutionized a large percentage of electronic products in a period of ten years.

2. The time lag between a new electronic invention and its commercial application seems to be shrinking rapidly. Fleming's basic invention of the electronic tube, which may be said to have ushered in the age of electronics, made radio broadcasting and reception possible. It was well over twenty years from the time of Fleming's invention until radio broadcasting became widespread. By contrast, the pioneering digital computers which were custom-built for scientific research around 1945 had become, ten years later, a widely accepted and mass-produced tool for government and industry. The rapid commercialization of transistors, already cited, is perhaps an even more dramatic example of this trend.

3. Virtually everything manufactured by the electronic industry, from simple components up to giant data-processing systems, is becoming technically more complex and sophisticated. Great efforts are being made to counter this tendency, but it appears that such efforts are not wholly successful, especially in the area of professional electronic equipment.

This tendency is partially due to the increasing number of functions which electronic equipment can perform as technology advances. For example, a combat aircraft in World War II used electronic equipment primarily for radio communication. Today's fighter aircraft uses not only multiple and complex radio systems but also intricate radar mechanisms, devices to guide the aircraft, devices to control and direct the plane's armaments, and other equipment as well.

This tendency towards increasing complexity is also due, quite often, to a desire for more sophisticated equipment. The usual home record player of thirty years ago had, as operating controls, the following: on-off, louder-softer, and (if a fancy model) bass-treble. As today's high-fidelity addict knows (and desires), a modern phonograph system may well have a dozen controls or more, most of them designed to make very minor adjustments to the system's performance.

4. Starting in the late 1930's, most of the major world governments became very interested in electronics as an aid to national defense. Today it is commonplace for many electronic companies to do a large part of their business with governmental agencies. Electronics and government agencies appear to be inextricably linked. One illustration of this is the fact that, in the United States and France, 75 per cent of sales of capital electronic goods are made to the armed forces.[3] The heavy in-

---

[3] Source: FNIE.

volvement of electronics in space exploration is strong assurance that the major world governments will be, for the foreseeable future, important customers of the electronic industry.

5. Micro-miniaturization of electronic components and products is one trend which has been notably fostered by military agencies, especially by air forces, where weight and volume are critical factors. This trend is also reflected in consumer goods: Today's TV set is considerably smaller, for any given picture size, than the set of 1945, and it is possible to buy a radio no larger than a pack of cigarettes.

6. One trend within micro-miniaturization is the continued research and development on transistors and other electronic devices which rely heavily on solid-state physics. Most of the solid-state devices have been developed for military requirements and have subsequently found many other applications. This general area of research is today receiving intense attention throughout the world electronics industry.

7. Computers are rapidly taking over many jobs formerly performed by people or by mechanical equipment; this is one of the best-understood trends in electronics today. Mostly a scientific curiosity before 1950, computers today have been assigned many basic business accounting functions, and coming years will see computers (and the techniques of operational research) used increasingly for making certain types of business and governmental decisions.

8. The control of industrial processes of all sorts is widely regarded today as an area of great growth for electronics in the immediate future. Some steps have already been taken in this direction, especially in the oil and chemical industries, for controlling continuous processes. Many industrial prophets predict that, in the not-too-distant future, the typical factory will present an eerie aspect: hundreds of machines will be busily at work turning out goods, but the only men in sight will be the engineers and technicians who watch over the electronic system which is controlling the entire manufacturing process. Some plants of this sort already exist, and more can be expected.

9. The forecast for electronic consumer goods appears to contain no outstanding innovations in the near future. There will certainly be a continual rise in the ownership of radio, TV, and home sound equipment, and color television may become commonplace if its cost is further lowered. At the moment, however, few industry observers predict any imminent and radical changes in the consumer market for electronic products. There are, indeed, electronic "homes of the future" often featured in magazines and other media, but the idea of a house where almost all

the normal housekeeping functions are under electronic control is unlikely to be a widespread reality by, say, 1975.

The fact that no major electronic consumer innovations are now foreseen as important within the near future is quite significant to the industry as a whole. Throughout most of the industry's history, production of consumer goods has been a major growth area. But today, in the United States and the United Kingdom, growth in consumer electronics has temporarily, at least, slowed drastically. Americans and Englishmen are better equipped with radios and TV sets than any other people (Table 2), and the primary demand for new radio and TV sets has accordingly dropped severely in both countries. Both the United States and the United Kingdom produced more TV sets in 1959 than in 1960. As the level of radio and TV set ownership rises in other countries, these countries' electronic industries will probably also find that their consumer sectors become less dynamic.

10. Some studies have recently been made which indicate the likely growth of the electronics industry in different areas. Table 3 gives a forecast for the United States electronic industry up to 1970; this forecast was made by 125 specialists on United States electronics and has been published by the FNIE.

Table 3

FORECAST PERCENTAGE SALES INCREASE OVER 1960 FOR THE
U.S. ELECTRONIC INDUSTRY

Sector	Per Cent by 1965	Per Cent by 1970
Defense equipment	50	92
Industrial equipment	83	177
Consumer goods	14	82

Source: FNIE.

Five European banks[4] have jointly prepared an analysis of, and forecast for, the European electronics industry. No specific time period has been assigned to this forecast, which is reproduced as Table 4.

As an adjunct to Table 4, the analysis continues by saying that, for the next few years, the European Gross National Product is expected to grow at an annual rate of about 5 per cent or slightly above and that European

---

[4] *L'Industrie Electronique en Europe*, prepared by: Banque Générale Industrielle La Hénin, Paris; Banque Mobilière Privée, Paris; Georg Hauck & Sohn, Francfort sur Main; Lombard, Odier & Cie., Genève; R. Mees & Soonen, Rotterdam. Privately printed, Geneva, January, 1962.

Table 4

EXPECTED DEVELOPMENT OF THE EUROPEAN ELECTRONIC INDUSTRY

Industry Sector	Size of Present Market	Growth Potential	Profit Potential	Expected Fluctuation of Sales
COMPONENTS:				
Tubes	Important	Fairly good	Fairly good	Small
Semiconductors	Fairly important	Good	Variable	Small
Other components	Important	Good	Good	Small
CONSUMER GOODS:				
Radio	Fairly important	(Mid-term): *fairly good* (Long-term): *fair*	(Mid-term): *fair* (Long-term): *mediocre*	Rather large
Television	Very important	Good	Fairly good	Rather large
CAPITAL GOODS:				
Defense	Rather small (except very important in France & U.K.)	Good	Very variable	Great
Public agencies	Important	Fairly good	Average	Rather large
Private sector	Small	Very good	Good	Small
*COMPUTERS & DATA PROCESS-ING:**				
Standard equipment	Fairly important	Good	Reasonable	Small
Automation	Small	Very good	Very good	Small
Data-processing	Very important	Very good	Variable	Small

* Separated from other capital goods because of this area's unusual importance.

Source: *L'Industrie Electronique en Europe*, prepared by: Banque Générale Industrielle Le Hénin, Paris; Banque Mobilière Privée, Paris; Georg Hauck & Sohn, Francfort sur Main; Lombard, Odier, & Cie, Genève; R. Mees & Soonen, Rotterdam. Privately printed, Geneva, Jan. 1962.

electronic production should grow, during the same period, at an annual rate of 10–15 per cent.

Finally, electronic production in Japan is expected to continue its rapid growth. The Japanese Ministry of Commerce and Industry has estimated that, by 1964, electronic production will be 82 per cent above its 1959 level.[5]

---

[5] Source: FNIE.

A NOTE ON THE FRENCH ELECTRONIC INDUSTRY

INTRODUCTION

This note describes, mainly in quantitative terms, the situation of the French electronics industry in the early 1960's. Most of the basic statistics used to compile this note have been taken from various reports and bulletins of the Fédération Nationale des Industries Electroniques (FNIE), the French industry syndicate which compiles and distributes comprehensive statistics on the electronics industries of France and other countries.

Little attempt has been made to present qualitative information on each individual sector of the industry; to do so in a thorough manner would, because of the industry's diversity, require a report vastly larger than this note. For such information, the reader is referred to the general trends in world electronics outlined in "ELECTRONICS: A SCIENCE AND AN INDUSTRY," pp. 674–79, and to the appropriate notes on narrow areas of the French electronics industry. This note follows the industry structure which has been established by the FNIE. The note contains six sections: a general view of the total industry, sections on each of the four sectors into which the FNIE divides the industry, and a final section which gives some forecasts for the future of the industry.

I: AN OVER-ALL VIEW OF FRENCH ELECTRONICS

INDUSTRY GROWTH

Table 1 gives some measure of the growth of the electronic industry in France since World War II. Because there has been considerable inflation in France during those years, certain of the figures are adjusted to constant francs.

Total industry employment in the period 1939–44 ranged from about 25,000 to 30,000, the high point being reached in 1941. It can be seen, thus, that, in terms of creating jobs, the industry was relatively static from 1939 until the early 1950's, at which time a period of steady expansion began. As an illustration of this expansion, total employment in the

Table 1

DEVELOPMENT OF THE FRENCH ELECTRONIC INDUSTRY, 1948–60

Year	Total Industry Sales (NF 000,000's)	Total Industry Sales in 1960 (NF* 000,000's)	Total Industry Employees	Annual Per Cent Increase in Sales 1960 NF*	Annual Per Cent Increase in Employment
1948..........	256	520	26,500	...	...
1949..........	269	487	28,900	6 decr.	9
1950..........	333	556	28,800	14	nil
1951..........	504	655	29,800	18	3
1952..........	590	732	31,000	27	4
1953..........	717	932	33,400	27	8
1954..........	919	1,223	41,500	31	24
1955..........	1,148	1,527	45,900	25	11
1956..........	1,424	1,807	51,000	18	11
1957..........	1,820	2,184	56,400	21	11
1958..........	2,100	2,245	59,400	3	5
1959..........	2,601	2,680	60,300	19	2
1960..........	3,203	3,203	69,200	20	15

* Computed from FNIE statistics by researcher. The price index used to adjust sales to 1960 francs was the general price index for France, computed by the International Monetary Fund and published in its periodical, *International Financial Statistics.*

French electronics industry rose, by 1960, to 262 per cent of 1948 levels (Table 1). By contrast, total employment in France rose only 111 per cent during this same period.[1]

THE INDUSTRY'S FOREIGN TRADE

Table 2 gives over-all statistics on exports and imports by the French electronic industry in recent years. In 1959, the latest year for which complete figures are available, total foreign exports of France were 18.705 billion NF and her foreign imports 16.567 billion NF. A comparison of these figures with those in Table 2 shows that the French electronic industry provided, in 1959, about 1 per cent of French foreign exports and accounted, in the same year, for about 0.75 per cent of foreign imports.

Table 2 does not include imports from the Franc Zone, because such imports have been very small; they reached a historical high of 810,000 NF in 1960. The foreign balance, rather than the over-all balance, is shown because exports to the Franc Zone do not earn foreign currencies for France and are, therefore, relatively unimportant from an international balance-of-payments viewpoint. It can be seen that, since 1955, the industry has not been an important earner of foreign currencies and that, in fact, in the first six months of 1961, the industry's imports were higher than its exports (if the Franc Zone is ignored).

---

[1] Source: Statistics published by International Monetary Fund.

Table 2

EXPORTS AND IMPORTS OF THE FRENCH ELECTRONIC INDUSTRY
(NF 000's)

	Exports		Foreign	Foreign
Year	*Foreign**	*Franc Zone*	*Imports*	*Balance†*
1948.................	3,862	16,754	14,519	(10,657)
1949.................	11,355	25,571	17,467	(6,113)
1950.................	21,473	20,795	21,991	(519)
1951.................	43,403	36,647	29,357	14,046
1952.................	49,267	42,339	33,256	16,011
1953.................	63,840	33,659	48,338	15,502
1954.................	109,717	38,695	51,208	58,509
1955.................	187,818	41,595	67,814	120,004
1956.................	68,516	51,166	81,795	(13,279)
1957.................	107,187	77,689	99,874	7,313
1958.................	130,076	108,668	102,873	27,203
1959.................	181,425	133,943	128,161	53,264
1960.................	282,057	141,497	246,550	35,507
1961‡................	180,714	94,616	203,840	(23,126)

* "Foreign" refers to all imports and exports not involving the so-called "Franc zone"; the latter was comprised of France's overseas territories and now consists chiefly of ex-French colonies.
† This is the net inflow (or outflow) of France's foreign exchange as a result of the balance between imports and exports.
‡ First six months only.
Source: FNIE.

The French electronic industry has traditionally been a good customer of the United States. For example, in 1960 about 50 per cent of the French electronic industry's total imports came from the United States, and about 30 per cent more from West Germany and Holland equally. Of its total 1960 foreign exports, the French electronic industry sent 18 per cent to Holland, 10 per cent to West Germany, 8 per cent to the U.S.S.R., and 7 per cent to Belgium and Luxembourg combined. The United States accounted for only about 4 per cent of the foreign total.

Table 3 shows, for the first six months of 1961, foreign imports and exports in each sector of the French electronic industry.

COMPOSITION OF THE INDUSTRY

The FNIE divides the French electronic industry into four sectors: (1) Consumer Goods, (also called Receiving Equipment); (2) Professional Equipment (mostly for business and government); (3) Tubes and Semiconductors; (4) Other Components. Those industry products which do not fit any of these categories are grouped under "Miscellaneous." Table 4 shows the development of each sector since 1948.

Since the industry's final products are those in the first two sectors— Consumer Goods and Professional Equipment—it can be seen that only about two-thirds of the industry's gross sales figure is accounted for by

Table 3

FOREIGN TRADE OF FRENCH ELECTRONIC INDUSTRY DURING THE
FIRST SIX MONTHS OF 1961
(NF 000's)

Sector of Industry	Foreign Exports	Foreign Imports	Foreign Balance
CONSUMER GOODS:			
Radio & TV sets	9,672	10,916	(1,244)
Home sound system	8,383	13,931	(5,548)
PROFESSIONAL EQUIPMENT	89,686	82,308	7,378
COMPONENTS:			
Tubes & semiconductors	42,295	54,283	(11,988)
Condensers	670	7,820	(7,150)
Other components	30,008	34,581	(4,573)
TOTAL INDUSTRY	180,714	203,840	(23,126)

Source: FNIE.

Table 4

DEVELOPMENT OF THE FRENCH ELECTRONIC INDUSTRY, 1948–60
(Sales figures in NF 000,000's)

Year	Sales in Each Sector					
	Consumer Goods	Profes- sional Eqpt.	Tubes and Semi- cond's	Other Com- ponents	Miscel- laneous	Industry Total
1948..............	110	57	48	41	...	256
1949..............	108	84	43	34	...	269
1950..............	132	95	55	51	...	333
1951..............	201	139	79	85	...	504
1952..............	186	230	79	95	...	590
1953..............	215	299	99	104	...	717
1954..............	256	420	96	147	...	919
1955..............	343	490	116	199	...	1,148
1956..............	500	500	143	274	7	1,424
1957..............	650	590	200	370	10	1,820
1958..............	758	638	255	404	45	2,100
1959..............	961	669	344	486	141	2,601
1960..............	1,186	822	413	609	173	3,203

Source: FNIE.

final products. The remaining one-third consists of the components to make these products.

As Table 4 shows, the Professional Equipment Sector became more important than the Consumer Goods Sector in the period 1952–56, after which time consumer goods regained their historical dominance of French electronic production. The growth in sales of consumer goods slowed down in the early 1950's because France lagged in establishing widespread television broadcasting, and sales of radios were made during this same period largely to a replacement market. When French television became widespread in the late 1950's, sales of consumer goods received a powerful impetus.

French production of professional electronic equipment appears, nevertheless, to be gaining on production of consumer goods. In 1938, sales of professional electronic equipment were 22 per cent of the sales of consumer goods. This ratio was 52 per cent in 1948 and 76 per cent in 1960. This trend towards an increasing proportion of capital to consumer production will continue for some time if the experience of other nations, with electronic industries more highly developed than the French industry, proves typical. In the United Kingdom, for example, 1959 sales of capital electronic equipment were 160 per cent of sales of consumer goods. One reason for the dominance of capital equipment in the United Kingdom electronic industry is that the British Consumer Goods Sector is producing TV sets largely for a replacement market.[2] Conversely, in France there is not yet widespread ownership of TV sets, so the French Consumer Goods Sector has still considerable room for growth in meeting primary demand for TV sets.

STRUCTURE OF THE INDUSTRY

Table 5 shows the composition of the French electronic industry, by size of individual firms, in 1960.

Table 5

STRUCTURE OF THE FRENCH ELECTRONIC INDUSTRY, 1960

Size of Firm (Number Employed)	*Number of Firms*	*Total Employees*	*1960 Sales (NF 000's)*	*Per Cent of Industry Sales*
Over 1,000	10	29,253	1,098,069	37.38
501–1,000	15	10,763	479,228	16.31
201– 500	29	10,112	496,610	16.90
101– 200	44	6,300	260,396	8.86
51– 100	70	5,138	308,401	10.50
21– 50	99	3,391	178,875	6.09
11– 20	65	997	75,444	2.56
Under 11	322	894	40,888	1.40
Total	654	66,848	2,937,911	100.00

Source: FNIE.

2 Precise statistics, found in Table 2 of "ELECTRONICS: A SCIENCE AND AN INDUSTRY," show that in 1960 the United Kingdom had 0.22 TV sets per capita compared with 0.04 in France.

II: CONSUMER GOODS

The French electronic industry has, since its beginnings, been dominated by the production of consumer products.[3] In recent years TV and FM radio broadcasting especially have provided great impetus for this sector. Also, there has been some growth in the number of normal "AM" radio sets. Table 6 shows the structure, in terms of products, of the Consumer Goods Sector in 1959 and 1960. TV sets form the most important branch within the consumer goods area, and the sector's over-all growth rate of 24 per cent is due primarily to the rapid sales increase of TV and home sound equipment.

Table 6

Consumer Goods Sector—French Electronic Industry, 1959–60

Type of Product	Units Sold 1960 (000's)	1960 Sales (NF 000,000's)	1959 Sales (NF 000,000's)	Percentage Change 1960/1959
Auto radios	88	20	16	25 up
Portable radios	1,564	264	189	39 up
Radio-phonographs	74	31	39	21 down
AM radios	450	76	101	25 down
AM-FM radios	38	14	17	18 down
Total radios	2,214	405	362	11 up
Television sets	655	635	487	30 up
Other products*	. . .	146	108	35 up
Total consumer goods.	. . .	1,186	957	24 up

* "Other products" consists mainly of tape recorders and high-fidelity components for home sound systems. This figure is slightly incomplete, but not significantly so.
Source: Compiled from FNIE statistics by IMEDE staff.

The statistics in Table 7 show the size of the firms which make up the Consumer Goods Sector of the industry.

III: PROFESSIONAL EQUIPMENT

There is no easy description possible of the products made by this sector of the industry. The electronics industry manufactures many tens of thousands of different types of products falling in the general area of professional equipment. "ELECTRONICS: A SCIENCE AND AN INDUSTRY" gives an indication of the variety of uses made of professional electronic equipment. The FNIE subdivides this sector in the manner shown in Table 8.

---

[3] As noted, consumer goods took second place to professional equipment in 1952–56, but this appears to have been an aberration in the normal relationship between the two sectors.

Table 7

STRUCTURE OF THE CONSUMER GOODS SECTOR OF THE
FRENCH ELECTRONIC INDUSTRY, 1960

Size of Firm (Number Employed)	Number of Firms	Total Employees	1960 Sales (NF 000's)	Per Cent of Sector Sales
Over 1,000 2		4,439	345,309	29.11
501–1,000 6		4,187	272,708	23.00
201– 500 8		2,532	180,106	15.18
101– 200 8		1,011	104,217	8.78
51– 100 23		1,644	135,072	11.38
21– 50 26		844	70,736	5.95
11– 20 24		367	51,788	4.36
Under 11		466	25,968	2.24
Total 97		15,490	1,185,904	100.00

Source: FNIE.

Table 8

PROFESSIONAL EQUIPMENT SECTOR—FRENCH ELECTRONIC INDUSTRY, 1959–60

Customer	1960 Sales	1959 Sales	Percentage Change 1960/1959
	(NF 000,000's)		
Government			
Defense 395		363	9 up
French radio-TV 25		30	17 down
P.T.T.* 6		13	54 down
Other agencies 111		64	74 up
Total government 537		470	14 up
Business (France) 91		69	32 up
Foreign exports 123		80	54 up
Franc-zone exports 55		51	8 up
Miscellaneous 16			
Sector totals 822		670	23 up

* Post, telephone, and telegraph services.
Source: FNIE.

In 1960, only 3 per cent of the French electronic industry's total production went to French business and industry, whereas 17 per cent of United States electronic production went to business and industry in the same year. It appears likely that, in the near future, sales of industrial equipment will be a major growth area for the French electronics industry. Sales to industrial customers rose 32 per cent in 1960 over 1959, well ahead of the rise for the sector as a whole.

The Professional Equipment Sector is dominated by a few firms, as Table 9 shows.

Table 9

STRUCTURE OF THE PROFESSIONAL EQUIPMENT SECTOR OF THE
FRENCH ELECTRONIC INDUSTRY, 1960

Size of Firm (Number Employed)	Number of Firms	Total Employees	1960 Sales (NF 000's)	Per Cent of Sector Sales
Over 1,000 5		16,982	514,878	62.80
501–1,000 3		2,149	78,419	9.56
201– 500 6		2,481	110,235	13.45
101– 200 14		1,981	48,869	5.96
51– 100 8		632	30,846	3.76
21– 50 23		804	28,286	3.45
11– 20 8		121	4,960	0.60
Under 11		90	3,210	0.42
Total 67		25,240	819,702	100.00

Source: FNIE.

IV: TUBES AND SEMICONDUCTORS

Tubes and semiconductors are vital components in virtually all electronic equipment. These devices are separated from other electronic components by the FNIE because of their special importance to the industry. Tubes and semiconductors, while markedly different from one another in design, size, composition, and other characteristics, are generally quite similar in function: they control electron flows with great precision. The demand for tubes and semiconductors is, of course, derived from the demand for finished electronic products, as is the demand for all electronic components.

The manufacture of tubes and semiconductors is work of high precision and must be carried out in spotlessly clean conditions. Since substantial cost savings can be made through mass-production techniques, the tube and semiconductor industry is dominated by a few large firms which make huge volumes of each of many different types of tubes and semiconductors. Few manufacturers of finished electronic products make their own tubes; they prefer to buy from specialists in this area. Only a few of the largest French electronic firms produce tubes and semiconductors and finished products as well. Table 10 shows the importance of large firms in this sector. Semiconductors (the most famous of which are transistors) were discovered as late as 1950, but since that time they have replaced electronic tubes in many applications, especially where low weight and reliability are critical. Table 11 shows the great growth in sales of semiconductors.

Table 10

STRUCTURE OF THE TUBE AND SEMICONDUCTOR SECTOR OF THE
FRENCH ELECTRONIC INDUSTRY, 1960

Size of Firm (Number Employed)	Number of Firms	Total Employees	1960 Sales (NF 000's)	Per Cent of Sector Sales
Over 1,000	5	7,832	237,883	57.61
501–1,000	2	1,408	49,416	11.96
201– 500	3	824	65,053	15.75
101– 200	2	357	8,826	2.13
51– 100	5	352	49,975	12.10
21– 50	1	34	43	0.01
11– 20	2	35	1,092	0.26
Under 11	..	24	613	0.18
Total	20	10,866	412,901	100.00

Source: FNIE.

Table 11

TUBE AND SEMICONDUCTOR SECTOR—FRENCH ELECTRONIC INDUSTRY, 1959–60

Product Type	1960 Sales	1959 Sales	Percentage Change
	(NF 000,000's)		1960/1959
Receiving tubes	126	115	10 up
Cathode-ray tubes*	107	95	13 up
Broadcasting tubes	44	39	13 up
Other tubes	6	10	40 down
Semiconductors	121	84	44 up
Parts of tubes	8	0.5	44 up
Sector total	412	343.5	20 up

* Mostly consists of picture tubes for TV sets, the rest being for oscilloscopes.
Source: FNIE.

V: OTHER COMPONENTS

Tubes and semiconductors can be regarded as the heart of most electronic equipment, but a wide variety of other components are nonetheless essential to almost any electronic circuit. Table 12 shows the diversity of components used in electronics. As might be expected from the diversity of its products, this sector of the industry is made up of many rather small firms. Many of these firms specialize in the production of only one or

Table 12

"OTHER-COMPONENTS" SECTOR—FRENCH ELECTRONIC INDUSTRY, 1959–60

Component Type	1960 Sales (NF 000,000's)	1959 Sales (NF 000,000's)	Percentage Change 1960/1959
Condensers	114	97	18 up
Coils	51	45	13 up
Transformers	80	52	54 up
Resistors	63	44	43 up
Mounting parts*	62	na	
Switches	17	na	
Fuses & circuitbreakers	3	na	
Vibrators†	0.5	na	
Wire bundles‡	18	na	
Antennae	51	na	
Crystals, etc.	46	na	
Microphones	5	na	
Loudspeakers	46	na	
Sound pick-ups§	24	na	
Other components	28	na	
Sector total	608.5	486	25 up

na: not available.
* Mainly tube-sockets and printed circuits.
† Used as power supplies.
‡ Used in connecting components within an electronic product.
§ Phonograph cartridges and pick-up heads on tape recorders.
Source: FNIE.

two types of components, and an even greater degree of specialization is not uncommon. For example, some firms will make only special types of loud-speakers, or resistors, or antennae, etc. Table 13 gives data on the size of individual firms in this sector.

Table 13

STRUCTURE OF THE FRENCH "OTHER-COMPONENTS" SECTOR OF THE FRENCH ELECTRONIC INDUSTRY, 1960

Size of Firm (Number Employed)	Number of Firms	Total Employees	1960 Sales (NF 000's)	Per Cent of Sector Sales
Over 1,000	0	0	0	0
501–1,000	4	3,019	78,684	15.14
201– 500	12	4,275	141,216	27.18
101– 200	20	2,951	98,484	18.96
51– 100	34	2,510	92,507	17.80
21– 50	49	1,709	79,810	15.36
11– 20	31	474	17,605	3.38
Under 11	...	314	11,097	2.18
Total	150	15,252	519,403	100.00

Source: FNIE.

VI: FUTURE DEVELOPMENTS IN THE FRENCH ELECTRONIC INDUSTRY

Only parts of the Fourth French Plan have, as of May, 1962, been published; currently available material on the Fourth Plan does not give a complete forecast for the electronic industry. But one French publication, *L'Usine Nouvelle*, has analyzed the future of French electronics and its relation to the Plan. Parts of this analysis are reproduced below.[4]

Three main problems [face] the French electronic industry: decentralization, recruiting of technical employees, and financing of research.

Electronics, which until recently was more or less included in the electrical-goods industry, now leads an independent existence. The annual growth in its sales has averaged about 15 per cent for some years. This growth has been achieved in the face of a ten years' lag, a lag due to the Second World War. This growth will continue when the present problems have been rationally resolved.

One of the first jobs of the French planners will be to organize the electronic industry's decentralization in an appropriate manner. Industry observers think that this drive towards decentralization is already late in starting.

Some firms have already "emigrated" towards outlying areas, but this industrial dispersion meets obstacles which must be thoroughly understood. [In the first place], the four main sectors of the industry are tightly intertwined; any given sector provides products for use by other sectors, so that real supply problems appear when decentralization is considered. Electronic products are often fragile, and shipping them long distances sometimes is a risky proposition.

Moreover, the industry flourishes when various manufacturers can easily exchange information with each other; this exchange becomes increasingly difficult as decentralization progresses.

For these reasons, industry observers point out that any move toward decentralization must take into account the interdependence of the various sectors.

Recruiting of technicians and skilled workers is another major problem. The industry is, above all, an industry where brain power is important, hence a great dependence on engineers, technicians, and skilled workers. Recruiting such employees is already difficult, and may become more so if decentralization takes most companies away from the major population centers. The electronic employee must have not only an excellent technical background but also a sort of vocation for this relatively new field.

Accordingly, many manufacturers have, on their own initiative, increased the number of training centers in hopes of inducing young people to plan careers in electronics. These efforts have, however, not provided enough technicians to keep up with the rapid growth of electronics.

Thus electronics experts are begging for very close cooperation between the University and the Factory, which is only possible if the Factory is not too far from the University. Moreover, in order to find enough skilled workers, a factory has to be located in an area where there is sufficient population density.

---

[4] *L'Usine Nouvelle;* June 1, 1961 and January 18, 1962; Paris.

Decentralization must, as a result, take into account not only the interdependence of the industry's sectors but also the problem of finding enough engineers, technicians, and workers.

Another obstacle to expansion is the financing of research. The rapid progress which other electronic industries have made is forcing France to devote enormous sums to pure and applied electronic research, lest France be left behind.

This problem is aggravated by the fact that total French electronic sales are not enormous, so that taking a fixed percentage of these sales for research may not provide enough funds to keep France abreast of other and larger electronic industries. The 1960 sales of the American electronic industry were about 20 times larger than those of the French industry; it is difficult to compete under this size disadvantage.

Industrialists have suggested that the government could contribute significantly by acting as a test market for new products and by contributing money for research into such new products.

The electronic industry's research funds depend on the Consumer Goods Sector of the industry, especially on the sale of TV sets, and at the present time there are some problems in this area. For example, the establishing of a second TV network is still 18 months from completion, and this is slowing down sales of TV sets. The Fourth plan forecasts that, in 1965, the industry will produce 2,100,000 radio sets and 1,470,000 TV sets, but this forecast presupposes that the second TV network be rapidly finished and that France continue to restrict the importing of transistorized Japanese radio and TV sets. [Table 6 shows that in 1960 France produced about 2,200,000 radios and 655,000 TV sets.—Ed.]

Despite all these problems, French electronic industrialists show no tendency to pessimism—quite the contrary. From their viewpoint, decentralization is perfectly feasible, provided that it is carried out under optimal conditions. Paying for research is a more serious preoccupation, but the general feeling in the industry is that, considering the industry's dynamism, all difficulties will be surmounted, no matter what their source.

A NOTE ON THE FRENCH ELECTRIC AND ELECTRONIC MEASURING-INSTRUMENT INDUSTRY

INTRODUCTION

This note is designed to be used in connection with IMEDE cases on the Galvor Company. The note provides factual background on the measuring-instrument industry in which Galvor competes.

Material for this note has been drawn from three sources: (1) the Syndicate Général de la Construction Electrique (SGCE), which collects data on the French electric-goods industry; (2) the Fédération Nationale des Industries Electroniques (FNIE), which collects data on the electronic industries of France and other nations; and (3) officials of the Galvor Company.

The note contains two sections: (1) a description of what measuring instruments are, what they are used for and by whom, and other characteristics of the instruments themselves; and (2) a description of the industry in France as of early 1962.

MEASURING INSTRUMENTS: DEFINITION AND DESCRIPTION

There are many types of measuring instruments, such as devices to measure heat, light, sound, and other physical phenomena. For the purposes of this note, the broad term "measuring instruments" refers *only* to devices which measure electric and electronic characteristics. The scope of this note is further limited by excluding a large class of products which are actually electric measuring instruments, namely, electric quantity meters. The most common electric quantity meter is the device, found in the household, which measures the amount of electricity consumed. Almost all French quantity meters are manufactured by one firm, and their design, manufacture, and sale bear little relationship to other electric and electronic measuring instruments. It is for these reasons that consumption meters are not included in this note.

THE PURPOSE OF MEASURING INSTRUMENTS

There are two main functions in which measuring instruments are employed: checking, and control.

The *checking* function is generally the more common one; it involves the testing, calibrating, servicing, and measuring of electric and electronic devices of all types. Such checking usually involves the measurement of physical characteristics, the most common of which are voltage, current, resistance, capacity, frequency, inductance, phase, and wave form. Other more specialized characteristics are also measurable by certain instruments.

Measuring instruments are used in their checking function to answer such questions about electric and electronic devices as the following:

1. Is the device working?
2. How well is it working?
3. Should adjustments be made? If so, of what sort?
4. How much voltage, or current, or resistance, etc., exists at a given spot within a circuit?

Measuring instruments used for checking are usually self-contained and portable. Occasionally they may be incorporated as part of an electric or electronic system and permanently mounted in the system, where their function is to give continuous checking on the system's operation.

The *control* function also usually involves the installation of the measuring instrument in a larger system. In this case, the instrument's function is not only to measure one or more physical characteristics, but also to make operating adjustments to the system based on the measurement performed.

THE USERS OF MEASURING INSTRUMENTS

Measuring instruments are used in many different fields and are, indeed, indispensable in the modern technological world. They are chiefly found in the following fields:

1. *Industry*, where they are used for controlling processes, for maintaining equipment, for checking product quality, and for performing research. They are also sometimes incorporated in industrial products for resale.
2. *Government*, for research, for maintenance of equipment, and for control.
3. *Laboratories* of such nonprofit institutions as universities and other schools, hospitals, and foundations, where they are used in research.
4. *Radio and TV* repair shops.
5. *Repair shops* for other electric and electronic goods.
6. The *home* of an electric/electronic amateur of some sort, such as a radio "ham." This use is uncommon, however.

As the foregoing suggests, the demand for measuring instruments is, to a certain extent, derived from the demand for other electric and electronic products. Accordingly, sales of measuring instruments are partially influenced by sales of electronic and electric equipment.

THE CONTENT OF MEASURING INSTRUMENTS

The process of manufacturing measuring instruments proceeds as follows. The manufacturer uses a few raw materials, mostly metal in various forms, which he manufactures into various components of the final product. He also buys many components from other manufacturers. (He typically makes parts which are relatively simple to construct, such as the sheet-metal chassis found in most measuring instruments.) All French manufacturers buy almost all their requirements of the complex electric and electronic components, such as tubes, condensers, resistors, and coils. Some manufacturers do virtually no manufacturing at all except assembly; they purchase all parts, and their manufacturing operation is purely one of mounting the parts.

As the above description suggests, the typical measuring instrument has a very small proportion of raw materials in its final cost, but it contains many purchased components. Purchases almost always account for the largest percentage of direct cost in a French measuring instrument. Assembly labor always accounts for a substantial proportion of direct cost, and other manufacturing labor may be considerable. Manufacturing labor never, however, exceeds assembly labor.

As for indirect costs, research and development expenses can be important, depending on the complexity and sophistication of the firm's products. Marketing costs depend largely on whether the firm attempts (as a few do) to sell to many small customers, or only to concentrate on the government and major corporations. Since manufacture of measuring instruments is dominated by assembly operations and since these operations are usually simple, the industry's capital investment per unit of sales is relatively low, a characteristic of many other branches of the electronic industry.

"ELECTRIC" VS. "ELECTRONIC" MEASURING INSTRUMENTS

Measuring instruments are generally classified as either electric or electronic. The distinction is one which has grown up over many years and is not always clearcut. As a rule, instruments containing electronic circuitry are called "electronic," and those lacking such circuitry are called "electric." Exceptions to this rule do, however, exist, as in the case of tube and transistor checkers, which contain no electronic circuits but which are called electronic devices because they are used only to check electronic products. Despite its limitations, this classification is used here because it frequently occurs in statistics on the industry.

The principal types of products which fall in each category are as follows:

Electric Instruments	*Electronic Instruments*
Galvanometers	Tube checkers
Multimeters	Tube analyzers
	Vacuum-tube bridges
	Transistor checkers
	Impedance bridges
	Vacuum-tube voltmeters
	Generators
	Oscilloscopes

These instruments are the basic ones used in measurement of electric and electronic characteristics. There are many other types of electric and electronic measuring instruments made, but such types are usually highly specialized, manufactured by only a very few firms, and not commonly used.

ELECTRIC MEASURING INSTRUMENTS

The GALVANOMETER (or "Galvano") is the most common measuring instrument used. It is simply a device which measures the amount of electric current passing through it. A galvano's findings are usually displayed in terms of current (amperes), voltage, or electric power (watts), since power and voltage can be ascertained by determining the current. Galvanometers are simple devices which are usually inexpensive, costing perhaps $10 to $30; they become more expensive as they are made more precise. As a rule, galvanometers are not used alone but are mounted in other measuring instruments, where they measure and display the findings of such instruments. Galvanos are also sometimes incorporated in electric and electronic systems, where they give continuous indications of the level of important characteristics. They are integral parts of multimeters and of vacuum-tube voltmeters.

The MULTIMETER is nothing but a very flexible galvanometer; where a galvanometer can be used only to measure one characteristic in one relatively narrow range (e.g., from 10 to 100 volts), the multimeter can, through elaborate circuitry, measure all the basic electric characteristics (voltage, amperage, resistance, and capacity) within rather broad ranges. Multimeters are technologically simple devices which, like galvanometers, are easily manufactured; they range in price from about $15 to $150. The precision of a multimeter depends primarily on the quality of the components used in its manufacture. As a rule, a multimeter is accurate to within 1–5 per cent. This accuracy suffices for most applications. When more accurate measurement is needed, a much more expensive instrument of a different type must be used, such as (for voltage measurement) a vacuum-tube voltmeter. The multimeter is the basic tool of electric and electronic technicians.

Other electric measuring instruments include FLUXMETERS, PHASE-METERS, and FREQUENCY METERS. Such devices are, however, much less widely used than galvanometers and multimeters. Only the latter two are important electric measuring instruments.

ELECTRONIC MEASURING INSTRUMENTS

Electronic measuring instruments can be roughly divided into two classes: those which measure components, and those which measure circuits.

Component Measurement. The most common instrument in this class is the TUBE CHECKER, sometimes called the TUBE TESTER. This is the basic instrument used in determining whether an electronic tube is operating. The simplest instrument of this sort will check only whether the tube is emitting electrons; more complex varieties measure several characteristics at once. A modern tube checker is generally sufficient to determine whether a tube is operating properly. Tube checkers contain relatively simple circuitry and are among the less costly[1] electronic instruments.

The TUBE ANALYZER is a complex and rather expensive instrument which measures with considerable precision certain operating characteristics of an electronic tube. Thus the tube checker will reveal whether a tube is functioning, and the tube analyzer gives further indication of how well the tube is operating.

The VACUUM-TUBE BRIDGE is a specialized and complex instrument which is used in connection with a tube analyzer, in order to measure additional operating characteristics of tubes. It is expensive and is not so widely used as are tube checkers and analyzers.

The TRANSISTOR CHECKER performs the same function for transistors that a tube checker performs for electronic tubes. It contains no electronic circuitry but is classified as an electronic product because, like the tube checker, it measures only electronic devices (transistors and other semiconductors). It is a technologically simple device and is inexpensive.

---

[1] In France, electronic measuring instruments range in cost from about $100 to perhaps $2,000. (Certain very specialized instruments cost well over $2,000.)

The IMPEDANCE BRIDGE is a technically uncomplicated instrument which can be made in varying degrees of precision, depending on the quality of components used in its manufacture. It measures three important electric-electronic characteristics with considerable precision: capacity, resistance, and inductance. It can be used either to check components (condensers, resistors, and inductors) or to measure circuits. The bridge is generally considered an electronic instrument, although it contains no electronic circuits. It is, as a rule, a medium- or low-cost instrument.

Circuit Measurement. The VACUUM-TUBE VOLTMETER (VTVM), as its name implies, measures voltages by means of circuitry involving electronic tubes. It measures voltage with much more precision than do galvanometers and multimeters. Depending on its precision, the VTVM is of low or medium cost.

GENERATORS form a family of apparati which have, in general, one chief purpose: to create the electromagnetic waves used in many electronic devices, notably in radio and television equipment. The members of this family are chiefly differentiated from one another by two main characteristics: the shape of the waves[2] generated, and the frequency range over which a given instrument produces these waves.

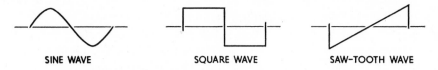

SINE WAVE   SQUARE WAVE   SAW-TOOTH WAVE

The AUDIO GENERATOR generates sine waves over a range of frequencies which corresponds approximately to the frequency range audible to the human ear: 50–20,000 cycles per second (cps).

AM and FM GENERATORS produce waves which are used to check the equipment employed in AM and FM radio broadcasting and reception. For AM radio, sine waves in the range 50,000–5,000,000 cps are used. Instruments for FM radio and for television testing usually create sine waves in the range of 5,000,000–250,000,000 cps. The AM, FM, SERVICE, and STANDARD SIGNAL GENERATORS are all used for AM and FM radio testing.

VHF (Very High Frequency) and UHF (Ultra High Frequency) GENERATORS are used in testing TV equipment and also for radar devices, microwave communication equipment, and other electronic products which operate with very—and ultra—high frequencies.

---

[2] There are three principal types of wave forms produced by most generators. They can be graphically represented in the manner shown below:

MARKER GENERATORS, PATTERN GENERATORS, WOBU-LATORS, and WOBULOSCOPES are special generators used in TV testing exclusively. (The wobuloscope also contains a built-in oscilloscope used in conjunction with the instrument).

All generators contain electronic circuitry, and most of them are fairly expensive instruments. They range in price from perhaps $100 to several thousand dollars, depending on their complexity, precision, versatility, and type.

The OSCILLOSCOPE is essentially a type of television set which displays a picture of an electromagnetic wave. This instrument contains fairly complex electronic circuits and ranges from low to high price, depending on its accuracy and flexibility. Like a TV set, its main component is a cathode-ray tube, (the "picture" tube of a TV set).

*   *   *   *   *

The foregoing description of the various types of electric and electronic measuring instruments gives only approximate indications of the cost of each type, because this cost can vary markedly within a single type. This variability is due to the fact that oscilloscopes, for example, while all similar in purpose and general design, can differ substantially in precision, sophistication of design, flexibility of measurement, convenience of operation, and elegance of finish.

In fact—and this is a striking characteristic of the French measuring-instrument industry—there is almost no direct competition among manufacturers in the electronic-instrument area. In galvanometers and multimeters, several producers may make some instruments which are essentially similar, but this is not always so. And in electronic instruments, it is rare to find two manufacturers making truly comparable products. Five different companies may produce oscilloscopes, but no two will produce identical ones, and it is unlikely that any two will produce oscilloscopes that are even reasonably similar in all respects. As a result, competition in the industry tends to be somewhat limited.

THE FRENCH MEASURING-INSTRUMENT INDUSTRY

GROWTH OF SALES

The French industry, which consists of only 12 firms of importance, has been growing very rapidly in recent years, but it is still a small one. Its total sales of electric and electronic measuring instruments were only

$27.6 million in 1960, compared with sales of $515[3] million by its U.S. counterpart in 1959. Table 1 shows the growth of the industry since 1956.

Table 1

SALES OF THE FRENCH MEASURING-INSTRUMENT INDUSTRY, 1956–60
(Figures in NF 000,000's)

Year	Sales of Electric Products	Sales of Electronic Products	Total Sales of Measuring Instruments
1956	49.14	19.30	68.44
1957	56.35	26.20	82.55
1958	62.38	37.23	99.61
1959	66.25	39.15	105.40
1960	89.55	48.58	138.13

Source: SGCE.

The industry's total sales had, by 1960, increased 102 per cent over 1956 levels (Table 1). Electronic instruments enjoyed a sales increase of 152 per cent during this time, and electric instruments an increase of 82 per cent. By way of comparison, sales of the French electronic industry as a whole rose 125 per cent during 1956–60.

FIRMS IN THE INDUSTRY

According to Galvor officials, there are twelve firms which are important in the industry. There are a few other French firms which make some measuring instruments, but only in insignificant quantities. The following information on the twelve major firms was obtained from various Galvor executives and represents their opinion on their competitors.

ALPHA CORPORATION[4] employs about 1,000 people. The company makes many types of industrial regulating and control devices, and it also produces a broad line of galvanometers and multimeters. The firm has recently made tentative efforts to enter the electronic measuring-instrument field. With its beginnings around 1920, ALPHA is one of the oldest and best-known companies in the industry. Its measuring instruments are sold to all types of customers; government, industry, radio and TV repair shops, etc. The company makes instruments of average quality and sells at average prices. It sells through about 10 wholly-owned sales agencies and through a small number of major wholesalers. Its reputation in measuring instruments is somewhat tarnished by its failure to give uni-

---

[3] Source: FNIE.
[4] All companies given fictitious names.

formly good repair service on its products. It is a major competitor in electric measuring instruments.

BETA CORPORATION is a large French company for which measuring instruments form only one of many product lines. It makes some high-quality and high-cost galvanometers for precision work and other galvanometers of average quality and competitive price. It sells through its large network of wholly-owned sales agencies, chiefly to the government and to large corporations. Its measuring instruments are mostly highly specialized; because of this specialization, BETA is not an important competitor in the industry.

GAMMA CORPORATION is a subsidiary of BETA CORPORATION, employs about 300, and makes only oscilloscopes. Like its parent, it makes high-quality and high-cost instruments which are sold through BETA'S agencies to government and industry.

DELTA CORPORATION, which employs 500, makes galvanometers (and also many devices which are not included in the measuring-instrument industry). It sells almost all of its output, which is of high quality and cost, through its Paris agency to government and industry.

EPSILON CORPORATION has 400 employees. It makes a rather broad line of electronic measuring instruments and concentrates on oscilloscopes; it also makes TV sets. It is especially well-known in production of TV testing instruments. It sells to all types of customers through a network of fifteen manufacturers' representatives and a Paris agency. Its products are of average quality and price.

ZETA CORPORATION employs 300 and makes electronic measuring instruments of high quality and price. It sells virtually its entire output through its Paris agency, mostly to the government. It makes a few products other than measuring instruments. It is most importantly a producer of highly specialized instruments manufactured in relatively small series and, as such, does not usually enter into intensive competition with the rest of the industry.

KAPPA CORPORATION employs 200; it is a major manufacturer of galvanometers and also produces some multimeters. All of its products are expensive and well made. It sells almost exclusively to the government and does so through its Paris office. Galvor executives consider KAPPA a serious competitor for them in galvanometers.

LAMBDA CORPORATION employs 100 and makes galvanometers and industrial control systems. It sells to industry through wholesalers and is not noted for the quality of its instruments. Galvor executives do not regard the firm as a serious competitor for them.

MU CORPORATION makes a wide range of electric and electronic measuring instruments of low quality and price. It sells them to radio and TV repair shops through 8–10 manufacturers' representatives and about 30 wholesalers. It is one of the few firms in the industry which offers one or more items in almost every product type. MU has 50 employees.

THETA CORPORATION was founded shortly after World War II and now employs 17. The company makes only one type of product: pattern generators for use in TV testing. THETA entered the pattern-generator field at a timely moment and has, as a result, captured virtually the entire market. Its products are of good quality and reasonable price; they are sold through a few manufacturers' representatives and through the sales network of the EPSILON CORPORATION. THETA's principal customers are radio and TV repair shops and manufacturers of TV equipment.

SIGMA CORPORATION, which has about 15 employees, makes a wide range of low-quality, low-cost electric and electronic measuring instruments. The company is able to span most of the industry's product line by confining itself to assembly operations only; no other manufacturing is done. SIGMA's customers are mostly radio and TV repair shops, who buy from about 5 manufacturers' representatives and 30 wholesalers.

The GALVOR COMPANY is located in Bordeaux and employs about 450. It sells a very complete line of electric and electronic measuring instruments which are of good quality and reasonable price. GALVOR is especially strong in multimeters, where it has over 80 per cent of the French market. It sells through 15 manufacturers' representatives and through its wholly-owned Paris agency; it sells to all of the typical groups of industry customers.

THE INDUSTRY'S FOREIGN TRADE

Table 2 shows the industry's foreign trade in 1960; the figures used include insignificant quantities of products other than measuring instruments.

The most striking fact revealed by Table 2 is that the French industry has been unable to meet the demand of French customers for electronic measuring instruments. The industry's 1960 production of electronic instruments was valued at about 48,500,000 NF (Table 1): 8,400,000 NF of this production was exported (Table 2), leaving about 40,100,000 NF for the French market. French customers imported an additional 24,100,000 NF worth of such instruments in the same year. The French

Table 2

FRENCH EXPORTS AND IMPORTS OF MEASURING INSTRUMENTS, 1960
(Figures in NF 000's)

Electric Instruments	*Electronic Instruments*
"Foreign"* exports 10,350	"Foreign" exports 7,450
"Foreign" imports 9,000	"Foreign" imports 24,100
"Foreign" balance 1,350	"Foreign" balance .... (16,650)†
Franc Zone exports 5,170	Franc Zone exports 950
Franc Zone imports .... neg.‡	Franc Zone imports .... neg.‡

* "Foreign" trade figures are those which are due to countries not in the Franc Zone.
† Shows negative trade balance.
‡ Negligible imports of measuring instruments from Franc Zone.
Computed from SGCE statistics by IMEDE staff.

industry filled only about 63 per cent of domestic demand. Of the 24,100,000 NF of imports, some 17,400,000 NF worth came from the United States alone.

This heavy reliance by French customers on imports, especially from the United States, of electronic measuring instruments is attributed by industry observers to the fact that the United States has a considerable technological lead in electronics over France and other countries. This lead appears to be shrinking as Western Europe rebuilds its industries, but it is still an important factor in the Free World's electronic industry. Galvor officials are confident that the French measuring-instrument industry will, in the near future, be able to supply most demands of French customers for all types of measuring instruments.

TRENDS IN THE FRENCH MEASURING-INSTRUMENT INDUSTRY

Since World War II, the industry has largely enjoyed a seller's market. There has been sufficient demand to keep the entire industry working at or near its productive capacity. Of equal importance, this high level of demand has enabled manufacturers in many instances to sell equipment at very profitable prices. There has been little price competition in the industry, not only because of the high level of demand, but also because so few of the industry's products enter into direct competition with one another.

This situation could change by 1964–65, for two reasons: first, because it appears that, by this time, the industry will have sufficient capacity, and second, because there is a trend toward increasingly direct competition among manufacturers in the products they offer. More and more frequently, a number of manufacturers will develop a new measuring instrument simultaneously, and their designs for such new products are becoming increasingly similar. For these reasons, there could be a natural tendency for most firms in the industry to compete more aggressively than ever for such new products as are designed.

As a result of these factors, Galvor officials expect to see, within the next few years, a period during which competition will become intense, but it appears likely that the Common Market, by opening a vast new clientele, will compensate for this intensive competition.

There is some possibility that a number of major French electronic corporations could enter the measuring-instrument field. Until recent years, these large corporations have ignored the commercial possibilities of measuring instruments, since total industry sales were rather small (e.g., only 82,550,000 NF in 1957). But, as French sales of measuring instruments have continued their rapid growth, the area has become increasingly attractive to other manufacturers of electronic products.

A final trend in the industry is the increasing complexity and sophistication of its products. This complexity has been necessitated by the tendency toward increasing complexity in electronic products of all kinds. The result of this trend is that research and development are becoming increasingly important, even vital, to the industry. Galvor officials believe that a company's success during the coming period will be largely determined by the extent to which the firm succeeds (*a*) in outstripping its competitors in research and development of new products and (*b*) in increasing productivity by means of new manufacturing techniques.

THE GALVOR COMPANY (B–1)

INTRODUCTION

As of early 1962, six men were mainly responsible for the management of Galvor: M. Georges Latour, president and owner of the company, and his five principal subordinates: Jean Chambertin (Administrative Director), Jacques Romanée (Manager of Manufacturing), Bernard Margaux (Manager of Commercial Service), Robert Meursault (Manager of Electronic Research), and Claude Pomméry (Manager of Electric Research). This case (*a*) gives a brief description of each man, including some of the impressions received about each by IMEDE researchers, (*b*) quotes some of the sentiments they expressed about one another, and (*c*) shows how each man viewed his role in the company and the problems associated with this role.

GEORGES LATOUR

In October, 1961, when IMEDE first proposed (by letter) to M. Latour the idea of doing case research on his company, he replied: "Since our company is of relatively small importance," he wrote, "and our organization far from perfect, I wonder if . . . our 'case' is worthy of special attention." When assured that these objections were of no consequence, M. Latour immediately agreed to the proposed extensive case research on Galvor. He promised to make all data available and to enlist the wholehearted support of his executives in this venture. He was as good as his word. By May, 1962, IMEDE researchers had spent about 50 man-days at Galvor; Galvor officials were at all times not only courteous and cooperative but also anxious to be of any possible help to IMEDE in this project. They were almost always available for interviews, even with as little as 24 hours' notice.

M. Latour was 53 years old; he was always immaculately dressed and of distinguished appearance and bearing. Researchers were struck by the extent to which his courtesy exceeded the demands of ordinary politeness. "I am always," he remarked, "entirely at your disposal. You have, by your research, contributed significantly to our company; you have asked

---

Copyright, 1962, by l'Institut pour l'Etude des Méthodes de Direction de l'Entreprise (IMEDE), Lausanne, Switzerland. Reprinted by permission.

us questions which we ought to have asked ourselves. Furthermore, you are involved in education, and it is our duty to do what we can to help you." Because M. Latour spoke English fluently, interviews with him were usually held in that language.

In the many hours that IMEDE researchers spent with M. Latour, he never raised his voice; he maintained a calm, formal, reserved air at all times. His elegant office, which contained a whimsical ceramic mural of the world on the wall behind his desk, was always uncluttered, and there were few papers on his desk. (Other Galvor executives had somewhat smaller offices, which were functional rather than lavishly decorated. M. Latour remarked that he hoped in the near future to be able to provide better offices for his colleagues.) He was always punctual for appointments with IMEDE staff and during such interviews was only rarely interrupted by his secretary or by one of his executives. One interruption occurred during a Saturday morning interview, when he answered a telephone call from a customer in Paris. The customer wanted to know why the invoice price of a Galvor instrument was higher than the catalogue price. M. Latour explained politely and patiently that the customer's catalogue was outdated and that the price used was that in effect on the day of delivery.

M. Latour frequently referred to his top executive group (the five men mentioned in the opening of this case) with pride and with concern for their welfare. He generally called them "my colleagues" or "my collaborators" and frequently remarked on the excellence of each man. He spoke often of the "team" consisting of all Galvor employees and of the importance of a team concept to him. He once mentioned that, on the occasion of his annual speech to Galvor exployees (December 31st), the employees collectively presented either him or Mme. Latour with a handsome gift.

M. Latour's hospitality towards IMEDE researchers was very generous. Lunches were always at one of the best restaurants in Bordeaux and always excellent; they generally lasted about two hours. On several occasions, he invited one or more IMEDE researchers to his home, which he had built in 1957–58. The house, perched on the side of a hill with a panoramic view, was modernistic in design and furnishings; it would have been an appropriate cover illustration for an architectural journal. In summary, IMEDE researchers were uniformly charmed by M. Latour.

*   *   *   *   *

When asked about the satisfactions he received from having built Galvor, M. Latour remarked: "You know, I suppose I could say simply that I have made a lot of money from the company, but it is much more than that. I like to think that we have built a company we can be proud of, one with a good reputation, and one which treats its employees well. I also think that, in a modest way, we have made some real contributions in our field, especially with special instruments for the French and foreign governments; this is a source of great satisfaction to us. This is a much different thing from just selling soap, or something like that. I think we all feel justifiably proud of Galvor.

"You know, in the old days it was an adventure to keep Galvor in business, a dangerous adventure. I used to worry about the fact that any sort of major crisis, particularly an economic crisis, could ruin the company overnight. But when Chambertin came in 1954, one of the things he did was to introduce the idea of routine into many of our operations, and this has profoundly changed the atmosphere of the company. Now things go along more or less according to routine. For example, in the old days there was a real question whether our growth would continue year after year, but now we have been growing at 15–20 per cent annually for so long that this rate of growth has itself become routine. As this has happened, much of the adventure has gone out of running the business.

"As to how I function as the general manager and owner, let me first point out that this is a "one-man company" *only* in the financial sense. In every other respect, this is a team effort. I prefer to think of myself not as the owner and the leader, but rather as the chief Galvor employee. I belong in this office only so long as I show that I am the best man to take charge of over-all company operations. Of course, I continually check up to see if things are going right in each area, but to me the word "leadership" implies dictatorship, and I don't want to be thought of as a dictator. I may own the company, but I cannot and do not want to run things all by myself. When we have specialized problems, I go out and find a specialist to take care of these problems.

"One day a close friend of mine, the director of a large British electronics factory, told me that I was running a so-called 'one-man company.' This shocked me greatly, because this is exactly the thing which I have tried to avoid. That is why we have the weekly management conference, where everybody in top management gets a chance to speak. And I listen to what my colleagues say.

"I have not stopped going to school; I continually attend the management seminars which are run by various French institutions, and one of the things I learned sometime ago is what a top manager is: he is a man who keeps on top of his work and who accordingly has time when he needs it. Every morning I have a certain number of things which I have to do that day, and when I leave at night, these things have been done.

"As the company grows, managing it becomes an increasingly difficult job, and for some time I have needed an assistant. I have just found this man, named Armagnac, and he reported last Monday [April 2d, 1962]. He will not only have line authority in certain areas, but he will be my personal assistant, and he will relieve me of a lot of the routine work I now have to do. This will leave me free for what I consider is my main job in the years to come: working for the long-term growth and success of Galvor. More specifically, I expect to spend an increasing amount of my time looking at new export markets and especially at how we will fit into the Common Market. Since my recent trip around the world, I have become convinced that Galvor has the ability to become one of the top four or five firms in measuring instruments in the world, and it is my intention to see that we attain this position. As soon as this new addition to the plant is finished, we will add 200 employees very quickly, and I can see us growing to 1,000 employees within a few more years.

"One of my dreams has been to erect a building to house our administrative and research staffs, five or six stories high, of square form and clad in glass. When we have the necessary capital, probably by 1964, this building will go up beside the plant. One reason I want it is so that I can give my executives nicer offices. I look on this building as being the crowning achievement of my life, but maybe I'll be able to go even further than this.

"Although I have not told any of them about this, I plan eventually to give my main executives stock in the company. This seems to me to be an obligation, because of all they have contributed. Until recently I have not considered such a move too seriously because, after all, my men were well paid, and Chambertin especially so. And I have always stood ready to make interest-free loans to all my employees for good purposes, especially for such things as building a house. My top men can live well; Romanée owns his own house and has a couple of cars, and the others are in equally comfortable circumstances.

"I think the chief reason that my executives enjoy working for Galvor is that they have, I hope, found the same spirit of adventure and enthusiasm that I have in being in this business and in making a famous product of high quality. I don't think that money is the chief attraction for them, although Chambertin is paid so much more than any of the others that this might be so in his case." [At 4:30 one Saturday afternoon, as M. Latour and several IMEDE people were leaving the plant, they met

M. Chambertin, who had been working at the office all day. M. Latour, after saying goodbye to M. Chambertin, remarked: "Chambertin pretends he's just killing time around here trying out a new secretary, and he pretends to grumble about having to do this, but he is just too modest to admit his devotion to his job and to the company."]

"When the company was small, I suppose that I was responsible for almost all of the new ideas which we followed, as was only natural. But as we have grown, it would have been foolish of me to pretend that only I had good ideas and not to listen to my colleagues.

"Now they provide as many ideas as I do, and I consider not only my own proposals, but those of the others as well." [M. Chambertin once remarked that M. Latour felt a great debt to his colleagues, especially to those who had been with him for many years, and that he was unwilling to impose his ideas on them. On another occasion, M. Meursault said that M. Latour never gave a direct order against his executives' wishes.]

"As to my colleagues' image of me," M. Latour continued, "this is obviously a difficult thing to judge. I hope they like and respect me. They are still with me after many years and they always show their respect in discussions with me, and I am doing all I can to keep Galvor a company of which they can be proud. Regarding their major problems, maybe they want more money, but I do not think this is really important to them. I don't know what problems they may have, if any. I would like to know, so that I could adjust to give them what they want. There is, as I have said, much routine, but there is adventure above that. I think that the company gives my colleagues a chance to live this adventure and that they consequently commit their goodwill and enthusiasm towards our success. There is no end to this adventure."

JEAN CHAMBERTIN

M. Chambertin was the only one of the main Galvor executives who had not risen through the ranks to his present position. For many years before coming to Galvor, he had been head of the Bordeaux office of Fiduciaire de France, a major firm of public accountants, where he had handled the Galvor account among others. In 1953, M. Latour proposed to M. Chambertin that he come to Galvor; after about a year, M. Chambertin accepted and was made Administrative Director of the company. (M. Chambertin's title of *Director* was equivalent to vice-presidential rank in the firm. The other four main executives had the title of *Manager*, which corresponded to the rank just below Director.)

M. Chambertin was the only Galvor employee beside M. Latour who wore a standard business suit while at the office. All the other executives wore white smock coats over their street clothes.

IMEDE researchers found that, with the exception of M. Latour, M. Chambertin was the only Galvor executive who would talk about the four Managers. M. Chambertin was always anxious to talk about company problems at great length with members of the IMEDE staff, and he sometimes quoted opinions of IMEDE researchers at the weekly management meetings. As case research progressed, M. Chambertin devoted more and more time to explaining, in great detail, the workings of the company to IMEDE people, and he often provided IMEDE with highly confidential documents which he had prepared for M. Latour on special problems and issues within the firm.

Although M. Latour referred to M. Chambertin as "the most intelligent of my colleagues, and the one who looks furthest ahead in his work," M. Chambertin himself said that he was probably not as intelligent as his assistant, Mme. Bollinger, a recent graduate of a large French graduate business school. "You know," remarked M. Chambertin, "even though I am ostensibly second-in-command here, I am 58 years old, and the company badly needs a younger man as the designated successor to M. Latour, I would happily be a subordinate to such a man, even if he were 20 years younger than I, just because it would be for the good of the company.

"I finally came to work for Galvor because in my previous job I had too many accounts to manage, and I was wearing myself out trying to do the job well. I felt that it would be considerably less of a strain to handle the affairs of only one company."

M. Chambertin described his role in the company as follows: "My most important function is taking care of Galvor's external affairs, notably our financial relations. Next in importance comes my responsibility for our accounting and statistical reporting services. I am also responsible for personnel. And, finally, I suppose that to some extent I act as adviser to M. Latour, but I should add that, except at critical moments, he usually doesn't solicit my opinion on an issue. It is well to remember that not only has M. Latour 97 per cent ownership of Galvor, but he also has 101 per cent of the responsibility. This responsibility extends all the way down in the organization, at least at some times; M. Latour even hires and fires the janitor. I think it is fair to say that nobody here so much as paints an arrow on the wall without M. Latour's approval. After all, why not? He owns the company."

When asked his opinion as to the most important factors in Galvor's success, M. Chambertin replied: "In the first place, it is important to remember that since the Second World War nobody in our industry has had any difficulty in selling instruments. We have been enjoying a seller's market since 1945. And also very important, the chief[1] has maintained a steady policy of expansion at a reasonable rate. He has made sure that when we make an expansion move, we digest the resulting growth before proceeding to the next stage. We have not gone madly ahead in an effort to grow regardless of the consequences. Another reason for our success is certainly the quality of our products, which keeps getting higher, and which we owe largely to Jacques Romanée. People are well aware of our quality, and so we never have trouble selling our instruments.

"As you know, I have often mentioned areas within the company where I think that we have some real problems, but it is important to keep these problems in perspective. I believe that Galvor today has attained such an eminent position in the industry that our continued success is assured. We may have small problems from time to time, even big ones, but people will always want Galvor products."

JACQUES ROMANÉE

Jacques Romanée, who was about 54, had been with Galvor since 1941 and was accordingly the oldest of the major executives in terms of service to the company. M. Romanée, who had had only a modest amount of formal education, had worked for about ten years in a galvanometer factory before coming to Galvor. While in this previous job he had invented an excellent moving element[2] for galvanometers, and he had further refined this design soon after coming to Galvor. This moving-element design was still used in most Galvor multimeters and galvanometers.

Although, as a rule, M. Romanée confined himself strictly, during interviews with the IMEDE staff, to remarks on manufacturing operations, he often commented on how overburdened he was with work.

M. Latour remarked: "Romanée came here twenty years ago as a worker, a foreman; I hired him especially because of his experience in galvanometers. As the company has grown and as he has moved up to become Manager of Manufacturing, I have had to bring him along. By this I mean that, every time we have moved up to a new platform in our growth, it has been difficult to get Romanée to accept the responsibilities

---

[1] M. Latour was usually referred to by his employees as *le patron*, which can be translated roughly as "the boss" or "the chief."

[2] The moving element of a galvanometer is the most crucial part of the instrument. It consists of a coil of wire very carefully wound around an axis and with a needle (to indicate on the dial) attached. The skill with which the moving element is manufactured largely determines the precision of the galvanometer.

which he must take on at this new stage. I have found, however, that, once I have brought him up to the new level, he then works well within his enlarged sphere of authority.

"But this indicates one real problem which I have had. When Galvor was young and small, it was natural and easy for me to supervise all the operations and to run the company by myself, and in those days I had all of the responsibility and authority. But the company is too big for that now, and I have to get my executives to take responsibility for themselves. Unfortunately, they are so used to the old days, when I *did* want to run everything, that now they find it difficult to change.

"In the old days, for example, at the end of every day Romanée would come to me with a list of problems which had built up during the day. For him, everything was a crisis: we were short of one little part, and so we were going to have to shut down the plant. He always wanted me to tell him what to do. Well, I managed to cure him of this to some extent; I went to America for a time, and in my absence my wife ran the company. When she was in my office, Romanée would come to her every night, but she would explain that she couldn't help him. The very first evening I was back, Romanée came to my office and told me I'd have to decide what to do with a whole group of problems which had accumulated during my absence. I told him I was no longer willing to do this, and he left. He never came to my office at the end of the day after that. This little story will give you some idea of the difficulty which I have had in getting some of my men to take on more responsibility for themselves. Chambertin is different; I recently noticed that we have a considerable number of new accounting machines in the office. I never heard anything about these machines, much less had anything to say about approving them; Chambertin just ordered them on his own authority, which is what he should have done.

"But when I tell Romanée that he is not to bother me with expenditures of less than X new francs, he just adds up things until they total more than X new francs and then asks for my approval because the amount is too large for him to approve alone. Or else he gets one large purchase, over X new francs, and tacks on a number of smaller machines to the same purchase request. He just doesn't want to decide for himself."

M. Romanée viewed this same problem differently, saying:[3] "Galvor's main problem is a simple one: the company is not run with a firm hand. M. Latour gives what one might call "semi-orders," where I am never sure what the order is because he is not explicit. I would much rather he

---

[3] This was the one occasion (occurring after five previous interviews) when M. Romanée made any personal comments of significance regarding other Galvor executives.

would figure out exactly what he wants and then give a definite and clear-cut order. Another problem sometimes is that I receive an order which is impossible; this is a terrible situation, and one which I never create when I give an order. I always make sure before giving an order that it can be carried out.

"The disease of our century, and one which we have at Galvor, is that responsibility is not clearly defined. We have a number of operating groups here in which we have problems, but before we try to fix these problems, we have to know who's in charge. I wish that M. Latour would set up a well-defined organization chart showing the exact responsibility of every executive."

M. Romaneé, it was agreed by all executives, was overloaded with work in early 1962. He was supervising the construction of the new factory and the plans to manufacture resistors. He was also partially responsible for liaison between the manufacturing and research groups, when it came to bringing a newly designed product into mass production. He had considerable methods work to perform and partial responsibility for inventories. And he was also responsible for seeing to it that he had enough workers with the proper skills to perform the manufacturing operations. Finally, he had all the other normal responsibilities associated with being Manager of Manufacturing.

"We know," remarked M. Latour, "that Romanée has far too much to do, and for that reason I have been urging him to hire an assistant to help relieve him of some of the detail work he now has. I have said that he can pay such an assistant as much as is necessary to get a good one. But somehow he never seems to find just the right man."

M. Romanée said: "I've been looking for years for a good assistant, but it's difficult to find the right man, I don't really have time to train him, and besides, you can't teach a man everything I've learned about this business in thirty years."

M. Chambertin said: "Romanée really needs a brilliant young engineer to assist him, because he does not have very strong technical background, especially in the electronic area. But I think Romanée is afraid that if he hires some bright young man, the new man will show him up, so he does nothing."

BERNARD MARGAUX

M. Margaux, who was about 35, had come to work for Galvor in 1957. M. Latour commented: "A friend of mine in Lyon told me about Margaux, who had been working in production up to that point and who was looking for another job. So I told him to have Margaux write me a letter stating what sort of things he might be interested in. I hired Margaux, and he went out on the road as a field engineer for us, dealing with our representatives and some of our clients. He did a good job, and so, soon after we brought him back to Bordeaux, I made him the Manager of our Commercial Service. I have hoped that eventually Margaux would grow sufficiently in stature to become our Commercial Director, that he would be in charge of our Paris agency and galvanometer sales as well as filling his regular role in the Commercial Service. But as time passes, I find two objections to his moving ahead: first, he does not seem to have the important qualifications of being able to keep on top of his job; he never is able to answer his mail the same day, he is always behind. Second, he has no great amount of formal education, and so he really lacks the technical background which is becoming increasingly necessary to handle our products, especially the electronic ones. I think that, in the long run, we need a man with engineering training as our Commercial Director." M. Chambertin also thought that M. Margaux lacked the necessary training and, to some extent, the ability to rise to Commercial Director.

In commenting on his role in the company, M. Margaux said: "My background is primarily technical; I suppose you could say that I am really a technician more than anything else, at least by previous experience. But now that I am Manager of the Commercial Service, I haven't enough time to deal with the many technical problems which arise in the course of my work. My role is as M. Latour's right-hand man for commercial problems. M. Latour himself is really the Commercial Director of Galvor. I must admit that at the moment I have far too much to do, because I am handling export sales myself, but I am looking for a man to take charge of exports; I must find this man no later than autumn. When I can unburden myself of export problems, I will be able to concentrate on more important things, such as over-all marketing problems, and especially the possibility of doing marketing research. I will also have more time to visit our agents and representatives here and in foreign countries.

"Before I came to work at Galvor, I was assistant to the Manufacturing Director of another company, and this man treated men like machinery. Things are completely different here. I enjoy working for Galvor (*a*) simply because I like the company and am proud to be associated with it and (*b*) because I have always had a pleasant relationship with M. Latour, quite unlike the experience in my previous job. M. Latour is courteous, polite, and very friendly, and he is always thinking of his colleagues' well-being. In the six years I've been here, I've never had any quarrel with M. Latour, except for normal disagreements on operating problems. That is why I like working here."

ROBERT MEURSAULT

M. Meursault, who was about 35, had gone to work for Galvor in 1943 as an apprentice. When the Messer brothers left the company in 1945 (as described in "The Galvor Company (A)"), M. Meursault left with them, but he returned to Galvor about a year later and was made Manager of Electronic Research within a few years. M. Meursault's training had been at a type of technical institute, which gave a minimal theoretical background and stressed practical applications of electricity and electronics.

"Meursault," remarked M. Latour, "is a brilliant man, and he has wonderful imagination when it comes to conceiving and designing new electronic products. He is working with very advanced technology, and he keeps abreast of advances in his field, but he is badly overloaded with work. He has too much administrative work to perform and really needs an assistant. But Meursault fears, I think, that if he hires some brilliant young electronic theoretician from Polythechnique, the assistant will outshine him and eventually get his job. I have promised Meursault that he will always be number one in electronic research at Galvor, but he does nothing. I have even told him that, if it is necessary in order to find the right man, he can pay an assistant even twice as much as he himself is earning. I try to give my executives all the support they need to find assistants for themselves, but I don't want to force assistants on them. These men have been with me for many years, and they have contributed greatly to Galvor's growth and success, so I don't want to force them to do anything they don't want to do."

In describing his job, M. Meursault said: "My primary function is to consider future developments in electronic equipment. I have to maintain customer contacts, in order to learn what the new instruments should be. I also have to maintain contact with my design engineers, in order to see that they are designing products which will meet future needs of our customers. It takes an engineer, and one intimately familiar with current developments, to be able to sense what kinds of instruments people will be wanting in the future, and this is my most important job.

"In order to give myself more time to do this type of exploration, I hope to bring in two assistants. One will be an administrative assistant to help with the routine work of the department. The other will be technical assistant to be in direct charge of the design men. I will hire one of these men fairly soon and try him out in both jobs; he will eventually take over the area for which he seems better suited.

"At the moment, my time is divided about as follows: 20 per cent on customer contact, 30 per cent on administrative work, 30 per cent on technical work, and 20 per cent lost time shifting from one job to another.

Once I have these two assistants, I expect to divide my time in this way: 60 per cent on customer contact, 20 per cent on technical work, 10 per cent on administration, and 10 per cent on lost time."

CLAUDE POMMÉRY

M. Pomméry, who was about 35, was an outstanding graduate of one of the great French scientific universities, and he had spent three years after graduation doing research and teaching at the university in the area of measuring instruments. M. Latour and M. Chambertin both observed that M. Pomméry's greatest difficulty was his inability to say "no" to anybody. "Pomméry," remarked M. Latour, "is simply too nice. He is anxious to please everybody, with the result that people bring him all sorts of petty problems to solve, and he never puts his foot down. Pomméry is a brilliant man, and he has done some remarkable work in designing new galvanometers and multimeters, but he wastes too much time in petty administrative detail. Now he is hiring an assistant, so I hope this will change somewhat."

M. Pomméry, who was always soft-spoken and formal in manner with IMEDE researchers, described the allocation of his time in this manner: "First of all, I have to do a lot of reading outside of working hours to keep up with the latest innovations in my area. As for time on the job, I ought to analyze it in terms of the demands made on my time. About 50 per cent of my time is theoretically necessary to work on our catalogue, on our commercial displays at trade fairs, and on working on models which we have developed, where it is a question of putting finishing touches on a new model. Another 30 per cent is demanded to supervise my share of the prototype and design services, where Meursault and I are jointly in charge. 20 per cent more is needed to provide answers to small technical problems which arise in my own research group, and I should spend another 20 per cent of my time doing basic research and development on new products. You will notice that this leaves no time for training my design technicians and no time for free-lance experimenting and engineering, and still the total demand is for 120 per cent of my time. I hope that my new administrative assistant will work on our catalogue (and the instruction books which go with each product), handle commercial inquiries about the possibility of designing a new product for a specific customer, do some of the technical administrative work, and supervise to some extent the prototype and design services."

* * * * *

When M. Latour had finished reading "The Galvor Company (B-1)" up to this point, he commented to the casewriter: "I am really very unhappy about one aspect of the B-1 case: it makes it appear that I am the 'star' of the company, and that the other men are not nearly so important as I am. This is an entirely false impression, and one which I would not want the reader to get. This is a team effort." Upon the casewriter's assurance that subsequent cases in the series would make it clear that the other Galvor executives were also very important, M. Latour agreed to release the B-1 case.

THE GALVOR COMPANY (C–1)
Distribution Policy

Galvor's distribution network was designed to handle all types of customers, from the small electrical repair-shop purchase of less than 100 francs to large industrial and government orders of several thousand francs. Company officials believed that their present sales network was best suited to their product line and their market. Table 1 shows the various channels through which Galvor products were sold.

Table 1
GALVOR DISTRIBUTION NETWORK, 1961

Distribution Channel	Per Cent of Total Sales
SALES IN FRANCE (83.9%)	
Manufacturers' representatives	32.4
Galvor Paris	42.3
Factory sales	5.9
Repairs	2.0
Sales to the TRONEX Corporation	1.3
EXPORT SALES (16.1%)	
COMOR S.A.	5.2
Importing agents	10.7
Repairs	0.2
	100.0

Source: Company records.

Factory sales were made to customers in those areas[1] of France where Galvor maintained no manufacturers' representative: such sales also included certain special-order products not included in the regular product line. The representatives were given a commission for any sale, whether by them or by the factory, of normal Galvor equipment in their assigned territories.

Although Galvor's products were exported to 43 countries, as can be seen from Table 2, only Europe, the Franc Zone[2], and the Americas ac-

---

This case was prepared by Mr. Warren J. Keegan under the supervision of Professor David S. R. Leighton.

Copyright, 1962, by l'Institut pour l'Etude des Méthodes de Direction de l'Entreprise (IMEDE), Lausanne, Switzerland. Reprinted by permission.

[1] These areas included 12 of France's 89 Departments.

[2] Mostly comprised of former French colonies.

counted for significant percentages of sales. (The 1961 percentages given in Table 2 were, M. Margaux asserted, about the same as those in previous years.)

Table 2
GALVORS EXPORT SALES ANALYSIS, 1961

Area	Per Cent of Total 1961 Sales
Export sales	
Europe	7.4
Franc Zone	4.7
The Americas	2.1
Asia	0.7
Africa	0.5
Australia/Oceania	0.5
Export repairs	0.2
Total	16.1

Source: Company records.

Galvor's biggest foreign markets were Italy, Spain, Belgium, the United States, the United Kingdom, and Australia. From 1957 to 1959, Galvor had a United States agency, owned equally by Galvor and an American partner. The arrangement had not been satisfactory, however, and, as of 1962, Galvor products were sold in the United States market through the sales force of a United States manufacturer of a related product line.

In early 1962, M. Latour was preparing to enter the German market. A Galvor sales engineer was going to spend six months prospecting the German market. According to M. Latour, "He will make a report on the requirements of the German market. When we can meet those requirements, we will set up our agency in a suitable location to direct a network of representatives just like our French network. We will repeat in Germany factors which made us successful in France, because I think the German market will be our second largest."

M. Latour felt that Galvor's biggest problem in exporting was price. When the company worked through a French exporter and then an importer in the foreign country (this arrangement accounted for 25 per cent of 1960 export sales), two margins were added to Galvor's prices. The only export markets with which M. Latour was satisfied were Italy and Belgium, where Galvor had exceptional agents.

Galvor grouped its French customers, who accounted for 84 per cent of 1961 sales, into ten categories, which were differentiated as follows:

1. *GRANDS ADMINISTRATIONS* included the large French gov-

ernment agencies, notably the armed forces; they typically placed very large orders. M. Latour commented: "The Government seldom buys directly from the catalogue. They prefer to deal with a company representative, usually M. Cliquot in Paris. The government has a technical staff which coordinates the requirements of all government agencies and then makes contact with the manufacturer. Often we find government specifications stating 'Galvor or equivalent.' When our salesmen work with government officials, they try to get these officials to specify Galvor." The government usually solicited bids for a given item from several manufacturers; the choice was made on the basis of price and on the supplier's reputation and reliability. Galvor had 10 customers in this category.

2. *ADMINISTRATIONS LOCALES* comprised French departmental and local governments, which had their own budgets. "This is one weak spot in our sales effort," commented M. Latour; "our salesmen don't usually call on these purchasers. Such sales as we make in this area are probably due to our good name, which people hear of in schools, in the armed forces, and in other companies." There were about 1,060 Galvor customers in this group.

3. *INDUSTRIES ELECTRONIQUES* included makers of electric and electronic products. Such customers, totalling about 450, generally bought Galvor products for (*a*) use in their laboratories, (*b*) maintenance of their equipment, or (*c*) incorporation in their products. M. Latour said: "With most of these firms, we must deal with their purchasing offices. This is a disadvantage when selling products like ours; I feel that if we could talk directly to their technical people, we should have greater success. We ought to visit each of these customers about 4–5 times per year."

4. *INDUSTRIES DIVERSES* included all other industrial users of Galvor products. Such customers bought Galvor instruments mostly for their maintenance work, occasionally for laboratory use. Galvor had about 1,950 customers in this category.

5. *GROSSISTES ELECTRICIENS*, or wholesalers of electrical goods, sometimes carried Galvor products in stock or would order such products at their customers' requests.

6. *GROSSISTES RADIOS*, radio and TV wholesalers, were important Galvor customers. There were about 700 customers in the wholesaler area, i.e., groups 5 and 6.

7. *GRANDES ECOLES* included the major French institutes and universities; although most of them theoretically belonged in one of the

government categories, these schools were treated separately because of their importance. Over 700 were Galvor customers. Not only were sales to this group considerable, but, even more important, Galvor executives considered it excellent publicity for the firm to have its products used by students.

8. *UTILISATEURS RADIOS* retailed radios and TV sets and used Galvor products in their repair shops. This group contained many individual customers, but the typical customer's account was a very small one. M. Margaux remarked that these customers, while individually unimportant, were very loyal to Galvor.

9. *UTILISATEURS ELECTRICIENS* included men who installed electrical goods of all sorts, i.e., electricians in general.

10. *UTILISATEURS PARTICULIERS* was somewhat of a "miscellaneous" group, including private "ham" radio operators, electronic hobbyists, and similar small customers. There were about 13,000 Galvor customers in groups 8, 9, and 10 combined.

The company did not maintain records on sales made to each customer group. Rather, groups 1 and 2 were called the "Government" sector, groups 5 and 6 the "Wholesaler" sector, and groups 3, 4, 7, 8, 9 and 10 the "Users" sector. An analysis of Galvor's French sales by customer type is found in Table 3.

Table 3
GALVOR SALES IN FRANCE, 1958–60

Sector	Percentage of Total French Sales		
	1958	1959	1960
Government:			
Special products	6.80	12.67	5.92
Catalogue products	25.46	24.17	26.90
Wholesalers	16.89	16.30	17.55
Users	35.15	31.78	32.02
Export	15.70	15.08	17.61
	100.00	100.00	100.00

Source: Company records.

The Commercial Service maintained an elaborate file on customers and potential customers. (Files on customers in the Paris area were maintained only by Galvor Paris.) M. Margaux described this file of customer cards as the Commercial Service's most important tool. He added: "A customer's card records every letter we have received from him, the number and type of Galvor products he has bought, the number of times this customer has been visited by our representative, and so forth. It is the customer's identity card. We can build up all sorts of useful statistics by using these cards."

THE SALES REPRESENTATIVES

As of early 1962, Galvor had 15 manufacturers' representatives, who covered most of France. In 1961, these representatives accounted for 32.4 per cent of Galvor's total sales. Some of these men had been Galvor agents for over twenty years, and M. Latour remarked on the debt which he owed many of them for having helped him to build the company. The typical representative also sold the products of two or more other manufacturers whose products were related to, but not competitive with, those of Galvor. The representative's entire line was, ideally, such that a customer for one of his product lines would be a potential customer for other lines as well. Galvor had used great care in selecting representatives whose product lines were complementary.

Most of these representatives had only a modest amount of technical knowledge; it was hoped that this knowledge would be sufficient to enable them to sell Galvor's products effectively, but, as the products became more complex, this aim was increasingly difficult to achieve. Galvor maintained two sales engineers who would help a representative on some of his customer calls, especially by providing expert technical information on Galvor products. The representatives generally appreciated the help, even though limited, which they received from this source.

"Depending upon how many other manufacturers' lines he carries," said M. Margaux, "a Galvor representative should expect to spend from two to six hours per day selling our products. If Galvor is his most important line, his time spent on Galvor should reflect this. Once we hire a representative on a permanent basis, he is protected by the French Representatives Indemnity Law, which normally requires that he be paid a sum equal to three years' commission if he is fired. Obviously, this law makes it very expensive to fire a man, so we give each representative a very careful and lengthy trial before we finally take him on. We have had very good luck with our representatives."

The representatives were paid on a straight commission basis. The rate, which was always paid on the list price before taxes and freight, varied, depending on the product, how much the representative discounted the list price, and the credit terms of the sale. For cash sales, the commission was 9.5 per cent for sales at list price, 7.5 per cent for sales at 10 per cent off list, 5.5 per cent for sales at 15 per cent off list, and

3.75 per cent for sales at 20 per cent off list. For credit sales (always at list price) the commission was always 8.5 per cent, regardless of whether the terms were six, nine, or twelve months. Exceptions to the above schedule were spare parts (always sold at list price), on which the commission was 4.75 per cent, and galvanometers (not sold on credit), on which a 7.5 per cent commission was paid regardless of the discount.

In 1961, commissions averaged about 6.3 per cent of a representative's net sales. For the same year, Galvor's commission payments to its agents ranged from 5,900 NF to 54,500 NF. A "typical" representative's commission totalled about 23,000 NF, M. Margaux estimated. The company's sales engineers, in both Bordeaux and Paris, were paid a straight salary.

Galvor had traditionally used manufacturers' representatives, a company document pointed out, because "the sale of measuring apparatus is difficult to accomplish in a single step. Rather, it requires several visits to the customer and perhaps some demonstrations. Thus it is difficult to organize our sales network except by means of manufacturers' representatives, who work from a fixed address in the appropriate region, where their clients can meet them and where operations can be based."

Each representative was given a small inventory of the principal Galvor products. This inventory was controlled by the Field Inventory Clerk of the Commercial Service. "This stock," commented M. Margaux, "serves three purposes. It helps a representative to speed delivery in urgent cases; it can be used for customer demonstrations; and with this inventory available in the field, we can lend a product to a prospective customer."

The performance of the representatives was not formally evaluated until 1960, when M. Margaux developed a measure of performance which he called the "fortune coefficient." This coefficient was based on the number of radios, number of TV sets, and the amount of industrial electricity used in France. The arithmetic mean of the percentages of these three factors in each territory was divided into the percentage of the total Galvor sales in France for the territory to obtain the performance coefficient for the territory. For example, if Britany had 3 per cent of France's radios, 2 per cent of France's TV's, and consumed 1 per cent of France's industrial electricity, then the representative for Britany needed sales equalling 2 per cent[4] of Galvor's total sales in France to

---

[4] $\dfrac{3\% + 2\% + 1\%}{3} = 2\%.$

have a fortune coefficient of 100. M. Margaux discussed the coefficient in detail with his representative and relied upon it to measure their selling performance. Whenever necessary, he made adjustments in the coefficient for factors such as how much time the representative could devote to Galvor and the general economic conditions in an area. M. Margaux considered a coefficient of 75 as an acceptable average for a good man in a typical territory. Exhibit 1 reproduces 1959 and 1961 sales, commissions, and fortune coefficients for France by distribution channel. Data on 1960 sales in France by distribution channel, with each channel ranked according to net return to Galvor as a per cent of list price, are shown in Exhibit 2. Exhibit 3 is an analysis of total 1960 Galvor sales by product category.

As can be seen from Exhibit 1, there was a wide variation in representative performance relative to fortune coefficient potential. In 1961 the coefficients ranged from 160 for the representative in Britany to 43 for the representative in Lille. When a representative's performance was below potential, M. Margaux attempted to get better performance from him. If this did not produce results, he sometimes reduced the representative's territory. On the other hand, when a representative was doing a good job, M. Margaux would sometimes reward him with a larger territory. When making adjustments, M. Margaux's objective was to match the representatives' selling ability with territory potential. The sales territory maps reproduced in Exhibit 4 reflect the territory reallocations during the 1959–61 period. M. Margaux's brief description of six representatives, selected at random by the researcher, is reproduced in Exhibit 5.

Although M. Margaux felt that it would be several years before direct sales offices would be economically feasible outside the Paris area, he did mention Lyon, Lille, Marseilles, Bordeaux, and Strasbourg as cities where it might someday be feasible to open direct sales offices. He gave the following approximate figures as the monthly cost of a direct sales office:

	NF per Month
Director's salary	2,500
Rent	500
Office expenses	150
Secretary	800
Commercial and travel costs	2,000
Total	5,950

Since the representative received an average commission of 6.3 per cent, M. Margaux reasoned that a direct sales office would have to have

Exhibit 1

1959 and 1961 Galvor Sales, Commissions, and Fortune Indexes in France by Distribution Channel*

Distribution Channel	Territory	Total Sales, All Taxes Included (NF)		Commissions (NF)		Fortune Index	
		1959	1961	1959	1961	1959	1961
Representative:							
A	Brittany	133,626	226,281	9,436	14,540	143.68	160.25
B	Pyrenée	55,465	124,867	3,568	8,402	37.72	78.76
C	Nice	.....	149,776	.....	10,199	.....	84.92
D	Vendée	162,819	227,755	11,118	14,963	77.90	105.42
E	Dijon	128,783	259,390	9,041	18,208	40.49	85.40
F	Herault	35,383	79,511	2,381	5,903	52.80	126.17
G	Lille	429,863	658,042	28,059	47,214	24.46	43.24
H	Marseilles	379,612	549,972	24,097	36,776	71.54	100.90
I	Normandy	224,037	321,602	14,106	21,400	46.87	63.04
J	Centre	110,920	190,363	6,453	12,468	51.59	62.11
K	Bordeaux	210,433	319,808	12,373	19,836	64.99	90.38
L	Lyon	515,603	793,074	34,362	54,546	63.34	115.12
M	Toulouse	232,877	385,560	13,815	22,973	85.61	120.46
N	Strasbourg	345,289	554,548	21,313	31,943	36.08	59.06
O	Nice	106,419	.....	7,473	.....	59.12	.....
X		20,136	14,148	1,271	806	.....	.....
Y		13,367	.....	997	.....	.....	.....
Total		3,104,632	4,854,670	199,863†	320,177	201.24	281.54
Galvor Paris		4,481,704	6,222,670	72,737			
Factory sales		580,049	806,434	.....	.....		
Sales engineer		28,413	14,220	.....	.....		
Grand total		8,194,798	11,897,994	272,600	320,177	.....	.....

* Not including sales to the Tronex Corporation (1.3% of total 1961 sales).
† In 1959, Paris sales were, for part of the year, made by a sales representative; hence the commission payments in that year.
Source: Company records.

Exhibit 2

1960 GALVOR SALES, COMMISSIONS, AND DISCOUNTS IN FRANCE BY DISTRIBUTION CHANNEL*
(Representatives Ranked According to Net Return to Galvor as a Per Cent of List Price)

Distribution Channels	Net Sales after Discounts (NF)	Commission Paid to Agent (NF)	Net Return to Galvor after Taxes and Commissions (NF)	Average Discount on List Price Given (%)	Average Commission Paid as a Per Cent of Net Sales	Net Return to Galvor as a Per Cent of List Price
Representative:						
A	169,844	11,925	124,176	4.31	7.02	69.82
B	92,793	6,464	67,769	4.42	6.97	69.80
C	109,195	7,370	80,135	5.42	6.75	69.27
D	205,301	12,726	151,514	6.90	6.20	68.71
E	158,574	11,038	115,821	6.11	6.96	68.57
F	75,468	4,433	55,941	7.66	5.87	68.45
G	492,111	34,499	359,218	6.94	7.01	67.92
H	416,919	26,502	307,430	8.52	6.35	67.35
I	236,429	14,636	174,566	8.88	6.19	67.25
J	179,145	11,148	132,209	9.14	6.22	67.03
K	263,332	16,006	194,982	9.43	6.08	66.92
L	738,004	48,482	541,920	9.57	6.57	66.40
M	274,610	15,881	203,807	11.36	5.78	65.79
N	462,053	25,688	349,192	11.81	5.56	65.28
X	52,953	3,135	39,228	12.77	5.92	64.62
Y	66,161	4,012	48,916	13.30	6.07	64.10
Total	3,992,890	253,945	2,946,824			
Galvor Paris	4,825,050	265,869	3,682,572	7.31	5.51	68.85
Factory sales	729,161	......	583,615	13.95	...	68.82
Grand total	9,547,101	519,814	7,213,011			

* Not including sales to the TRONEX Corporation.
Source: Company records.

Exhibit 3

ANALYSIS OF TOTAL 1960 GALVOR SALES BY DISTRIBUTION CHANNEL AND PRODUCT CATEGORY

DISTRIBUTION CHANNEL	ELECTRONIC PRODUCTS		ELECTRIC PRODUCTS		GALVANOMETERS		TOTAL		
	Net Sales (NF)	Average Discount (%)	Net Sales (NF)	Average Discount (%)	Net Sales (NF)	Average Discount (%)	Net Sales (NF)	Average Discount (%)	Per Cent of Total Net Sales
Representative									
A	90,422	2.24	70,837	6.62	8,584	6.08	169,844	4.31	1.454
B	35,388	1.99	53,369	5.82	4,035	6.27	92,793	4.42	0.795
C	36,846	3.59	53,883	7.14	18,464	3.84	109,195	5.42	0.935
D	111,346	2.30	89,769	11.70	4,185	14.20	205,301	6.90	1.757
E	67,342	2.13	75,940	7.27	15,291	15.97	158,574	6.11	1.357
F	32,789	4.44	40,874	10.36	1,804	0.85	75,468	7.66	0.646
G	175,681	4.84	290,887	8.07	25,542	7.99	492,111	6.94	4.212
H	143,881	4.24	229,965	11.10	43,069	8.04	416,917	8.52	3.568
I	80,033	5.59	139,565	11.32	16,831	2.88	236,429	8.88	2.024
J	92,078	7.09	79,651	11.37	7,415	9.47	179,145	9.14	1.533
K	120,398	5.95	129,408	12.08	13,525	13.07	263,332	9.43	2.254
L	287,625	5.94	288,700	9.75	161,678	15.11	738,004	9.57	6.317
M	123,059	9.67	130,325	12.63	21,225	12.97	274,610	11.36	2.350
N	191,497	10.53	255,133	13.09	15,422	5.47	462,053	11.81	3.954
X	21,404	12.61	27,701	12.40	3,848	16.17	52,953	12.77	0.453
Y	27,173	5.39	25,387	10.74	13,599	28.97	66,161	13.30	0.566
Total representatives	1,636,962	….	1,981,394	….	374,517	….	3,992,890	….	34.175
Galvor Paris	2,159,494	5.45	2,038,117	6.23	627,439	16.14	4,825,050	7.31	41.298
Factory sales	411,964	17.39	319,494	14.90	129,939	24.86	861,397	23.03	7.732
Comor S.A. (French Export Co.)	224,177	19.73	208,434	29.76	….	….	432,611	24.90	3.702
Importing Agents									
Franc Zone	240,422	14.02	285,280	15.75	….	….	525,702	14.97	4.500
Others	275,870	13.54	436,189	13.97	51,328	20.00	763,388	14.25	6.534
Sales to the Tronex Corp.									
Tronex sales in France	226,977	18.60	11,812	23.11	….	….	238,789	18.84	2.044
Tronex Franc Zone sales	20,405	25.54	2,945	25.88	….	….	23,350	25.58	0.200
Tronex export sales	17,482	19.51	3,130	12.16	….	….	20,612	18.47	0.176
Grand total (weighted average discount shown)	5,213,753	8.68	5,286,795	10.61	1,183,223	16.29	11,683,789	10.38	100.000

Source: Company records.

sales of more than 1,000,000 NF per year in order to pay expenses. In the long run, M. Margaux thought it would be advantageous to have direct sales offices, because he felt that a Galvor agent with technical training would sell much better than most representatives, who had little technical training.

When asked about the possibility of a direct sales force, M. Latour replied: "Before we can use our own sales force, we need a broader product line. And anyway, we would use such a sales force only in the major industrial centers of France. M. Margaux's dream is to eliminate the representatives and replace them by a direct sales force, but this is a long way away."

Exhibit 4

1959 SALES TERRITORY MAP WITH FORTUNE COEFFICIENTS

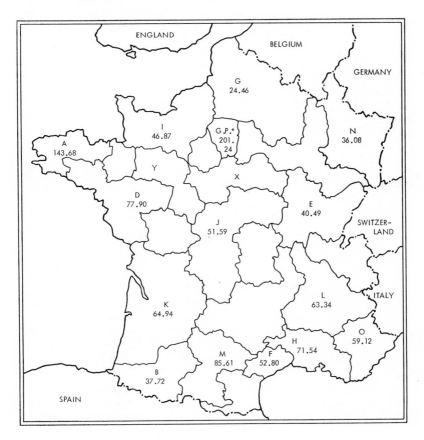

* G.P. = Galvor Paris.

Exhibit 4—Continued

1961 SALES TERRITORY MAP WITH FORTUNE COEFFICIENT

Exhibit 5

M. MARGAUX'S DESCRIPTION OF SIX REPRESENTATIVES*

Monsieur N.

	Total Sales	Commissions	Fortune Coefficient
1959	345,289 NF	21,313 NF	36.08
1961	554,548 NF	31,943 NF	59.06

Territory   :   Strasbourg
Age   :   58 years
Years with
Galvor   :   15
Percentage of Galvor products in total
sales   :   40%

Annual sales potential (estimated) for his territory if he devoted 100% of his time to Galvor: 1,600,000 NF.

---

* Selected at random by researcher. Arranged in order of estimated sales potential for their territories.

Exhibit 5—Continued

Technical knowledge : None
Qualifications : Personal charm
General remarks : Sells to wholesalers only. Does not try to sell to individuals. This is bad, because he has no direct contact with clients.

Monsieur L.

	Total Sales	Commissions	Fortune Coefficient
1959	515,603 NF	34,362 NF	63.34
1961	793,074 NF	54,546 NF	115.12

Territory : Lyon
Age : 40 years
Years with Galvor : 25
Percentage of Galvor products in total sales : 60%

Annual sales potential (estimated) in his territory if he devoted 100% of his time to Galvor: 1,400,000 NF.

Technical knowledge : None
Qualifications : A good salesman, knows his area well, dynamic.
General remarks : No technical knowledge. Whenever he gets a technical letter, he just sends a catalogue. Can't give technical advice to customers, we have to do it for him.

Monsieur H.

	Total Sales	Commissions	Fortune Coefficient
1959	379,612	24,079	71.54
1961	549,972	36,776	100.90

Territory : Marseilles
Age : 34 years
Years with Galvor : 12
Percentage of Galvor products in total sales : 50%

Annual sales potential (estimated) if he devoted 100% of his time to Galvor: 900,000 NF.

Technical knowledge : A little. Can demonstrate.
Qualifications : Good personality, aggressive, dynamic, some technical knowledge.
General remarks : Very good. Tries hard, and is a good Galvor man.

Monsieur M.

	Total Sales	Commissions	Fortune Coefficient
1959	232,877 NF	13,815 NF	85.61
1961	385,560 NF	22,973 NF	120.46

Territory : Toulouse
Age : 60 years
Years with Galvor : 18
Percentage of Galvor products in total sales : 50%

Annual sales potential (estimated) if he devoted 100% of his time to Galvor: 600,000 NF.

Technical knowledge : Electrical engineer
Qualifications : Very dynamic, good technical knowledge, agreeable, well known.
General remarks : Hired an assistant to help him sell. Very good, has the Galvor spirit.

Exhibit 5—Continued

Monsieur E.

	Total Sales	Commissions	Fortune Coefficient
1959	128,783 NF	9,041 NF	40.49
1961	259,390 NF	18,208 NF	85.40

Territory : Dijon
Age : 50 years
Years with
Galvor : 3
Percentage of Galvor products in total
sales : 35%

Annual sales potential (estimated) if he devoted 100% of his time to Galvor: 450,000 NF.

Technical knowledge : None
Qualifications : Hard prospector
General remarks : Tries hard, but doesn't work in depth. In general, however, we are satisfied.

Monsieur C.

	Total Sales	Commissions	Fortune Coefficient
1960	109,195 NF	7,370 NF	NA
1961	149,776 NF	10,199 NF	84.92

Territory : Nice
Age : 42 years
Years with
Galvor : 2 (previously 8 years as salesman for the Galvor representative in the Nice area).
Percentage of Galvor products in total
sales : 30%

Annual sales potential (estimated) if he devoted 100% of his time to Galvor: 200,000 NF.

Technical knowledge : Knows what electricity is, and can demonstrate.
Qualifications : Some technical knowledge. Formerly with electrical wholesaler.
General remarks : Hard worker, truly digs for business. Has to prospect hard because his area potential is small. In general, we are very satisfied with C.

THE GALVOR COMPANY (C–2)
Pricing Policy

Galvor prices were established by decision of the pricing committee, which consisted of M. Latour and M. Margaux (Commercial Manager). As a basis for the price, the committee used a formula consisting of three stages. The stages were (1) determination of a product factory cost; (2) addition of an allowance for profit; and (3) allowance for direct sales expenses, discounts, and sales taxes. The price resulting from the above formula was almost always used without adjustment. Occasionally, however, MM. Latour and Margaux increased or reduced the formula price, depending on the competitive situation.

Determination of factory cost began by establishing standard charges for material and direct labor. The cost of purchased materials was obtained from the Manufacturing Department's bill of materials for each product. M. Romanée, Manager of Manufacturing, arrived at the direct labor cost by (*a*) setting up production techniques and methods to be used in manufacturing and assembling a product, (*b*) determining total standard hours needed to make a product, and (*c*) applying the appropriate wage rates to these standard times. Total factory cost was then arrived at by the following calculation:

Cost of purchased material
PLUS : 12% of purchased material cost to cover purchasing expense
PLUS : Direct labor cost
PLUS : *310% of direct labor* (to cover all overhead)
Equals : Factory cost.

The 12 per cent figure for purchasing costs was an estimate of actual costs. The 310 per cent of direct labor, designed to cover "overhead," was intended to cover factory overhead, depreciation, research and development costs, administrative expenses, miscellaneous charges, and indirect selling costs. "I have been using this 310 per cent for many years," said M. Latour, "and it seems to work out pretty well, so I see no reason to change it."

This case was prepared by Mr. Warren J. Keegan under the supervision of Professor David S. R. Leighton.

Copyright, 1962, by l'Institut pour l'Etude des Méthodes de Direction de l'Entreprise (IMEDE), Lausanne, Switzerland. Reprinted by permission.

The allowance for 20 per cent gross profit on factory cost was made simply by multiplying 120 per cent times the factory cost previously computed.

The allowance for direct sales expense, discounts, and French sales tax was arrived at by multiplying the amount (120 per cent of factory cost) by 1.63, in order to arrive at a final list price. This 1.63, called the "K" factor was arrived at in the following manner. First, the final list price (the catalogue price) was set at 100 per cent for purpose of computation. Galvor gave discounts ranging up to 20 per cent off list; it was assumed that the maximum (20 per cent) discount would always be given. After the assumed discount, the proceeds to the company would be 80 per cent of the list price (100 per cent — 20 per cent discount).

Under French law, 20 per cent of net sales had to be paid to the government as a sales tax. This meant that, after the assumed 20 per cent discount, the sales tax would be an additional 16 per cent (20 per cent × 80 per cent) off the list price. Thus the proceeds to the company after discounts and taxes would be 64 per cent (100 per cent list — 20 per cent discount — 16 per cent sales tax).

The final costs accounted for in the "K" factor were the commissions paid to representatives and the cost of operating Galvor Paris. The representatives were paid commissions which varied inversely with the discount given: the higher the discount, the lower the commission. At the assumed 20 per cent discount, sales commissions would be approximately 4 per cent. This was the most "expensive" Galvor sale possible. At lower discounts, higher commissions were paid, but not sufficiently high to equal the savings of lower discounts.

Thus the commission assumed was 2.56 per cent (4 per cent of 64 per cent, since commissions were paid on the basis of net sales after discounts and taxes), which left 61.44 per cent of list price to cover factory cost and profit on factory cost. This meant that if the amount (120 per cent of factory cost) was multiplied by 1.63 (100 per cent divided by 61.44 per cent), after paying sales taxes, and the maximum discount-commission combination, Galvor would have left a sum exactly large enough to cover its computed factory cost and to provide pretax profits of 20 per cent of factory cost. In reality, Galvor gave discounts averaging about 10 per cent of list price, and direct sales expense (representatives' commissions plus the total operating cost of Galvor Paris) averaged 6 per cent of net sales after discount and sales tax. As a result, Galvor's "K" factor of 1.63 actually contained some allowance for profit. The following table summarizes Galvor's pricing formula:

Purchased material + 12% purchasing expense   = A
Direct labor cost   = B
310% (B) to cover all overhead   = C
A + B + C   = (FC) (Factory cost)
FC + 20% (FC) for profit   = D
1.63 (D) to allow for sales taxes, commissions, and discounts = List price

In commenting on the "hidden profit allowance" in the "K" factor, M. Chambertin said: "It would appear that we are over-pricing our products by leaving in this hidden margin. However, we find that the 310 per cent overhead allowance is inadequate to cover our actual overhead, so that the hidden profit allowance tends to compensate for the fact that our true factory costs are higher, on balance, than we compute. We produce over 150 models of 40 basic items, and I suspect that we are losing money on many of the slow-selling models. There are 'hidden costs' in carrying an extensive product line which we do not account for." As an illustration of such hidden costs, M. Chambertin mentioned the cost of maintaining parts inventories to build so many instruments and the increased production difficulties due to more complicated scheduling.

M. Margaux commented on the pricing system as follows: "It is no secret that most of our competitors overcharge for their products. The fact is, we overcharge less than they do, if at all. This is clearly indicated by the fact that nobody offers Galvor quality at our prices. Maybe this pricing method won't work in the future, but Galvor has always operated at capacity; we can sell everything we can produce."

When asked about competitive prices, M. Margaux replied: "We do have perhaps some competitors who sell similar equipment at a similar price, but generally only for a small part of our line. In our industry, especially in measuring instruments, there are almost literally no identical products. There is competition, but mostly in small, overlapping areas. An example of overlapping competition is our No. 462 pocket multimeter which we sell for 170 NF. In 1958, when we introduced this product, we received 133 orders. In 1959, we received 3,068 orders, and in 1960 orders increased to 4,546. The Alpha Corporation,[5] our largest competitor (1,000 employees), tried to move into this market in 1961 by introducing a similar model at exactly the same price as our Model 462. They have not had any success with their model except insofar as they are filling orders we can't supply. Our repair service is better than theirs, and much cheaper."

M. Latour made the following remarks about foreign competition:

---

[5] Fictitious name.

"The Japanese are starting to enter some markets with products competitive to ours. They produce a good-quality product, but to date they have not offered precision as high as ours. Their prices are very low. I bought a Japanese multimeter with precision of 2½ per cent and showed it at our management conference. We came up with the following price comparisons:

Item	*NF*
Galvor's catalogue multimeter (1% precision)	100
Similar Japanese meter (2½% precision)	26
Galvor's price (using price formula) for a comparable multimeter of 2½%) precision	76

This comparison shocked us. We were quite relieved last year when a delegation of Japanese businessmen visited us and asked for rights to sell our products in Japan. I asked them how this would be possible when our products were so much more expensive. They showed me that Japanese products of similar precision and quality to Galvor products were actually priced higher in Japan. In my opinion the Japanese cannot manufacture quality and precision at low cost. Their forte is in mass production; when it comes to high-precision instruments such as our multimeters, their costs go up sharply. We sell precision and reliability. Our production is always small, and therefore we are not susceptible to mass-production competition.

"Production costs in the United States are so high that American companies should not be difficult competitors in the European market, except when they have a unique product. As tariffs go down, Germany will be a stronger competitor in the electronic area. However, we are not worried about German competition. We look at the opening of the Common Market as an opportunity."

ALLOCATION OF RESEARCH AND DEVELOPMENT COST

M. Chambertin had long argued that the simple electric products were being unfairly burdened with R&D (research and development) overhead. Electronic products, he said, should carry more overhead. To support his argument, in mid-1962 M. Chambertin analyzed cost data to determine the actual R&D and factory cost of the two Galvor product categories: electric equipment and electronic equipment. He discovered that the actual cost of R&D and factory overhead for electric products was 177 per cent of direct labour. The same figure for electronic products was 245 per cent. With these figures, M. Chambertin developed the tentative pricing system shown in Table 1.

Table 1

M. CHAMBERTIN'S TENTATIVE PRICING SYSTEM

Electric Products	*Electronic Products*
Net cost of Purchased Material	Net cost of Purchased Material
Add: 11% of Purchased Material Cost to cover purchasing expense.	Add: 11% of Purchased Material Cost to cover purchasing expense.
Add: Direct Labor Cost (Y).	Add: Direct Labor Cost (Y).
Add: 177% of Y above to cover factory overhead and R&D costs.	Add: 245% of Y above to cover factory overhead and R&D costs.
Equals: Basic Manufacturing cost (BMC).	Equals: Basic Manufacturing Cost (BMC).
Add: 25% of BMC to cover Commercial and Administrative Overhead.	Add: 25% of BMC to cover Commercial and Administrative Overhead.
Equals: Total Product Cost (TPC) (125% BMC).	Equals: Total Product Cost (TPC) (125% BMC).
Add: 14% TPC to cover profit.	Add: 14% TPC to cover profit.
Equals: Final Price *before* allowance for Sales Taxes, commissions, and discounts (114% TPC).	Equals: Final Price *before* allowance for Sales Taxes, commissions, and discounts (114% TPC).

Source: Company officials.

The "final" price (not yet the list price) at the bottom of Table 1 is at that point directly comparable with the price of a product priced under the actual Galvor system before the multiplication, in the actual system, by the "K" factor of 1.63 to allow for discounts, sales taxes, and commissions.

The main difference between M. Chambertin's pricing system and the actual Galvor system was in the handling of overhead costs. Instead of taking 310 per cent of direct labor to cover all overhead, M. Chambertin determined R&D and factory overhead for the electric and electronic product categories, and he made a separate allowance for commercial and administrative overhead. Because 12 per cent of raw-material costs over-allowed for purchasing expense, he reduced this allowance to 11 per cent, the actual cost to Galvor. The 14 per cent profit allowance in Table 1 was arrived at empirically by M. Chambertin. He assumed that 1960 had been a normal year in terms of profitability. He then analyzed the 1960 profit and loss statement to find out how much the company earned on its operations excluding windfall losses and gains. The mechanics of what he did were very complex, but the end result was that, had his system been used to price 1960's sales, he believed that Galvor's total revenue and net profit would have been unchanged.

The impact of M. Chambertin's pricing system on several typical electric and electronic products is illustrated in Table 2.

Although M. Chambertin did not advocate an immediate change in Galvor's pricing system, he was convinced that eventually Galvor would be forced by competitive pressure to allocate its costs more realistically.

Table 2

GALVOR: COMPARISON OF ACTUAL WITH THEORETICAL PRICES

ELECTRIC PRODUCTS

CATALOGUE NUMBER	PRODUCT DESCRIPTION	FINAL LIST PRICE (IN NF)	
		List Price 1961	With Chambertin's System
400	Transclip	140.00	120.00
410	Electrician's multimeter	89.50	86.00
430	Multirange meter	250.00	234.00
453	Pocket multimeter	129.50	126.00
460	Multimeter	119.50	119.00
462	Pocket multimeter	170.00	142.00

ELECTRONIC PRODUCTS

CATALOGUE NUMBER	PRODUCT DESCRIPTION	FINAL LIST PRICE (IN NF)	
		List Price 1961	With Chambertin's System
231	Wobuloscope	1,950.00	2,297.00
310	Tube checker	545.00	636.00
626	Precision impedance bridge	1,515.00	2,056.00
661	Vacuum-tube bridge	2,230.00	2,593.00
742	Vacuum-tube voltmeter	350.00	410.00
744	Vacuum-tube voltmeter	735.00	807.00
931	Standard signal generator	1,805.00	2,198.00
936	VHF generator	1,665.00	1,730.00

Source: Company records.

M. Latour, in commenting on M. Chambertin's pricing system said: "I have suspected that our electric products are too high-priced, and our electronic products are too low-priced. So what does this mean? Why should we lower our prices for multimeters and galvanos? At our current prices we can easily sell our entire production of electric products."

THE GALVOR COMPANY (C–3)
Product Policy

One of the major issues at Galvor was the question of catalogue size, or product diversity. As Table 1 shows, the company carried a broad line of measuring instruments, and there was disagreement among company officials as to whether this line was too broad.

M. Margaux summarized the commercial point of view as follows: "Galvor's fame is largely due to the diversity of products it sells. In the six years I've been here, I've noticed that our customers have changed from technicians to high-class engineers. Doors open to us now because of the size and diversity of our catalogue. People come to us because we can meet a broad range of needs. Also, those who are customers for only one of our products at the outset may later need other products that we sell. When this happens, they think of us immediately. There is a big difference, I suppose, in the profitability of our different products. However, we always sell at a profit, because a profit allowance is included in our pricing formula. We almost never make a product at an unprofitable price. When we do so, it is usually to accommodate a government agency."

M. Chambertin, Administrative Director, disagreed with the proponents of a broad product line, saying: "One of our problems is that we make a number of products which have very small sales volumes. I am fairly certain that many of these products are unprofitable. The real reason we make these products is that M. Latour likes a fat catalogue and will sometimes add a new product to the line for reasons of prestige."

The technical point of view was expressed by M. Meursault, Manager of Electronic Research: "Our R & D effort is too spread out. In an attempt to build a thick catalogue, we have produced a large number of products which have little in common. Instead of specializing in a single product area, we have become so diversified that R & D we do for one type of product has little applicability for other products. For example, the men working on the FM generator are doing work that has no value to the

This case was prepared by Mr. Warren J. Keegan under the supervision of Professor David S. R. Leighton.

Copyright, 1962, by l'Institut pour l'Etude des Méthodes de Direction de l'Entreprise (IMEDE), Lausanne, Switzerland. Reprinted by permission.

Table 1

THE GALVOR PRODUCT LINE, 1961

PRODUCT GROUP	NUMBER OF MODELS	PRICE RANGE (NF)	1961 SALES* (NF 000's)	PERCENTAGE OF TOTAL 1961 SALES
Electric products:				
Multimeters................	15	100–550	5,188	36.2
Galvanometers.............	Over 100	60–150	1,412	9.8
Milliammeters.............	2	200–230	105	0.7
Special products...........	..	....	275	1.9
Accessories and spare parts....	..	....	795	5.5
Total electric...........			7,775	54.1
Electronic products:				
Tube and transistor checkers and analyzers.............	5	250–2,340	881	6.1
Generators:				
Wobulator................	2	700–1,800	67	
Pattern generator.........	1	1,100	153	
Audio generator..........	1	680	156	
Service..................	1	670	191	
HF.....................	2	1,850–2,250	1,073	15.7
VHF....................	2	1,665	127	
UHF....................	1	n.a.	227	
AM and FM.............	3	1,200–2,000	245	
Marker.................	2	800–2,000	11	
Total generators........	15	680–2,250	....	....
Wobuloscopes.............	2	1,320–2,050	986	6.9
Oscilloscopes.............	3	1,115–2,200	321	2.3
VTVM's†................	3	365–1,300	781	5.4
Impedance bridges..........	3	n.a.	417	2.9
Vacuum—tube bridge.......	1	3,800	126	0.9
Accessories and spare parts....	..	....	344	2.4
Equipment racks...........	..	....	11	Nil
Total electronic........	..	....	6,117	42.6
Sales to Tronex...............	..	....	192	1.3
Equipment repairs............	..	....	281	2.0
Total.................	..	....	14,365	100.0

* Including all taxes.
† Vacuum-tube voltmeters.
Source: Company officials.

transistor research team. Our effort is so divided that, instead of having a company of 450 employees, we have three companies of 150 employees each. This has been all right so far, but what worries me is that, in two years, the French measuring-instrument industry will have enough capacity to serve all its customers. When that day comes, there will be a shakedown in the industry just like the one we are seeing in the French automobile industry today. Only the best companies will survive and, to be really good, a company must concentrate its effort."

M. Romanée, Manager of Manufacturing, remarked: "In my opinion, we could easily manufacture a broader product line if we could eliminate some problem areas within the company. In the first place, we have no Methods Staff, which loads me and my foremen with methods work. Second, liaison between R & D and manufacturing is not working smoothly, which further complicates life. Third, the R & D groups keep modifying products which have been approved for production, and this means that our manufacturing activities are constantly being disrupted and schedules changed. When we can iron out these problems, we can handle a much broader product line, but at the moment even our present line is far too broad for smooth operations."

The most important products in the line in terms of volume were multimeters. As Table 1 shows, 15 multimeters accounted for 36.2 per cent of Galvor's total 1961 sales. Table 2 gives the unit orders received for all types of multimeters which Galvor manufactured between 1954 and 1960, and the list price value of the 1960 orders.

Table 2

UNIT ORDERS RECEIVED FOR GALVOR MULTIMETERS, 1954–60, AND
LIST PRICE VALUE OF THESE ORDERS IN 1960

MODEL	1960 LIST PRICE (NF)	ORDERS RECEIVED (UNITS)							LIST PRICE VALUE OF 1960 ORDERS (IN NF)
		1954	1955	1956	1957	1958	1959	1960	
A.........	140	1,591	1,484	2,232	2,195	2,227	3,000	4,866	681,240
B.........	304	....	....	....	....	....	130	434	131,936
C.........	100	243	647	1,071	1,347	1,530	1,813	1,565	156,500
D.........	...	465	147	247	412	2	....	....	....
E.........	370	200	221	84	335	298	349	402	148,740
F.........	...	22	1	....	....	....	....	....	....
G.........	255	988	2,036	2,871	3,347	2,851	3,056	2,887	736,185
H.........	375	....	....	....	....	2	253	869	325,875
I.........	n.a.	....	....	....	....	....	30	25	n.a.
J.........	212	67	57	106	53	135	142	217	46,004
K.........	220	236	85	369	230	200	267	122	26,840
L.........	...	....	26	....	120	....	....	....	....
M.........	273	....	193	310	386	365	377	717	195,741
N.........	n.a.	....	....	....	125	....	150	386	n.a.
O.........	136	....	....	....	1	678	985	1,384	188,224
P.........	124	6,425	7,748	9,516	11,034	9,961	10,411	11,387	1,411,988
Q.........	...	....	....	....	....	....	100	....	....
R.........	170	....	....	....	....	133	3,068	4,546	772,820
S.........	250	....	....	....	....	....	1,500	....	....
T.........	n.a.	1,144	809	1,370	1,663	1,096	895	762	....
U.........	535	....	....	....	....	1	146	593	317,225
V.........	380	....	....	....	....	....	....	68	25,840
Total List Price Value of 1960 orders..									5,165,158

Source: Company records. n.a.: not available.

One company official, upon examining Table 2, observed that five models (A, G, H, P, and R) accounted for over 75 per cent of the total list-price value of 1960 multimeter orders. (This ignores minor list-price values for types I and N, for which data were not available.) He pointed out that, by eliminating many of its small-volume multimeters, Galvor could reallocate its marketing, production, and R&D efforts over its large-volume items. This, he argued, would have three main effects: (*a*) a concentrated R&D effort would result in better product design for the remaining multimeters; (*b*) a smaller and better product line would be sold more intensively by the marketing organization, resulting in greater unit sales volumes; and (*c*) factory costs would be cut by longer and more efficient production runs. He concluded by saying: "I think that, by gradually cutting our product line, we could continue to increase our sales as much as we have in the past, if not more. The big difference would be in our profitability, which would be much greater due to lower factory costs."

M. Latour replied to this argument as follows: "I know that not all of my colleagues agree with me that we should carry so many multimeters, but I have four arguments in favor of keeping our line as broad as it now is. First of all, I want our customers to think of Galvor as the company which can provide *any* type of multimeter, not just the few most common ones. I want engineers and technicians to identify Galvor and measurement as being synonymous. Second, I want our customers to be able to come to Galvor for any multimeter, even if an uncommon type; if one of our customers has to go to a competitor for a special multimeter, maybe he'll try some other products of that competitor, instead of dealing exclusively with us. Third, if we didn't offer every type of multimeter, some of our competitors would be encouraged to try to fill demands we weren't meeting; they would start making these special multimeters, and I don't like to give my competitors such encouragement. And, fourth, it doesn't cost us much to do the research on these special types, and they don't require expensive tooling. We indeed do devote our main efforts to the high-volume types; it would be unthinkable to do otherwise. So it doesn't cost us much to make these special types. And remember, since we allocate overhead on the basis of the amount of direct labor used for a given product, we always make a profit. I admit that if we made these special types in larger quantities, we could lower the labor hours on some of them, but, since we put overhead right into labor, we always make a profit. When all is said and done, however, I will be interested to hear what students of business have to say about this question."

M. Latour remarked: "Our policy on product quality is very important to us. As I have mentioned, from Galvor's early days we have continually upgraded the quality of our products. Today all Galvor products are of very high quality, and they are very reasonably priced as well. On my recent trip around the world [which occurred during March, 1962], I visited a number of measuring-instrument plants, especially some of the famous ones in the United States. I came back from this trip convinced that Galvor is today in a position to aim for being one of the top four or five companies in the world in measuring instruments. This will be possible only if our quality is impeccable, and I have urged all our employees to concentrate on quality above all.

"As you know, in 1957 we set up the TRONEX Corporation to manufacture measuring instruments of modest price and quality. But this decision was in no way inconsistent with our aim to make Galvor first class in quality, quite to the contrary. I set up TRONEX for two main reasons. First, and most important, I wanted to discourage our competitors from trying to undercut our prices for Galvor instruments with their low-price and low-quality equipment. Two of these competitors, the MU[6] and SIGMA[7] Corporations, were at that time especially aggressive in pushing their equipment, and our salesmen were beginning to complain about this. The instruments manufactured by these two firms were of cheap quality, but they were nonetheless taking some sales away from us. I thought that, by starting our own company in their specialty, we might dissuade them from trying to make further inroads into our business. The second reason I started TRONEX was to introduce a line which might, some day, become a major part of our business. I foresaw that we might eventually sell TRONEX products in kit form to reach an even broader market.

"As time passed, we found that MU and SIGMA were not causing us serious problems, so today that reason for TRONEX' existence has disappeared. I am afraid that, at the moment, we all tend to regard TRONEX as a 'poor relation' of Galvor. I am the only one here who thinks it worthwhile to keep TRONEX alive; it would have disappeared long ago if I weren't president of the company. And I must admit that we haven't had the time we need to give TRONEX a real push. But I am maintaining the corporation nonetheless, because some day it may be valuable to us. Perhaps eventually we will give it a complete organization of its own, and set it up in a plant away from Bordeaux, where TRONEX can operate independently of Galvor influence; this is how our INDICA S.A. operation is run in Paris. Besides, with our pricing system, we make money on every TRONEX product we sell, so why not keep it going?"

SELECTING NEW PRODUCTS

When asked what criteria were used to select new products for manufacture at Galvor, M. Latour replied: "We try to find a product in an area where we have a strong technical background, because without this

---

[6] Fictitious name.
[7] Fictitious name.

background we cannot really compete. Second, having found such a product, we try to determine whether we can sell it in profitable quantities. This means finding out (*a*) if the total market is large enough to justify our entry and (*b*) how much of the total market we can capture for ourselves. We must, however, also pay attention to customer demands. We may develop products for customers without full confidence in the commercial prospects for these products.

"The future growth and development of the electronic industry will continuously open new product opportunities for us. For example, the complicated and extremely accurate generator which we are building for the Air Force is an entirely new product that was unnecessary before the jet plane came into use.

"We try to be first with products and features, and we continuously watch competitors to maintain this lead. Trade shows are very useful in this regard. I attend all the important shows (Paris, New York, Hanover, etc.) from the minute they start until they end. The chief engineers attend to find out what other manufacturers are doing and to look for parts that we might use.

"Generally speaking, the representatives are not a good source of product ideas. Usually, they wait until a competitive product is hurting their sales before they report anything to us. Our sales engineers are far more useful, for they react to changes, demands, and needs faster than the representatives. They have a real technical curiosity to find out what is going on and what is needed. The foreign agents are, for the most part, too far out of touch with over-all market consideration to be of much help in product development.

"At the management meetings when we are considering a product, we discuss what quantities might be sold. Occasionally we have the Paris sales force conduct a survey. Then we roughly try to determine what we could sell the product for, and what it would cost to make, and how much we might have to invest. After these considerations, we discuss the product until we come to a unanimous decision on whether to adopt it.

"After deciding upon a new product, we develop a prototype model. This prototype will be identical in all respects to the mass-produced instrument. If we have done all of the research needed to develop a finished prototype, it is almost 100 per cent sure that we will go into production of the instrument. After an engineer has spent one or two years developing a product, it is a great blow to him if the product is never put on the market. Occasionally I have to veto production. An example of this was a photoelectric cell we developed. After the prototype was completed, we discovered that it would have to be sold at double the price of comparable models already available in the market. It was clear that we would have to drop our cell.

"We do not make elaborate cost calculations when we are considering a product. We determine costs in the usual manner—by estimating direct labor costs and allocating overhead on this basis and adding in the cost of the necessary purchased materials and parts. The result of this system is that the small, low-priced units sold in volume are overpriced, while the large individual units, which sometimes require years of development work, are underpriced. This system has worked up to now, however, and I am not going to bring in a bevy of accountants until I have to, which will be when the market gets much tougher than it is now. We make no payback on investment calculations."

M. Meursault, Manager of Electronic Research, when questioned upon product policy, emphasized the importance of market demands in guiding preliminary research efforts. He remarked: "I try to get to Paris often enough to visit top-notch engineers in order to find out what kinds of new instruments they would like to have. I ask them about the physical specifications of the instruments, the characteristics they want to measure and how they would like to measure them, and what degree of precision is required. After gathering this information, I estimate the requirements for such an instrument. If it appears that the instrument is of a type for which we are well equipped to do research and which is suitable to our manufacturing operation, I will make a rough cost and price estimate. I then return to the engineers I first queried and ask them if they would be interested in an instrument with X precision, Y specifications, and costing Z NF. This is the kind of market research which I find most useful, and it can be done only by an engineer who is intimately familiar with current technology. A man doing this job has to be able to distinguish between the usual customer request, which is simply a 'one-shot' application, and the unusual request which indicates a widespread new need for an instrument.

"As you know, up to the present time we have tried to sell Galvor products to all customer sectors, from the home electronic hobbyist up to the French Air Force. This has been a very sound policy while we have been building the company, but in recent months I have become convinced that, for the future, we should concentrate all our efforts on a narrower range of customers, rather than attempting to sell to all. More specifically, I think that Galvor's true vocation will be to equip manufacturers of electronic goods with measuring and control equipment. So far, this group of customers has been only one segment of our business, but this sector is going to grow enormously in coming years, and we can become dominant in this sector if we start now. For this reason, in my thinking about new products, I keep in the back of my mind the idea that ultimately we will concentrate on instruments for the electronic industries."

Ideas for new products came to Galvor mainly from two sources. The most frequent source was a specific customer request for a special modification of an existing instrument or for an entirely new instrument which did not yet exist. Galvor received hundreds of such requests each year, either in writing or in interviews with customers, and there was a considerable problem of sorting out such requests. Most requests were for instruments so specialized that there would be no real market for the product. Company officials were always looking for the less common request, one which signalled a major new demand which Galvor could profitably fulfill. The second source of new-product ideas was the Galvor executives themselves, especially the engineers, who in the course of their talks with various people in electronics might hear of some new problem which was as yet unsolved. For example, in the mid-1950's Galvor executives heard from many customers about the problem of defective transistors. Because transistor sales were growing rapidly, company officials began to think about how to develop a transistor checker. In this case, the engineers worked only with an idea of what had to be done, not with a set of specifications submitted by the customer.

A PROPOSED NEW PRODUCT

"For about three years," remarked M. Latour, "I have been asking my engineers, 'How about making a digital voltmeter?' But they kept putting me off and saying it was unfeasible, so I did not press the point. But when I was at the I.R.E.[8] show in New York last month [March, 1962], I noticed that in about half of the booths there was seen to be a digital voltmeter on display. Everybody is making them, and I am beginning to be a little more concerned about whether we should get into this area; it may be the coming thing."

A digital voltmeter (DVM) was a measuring instrument which, like the conventional vacuum-tube voltmeter (VTVM), measured voltages by means of electronic circuitry. But whereas the VTVM was read by observing the position of a moving needle on a dial, the DVM had on its face a panel in which numbers appeared and indicated the size of the voltage being measured. These numbers were typically 2–4 cm.

---

[8] The Institute of Radio Engineers (I.R.E.) included a large number of United States electronic engineers; the Institute sponsored an annual trade show, where many electronic manufacturers displayed their new products.

in height. Another significant difference between the two was in precision. A VTVM usually had a precision on the order of plus-or-minus 1–1.5 per cent. A DVM was accurate to within 0.01–0.001 per cent, or about 100 to 1,000 times more precise than a VTVM.

As for the comparative advantages of the DVM, M. Meursault mentioned these facts: First, it was much easier to read a DVM than a VTVM. A DVM could also be read from a distance of several meters, whereas a VTVM had to be read from a distance of 50 cm. or less. Furthermore, an unskilled person could read a DVM with ease, while some training was required to operate a VTVM. On many DVM's the decimal point was automatically positioned when the voltage measurement was displayed; on a VTVM, the reader had to have some idea of the size of the voltage being measured, in order to read the actual voltage on the appropriate scale. VTVM's often had seven or more scales on their faces. The next most important advantage of the DVM, M. Meursault asserted, was its extreme precision, which was useful in some applications. He added, however, that precision requirements on the order of 0.01–0.001 per cent were unusual and that a VTVM's precision sufficed for most applications.

A third advantage of the DVM was its suitability for incorporation in control systems. For example, a machine could be linked to a DVM, and the DVM could then be used to control the machine's operation: if voltage were from 7,500 volts to 9,500 volts, say, the machine could be speeded up or otherwise given commands. This sort of operating control was impossible, as a rule, with a VTVM. Related to this function was the ability of the DVM to accept or reject within precise error limits. A DVM could be connected to a scale on a conveyor which was carrying, for example, cans of food. The weight registered by the scale could be expressed in terms of voltage on the DVM, and the DVM could signal when an underweight can was sent through. This was especially valuable in the case of untrained personnel, who could easily read several digits of a DVM, but who might have difficulty (and eyestrain) in trying to make the same readings on a VTVM. M. Meursault added that, in general, the DVM was useful for making rapid readings and decisions based on these readings, especially where people without electronic training were involved.

As for the advantages of the VTVM over the DVM, M. Meursault cited two. Most important, the VTVM was much cheaper. The typical VTVM cost from 500 to 1,000 NF, depending mostly on its precision and flexibility. The DVM cost from about 2,500 to 5,000 NF, again depending on its precision and flexibility. A second major advantage of the VTVM was its "analogue" feature. The swinging needle of the VTVM exactly traced the speed and range of voltage changes, so that, by observing this swing, the electronic technician or engineer could make very precise adjustments and gain considerable insight into the workings of the system on which voltage measurement was being performed. The DVM had no analogue feature; it was impossible to observe the rate and degree of change of a continuously varying voltage.

As of early 1962, there were several DVM's available on the French market, but all of them were made by foreign firms or by French subsidiaries of foreign firms; none was made by any of the French measuring-instrument companies which Galvor officials thought of as competitors. Galvor had no information available as to the total size of the French market for DVM's, but knew there was a very active sale of this product in the United States.

M. Meursault said: "I don't think we ought to make a DVM, mainly because this instrument is useful mostly outside the electronic industry. An electronic engineer or technician will generally prefer to use a VTVM, because of its analogue feature. Since I think we ought to concentrate on the electronic industry in the future, I can't see much future for us in making a DVM. I am also opposed to the DVM because it would not fit into our distribution network very well. Nonetheless, I have made a preliminary estimate of the cost to develop a DVM at Galvor." M. Meursault's estimate is found in Table 3. "The 250 per cent of straight salary as an allowance for overhead is just a rough estimate, but I think it gives a fair idea of what our overhead really is. Now, you can see that I estimate about 54,000 NF to develop two prototypes of a DVM, but engineers tend to be a bit optimistic, and I am probably no exception. Let's say that a more realistic figure might be around 60,000 NF. After spending this money, we would have two finished prototypes and the necessary manufacturing plans to put these prototypes into production. As to the time for this project, my cost estimate shows a total of about 9 months: the first 6 months for R&D, then 3 successive months for designing, building, and writing the manufacturing documents for the prototypes. In reality, the R&D would probably not be done in one concentrated 6-month period, but spread out over an interval of perhaps a year, and the same slowing-down would occur in the prototype stage. Thus it would take us about 1½ to 2 years to get a prototype, after which it would be another 9 months before the first models would come off the production line. Finally, I estimate that we would sell this instrument for a list price of about 3,000 NF, which would be a fair price for a good instrument such as we would try to design.

"We have the background to do this research project, and the DVM

Table 3

ESTIMATED DEVELOPMENT COST OF A DIGITAL VOLTMETER

Mockup development costs	*Cost*
6 mo. R&D work by research technician	7,800 NF*
2 mo. work by lab. technicians who would help the research technician to make a preliminary mockup of the DVM	2,000 NF*
Overhead on the above research time, at 250% of straight salary (2.5 × 9,800 NF)	24,500 NF
New lab. instruments needed for research on this project	2,000 NF
Purchased DVM made by some other firm, to give us an idea of how others do the job	3,000 NF
Total cost to develop mockup	39,300 NF

Prototype development costs	
1 mo. of designer's time (to design a prototype from the mockup)	1,000 NF*
1 mo. of prototype builder's time	1,000 NF*
1 mo. of clerk's time (to draw up papers for manufacturing the DVM)	1,000 NF*
Purchased components used to make one mockup and two prototypes	3,750 NF
Overhead on time of designer, prototype builder, and clerk (250% × 3,000 NF)	7,500 NF
Total prototype development costs	14,250 NF
Total development cost	53,550 NF

* These were the straight salaries paid these men for the period of time indicated.

would fit in reasonably well with our other manufacturing operations. I think we could cover our R&D costs of 60,000 NF by selling from 100 to 200 DVM's at 3,000 NF each, and I think we could sell this many. I am nevertheless not very enthusiastic about doing this job. First of all, I don't yet see any strong market for this instrument in France, and merely covering our R&D costs is not worth the effort. We could spend this R&D time better, I think, on another instrument which would have a wide appeal. We don't have many industrial customers outside the electronic industry, and it is precisely these non-electronic manufacturers who would be the best customers for a DVM. Our sales network is not set up to concentrate on non-electronic manufacturers, nor do I think it should be. We ought to concentrate on electronic manufacturers, so I disagree with M. Latour: we should not develop this instrument, at least at this time."

In commenting on M. Meursault's arguments, M. Latour said: "Well, I don't want to force my engineers to study something which doesn't interest them, and I know that their technical backgrounds are very strong, but I still am not convinced that we shouldn't make a DVM. Judging from what I saw, it's one of the coming things in instrumentation in the United States."

THE GALVOR COMPANY (D)

"We have had no serious problems in the area of finance since 1948. At that time, we were a little short of funds while building our first large factory, but we came through fine. Since then, we have never been short of money, because internally generated funds have been ample to finance our growth." So said Mr. J. Chambertin, Administrative Director of Galvor Company, in early 1962.

Since no serious financial problems were apparent early in 1962, this case describes the financial condition and financial policies of Galvor as they existed at that time. The company's balance sheet is used as a "map" to organize this description. Table 1 is the asset side of Galvor's balance sheet and is followed by comments on its individual segments; Table 3 represents the liability side and is similarly treated. Later in the case, some further comments are made on financial policies; profit and loss statements are found in Exhibits 1 to 5.

FIXED ASSETS

LAND

Until 1960, the Galvor Company owned only part of the land upon which it is situated, and this land was carried on the books at 105,000 NF (New Francs). The rest of the land was owned by M. Latour, the President and principal stockholder of Galvor. During 1960, M. Latour sold the land which he owned as an individual to the company for 160,000 NF to obtain some cash to finance the construction of his home.

BUILDINGS

Galvor's first large factory was built in 1948, and additions were completed in 1953, 1956, and 1958. In early 1962, construction of a new wing was begun; it was designed to increase floor space by approximately 70 per cent, to a total of 8,917 square meters. Its cost was estimated by M. Chambertin to be between 1 million and 1.2 million NF. When asked what the production capacity of the company would be with the new

This case was prepared by Mr. James Hugon and Professor Vincent M. Jolivet.
Copyright 1962 by l'Institut pour l'Etude des Méthodes de Direction de l'Entreprise (IMEDE), Lausanne, Switzerland. Reprinted by permission.

Table 1

ASSET SIDE OF GALVOR'S BALANCE SHEET, DECEMBER 31, 1961
(In 000's of NF)

	Gross	Depreciation and Amortization	Net	Subtotals
Fixed assets:				
Land	265	. . .	265	
Buildings	1,849	430	1,419	
Equipment	754	586	168	
Transportation equipment	94	60	34	
Furniture and fixtures	590	332	258	
Patents and trademarks	31	10	21	
				2,165
Other fixed assets:				
Loans (over 1 year)	24	. . .	24	
Subsidiaries	127	7	120	
Deposits	9	. . .	9	
				153
Inventories:				
Raw materials and packing	148	. . .	148	
Parts	1,239	. . .	1,239	
Finished goods	963	. . .	963	
Work in process	898	. . .	898	
				3,248
Quick assets:				
Due from others:				
Accounts receivable on "open-book" credit	2,406	40	2,366	
Advances to suppliers	40	. . .	40	
Loans to employees	26	. . .	26	
Tax refund	126	. . .	126	
Prepaid items	30	. . .	30	
Financial assets:				
Time drafts	390	. . .	390	
Bonds	1	. . .	1	
Bank and post deposits	271	. . .	271	
Cash on hand	3	. . .	3	
				3,253
				8,819

wing, M. Chambertin and Mme Bollinger (the head of the Statistical Department) answered that no exact estimates had been made, but they guessed that with the new floor space, Galvor's ultimate capacity would be 18 million NF per year (net of sales tax). This represented a 50 per cent increase over the 1961 sales volume of 12 million NF.

EQUIPMENT

Galvor's balance sheet separated equipment into three categories: (1) "equipment" (which meant equipment used in production and in research), (2) transportation equipment, and (3) furniture and fixtures. The production equipment was shown on the books at a gross value of 754,000 NF, with a depreciation reserve of 586,000 NF, giving it a net value of 168,000 NF. Late in 1961, however, company officials appraised the real value of this equipment at approximately 675,000 NF (466,000 NF for machine tools and 209,000 NF for scientific instruments used in testing and research). M. Chambertin estimated that approximately 500,000 NF's worth of equipment would eventually have to be purchased to equip the new wing under construction.

PATENTS AND TRADEMARKS

The net value of patents and trademarks shown on the balance sheet was 21,000 NF. Inasmuch as Galvor had spent 645,000 NF on research and development during 1961 alone, it is obvious that the value of patents and trademarks exceeded their book value.

OTHER FIXED ASSETS

LOANS (over One Year)

The 24,000 NF loan shown under this heading was to the building subsidiary which owned housing for Galvor employees and which is described below.

SUBSIDIARIES

The subsidiaries owned by Galvor were Indica, S.A., a Parisian corporation engaged in manufacturing dials and faces for measurement and indicating instruments, and the building subsidiary created to hold title to housing for Galvor employees.

Galvor purchased full ownership of Indica, S.A., in 1955, when the latter firm was in bankruptcy. Galvor had been buying meter faces from Indica, and M. Latour felt that it could be put on a profitable basis. The reason for Indica's bankruptcy was that the owner had been indulging in personal eccentricities, such as buying old warships. The trustee of the bankrupt firm did not think it could be revived, but M. Latour offered to take it over, and Galvor purchased the firm's assets for 60,000 NF. In a few months, Indica was showing a profit, and since that time Galvor owned Indica outright. Indica had not been consolidated or merged with

Galvor, because many of its customers were competitors of Galvor, and these customers were not aware of the fact that Galvor owned Indica. In 1955, Indica's sales (net of sales taxes) were 388,000 NF; during the year ending March 31, 1961, its sales were 1,568,000 NF; during the first nine months of the 1961–62 year, sales were going at a pace approximately 30 per cent ahead of the previous year. For the year ending March 31, 1961, Indica's net profits after taxes were 95,840 NF; M. Chambertin estimated that, for the current year, Indica's profits would be about 130,000 NF after taxes. On March 31, 1961, Indica's total assets were 814,566 NF. It had approximately 50 employees, including a manager sent there by Galvor, two of the prior owner's sons, and one of his nephews. Indica used a rented building which was rather old, and M. Chambertin stated that in the near future it would need new quarters. For this reason, Indica's profits were being left in the firm to build up a fund which might then be used to purchase new quarters. M. Chambertin pointed out that, although Galvor carried Indica on its books at 60,000 NF, the book value of the equity in Indica's books was close to 300,000 NF.

Galvor's other subsidiary was a company which owned apartments to be leased to employees. Under French law, all firms having over ten employees must take 1 per cent of salaries paid and use this money to build housing. The obvious purpose of this law is to encourage the building of lodgings, which are in short supply in France. A company has two choices as to how it will spend this money. It can either make an outright grant of this amount to a legally acceptable firm which is building housing, and in this case the firm can deduct this as a business expense for tax purposes; or the firm can take this 1 per cent and invest it in the ownership of apartments or houses to be leased to employees. This latter alternative does not allow the firm to deduct this investment in housing as a tax-deductible expense, but a special tax regulation exempts the firm from paying any taxes on the income received from such property for a period of 25 years. The reason for forming a separate building subsidiary was that Indica was subject to the same regulation as Galvor, but it was too small to purchase apartments on its own, inasmuch as 1 per cent of its salaries would not have gone very far in that direction. Therefore, the building subsidiary was formed to take contributions from both Galvor and Indica, and at the end of 1961 it owned two apartments in Paris and four in Bordeaux (where Galvor is located). In addition, Galvor itself directly owned three apartments and one house in Bordeaux. Galvor thus, either directly or indirectly, owned ten lodgings which it rented to its employees.

INVENTORIES

At the end of 1961, inventories accounted for approximately 37 per cent of the total book value of Galvor's assets. M. Chambertin estimated that approximately 15,000 different items were kept in inventory, many of them very small parts. M. Chambertin was concerned about the level of inventories. He felt that in some cases the manufacture and sale of products which had a very low sales volume required the maintenance of a stock of parts out of proportion to the sales value of these products.

Of total 1961 purchases, 8 per cent of the New Franc volume was for raw materials, 87 per cent for partially or wholly finished parts, and 5 per cent for products for resale (e.g., leather carrying cases). The way in which purchases were made was as follows: Every two months, the Statistical Department prepared a production schedule for a two-month period starting eight months later. On the basis of this production schedule, purchase orders were issued for the necessary parts and materials, and four months before the beginning of this production a check was made to make sure that no changes were necessary. No studies of economic ordering quantities or minimum base inventory amounts had been made, but M. Chambertin stated that such studies were to be made in the future.

The inventory figures on the balance sheet were broken down into four categories: (1) raw materials and packing, (2) parts, (3) finished goods, and (4) work in process. Quantities were established by physical count at the end of the year. For raw materials and packing and for parts, the price per unit was established by looking over recent invoices to see what the average recent price was, and this figure was used to price the unit amounts. Purchasing and transportation expenses were not included in the price of the inventory—these were written off as operating expenses. The value of finished goods was established by adding the cost of materials and parts, plus 7.92 NF per hour of direct labor to cover both the direct labor and manufacturing overhead (in 1961). This overhead did not include administrative expenses or research costs; as in the pricing of raw materials and parts, no allowance was made for purchasing or transportation expenses. Work-in-process inventory was priced in the same manner as finished goods, except that the direct labor content was estimated on the basis of judgment of those making the count.

QUICK ASSETS

ACCOUNTS RECEIVABLE ON "OPEN-BOOK" CREDIT

It was customary for Galvor's customers to state what credit terms they would like when they first began buying from Galvor, and Galvor could either accept these terms or insist on different terms. Generally, these terms extended from 30 to 90 days. Galvor did not, as a rule, grant cash discounts, although on some occasions very large customers would insist on one; in this case, Galvor might grant a 2 or 3 per cent cash discount if these very large customers paid within a week. Export sales made through Comor, S.A., were paid by Comor itself directly to Galvor, and it received a 3 per cent cash discount for payment within 15 days.

Credit information on new customers was obtained from Galvor's agents or Galvor's bank. This information was not detailed, but it was enough to establish a credit limit for the new customer until collection experience had been accumulated. If the customer had not paid by the end of his credit term, he was sometimes given extra time to pay, but when Galvor decided that enough time had passed, a series of three letters was sent to the delinquent debtor. Each letter was in stronger terms than the prior one, and if the customer still had not paid within a week or two of the third letter, Galvor usually took advantage of a law passed in France in 1953. Under this law, Galvor filled out a form stating the customer's name, the amount owed, and other pertinent information, and this was forwarded to a judge in the customer's district. The judge would sign the form and send it to the customer, who had 15 days to reply. If the customer had not replied within 15 days, judgment was automatically entered in Galvor's favor, and Galvor could then foreclose on the debtor. Total bad debts during 1960 amounted to 19,000 NF. Table 2 is an aging schedule of Galvor's accounts receivable as of September 30, 1961.

Although many customers owed Galvor on "open-book" credit, many deliveries of Galvor's products were accompanied by a time draft ("trade acceptance") which the customer signed upon receipt of the goods. At maturity, Galvor merely had to present the draft to the customer's bank to collect the money it was owed. M. Chambertin estimated that approximately one-half of Galvor's customers accepted drafts as opposed to using "open-book" credit.

A different type of credit arrangement was available for radio repair shops. Shop owners who wished to purchase equipment but could not pay for it under normal terms were granted credit for 6, 9, or 12 months. A 20 per cent down payment was required, with monthly payments for the balance. The credit charges for such arrangements were as follows:

6 months.................3.5% of original amount owed
9 months.................5.0% of original amount owed
12 months................6.5% of original amount owed

This type of sale was not based on a conditional sales contract, which has no legal validity in France; if the debtor did not make his payments,

Table 2

AGING SCHEDULE OF ACCOUNTS RECEIVABLE
AS OF SEPT. 30, 1961

	NF
Owed by French government	505,839
Owed by schools	232,366
Exports—COMOR, S.A.	78,312
Other exports	235,507
Owed by TRONEX	31,942
Time drafts in process	112,028
Other accounts receivable:	
September, 1961	508,678
August	86,601
July	76,526
June	144,617
May	9,385
April	1,524
March	76
February	1,670
January	92
December, 1960	1,466
November	15
October	100
Over one year	4,097
In court	7,938
Bankrupt	40,413
Total	2,079,192

Galvor did not have a legal right to repossess the equipment (although in some cases this could be done). The decision whether or not to grant such credit had, in the past, been made by Galvor salesmen, but this had led to some collection difficulties. Recently, Galvor had changed to a new system under which the salesmen could no longer make the decision on the spot, but had to refer it to the head office first.

LOANS TO EMPLOYEES

As a service to its employees, Galvor made loans for the purpose of financing the construction of houses until the time when a mortgage could be obtained. Such construction loans usually amounted to around 5,000 NF to any one employee, and no interest was charged by Galvor.

TAX REFUND

Galvor had to charge the French sales tax on its own sales, and similarly it had to pay this tax on its purchases. Since sales tax is levied only once on the finished article, Galvor was entitled to a refund of sales taxes it paid to its suppliers, but this refund came one month later. For this reason, it was shown on the asset side of the balance sheet.

TIME DRAFTS

As mentioned above, many of Galvor's customers accepted time drafts upon receipt of goods. At their maturity, these drafts could be presented to the customer's bank for payment by way of Bertrand et Cie., Galvor's principal bank. Alternatively, if Galvor needed funds, these drafts could be discounted with the Banque Bertrand. In other words, Galvor could sell these time drafts to its bank before their maturity; this is the French method of borrowing on or against accounts receivable and is actually very convenient. The rate charged by the bank for this service was 3½ per cent per annum on the amount discounted (for the period until maturity), plus a 1 per cent service charge per annum on the same basis, for a total of 4½ per cent per annum. In addition, there were a number of service charges which were the same whether Galvor discounted the draft or whether it gave it to the Banque Bertrand to be presented for payment to the customer's bank at maturity. M. Chambertin estimated that, on the average, Galvor discouned 500,000 NF's worth of time drafts a month; during 1961, a total of 5,580,000 NF's worth was discounted. He also estimated that the average remaining time until maturity on these drafts was about 45 days.

*   *   *   *   *

The liability side of Galvor's balance sheet is shown in Table 3.

CAPITAL AND RESERVES

RESERVES REQUIRED BY LAW

Under French law, every société anonyme is required to take 5 per cent of its net annual profits to a statutory reserve until that account reaches 10 per cent of the authorized share capital. When this has been reached, no further appropriations to the legal reserve are required until there is an increase in capital.

SPECIAL REVALUATION RESERVE

French companies were allowed in the past by the fiscal authorities to revalue fixed assets in accordance with government-decreed indices. This revaluation was achieved by multiplying the original cost of the asset by the index appropriate for the year of its acquisition, and multiplying the actual depreciation used in each year by the index for that particular year. For example, in 1960 the treatment of an asset purchased in 1956 for 1,000 NF and depreciated on a five-year straight-line basis would have

Table 3

LIABILITY SIDE OF GALVOR'S BALANCE SHEET, DECEMBER 31, 1961
(In 000's of NF)

		Subtotals
Capital and reserves:		
Common stock par value	2,500	
Reserves required by law	196	
Retained earnings	1,852	
Special revaluation reserve	164	
Inventory revaluation reserve	85	
		4,797
Intermediate-term debt:		
Mortgages on housing	57	
Bank term loan	90	
		147
Short-term debts:		
Bank loan on exports	75	
Accounts payable, suppliers	1,110	
Accrued wages and commissions	140	
Accrued taxes	1,031	
Welfare contributions	131	
Owed to customers	54	
Other accounts payable	16	
Other accruals	192	
		2,749
Provision for price increases:		
Allowance for 1961		64
Net profits after taxes, 1961		1,062
Total		8,819

been as shown in the accompanying table. Thus, in the example given, the asset's net book value would have been increased from 200 to 370 NF. The net increase on the asset side was balanced by an entry on the liability side called the "special revaluation reserve." Such revaluation of assets allowed Galvor greater depreciation allowances for the future (e.g., 170 NF more in the example given) and thus reduced income taxes.

Year	Revaluation Index	Cost	Actual Depreciation	Revalued Cost	Revalued Depreciation
1956	1.25	1,000	200	1,250	240
1957	1.15		200		230
1958	1.05		200		210
1959	1.00		200		200
		1,000	800	1,250	880
Net		200		370	

INVENTORY REVALUATION RESERVE

Under a law no longer in existence, Galvor had been allowed to re-value its inventory and set up a reserve of 85,000 NF, as shown on the liability side. A new law passed in 1960 changed the system and is described below.

INTERMEDIATE-TERM DEBT

MORTGAGES ON HOUSING

This entry on the balance sheet reflects mortgages on the houses Galvor owned directly.

BANK TERM LOAN

Galvor borrowed 250,000 NF from the Banque Bertrand at the end of 1959. This amount was used to finance half of the cost of acquiring the new Paris sales office. The loan was a three-year term loan, unsecured, with an interest rate of 7 per cent. Eighty thousand New Francs were repaid at the end of 1960, 80,000 NF were repaid at the end of 1961, and the final 90,000 NF repayment was scheduled for the end of 1962.

On February 23, 1962, Galvor was granted another term loan, which was not shown on its December 31, 1961, balance sheet. This new loan from the Banque Bertrand was for 600,000 NF and was for the purpose of financing part of the cost of construction of the new wing on the factory. The interest rate on this loan was 6 per cent per annum. Galvor paid a commitment fee of 1.25 per cent whether it borrowed the money or not, and when it did borrow, it paid an additional 4.75 per cent on the amount borrowed, bringing the total to 6 per cent. This loan had a three-year maturity, but at least 200,000 NF had to be repaid during the first two years, so that the loan would not exceed 400,000 NF by February 23, 1964, and would be completely repaid by February 23, 1965. Galvor had originally requested a loan of 900,000 NF but was quite happy with the 600,000 NF loan. The national credit policy of France was to discourage term loans to companies which had adequate internal funds for expansion, and, since Galvor had always been in this category, it had always had difficulty in obtaining term loans.

SHORT-TERM DEBTS

BANK LOAN ON EXPORTS

Galvor was allowed to borrow from the Banque Française du Commerce Extérieur up to 350,000 NF. Such loans were unsecured and carried a 4 per cent interest rate per year; the only requirement was that Galvor show that, on the average, its accounts receivable on export sales were approximately equal to the loan. Such loans were very advantageous for Galvor, and 75,000 NF of the available amount were being used at the end of 1961. The reason for such a low interest rate on an unsecured loan was that the B.F.C.E. is a government-owned bank whose purpose is to encourage the export of French goods.

ACCOUNTS PAYABLE, SUPPLIERS

In the same way as Galvor's customers normally stated the credit terms which they expected, Galvor told its suppliers that it would pay 60 days from the end of the month during which the purchase was made, on the 15th. In other words, if a purchase was made on April 10, the 60 days would start from the end of April and run to July 1; payment would be made only on July 15. Effectively, although Galvor's terms included the words "60 days," this meant that Galvor, on the average, had 90 days in which to pay its accounts payable. When suppliers requested that Galvor sign drafts, Galvor did this willingly. On the other hand, Galvor had obtained from many of its suppliers the privilege of paying cash and obtaining a cash discount of 2 or 3 per cent; 45 per cent of Galvor's purchases were paid for in this manner. M. Chambertin stated that Galvor's time drafts, which could be discounted at a bank, were more advantageous for suppliers than cash payment with a discount, and new suppliers were unwilling to give the cash discount. Those suppliers who did give a cash discount were those who had been giving it for years and had started this practice at a time when they were glad to get Galvor's business and its money.

PROVISION FOR PRICE INCREASES

ALLOWANCE FOR 1961

Reference has been made above to revaluation reserves on property and inventories prior to 1961. Both of the latter revaluation policies were discontinued by the French government in 1961, and in their stead a new law was passed. The new law applied only to inventories and worked as follows: At the end of 1961, the difference between the current price of an item in inventory and the sum of its 1959 (end of year) price plus 10 per cent was calculated. This difference was multiplied by the number of units of the item in stock at the end of 1961. The total amount thus obtained was deducted from profits before the calculation of income taxes; it was then segregated on the liability side of the balance sheet. Six years later (i.e., in 1967), this amount was to be taxed at the prevailing rates. This new system was a permanent one which would be used every year. Effectively, it amounted to a six-year postponement of taxes on part of the company's annual inventory profit.

NET PROFITS AFTER TAXES, 1961

As is customary in many European countries, French balance sheets showed the current year's profits separate from capital and reserves.

*   *   *   *   *

Exhibit 1

PROFIT AND LOSS STATEMENT, 1961
(in 000's of NF)

Sales:

Apparatus sold in France	12,172	
Export sales (incl. Franc Zone) of apparatus	1,912	
Repairs—France	260	
Repairs—export (incl. Franc Zone)	21	
Services billed to TRONEX (subsidiary)	24	
	14,389	
Minus sales tax	2,359	
Net Sales	12,030	100.0%
Cost of goods sold	7,074	58.8%
Gross margin	4,956	41.2%
Research and development	645 (5.4%)	
Sales expenses	1,421 (11.8%)	
Administration expenses	645 (5.4%)	
Income taxes and miscellaneous*	1,184 (9.8%)	
	3,890	32.4%
Net Profit After Taxes	1,062	8.8%

* Income taxes accounted for 1,031 of the total.

Exhibit 1 shows the 1961 profit and loss statement for the Galvor Company, and Exhibit 2 shows the calculations used to arrive at the cost of goods sold. Exhibit 3 gives comparative profit and loss data for the years 1950 through 1961, and Exhibit 4 gives comparative balance-sheet data for selected years during the same period. Exhibit 5 gives selected profit and loss and balance-sheet figures adjusted for price changes during the 1950–61 period, plus selected ratios.

*   *   *   *   *

Two aspects of Galvor's financial policy deserve special mention. First of all, M. Latour owned 97 per cent of the common stock of Galvor, and

Exhibit 2

DETERMINATION OF COST OF GOODS SOLD, 1961
(in 000's of NF)

	Raw Materials	Parts	Apparatus in Process	Finished Goods
Inventories, Jan. 1, 1961...........	141	936	954	661
Purchases	331	3,638	—	344
Costs of purchasing	16	179	—	17
	488	4,753	954	1,022
Inventories, Dec. 31, 1961..........	147	1,239	898	962
Inventories used	340	3,514	56	60
Direct labor	313		810	
Work subcontracted	52			
Overhead	538		1,391	
	1,243			
	→	1,243		
		4,757		
		→	4,757	
			7,014	
			→	7,014
		Cost of goods sold, 1961		7,074

the remaining 3 per cent was owned by M. Romanée, the Production Manager, who had been with M. Latour for many years. Although many people had expressed a desire to purchase equity in Galvor, M. Latour firmly declared that under no circumstances would he sell stock to get new capital for the firm, nor would he sell any of his own stock. He felt that complete control of the enterprise was necessary to continue his dynamic policies without outside interference. Actually, M. Latour's stock was held jointly by him and his wife, inasmuch as they had a community property marriage. M. and Mme Latour had three daughters, to whom the stock was willed. French estate taxes were considerably lower when the inheritance went to direct heirs as opposed to nonrelated heirs. For this reason, the inheritance tax on M. Latour's share of the stock was estimated to be about 250,000 NF as of 1961, with the same tax on Mme Latour's share. The problem of paying inheritance taxes in case of their deaths had been taken care of by means of life insurance policies.

M. Latour was equally set against selling long-term bonds, as he felt that the owners of such securities might try to influence his management of the firm. Galvor's sources of capital funds were therefore restricted to retained earnings, depreciation funds, bank loans, and short-term obliga-

Exhibit 3

COMPARATIVE PROFIT AND LOSS DATA, 1950–61
(in 000's of NF)

	1950	1951	1952	1953	1954	1955	1956	1957	1958	1959	1960	1961
Sales and repairs:												
Domestic	1,020	1,257	1,350	2,510	3,010	3,629	3,698	6,458	6,379	9,084	10,201	13,456
Export	437	611	442	486		707	1,224	1,067	1,013	1,890	1,760	1,933
Less sales tax	148	199	223	412	391	530	688	1,025	1,195	1,580	1,916	2,359
Net sales	1,309	1,669	1,569	2,584	2,619	3,206	4,234	5,600	6,197	8,404	10,045	12,030
Cost of goods sold	934	1,144	1,007	1,496	1,632	2,010	2,678	3,497	3,835	4,861	5,952	7,074
Gross profit	375	525	561	1,088	987	1,196	1,556	2,103	2,362	3,543	4,093	4,956
LESS:												
Research and development*	....	....	....	....	....	....	....	....	....	552	561	645
Sales expenses	129	147	184	257	288	392	491	708	727	1,040	1,205	1,421
Administration expenses	138	190	193	197	186	223	262	332	520	489	573	645
Income tax and other expenses	37	62	63	200	216	227	378	543	630	796	978	1,184
Net profits after taxes	71	126	122	434	297	354	425	520	485	666	776	1,062

* Included with "Administration Expenses" until 1959.

Exhibit 4

COMPARATIVE BALANCE SHEETS
(in 000's of NF)

	1950	1953	1956	1959	1960	1961
Assets:						
Land.....................	....	....	105	105	265	265
Buildings................	154	299	408	1,078	1,792	1,849
Minus depreciation......	15	53	111	256	358	430
Net buildings............	139	246	297	822	1,434	1,419
Equipment...............	179	359	512	1,024	1,312	1,438
Minus depreciation......	67	216	375	679	850	978
Net equipment...........	112	143	137	345	462	460
Other net fixed assets*......	8	7	239	581	166	185
Inventories...............	132	349	891	2,378	2,692	3,248
Net accounts receivable and drafts..............	265	564	1,052	1,737	2,130	2,746
Miscellaneous current assets..	13	46	150	106	114	223
Cash....................	40	380	312	249	279	274
Total................	709	1,735	3,183	6,323	7,542	8,820
Liabilities and net worth:						
Capital Stock.............	70	500	1,000	2,500	2,500	2,500
Reserves & retained earnings.	182	661	1,213	1,408	2,305	3,425
Total net worth........	252	1,161	2,213	3,908	4,805	5,925
Intermediate—term debt.....	83	40	10	270	190	147
Accounts payable...........	152	169	315	897	1,006	1,110
Accrued taxes.............	115	365	357	742	717	1,031
Other current liabilities†.....	107		288	506	824	607
Total................	709	1,735	3,183	6,323	7,542	8,820

* Includes net patents and trademarks, loans, subsidiaries, and deposits.
† Includes customer advances, welfare, and accruals.

tions. Galvor had never paid a dividend, and M. Latour had no intention of changing this policy.

The other area which deserves special mention is Galvor's capital budgeting policy—or perhaps the lack of such a policy. M. Latour made all decisions on new capital investments himself. His approach to such investments was pragmatic. Essentially, new capital investments were made only when they were obviously necessary. As a result of its rapid growth, Galvor had never lacked needed capital expenditures to absorb all of the available funds easily. As an illustration of this policy, the decision to expand the factory (made in 1961) was forced upon Galvor because all space was already in use, and it was obvious that greater sales could be achieved if production facilities were increased. Only rough estimates of the cost of expanding were made: the architect provided an estimate of the cost of the building; the amount to be invested in equipment was estimated without detailed calculations; no forecasts of addi-

Exhibit 5

SELECTED FIGURES ADJUSTED FOR PRICE CHANGES AND SELECTED RATIOS, 1950–61

Year	Price Index*	Sales in 000's of 1961 NF (Adjusted)	Profits in 000's of 1961 NF (Adjusted)	Total Assets in 000's of 1961 NF (Adjusted)	Equity As Per Cent of Long Term Capital	Equity As Per Cent of Total Assets	Profits As Per Cent of Equity (End of Year)	Profits As Per Cent of Sales (Net of Taxes)	Gross Margin as Per Cent of Sales (Net of Taxes)
1950	78	2,210	120	1,200	75	36	28	5.4	29
1951	100	2,203	166	1,362	89	57	22	7.6	31
1952	105	1,969	153	1,595	93	58	17	7.8	36
1953	100	3,420	574	2,290	97	67	37	16.8	42
1954	98	3,530	400	2,594	98	75	21	11.3	38
1955	98	4,180	477	3,431	99	70	20	11.4	37
1956	102	5,485	550	4,122	99	70	19	10.0	37
1957	108	6,835	635	4,753	100	70	19	9.3	37
1958	121	6,760	529	5,291	100	66	15	7.8	38
1959	126	8,820	699	6,628	94	62	17	7.9	42
1960	130	10,200	787	7,654	96	64	16	7.7	41
1961	132	12,031	1,062	8,819	98	67	18	8.8	41

* French Price Index computed by the International Monetary Fund and published in IMF's *International Financial Statistics*.
† Net of sales tax.

tional working capital needed were made; and it was assumed that working capital would be required in the same proportion to sales as before. As another illustration of this policy, Galvor decided to manufacture a new product (resistors) in 1962 which it had never produced before, but no forecasts of estimated profitability were made in arriving at this decision.

Although detailed sales forecasts were made for each coming year, no cash budget was prepared, nor were detailed projected balance sheets and profit and loss statements prepared.

THE GALVOR COMPANY (E)
The Galvor Inventory-Control System

"I am not happy with our present inventories, especially of raw materials and purchased parts," said M. Latour in commenting on Galvor's current stock levels early in 1962. "Whenever I ask why our stock of a given item is so high, I get a wonderful explanation. But this fact remains: I would like to have two months' supply of purchases on hand, not what we now have. One of these days I am going to fix this inventory problem, and I'll tell you how: I'll hire a strong man, give him a pistol, and set him on our receiving platform. He'll be told how much we have on hand of every item, and when a supplier tries to deliver more than we need (a two months' supply), he'll refuse the excess."

M. Chambertin stated: "I disagree with M. Latour. We don't need a man with a pistol, we need a man with a machine gun, because there are so many different problem areas in our inventory control system."

THE NATURE OF GALVOR INVENTORIES

Galvor's purchases were in three major categories: (1) wholly finished components, such as electronic tubes, to be mounted directly in the instruments; (2) partially finished products which would undergo further manufacturing operations at Galvor; and (3) raw materials, such as sheet metal, where all manufacturing operations were done by the company. In 1961, of Galvor's total purchases from outside suppliers, 8 per cent were raw materials, 87 per cent were partially and wholly finished products (mostly components), and 5 per cent were products to be resold directly to Galvor customers, such as leather carrying cases for multimeters. These percentages had not, company officials stated, changed much in recent years.

About 15,000 different parts were used in making the products in the Galvor line; some 10,000 of these were purchased in a partially or wholly finished condition. The typical Galvor electric product, such as a multimeter, contained 2–3 times as much purchase content as direct labor content, while the typical electronic product contained 3–5 times as much

---

This case was prepared by Professor Rufus Wixon and Mr. Robert C. K. Valtz.

Copyright 1962 by l'Institut pour l'Etude des Méthodes de Direction de l'Entreprise (IMEDE), Lausanne, Switzerland. Reprinted by permission.

purchase content as direct labor. This was due to the fact that most electronic products contained a considerable number of relatively complicated and expensive components, such as electronic tubes and transistors, while electric products generally contained few sophisticated components. In 1961, purchased parts accounted for almost 50 per cent of total manufacturing cost, and raw materials accounted for an additional 5 per cent.[1]

Table 1 shows the size of Galvor inventories in recent years as a percentage of net sales.

Table 1

GALVOR INVENTORIES AT YEAR END AS A PER CENT OF NET SALES

Year	Raw Materials and Purchased Parts	Work in Process	Finished Products	Total
1956	13.3	4.3	3.4	21.0
1957	9.5	3.8	4.1	17.4
1958	12.0	8.5	7.3	27.8
1959	15.4	9.2	4.2	28.8
1960	10.7	9.5	6.6	26.8
1961	11.5	7.5	8.0	27.0

Computed from company records by IMEDE staff.

Table 2 gives the percentage relationship of these same three inventory categories to total assets since 1956.

Table 2

GALVOR INVENTORIES AT YEAR END AS A PER CENT OF TOTAL ASSETS

Year	Raw Materials and Purchased Parts	Work in Process	Finished Products	Total
1956	17.6	5.7	4.5	27.8
1957	13.7	5.5	5.9	25.1
1958	15.3	10.8	9.3	35.4
1959	20.5	12.2	5.6	38.3
1960	14.2	12.6	8.8	35.6
1961	15.8	10.3	11.0	37.1

Computed from company records by IMEDE staff.

PRICING OF INVENTORIES

Galvor's inventory of purchased materials and parts was priced annually when the physical inventory was taken. (This inventory was taken soon after the close of Galvor's fiscal year on December 31st.) The

---

[1] Computed from figures in Table 7 of "The Galvor Company (A)."

price of a given item was set by estimating what the recent price of the part had been and what it was likely to be in the near future. The cost of freight was not added into this price. For example, if a given tube had recently been purchased for about 5 NF per piece and if it appeared that the price would remain there for some time to come, the price was set at 5 NF in valuing the inventory of this tube.

The pricing of the work-in-process inventory proceeded by adding together, for a given instrument, the total purchased parts actually installed in the instrument (without purchasing cost), plus an allowance of 7.92 NF per estimated hour of direct labor to cover direct labor cost and overhead charges.

Finished instruments were priced in a manner similar to that for work-in-process, the only difference being that, for a finished product, the exact direct labor hours were known. Thus a finished product was priced at the cost of the purchases it contained, plus 7.92 NF per hour of direct labor. Purchasing cost was not included in the calculation.

As can be seen from an analysis of Galvor's true product costs, the method of pricing work-in-process and finished goods made insufficient allowance for the total overhead costs applicable to each product. The inventory pricing method allowed 7.92 NF for each hour of direct labor. Since the average hourly direct labor cost was, company officials estimated, about 3 NF, this left about 5 NF per direct labor hour to cover all overhead, or 100 per cent of direct labor cost. Galvor officials estimated that true overhead was something in excess of 310 per cent of direct labor charges.

INVENTORY TURNOVER

In 1961 Galvor used, in order to make the products which it sold, about 3,660,000 NF worth of purchased materials and parts. (This figure does not contain purchasing expense.) At the end of that year, the company valued its inventory of such materials at about 1,387,000 NF (again not including purchasing expense). Assuming, as company officials said was correct, that both parts used and the parts valued in inventory were costed on the same bases, it can be seen that in 1961 the company turned over its inventory of purchases approximately 2.64 times (the result of dividing 3,660,000 by 1,387,000). In other terms, the company was maintaining, at the end of 1961, approximately a 4½ months' supply of such materials.

In the same year, the company's total factory cost, or cost of goods sold, was about 7,074,000 NF. The finished-goods inventory on hand at the end of the year was valued at 963,000 NF. This inventory was turned over 7.35 times in 1961 (7,074,000 divided by 963,000). It follows that, in 1961, the inventory at year's end represented about 1.6 months' cost of goods sold.

INVENTORY-CONTROL PROCEDURE FOR PURCHASED MATERIALS AND PARTS

Two systems of inventory control were employed by Galvor for purchased materials and parts. If a given item was used for only one product, its inventory was controlled by the "Program" system. If it was used in more than one product, it was controlled by the "Mini" system. Of total 1961 purchases, 72 per cent were made under the Program system and 28 per cent under the Mini system.

The *Program System* was based on the production schedule prepared by Mme. Bollinger for a two-month period beginning eight months hence. Upon receipt of this schedule by M. Gevrey (Assistant to M. Romanée for Production Scheduling), he and his clerks drew up a list of the parts which would have to be purchased to fulfill the program's requirements. Some of these parts would be needed not only for the planned manufacturing but also for making repairs and for sale as spare parts. Accordingly, the stock of a given part under the Program system was determined not only by the production schedule's requirements, but also by an estimate made by the appropriate inventory clerk of the extra parts which would be required to cover repairs and sales of spare parts. These latter two needs were determined largely on the basis of past experience.

Under the *Mini System,* the stock of a part was set at a four months' supply. This period was based on an allowance of three months to cover the time from placing an order until delivery, plus a one-month safety margin. All parts controlled under this system used the same four months' minimum stock level, except for a very few where lead time was known to be significantly longer than three months; in these few cases, a larger minimum stock was maintained.

THE REORDER POINT

The two inventory-control systems described above determined the reorder points. For those stocks controlled by the Program system, materials and parts were ordered as needed every two months. For parts controlled by the Mini system, pieces were reordered when the supply was down to the minimum four months' level. In practice, according to M. Chambertin, nearly all parts were ordered about every two months, regardless of the system of control used. No formal study had been made of the order frequency for individual parts.

The company's programs did not vary significantly with the value of the item stocked. While lead times for ordering might vary from four weeks to six months, as far as was known there was no relationship between the item's value and the lead time necessary for ordering and receipt. Some complicated and expensive parts, which were manufactured outside to special order, might have higher lead times, on the average, than other parts. Purchases from suppliers were never on a contractual basis but were made by individual orders. The cost range for various parts ranged from about 0.001 NF to a realistic maximum of about 20 NF. A few parts might cost as much as 100 NF or so. Cost of the part played no role in its treatment. No data existed on the cost of carrying various items in inventory. In this connection, M. Chambertin stated: "Because we have had for many years plenty of ready cash, with no particularly good alternative use for it, this cost has not seemed important to us. We are usually not borrowing and paying interest, so it's not worth figuring out."

Virtually no parts were individually analyzed, although up-to-date inventory records were kept for every part. M. Chambertin remarked that standardized parts could be much more widely used in Galvor products than was being done. Mme. Bollinger commented: "The two steps we could take which would most cut down our inventory are: increased standardization, and individual minimum stock levels for Mini-controlled items."

M. Romanée remarked that, in general, there were sufficient stocks on hand to insure a stead manufacturing operation. He continued: "As long as we will ultimately be able to use it, it's no terrible handicap or error to keep a part in stock for six months, especially if lack of a certain part can delay finishing a very valuable product for delivery. But our engineers are modifying products so continually, and changing the necessary parts as they go along, that we end up with lots of pieces which we'll never use. The storeroom is full of such pieces—God only knows how many."

STOREROOM FACILITIES AND PROCEDURES

Separate storerooms existed for finished instruments and for purchased materials and parts. Both storerooms were kept under lock and key. The man in charge of the parts and raw-materials storeroom, a foreman, was, according to M. Chambertin, "Pretty good—he knows all about every product we make and the parts required, but since he has nothing to do with ordering, he has not the responsibility and importance often enjoyed by his counterpart in other firms. He is not brilliant, but he works 65 hours a week, and he knows exactly where every part is and how many of each we have in stock—he'd be a difficult man to replace, almost impossible.

"One problem we have is that sometimes parts are taken out of stock to make repairs or to sell as spare parts, when we have only enough on hand for manufacturing requirements. When this happens, we are out of luck; we may not be able to finish our production run of an important product until a new supply comes in. To avoid this eventuality, the ordering clerks load us up on parts to make sure we won't run out, and inventory goes up way too much."

Parts and materials were issued from the storeroom only upon receipt of a ticket, which the appropriate workman and his foreman both initialed. This ticket listed the code number of the piece being requisitioned, the units needed, the purpose of these pieces (i.e., for a given production run, or for repairs, or for sale as spare parts), and the date. The storeroom accumulated throughout the day all of these tickets, and the next morning the tickets were taken to the inventory records rooms and used to adjust the stock cards for the appropriate pieces.

MAINTENANCE OF INVENTORY RECORDS

The inventory records for all purchased parts and materials were kept in files in a special room set aside for the purpose. Each item had its own stock card; the cards were coded in different colors to distinguish between various categories of materials.

The card, when properly used, showed how many units were on hand, how many of these units were necessary for each of the production schedules which had been processed, how many units were on order, how many of the units on hand were available for resale or making repairs, and if appropriate, the reorder point (in number of units) for those items controlled by the Mini system. Every time pieces were put into inventory (through receipt of an order) or taken out (through requisition from the storeroom), the card was updated, so that at all times it theoretically showed the company's exact stock and the availability of this stock for different purposes.

CAUSES CITED FOR EXCESS INVENTORY

Only recently had Galvor officials become concerned with the problem of inventory control. In commenting on the problem, M. Chambertin stated, "I am not convinced that M. Latour fully understands the dimensions of our inventory problem. He thinks that it is a simple thing, that it has only one cause. The other day I took a walk in the woods, and I came up with 17 reasons why we have too much inventory. When I showed this list to Romanée, he added another cause, and Mme. Bollinger added eight more. I have just prepared a memorandum which discusses the problem and gives these 26 causes." Mr. Chambertin's memorandum is reproduced below.

MEMORANDUM ON INVENTORIES

I. INTRODUCTION

We must not underestimate the long-term problems which can arise from having our cash tied up in inventories of all types. We can measure the extent of this problem by noting that from Jan. 1, 1960, to Dec. 31, 1961, we had within 10% as much money tied up in inventories as we spent in erecting the new factory addition. This has created some problems in our cash budgeting for 1962, since aside from our investment in the new plant (only 60% of which was covered by outside credit), we have needed funds to pay for an apparently irreversible increase in our inventories.

The rise in our inventories is almost exactly parallel to our sales increase, and as a result we must note that it would be difficult to increase sales if our inventories did not rise at the same rate. All the same, even if we accept this relationship between sales and stocks, we should be certain that the inventory curve, no matter how exactly it follows sales, does not start from a bad base point—this error, if made, would be difficult to correct. Thus, we ought to do at least a summary analysis of our inventory position.

Based on our balance sheet as of Dec. 31, 1961, we have on hand a 1.5 months' supply of finished instruments, about 1.5 to 2 months' worth in process, and 4 months' supply of purchased materials. We must remember that these are only overall figures, and that we can easily have, in finished goods, no stock at all of some items and be vastly over-stocked in others. Accordingly, one can easily make a commercial error in holding back deliveries and uselessly tying up for months capital which could be better used in productive investments.

On this last point, we can make four important observations:

—The growth of the company is the fruit of its investments in physical plant and research.
—Management's most difficult problem is in choosing the proper investments.
—Return on investment ought not to be below 20% (or, at worst, 15%).
—According to most experts, the cost of carrying inventory is 1% per month, or 12% per year.

Which four observations lead to the conclusion that:

—1,000,000 NF invested in inventories has a value, one year later, of 880,000 NF.
—The same 1,000,000 NF, invested rationally, would grow to 1,200,000 NF within the same year's time.

The solution of any difficult problem demands an intensive preliminary study.

It therefore seems wise to recapitulate the reasons for which our inventories have been rising.

II. REASONS FOR INCREASE IN OUR INVENTORIES
A: STOCKS OF PURCHASED MATERIALS AND PARTS and STOCKS OF WORK IN PROCESS.

Increases Due to Our Suppliers:

1: The quantity delivered is larger than ordered. (We even find this happening in the case of our own subsidiary, Indica, S.A.)

2: Delivery ahead of schedule. (We usually take care of this problem by holding back payment.)

Increases Due to Our Purchasing Department:

3: We increase the theoretically necessary quantity if it is too small. (This often occurs when ordering metal bar and tube stock.)

4: We increase the order at the supplier's request.

5: We increase the order to avoid paying a premium for very small orders.

Increases Due to Our Production Scheduling and Inventory-Control Departments:

(under the MINI system):

6: A tendency to round off (upwards) the number to be ordered.

7: The fact that all parts have a minimum stock level of four months' supply, when for many parts much less is needed.

(under the PROGRAM system):

8: The impossibility of finding out how many have been set aside for sale as spare parts, which quantity must be added to the number ordered for production runs, causes the clerk to buy too many in order to avoid running out. This observation is equally true of parts needed for repairs, and also to replace parts wasted during the manufacturing process.

Increases Due to Production Scheduling Procedure:

9: Failure to use parts which have been ordered, when the initial production schedule is changed after orders have been placed on the basis of its requirements. Schedules are changed in this manner when we find that our sales forecast, on which the original production schedule was based, is too optimistic for a given product, so we change the schedule in order to make less of that product.

Increases Due to Manufacturing:

10: We are steadily increasing the number of types of instruments which are in process at a given time; this is probably unavoidable as our company expands.

11: As the number of types in process increases, we find that we have to keep more and more parts on hand in the storeroom.

12: The time during which an instrument is in manufacture sometimes is unusually long. This often happens if the manufacturing process is interrupted for some reason.

Increases Due to Our Research Groups:

13: We throw away parts we have ordered. This occurs when the Research Groups modify an instrument after we have bought the parts to make it, and when they label this modification "Top Priority." Top Priority means that the change *must be made immediately*, regardless of what parts have already been bought.

14: When we get a "Second Priority" modification, it allows us to finish production of all series we have started. However, we may have ordered surplus parts for sale as spares and for use in repairs, and this surplus becomes valueless.

15: When we make a modification, it usually involves not just one part, but an entire group of parts which depend on one another. Thus, a minor modification may result in our having to abandon many parts.

16: Since we have no expert on product standardization, diversity of parts is our law.

17: When a new product is insufficiently prepared for manufacturing, this product may spend an unusually long time in the manufacturing process. This is the case of Model 404, for example, where the first series has not yet been finished, although we have already parts on hand for the second and third series.

Increases Due to Our Commercial Service:

18: We sometimes agree to manufacture for one customer a new product type which has no commercial value except for this customer.

19: Our policy of repairing even our very old models means that we have to stock parts which cannot be used for any other purpose.

20: Our catalogue is steadily expanding. This policy, which we will not discuss here, obviously bears on all the 19 reasons previously cited in this memorandum.

B: STOCKS OF FINISHED INSTRUMENTS AND ACCESSORIES

1: Our sales of a product may be far below the forecast level on which the manufacturing program was based.

2: Our Manufacturing Department may request the right to make more units of an instrument, in a given production run, than the Commercial Service wants; this is done in order to make economic production runs.

3: Delivery of products we are holding in stock may be slowed down through no fault of ours. For example, delivery of an export license may be retarded.

4: Sometimes we keep in stock instruments for special customers, when we could easily sell these instruments elsewhere.

5: Since in large unit orders (especially from the Government), we may have to pay a penalty if we deliver late, we sometimes keep a heavy stock of the item on hand, just in case the production run from which the order should be filled is slowed down.

6: We sometimes set aside, for our sales representatives, excessive quantities of products which are low-volume items.

THE GALVOR COMPANY (F)
International Operations

✿✿✿

At the end of 1961, Galvor's export sales were under the supervision of M. Margaux, although there was no real export department. Exhibit 1 shows the exports to various countries. Exhibit 2 shows the percentages of total sales represented by exports.

Question 1: How have Galvor's exports developed, and what is your present export policy?

M. Latour: "Before the War some export orders came in but they were not actively solicited. They usually resulted from contacts with our suppliers or their agents. Just after the War our quality, and, in fact, the quality of French manufacturers generally, was not of international class, so that at that time our first and most important problem was to improve the quality of our products.

"I am an exporter at heart and have always had a personal 'mystique' for export sales. Galvor has always given preference to exports and the only reason that they did not, in the past, grow as fast as domestic sales is because we did not have the means to compete abroad as we did in France. I have hired M. Armagnac to lighten my work-load so that I can do the travelling which is required to sell in the world market. I do not think that my export-mindedness is shared by my collaborators. Export matters must be dealt with as soon as they are received; some departments do not always seem to understand this and consider such business of secondary concern."

M. Chambertin: "M. Latour likes to think of himself as a great exporter. In fact, exports have only once exceeded 20 per cent of our sales, and that was in 1957, just after we started the United States venture. There is no question that M. Latour really wants to export, although this desire is not based on any market research but is merely a reflection of his personal interest and optimism. For many years we have exported just because orders from foreign countries happened to come in. There has never been any real sales policy for exports, and we have had to deal

This case was prepared by Mr. Harold Ehrenstrom under the Supervision of Professor Pierre Goetschin.

Exhibit 1

EXPORTS BY MAJOR COUNTRIES
(NF 000's)

Foreign Exports	1958	1959	1960	1961
Europe				
Italy	34	72	93	213
Spain	102	83	105	175
Belgium	64	118	103	127
Portugal	22	43	61	97
Germany	17	23	34	74
England	33	68	38	58
Switzerland	32	33	57	50
Eastern Bloc	13	21	36	36
Other Europe	42	73	90	61
Total Europe	359	534	617	891
Africa				
Nigeria	11	16	17	33
Union of South Africa	2	6	44	19
Other Africa	8	13	4	9
Total Africa*	21	35	65	61
North and South America				
U.S.A.	32	85	159	188
Other	11	18	63	62
Total N. & S. America	43	103	222	250
Asia				
Israel	1	37	70	20
Lebanon	8	11	22	16
Viet-Nam	3	2	81	5
Cambodia	19	36	38	6
Other Asia	19	21	37	31
Total Asia	50	107	248	78
Total Australia	54	51	44	66
Total Foreign Exports	527	830	1,196	1,346
Franc Zone	422	407	526	566
Foreign exports	527	830	1,196	1,346
Total Exports	949	1,237	1,722	1,912
Total sales	6,197	8,403	10,045	12,030

* Excluding Franc Zone.

through agents or representatives with very limited abilities. We have always been hampered by the fact that we know almost nothing about our competitors in other countries."

M. Margaux: "Galvor's exporting policy so far has been to navigate by following the wind. There is no real sales effort abroad but rather a technical effort to help the distribution process. There has been some publicity, although on a very modest scale; we do not really sell because

Exhibit 2

EXPORTS AS A PERCENTAGE OF TOTAL SALES

	Franc Zone	Other Exports	Total
1958	6.8	8.6	15.4
1959	4.8	9.9	14.7
1960	5.3	11.0	16.3
1961	4.7	11.4	16.1

France	1961
Sales	81.9
Repairs	2.0

Exports

Franc Zone	4.7
Europe	7.4
Americas	2.1
Africa	0.5
Asia	0.7
Oceania	0.5
Repairs	0.2
	100.0

of our price, we sell because of our quality and our product line. If we have what people need, we will sell it.

"Export sales are mainly generated by our company's reputation. Galvor exhibits in specialized electronics shows and fairs, and in most foreign countries the equipment is purchased by importers for their own account and then resold by them. Whenever we approach a new market, and after the initial contact, we usually felt our way and tried some distribution by appointing an agent. The choice of an intermediary is always a very delicate one because many representatives will sell anything. As a consequence, we often had to deal with agents who know a great deal less than the potential customers about the technical characteristics of our products. The company only started to attack export markets last year. In the past we have worked through contacts which we got from suppliers or other firms operating in different countries. This takes a lot of flair. Sometimes we get addresses of importers from French embassies. For instance a few months ago two Japanese engineers came to visit us as a result of a contact which we got from our Indonesian importers.

"We have not done much to expand exports so far because of our limited production capacity. With the new production facilities we are building, however, there is no question but that we shall be able to expand sales in all our markets. I am hoping eventually to be able to delegate my present routine work and take a more personal interest in our exports."

Question 2: What are the main limitations to the expansion of your exports?

M. Chambertin: "One of our problems is that M. Latour does not want to hurt or irritate his long-standing agents or representatives. For instance, the president of COMOR, in Paris, controls Galvor sales to 17 countries (see THE GALVOR COMPANY (A), p. 650), and in those countries we can do nothing, not even control the sales price of our product. I think that we should try to sell more in Italy, but there is little we can do unless M. Latour agrees to take that market away from COMOR. At the moment Germany is the only place in which an effort is being made. We just send our catalogues and price lists to other countries. The price list, by the way, is always the same as the French one, except that prices are expressed in the local currencies.

"COMOR gets the normal trade discounts of 20 per cent on all sales of Galvor products, and it receives an additional 3 per cent for paying us within 15 days. I am afraid that we will lose sales in the Common Market because of the high prices charged by COMOR's agents.

M. Latour: "It is an unfortunate state of affairs that we have no control over the prices at which COMOR's agents sell our equipment, although I expect that this will remedy itself in the long run. Italian and Belgian buyers already get the French price list and compare it with the prices charged by COMOR's Italian and Belgian agents. Those two, by the way, are excellent agents and sell quite a few of our instruments. I do not think that they will be able to charge such high prices for very long. Our export prices are normally list price minus 20 per cent (a rebate on the French sales tax), but the prices in Belgium are 50 per cent higher than the French list prices. This cannot go on in the Common Market.

"Because of the cumbersome manner in which exports are being dealt with, our delivery prices in certain countries are sometimes so high that we cannot compete effectively: here in France we often work through an exporter (COMOR S.A.), who then, in turn, sells to importers in the foreign country. This adds two margins to our prices. In the future, we will have to try to eliminate one or both of these."

M. Margaux: "I do not think our exports can expand very much at the moment. Our production capacity is barely sufficient for sales in France, so we should not rush out into the world before we can take care of our domestic orders. In my case I think it would be better to have a high sales volume in markets that have great potential, and which are nearby, such as the Common Market, rather than to get small sales volumes in far away and exotic countries. In the Common Market, at least, we could eventually make a substantial and complete effort. We cannot possibly send technically qualified men to prospect all round the world, as we have done in Germany. In many countries, of course, we can do nothing because these countries have been given to COMOR."

Question 3: The German venture seems to be your first real effort in a foreign market. How are you going about it?

M. *Latour:* "I took the precaution of not conceding the German market to COMOR; it was purposely kept free for the day when we could attack it ourselves. There are few competitors in Germany, with the exception of Rhode & Schwarz, who sell very high-quality and high-priced equipment. I see great potential for us in Germany and few problems, because our distribution system there will eventually be similar to the one in France. We have hired an engineer from Alsace who speaks fluent German and who is going to travel around the country for 4 to 6 months to explore the market. He will observe the reactions of potential customers to our products, our quality, and our prices. We will give him a small truck which has been transformed into a demonstration laboratory, and which is similar to those which Hewlett-Packard sends out on the road in the United States and Europe. The sales engineer's job is also to report on any special needs of the German market. If the situation looks encouraging, we shall install an agency as we have done in Paris. This agency will probably be located in Frankfurt and will then sell through a network of manufacturers' representatives."

M. *Margaux:* "The decision to attack the German market was naturally helped by the advent of the Common Market, although customs' tariffs were not a very significant factor [Exhibit 3]. The decision, however, was taken mainly because Germany was thought to be the most important

Exhibit 3

TARIFFS AND TAXES FOR ELECTRICAL AND
ELECTRONIC MEASURING INSTRUMENTS IN
THE COMMON MARKET (AS OF 9.30.61.)

	Import Duty	Sales Tax	Compensation Tax
France	12%	25%	—
Germany	5.5%	4%	6%
Belgium	7%	6%	—
Holland	7%	5%	2%
Italy	14.7%	3.3%	5%

potential market. We will need excellent salesmen to show them the technical advantages of buying our products. We are using our French experience, that is, we are interviewing the potential customers to find out what their needs are. We will then look for good representatives, beginning probably with the Ruhr and Saar areas. It may well be that we shall end up by having one centrally-located sales agency. German sales will not amount to much until there is a Galvor sales agency there. We shall, of course, have to sell them instruments which are duty-paid and which they can buy on the same terms as their own. Our sales engineer may come back to Bordeaux, once he is thoroughly familiar with the German market, to direct the German representatives, as M. Matté is now doing for France.

"The German experience seems to be taking a favorable turn. It appears that we may be able to sell quite a lot of multimeters and some generators, but probably no voltmeters. The sales engineer sends daily reports of his visits and also his impressions of each region's potential. Only at the end of the 4–6 month prospecting period will we know for sure what the possibilities are. We will then have to decide whether to work only through representatives, or whether it will be worth our while to establish a Galvor sales agency. The Germans seem to be particularly interested in our No. 462 multimeter. It is unfortunate that there is a 4-month delay in deliveries on that item. That is not the way to make a good impression on a new market."

Question 4: In what way do you expect the advent of the Common Market to affect your exports, or even your sales in France?

M. Latour: "After a period of apprehension, experience has shown French industry that the Common Market is not as serious a threat as had been expected, and that it even increases their opportunities for exports. Galvor has few real competitors, either in France or in the Common Market, and thus has little to fear, British entry into the Common Market may well create some problem, however, because of the tougher competition from such companies as Marconi Instruments and AVO (multimeters).

"One positive feature is that a large part of our output goes to the French Government; those sales are not likely to be subject to foreign competition, although national preferences will probably weaken within the Common Market, due to the fact that public tenders may become open to competitors in other Common Market countries. This would mean that foreign companies might, in time, be able to submit bids to the French Government, although we should then be in a good position to sell to other Common Market government agencies. The big problem there will be to adapt our products to those agencies' norms and specifications. On the other hand, many of the French Government agencies' specifications are patterned after our own norms, so that our foreign competitors would have to make costly changes in their products. In many ways, the German venture will prepare us for the exploration of other Common Market countries."

Question 5: What are your impressions of the possibilities resulting from M. Latour's recent trip around the world?

M. *Chambertin:* "One day someone from India came to France to visit some electronic-instrument manufacturers. This man got an excellent reception at Galvor. He wanted a licence to manufacture our products in India but wanted us to assume responsibility for building the plant. I persuaded M. Latour that this was sheer folly, and the result is that we now only have a licencing agreement with them. The Indian Company, Galmount (Private) Limited, is going to send two or three Indian technicians to Bordeaux for 6 months to learn how to assemble controllers. At the beginning, Galmount will import complete instruments and then start assembling parts, until they have acquired the necessary skills for complete manufacture. The contract, which was inspired by the Indian Government, is an agreement for technical collaboration, consulting engineering service, and manufacturing assistance. For this Galmount is to pay a royalty on net sales and a small lump sum. The contract also includes a trading agency agreement covering 10 countries.[1] I frankly do not think that this venture is going to be profitable enough to warrant the effort, but M. Latour hopes that the fact that Galvor products are manufactured in India will generate business for our larger instruments. In any case, it should certainly help them to get import permits for our equipment.

"M. Latour also visited Japan and thinks that some of the high-precision instruments we make could be sold there. He also mentioned something about the possibility of importing cheap instruments from Japan to sell them here, but I told him that this was none of our business; I was quite vehement about it. I do not know whether he appreciates my position, but I think Galvor as a company should do everything in its power to prevent such a project.

"M. Latour then went to the Institute of Radio Engineers' Show in New York. M. Pomméry was also at the Show, after having spent 10 days in Brazil on his way over, because COMOR's president suggested that Brazil might be an interesting market. With the depreciation of the cruzeiro, I do not think it is interesting to anyone anymore, but this is

---

[1] Ceylon, Nepal, Burma, Thailand, Malaya, Iraq, Pakistan, Afghanistan, Egypt, and Sudan.

typical of M. Latour's attitude towards his agents. He will do anything they ask him."

M. Pomméry: "As you know, I spent 10 days in Brazil before meeting M. Latour in New York. I saw several plants both of Brazilian and foreign companies. I also visited some laboratories and saw the kind of instruments they were using. I saw a lot of American and German instruments as well as a few very old Galvor meters, but not a single Japanese one. I do not think we could sell any of our smaller instruments in Brazil; our prices would be too high. If we wanted to penetrate this market, we should probably have to assemble in Brazil, because customs duties are about 90 per cent."

M. Latour: "I see a great potential in the high-quality, high-precision export market. In this market the Japanese cannot compete with us. For instance, a while ago a delegation of Japanese businessmen visited us and asked for the rights to sell our products in Japan. I was surprised, and asked them how this could be possible when our products were so much more expensive. They then showed me that Japanese products of similar precision and quality to Galvor products were actually priced higher in Japan. In my opinion the Japanese cannot manufacture quality and precision at a low cost. Their strength is in mass production; when it comes to high-precision instruments like our signal generators, their costs go up sharply. We sell precision and reliability. We are in a specialty market, quantities are always relatively small, and therefore we are not susceptible to mass-production competition.

"On my way to India, I stopped for two days in Beirut. There I met our agents in Syria and in Lebanon who know each other very well. Their big problem is that they do not sell any of our larger instruments; in fact, we have not done very well in the Middle East due to lack of technical abilities in our sales force. I told them that I saw no reason why Galvor should not have a share of the large instrument market and suggested that they hire professors of technical subjects to help them raise the technical quality of the sales effort.

"In the plane between Beirut and Bombay I happened to meet an Indonesian engineer who had studied in Germany. I am hoping that we may be able to get an agent in Indonesia through this man."

Question 6: Could you tell us something about the progress of your Indian venture and the reasons behind it?

M. Latour: "The Indian venture was started mostly for humanitarian reasons, and also because it serves the prestige of France. It is our duty to help the underdeveloped countries to acquire the necessary skills for industrialization. Galmount has a plot of land with an old hexagonal building in which a shop and the assembling operations for galvanometers will be installed. Three people are already working there, one of whom teaches at the local technical college and has had experience with galvanometer manufacturing in England. Another appears to be a very able mechanic and technician. These two men will be coming to Bordeaux for a training period of a few months and are now trying very hard to learn French.

"We will start by selling them finished instruments for resale, but we should not expect too much, since they have no sales organization as yet, and import licences are almost impossible to get."

Question 7: What other countries did you visit on your trip?

M. Latour: "I spent a few days each in Saigon and in Hong Kong. We have a very good agent in Viet-Nam, although the market, of course, is very limited. It has lately become very difficult to get import licences for anything other than U.S. equipment.

"As for Hong Kong, there is a very limited market unless you want to sell to Red China. I am not interested in selling behind the Iron Curtain, but my curiosity about the Chinese purchasing system led me to go and see their buying and trading organization in Hong Kong. There I was met by an apparently well-qualified Chinese who said that they might be very interested indeed in Galvor products, but that he would also like us to supply material which we do not make. By playing dumb, I found out that he was referring to certain strategic materials. I do not think we shall do any business with them, although there would certainly be possibilities. As for sales to other East Bloc countries, I have been happy to leave these to COMOR, because I am not very keen in trading with them.

"One of the high points of my trip was my visit to Japan. I was able to visit several plants and was very much impressed with what I saw. I was surprised to see that they produced a lot of high-precision equipment. Of course they still use a lot of manual labor, and most of their methods of fabrication are old-fashioned. Furthermore, their wage rates have increased three-fold in as many years. Prices are very high for high-precision instruments and very low for those which are mass-produced. I should think there would be many possibilities for selling our equipment in Japan, especially in the high-precision field. This, however, would necessitate frequent trips, because it is a market with very particular characteristics. I was very impressed by the reception I received. When I visited one company, they had a French flag in the reception-room and a sign saying 'Welcome to our visitor of today: Monsieur Latour.' "

Question 8: What are your plans for the American market?

M. Latour: "Next to Germany, I think the United States is potentially our best export market. I tried to form a 50-50 partnership with an agent a few years ago, but the man proved incapable and the company had to be liquidated; I lost about $30,000 on the deal. We were planning to assemble multimeters over there and sent one of our foremen over at that time. He met some people from Random Controls, Inc., who later proposed that they should manufacture some Galvor instruments on licence and that this foreman should stay with them. Three years ago we made an agreement with them for partial manufacture of our galvanometers. This agreement was recently extended so that Random will now sell all Galvor products in the United States, besides manufacturing our galvanometers and assembling our multimeters under their trade-name. I wonder if they are doing all they can, but, of course, they must be given time to get their production under way."

Question 9: How will you organize for future exports?

M. Latour: "I am thinking of devoting most of my time to exports. My role is to see that things develop in an orderly fashion. I want Galvor to become one of the leaders in the high-precision and high-quality market, but I do not want to expand too much or too fast, if I can help it. In any case, we are in no hurry to increase exports because our instruments have to be in the Hewlett-Packard class if we are to compete on the world market. When we get to that point, we will have no problems in selling them, because the company which produces the best quality does not need to make so much of an effort to sell, and its prices will generally be accepted if they are not exorbitant. I think we have reached this stage in the French market, but we have to improve the quality and finish of our products for the international market.

"In the future, we may well have sales engineers travelling throughout the world. Think of it: the man in Beirut has been our agent for 15 years, and my recent trip was the first direct contact we have had with him! Imagine how it would be if someone visited him once a year! We shall probably create an export department in the near future, but I have yet to find someone who is export-minded enough to take care of it under my direct supervision. There are many possible markets in Latin America, in Australia, etc., but we should have to send someone over there if we really wanted to sell.

"I visited the Hewlett-Packard plant in California and was extremely impressed with their manufacturing standards. The way they do it is the way instruments should be produced for the world market. We should pay higher salaries to get the cream of the crop of workers. It should be our policy in the future to get additional excellent and highly-paid engineers in order to develop superlative products. We have to make an effort now to improve our quality and use the ideas which we got from our recent trip to the United States. We have what it takes to reach Hewlett-Packard's level. I shall have to buy some of their instruments to use as an example for our Manufacturing Department."

THE GALVOR COMPANY (G–1)

INTRODUCTION

Galvor had expanded very rapidly throughout its history, and especially during the 1950's. Company officials remarked that this rapid growth had imposed some strains on the organization. At the outset of IMEDE's research at Galvor, M. Latour pointed out that "our organization is far from perfect"; soon afterwards M. Chambertin observed that Galvor's most interesting problems were organizational in nature.

This case contains two sections. Section I briefly describes the way in which the Galvor organization evolved from 1936 until the end of 1961. Section II contains (*a*) an analysis by company officials of the total organizational structure at the end of 1961; (*b*) similar analyses of each of the company's major departments; and (*c*) remarks as to the manner in which the company officials hoped to develop the organization in coming years.

I. A SHORT HISTORY OF THE GALVOR ORGANIZATION

During Galvor's early years, M. Latour managed the company with a minimum of formal organization. In 1941, at which time the company had 20 employees, Mr. Romanée was brought in to take charge of manufacturing and especially to supervise manufacturing of galvanometers. During the Second World War, research and development were under the responsibility of the Messer brothers, but when they left the company in 1945 (as described in "GALVOR (A)"), M. Latour resumed direction of research and development. By 1948, when the company had 50 employees, M. Meursault had taken charge of electronic research, and M. Pomméry was employed in 1951 to oversee electric research, at which time about 100 people were employed in the company. After M. Pomméry arrived, M. Latour concentrated his activities on commercial affairs and on the financial management of Galvor. During all of the company's history, M. Latour always supervised to some extent every department of the company, but as the organization grew, he was able to delegate more and more responsibility: first in manufacturing, to M. Romanée, and next in research and development, to MM. Meursault and Pomméry.

This process of delegation continued with the addition, in 1954, of M. Chambertin as the Administrative Director. Despite his title, M. Chambertin's primary responsibilities were in finance and accounting. "I brought in Chambertin," M. Latour said, "because our financial problems were becoming very complex, and I needed an expert in this area. Furthermore, I was not very interested in finance; I wanted to concentrate more on the commercial side of the business, and Chambertin's coming really freed me to do so."

M. Latour created more assistance for himself when he promoted M. Margaux to Manager of the Commercial Service in early 1958. Prior to this time M. Latour himself had been in charge of all commercial activities. M. Margaux was added to the Galvor staff in February, 1956, and spent his first two years with the company as a travelling sales engineer, visiting sales representatives and customers. After M. Margaux's promotion in 1958, no important changes occurred in the formal organization through the end of 1961.

In describing the way in which he had built up what he referred to as his "executive team," M. Latour said: "As the company grew, it was naturally necessary to find experts to assist me, and I found these men, beginning back in 1941 with Romanée. I cannot stress enough that my success would not have been possible without this team of experts."

II. THE GALVOR ORGANIZATION, DECEMBER 1961

A. THE OVER-ALL ORGANIZATION

The following comments on the Galvor organization were made during November–December, 1961:

M. Latour: "We certainly have some organization problems, especially insofar as my colleagues are generally over-loaded with work and don't have good assistants to help them. Furthermore, I find some unwillingness, especially in Romanée's case, to take on added responsibilities as the company grows. In general, however, we have a very solid executive team whose members work well together. For myself, I am trying more and more to work on long-range policies of the company, such as the development of our export markets. I am trying to leave more and more of the detail work to my colleagues. I manage to keep on top of my work, which I think is one important sign of a good manager; I finish by night all the jobs that were waiting for me when the day started."

M. Chambertin: "M. Latour makes all our major policy decisions alone; since he is not always in touch with daily operating details, he sometimes creates problems. As for our other executives, I think that they suffer from what seems to me a common administrative problem: all of them have too much to do, because they haven't the assistants they need, so they do the easy jobs first and leave the difficult problems unsolved. As a result, our executives don't always deliver the value for which they are paid: they are supposed to make the important and difficult decisions, but they often just do detail work that any clerk could do.

"Our major problems here are probably organizational. We do not have a good organizational structure, and we badly lack depth in our management. This is because the company has grown rapidly; the organization has not kept pace with this growth. The organization which we have today is much too weak: it would have been insufficient at our operating level of two years ago.

"The weakest point in our structure appears in the question of a true second-in-command for M. Latour. At the moment, we have nobody who can run the company except M. Latour. I suppose that I am ostensibly the second man here, but I am 58 years old, and I have no technical background at all, so that some of the other executives would not consider me a very good leader. Margaux is probably the best-suited of the other executives to run the company, but he would never be accepted by the others.

"We have never had any true forward planning in the company, with the possible exception of our 12-month sales forecasts. We have operated pragmatically, and this policy has clearly worked well, at least judging by our results. We feel that this has been the best policy, because we have had to go where technology has taken us, but in the future we will probably need to do more long-range planning."

M. Romanée: "I am afraid that we have some real organizational problems here. In the first place, M. Latour gets involved far too deeply in the trivial operating details of the company. This is probably unavoidable, when you consider that in Galvor's early days he *had* to run all aspects of the business, but it is a real problem nonetheless. Because M. Latour does get involved in such detail work, our responsibilities and chains of command are very unclear. I am not really sure what our true organization chart should look like, but it would certainly show that M. Latour's role extends from the top of the structure to the bottom. If we cannot improve our organization, and do so rapidly, I fear that we shall miss our chance to capitalize on the opportunities for growth and success which are open to us."

M. Margaux: "There are three reasons for Galvor's success. First, we give excellent technical support to our customers in helping them to solve their measuring problems. Second, M. Latour's basic policy has been steady and prudent; we have moved ahead consistently, and he has been willing to alter his policies to meet the demands of special situations, but he keeps a firm and steady hand on the rudder. Third, we have a fine organization whose members work very well together."

Messrs. Meursault and Pomméry never commented on the over-all organization of Galvor during interviews with IMEDE researchers. They confined themselves to remarks on the functioning of their own departments.

B. DEPARTMENTAL ORGANIZATIONS

I. *The Research Departments,* one for electronic research (under M. Meursault) and the other for electric research (under M. Pomméry) suffered from two main organizational problems, according to company executives.

The first problem was that MM. Meursault and Pomméry both had too many responsibilities and badly needed assistants. This problem was mentioned not only by MM. Latour and Chambertin, but also by MM. Meursault and Pomméry themselves. M. Chambertin commented: "I suspect that the real problem here is that, despite the fact that Meursault and Pomméry are well aware that they have too much to do, they enjoy the wide responsibilities which accompany this situation, so they don't want to hire assistants and give up even some petty responsibility for detail work."

"Meursault," remarked M. Latour, "really needs a brilliant young engineer as an assistant, but he is afraid that such an assistant might show him up. Thus, although I have promised to write him a contract guaranteeing that he will always be Manager of Electronic Research, and although I have said that he may pay an assistant as much as necessary, even twice what he himself makes, he does nothing. I don't want to push him into anything, because he has been with me since he was a boy, but if I find a man I think would make a suitable assistant for him, I'll hire the man on the spot and worry later about how to sell him to Meursault."

As described in "GALVOR (B-1)," MM. Meursault and Pomméry were both keenly aware that they needed assistants, and as of late 1961 both claimed that they were searching intensively for such men.

The second problem in the research groups was in their liaison with the Manufacturing Department. Under the system in effect as of late 1961, the Research Services were responsible for carrying new product research to the point of building and testing a prototype of the product. They also had to draw up the necessary documents for putting this product into manufacturing: such documents included, for example, a list of parts to be purchased for assembly work and a list of parts to be manufactured in the factory. The Manufacturing Department entered the process of accepting the prototype (which was supposed to be identical in all ways to the mass-produced product) and the accompanying documents. The Manufacturing Department would then determine how the manufacturing and assembly operations were to be handled in the plant.

Problems arose frequently between Manufacturing and Research. According to M. Meursault, after the prototype of a new product had been tested, finished, documented, and turned over to Manufacturing, the latter department would request minor modifications in order to simplify certain manufacturing processes. This meant, claimed M. Meursault, that he was constantly being called away from his important duties in order to supervise such minor changes required by Manufacturing.

M. Pomméry added that the Research Departments were often asked to update existing Galvor products; such requests normally came either from M. Latour or from the Commercial Service. "As a result of these demands by the Manufacturing Department and the Commercial Service," said M. Pomméry, "we fall far short of our true potential for developing new products. We have on hand a huge backlog of desirable new products to develop, but we simply have too much updating and modifying to do." During the approximately seven interviews held by IMEDE researchers with M. Meursault and/or M. Pomméry, neither man ever commented on the other except insofar as described in the "GALVOR" series.

2. *The Manufacturing Department,* under M. Romanée, viewed this liaison problem with the research groups somewhat differently. M. Romanée said: "There certainly is a big problem in getting new products from research into manufacturing. The chief difficulty is that after a design has been 'frozen' for manufacturing, the research people will decide that they have to make some further modifications in order to improve the product. This makes it difficult to plan a smooth work flow in the plant, and it also creates inventory problems: we end up having parts on hand which we'll never use, and then there is a big rush to get the new parts required for the modification. We really need a special service to take charge of transferring new products from design to manufacturing.

"Another problem in our department is that my foremen have far too much responsibility, especially in that they have to devise many of the manufacturing methods and techniques. We have no Methods Department, which we badly need. I full realize that I need an assistant, because I have far too much to do, but I can't teach such a man everything he would need to know to be truly valuable to me.

"I view my role as that of being a coordinator for the various manufacturing departments, and also for getting new products through the manufacturing process. When problems arise, I look at the trouble and take the necessary steps. The difficulty with the Manufacturing Department's organization is that we have had to expand our operations so rapidly that we have not been able to develop the staffs of specialists, in methods, coordination with research, and other areas, which we need today.

"My other major problem is in factory equipment. M. Latour does not like to buy machinery until evey machine we have is being used 100 per cent of the time; this means that we often go on using machinery long after it should be replaced. I have no authority to buy new equipment myself; I have to ask M. Latour for his approval first. This often means a delay of several months before I can get the machine I want."

Speaking on this point, M. Latour said: "I cannot get Romanée to buy machinery on his own authority. He refers virtually all his purchase requests, no matter how small, to me."

3. *The Commercial Service,* under M. Margaux, actually controlled only about 50 per cent of Galvor's total sales. The rest of the company's sales were accounted for by Galvor Paris (42 per cent of 1961 sales) and the Galvanometer Sales Department (10 per cent of 1961 sales), supervised by MM. Cliquot and Lanson, respectively. MM. Margaux, Cliquot, and Lanson all reported directly to M. Latour.

"In effect," M. Chambertin said, "M. Latour is really our Commercial Director, although the official post does not exist, because he is in general charge of *all* sales activities. I doubt that M. Margaux has the ability to fill the job of Commercial Director, although I may be wrong."

M. Latour commented that one of M. Margaux's difficulties was that the latter had too many things to do and that he needed an assistant. M. Latour continued: "Margaux is the only one of my colleagues who has come to me and admitted that he needs an assistant; this pleases me very much, because it shows that he is beginning to understand the responsibilities of a real manager." As of late 1961 M. Margaux was personally supervising the Export Department, since he had not yet found an assistant to supervise this department for him.

"In general," commented M. Margaux, "the Commercial Service is in good shape, and things will be even better when I can find a suitable assistant for exports."

4. *The Administrative Department,* under M. Chambertin, had four main functions: bookkeeping, financial management, personnel, and statistical reporting. M. Chambertin had assistants in charge of Personnel (starting January 1, 1962), Accounting, and Statistical Services (under Mme. Bollinger). He also created, effective January 1, 1962, a special group of several men to analyze factory costs, because he hoped to do intensive research into Galvor's direct and indirect cost structure during 1962.

"I have all the help I need," M. Chambertin said. "Mme. Bollinger is a superb assistant, because she is brilliant and well-educated in statistics and other areas of management." [Mme. Bollinger was a recent graduate of INSEAD, a new graduate school of business administration located in Fontainebleau, France.] I try to make sure that I have a good staff to help me, and, as you can see, I have just created two new departments to relieve me of additional detailed work. I myself supervise our financial management, in cooperation with M. Latour, and I also maintain our external financial relations, such as those with our bankers." As far as IMEDE researchers could determine, the Administrative Department had no organizational difficulties.

5. *The Weekly Management Conference* was, company officials said, an important element in Galvor's organization and operation. This conference, which met starting at 8:30 every Tuesday morning, brought together M. Latour and his five main executives for a general discussion of technical, manufacturing, and commercial problems. The conference had been instituted in 1959; prior to this time M. Latour had discussed such problems only with the specific executive whose area was involved. "Our first conferences," said M. Latour, "dealt only with technical matters, but after a year or so we enlarged the scope of this meeting to include manufacturing and commercial problems as well. It is a very effective way of maintaining our executive team."

M. Chambertin observed: "The only trouble with the conference is that we spend hours discussing details which ought not to concern the upper level of management. The conference seldom lasts less than four hours, and it has on occasion been known to run the whole day. I think that M. Latour involves himself unnecessarily in details, especially in technical matters."

In March, 1962, while M. Latour was on his trip around the world, no management conferences were held at Galvor, M. Chambertin said:

"When the first Tuesday after M. Latour's departure arrived, we suddenly realized that there was no real purpose in holding the conference—we had nothing to talk about, so we abandoned it until his return."

C. ORGANIZATIONAL PLANS AS OF DECEMBER, 1961

"In the long run," said M. Chambertin, "we know how we would like to develop the organization; M. Latour and I have already talked about this at some length. We envision the company as being organized into three main departments, Technical, Commercial, and Administrative, with a Director at the head of each. The Administrative Department and its Director already exist, of course. The Commercial Department would unite under one Director the Commercial Service, Galvanometer Sales, and Galvor Paris. The elements of this department already exist, as you know, but the true Director is M. Latour.

"The major change would be in gouping both the Research Services *and* the Manufacturing Department under a single Technical Director; this man would have complete responsibility for designing and producing all Galvor products. In my opinion we have nobody in the company who meets the specifications for Technical Director, nor have we a solid candidate for Commercial Director.

"This new Technical Director, whoever he is, ought to be (*a*) a brilliant engineer, with a sound theoretical background; (*b*) a first-class administrator who can take all of research and manufacturing under his control; (*c*) about 35 years old. I suggest age 35 because, in my opinion, this is the man we ought to train to be M. Latour's successor."

*   *   *   *   *

In speaking of future developments in the Manufacturing Department, M. Romanée said: "We are planning to bring two new staffs into existence: first a Manufacturing Bureau, in about two years, and then a Methods Staff perhaps a year later. The Manufacturing Bureau, which will be under my charge, will be responsible for transferring a new product from research to manufacturing. The Methods Staff will relieve me and my foremen of a lot of the methods work we now have to do. With these two services, I think we can significantly reduce the time now required to move from a finished prototype to a mass-produced instrument. This time lag is now 9–12 months, depending mostly on the instrument's complexity and whether we encounter many modifications and other problems."

M. Chambertin said: "Only in recent months has M. Romanée begun to admit that he and his foreman have too much work to do and badly need to enlarge the Manufacturing Department's staff services."

*   *   *   *   *

M. Margaux spoke of his search for an assistant as follows: "I am now looking intensively for a man to take charge of our Export Department, and I must have this man not later than the autumn of 1962. His arrival will free me from a large part of the detail work I now have to do, so that I can concentrate on the two things which seem to me most important: (1) doing more intensive analyses of our marketing procedures, especially determining the feasibility of marketing research in our industry; (2) developing the technical side of our commercial organization, first in France, and afterwards abroad. By this I mean building up our staff of sales engineers and using other means to strengthen the technical support we can give to our sales representatives."

*   *   *   *   *

"All in all," said M. Chambertin, "I think that our organizational structure is slowly being developed along desirable lines, but we are far from being where we should be in this area. In my opinion, the other executives badly need assistants, we certainly need a thoroughly accepted second-in-command to M. Latour, and we ought to define our organization more sharply by getting competent Technical and Commercial Directors."

THE GALVOR COMPANY (G–2)

On January 2, 1962, M. Latour announced at the weekly Management Conference that he had just employed a new man, M. Roger Armagnac, to assist him in his work. M. Latour added that M. Armagnac would begin in his position on April 2. "For ten years," remarked M. Latour, "I have been looking for a high-level assistant for myself; the need for such a man became especially obvious during the last three months of 1961. I think that M. Armagnac is just the man we need; he ought to work out very well."

$*$ $*$ $*$ $*$ $*$

In explaining the circumstances which led to his coming to Galvor, M. Armagnac said: "I was educated by the French Navy as an engineer from 1942 to 1950, at the end of which time I was 23 years old. After finishing my education, I had a contract to serve eight years as a Naval officer, and I expected to spend all my working life in the Navy. By 1961, I was in charge of Electronic Research and Development at the Toulon Naval Base; I had slightly more than 100 engineers and technicians under my command. By this time, however, I began to consider the possibility of leaving the Navy to go into industry. When I was in Paris in April, 1961, I looked up my old schoolfellow Cliquot, who is the Manager of Galvor Paris. He had also been a Naval officer before going to work for Galvor. Cliquot knew of my interest in industry, and he suggested that I consider Galvor as a place to work. Naturally, everything was very tentative at this time, because I was still in the Navy. I was not sure I could get a discharge on short notice.

"Cliquot suggested that I send my dossier to Galvor, which I did in May. Aside from the usual background information, I also included an explanation of why I was thinking of leaving the Navy." This explanation is reproduced below:

The following ideas are strictly personal and apply only to one particular case: mine. It is difficult to analyze one's self objectively; I hope I can do so without either boasting or excessive modesty.

I think that a private corporation to which a military engineer is offering his services should ask the following questions:

What are the engineer's motives? Why is he considering abandoning a stable and comfortable career, with a well-defined place in the hierarchy, with almost mathematical rules for promotion, and with many honors and social advantages, for a career which, while offering significant material advantages, must be at the outset, at least, riskier and less well defined?

To understand the answers to these questions, the following must be borne in mind:

The Navy is structurally very compartmentalized in each branch, and the functions within each branch are narrowly and precisely defined. In certain branches, including mine, and especially in electronics, many men reach at an early age the highest post attainable within the branch. I have been at the top for two years, and the rules do not allow me any chance of rising higher.

I think (as do my superiors) that private industry, which is growing and is less compartmentalized than the Government, would permit me to develop more broadly in the future.

"In short," added M. Armagnac, "I had gone about as high as I could for the foreseeable future. That is why I considered a career change. I sent M. Cliquot my dossier, which he forwarded to Bordeaux. I received a reply suggesting a visit to the factory, which took place in November."

M. Latour said: "My preliminary reaction to Armagnac's résumé was favorable, so I thought it would be wise to talk to him here and to show him the plant. During this tour of the plant, he asked many intelligent and penetrating questions about various operations; I was impressed by the perception which these questions revealed. After the visit, I suggested that he write me a letter outlining where and how he saw himself fitting into our organization. Various people who had known Armagnac told me that he was brilliant, an outstanding man in his field. He had earned a fine reputation as an administrator while at Toulon."

M. Armagnac said: "After the visit to the plant, I considered things for a month before I decided to make a written proposal to Galvor. I don't like to make up my mind in a hurry, and I still had to decide whether I would leave the Navy. So I talked things over with my wife. I also found out that I could get a discharge from the Navy, on a so-called 'temporary' basis, to work in industry. If things didn't work out I could return to the Navy.

"After considering all aspects of the decision carefully, I decided to propose myself for a position at Galvor. I wrote to Galvor on December 26th, as follows:

DEAR MONSIEUR LATOUR,

I very much appreciated the visit to your factory, for which my warm thanks. I came away with an excellent impression of your plant.

1) As a result of this visit and the information given me on the organization structure of the company, it seems to me that Galvor's management could be

strengthened by the addition of an engineer as Technical Director; the role of this man would be to oversee the various research teams and especially, for a given manufacturing program, to:

—keep an eye on the jobs being done by the research engineers, give them advice, coordinate their activities and, in time, to improve their relationships;
—organize manufacturing operations (which would require a complete understanding of potentialities), to keep general control over manufacturing, and to improve the workings of this department if possible;
—control and coordinate the job of transforming a prototype into a mass-produced instrument;
—cooperate actively with the other staffs of the company which would not be directly under my command, such as:
—defining the stocks of raw materials and components needed to make a given product;
—issuing a memo giving my opinion on the value of various personnel;
—etc.

In short, the Technical Director would have to be the administrator of the technical side of the business.

2) The foregoing definition of the job of the Technical Director is clearly not exhaustive. Nevertheless, using it as a general guide, and assuming you should be interested, I would be happy to enter your team in this capacity.

The rest of M. Armagnac's letter dealt with the exact terms of employment and with the formalities which would be required to secure his release from the Navy. M. Latour considered M. Armagnac's application and accepted his proposal. On January 2, 1962, M. Latour informed his colleagues that M. Armagnac would be joining the staff around April 1st, as an assistant to himself. He did not at that time discuss M. Armagnac's role and title in the company.

＊　　＊　　＊　　＊　　＊

During the negotiations with M. Armagnac, M. Latour discussed M. Armagnac's possible function and role in Galvor only with M. Chambertin. M. Armagnac was to be given the title of Technical Director, but as of January 2, 1962, the place of the Technical Director in the organizational structure had not been established.

"Chambertin," commented M. Latour, "looks to the future more than any of the other executives, and the first thing he said at the January 2 meeting was that we must define M. Armagnac's position very carefully. I generally agreed with M. Armagnac's definition of his job in the letter of December 26th, 1961, that is, I agreed that he would have responsibility over research and manufacturing. Chambertin said that if we put Armagnac *only* in charge of R&D and Manufacturing, we might create some human problems, notably in the case of Romanée, who might well not want to be under a much younger man. Chambertin then suggested that Armagnac might conceivably be appointed the executive vice-president, or assistant managing director, which would mean being second-in-command of the company. It is typical of Chambertin's selflessness that he was willing to subordinate himself and give up being second man at Galvor. I replied that I did not propose to give Armagnac control over finances, that his excellence was in manufacturing and research—he is not a financial expert, after all."

M. Chambertin said: "On February 7th, 1962, I sent M. Latour a memorandum outlining my thoughts on the way in which M. Armagnac might be fitted into the organization structure. Mme. Bollinger and I did some preliminary research on the subject of organizational structure and the usual responsibilities of Manufacturing and Technical Directors. This research suggested that it would be appropriate to have both a Technical Director and a Manufacturing Director; one would be in charge of conceiving the product, the other of manufacturing it. We did recognize, however, that one problem at Galvor was the poor liaison between research and manufacturing and that we also had difficulties with purchasing, production scheduling, and methods. We saw that, because of their interdependence, purchasing and production scheduling should be under the control of the same man, and we realized that both of these staffs were inadequate for our current level of operations.

"Recognizing as we did that Romanée already had far too much to do, we questioned whether M. Armagnac might not assume control of scheduling, purchasing, and methods. It was clear that Armagnac would have to be given *formal* authority over these three areas if he was to improve them; he could not do the job as a trespasser on another man's domain.

"We concluded that M. Armagnac must be given explicit responsibility in every area where he expected to make changes. If he were only a staff assistant to M. Latour, without real power, he would be useless. Therefore, if we wanted Armagnac not only to supervise research, but also to attack the problems in some of our services (purchasing, scheduling, and methods), M. Romanée would have to turn over control of these services to M. Armagnac. We suggested that this be done, that Romanée, Armagnac, and I be on the same level and, most important, that Armagnac be given a position with well-fined authorities and responsibilities. It would not work if M. Armagnac were just a high-level trouble shooter for M. Latour."

M. Latour said: "Although it would have been possible, as suggested by this memo, to put Romanée on the same level with Armagnac and Chambertin, I knew that Romanée's technical background was not strong. On my recent trip around the world, I observed that the companies which are world leaders of our industry are very technically oriented. It seemed to me that if we wanted to become one of the industry leaders it might not be appropriate to elevate Romanée to the same rank as Chambertin and Armagnac. So I finally decided that Armagnac should be Technical Director in charge of all manufacturing and research. On April 2d, when M. Armagnac arrived and was formally introduced to his colleagues, I described very precisely M. Armagnac's position in our company. There were no problems; the whole thing was done and accepted within a minute.

"Our next major organizational development will probably be to find a Commercial Director to run the Commercial Service, Galvanometer Sales, and Galvor Paris. I am in no great hurry to find this man, who must really be superb, because, now that Armagnac is here, I can concentrate more and more on the commercial side of the business, especially on exports. This Commercial Director will have to have a very strong technical background, because our product line is becoming steadily more complex, and this probably means that Margaux will not be able to fill the job, but we shall see."

*   *   *   *   *

Until April 2d, 1962, when M. Armagnac arrived, only two executives besides M. Latour made any comment to the IMEDE researchers on M. Armagnac's probable role in the company: Messrs. Chambertin and Romanée.

On February 13, M. Chambertin said: "As you can see from the memo I wrote, I was worried lest M. Latour use Armagnac merely as an errand boy in solving minor problems. If this were done, Armagnac would be worthless, and he would quit very soon. I was therefore happy to see M. Latour define very carefully what he expected of Armagnac; I just hope things work out as planned."

Late in March, M. Romanée said: "It's no use asking me what M. Armagnac will do when he gets here; we have not discussed it at all, which seems to me a strange state of affairs. I haven't the least idea as to how he will fit into the company; you had better see M. Latour on this subject."

*   *   *   *   *

On April 26th, after M. Armagnac had been at Galvor about three weeks, IMEDE researchers asked each executive for his reactions to the way in which M. Armagnac was proceeding in his work. The following replies were received:

M. Margaux: "I think that Armagnac's presence here will be exceptionally valuable. M. Latour can no longer be expected to have the technical knowledge which is becoming increasingly important, and Pomméry and Meursault have far too much to do without providing M. Latour with technical assistance, so M. Armagnac will help to fill this gap. I am also pleased because M. Armagnac will be able to help me with the many technical problems which arrive in the course of my work, whereas Pomméry and Meursault are so busy that they cannot always give me this assistance. If I have a pressing technical problem of importance, now I can take it to the chief's right-hand technical man.

"I suspect, although this is only my opinion, that Pomméry and Meursault will be less enthusiastic than I about M. Armagnac's arrival. This is only natural, because now they are no longer directly below the chief, but must work through M. Armagnac. I think, however, that they will find Armagnac relieving them of many of their problems, and their departments will probably produce more high-quality products. I must also admit that there may be some real problems in having M. Romanée under M. Armagnac. M. Romanée is a self-taught man who has learned by experience, and he's been in this industry a long time, so there may be some friction here."

M. Romanée: "My first reaction to M. Armagnac is very favorable. He has started already to analyze some of our difficult problems, especially in the relationship between manufacturing and research. Obviously it is too soon to judge him, but I find him to be a real leader, a man who can and will make decisions on his own responsibility. He will also serve to screen M. Latour from the petty problems which are always appearing. I think he will prove a big help to the company."

M. Chambertin: "I think Armagnac will be a real manager and decision-maker. He and I together have planned a new system of management conferences which M. Latour has approved. Under this system there will be two Management Committees: a Technical Committee and a General Management Committee. The Technical Committee will include Armagnac, Cliquot, Meursault, Pomméry, and Romanée; it will meet around the 9th of each month (except for its first meeting, which began April 25th). This group will study all manufacturing and research problems and decide which are worth presenting to the General Management Committee, which will meet on the next day. The General

Management Committee consists of MM. Latour, Armagnac, Chambertin, Cliquot, Meursault, Pomméry, Romanée, Margaux, and Mme. Bollinger. This group will consider developments of importance during the previous month, the state of the market for our products, such technical problems as are brought up by the Technical Committee, and administrative problems if any. If at some time we need more than one meeting a month, this will be easy to arrange.

"I think that Armagnac will avoid getting involved in detail work; he wants to stay at the policy level, which is certainly a wise decision. He has the important talent of getting the men under him to come to a unanimous decision where before they could not agree. From what Cliquot has said, Armagnac will never have to rush; he is well-organized. The only problem which might arise would occur if he and M. Latour were to disagree on an important issue."

M. Meursault: "It is far too early to judge, but I am already beginning to wonder if M. Armagnac may not get too involved in the detail work of research, rather than staying up top as general coordinator."

M. Pomméry was unavailable at the time of this interview.

M. Latour: "I am very satisfied with the way Armagnac has come in and started to work on our problem areas."

*   *   *   *   *

In speaking of his activities since arriving at Galvor, M. Armagnac said:[1] "Although I was educated as an engineer, I have had considerable experience with administrative problems. It appeared to me that the major problems at Galvor were administrative in nature, and so I saw my role primarily as that of an administrator, a sort of orchestra conductor, helping to coordinate production and research activities. My proposal to M. Latour in December was made with this basic idea in mind. I did not want to get into detailed technical matters; I knew that we already had good men in this area, and that my value would be as an administrator.

"The first job I set for myself was to define the boundary between research and manufacturing. As you know, this has been a constant problem at Galvor, and I might add that it seems to be common to many other technically oriented companies. After I had considered the subject for some time, I felt that I knew where this boundary should be set. I did not want, however, to set it by dictatorial decree, to impose my will on my colleagues. Obviously, if the research and manufacturing people were to work willingly within this boundary definition, they would have

---

[1] This interview took place on May 7th, 1962.

to participate in its creation. I therefore made this question the major topic for discussion at our first Technical Committee meeting, which took place during April 25–27.

"In this meeting, my colleagues pointed out to me some details of company operations which I had not known and which affected our decision. I am happy to say that, as a result of this meeting, we were able to agree unanimously on a precise definition of the boundary between research and manufacturing. I also found that, with minor changes, the definition we arrived at was basically the one which I had initially felt to be the best.

"Our definition is as follows: the research process ends when there are two finished prototypes produced, both of which are *exactly* what we want in the mass-produced instrument. The prototypes will be identical. One will be called the 'reference' prototype; it cannot be taken apart under any circumstances by the manufacturing people. The other prototype may be disassembled for study if desired.

"The Manufacturing Department will have *no* responsibility for, or authority over, the technical functioning of the instrument. This responsibility rests solely with the research groups. The research groups, on the other hand, have no say in how the instrument is to be manufactured.

"Now in order to smooth out liaison between research and manufacturing, around the end of 1962 we will initiate a 'Staff for Preparation for Manufacturing,' which we will call the Manufacturing Bureau. This staff will receive from the research group the two prototypes of a new product. It will then dissect one of these prototypes and decide what the tooling requirements will be and what parts are to be purchased. This staff will *not* judge the instrument's performance: it will merely decide how to make it. Obviously, we will need experts to serve on this staff, men who know the factory and our production capabilities perfectly.

"At some time in the future we shall add a Methods Staff; this will consist largely of experts in production methods and time study. These men will analyze every factory operation, tell us how to do it most effectively, and how much time it should take. Eventually this staff will analyze the entire production line which is set up to make an instrument.

"Up to now, there has been a wonderful spirit, almost a family feeling, at Galvor, but I thing this will have to change in the future. The Methods Staff, for example, will be oriented towards worker efficiency and performance. Unpleasant as these changes may seem at first, I am sure they are necessary if Galvor is to realize its potential for becoming an industry leader.

"My first objective at Galvor is to establish a good working relationship with my colleagues, and especially with Pomméry, Meursault, and Romanée. You know, I am a newcomer to the company, and I am just under 35 years old. It seems to me that I will have to walk a narrow line between exercising too much authority and not exercising enough. If I always insist on making decisions myself, my colleagues will resent me. On the other hand, if they don't realize that I can and will make decisions when necessary, then I will be useless here. I don't want to have to use my authority, but I want them to know it exists. My most important task here will be in creating teamwork between manufacturing and research.

*   *   *   *   *

On April 7th, M. Latour summarized his views on M. Armagnac's role within the company, saying: "I long ago saw the need for a highly qualified man to assist me by supervising manufacturing and research. I belive I have found this man in M. Armagnac; my first impression is that he is highly capable, has a solid technical background, has solid administrative ability, and has a strong character.

"His position as Technical Director gives him the responsibility and authority to work on our difficult problem areas. And he will not only coordinate research and manufacturing, but he will also relieve me of much of the detail work I now have to do. The men under him will no longer have to come to me with trivialities: they will discuss them with Armagnac, who will then report to me on significant issues. This is the way in which he will assist me.

"In my opinion, hiring Armagnac means more than merely finding an assistant for myself: it is a basic change in our policy. For the first time, somebody will really be taking over-all charge of our research and manufacturing.

"As to my colleagues' reaction to Armagnac's being brought in, I believe that they will not fight him but will recognize that he can be a great help to them, and that we badly need the type of assistance he can give us. I think that, from a human point of view, Armagnac will work out very well. I have a sixth sense which tells me if problems are arising with my colleagues. We always have free and open discussions, so I will be able to find out what his colleagues think of him and whether he is making any mistakes. I will pass this information on to him so that he can make the necessary adjustments.

"I admit that if Armagnac is not both strong and very competent, the men under him will destroy him, but I am confident that he can handle himself.

"I have already told Armagnac that, because he is my assistant, he must not fail; his failure would be very bad for morale. I am 53 years old, and I need this man's assistance, so I shall give him my full support. Little by little, as he proves himself here, I shall give up research and manufacturing completely to his control. I must foresee the day when I shall have to give up my whole job to a younger man."

Appendix

SELECTED STATISTICS, THIRTEEN WEST EUROPEAN NATIONS

AND THE UNITED STATES, 1960

	(1)	(2)	(3)	(4)		(5)
				Currency		
	Area (*Thousands of Sq. Km.*)	*Population* (*Millions*)	*Index of Industrial Production* (*1958=100*)	*National Unit*	*Value of U.S. $1.00*	*Gross National Product* (*Billions*)
Austria*	83.8	7.08	117	Schillings	26.04	148.20
Belgium†	30.5	9.17	111	Francs	49.88	608.00
Denmark*	43.0	4.58	112	Kroner	6.91	41.23
France†	551.2	45.73	116	New Francs	4.91	286.00
West Germany† ..	248.0	53.75	119	Deutsche Marks	4.17	282.40
Italy†	301.2	49.51	128	Lire	620.60	19,937.00
Netherlands†	32.4	11.35	124	Guilder	3.76	42.47
Norway*	323.9	3.59	117	Kroner	7.15	31.73
Portugal*	92.2	9.12	117	Escudos	28.83	69.10
Spain	503.5	30.13§	111	Pesetas	60.15	583.50
Sweden*	449.7	7.48	112	Kronor	5.18	63.50
Switzerland*	41.3	5.30	n.a.	Francs	4.29	36.80
United Kingdom*.	244.8	52.54	112	Pound	.36	25.31
United States	8,362.85¶	179.32	116	Dollar	1.00	503.40
EFTA	1,278.7	89.69				
EEC	1,165.9‡	170.02				

* Member of the European Free Trade Area (EFTA).
† Member of the European Economic Community (EEC), which also includes Luxembourg.
‡ Including Luxembourg.
§ Estimate for 1961.
‖ Estimated (United Nations figure).
¶ Or 3,615,200 sq. mi. at 2.5899 sq. km. to the sq. mi.
** Total world-trade figures for all member nations. Exports for EFTA include $3.46 billion within the Association and $4.3 billion to members of EEC; exports of EEC include $10.24 billion within the Community and $6.52 billion to members of EFTA.

Source: Columns 1, 2: *The Europa Year Book, 1962* (London, Europa Publications Limited, 1962). Columns 3-6, 8, 9: International Monetary Fund, *International Financial Statistics* (Washington, D.C., February, 1963) and United Nations, *Statistical Yearbook, 1961* (New York, 1961). Column 7 was derived from Columns 2 and 6. All dollar figures derived from Columns 4-9, except import and export figures, which are from United Nations, *op. cit.*

(6)	(7)	(8)	(9)

Financial Statistics in National Currencies				Financial Statistics in U.S. Dollars				
National Income (Billions)	*Per Capita Income*	*Exports (Billions)*	*Imports (Billions)*	*Gross National Product (Billions)*	*National Income (Billions)*	*Per Capita Income*	*Exports (Billions)*	*Imports (Billions)*
118.30	16,709	29.13	36.81	5.69	4.54	642	1.12	1.41
447.00	48,746	188.80‡	197.90‡	12.19	8.96	977	3.79‡	3.97‡
33.18	7,245	10.32	12.47	5.97	4.80	1,049	1.49	1.81
216.20	4,728	33.87	30.98	58.31	44.08	964	6.91	6.32
219.40	4,082	47.93	42.44	67.80	52.68	980	11.51	10.19
15,692.00	316,946	2,280.00	2,953.00	32.13	25.29	511	3.67	4.76
34.84	3,066	15.31	17.22	11.31	9.28	816	4.08	4.58
24.59	6,850	6.29	10.45	4.44	3.44	958	0.88	1.46
60.20	6,601	9.41	15.68	2.40	2.09	229	0.33	0.54
495.80	16,455	43.91	43.31	9.70	8.24	274	0.73	0.72
56.70 ‖	7,580 ‖	13.27	15.01	12.26	10.95 ‖	1,463	2.56	2.90
31.50	5,943	8.07	9.64	8.57	7.34	1,385	1.88	2.25
20.43	389	3.70	4.54	70.90	57.23	1,089	10.36	12.72
415.50	2,317	20.58	15.07	503.40	415.50	2,317	20.58	15.07
				110.23	90.39	1,008	18.2**	22.7**
				182.17‡	140.64‡	828	29.7**	29.6**

Index of Cases

This book has been set in 12 and 10 point Intertype Garamond, leaded 1 point. Part numbers and titles are in 24 point Deepdene italics; case titles are in 12 point Palatino italics. The size of the type page is 27 by 46½ picas.